Greek Generations

A Medley of Ethnic Recipes, Folklore, and Village Traditions

Susie Atsaides

Baltimore, Maryland

Greek Generations:
A Medley of Ethnic Recipes, Folklore, and Village Traditions

Copyright © 2003 Susie Atsaides

All rights reserved under International and Pan-American copyright conventions. No part of this book may be reproduced, stored in a retrieval system, or transmitted in any form, electronic, mechanical, or other means, now known or hereafter invented, without written permission of the publisher. Address all inquiries to the publisher.

Library of Congress
Cataloging-in-Publication Data
ISBN 1-56167-718-3

Library of Congress Card Catalog Number:
2002091512

Published by

8019 Belair Road, Suite 10
Baltimore, Maryland 21236

Manufactured in the United States of America

*For Stamati,
and our own generations
Mary, Petra, and Ianni,*

I Love You!

Contents

Prologue xvii
Lessons & Legacies xviii
Measure?...What's A Measure? xx
A Note About Restaurant Recipes xxii
Notes for Using the Recipes xxiii

Sauces & Dressings / Sáltses
    Introduction to Sauces & Dressings 1
    Soggy Bread 2
    Egg-Lemon Sauce / Avgolémono 3
    Egg Lemon Sauce - Traditional / Avgolémono Paradosiakó 4
    Egg Lemon Sauce - Creamy Version / Avgolémono Kréma 4
    Béchamel Sauce / Kréma Bechaméla 5
    Lemon Oil Dressing / Ladolémono 6
    Orange-Pepper Dressing / Sáltsa Piperioú me Portokáli 6
    Greek Vinaigrette Dressing / Ladóxido 7
    Garlic Sauce / Skordaliá 8
    Garlic Sauce -Thin Version/ Skordaliá Pihtí 8
    Garlic Sauce -Thick Version/ Skordaliá Lafriá 8
    Almond-Garlic Sauce / Skordaliá Amygdálou 9
    Walnut-Garlic Sauce / Karidoskordaliá 10
    Herb Mayonnaise / Mayonéza me Vótana 11
    Minute Mayonnaise / Mayonéza tis Stigmís 12
    Greek Hummus - Chickpea and Sesame Sauce 13
    Sesame Sauce / Sáltsa me Tahíni 13
    Greek Tahíni Dip 14
    Cold Tomato Sauce / Kría Sáltsa Tomátas 15
    Basic Meat Sauce for Casseroles / Sáltsa Kimás 16
    Zesty Tomato Sauce / Sáltsa Pikántiki 17
    Tomato-Dill Sauce / Sáltsa me Ánitho 18
    Tomato and Rosemary Sauce / Sáltsa Marináti 18
    Tomato-Pepper Sauce / Sáltsa Tomatopiperiás 19
    Tomato-Onion Sauce / Sáltsa Kremidáti 19
    Tomato-Vegetable Sauce / Sáltsa me Hortariká 20
    Tomato Gravy for Meatballs / Sáltsa gia Keftédes 20
    Village Gravy / Sáltsa Psitoú 21
    Mustard Sauce / Sáltsa Moustárdas 21
    Red Sauce for Fish / Sáltsa gia Psári 22
    Rosemary Sauce / Sáltsa Dendrolívano 22
    White Sauce for Meats / Áspri Sáltsa giá Kréata 23
    Yogurt Sauce / Sáltsa me Yiaoúrti 24
    Yogurt - Spinach Sauce / Sáltsa Yiaoúrti me Spanáki 24
    Yogurt and Mint Sauce / Taratoúri 25
    Yogurt and Pimento Sauce / Sáltsa Yiaoúrti me Páprika 25
    Batter / Kourkoúti 26

Marinades / Marinádes
    Spicy Fish Marinade / Pikántiki Marináda gia Psári 29
    Marinade for Pork or Lamb Chops 29
    Herbal Marinade for Poultry and Roasts 30
    Lemon Marinade for Poultry 30

Marinade for Beef Cuts 31
Basting Marinade for Game and Lamb 31
Basting Marinade for Goat or Kid Chops 32
Marinade for Oven Roasted Lamb 32

Appetizers / Mezédes

Introduction to Appetizers / Mezédes 35
The History of the Mezé 37
Feta & Hot Pepper Dip / Ktipití, Tirokauterí, or Kopanistí 38
Tzatzíki 38
Tarama (Roe) Salad / Taramosaláta 39
Fish Roe Fritters / Taramokeftédes 39
Charcoal Grilled Eel / Souvlomoutariá 40
Eel with Eggs and Vinegar / Héli me Avgá ke Xídi 40
Fried Mussels / Mídia Tiganitá 41
Charcoal Grilled Octopus / Htapódi sta Kárvouna 42
Sun Dried Octopus in Garlic Sauce / Htapódi Xiró Skordaliá 42
Octopus in Wine / Htapódi Krasáto 43
Grilled Sun Dried Fish / Psária Heliókafta 44
Salt Cod with Garlic Sauce / Bakaliéros Skordaliá 44
Salt Cod Croquettes / Bakaliéros Krokétes 45
"Singing" Sardines / Sardéla pou Keladái 46
Fried Whitebait / Marídes Tiganités 47
Shrimp Cocktail - Greek Style / Garídes me Kókkini Sáltsa 48
Shrimp in Wine / Garídes Krasátes 49
Squid Rings / Kalámari Tiganitó 50
Squid in Spicy Batter / Kalamári Tiganitó Pikántiko 51
Cheese Saghanaki / Tirí Saghanáki 52
Greek Meat Balls / Keftédes 52
Tomato Balls / Tomatokeftédes 53
Stuffed Cucumbers / Agourákia Gemistá 53
Fried Stuffed Olives / Tiganités Gemistés Eliés 54
Peppers Stuffed with Feta / Piperiés me Féta Tiganités 54
Ptolemies' Tomatoes / Tomátes tis Ptolemaídas 55
Batter Fried Broccoli & Cauliflower / Tiganitó Mbrókolo & Kounoupídi 56
Fried Pumpkin / Kolokítha Tiganití 57
Savory Pumpkin Pancakes / Kolokithópites 58
Onion Fritters / Kremidokeftédes 58
Spicy Pickled Eggplants / Pikántikes Melintzánes 59
Zucchini Blossoms / Anthoús Kolokithiás 60
Stuffed Zucchini Blossoms / Anthoús Kolokithiás Gemistá 60
Zucchini Pancakes / Kolokithokeftédes 61

Salads / Salátes

Introduction to Salads / Salátes 65
The Greek Village Salad 67
Greek Village Salad / Horiátiki Saláta 68
Tomato and Feta Salad / Tomáta me Féta Saláta 69
Spicy Tomato Salad / Pikántiki Tomatosaláta 69
Crab Salad / Kavourosaláta 70
Herring Salad / Renkosaláta 70
Shrimp Salad / Garidosaláta 71
Shrimp and Artichoke Salad / Garídes me Agináres Saláta 71
Artichoke Salad / Saláta Agináres 72
Beets in Garlic Sauce / Patzária Skordaliá 72
Stuffed Beets / Patzária Gemistá 73

Green Bean Salad / Fasolákia Saláta 73
Attica Green Bean Salad / Saláta Fasolákia Attikís 74
Kidney Bean Salad / Saláta Mavrofásoula 74
Lima Bean Salad / Gígantes Saláta 75
Lettuce Salad / Maroulosaláta 75
Radish & Feta Salad / Rapanáki me Féta Saláta 76
Dandelion Salad / Radíkia Saláta 76
Poor Mans' Cabbage Salad / Lahanosaláta 77
Russian Salad / Rósiki Saláta 77
Olive Salad / Saláta apo Eliés 78
Macedonian Taratór / Saláta Taratór 78
Mixed Boiled Vegetables / Saláta Vrastí 79
Boiled Zucchini Salad / Saláta apó Vrastá Kolokithákia 79
Island Potato Salad / Patatosaláta Vrastí 80
Potato Salad from Attica / Patatosaláta Attikís 80
Red and Green Pepper Salad / Kókkines ke Prásines Piperiés Saláta 81
Roasted Eggplant Salad / Melintzanosaláta 81
Fruit with Feta Cheese 82
SALAD COMBINATIONS
Tomato and Herb Salad / Tomatá me Vótana Saláta 82
Farmers Salad / Saláta Laikí 82
Winter Salad / Saláta Himoniátiki 83
Tuna-Bean Salad / Saláta me Tóno ke Fasólia 83
Tomato-Green Bean Salad / Tomáta me Fasolákia Saláta 83
Peasant Pasta Salad / Makaronáki Saláta 84
January Salad / Saláta tou Yianári 84
Chickpea Salad / Revithosaláta 84
Herbal Rice Salad / Rizi me Vótana Saláta 85
Cabbage Salad / Lahanosaláta 85
Bean & Rice Salad / Fasólia me Rízi Saláta 85
Garden Salad / Saláta tou Kípou 86
Colorful Salad / Saláta Chromatistí 86
Green Salad / Saláta Prásini 86

Savory Pies / Pítes
Introduction to Savory Pies / Pítes 89
Traditional Cheese Pie / Tirópita Paradosiakí 91
Plain Cheese Pie / Tirópita Aplí 92
Rich Cheese Pie / Tirópita Ploúsia 93
Ragged Cheese Pie / Patsavoúra Tirópita 94
Simple Chicken Pie / Kotópita Aplí 95
Chicken Pie / Ornithópita or Kotópita 96
Turkey Pie / Galópita 97
Ham Pie / Zambonópita 98
Sausage Pies / Loukanópites 99
Lamb and Feta Pie / Píta me Arní ke Féta 100
Lamb Pie from Cephalonia / Kreatópita Kefalonítiki 101
Cretan Lamb Torte / Toúrta Krítis me Arní 102
Leek and Beef Pie / Prasópita me Kréas 103
Leek and Egg Pie / Prasavgópita 104
Basic Meat Pie / Kreatópita Aplí 105
Beef and Cheese Pie / Kreatópita me Tirí 107
Fried Sweet Meat Pies / Pitákia me Kimá 108
Rice Pie / Rizópita 109
Eggplant Pie / Melintzanópita 110
Spinach Pie / Spanakópita 111

Wild Greens Pie / Hortópita 112
Zucchini Pie / Kolokithópita 113

Stuffed Vegetables / Gemistá and Dolmáthes
Village Secrets of Dolmáthes 117
Making Stuffed Vegetables / Gemistá 118
Vegetable Preparation for Gemistá 118
Working with Fresh Grape Vine Leaves 120
Step by Step Dolmáthes Making 121
Stuffed Grape Leaves with Meat / Dolmáthes or Giaprákia me Kréas 124
Vegetarian Stuffed Grape Leaves / Dolmáthes Pseútiki or Giaprákia Pseútika 124
Stuffed Vegetables with Meat / Gemistá 125
Stuffed Vegetables Vegetarian Style / Gemistá Pseútika 125
Stuffed Cabbage Rolls with Meat / Lahanodolmáthes 126
Stuffed Cabbage Rolls - Vegetarian Style / Lahanodolmáthes Pseútiki 126
Tomato-Onion Dolmáthes / Dolmáthes Nistísimi 127
Bulgur Wheat Dolmáthes / Dolmáthes me Pligoúri 127
Pine Nut Stuffing / Gémisi me Koukounária 128

Pilafs and Pastas / Makarónia
Aegean Pilaf / Piláfi tou Aegéou 131
Lemon Pilaf / Piláfi Lemonáto 132
The Bride's Pilaf / To Piláfi tis Nífis 132
Lentils with Rice and Onions / Fakórizo me Sívrasi 133
Bulgur Wheat Pilaf / Pligoúri Piláfi 133
Orzo in Tomato Sauce / Kritharáki 134
Pasta Imam / Makarónia Imám 135
Pepper Pilaf / Piláfi me Piperiés 136
Spinach Rice / Spanakórizo 137
Tomato Rice with Garlic / Tomatórizo me Skórdo 137
Lenten Spaghetti / Makarónia Nistísima 138
Spaghetti from Hálki / Halkítika Makarónia 139

Vegetables / Lahaniká
Greek Seasons and the Vegetable 143
Boiled Vegetables 144
Sívrasi 144
Artichokes with Egg Lemon Sauce / Agináres Avgolémono 145
Artichokes with Tomatoes / Agináres me Tomáta 146
Baked Beans in Tomato / Fasoláda tou Foúrnou or Lópia 147
Baked Eggplant with Cheese / Melintzánes Foúrnou me Tirí 148
Fried Vegetables / Tiganitá 149
Greek Green Beans / Fasolákia Giahnistá 150
Spinach with Onions / Spanáki Sívrasi 150
Zucchini Stew / Kolokithákia Giahnistá 151
Green Beans with Zucchini and Feta / Fasolákia me Kolokitháki ke Féta 151
Okra with Potatoes / Mbámies me Patátes 152
Sponge with Lettuce and Onions / Sfouggáto me Maroúli ke Kremídi 153
Tomato-Egg Omelet / Tomáta me Avgó 154
Village Omelet / Omeléta Horiátiki 154
Peas with Dill Sauce / Mbizélia me Ánitho 155
Thessalonian Peas / Arakás Thessalías 155
Lemon Roasted Potatoes / Patátes tou Foúrnou Lemonátes 156
Mint Roasted Potatoes / Patátes me Diósmo 156
Potatoes with Rosemary / Patátes me Dendrolívano 157
Tomato Roasted Potatoes / Patátes toú Foúrnou Kokkinistés 157

Vegetables Imam Baildi / Imám Baildí 158
Oven-Baked Imam / Imám tou Foúrnou 159

Soup / Soúpes
The Perfect Soup - Soúpes 163
The Soup Stocks 165
Beef Stock / Zomós Vodinoú 166
Chicken Stock / Zomós Kótas 166
Fish Stock / Zomós Psarioú 167
Vegetable Stock / Zomós Lahanikón 167
Bean Soup / Fasoláda or Lópia 168
Lentil Soup / Fakés 169
Greek Chickpea Chili / Revíthia 170
Spinach and Lentil Soup / Spanáki me Fakí 170
Village Vegetable Soup / Soúpa Horiátiki 171
Tomato Soup - Tomatósoupa 171
Chicken-Vermicelli Soup / Soúpa Fidés 172
Chicken Egg Lemon Soup / Soúpa Avgolémono 172
Rooster Soup / Soúpa Petinoú 173
Greek Beef Soup / Kréas me Kritharáki Soúpa 173
Poached Meatball Soup / Youvarlákia Soúpa 174
Traditional Easter Soup / Magirítsa 175
Tripe Soup / Patsás 176
Greek Bouillabaisse / Kakaviá 176
Island Fish Soup / Psarósoupa 177
Cheese Soup Santorini Style/ Tirávgoulo Santorinítiko 178
Yogurt Soup / Yiaourtósoupa 178
Sesame Soup / Tahinósoupa 179

Meats / Kréata
Introduction to Meats 183
BEEF
Beef with Orzo Macaroni / Moscári Giouvétsi 185
Beef Stew with Peas / Moscári me Mbizélia 186
Beef Stewed with Potatoes / Moscári me Patátes Giahní 186
Stuffed Beef Rolls / Skartotséta apó Moscári 187
Veal Roll with Feta / Moscári Tiliktó me Féta 188
Boiled Beef and Vegetables / Vrastó Moscári me Lahaniká 189
Pastitsáda from Kerkyra / Kerkiráiki Pastitsáda 190
PORK
Baked Pork with Lima Beans / Hirinó me Gígantes 191
Pork Aspic / Pihtí 192
Pork Roast / Hirinó sto Foúrno 193
Stuffed Suckling Pig / Gourounópoulo Gemistó 194
LAMB
Charcoal Grilled Lamb Chops / Arnáki sta Kárvouna 196
Easter Lamb on a Spit / Arní Soúvlas 197
Easter Stuffed Lamb / Lambriátiko Arní Gemistó 198
Lamb with Lettuce Fricassee / Arní Frikasé 199
Lamb In Paper - Kleftiko Style / Arní Kléftiko se Hartí 199
Lamb In Pastry Country Style - Arní Exohikó 200
Lamb Kleftiko - Traditional / Arní Kléftiko Paradosiakó 201
Lamb Stew / Arní Giahní 202
Lamb with Green Beans / Arní me Fasolákia 202
Roasted Leg of Lamb / Arní tou Foúrnou 203

GROUND MEAT
- Eggplant-Potato Casserole-Mousaká 204
- Mousaká with Yogurt / Mousakás me Yiaoúrti 205
- Macaroni Casserole / Pastítsio 206
- Goat Herder's Pie / Pastítsio me Pouré 207
- Beef Rolls from Smýrni / Souzoukákia Smyrnéika 208
- Beef Rolls from Smýrni 208
- Poached Meat Balls / Youvarlákia 209
- Greek Hamburgers / Mpiftéki 210
- **THE INFAMOUS GÝRO** 211
- **THE ART OF SOUVLÁKI MAKING / SHISH KEBOB** 214

Poultry / Pouleriká
- The Village Chicken / Pouleriká 219
- Chicken in Tomato / Kotópoulo Kokkinistó 221
- Chicken Baked with Vegetables / Kotópoulo sto Foúrnou 222
- Lemon Baked Chicken / Kotópoulo Lemonáto 222
- Chicken with Lentils / Kotópoulo me Fakés 223
- Chicken with Quince / Kotópoulo me Kidónia 224
- Herbed Chicken Breasts / Kotópoulo Rigganáto 224
- Island Chicken with Orzo / Kotópoulo me Kritharáki 225
- Marinated Chicken / Kotópoulo Marinátha 225
- Sesame Fried Chicken / Kóta Tiganití me Sisámi 226
- Stewed Chicken and Macaroni/ Kotópoulo me Makarónia 227
- Stuffed Chicken / Kotópoulo Gemistó 228
- Duck with Olive Stuffing / Pápies me Eliés 229
- Turkey with Potatoes and Onions / Galopoúla me Patátes Stifádo 230
- Holiday Stuffed Turkey / Galopoúla Gemistí 231

Game Meats / Kinígi
- Game Meats - Kinígi 235
- Pit Roasted Baby Goat / Katsikáki - Rifáki Soúvla 237
- Baby Goat Stuffed with Rice / Katsikáki - Rifáki Kapamá 238
- Spit Barbequed Hare / Lagós stin Soúvla 239
- Hare in Garlic / Lagós me Skórda 240
- Hare in Onions / Lagós Stifádo 240
- Partridge Pilaf / Pérdika Piláfi 241
- Partridges with Wheat Stuffing / Pérdikes Gemistés 242
- Partridges in Vine Leaves / Pérdikes se Ambelófila 243
- Stuffed Pigeon / Peristéria Gemistá 244
- Eggplants Stuffed with Quails / Melintzánes Gemistés me Ortíkia 245
- Quails in Tomato and Wine / Ortíka me Tomáta ke Krasí 246
- Rabbit in Yogurt / Kounéli me Yiaoúrti 247
- Rabbit with Walnut Stuffing / Kounéli Gemistó me Karídia 248
- Wild Boar in Wine / Agriogoúrouno Krasáto 249
- Baked Venison / Eláfi sto Foúrno 250
- Stewed Land Snails / Karavóli Giahní 251

Organ Meats / Entóstia
- Organ Meats - Entóstia 255
- Beef Tongue with Olives / Glósa Moscarísia me Eliés 256
- Heart and Kidney Pilaf / Piláfi me Nefrá ke Kardiés 257
- Chicken Livers in Vinegar / Sikotákia tis Kótas Xitháta 257
- Liver Roúmelis in Paper / Sikóti se Hartí 258
- Liver with Leeks / Sikotariá me Prása 259
- Liver with Rosemary / Sikotákia me Dendrolívano 259

Roasted Pig's Head / Kefáli Gourounioú Psitó	260
Baked Beef Head / Kefáli Moscarísia sto Foúrno	261
Village Mountain Oysters / Amelétita	261
Fried Brains / Mialá Tiganitá	262
Stewed Lung / Pnevmóni Giahní	262
Pork and Rice Sausages / Kolousafádes	263
Garlic Rice Sausages / Kolousafádes Skordáti	264

Seafood / Thalassiná

Seafood - Thalassiná	267
Stewed Cuttlefish / Soupiés Giahní	269
Cuttlefish in Wine and Sepia / Soupiés Krasátes me Meláni	269
Baked Grouper / Orfós sto Foúrno	270
Simple Poached Fish / Psári Vrastó	271
Spicy Fish in Tomato Sauce / Pikántiko Psári me Tomáta	272
Fish in Rosemary and Garlic / Psária Skordaliá me Dendrolívano	272
Tuna in Tomato Sauce / Sáltsa me Tóno	273
Mussels and Feta in Tomato Sauce / Sáltsa Mídia ke Féta	274
Mussels with Rice / Mídia Piláfi	274
Octopus with Macaroni / Htapódi me Makarónaki	275
Steamed Crayfish / Karavída	275
Baked Shellfish Casserole / Thalassiná tou Foúrnou	276
Shrimp with Rice / Garídes Piláfi	277
Shrimp Saghanaki / Garídes Saghanáki	278
Stuffed Squid / Kalamarákia Gemistá	279
Moray Eel in Tomatoes / Smírna Plakí	280

Bread Making

The Village Foúrno	283
The Foúrno Tutorial	284
The Praxis of Prozími	286
Village Sour Dough Starter / Prozími Horiátiko	287
Step by Step Village Bread Making	288
Village Bread Making Tips	291
The Bread Glazes	293
Mpouloumasí / Serbian Bread Glaze	293

Breads / Psomiá

The Bread Stamp - Tipári or Sfragítha	297
Greek Pita Bread / Pítes	299
Greek Village Bread / Psomí Horiátiko	300
Bread from Kárpathos / Karpáthika Glykanálata Psomiá	301
Stuffed Olive Bread / Eliópsomo Gemistó	302
Ground Sesame Bread / Tahinópsomo	303
Sesame Breads for Fasting / Sisamotá Psomiá Nistísima	304
Seven Seed Bread / Eptásporo Psomí	305
Herbal Bread / Áspro Psomí me Vótana	306
Black Garlic Bread / Mávro Skordópsomo	307
HOLIDAY AND CELEBRATION BREADS	
St. Basil's Bread / Vasilópita	308
Christmas Bread from Constantinople / Christópsomo Constantinoúpolis	310
Sweet Christmas Yeast Bread / Christópsomo	311
Easter Bread / Lambrópsomo	312
Lenten Flat Bread / Lagána	313
The traditional Clean Monday bread	313
Sweet Easter Bread / Tsouréki	314

Bread of Seven Fermentations / Eptázima ... 315
Church Bread from Crete / Ártos Kritikós ... 316
Holy Communion Bread / Prósforo or Liturgiá ... 317
The Five Church Breads / Pentárti ... 318
Lazarus Bread Cookies / Lazarákia ... 319
Wedding Breads / Kouloúres tou Gámou ... 320

ZWIEBACK / RUSKS
Notes on Making Zwieback or Rusks—Paximádia ... 321
Lenten Zwieback or Rusks / Paximádia Nistísima ... 322
Riganáda - A Paximádi Snack ... 323
Raisin Filled Rusks / Paximádia me Stafídes ... 324
Sesame Rusks / Sisamotá Paximádia ... 325
Oil Rusks from Smýrni / Smyrnéika Paximádia me Ládi ... 326
Barley Bread Wreaths / Kritharénies Kouloúres ... 327

LEFTOVER BREADS
Using Left-over Breads and Mistakes ... 328
Salted Fried Bread / Tiganópsomo Almyró ... 329
Sweet Fried Bread / Tiganópsomo Glykó ... 329

PASTRY DOUGHS
Rich Short Crust Pastry ... 330
Home Made Phyllo Pastry Sheets / Phýllo Spitísio ... 331
Home Made Phyllo Pastry Sheets with Egg / Phýllo Spitísio me Avgó ... 331
Butter Pastry for Pies / Zími Voutírou yia Pítes ... 332
Pastry Dough - Savory Style ... 333
Lemon Pastry / Zími me Lemóni ... 333

Desserts / Glyká

The Greek Sweet Tooth ... 337
The Legend of St. Fanourios' Cake - Fanourópita ... 339
St. Fanourios Cake / Fanourópita ... 340
St. Basil's Cake / Vasilópita Glýkisma ... 341
Custard Pies / Mpougátsa ... 342
Cretan Almond Torte / Amygdalópita Krítis ... 343
Byzantine Rice Cake / Vizantiní Rizópita ... 343
Lemon Cake / Lemonópita ... 344
Ouzo-Coconut Cake / Revaní me Oúzo ke Karída ... 345
Raisin Cake / Stafidópita ... 346
Island Cheese and Honey Pie / Melópita Nisiótiki ... 347
Sweet Cheese Tart / Tárta me Mizíthra ... 348
Apricots and Cream / Chrisómila Poltós ... 349
Rice Pudding - Traditional Style / Rizógalo Paradosiakó ... 349
Custard Style Rice Pudding / Rizógalo ... 350
Pasta Pudding / Matsógalo ... 350
Grape Pudding / Moustoaleuriá ... 351
Bread Pudding / Poutínga ... 352
Figs Stuffed with Nuts / Síka Gemistá me Xiroús Karpoús ... 353
Stuffed Melon / Piponáki Gemistó ... 353
Mastic Ice Cream / Pagotó Mastíhas ... 354

THE FRIED DOUGHS AND DESSERTS ... 355
Deep Fried Apple Rings / Tiganítes me Míla ... 355
Díples ... 356
Fried Almond Fingers / Amygdalotá Tiganitá ... 357
Fried Dough Balls / Loukoumádes ... 358
Fried Cheese Pies / Mizithrópites ... 359
Cheese Filled Crescents from Crete / Kaltsounákia Kritiká ... 360
Fried Phyllo from Thrace / Kourkoumpínia Thrákis ... 361

Crispy Pastry in Syrup / Xirotígana	362
Fried Rice Balls / Akoúmia	**363**

The Syrup Pastries and Cakes 364

Almond Cake in Syrup / Amygdalópita Ípirou Siropiastí	364
Almond - Brandy Cake / Amygdalópita Siropiastí	365
Baklavá	366
Kataífi	367
Ekmék Kataífi	368
Milk Custard Pie / Galaktomboúriko	369
Macedonian Semolina Halva / Makedonikós Halvás apó Simigdáli	370
Walnut Cake / Karidópita	371
Yogurt Pie / Yiaourtópita	**372**

Cookies, Sweet Biscuits, and Bars 373

Chocolate Chestnut Bars / Glykó me Kástana Attikís	374
Easter Cookies / Koulourákia Pascaliná	375
Short Bread Biscuits / Kourambiédes	376
Sesame Honey Bars / Melekoúni	377
Phoenician Stuffed Biscuits / Finíkia	378
Honey Macaroons / Melomakárouna	380
Almond Meringue Biscuits / Amigdalotá	381
Oil cookies / Koulourákia Ladioú	381
Moonshine Cookies / Kouloúria me Rakí	382
Loukoúmia	383

THE SPOON SWEETS 384

Whole Apricot Preserves / Chrisómila Glykó	385
Bergamot Spoon Sweet / Pergamónto Glykó	386
Bitter Orange Spoon Sweet / Nerantzáki Glykó	386
Cherry Spoon Sweet / Kerási Glykó	387
Dry Fruit Sweet / Glykó apó Xirá Froúta	388
Eggplant Spoon Sweet / Melintzanáki Glykó	388
Fig Spoon Sweet / Síko Gkykó	389
Grape Spoon Sweet / Stafíli Glykó	389
Pear Spoon Sweet / Ahládi Glykó	390
Quince Spoon Sweet / Kithóni Glykó	390
Strawberry Spoon Sweet / Glykó Fráoulas	391
Green Walnut Spoon Sweet / Karidáki Glykó	392
Walnut Meats in Syrup / Karídia Glykó	393

Preserving and Pickling / Toursés

The Greek Olive	397
Green Olives in Vinegar / Eliés Xitháres	399
Green Cracked Olives / Eliés Tsakistés	400
Olives in Bitter Orange / Eliés Nerantzátes	401
Black Wrinkled Olives / Eliés Zoúpes	401
Spicy Olive Oil / Pikántiko Eleólado	402
Sun Dried Tomatoes / Tomátes Xerés	402
Sun Dried Octopus	403
Peppers Stuffed with Anchovies / Piperiés Gemistés me Antzoúgies	404
Pickled Peppers / Piperiés se Salamoúra	404
Sinking Sauce for Fish / Sáltsa Savoúro	405
Home-made Feta Cheese / Tirí Féta Spitísia	406
Village Raisins / Stafídes	407
Preserved Pork Fats / Míla and Tsirígia	407
Preserved Pork in Lard / Kavroumás	407
Wheat Baby Cream / Kréma gia Morá	408
Home-Made Pasta / Mátsi	408

Beverages and Bottling / Potá
Súma, Rakí, and Tsípouro 411
Village Wine Making 412
Village Style Home-made Wine 412
Greek Coffee / Kafés Ellinikós 412
Apricot Pit Liqueur / Likér apó Koukoútsia Veríkoko 414
Blueberry or Raspberry Liqueur / Likér apó Vatómoura 414
Mandarin Liqueur / Likér apó Mandaríni 414
Morello Cherry Liqueur / Likér apó Víssino 415
Walnut Liqueur / Likér apó Karídia 415
Orange Liqueur / Likér apó Portokáli 415
Spearmint Liqueur / Likér apó Diósmo 416
Village Hangover Cure / Stomahikó 416

Greek Cooking for Children
Introduction to Greek Cooking for Children 419
Pies - Pítes 420
Short Cut Savory Pítes 420
Short Cut Sweet Pies 421
Short Cut Syrup Cakes 422
Short Cut Cakes 423

Kitchen Techniques
Working with Pastry Dough 427
Working with Phyllo Pastry Sheets 429
Basic Seed and Nut Knowledge 432
Whitening Sesame Seeds 433
Toasted Chickpeas / Stragália 433
Preparing Fresh Vegetables 434
Roasting Vegetables 436
The Mysterious Bean 436
Plucking, Cleaning & Preparing Fresh Birds 438
Cleaning and Preparing Heads for Soups and Roasts 439
Cleaning Intestines 440
Cleaning and Preparing Tripe 440
Preparation tips for Open Pit Barbeques - Soúvles 441
Herbal Basting Brushes 443
The Do's and Don'ts of Fish Preparation 444
Fish Variety List 446
Preparing Fresh Squid and Cuttlefish 447
Preparing Fresh Octopus 448
Preparing Fresh Moray Eels 450
Preparing Other Fruits Of The Sea 452
Preparing Land Snails 453

The Greek Pantry
Introduction to the Greek Pantry 457
Herbs and Spices for the Greek Kitchen 459
Mystic Mastic 462
What is Mahlep or Muhlep - Mahlépi? 462
Concoctions For The Greek Kitchen 463
Lime Water / Asvestónero 464
Blossom Water - Anthónero 465
Homemade Village Rose Water 465
Home Made Yogurt / Yiaoúrti 466

Strained Yogurt / Yiaoúrti Stragistó 466
Greek Cheeses 467

The Greek Menu Planner

Menu Suggestions 471
A Mezé Style Dinner Party 471
The Greek Barbeque 473
Clean Monday Picnic 474
Holy Saturday Night 475
Easter Dinner 475
Christmas Dinner 476
New Year's Eve Party - Revegión 477
Children's Name Day or Birthday Celebrations 478
THE GREEK ORTHODOX FASTING PERIODS 479
Fasting Menus - Nistísima 481
The Lentient Fast 482
The Semi-Rigid Fast 483
The Rigid Fast 484

Superstitions, Traditions, and Legends

Introduction to Superstitions, Traditions, and Legends 487
The Story of O.K. 488
The Evil Eye - To Máti 489
Knot Ropes - Komboskínia 491
Talismans - Filahtá 492
Breaking Plates 493
Incense Burning - Thimíama or Thímiasma 494
Holy Water - Agiasmós 495
Buildings, New Homes, and Businesses 496
Worry Beads - Kombológia 498
Promise to a Saint - Táma or Táximo 499
The Village Cures 500
Other Greek Superstitions and Religious Beliefs 503

Holiday Celebrations

The Name Days 511
Spring and Easter Traditions and Celebrations 513
Christmas - New Year - The Epiphany 520
The Summer Festivals 522
October 28th - Ochi Day 522

Men and Women

Village Babies 525
The Village Woman 529
The Village Launderette 534
The Village Man 536
The Games They Played 540
Grandmom's Dolls 543
The Elders 545
Greek Men and Women Today 547

The Ceremonies
WEDDINGS
Engagements - Aravónes 551
Dowries 554
Village Weddings 556
BAPTISMS
Greek Baptisms 571
FUNERALS
Greek Funerals 577
Memorial Wheat - Kóliva 582
Index 584

Prologue

I have been asked many times by my readers as to what exactly my qualifications are for writing about cooking and folklore of Greece and her Islands. Let me begin by saying that I am not a historian nor am I an expert on Greek culture. And although I have worked in commercial kitchens for the past twenty-five years, I am not a professional chef. I am simply an American woman of Greek descent who now lives in the Greek Islands.

The recipes and tales of folklore that are in the following pages have been given to me by simple Greek village men and women, who themselves are not historians or culture experts either. Although you may find some of the more prominent information in history books and encyclopedias, most of the contents on these pages are about the quirks, superstitions and ways of life that these villagers have grown up with or what I would call, Grandmom's *Paramíthia*—tall tales.

Given the opportunity to visit and speak to these people, I found a wealth of information that is not only amusing, but just plain interesting as well. I'm the kind of person that always asks "Why?" and you'll find that out as you read along. Unusual customs and recipes are explained with as much information as I could gather.

This wonderful collection is presented in an easy and familiar way, just as it was given to me, so it can be shared with other Greek descendants or people who may be close to, involved with, or married into a Greek family.

Some of these villagers are still with us and others, have moved on to a better place. This book is dedicated to these fantastic men and women who raised our forefathers and gave us what is our heritage today. It is my hope that in some small way, they will be honored and remembered not only by me, but by future Greek Generations too.

Lessons & Legacies

**Pictured are three generations of my ancestral family
taken in the village of *Kalithiés*, Rhodes in the early 1900s.**

Born as the only daughter of Greek immigrants living in a big city like Baltimore, my upbringing was on the strict side. Although we were thousands of miles away from the home-land, the traditions and customs were kept alive in our home along with a strong sense of family. I had never stepped foot on Greek soil yet my parents made sure that I was exposed to the Greek culture as much as possible. English was never spoken in our home, Greek school was attended on Tuesday nights, we sang in choir every Sunday and occasionally, we would go to a Church club social with the fellow Greeks who lived in 'Greek Town'.

There was a lot of comradeship amongst the Greek immigrants in Baltimore. Although we were of no relation nor from the same island, we considered each other as family, very much like the villages in Greece. In fact, I had always referred to my Greek girlfriends as my 'cousins' when I lived in the States.

The first time I came to visit the Island of Rhodes, I was a young teenager. Instantly, I fell in love with the island life style. Speaking the language and growing up with the customs at home helped me to fit in and adapt easily. And here, I found even more family. It seems that everyone in your village is somehow related to you in one way or another.

During the day, I went for walks through the village and visited with my new-found relations and in the evenings, I had discovered that the open air cinema in the village square always had the most recent *Finos Film* showing. Hours upon hours were spent at the beach with more cousins. Swimming and snorkeling were our big activities in hopes of getting a fresh octopus. We slept with the doors and windows open. Many times we would sleep on the front porch, completely at ease and never with a sense of fear or danger.

Our daily bathing ritual consisted of donning a bathing suit and going out to the back yard where the water barrels were kept. My Aunt Leukothéa—God rest her soul, kept the full barrels heating in the sunshine. They contained the freshest, purest water I had ever known that was used for a variety of things, including showers. Armed with a small cooking pot, we would scoop out the clean water and dump it over our heads. A vigorous shampoo was followed with a good dousing to rinse off. Of course it helped greatly if you took joint showers with a cousin so they could give you a hand if soap got in your eyes.

Saturdays were always looked forward to as this was the day that Aunt Leukothéa would light the *foúrno* or beehive oven and bake the family's weekly bread supply. Along with the baking bread, she would push in a pan of *fasoláda* or beans to cook along side. Oh, those beans! I can still remember the taste of those plain old beans in tomato. When they came out of a Greek *foúrno*, no gourmet meal could match the deliciousness.

All these memories of tastes and experiences stayed with me through the years. Then one day, my family decided to move back to the home-land. I didn't give the move a second thought as I followed close behind.

Not long ago, I began writing about Greek cooking for the internet. Unknowingly to me at the time, I published the basis of what turned out to be a labor of love. As the web site took off, I had more and more requests from fellow Greek generations not only for recipes but for answers to questions about our culture and traditions. I slowly came to realize that there were so many Greek descendants that didn't know much about their homeland and it's ways. I, on the other hand, was living right in the thick of it - spinach pie, evil eyes, ...and all.

Living on a small Island does have its advantages as I had the opportunity to get first hand information about our *parádosi* or tradition. After asking around the villages, I tracked down some of the old women— and I do mean old. These ladies were said to have all sorts of knowledge about long-forgotten recipes as well as certain strange customs and traditions that baffled even me.

Unless these women have large families with children or grand children, they don't get many visitors, so when company calls, they are so very pleased. One of these outstanding ladies could barely stand up, yet somehow she managed to make Greek coffee and served me a dish of Grape Spoon Sweet. After some light conversation, she began sharing with me the most wonderful lessons of cooking and amusing tales of our folklore. I learned many stories of bygone days that even my parents had long forgotten about. After receiving her blessing, I left her home with a great feeling of satisfaction, as though I had saved a small piece of my ancestry from extinction.

Another lesson that I learned on my quest for knowledge was that recipes and customs not only vary between the mainland and the islands, or from island to island, but from village to village as well. A mere distance of 10 kilometers can make the difference between using lemons or almonds in a certain cake recipe or if a black cat is meant as a bad omen or a good one. Each village has its own characteristics and is very individual and very special. If you know the name of your home village, I would suggest writing it down and keeping it someplace safe, like in a photo album for future generations to find. Greek village names can be complicated and are easily forgotten.

Even here in Greece, many of our customs are being forgotten as we become more and more westernized and our traditions seem to be dying out along with the old ladies of the villages, lost in time forever. Although geographical and language barriers may stop many Greek generations from ever visiting their home land, we can still share some of the heritage that is our legacy. Our recipes, customs, and superstitions can be preserved and remembered so that our own younger generations will also come to realize some of the wonderful things that make the Greeks the unique breed that they are.

Measure? ....What's a Measure?

It has been on a rare occasion that I have found a true traditional recipe that includes with it exact measurements for ingredients. It was something that just wasn't done. "A bit of this and a dash of that" is the way that the recipes were handed down from generation to generation.

This disregard for using measurements does not mean that our ancestors were careless or thoughtless. You have to keep in mind the history of Greece and remember how poor and war-torn she had been for centuries. It wasn't until well after the second world war that village girls commonly began attending school. Although some did study and were educated enough to become teachers or mid-wives, as my mother, the majority of the girls remained at home doing household chores.

Since few women were schooled, recipes were just not written down. Who would have been able to read them anyway? The equivalent of what would be entire volumes of our modern cookbooks today, were memorized and remembered right down to the pinch of salt.

Imagine a little girl sitting in the preparation area of the *esóspito* or inner house. Diligently, the little girl would watch her mother make up a recipe, paying keen attention to the handfuls of ingredients as well as the techniques used. After having watched the ritual over and over again, she would learn the recipe.

Measuring cups and measuring spoons simply did not exist. The most common cooking measure was the *hoúfta* or hand full. "One *hoúfta* of rice for every serving," was one of my mother's basic cooking lessons to me. Many times, a household utensil such as a particular glass, clay pot, jug or basket would be used as a measure within a home, but there was no common standard measurement that would be used from household to household. A cup of flour may have been measured in a favorite glass in one home, where as another would use a small coffee cup. This is probably why the recipes differ so much between village to village, today.

No thermometers or timers existed for cooking. When heating the *foúrno*, a village woman would "feel" for the right temperature with her hand. She knew when the heat was too high or too low simply by sticking her hand into the opening.

Another kitchen measurement technique used is called *me to máti* or "with the eye." Cooking utensils were few within a home. They didn't have sets of pots and pans like we do today so they became very familiar with the quantities and capacities of their particular utensils. A village woman could tell just by looking if the amount of liquid was enough to cook *Giahní* (stew) or if the oil was enough to fry *Loukoumádes* (dough balls).

Don't think that the lack of measurements stops at cooking. There are still women around today that use what's called the *pithamí*. What exactly is a *pithamí*? Hold your hand out in front of you and stretch your fingers apart. The distance between the tip of your thumb and the tip of your pinky is a *pithamí*. This was commonly used to measure small distances such as hem length on a skirt or the width of a table or curtain.

There was also what I like to call "The Finger Method" or *me to dáhtilo*, that had many uses through out the house. Heat two fingers of oil.....trim the hem of a skirt to three fingers....cut bread slices one finger thick.... All very common ways of measuring that are still in use by some old village folk even today.

When calculating greater distances such as land area, they used what's called the *víma*. A *víma* is very simply, a long stride. By taking long strides and counting them, the villagers knew just how many *vímata* their property lines were.

A trip to the tailor would pose another problem. Since the basic transportation of the village was by donkey or mule, it wasn't very easy to take the whole family to get fitted for their holiday clothing. A typical village mom could order her children's new trousers and skirts by using the *klostí* or thread. A child's waist line would be measured with a piece of thread that was cut with maybe an inch or two to spare—giving the child room to grow. The inseam for a new pair of trousers was measured by another piece. How do you tell the threads apart? Tie one knot in the waist *klostí* to tell it apart from the inseam one.

Have more than one child?—use different color threads for each one.

The depth of a water spring or sea bank could easily be measured by using a *vítsa*, which is nothing more than a long cane made from the trunk of a small pine tree. For deeper measurements, a rock could be tied to the end of a rope and thrown into the water. Once it sank to the bottom, the rope would become slack and you would begin to wind it back up, looping it over your hand and elbow. By simply counting the loops, you would know the depth.

I know that common sense tells us that some people have larger hands, wider fingers and longer legs than others, but somehow, these units of measurement worked for our forefathers, and believe it or not, many of these village methods are still in use today. My mom still uses the *pithamí* and my dad is renowned for using the *víma*. And I too confess, that very often I use the *hoúfta* instead of actually measuring ingredients.

Although you'll find that I have given you measurements for spices, herbs and seasonings through out this book, remember that village cooking is done without a measuring spoon, it's not an exact science. The final taste test relies on you and your family's preferences. Go ahead and alter recipes to suit your tastes. Use more pepper or add a dash of oregano for a variation to spice something up. A bit of this, a hand full of that and a few basic ingredients make a marvelous meal, Greek Style.

A Note about Restaurant Recipes

I've received many requests from my readers requesting a particular recipe that they've enjoyed in a Greek restaurant that they want to duplicate at home. They describe the dish as it was served to them and often believe that the recipe used was a traditional one.

Let me try to clarify the difference between a restaurant recipe and a traditional recipe. Most of the Greek foods that you enjoy in Greek restaurants in countries outside of Greece have been altered in one way or another. This is due to the fact that it's difficult to get certain ingredients and many of them, which would be used in their fresh state in Greece, come preserved or canned in other markets.

Having been a restaurateur myself, I know that it's not cost effective to get some of the special ingredients that a recipe calls for only for it to be traditional. Instead, alternatives are used so a dish can be served by the restaurant that can be offered in an economical way to the customer.

Take for instance the dessert *Ekmék Kataífi*. I have been told by one reader that the dessert she had eaten was made with a nut base, another reader says that it was made with short-crust pastry and yet another, said that they enjoyed it with a firm, pound cake like bottom.

Although the traditional dessert is made with *Kataífi*, a thin, angels' hair like pastry, all these variations do give you *Ekmék*. The *Kataífi* pastry is not used simply because it's difficult to find. Even if the restaurant is next door to a Greek or Middle eastern grocer, the extra cost of this ingredient will have to be charged to the customer, making it an expensive menu item.

Since the traditional recipes can and do become altered, I've given you as many of the variations on each recipe as I've come across during my years at this. If not the recipe itself, one of these changes may suit your tastes or at least guide you in the right direction of duplicating a restaurant recipe.

Your friend in Greek cooking,

Susie Atsaides

Notes for Using the Recipes

Cook Ware

Instead of stating exact measurements for cooking pots and pans, I refer to them in the sizes of small, medium, and large. We all have favorite pots that we like to use and for most recipes, it doesn't matter if you use a round pan or a square pan. Personally, I think that if you use the pots and pans that you are comfortable with, you'll be more at ease with the process of cooking to begin with. Since some people NEED a measurement, use this as an approximate gauge for the cookware that I refer to:

Small:
Use approximate sized 8" x 8" square or 9" round pans.

Medium:
Use approximate sized 9" x 13" rectangular or 11" round pans.

Large:
Use approximate sized 12" x 15" rectangular or 13" round pans.

Oil For Frying

Many recipes call for the ingredient "oil for frying." The Greek villagers use pure olive oil for most of their recipes including home fried potatoes. For some palettes, I think that this is too heavy of an oil to use, especially when making the sweet fried doughs. Personally, I'll mix half and half, olive oil with a light cotton or soy oil and use that for any savory foods. For sweet recipes, I use plain corn oil for a lighter flavor. The choice is yours as to your preference.

Basic Thickener

Some people prefer their soups, stews and gravies to be very thick but on some occasions, depending on many factors, the cooking process alone won't give you the consistency that you're looking for. For these times, use a basic thickener such as flour and water to thicken up your gravies. Whisk together 3 tbs. of cold water with 1 tbs. of flour, getting rid of any lumps and stir it into the stew. Let it simmer for a moment, and you'll see that it's thicker. This also works wonderfully to make plain meat drippings into a gravy. You may have to adjust the amounts, but the ratio of 3 parts cold water to 1 part flour remains the same.

Sauces & Dressings
Sáltses

Sauces & Dressings - *Sáltses*

**The *piatothíki* or dish-keeper hangs on the wall of the village home.
Here, the dishes of a household could be arranged and kept easily at hand, ready for use.**

You'll be surprised at the simplicity of the Greek sauces. By using basic ingredients that are often on hand, you can make spectacular toppings and additions that bring out and accentuate the flavors of a dish. Although some of these recipes may seem very simple to you, it's the combination that's great. Don't be fooled because there aren't long lists of ingredients. You don't need a lot of ingredients for authentic Greek cooking to taste good. Something as easy as olive oil & fresh squeezed lemon can turn plain sliced cabbage into a delicious salad.

There are certain recipes that call for sauces that may seem more complicated to make and you may be tempted to skip them. Don't. When you taste the finished product, you'll realize that these dishes would be incomplete or naked without the extra effort. Chicken soup would just not be the same without its *Avgolémono* nor would *Mousaká* enjoy its popularity without its crowning glory, the *Béchamel* Sauce.

Most sauces and dressings can be made ahead of time and refrigerated until you're ready to use them. When making a vinaigrette dressing, for added convenience, I double or triple the given recipe and store it in an old wine bottle in the refrigerator. The vinaigrette keeps for a long, long time and all I have to do is shake it up and I have home-made dressing readily on hand. Another bonus that I have found is that by using this method, the flavors of dried herbs really come out, so the longer it sits, the better.

Traditionally, these recipes were made by using a *gouthí* and *gouthohéri* or mortar and pestle, or what I lovingly call the village food processor. The ingredients were grinded together by hand until they became a very smooth and creamy mixture. I don't think that our ancestors would object if you used a modern day food processor or blender to get the same results.

Soggy Bread

Some recipes call for bread as an ingredient. Remember, that in the village homes, nothing is thrown away, so stale bread is used quite often as a base ingredient. It has to be soaked and the excess moisture squeezed out so that it can be incorporated into the recipes.

Don't use just any bread. Using rye bread, onion bread or garlic bread will give the recipe a distinct flavor that you may not want. Whole wheat breads can have a mild flavor, so use them at your discretion. The best kind of bread that I have found to use in these recipes, is plain old white bread. It can be a sliced sandwich loaf or a baguette. Remove the crusts and use only the white part.

A basic method for preparation is as follows:

Take seven slices of white bread and cut off the crusts.

Soak the bread in plain water for about 15 minutes—longer if it's very stale.

Remove the bread to a mesh strainer and press it against the sides to remove as much water as possible. It will have the consistency of clay or putty.

The bread is now ready to be used in the recipe of your choice.

Egg-Lemon Sauce / *Avgolémono*

This simple sauce is used quite often in Greek cooking. It may seem complicated, but once you get the hang of it, it's easy to make and tastes delicious. Some villagers still use a table fork as the 'whisk' to beat the egg whites and surprisingly, they get beautiful results. I, on the other hand, am all for convenience, so if you own an electric mixer—use it.

The traditional recipe is used more for soups and stews. Although it can be used with other foods as a topping, there is a sister version that is made with corn flour and is very creamy and rich. It's more thicker and can be served over *Dolmáthes,* poached meatballs, fish and other vegetables.

Which ever version you choose to make, keep a few tips in mind about this sauce: Never add boiling hot broth or juice to *Avgolémono*. Since it's made with egg, a high temperature will curdle or cook it and you'll get scrambled eggs instead of thick and frothy sauce. Always let your broth cool down a bit before you use it in the recipe. Or if you're in a hurry, use a few ice cubes to cool it down. Don't worry, I won't tell your great-grandmothers about the short cut.

Never boil a soup once it has *Avgolémono* in it. Again, the eggs will cook and although it may taste good, it will look terrible. Re-heat any recipe that contains *Avgolémono* gently and slowly, only to the point where it's almost hot.

Once the *Avgolémono* has been added to a soup or stew, you should serve it immediately. The foaminess of this sauce is caused by the air that is incorporated into the egg, so you'll lose the effect if you wait too long. Make your soup ahead of time as it can be re-heated easily, but wait to make the *Avgolémono* sauce until you know that everyone is ready to sit at the table.

Egg Lemon Sauce - Traditional / *Avgolémono Paradosiakó*

Ingredients:
5 eggs, separated
juice of 2 lemons
2 cups broth from your soup or stew, allowed to cool for about 20 minutes or longer.

In a large bowl, beat the egg whites at high speed until almost stiff. Reduce your speed to medium and add one yolk at a time, beating well after each addition.Beat in the lemon juice.The egg-lemon sauce should be thick and foamy.

Reduce the speed to low and add some broth to the mixture, slowly while beating the whole time.Add more broth and keep beating gently so the sauce stays foamy. Slowly pour the hot mixture to the pot of soup, stirring the soup so the egg doesn't separate. Serve immediately.

Egg Lemon Sauce - Creamy Version / *Avgolémono Kréma*

Ingredients:
2 tbs. corn flour combined with 1½ to 2 cups cooled vegetable, chicken or beef broth, depending on what you'll be serving the *Avgolémono* with.
5 eggs, separated
juice of 2 lemons

In a small sauce pot, cook the corn flour and broth mixture until it thickens. Remove it from the heat and allow it to cool. In a large bowl, beat the egg whites at high speed until almost stiff. Reduce your speed to medium and add one yolk at a time, beating well after each addition. Beat in the lemon juice. The egg-lemon sauce should be thick and foamy.

Reduce the speed to low and add some of the cooled corn flour mixture, slowly while beating the whole time. Continue adding it until it has all been incorporated. To serve the sauce with entrees such as meats and *Dolmáthes*, simply spoon it over the servings. Serve immediately.

Béchamel Sauce / *Kréma Bechaméla*

Béchamel has long been used as the crowning touch to casseroles. It involves a bit of work, but is truly worth the extra effort. You have the option of using nutmeg when making this sauce. It will give the cream a distinct aroma and flavor toward the sweet side, so if you prefer a more savory taste, don't use it.

Ingredients:
2 tbs. butter
2 tbs. flour
2 cups milk
salt and pepper
pinch ground nutmeg - optional
2 beaten egg yolks - optional

To make the *Béchamel* Sauce, you have to begin by making what's called a roux. Melt the butter in a deep pot. Add the flour and mix constantly with a wire whisk. It will look like bubbling cake batter - roux. Add the salt and pepper, and a dash of nutmeg, if you prefer. While whisking the roux mixture, add the milk. It may become lumpy initially, but continue to whisk the mixture and the lumps will dissolve. Be careful as *Béchamel* has a tendency to scorch.

You have to whisk the thickening sauce constantly while it's over the heat—don't walk away from it. If you see that the sauce is at a boil but it has not thickened, remove the pot from the heat source. Mix a little flour with some water and whisk it in and then return the pot to the heat, whisking again continuously. Once it has become creamy and thick like a custard, remove it from the heat and use it as your recipe directs.

Some people prefer to use egg yolks in this recipe as they make the cream denser. If you choose to add the yolks, remove the cream from the heat source and mix a bit of it into the beaten yolks while whisking constantly so they don't cook and separate. Repeat the step, by adding more cream and mixing it with the yolks thoroughly. Once the temperature of the yolks seems hot, pour it into the *Béchamel* cream and return the pot to the heat. Cook it for one or two minutes, again, whisking continuously. The sauce is ready to use in the recipe of your choice.

Lemon Oil Dressing / *Ladolémono*

Vegetables, served hot or cold such as lettuce, broccoli, cauliflower, cabbage, spinach and all the kinds of *hórta* or greens, are just a few of the winter crops that this tangy dressing is used with. Lemon oil is also used when baking fish and game meats as a marinade or as a basting sauce.

Ingredients:
1 cup olive oil
¼ to ⅓ cup fresh squeezed lemon juice
⅛ tsp. salt
⅛ tsp. pepper

Mix all ingredients together. For more of a tang in the taste, grate the rind of one lemon and add that as well. The dressing can be stored in a covered jar in the refrigerator, but because of the fresh lemon juice, don't keep it longer than a day or two.

Orange-Pepper Dressing / *Sáltsa Pipernoú me Portokáli*

This spicy dressing can be served with any combination of vegetables, hot or cold. It's also a delicious marinade to use for charcoal grilled pork chops and *Souvlákis*.

Ingredients:
1 cup olive oil
½ cup lemon juice
¼ cup vinegar
2 tbs. grated orange rind
½ tsp. flaked hot peppers
¼ tsp. cayenne pepper
salt

Mix all the ingredients together and refrigerate overnight. Toss the dressing with your favorite vegetables or use it as a marinade, allowing the meat to soak up the flavors for 1 to 3 three hours prior to grilling.

Greek Vinaigrette Dressing / *Ladóxido*

More and more vinegar is used in cooking in the spring and summer months in the islands. When the home-made wines of the previous winter are beginning to sour, a bit of *mána* or "mother" is added to ferment them into vinegar. Since the coming fall season will bring with it a fresh crop of grapes to be made into wine and vinegars, the old stock is used up to make room for the new.

Ingredients:
1 cup olive oil
⅓ cup white wine vinegar
⅛ tsp. garlic powder or 1 crushed clove
⅛ tsp. paprika
⅛ tsp. salt
⅛ tsp. pepper
1 pinch dried basil
1 pinch dried oregano
2 tsp. grated Parmesan cheese
⅛ tsp. sugar – optional

Mix all ingredients together and refrigerate. This delicious salad dressing can be served with any combination of fresh vegetables so make extra. It's convenient to use and you'll always have some on hand for when company calls.

Garlic Sauce / *Skordaliá*

The traditional *Skordaliá* is a time-honored sauce. Through the generations, this recipe has been handed down consistently and is used in every Greek home today. There are two basic variations to this recipe: Thin Style, which can be tossed with vegetables or used as a marinade and Thick Style which is much more spread-able and is used with fried fish and fried vegetables.

Garlic Sauce-Thin Version/ *Skordaliá Lafriá*

Ingredients:
6 tbs. olive oil
2 tbs. vinegar
2 crushed garlic cloves
salt and pepper

Mix all the ingredients together and pour over fish or toss with vegetables. For a stronger taste, let the sauce stand for a few hours or over night before using.

Garlic Sauce -Thick Version/ *Skordaliá Pihtí*

Ingredients:
3 mashed garlic cloves
⅓ cup white vinegar
½ cup olive oil
1½ cup soggy bread (see recipe) or 1½ cup mashed potatoes
salt to taste

Mix together all the ingredients, blending until the sauce is smooth. If you find that it is too thick or prefer a thinner version, use a bit of water to get the consistency that you like.

I prefer to use the mashed potatoes because I think that it gives the sauce a much creamier texture and if I make a mistake and it's too thin, I can always mix in a bit of instant potatoes to thicken it.

Almond-Garlic Sauce / *Skordaliá Amygdálou*

A variation of the traditional *Skordaliá* sauce, the almonds give this recipe a "something special" flavor. It's easy to make and tastes like you have fussed for hours. Serve it with fried vegetables or seafood such as fish or salt cod.

Ingredients:
1½ cups soggy bread - see recipe
5 cloves garlic, mashed
1 cup olive oil
3 tbs. vinegar
1 cup ground almonds
1 cup strained yogurt - see "Concoctions for the Greek Kitchen"
salt to taste

In a mixer or food processor, combine the soggy bread with the garlic. Add the oil, vinegar and almonds and mix thoroughly until creamy. Stir in by hand the yogurt and season it with salt. Don't over mix or it may become thin and runny. Refrigerate it for at least one hour before serving or overnight for a stronger taste.

Walnut-Garlic Sauce / *Karidoskordaliá*

This easy to make recipe will give your plain veggies and seafood a gourmet touch. If you have a food processor or blender - use it. It will make the sauce much more creamier and smoother. This sauce is wonderful over plain boiled vegetables such as green beans or you can try it over seafood such as fried or baked fish.

Ingredients:
4 garlic cloves
2 cups ground walnuts
½ cup dry bread crumbs
salt and pepper to taste
1 cup olive oil
⅓ cup vinegar

In a food processor, mix together the garlic, ground walnuts, bread crumbs and salt. Stir together the olive oil and vinegar and add it to the dry ingredients a little at a time, mixing thoroughly as you go along. Keep adding the oil and vinegar until you have a smooth and creamy sauce. Cover the sauce and chill it. When you're ready to use it, the sauce may have thickened as the bread crumbs will absorb a lot of moisture. You can add more oil and vinegar or a bit of warm water to get it to pourable consistency again. Make sure you taste it too, because if you add more liquid you'll probably need a bit more salt and pepper as well.

Herb Mayonnaise / *Mayonéza me Vótana*

Mayonnaises are often used to add flavor when serving boiled meats and poultry. Poached fish are especially delicious when served with the creamy topping. Any entree you choose can take on a whole new appearance as they can be garnished by pressing capers, carrot slices, parsley and other herbs into the mayonnaise, making a simple dish very elaborate.

Ingredients:
1 egg
¼ tsp. dry mustard
⅓ tsp. salt
2 tbs. lemon juice
⅓ cup chopped fresh tarragon
⅓ cup chopped fresh thyme
1 cup olive oil

Combine all the ingredients with ½ cup of the olive oil in a blender or a food processor. Blend for 15 to 30 seconds or until the mixture is smooth. Uncover the blender and add the remaining ½ cup of olive oil in a slow, thin, steady thread while blending. Increase the speed to high and blend for a few seconds more just until it thickens. Store the mayonnaise in a covered jar in the refrigerator until you're ready to use it.

Minute Mayonnaise / *Mayonéza tis Stigmís*

This recipe is a simplified way of making a delicious home-made version of the popular mayonnaise. For gourmet variations, try stirring in a handful of chopped fresh herbs such as parsley, dill weed or rosemary to the finished sauce.

Ingredients:
1 cup water
3 tbs. corn flour
½ tsp. salt
2 tsp. lemon juice
1 tsp. yellow mustard
1 cup olive oil
2 eggs

In a sauce pan, mix together the water, corn flour, salt, lemon juice, and mustard. Place it over medium heat and stir it together until it thickens. Remove the mixture from the heat, and set it aside to cool completely. Occasionally, give it a stir so it doesn't form a skin on the surface. In the bowl of a mixer, beat the eggs on high with the oil until it's thick. Reduce the speed to low and add the cooled corn flour mixture, a little at a time, until it's all been incorporated. Refrigerate until you're ready to use it.

Greek Hummus - Chickpea and Sesame Sauce

Ingredients:
3 tbs. *tahíni**
1 tbs. olive oil
juice of ½ lemon
½ cup water
1 crushed garlic clove
salt and pepper
1 cup cooked chickpeas, ground to a paste
chopped fresh parsley

Combine the *tahíni* and the olive oil in a bowl. Mix in the lemon juice and add the water while mixing constantly. You want the mixture to turn almost milky white, so keep mixing it. If the *tahíni* curdles on you, don't worry, add a bit more water and keep mixing. Add the garlic, salt and pepper and the chickpea paste. Mix well and sprinkle with parsley. Refrigerate.

Sesame Sauce / *Sáltsa me Tahíni*

Fried foods such as zucchini or eggplant as well as fried fish take on a new flavor when served with this sauce. It can also be used as an accompaniment to *Dolmáthes* or eaten as is with some fresh, crusty bread.

Ingredients:
1 cup *tahíni**
¼ cup parsley
3 cloves garlic
juice of 2 lemons
salt to taste

Blend all the ingredients together until the mixture is smooth and has turned a whitish color. You can refrigerate the sauce for later use and to give it time for the flavors to blend, but you'll need to mix it again before serving.

*A paste made from ground sesame seeds that can be bought at a Greek or Middle Eastern specialty shop.

Greek Tahíni Dip

This great short cut recipe was given to me by a village friend. For the hummus lover, this is a very simple and fast way to make a great dip.

Ingredients:
½ cup *tahíni**
2 - 16oz. cans garbanzo beans or chickpeas
½ cup olive oil
1 tbs. white vinegar
¼ cup chopped onion
2 garlic cloves
pinch cayenne pepper
salt to taste

Drain the garbanzo beans and reserve the liquid. Put all the ingredients into a food processor and puree, adding enough of the reserved liquid until you get a smooth and creamy consistency.

*A paste made from ground sesame seeds that can be bought at a Greek or Middle Eastern specialty shop.

Cold Tomato Sauce / *Kría Sáltsa Tomátas*

This refreshing sauce is made often in the summer when tomatoes are plentiful. It's served with other summer foods such as fried vegetables and Greek meatballs.

Ingredients:
4 cups fresh chopped tomatoes
1 cup olive oil
4 cloves garlic, chopped
2 tbs. lemon juice
1 tbs. oregano
2 tbs. chopped parsley
salt and pepper

Strain the tomatoes in a sieve for two hours or better yet, over night in the refrigerator to get rid of as much moisture as possible. Mix all the ingredients together and it's ready to serve as a dip, or topping for hot or cold foods. You can also refrigerate the sauce and serve later so that the flavors will have time to blend, but you'll have to mix it again before you serve as the oil will separate from the tomatoes.

Basic Meat Sauce for Casseroles / *Sáltsa Kimás*

This meat sauce is used for casserole dishes such as *Pastítsio* and *Mousaká*. It's made simply, without many herbs and spices, so the flavors in the casserole can come out.

Ingredients:
½ cup olive oil
2 lbs. ground beef, pork or lamb
1 cup chopped onions
2 crushed garlic cloves - optional
2 cups crushed tomatoes
bay leaf
salt and pepper
chicken or vegetable stock

Heat the oil in a skillet. Brown your ground beef with the garlic and onions. Add the tomatoes, bay leaf, salt and pepper. Simmer on low heat for 40 minutes. The sauce should be juice and not dry, so if it seems too thick, add a bit of stock.

Zesty Tomato Sauce / *Sáltsa Pikántiki*

Small, whole chili peppers give this tomato sauce an added lift. Serve over spaghetti, pilaf or as a topping for fried vegetables.

Ingredients:
1 cup olive oil
1 chopped onion
1 chopped green pepper
2 cups chopped fresh tomatoes
1 cup chicken, vegetable or beef stock
1 tbs. whole black pepper
1 bay leaf
3 small dried chili peppers
salt to taste

In a sauce pot, heat the oil and fry the onions until translucent. Add the green peppers and fry until they have softened. Add the rest of the ingredients and simmer over medium heat for 40 minutes or until the sauce is thick. Before serving the sauce remove the bay leaf and the chili peppers.

Tomato-Dill Sauce / *Sáltsa me Ánitho*

This sauce can be served over pasta, pilaf or fried vegetables such as eggplant, peppers, zucchinis and potatoes.

Ingredients:
1 cup olive oil
1 cup chopped onions
2 minced garlic cloves
2 cups chopped fresh tomatoes
1 cup chicken, vegetable or beef broth
¼ cup chopped fresh dill weed
salt and pepper

Heat the olive oil in a deep skillet and fry the garlic and onions until translucent. Add the tomatoes, broth, dill and season with salt and pepper. Simmer for 40 minutes until the sauce is thick.

Tomato and Rosemary Sauce / *Sáltsa Marináti*

Steamed or boiled shellfish as well as plain fried fish are made something special when the flavor of tomato and rosemary are used to accompany them.

Ingredients:
½ cup olive oil*
4 tbs. flour
2 cups of water
¾ cup vinegar
1 ½ cups fresh pureed tomatoes
2 tbs. dry rosemary
salt and pepper to taste

Heat the oil and add the flour, whisking it for a few minutes until it turns slightly tan in color. Mix in the rest of the ingredients and cook it for 20 minutes, stirring it occasionally as it bubbles and thickens. Season the sauce with salt and pepper as to your preference. Serve immediately.

*If you are making the sauce to accompany fried fish, reserve the oil from the skillet that you fried in, including the crusty, brown bits on the bottom.

Tomato-Pepper Sauce / *Sáltsa Tomatopiperiás*

This is the Greek version of Salsa. This sauce can be used as a party dip with vegetables and cheeses or as an accompaniment for your favorite cuts of meats and roasts.

Ingredients:
1 cup olive oil
4 crushed garlic cloves
½ cup chopped onions
2 cups chopped fresh tomatoes
1 cup chopped, red roasted pepper - see "Kitchen Techniques"
2 tbs. parsley
salt and pepper
¼ tsp. dry red pepper or cayenne
pinch basil
pinch oregano
pinch ground cumin

In a sauce pan, heat the oil and add the garlic. Sauté it lightly, then add the onions and fry them until translucent. Add the tomatoes and reduce the heat. Simmer it gently until most of the liquid has evaporated. Add the rest of the ingredients and simmer the mixture until it's thick. Remove from the heat, let it cool down and then refrigerate. If you prefer a smoother version, transfer the cooked sauce to a food processor after it's been cooked and puree it.

Tomato-Onion Sauce / *Sáltsa Kremidáti*

A very easy to make, great tasting tomato sauce that can be used with pasta, pilaf or for vegetarian versions of casseroles such as *Mousaká* and *Pastítsio*.

Ingredients:
1 cup olive oil
2 cups chopped onions
4 cups fresh chopped tomatoes
1 cup vegetable stock
¼ tsp. sugar
2 bay leaves
salt and pepper to taste

Heat the oil in a sauce pan and fry the onions until translucent. Add the rest of the ingredients and reduce the heat. Simmer it all together until the sauce thickens - about 30 minutes.

Tomato-Vegetable Sauce / *Sáltsa me Hortariká*

The carrots and celery in this recipe lend a mild flavor to the tomato base. Use this sauce with any rice or pasta of your choice. It's also a great substitute for meatless versions of *Mousaká* and *Pastítsio*.

Ingredients:

2 tbs. butter
½ cup olive oil
2 large onions, chopped
1 cup dry white wine
2 cups fresh chopped tomatoes
1 large carrot, sliced thinly
1 stalk celery, chopped
2 tbs. chopped parsley
2 bay leaves
salt and pepper to taste

Heat the butter with the oil in a skillet. Fry the onions until translucent. Reduce the heat to medium and add the rest of the ingredients. Simmer for 40 minutes or until the vegetables are tender. Remove the bay leaves and put it in a blender and puree. Return the sauce to the heat and simmer until it's as thick as you prefer.

Tomato Gravy for Meatballs / *Sáltsa gia Keftédes*

Although Greek Meatballs are a wonderful summer dish by themselves, you can choose to serve them drenched in this light tomato sauce for a more elaborate meal. A side dish of pilaf or fried potatoes and a Greek Village Salad complete the menu.

Ingredients:
½ cup oil reserved after frying Greek meatballs, strained from any brown bits.
3 tbs. flour
3 cloves garlic, crushed
1 tbs. tomato paste diluted in 1½ cup beef stock
salt and pepper to taste

Heat the oil in a skillet, add the flour and whisk it together. Add the rest of the ingredients and let it all bubble together and thicken, whisking occasionally so it doesn't scorch. When the sauce has thickened, remove it from the heat and season it with salt and pepper. Gently stir in the meatballs, coating them with the sauce and serve.

Village Gravy / *Sáltsa Psitoú*

Gravy isn't just for westerners—villagers enjoy it too. Any roast can be used, but keep in mind that the herbs used in a particular recipe, such as lamb in rosemary, would give your gravy a very distinct flavor.

Ingredients:
2 tbs. butter
2 tbs. flour
1½ cups drippings from a roast
salt and pepper to taste

Melt the butter in a skillet and whisk in the flour. Stir in the drippings. Simmer it all together until it thickens. Serve hot as an accompaniment to the roast.

Mustard Sauce / *Sáltsa Moustárdas*

When poaching fish or seafood, don't discard the broth. Use it to make this fantastic sauce that turns even plain boiled fish into something special.

Ingredients:
2 tbs. butter
2 tbs. flour
2 cups broth from boiled seafood such as shrimp, lobster or fish
½ cup white wine
1 tbs. chopped parsley
2 tbs. yellow mustard
¼ cup cream
salt and pepper

Melt the butter in a skillet. Add the flour and fry it until it turns slightly tan in color. Add the broth and cook for 15 minutes. Add the wine, parsley and mustard and cook for another 15 minutes. Remove the sauce from the heat and stir in the cream. Season with salt and pepper and it's ready to serve.

Red Sauce for Fish / *Sáltsa gia Psári*

This sauce can be used over any variety of fish and seafood. For some added spiciness, stir in a spoon full of grated horseradish.

Ingredients:

½ cup olive oil
1 chopped onion
1 clove garlic
2 carrots, chopped or shredded
½ cup chopped fresh parsley
¼ cup chopped celery
1 tbs. flour
4 chopped fresh tomatoes
1 cup fish stock
juice of 1 lemon
salt and pepper to taste

In a pot heat the oil and sauté the onions with the garlic. Add the carrots, parsley and celery and cook for 5 minutes. Add the flour and stirring constantly, sauté for a few minutes longer. Add the tomatoes and the fish stock and cook over medium heat until the vegetables are very well done.

Using a blender or food processor, puree the mixture and return it to the pot and cook it down, over medium heat until it is thick. Remove from the heat and stir in the lemon juice.

Rosemary Sauce / *Sáltsa Dendrolívano*

This is a wonderfully aromatic sauce for fish or liver. You can use the same oil in which you fried in. Just pour off all but half a cup of oil and use that - even the brown, crusty bits at the bottom.

Ingredients:
½ cup olive oil
3 tbs. flour
1 cup water
2 tbs. vinegar
3 bay leaves
fresh rosemary sprigs or 1 tbsp. dried

Heat the oil or use reserved oil from frying. To the oil in the skillet add the flour and the vinegar, whisking it together. Add the water and stir so you have a creamy mixture. Add the bay leaves and the rosemary and let it all bubble together for 10 minutes. If needed, add more water to keep it smooth. When ready, pour over the fish or liver and serve.

White Sauce for Meats / *Áspri Sáltsa giá Kréata*

This sauce nicely dresses up boiled meats and poultry. It can be served on the side, in a gravy boat or poured right over de-boned chicken or slices of beef arranged on a platter.

Ingredients:
2 tbs. butter
2 tbs. flour
1 grated onion
1 cup beef or chicken stock, depending on what you serve with it
1 egg
juice of one lemon
salt and pepper to taste

Melt the butter in a skillet. Whisk in the flour and onion and fry for two minutes. Mix in the beef stock, stirring constantly so it doesn't become lumpy. Cook the mixture for 10 minutes. Remove it from the heat and set it aside to cool down. In a mixing bowl, beat the egg until frothy then add the lemon juice. Gradually mix the egg-lemon mixture to the cooked sauce, stirring the whole time so the egg doesn't cook and separate. Season with salt and pepper and serve.

Yogurt Sauce / *Sáltsa me Yiaoúrti*

Islanders often use plain yogurt as a topping on their foods. This recipe turns the basic yogurt into a wonderful sauce. Serve it with Greek meatballs, *Dolmáthes, Gemistá* or any pilaf of your choice.

Ingredients:
¼ cup olive oil
2 tbs. flour
¼ tsp. dry mustard
1 cup beef broth
1 cup strained yogurt - see "Concoctions for the Greek Kitchen"
2 tbs. chopped parsley

Heat the oil in a skillet. Add the flour and mustard and fry for 2 minutes. Add the broth and cook it together until the sauce thickens. Remove it from the heat to cool completely. In a small bowl, mix the yogurt with the parsley. Add the cooled broth mixture and fold in gently until it's incorporated. Serve immediately.

Yogurt - Spinach Sauce / *Sáltsa Yiaoúrti me Spanáki*

A variation of the traditional *Tzatzíki*, this sauce uses hot peppers to add a bit of spice. Make this up a day or two ahead of time and refrigerate it so the flavors have time to meld. It's especially good when served with toasted *pítes* or garlic bread and its also a great accompaniment to seafood and poultry dishes whether they be fried, baked, or grilled.

Ingredients:
1 lb. spinach leaves
1 cup chopped parsley
1 clove garlic, minced
1 tbs. dry pepper flakes
salt and pepper to taste
3 cups strained yogurt - see "Concoctions for the Greek Kitchen"
toasted pine nuts - optional garnish

Wash and rinse the spinach leaves but don't drain them. Coarsely chop them up and put them into a pot. Set it over high heat and cover. Cook the leaves until they are well wilted - about 3 or 4 minutes, shaking the pot occasionally. Don't add any more water. Since you haven't drained the leaves, there should be enough moisture in the pot to cook them sufficiently.

Remove the spinach to a strainer and let it drain and cool down. Press the leaves against the side of the strainer to release as much water as possible. Chop the cooked spinach into small pieces.

Put the spinach in a mixing bowl along with the parsley, garlic and peppers and season with salt. Mix it all together thoroughly. Gently fold in the yogurt, stirring only until it's been incorporated. Refrigerate the mixture for a few hours or overnight. When ready to serve, spoon the sauce onto a small appetizer platter and sprinkle with the toasted pine nuts or chopped parsley.

Yogurt and Mint Sauce / *Taratoúri*

This Cypriot recipe makes a sauce very much like *Tzatzíki*, but without the worry of garlic breath. The flavors of mint and yogurt make a refreshing combination that can be served as a bread spread or with all kinds of roasts and vegetables. It's also delicious in píta sandwiches such as *Souvláki* or *Gýro*.

Ingredients:
1 cucumber, grated
3 tbs. dried spearmint
3 tbs. olive oil
1 tbs. vinegar
salt and pepper
3 cups strained, yogurt - see "Concoctions for the Greek Kitchen"

Set the cucumber in a sieve and drain it over night.
Put the cucumber, spearmint, oil, and vinegar in a bowl. Season it with salt and pepper and mix it all together. Lastly, fold in the yogurt and gently stir it together until it's all mixed. Don't over mix it or the yogurt will get watery. Refrigerate the sauce for at least one hour. It keeps well, so you can make extra and store it in a covered container for a week.

Yogurt and Pimento Sauce / *Sáltsa Yiaoúrti me Páprika*

Use this delicious sauce as an accompaniment for roasts or barbeques. It's great as a dip with fresh vegetables or as a snack with some fresh bread.

Ingredients:
3 tbs. olive oil
1 cup chopped spring onions
1 cup chopped pimento
2 cups strained yogurt - see "Concoctions for the Greek Kitchen"
½ tsp. hot paprika
salt and pepper to taste
chopped parsley - optional

Heat the oil in a skillet. Sauté the onions and pimento until they are softened and set them aside to cool down completely. Stir together the yogurt, paprika and parsley - if you're using it, in a small bowl. Add the cooled onion mixture and season with salt and pepper. Refrigerate for 3 hours or more before use.

Batter / *Kourkoúti*

Some recipes call for the use of a batter when frying. Use your choice of the following recipes to customize your meals.

Simple Batter Ingredients:
1 cup flour
¾ cups warm water
1 beaten egg
1 tbs. olive oil
1 tsp. salt
pepper to taste

Whisk together all the ingredients and use it for your favorite recipes.

Spicy Batter Ingredients:
1 cup flour
¾ cups warm water
1 beaten egg
dash oregano
dash thyme
dash paprika
dash red pepper
dash garlic powder - optional
salt and pepper

Use this batter with any vegetable or meat recipe that calls for it. The herbs give it a savory taste that is great when accompanied by a tomato sauce.

For more great Sauces and Dressings, see these recipes in other sections:

Tzatzíki
Feta and Hot Pepper Dip / *Ktipití - Tirokauterí - Kopanistí*
Tuna Sauce / *Sáltsa Tóno*
Mussels and Feta in Tomato Sauce / *Sáltsa Mídia me Féta*
Lenten Spaghetti / *Makarónia Nistísima*
Macedonian *Taratór* / *Saláta Taratór*

Marinades
Marinádes

Spicy Fish Marinade / *Pikántiki Marináda gia Psári*

This wonderfully spicy marinade can be used with any whole fish or fillet of your preference.

Ingredients:
½ tbs. dry pepper flakes
2 cloves crushed garlic
1 tsp. dry spearmint
3 tbs. fresh lemon juice
5 tbs. olive oil
salt to taste

Mix together the marinade ingredients. Cover the fish of your choice in the marinade and refrigerate it for at least one hour for the flavors to blend. Use the marinade to baste the fish as it bakes or grills over charcoal.

Marinade for Pork or Lamb Chops

Ingredients:
2 cups olive oil
1 cup fresh lemon juice
1 tsp. salt
1 tsp. black pepper
2 tsp. ground cumin
2 crushed garlic cloves
1 tbs. minced fresh parsley

Mix all the ingredients together. In a pan or bowl, arrange the meat cuts of your choice. Pour the marinade over the meat and cover with cling wrap. Let it set at room temperature for three hours or refrigerate over night.

Drain the meat from the marinade, reserving the liquids. Cook the meat using your preference by frying, baking, broiling, or charcoal grilling. Baste the meat with the reserved marinade, using a pastry brush or see the Kitchen Techniques section for the details on making an herbal brush that can be used to add more flavor.

Herbal Marinade for Poultry and Roasts

Ingredients:
2 cups olive oil
1 cup fresh lemon juice
3 cloves crushed garlic
¼ cup chopped parsley
¼ cup chopped dill weed
1 tbs. grated lemon rind
1 tbs. chopped fresh basil
1 tbs. oregano
1 tbs. thyme
1 tbs. paprika
1 tsp. salt
1 tsp. black pepper
½ tsp. dry spearmint

Mix together all the ingredients. Place the meat in a pan and cover it with the marinade. Wrap it with cling film. Let it set at room temperature for three hours or refrigerated overnight. Drain the meat from the marinade, reserving the liquid. Broil or bake the meat, using the reserved marinade to baste it.

Lemon Marinade for Poultry

Ingredients:
1 cup olive oil
1 cup fresh lemon juice
1 tsp. salt
1 tsp. black pepper
3 tbs. oregano
5 crushed garlic cloves

Mix together the ingredients. Arrange the poultry in a bowl and cover with the marinade. Wrap it with cling film and let it set at room temperature for three hours or refrigerated over night. Drain the meat from the marinade, reserving the liquid. Roast the meat as per your recipe directions, using the reserved marinade to baste it.

Marinade for Beef Cuts

Ingredients:
2 cups olive oil
1 cup fresh squeezed lemon juice
3 crushed garlic cloves
1 tsp. salt
1 tsp. black pepper
1 tsp. oregano
1 tsp. ground cumin
1 tsp. thyme
1 tsp. paprika - optional
1 tbs. chopped fresh parsley - optional

> **Menu Idea**
> Grilled Marinated Steak
> Tomato Roasted Potatoes
> Fried Pumpkin
> Greek Village Salad
> Yogurt and Pimento Sauce
> Feta Cheese
> Olives
> Fresh Bread

Mix all the ingredients together. Place the meat in a pan and cover it with the marinade. Wrap it with cling film. Let it set at room temperature for three hours or refrigerated overnight. Drain the meat from the marinade, reserving the liquid. Grill, Broil or bake the meat, using the reserved marinade to baste it.

Basting Marinade for Game and Lamb

Ingredients:
1 cup olive oil
1 cup butter at room temperature
1 tbs. chopped rosemary
1 tbs. cumin
1 tbs. oregano
1 crushed garlic clove - optional
1 tbs. chopped fresh parsley - optional
Lemon or Herbal Brush - see "Kitchen Techniques"

Mix all the marinade ingredients together. Use it to baste lamb and game meats that are roasting over a barbeque or in the oven. The subtle flavors of the marinade will help to reduce the gamy or wild taste of the meats.

Basting Marinade for Goat or Kid Chops

Ingredients:
1 cup olive oil
1 cup butter at room temperature
1 tsp. salt
1 tsp. black pepper
1 tsp. cumin
2 tbs. grated parmesan cheese
Lemon Brush - see "Kitchen Techniques"

Mix together the marinade ingredients. Use the lemon brush to smooth it over the delicate chops as they are broiling or roasting.

Marinade for Oven Roasted Lamb

Ingredients:
1 cup olive oil
⅓ cup fresh lemon juice
2 crushed garlic cloves
½ tsp. salt
½ tsp. black pepper
½ tsp. oregano
1 tbs. chopped rosemary
1 tbs. chopped parsley

Mix all the ingredients together. Place your cut of meat in a bowl or pan and cover with the marinade. Wrap it with cling film and let it set at room temperature for three hours or refrigerated over night.
Drain the meat from the marinade, reserving the liquid. Roast the meat as per your recipe directions, using the reserved marinade to baste it. An herbal or lemon brush can be used to add more flavor. See the Kitchen Techniques section for details on how to make this great home accessory.

More great marinade ideas can be found in the following recipes and sections:

Charcoal Grilled Lamb Chops / *Arní sta Kárvouna*
Easter Lamb on a Spit / *Arní Soúvlas*
Pit Roasted Goat / *Katsikáki* or *Rífi Soúvlas*
Lamb *Kléftiko* - Traditional / *Arní Kléftiko Paradosiakó*
Chicken *Lemonáto* / *Kotópoulo Lemonáto*
Marinated Chicken / *Kotópoulo Marináda*
The Art of *Souvláki* Making

Appetizers
Mezédes

Appetizers - *Mezédes*

An appetizer or *mezé* means much more to a Greek than just the beginning of a great meal. *Mezédes* very often are the meal itself and a wonderful one at that. Because of the variety that is in a *mezé* dinner, there are tastes to please everyone. Offerings of plain boiled greens to seafood to the richest of meat cuts can be served. It's not a meal to be rushed through. Sip the ouzo, retsina or house wine slowly because depending on how good the conversation of your dinner companions, a *mezé* dinner can last for hours.

There is no mystery to putting together a *mezé* dinner or ouzo party. The simple place setting consists of an Ouzo or wine glass, an appetizer plate, a fork and a knife. Dishes of *mezédes* are placed in the center of the table where anyone can reach for a forkful of this or a forkful of that, very much like a sit down buffet. Personally, I place small portions of everything on my appetizer plate and eat from there, but I do know of people that can go through hours of eating *mezédes* and never get their plate dirty because they eat right off the serving dishes. Other than a catcher for a few fallen bread crumbs, they use their plate only as a fork rest.

Traditionally, *mezédes* are eaten to accompany an alcohol such as ouzo, retsina, or home-made wine. They help absorb the alcohol so you can keep your wits as well as coat your stomach. When our grandfathers would take a walk to the village café to see their friends and have a drink, it always included a *mezé* ... "for the stomach." Nothing lavish, some bread, olives, salted sardines and cheese are good companions to drinking. Or, if he was lucky enough to have a fresh catch of fish or game, the café owner would prepare it and it was enjoyed along with his friends.

Mezédes are meant to be nibbled at while you're sipping the libation of your choice for as long as you are drinking. This can mean hours and hours so be prepared and don't rush your guests. The first time that I had friends over for drinking and *mezédes*, I tried to clear away the plates after two hours of eating but ended up very embarrassed because they weren't finished. In fact, as I remember, it wasn't until four hours later that I was given the green light to clear away the table. To avoid the same mistake that I made, wait to clean up until your guests leave the table or go home. As a note, although *mezédes* are meant to be served in small quantities, do make up more of a favorite dish, especially if you know that your guests enjoy it.

I've often been caught off guard by friends that have stopped by for a few drinks and have had nothing prepared. These situations are easily handled and relatively fast and stress free if you keep your thinking clear. Bread is a must for Greeks so I always have a loaf frozen in the freezer. I place it in the microwave on defrost setting for a few minutes while I'm getting the rest of the goodies ready.

Then, I basically empty out the refrigerator and the pantry. Offer variety, lots of dishes of anything that you have on hand... olives, pickles and pickled veggies, canned or salted sardines, canned tuna with a squeeze of lemon juice, cut up fresh vegetables such as tomato wedges, whole spring onions, cauliflower, cucumber, assorted cheeses, sliced hardboiled eggs, sliced lunch meats and etc. Leftovers from another meal make a good *mezé*, so serve them too. Following this advice, you'll have a table full of *mezédes* that would make your grandmother proud and you'll still have the time and energy to enjoy a drink or two yourself.

The History of the *Mezé*

Mezédes were not a planned happening, they just sort of came to be. Our grandmothers did not sit down and try to think up new recipes to serve as appetizers because they thought that a meal needed an extra course nor did they struggle with the thought of what to serve with a good batch of Retsína wine. That was a luxury that was not available to them. Instead, they tried to do the best with what was available from their homes, fields and from the mountains and seas. They were very frugal when it came to cooking and wasted nothing in their effort to provide good nutritious food to raise their families on.

Imagine the days of less abundance when our grandmothers, perhaps while herding the goats, would find a handful of fresh mushrooms and dandelion greens growing near by. Alone as a side dish, there would not be enough for everyone—especially for the large families of our ancestors, but they would be prepared and served at the table anyway. Accompanying a main course made from household staples such as rice or beans would be these "found" edibles, as well as a salad of some sort depending on the season, bread, olives, pickled vegetables, and feta cheese.

When available, there was a lot of variety but the quantities of these dishes were limited to only a forkful or two for each person at the table. And remember that these were times of hardship so the main course wasn't a whole lot either. Looking at each dish individually, the servings would be very sparse, but when they were served as a group, they were more than enough for a growing family.

Since our grandmothers didn't have a "Frigid-air" in their home, leftovers couldn't be kept for more than maybe a day or so. When cooking, they estimated the appetites of the family rather precisely. If something was leftover, it would be added as a *mezé* to the following meal even though it may have been no more than a third of a serving. A forkful of leftovers for each family member and it would get eaten. Even today, this thinking still exists and you'll find that many households serve their meals in the same fashion. You'll also find that many of the entrees that we consider main course dishes still take their place amongst the *mezédes* as well, reminiscent of days gone by.

Feta & Hot Pepper Dip / *Ktipití, Tirokauterí,* or *Kopanistí*

An easy substitution for the popular Greek cheese can be made at home using this little known secret. This is a great party dip that can be used with any array of fresh vegetables or just as a spread on saltines. The recipe is known by many names but has the same great taste. Mind you, this is spicy!

Ingredients:
1 cup crumbled feta cheese
¼ cup finely chopped pepperoncini
½ tbs. ground oregano
water or brine from the pepperoncini, depending on how hot you want it.

Just mix all of this together for a fantastic dip. Use the water sparingly, just enough to get the right consistency for spreading.

Tzatzíki

This fantastic appetizer is a great accompaniment with roast meats, salads, entrees, vegetable dishes, or just as a bread spread. It's the secret ingredient of the infamous *Gýro*.

Ingredients:
1½ cups strained yogurt - see "Concoctions for the Greek Kitchen"
1 tsp. salt
2 medium sized cucumbers, peeled and shredded
3 tbs. olive oil
4 to 6 crushed garlic cloves, depending on how strong you want the taste
1 tbs. vinegar

Put the cucumber in a strainer and sprinkle with the salt. Using your hands, squeeze the cucumber, trying to release as much liquid as possible. In a separate bowl, mix the crushed garlic with the oil and vinegar. Add the drained cucumber and mix. Add in the yogurt, folding it in carefully. Don't stir vigorously, or you will make it watery. Chill for a few hours or overnight to meld the flavors. Enjoy !!

Tarama (Roe) Salad / *Taramosaláta*

This is a popular appetizer in Greece and it is served quite often during the Lent season with toasted pita bread. You can use your mixer for this instead of using a spoon. Some people also prefer to use fresh boiled potatoes that have been mashed instead of the bread. Try it both ways and see what you like.

Ingredients:
½ jar (4oz.) *Taramá* or Mullet Roe - available at Greek Specialty Shops
1½ cups fresh mashed potatoes or 1½ cups soggy bread - see recipe
1 tsp. grated onion -optional
¼ cup water
juice of 1 lemon
½ cup olive oil

Put the *Taramá* in a bowl and crush the little eggs with the back of a spoon. Slowly mix in the water and add the pieces of bread while continuously crushing and mixing. Alternately add small amounts of oil and lemon, mixing until it has all been incorporated and stir in the onion. The *Taramosaláta* should be smooth and salmon pink in color.

Fish Roe Fritters / *Taramokeftédes*

Ingredients:
1 cup thinly sliced green onions
½ cup *Taramá* or Mullet Roe - available at Greek Specialty Shops
¼ cup chopped dill weed
1 tbs. dry spearmint
2 cups soggy bread, well drained - see recipe
salt and pepper
olive oil for frying
flour

Heat enough olive oil in a skillet to cover the bottom. Add the onions and dill weed and sauté them until the onions are soft. Put the soggy bread into a bowl and add the onion mixture. Mix in the mint, roe, and season with salt and pepper. Form the mixture into small balls and roll them in flour. Heat oil in a skillet and fry the balls until they are golden on each side.

Charcoal Grilled Eel / *Souvlomoutariá*

Ingredients:
1 large fresh or salt water eel

Marinade:
1 cup olive oil
½ cup vinegar
2 bay leafs
1 tbs. oregano
salt and pepper

See the directions for cleaning and preparing eel in the Kitchen Techniques section. Slice the cleaned eel into 1-inch thick pieces and put them into a bowl. Mix together the marinade ingredients and pour it over the eel. Cover it and refrigerate over night.

Drain the eel slices from the marinade, reserving the liquid. Place the eel on a grill over hot charcoals. Baste it with the marinade as it cooks. Use an Herbal Basting Brush for added flavor.

Eel with Eggs and Vinegar / *Héli me Avgá ke Xídi*

Considered a delicacy, this *mezé* can be made with fresh or salt water eels.

Ingredients:
one small eel, about 2 lbs., cleaned - see "Kitchen Techniques"
salt and pepper
olive oil
3 bay leaves
2 eggs
¼ cup vinegar

> *Mezé* **Menu Idea**
> Eel with Eggs and Vinegar
> Peppers Stuffed with Feta
> Greek Village Salad
> Boiled Green Beans
> Lemon Oil Dressing
> Pickled Vegetables
> Fresh Green Onions
> Lemon Wedges
> Olives
> Fresh Bread

Preheat your oven to 350°F. Partially slice through the body of the eel at 2 inch intervals, but without severing the slices completely as you want the eel slices to fan out. Sprinkle the flesh with a little salt and pepper. If the eel you are using is from the sea, use the salt sparingly until it's cooked and you can taste it first.

Arrange the eel in a coil in a small baking pan or casserole dish that's just the right size to fit it. Add the bay leaves and drizzle olive oil over it. Don't use too much as eel is an oily fish to begin with. Bake for 30 minutes or until done. Use a fork to test the meat. It should be flaky and all white in color with no traces of translucent flesh.

Beat the eggs with vinegar and pour it over the eel. Return it to the oven and bake it until the eggs have set.

Fried Mussels / *Mídia Tiganitá*

A great *mezé* to be served with a selection of hot and cold vegetables and of course... chilled ouzo. I have also seen this dish made by just rolling the mussels in flour that has a little salt and pepper added. It makes the mussels crunchier—try it both ways and see what you like.

Ingredients:
3 lbs. fresh mussels, shelled - see "Kitchen Techniques"
oil for frying
chopped parsley
lemon wedges

Batter:

1 cup milk
1 egg, beaten
1 tbs. olive oil
flour
salt and pepper

Make your batter by mixing the milk, egg, olive oil, salt and pepper and enough flour to make it smooth. Heat an inch of oil in a deep skillet. Dip the mussels one by one into the batter and gently drop them into the hot oil to fry. Serve them with a sprinkling of parsley and lemon wedges on the side.

Charcoal Grilled Octopus / *Htapódi sta Kárvouna*

A very common appetizer, you will find this dish offered in most restaurants as well in many homes especially when chilled ouzo is served. It is delicious just plain grilled and served with a good squeeze of lemon juice. Try it both ways and see what you like.

Ingredients:
1 octopus (2 to 4 lbs.), cleaned - see "Kitchen Techniques"
olive oil
vinegar
pepper
oregano

If you are lucky enough to find fresh octopus at the fish market, ask the fish monger to clean it for you. For all of those who don't live near warm seas, frozen octopus works just as well in this recipe.

Rinse the cleaned octopus under cold running water and set it into a pot without draining off the water. Cover the pot tightly and set on medium heat. You will steam the octopus in its liquid until it has all been absorbed.

Remove the steamed octopus from the pot and rinse again under cold water and set aside to drain. Cut it up into 3 or 4 pieces and spread olive oil over them. Set the pieces on a grill over hot coals and cook it. Careful, you want the heat to be medium hot or else you will char the meat too much.

To serve, chop up the octopus into bite size pieces. Add olive oil, vinegar, a good sprinkle of oregano and pepper to taste. Salt is not used because octopus tends to be salty from the sea. If you do choose to use it, do so very sparingly.

Sun Dried Octopus in Garlic Sauce / *Htapódi Xiró Skordaliá*

From the Ionian island of Cephalonia, this recipe is an easy and simple way to enjoy this delicacy.

Ingredients:
1 lb. dried octopus-see recipe
Garlic Sauce - thin version - see recipe

Put the octopus in just enough water to cover it and let it soak over night. The next day, put the octopus and the same soaking liquid in a pot and bring it to a simmer. Cover the pot and cook the octopus until it's tender and there is little liquid left. Cut it into bite sized pieces and arrange it on a platter. Cover it with garlic sauce and serve.

Octopus in Wine / *Htapódi Krasáto*

Traditionally this is served as a *mezé* or appetizer dish. Make sure you have lots of other *mezédes* and a chilled bottle of ouzo on hand.

Ingredients:
1 octopus (2 to 4 lbs.), cleaned - see "Kitchen Techniques"
2 bay leaves
1 bottle dry red wine - 750ml.
olive oil
2 tbs. black pepper corns

    If you are lucky enough to find fresh octopus at the fish market, ask the fish monger to clean it for you. For all of those who don't live near warm seas, frozen octopus works just as well in this recipe.
    Cut the cleaned octopus into one inch pieces. Heat the wine in a deep pot with all the spices. Bring to a boil and add the octopus pieces. Reduce the heat and simmer covered until the meat is tender - about 1½ hours.
    Strain the meat and spices from the wine and let cool. Put it into a large jar and cover with olive oil. This can be kept in the refrigerator for a few days. To serve, spoon out some of the meat and oil, and sprinkle with vinegar.

Grilled Sun Dried Fish / *Psária Heliókafta*

Ingredients:
fish such as large mackerel or bogue
oregano
salt and pepper
olive oil

Scale and clean the fish. If you need help in doing this, see the "Kitchen Techniques" section for "The Do's and Don'ts of Fish Preparation."

Slice the fish carefully from the stomach cavity so you can remove the spine and as many bones as possible but don't cut it into two pieces. You want to form a pocket. Sprinkle the insides with oregano, salt and pepper and brush them with oil. Tie the fish from their tails with a piece of butchers cord and hang them outside to dry, using tooth picks to keep the pockets open . Cover the fish with a piece of tulle to keep insects away and let them dry for 12 to 24 hours.

When they are ready, remove the toothpicks and cord. Brush the fish with more olive oil and sprinkle them with more spices. Cook the fish over medium heat charcoals. Serve with fresh lemon wedges.

Salt Cod with Garlic Sauce / *Bakaliéros Skordaliá*

This is another village favorite. It dates back to days of old when refrigeration was non-existent and salt was used as a preservative. Though we live in modern times, it is still enjoyed quite often and you will find it on any Greek restaurant menu. When serving this dish, make sure that everyone at least tastes the *Skordaliá* sauce or else they'll have to put up with the diners' garlic breath.

Ingredients:
1 lb. salt cod
1 cup flour
1 cup water or beer
1 egg
pinch salt
pepper
olive oil
Garlic Sauce - thick version - see recipe

> **Menu Idea**
> Salt Cod with Garlic Sauce
> Fried Vegetables
> Spinach Pie
> Greek Village Salad
> Lemon Wedges
> Feta Cheese
> Olives
> Fresh Bread

Cut the cod into pieces about 2 inches square. Place it in a bowl of water and let it set refrigerated at least overnight, changing the water a couple of times to get rid of the salt. For a less salty version, two nights are better.

Wash the cod under running water. Remove any loose bones or skin and set it in a strainer to drain. In a bowl, mix the flour, water, egg, pepper and just a pinch of salt until it is a smooth batter.

Heat an inch of oil in a large skillet. Dip the cod pieces into the batter and fry on both sides until they are golden brown. Make the garlic sauce and serve as an accompaniment.

Salt Cod Croquettes / *Bakaliéros Krokétes*

Very much like its sister version, this recipe blends the tastes of Salt Cod with the traditional Garlic Sauce. The difference is that these cod balls are bone and skin free, making them much easier and less messier to enjoy.

Ingredients:
1 lb. salt cod
2 cups mashed potatoes
3 eggs
1 tbs. olive oil
¼ cup butter
1 cup fine bread crumbs
salt and pepper
oil for frying

Garlic Sauce - thick version - see recipe

Place the salt cod in a bowl with enough water to cover it. Let it soak for 24 hours, changing the water 2 or 3 times. Drain the salt cod and boil it in clean water for 5 minutes. Strain it and let it cool enough so you can handle it. Remove the skin and bones so you have very clean flesh. Chop the cod into small pieces.

In a bowl, mix together the salt cod, mashed potatoes, two egg yolks, olive oil and butter. Season it with salt and pepper. Form the mixture into small pancakes.

In a separate bowl, beat the two egg whites with the remaining egg. Dip each pancake into the egg mixture and then roll it in the bread crumbs. Fry them in hot oil until golden brown on each side.

"Singing" Sardines / *Sardéla pou Keladái*

The island of *Kíthira* is known in Greek mythology as the birth place of Aphrodite, the goddess of love, so it's no wonder that this local recipe has such a romantic name. The packages of foil and wax paper are referred to as cages for the sardines. As the fish are cooking slowly in hot ashes, they make a humming and crackling noise, so they are said to sing in their cages.

Ingredients:
2 lbs. fresh sardines
3 tbs. olive oil
1 tbs. salt
1 tbs. pepper
1 tbs. lemon juice
fresh lemon slices

Scale and clean the sardines. If you need help in doing this, see the "Kitchen Techniques" section for "The Do's and Don'ts of Fish Preparation."

Toss them with all the ingredients. Cut a piece of wax paper and place two sardines, side by side in the center. Add a slice or two of lemon and wrap it up, sealing the edges so it's a parcel. Wrap the whole thing up in aluminum foil. Continue until you've prepared all the sardines. Place the foil wrapped parcels into hot ashes and let the sardines cook slowly for 15 to 30 minutes.

Carefully unwrap the foil and discard it. Remove the ash free wax paper while holding it over a platter so any hot juices will be caught. Serve with fresh lemon wedges.

Fried Whitebait / *Marídes Tiganités*

This is what my best friend affectionately calls "Greek French Fries." The little fish are left whole and fried with their heads, fins and innards. It may sound strange, but I have to admit that these are really tasty. And I have also found that the smaller the whitebait, the better because they get really crispy.

Ingredients:
2 lbs. small to medium sized whitebait
olive oil for frying
1 cup flour
lemons
salt and pepper

Wash the whitebait and let them drain. In a deep skillet, heat the oil - it has to get really hot. Put the flour in a bowl and season with some salt and pepper. Coat the whitebait with flour, shake them a little to remove any excess and fry. When they brown, they're ready. Serve them with lemon juice squeezed over them. To eat them, just pop the whole thing in your mouth.

Shrimp Cocktail - Greek Style / *Garídes me Kókkini Sáltsa*

If you have Old Bay™ seafood seasoning, add just a dash of it to give the sauce and shrimp some kick. Also, as a garnish, you can get creative with the shrimp heads, whiskers and all, as few people have ever seen them. This is a great make ahead party dish. Serve saltines or bread rounds on the side for your guests to help themselves to the excellent sauce.

Ingredients:
3 lbs. shrimp, with shells on and preferably with the heads
1 cup olive oil
4 tbs. flour
4 cups of liquid from the shrimp
1 cup tomato juice (V8™ can be substituted)
¼ cup red wine vinegar
3 cloves garlic, crushed
1 tbs. fresh rosemary, chopped finely
red cayenne pepper
salt

In a large pot, boil the shrimp with enough water to cover them. Cook them for 5 to 8 minutes then remove them and set aside to cool. Remember that you want to reserve 4 cups of this liquid for the sauce, so if it seems like too much, just keep boiling the water to reduce it. When you have your 4 cups of shrimp juice, pour it through a strainer and set it aside.

Making the sauce: Have all your ingredients measured and handy, as you will have to move quickly. In a medium saucepan, heat the oil and add the flour, stirring constantly to make a roux. You want it to turn slightly golden but not burn. Pour in the shrimp juice, whisking continuously as the flour will make it into a thick custard in no time. Add the vinegar, tomato juice, garlic, rosemary, pepper and salt. Keep whisking as the mixture cooks and thickens. Remove from heat.

Peel your shrimp and arrange them in a serving dish. Spoon the sauce over them and let them cool. The shrimps will absorb the flavor of the sauce. This dish is served cold, so it can be made ahead of time and refrigerated overnight.

Shrimp in Wine / *Garídes Krasátes*

This is a very easy recipe for the basic steamed shrimp but with a touch of Greek zing added. Prawns, mussels or any kind of shell fish can be easily substituted.

Ingredients:
2 lbs. shrimp with their shells
2 minced garlic cloves
1 onion, cut into wedges
¼ cup chopped celery
2 tbs. chopped parsley
1 cup dry white wine
½ cup olive oil
1 bay leaf
sprig of fresh rosemary or 1 tsp. dry
salt and pepper

Rinse the shrimp under cold running water and set them in a colander to drain. In a large sauce pan add everything but the shrimp and bring it to a boil over medium heat. Cook the mixture for one minute then add the shrimp. Toss the shrimp with the liquid then cover the pot. Let it boil a minute or two, then remove the cover, toss the shrimp once more and then cover again. Continue until the shrimp have turned pink and are done.

Remove the pot from the heat and let it all cool down. Using a slotted spoon, put the shrimp into a deep container and cover them with the juice. Let the shrimp cool down slightly before removing them from the juice to serve.

If you have time, let the cooked shrimp refrigerate in the marinade over night, soaking up the flavors.

Squid Rings / *Kalámari Tiganitó*

To some people, the thought of eating squid is a complete turn off. Many of my friends refer to it as "eating bait." And though I never thought that I would eat the things myself, I do have to admit that this is a delicious seafood. This dish is served with a Greek Village Salad, fried potatoes, and lots of *Tzatzíki*.

You can purchase frozen squid that has already been cleaned and cut up into rings. If you are using fresh squid, you must clean them before you can use them in this recipe. See the Kitchen Techniques section for details and tips on how to do this yourself.

Ingredients:
2 lbs. squid cut into rings
salt and pepper
1 cup flour
oil for frying

> *Mezé* **Menu Idea**
> Squid Rings
> Greek Meatballs
> *Tzatiki*
> Greek Village Salad
> Lima Bean Salad
> Fresh Fried Potatoes
> Lemon Wedges
> Feta Cheese
> Olives
> Fresh Bread

Heat an inch of oil in a deep skillet. In a shallow dish, mix flour with some salt and pepper—not too much salt as the squid is already salty from the sea. Toss the squid pieces with the flour mixture, and tap lightly to remove any excess. Gently drop into the heated oil, and fry until golden brown. It doesn't take long. Remove and drain on paper towels. Serve it with fresh lemon wedges.

Squid in Spicy Batter / *Kalamári Tiganitó Pikántiko*

Fried squid is a specialty that is served all through the Greek Islands. This recipe makes for a spicier version that is great as an ouzo party *mezé*.

Ingredients:
1 lb. squid, cleaned and cut into rings - use the legs too
4 tbs. corn meal
4 tbs. bread crumbs
3 tbs. ground almonds
3 tbs. hot pepper flakes
1½ tsp. oregano
oil for frying
2 eggs
2 tbs. milk

Mix together the corn meal, bread crumbs, almonds, pepper flakes, oregano and salt. Add the squid and toss with the mixture so they get floured completely.

In a deep skillet, heat one inch of oil. Beat together the eggs and the milk. Dip the floured rings into the egg mixture and drop them into the hot oil. Make sure that you've heated the oil enough and the rings sizzle when they hit the oil or else you'll get soggy squid. Fry until golden brown. Remove the rings to paper towels to drain and then serve with fresh lemon wedges.

Cheese Saghanaki / *Tirí Saghanáki*

Ingredients:
1 lb. Greek *kaséri* cheese
butter for frying
2 eggs, beaten
flour

Cut the *kaséri* into slices about ½ inch thick. Dip each slice into the egg then coat them with flour. Fry the cheese in the butter until golden brown on each side. Serve it hot with a squeeze of lemon juice.

Greek Meat Balls / *Keftédes*

Greek meatballs, fried potatoes and a Greek Village Salad are a traditional summer meal. Have lots of fresh bread on hand and a chilled bottle of wine.

Ingredients:
2 lbs. ground beef or a mixture using pork or lamb as to your preference.
1 cup dry bread crumbs
2 cups fresh crushed tomatoes
1 large onion, minced
¼ cup parsley, finely chopped
1 tsp. dried mint
1 egg
3 tbs. grated parmesan or Greek *kefalotíri*
1 tbs. vinegar
salt and pepper
oil for frying
flour for rolling

> *Mezé* **Menu Idea**
> Greek Meatballs
> Tomato Gravy
> Plain Buttered Rice
> Greek Village Salad
> Fresh Fried Potatoes
> *Tzatiki*
> Grated Cheese
> Feta Cheese
> Olives
> Fresh Bread

Mix all the ingredients together. Using your hands, form the mixture into one inch balls. Heat ½ inch of oil in a skillet. Roll the balls into the flour to coat and gently drop them into the hot oil. Fry until brown on both sides. Easy!!

Tomato Balls / *Tomatokeftédes*

A meatless version of Greek meatballs, this appetizer is very easy to make and can be served hot or cold. When accompanied with a green salad and *Tzatziki*, they make a great meal especially for the meatless religious fasting days.

Ingredients:
2 cups pureed fresh tomatoes
2 cups chopped fresh tomatoes
2 zucchinis, shredded
2 onions, minced
salt and pepper
1 tbs. dried mint
½ cup grated Greek *kefalotíri* or parmesan
2 eggs, beaten
flour
olive oil

In a large bowl, mix the veggies together with the spices, the cheese and the eggs. Add enough flour to make it into a stiff mixture, like a thick cake batter. Heat olive oil in a skillet and drop the mixture by teaspoonfuls into the hot oil. Fry them gently on one side then the other.

Stuffed Cucumbers / *Agourákia Gemistá*

These simple appetizers are a great addition to any *mezé* table.

Ingredients:
4 small cucumbers, peeled
1 cup crumbled feta cheese
5 tbs. olive oil
1 tbs. dry spearmint
juice of 1 lemon
black pepper

Slice the cucumbers in half and using a knife, spoon, or apple corer remove the seeds. The cucumber halves should resemble a celery rib. Cut the cucumber shells so they are 3 to 4 inches longs.
In a small bowl, mash together the remaining ingredients and season with black pepper. Spoon the mixture into the cucumber shells and arrange them on a platter.

Fried Stuffed Olives / *Tiganités Gemistés Eliés*

Ingredients:
½ lb. large green pitted olives
½ cup minced onion
¼ cup minced parsley
pepper
oil for frying
flour
1 egg, beaten
fine bread crumbs

In a small bowl mix together the onion and parsley and season it with pepper. Mix in a little bit of olive oil so you get a paste. Using a small spoon or paring knife, stuff each olive with the mixture. A pastry bag also works. Heat an inch of oil in a skillet. Roll the stuffed olives in flour, dip them into the egg and then roll them in the bread crumbs. Fry them in the hot oil until they are golden. Remove them to paper towels to drain and serve.

Peppers Stuffed with Feta / *Piperiés me Féta Tiganités*

Ingredients:
8 medium sized green peppers
1 cup crumbled feta cheese
¼ cup chopped parsley
2 tbs. butter
pepper
oil for frying
vinegar - optional

Slice each pepper down one side and remove the seeds. Rinse the pepper inside and out and set it aside to drain. In a small bowl, mix together the feta, parsley and butter and season it with pepper. Stuff each green pepper with the mixture. Heat a half inch of oil in a skillet and fry the peppers on each side, taking care that the stuffing doesn't come out. Remove them to a serving platter and sprinkle them with vinegar if you wish.

Ptolemies' Tomatoes / *Tomátes tis Ptolemaídas*

Near the northern border of Greece, between *Kozáni* and *Flórina*, is the village of *Ptolemaídas*. Its name is given in honor of Alexander the Great's general, Ptoleméous the First, who went on to become the first of a long line of Greek kings that ruled Ancient Egypt.

Ingredients:
2 lbs. fresh ripe tomatoes
5 crushed garlic cloves
1 cup finely chopped parsley
½ cup olive oil
salt and pepper
½ cup vegetable stock

Wash the tomatoes to get rid of any dust and pesticides. Drain them and pat them dry with paper towels. Cut them in half and arrange them cut side up in a skillet. In a small bowl, mix the parsley and garlic with just enough olive oil so it becomes a paste. Sprinkle the tomato halves with salt and pepper and spread the parsley mixture over the top. Pour the vegetable stock into the bottom of the skillet along with the remaining olive oil. Simmer the tomato halves, partially covered for 30 to 40 minutes. Remove the lid and let all the liquid evaporate so you are left with the oil.

Batter Fried Broccoli & Cauliflower / *Tiganitó Mbrókolo & Kounoupídi*

This is a tasty way to do something different with plain broccoli and cauliflower. These vegetable fritters are a wonderful accompaniment to hot soup as well as a *mezé*, served with one of the cold tomato dips.

Ingredients:
2 lbs. fresh or frozen broccoli or cauliflower cleaned
and separated into clusters.

Batter:
2 cups all purpose flour
1 cup milk
1 tsp. salt
1 egg
1 tsp. paprika
1 tsp. baking powder
oil for frying

The broccoli and cauliflower have to be pre-cooked. If you have leftovers, great – use them, if not, par-boil the fresh or frozen vegetables in salted water for a few minutes, just to soften. Drain well. In a large bowl, mix together all your batter ingredients. You may need more milk so add it accordingly. You want the batter to be light, not thick and lumpy.

Heat a good two inches of oil in a deep skillet. Salt and pepper your vegetables. Dip a cluster into the batter, and tap against the side of the bowl to remove any excess. Drop it into the hot oil and fry until golden brown. Repeat with the rest of your vegetables. When they are done, remove to drain on paper towels.

Fried Pumpkin / *Kolokítha Tiganití*

This is another village secret that you just have to try. I lived in the States most of my life, surrounded by pumpkins but never knew what to do with them. The secret to this wonderful side dish is to fry the pumpkin in hot oil and let it brown. The browner it gets, the sweeter it gets. I prefer mine almost burnt.

Ingredients:
1 ripe pumpkin
salt
olive oil for frying

First, wash the pumpkin before cutting to remove all traces of dirt. Using a sharp knife, quarter the pumpkin. Depending on the size, you may have to quarter it again. You want to get it into manageable wedges so you can slice it into thin strips – about ½ inch thick. Remove the hard peel after it's been sliced. It's easier!

Sprinkle the pumpkin slices with salt. Heat oil in a skillet and fry it until brown on both sides. Patience though, it takes a while to brown but it's worth the wait. That's it. Very easy and great as a side dish or alone with fresh bread.

Savory Pumpkin Pancakes / *Kolokithópites*

The fall season brings with it an abundance of pumpkins. These pancakes or fritters are a wonderful way to use up this versatile vegetable. Serve them as a *mezé* or as an accompaniment to hot soup.

Ingredients:
4 cups mashed boiled pumpkin
1 cup olive oil
1½ cups chopped onions
½ cup chopped green onions
1 cup chopped dill weed
2 cups grated cheese
4 eggs, beaten
1 tsp. oregano
1 tsp. spearmint
1 cup flour
salt and pepper to taste
oil for frying

Begin by setting the pumpkin in a fine sieve to drain. You want to get rid of as much moisture as possible, so if you have the time, let it strain for a few hours or over night.

Heat the olive oil in a skillet. Sauté the chopped onions with the green onions and dill until they are translucent and tender. In a large bowl, mix together the pumpkin, cheese, eggs, oregano, spearmint and the flour. Stir in the onion mixture. Season it with salt and pepper. The mixture should be the consistency of thick cake batter. If it looks too loose, stir in more flour.

Heat ½ inch of olive oil in a skillet. Add the pumpkin batter by tablespoons and fry on one side then turn them over to fry on the other. Remove them to paper towels to drain.

Onion Fritters / *Kremidokeftédes*

When you're stuck for a side dish or a snack, this is great. It seems there are always onions on hand.

Ingredients:
1 lb. onions – ½ grated finely and ½ chopped coarsely
1 lb. all purpose flour
½ cup finely chopped fresh mint
salt and pepper
oil for frying

In a mixing bowl, toss together the onions, mint, flour and salt and pepper. Add enough water to make it into a paste. Heat oil in a skillet. Drop by spoonfuls into the hot oil and fry until golden.

Spicy Pickled Eggplants / *Pikántikes Melintzánes*

This recipe requires a bit of planning ahead and preparation, but the results are delicious. Serve these babies as part of a *mezé* dinner party or as a side dish for charcoaled poultry and seafood.

Ingredients:
2 lbs. small eggplants - about 6 inches in length.
salt
2 cups chopped fresh parsley
4 cloves garlic, minced
2 chili peppers, chopped
½ cup red wine vinegar
3 tbs. vinegar
½ cup olive oil

Cut the stems off of the eggplants and wash and rinse them. Slice each eggplant down the length on one side forming a pocket. Sprinkle the insides with salt and set them aside to drain for one hour. Bring two quarts of water to a boil. Add the eggplants and boil them for 20 minutes or until a fork pierces through them easily. Remove them to a strainer and let them drain overnight.

In a bowl, mix together the parsley, garlic, and peppers with two teaspoons salt. Mix it together until the parsley has begun to wilt. Stuff each of the eggplants with a spoonful of the mixture and lay them sliced side up, side by side, in a Pyrex or enamel pan. Mix the oil with the vinegars and pour over the eggplants. Cover them and refrigerate at least overnight before serving. They keep for up to two weeks in the refrigerator.

Zucchini Blossoms / *Anthoús Kolokithiás*

In the summer months, the zucchini plants will produce their tender blossoms. If left on the vine, the blossoms will become the vegetable. Often in the Greek islands, these blossoms are picked just as they begin to open. They are used for stuffing, as in *Gemistá* or they can be pan fried in batter. If you're lucky enough to have your own zucchini plants, try this recipe using the fresh blooms and serve them up as a different *mezé*.

Ingredients:
zucchini blossoms
salt and pepper
oil for frying

Batter:
1 cup milk
1 egg
salt and pepper
dash paprika
dash oregano
flour

Rinse the blossoms in cold water and set them aside to drain. Prepare the batter by mixing together all the ingredients and adding enough flour so it's thick but not pasty.

Heat two inches of oil in a skillet. Sprinkle the blossoms with salt and pepper. Hold each blossom by it's stem end and dip it into the batter. Tap it on the side of the bowl to get rid of any excess and drop it into the hot oil. Let them fry until golden brown. Remove them to paper towels to drain.

Stuffed Zucchini Blossoms / *Anthoús Kolokithiás Gemistá*

A variation of the above recipe, this dish stuffs the blossoms with feta cheese.

Ingredients:
1 cup feta cheese
1 egg
dash black pepper

Mix the feta with the egg and the pepper. Fill the zucchini blossoms and then fry them in batter, following the directions above.

Zucchini Pancakes / *Kolokithokeftédes*

Ingredients:
4 cups shredded zucchini
1 cup feta cheese
½ cup grated Greek *kefalotíri* or parmesan cheese
2 cups mashed potatoes
3 eggs, beaten
½ cup bread crumbs
2 tbs. fresh spearmint–dry can be substituted
salt and pepper
flour
oil for frying

Salt the zucchini and set in a strainer for one hour to drain. In a mixing bowl, toss the zucchini with the feta, cheese, mashed potatoes, breadcrumbs, mint and pepper. Add one tablespoon flour to the mixture and refrigerate for one hour. Heat oil in a skillet. Shape the mixture into small pancakes and dip them into flour. Fry them in oil until golden on both sides.

For more *Mezédes* or appetizers see the following:

The Salads & The Savory Pítes
The Game Meats & The Organ Meats
Stuffed Vegetables and *Dolmáthes*
Fried Vegetables / *Tiganitá*
Mussels and Feta in Tomato Sauce/ *Sáltsa Mídia me Féta*
Shrimp Saghanáki / *Garídes Saghanáki*

Salads
Salátes

Salads - *Salátes*

The most popular space of a village home was the *soufá* or the area in front of the fireplace. Used as a living room and dining room, the *soufá* was also the area for much preparation of meals since the utensils and supplies were kept nearby. And when the day was done, many villagers would lay blankets or mats on the floor and convert it into a child's bedroom since it was kept warm by the fire.

Salads take their place on the Greek table along with the appetizers or *mezédes* because they are often considered appetizers themselves and vise versa. The traditional *Taramosaláta* or Fish Roe Salad is a fine example of this. Although, I would have preferred to group these two categories together, for convenience sake and ease of reading, they've been separated.

When living in the Greek Islands, you are limited by the seasons as to what you're going to be serving as a vegetable salad. Winter is a time of cabbage, lettuce, cauliflower and the green vegetables such as spinach and kale, where as the summer months are abundant with tomatoes, green peppers, cucumbers, eggplants and green beans. Because of these seasonal variations, we've learned to improvise on our salad making.

Sure, there are common salad recipes that we follow, such as the traditional Greek Village Salad, but to believe that this is where the imagination of the Greeks stops, would be a mistake. Many combinations of vegetables, legumes, meats and seafood are used in salad making. Some ingredients are common and maybe some are not, but they make for flavorful accompaniments to any meal.

Other than garden grown vegetables, we often use wild vegetables in our salads as well. Sometimes, salad making depends on what's been collected from the hill side, if anything at all. Many villagers go to the mountains to collect *manítes*—wild mushrooms and *hórta*—greens in general. I can remember when I lived in the States, my aunt would go outside to the back yard with a plastic bag and a small knife and collect dandelion greens. Unless you are a seasoned collector, I wouldn't recommend hunting for wild vegetables. My mother-in-law can spot a poisonous mushroom a mile a way, while I, on the other hand, have no idea what the difference is.

Since any cooked vegetable and legume can be used for a salad, let me give you a tip in case you decide to make up your own recipe. Marinate... Marinate... Marinate! Beans and cooked veggies are wonderful when they've been soaking up the flavors of an herbal dressing. If you have the time, soak or toss them in the dressing for an hour or longer before finishing the salad to be served.

Also, let me suggest that you try to keep your vegetables uniform in size when you are preparing a salad. For instance, a white bean salad would not be easy for your guests to eat if it had strips of green peppers or rings of onions in it. But if the vegetables were chopped up about the same size as the beans, it'd be beautiful.

Salad making is one of the easiest things to do. Take a lesson from your grandmother and throw together a handful of this and a handful of that. Use your imagination to come up with combinations that lend themselves to the particular tastes of your family. Try using left over pita bread in your salads as "Greek croutons" or try a different dressing or sauce on the traditional Greek Village Salad. The themes and combinations are endless.

The Greek Village Salad

On one occasion, I was asked about the history of the Greek Village Salad. Where did it originate and how did it become so popular? Unfortunately, there really isn't a history for the 'salad', per say, but if you look at the history of Greece itself, then you may be able to understand how and why some things about our culture came to be.

Greece, historically, has been a poor country. The various war conflicts - World and Civil as well as the occupations such as those of the Turks and Italians all took their toll on the progress of the nation. Traditionally, villagers and islanders had large families. With many mouths to feed and almost no income, they depended on their lands and crops to survive and raise their families. Each family and homestead always strived to be completely self sufficient. These were times of no modern conveniences, much less supermarkets, so a donkey ride to Giant™ or Safeway™ just didn't exist. What necessities they lacked, they bartered for with other families. Perhaps something like..."I'll give you a basket of flour if you give me a basket of potatoes".

Almost all village homes had a garden of sorts so they could raise their own vegetables. Seeds were a special commodity and were often traded amongst households. And always, a particular amount of each crop were left to seed for the next season. Farm animals were also raised on a family homestead, but they were only slaughtered for special occasions such as Easter or Christmas. Sometimes an animal might get hurt and have to be taken out of it's misery, but again, these were times of no refrigeration so you couldn't keep a freezer full of pork chops. The families estimated their needs and what meat could not be eaten within a few days was traded or sold for some other commodity.

Although having a large family meant many mouths to feed, our ancestors considered it a blessing. The more children that a family had, the more hands that were available to help with the fields and crops.

Very often, a salad was dinner. A village woman would collect what was available in her garden - tomatoes, cucumbers, onions, lettuce, basil, etc., and if she had something preserved at home, she would add that, too. In the Islands especially, every family had their own goats and olive trees. So feta cheese, olives in brine and olive oil were commonly found in each home. A walk in the mountains could supply extras like fresh capers, dandelion greens, mushrooms, pine nuts and all sorts of herbs so these were added to the dinner as well.

Anchovies, sardines and mackerel could be caught in our seas and easily preserved in salt. These salted fish were a popular staple and kept on hand in every Greek village home. The same holds true for bread. Considered an absolute necessity, bread always played a major role during meal time. Again, if you didn't have a wheat crop, you could trade what you did have for the flour.

By looking at a Greek Village Salad in a more defined, modern way, you'll see that you have your proteins, carbohydrates and fats all mixed into one dish. Add some wheat bread to it and you have a meal that many, many of our ancestral families were raised on.

Greek Village Salad / *Horiátiki Saláta*

A true Greek Village Salad is served with only a sprinkling of olive oil. The oil mixes with the juices of the vegetables and makes a flavorful dressing for you to dip your bread into as you eat.

You can add any variety of chopped vegetables that you have a fondness for or you can delete an ingredient as well. Just because you don't have cucumbers on hand does not mean that the salad will not be delicious.

Many people will add capers or chopped *glistrída* - purslane as well as chopped fresh basil and pepperoncinis. The salad can be made with many variations and is offered in most Greek restaurants in the range of a simple tomato salad to the most elaborate 'kitchen sink' concoctions.

Tomatoes, onions, feta cheese, olives and olive oil make up the basis of a Greek Village Salad and the recipe for Tomato-Feta Salad is and example of this. After those ingredients are in your salad bowl, use your own preferences and enjoy!

Ingredients:
3 tomatoes, cut into wedges
1 green pepper cut into thin rings
1 medium onion, sliced thinly
1 cucumber peeled and sliced
green and black olives
feta cheese cut into chunks
olive oil
salt and pepper
dry or fresh chopped spearmint
oregano
vinegar – optional
anchovies or salted sardines – optional

Place the cut vegetables into a salad bowl, sprinkle with salt, pepper, mint and oregano and toss them. Arrange the olives and feta cheese over the vegetables and pour a generous amount of olive oil over the salad. If you prefer, add some vinegar.

Tomato and Feta Salad / *Tomáta me Féta Saláta*

A simpler version of the Greek Village Salad but just as delicious. Make this salad with fresh, plump tomatoes and lots of feta cheese.

Ingredients:
3 fresh tomatoes cut into wedges
1 onion halved and cut into wedges
salt and pepper
feta cheese
olive oil
olives

In a bowl, mix together the tomato and onions. Season it with salt and pepper and toss in the feta cheese. Sprinkle it with olive oil and garnish with olives.

Spicy Tomato Salad / *Pikántiki Tomatosaláta*

This recipe hails from Constantinople. As many Middle Eastern dishes, the ingredients for this salad are chopped into small, spoon sized bits. This salad can be used as an appetizer or as a side dish for seafood and poultry.

Ingredients:
4 medium tomatoes, diced
1 chopped cucumber
1 cup chopped parsley
3 tbs. chopped fresh spearmint
1 chopped green pepper
2 chopped chili peppers or ½ tbs. dry flakes
3 tbs. capers
1 cup feta cheese, cubed
1 cup chopped pita bread - optional
Orange-Pepper Dressing - see recipe

In a bowl, toss together all the chopped vegetables and the feta cheese. You can control how hot and spicy you want this salad by adding more or less chili peppers. Season it with salt and pepper and top it off with Orange-Pepper Dressing.

Crab Salad / *Kavourosaláta*

Ingredients:
1 cup crab meat
1 cucumber, chopped and drained
2 tbs. chopped parsley
juice of 1 lemon
salt and pepper
Minute Mayonnaise - see recipe
3 tomatoes, cut into wedges
3 hard boiled eggs, cut into wedges

Line a platter with fresh lettuce leaves. Toss together the crab, cucumber, parsley, lemon juice and season it with salt and pepper. Add enough mayonnaise so the salad is creamy. Arrange it in the center of your platter and use the tomato and egg wedges as garnish.

Herring Salad / *Renkosaláta*

Herrings have very fine bones in the flesh. If you can get ready-filleted smoked herring, go ahead and use it.

Ingredients:
4 smoked herrings
milk
1 lb. potatoes, cubed and boiled
1 onion, thinly sliced into rings
1 green pepper, thinly sliced into rings
⅓ cup chopped parsley
4 tbs. olive oil
2 tbs. vinegar

Soak the herring in enough milk to cover them for 8 hours. Drain them; remove the skin and bones then cut the fillets into small pieces. In a mixing bowl, toss the potatoes, onions, green peppers and parsley with the herring and the oil and vinegar. You may add salt and pepper to taste but smoked herring is a very salty fish so try it first.

Shrimp Salad / *Garidosaláta*

For a spicy variation, try some seafood seasoning such as Old Bay™ in the shrimp when you steam them. It really gives it a spicy kick. Serve the salad over a bed of cut lettuce leaves that have been tossed with some chopped spring onions and fresh dill weed. Delicious !

Ingredients:
2 lbs. shrimp
1 small beer
1 lb. potatoes, cubed and boiled just until tender
½ cup capers
5 hard boiled eggs, chopped
½ cup chopped parsley
salt and pepper
mayonnaise

Clean the shrimp under cold running water, drain them and put them in a large pot. Sprinkle with salt and add the beer. Cover the pot and bring to a boil over high heat. Cook the shrimp for 5 to 10 minutes or until they are pink. Remove from the heat and set them in a strainer to drain. When they are cool enough to handle, peel off the shells. Chop the shrimp into fork sized pieces.

In a large mixing bowl toss the shrimp with the potatoes, eggs, parsley and capers. Sprinkle it with salt and pepper and use enough mayonnaise so the salad holds together. Refrigerate the salad covered until you're ready to serve it.

Shrimp and Artichoke Salad / *Garídes me Agináres Saláta*

Ingredients:
2 lbs. shrimp
1 lb. boiled artichoke hearts
2 hard boiled eggs, sliced
1 tsp. mustard
juice of 2 lemons
3 tbs. olive oil
parsley
salt and pepper

Steam the shrimp using your favorite recipe or try the recipe for Shrimp in Wine. Arrange lettuce leaves on a platter. Quarter the artichoke hearts and arrange them in the center. Peel the shrimp and cut them into bite sized pieces or leave them whole if they're small. Arrange them on top of the artichokes and garnish the platter with the hard boiled egg slices.

Whisk together the mustard, lemon juice, olive oil and parsley. Season it with salt and pepper and pour it over the shrimp and artichokes.

Artichoke Salad / *Saláta Agináres*

Ingredients:
1 lb. boiled artichoke hearts
½ cup chopped pimento
Greek Vinaigrette Dressing - see recipe

Quarter the artichoke hearts and toss them with the pimento. Add the vinaigrette and let them marinate for at least one hour, tossing them occasionally.

Beets in Garlic Sauce / *Patzária Skordaliá*

A nice salad dish that can be eaten hot or cold. The beet greens make a tasty addition. Just boil them lightly in salted water until tender and mix them into the beet roots. The beets marinate in the garlic sauce, so this dish could be made well in advance and will taste that much better.

Ingredients:
2 lbs. beets
salt
Garlic Sauce - thin version - see recipe

Remove the stems and leaves from the beets. Wash them under running water, removing all traces of mud and dirt. Boil them with their skins for 40 to 50 minutes or until tender. Strain them and let them cool down a minute or two. Using your fingers remove the skins. They should slide off easily. Any blemishes can be cut away with a knife. Slice them into rounds into a bowl. Pour the sauce over the beets and toss it all together. Add salt accordingly.

Stuffed Beets / *Patzária Gemistá*

Ingredients:
2 lbs. boiled whole beets, skinned
vinegar
2 chopped hard boiled eggs
4 anchovy fillets, chopped
2 cucumbers, chopped
2 tbs. capers
chopped parsley
Greek Vinaigrette Dressing - see recipe

Cut the beets in half. Take each half and slice off a bit of the rounded side so it will sit easily. Using a spoon or a knife, hollow out the centers of the halves. Sprinkle them with vinegar and let them stand for 30 minutes, then turn them upside down to drain.

Mix together the eggs, anchovies, cucumbers and capers and fill the hollows. Top the stuffing with some chopped parsley and spoon some vinaigrette over it all.

Green Bean Salad / *Fasolákia Saláta*

Ingredients:
1 lb. fresh green beans, washed & trimmed
1 tbs. chopped parsley
1 garlic clove, crushed
salt and pepper
Lemon-Oil Dressing - see recipe

Bring a pot of salted water to a boil. Add the beans and cook them until they are tender as to your preference. Drain them and set them aside. In a medium sized bowl, mix all the remaining ingredients together. Add the beans and toss to coat. Refrigerate them for at least an hour so the flavors meld. Serve cold.

Attica Green Bean Salad / *Saláta Fasolákia Attikís*

Ingredients:
1 lb. cooked green beans
1 cup capers
1 cup chopped arugula
1 cup chopped dill pickles
pepper
Minute Mayonnaise - see recipe

Soak the capers in water for 1 hour to remove any saltiness and drain. Toss all the ingredients together and season with black pepper.

Kidney Bean Salad / *Saláta Mavrofásoula*

Ingredients:
2 cups cooked kidney beans, drained
Garlic Sauce - thin version - see recipe
1 tbs. chopped parsley

Toss the beans in garlic sauce and let them marinate for 2 hours. Arrange them on a platter lined with green vegetable leaves and sprinkle with parsley.

Lima Bean Salad / *Gígantes Saláta*

Legumes of all kinds are eaten during the Lent season. This is a delicious variation for Limas. You could use a pressure cooker to speed up the cooking time, but be careful that you don't over cook the beans and they split. You want them whole for this salad.

Ingredients:

1 lb. dry lima beans, soaked over night
1 chopped onion
1 cup chopped celery
2 tbs. tomato paste
salt and pepper
chopped parsley
Lemon Oil Dressing - see recipe

Boil the beans in enough water to cover them for 10 minutes. Drain the beans and rinse them. Return the beans to your pot along with the onions, celery, and tomato paste and add your salt and pepper. Add enough water to cover the beans and cook over medium heat for 1 to 2 hours, or until tender. When they are done, drain off the liquid and put the beans in bowl. Add the lemon oil dressing and sprinkle them with parsley. Toss it all together, and chill.

For more tips on cooking beans and legumes, see the Kitchen Techniques section.

Lettuce Salad / *Maroulosaláta*

This simple yet tasty salad is served in the winter months with soups, stews or roasted meats. Croutons, though not traditional, make an excellent addition to this salad.

Ingredients:
1 head romaine lettuce
2 tbs. fresh chopped dill weed
¼ cup fresh chopped spring onions
2 cloves finely chopped garlic
salt and pepper to taste

Wash the romaine lettuce and cut it thinly or tear the leaves into bite sized pieces. Toss all ingredients together with Greek Vinaigrette or Lemon-Oil dressing.

Radish & Feta Salad / *Rapanáki me Féta Saláta*

The fresh vegetables in this salad give you the taste of Mediterranean springtime. If you don't like the traditional parsley in this recipe, you can use fresh dill weed or a combination of both.

Ingredients:

1 head romaine lettuce
5 spring onions, cleaned and thinly sliced
10 radishes
½ cup feta cheese, crumbled
¼ cup chopped parsley
Lemon Oil Dressing - see recipe
salt and pepper

Wash and drain your vegetables. Bunch the lettuce leaves together and cut them cross wise into ¼ inch wide strips into a salad bowl. Cut both ends off the radishes, but don't peel them. Slice them into thin circles. Add them to the salad bowl along with the spring onions, feta, parsley, pepper and the dressing. Toss it all together and taste it for saltiness. Feta is a salty cheese, so don't add more salt unless you're sure it needs it.

Dandelion Salad / *Radíkia Saláta*

When writing this recipe, I couldn't help but remember the years that I lived in the United States. Even in America, my family kept up with the Greek ways, so much, that our back yard was always kept clean from dandelions because we would pick the greens for salad.

Ingredients:
½ lb. dandelion greens
½ cup fried bacon cut into small pieces - bacon bits can be substituted
salt and pepper to taste
Lemon Oil Dressing - see recipe

Wash and drain the dandelion greens. If they are large leaves, cut them into smaller, fork-sized pieces. Toss all the ingredients together and serve.

Poor Mans' Cabbage Salad / *Lahanosaláta*

Another traditional Greek salad that's as colorful as it is delicious. The assortment of fresh vegetables greens that can be used is limitless. This salad gets its tastiness from the texture of crunchy vegetables. Use your imagination and enjoy!

Ingredients:
4 cups shredded cabbage
1 cup shredded red cabbage
1 grated carrot
salt and pepper to taste
Lemon Oil Dressing or Orange Pepper Dressing - see recipe

Toss together all the salad ingredients with a generous amount of dressing.

Russian Salad / *Rósiki Saláta*

This easy salad is a popular appetizer dish in the islands. It's great as a side dish or as a *mezé* when ouzo is served. For added convenience, use frozen mixed veggies that have been cooked and drained.

Ingredients:
1 cup boiled white beans
1 cup cooked peas
1 cup diced carrots
2 cups cubed boiled potatoes
3 chopped hard boiled eggs
½ cup chopped dill pickles
salt and pepper
1 tsp. paprika - sweet or hot as you prefer
mayonnaise - see recipes for home made versions or use store bought.

Make sure that all the vegetables have been drained well and are as dry as possible. Simply combine all the ingredients together and mix them with enough mayonnaise so that it holds together. For a gourmet version of the salad, use an herbal mayonnaise. Refrigerate the salad covered for one hour before serving.

Olive Salad / *Saláta apo Eliés*

This easy, festive salad is great to serve as an appetizer or cocktail party snack. Serve it with bread or crackers and it's also wonderful when accompanied with a yogurt sauce, such as *Tzatzíki* on the side.

Ingredients:
2 cups cubed boiled potatoes
½ cup chopped pitted black olives
½ cup chopped pitted green olives
½ cup sliced pimento stuffed olives
½ cup minced red pepper
½ cup minced green pepper
½ cup chopped green onions
½ cup chopped dill weed
1 tbs. dry spearmint
black pepper
Greek Vinaigrette - see recipe

Mix together all the ingredients and chill.

Macedonian Taratór / *Saláta Taratór*

Ancient Macedonia was home to Mount Olympus, the seat of the mythological Greek gods as well as the birth place of Alexander the Great. Perhaps this recipe was a secret handed down through the ages. Use this delicious spreadable salad as a dip or as an appetizer.

Ingredients:
1 cup finely chopped walnuts
5 minced garlic cloves
1 grated cucumber, drained
¼ cup bread crumbs
salt and pepper
½ cup olive oil
¼ cup vinegar

Toss together the walnuts, garlic, cucumber and bread crumbs with a bit of salt. Stir in the olive oil and vinegar with some water, if needed to make it into a very thick paste. Season it with salt and pepper. As the salad sits, it will thicken so add more water if needed.

Mixed Boiled Vegetables / *Saláta Vrastí*

Ingredients:
1 lb. Swiss chard, boiled
2 cups sliced boiled potatoes
2 cups sliced boiled zucchini
2 cups sliced boiled beets
1 cup boiled green beans
1 cup sliced boiled carrots
2 tbs. capers
olives with pimento stuffing
Lemon- Oil Dressing - see recipe

Make sure that all the vegetables have been thoroughly drained. Layer each vegetable on a large salad platter, beginning with the Swiss chard. Spread out the potato slices over it, continuing with the zucchini, beets, green beans and carrots. Sprinkle the top with the capers and arrange the olives on the salad. Top the whole thing with dressing.

Boiled Zucchini Salad / *Saláta apó Vrastá Kolokithákia*

Ingredients:
2 lbs. small zucchinis
1 tbs. dried spearmint
½ cup olive oil
1 cup vinegar
salt and pepper

Rinse the zucchini, cut off the stems and quarter them. Put the zucchini in a pot and add a little water. Cover them and bring to a boil. You want to steam the zucchini for 10 to 15 minutes to tenderize it, but without a lot of liquid.

Remove the cover to let as much liquid as possible steam away. Pour in the olive oil, vinegar and spearmint and stir it together. Season it with salt and pepper and let it simmer for another 2 to 3 minutes. Remove the salad to a platter and serve.

Island Potato Salad / *Patatosaláta Vrastí*

A simple but flavorful side dish that's great when served warm. Fresh tomato wedges can be added to this salad as a delicious variation.

Ingredients:
2 lbs. potatoes
1 cup chopped onions
½ cup chopped parsley
salt and pepper
olive oil

Peel and boil the potatoes until tender. Strain and let them cool down enough so you can handle them and cut them into one inch chunks. In a large bowl toss together all the ingredients with enough olive oil to coat. Add salt and pepper to taste.

Potato Salad from Attica / *Patatosaláta Attikís*

Ingredients:
2 lbs. sliced boiled potatoes
1 cup chopped beets
½ cup olive oil
2 tbs. vinegar
1 tbs. dry white wine
1 tsp. yellow mustard
salt and pepper

Line a platter with lettuce leaves. Toss the potatoes with salt and pepper and arrange them over the lettuce. Sprinkle the beets over the potatoes. Mix together the remaining ingredients and pour the sauce over the salad.

Red and Green Pepper Salad / *Kókkines ke Prásines Piperiés Saláta*

Ingredients:
1 lb. green peppers
1 lb. red peppers
Garlic Sauce - thin version - see recipe

Roast the green peppers in the oven following the directions for Roasting Vegetables in the Kitchen Techniques section. When they are done, remove the peels and chop them into bite sized piece. Toss the peppers with the garlic sauce and serve.

Roasted Eggplant Salad / *Melintzanosaláta*

This is terrific served with feta cheese, a Greek Village Salad and of course – ouzo. As an alternative, you can try roasting the eggplants and peppers in a corner of the fireplace or barbecue. This is my preference as the coals give the salad a charred taste. Look in the Kitchen Techniques section for tips on how to prepare the vegetables.

Ingredients:
3 large eggplants, washed
2 large green peppers, washed
white vinegar
olive oil
1 crushed garlic clove
salt and pepper

Wrap the eggplants and peppers individually in aluminum foil. Bake them at 350°F for an hour or more, depending on the size of the eggplant. They are done when you squeeze them and they are very soft and mushy.
Remove them from the oven and let them cool off enough so you can handle them. Slice the eggplant down the middle and scoop out the pulp. Do the same for the peppers, discarding the skins.
Put the eggplant and pepper pulp on a cutting board and chop it finely. Return it to the bowl and add the garlic, salt and pepper, oil and some vinegar. Mix it up and give it a taste. You can add more oil or vinegar according to your preference.

Fruit with Feta Cheese

This snack is not necessarily a salad , although you could call it a Greek fruit salad. Fresh fruit is quite abundant here in the Islands during the summer months and because of this, it may make for some strange sounding combinations. Here, salty feta cheese is served with sweet fruit - and it's great!

My mom's favorite is watermelon with feta cheese. She arranges watermelon pieces on a large plate with a few slices of feta next to it or you can choose to crumble the cheese right over the fruit if you prefer. Taking hold of a crusty loaf of fresh white bread, she'll cut it apart with her hands and dig in.

Tried and true combinations that go together well with feta cheese include watermelon, pears, cantaloupe and honeydew melons. Don't forget the bread, it goes beautifully with this snack.

Salad Combinations

Instead of dwelling on exact measurement, since Greek cooking doesn't rely on it any way, I'm giving you some combinations that go together wonderfully. Again, don't be afraid to experiment - you'd be missing out on the fun part that make us Greeks. A handful of dandelion greens tossed in a Greek salad makes a great addition. Have veggies left over from last nights dinner? Try marinating them in some dressing then adding them to a salad too. The dressings that I list are suggestions so don't be afraid to try some other great sauces on your salad.

Tomato and Herb Salad / *Tomáta me Vótana Saláta*

sliced tomatoes
sliced onions
chopped parsley
basil - fresh or dry
thyme - fresh or dry
salt and pepper to taste
plain olive oil or Greek Vinaigrette - see recipe

This salad can be beautifully presented by layering the tomatoes and onions on a serving platter. Sprinkle the herbs as a topping and pour the dressing over it all.

Farmer's Salad / *Saláta Laikí*

cooked sliced potatoes
cooked sliced carrots
cooked peas
chopped parsley
chopped pitted olives
salt and pepper to taste
Herb Mayonnaise - see recipe

This recipe is very much like the Russian Salad. For added convenience, go ahead and use frozen mixed vegetables that have been cooked and drained. Simply toss together all the ingredients and serve.

Winter Salad / *Saláta Himoniátiki*

cooked cubed potatoes
cooked peas
chopped green peppers
chopped onions
chopped celery
minced garlic
salt and pepper to taste
Greek Vinaigrette Dressing - see recipe

Serve this exceptional salad warm. Toss just cooked potatoes with all the ingredients. This salad can be served with tomato slices or as a side dish for pork chops or steaks.

Tuna-Bean Salad / *Saláta me Tóno ke Fasólia*

cooked white beans
canned tuna
chopped onions
grated carrots
thyme, fresh or dry
chopped parsley
minced garlic
salt and pepper to taste
Lemon Oil Dressing - see recipe

Use canned beans in this recipe for added simplicity. Drain the beans and the tuna. Toss them with the rest of the ingredients and serve. For a change of pace, serve this as a lunch salad in hollowed out tomatoes using a vinaigrette dressing.

Tomato - Green Bean Salad / *Tomáta me Fasolákia Saláta*

tomato wedges
chopped onions
cooked green beans
chopped olives
minced garlic
salt and pepper to taste
Greek Vinaigrette Dressing - see recipe

For added taste, marinate the green beans over night in the vinaigrette, olives and garlic. The next day, mix in the rest of the ingredients when you're ready to serve it.

Peasant Pasta Salad / *Makaronáki Saláta*

any small, cooked pasta of your choice
tomato wedges
chopped anchovy fillets
minced garlic
grated cheese
chopped fresh basil
salt and pepper to taste
Greek Vinaigrette Dressing - see recipe

Small, bite sized pasta such as macaroni, penne or shells work nicely in this recipe. Toss together all the ingredients.

January Salad / *Saláta tou Yianári*

cooked diced potatoes
cooked diced carrots
chopped green onions
chopped dill weed
salt and pepper to taste
A cold yogurt sauce such as *Tzatzíki* or *Taratoúri* - see recipes

Combine the vegetables and dill weed together. Serve the salad on a platter, with a dish of yogurt sauce on the side.

Chickpea Salad / *Revithosaláta*

cooked chickpeas
chopped onions
chopped hard boiled eggs
crumbled feta cheese
salt and pepper to taste
Lemon- Oil Dressing - see recipe

Canned chick peas can easily be substituted here. Just drain the beans and toss all the ingredients together for a fast salad dish or *mezé*.

Herbal Rice Salad / *Rízi me Vótana Saláta*

cooked rice
chopped raw spinach
chopped onions
rosemary, dry or fresh
thyme, dry or fresh
sage, dry or fresh
minced garlic
grated lemon rind
salt and pepper to taste
Greek Vinaigrette Dressing - see recipe

This rice salad is better if made ahead. Simply mix together all the ingredients and refrigerate covered, overnight. It's a great side dish for a summer barbeque.

Cabbage Salad / *Lahanosaláta*

sliced cabbage
chopped parsley
chopped green and red peppers
minced garlic
crumbled feta cheese
salt and pepper to taste
Lemon Oil Dressing - see recipe

Combine all the ingredients together in a large salad bowl. This salad is traditionally served in the winter months with roasts and chops.

Bean & Rice Salad / *Fasólia me Rízi Saláta*

cooked beans of your choice
cooked rice
chopped onions
chopped celery
chopped green pepper
chopped cucumber
chopped parsley
salt and pepper to taste
Greek Vinaigrette Dressing - see recipe

For added ease, use canned beans that have been drained. If you have the time, soak them overnight in some dressing. The next day, toss together all the ingredients and serve.

Garden Salad / *Saláta tou Kípou*

tomato wedges
zucchini slices
cucumber slices
chopped green pepper
chopped green onion
green olives and capers
chopped fresh spearmint
salt and pepper to taste
Greek Vinaigrette or Tzatzíki - see recipes

This is your basic Greek summer "kitchen sink" salad. Combine all the vegetables together and serve with a vinaigrette. For a fresh, creamy taste, serve the salad with a yogurt sauce such as *Tzatzíki* on the side.

Colorful Salad / *Saláta Chromatistí*

sliced cabbage
sliced cucumber
sliced mushrooms
chopped red pepper
chopped parsley
grated carrots
chopped fresh spearmint
salt and pepper to taste
Lemon-Oil Dressing - see recipe

Another winter salad that can be served as a side dish or as a *mezé* for ouzo. It's colorful appearance makes it a nice party dish as well. Simply toss together all the ingredients and serve.

Green Salad / *Saláta Prásini*

chopped lettuce
sliced cabbage
chopped parsley
chopped green onions
chopped fresh dill
chopped anchovies
olives
salt and pepper to taste
Greek Vinaigrette - see recipe

As the name implies, this salad is made from various green salad vegetables. Combine them all together and use a vinaigrette. Pieces of soft pita bread go wonderfully in this salad.

Savory Pies
Píbes

Savory Pies-*Pítes*

Another category of Greek cuisine that could easily be classified as a *mezé* or a main course would be the savory pies or *pítes*. Don't go thinking pita bread and the drippy, saucy *Gýro*. The savory *pítes* of Greek cooking are so much more than just a sandwich. They are an entire meal that fits right into the palm of your hand and other than a few crumbs, makes almost no mess.

Traditionally, these *pítes* were made to take on an outing such as olive picking or for a meal along the donkey path to another *horáfi* or piece of land. They were also a good way to use up any leftovers from previous meals by wrapping them up in flaky pastry. For a poor family, a *píta* was a way to stretch a few ingredients into a delicious and nutritious a meal.

The savory *pítes* can be made two ways. There is "pan style," which is the easiest method of making these treats. The *píta* is made as one whole pie where you cut serving sized pieces. For the more ambitious, there are the individual, single serving versions where the phyllo or pastry is folded into triangles, squares or cut into circles and encloses the filling completely. If you do make individual pies, make sure that you cook the fillings longer so that there is less moisture and they are easier to wrap up.

The individual pies are more convenient when you don't have the luxury of a dinner table and are on the run, because they don't make a mess. They are great to have in the car as breakfast on your way to work or as a school lunch.

The *pítes* use ingredients such as vegetables, dairy products, meats and poultry. The vegetables and meats have to be pre-cooked so using leftovers in these recipes is a time saver. For convenience, the crust can be made easily with ready bought phyllo pastry sheets or a ready bought pastry dough of your preference. If you'd rather make your own crust, I've got a variety of pastry recipes for you in the breads section.

For most of the *pites*, you'll have the choice between using butter or olive oil as the fat in the recipe. The finished product is delicious either way, but butter will thicken when served cold or at room temperature where as olive oil will stay moist and not taste so greasy. The choice is up to you. If you want your spinach pies available to take on an outing, I would use the oil. When butter is your choice of ingredient, the simplicity of using a modern day microwave for a minute or two to heat them up makes a hot meal very easy and very fast.

Basic lessons as well as tips and shortcuts to working with phyllo and pastry dough are available in the Kitchen Techniques section. Take the time and read over it as you'll find detailed instructions on the various ways of making the individual treats as well as the pan versions, so you don't have to spend all day in the kitchen.

The *petrómilos* or stone mill could be used by the village woman to grind fresh flour from wheat, barley or rye as well as dried legumes and seeds for use in a recipe.

Traditional Cheese Pie / *Tirópita Paradosiakí*

The cheese pies that are served in our open-air markets are very popular in Greece and simple to make. This recipe can be made as individual pies or as a large pan pie that can be cut into serving size pieces. Pastry dough can easily be substituted for the phyllo.

Ingredients:
phyllo pastry sheets
melted butter

Filling:
2 cups crumbled feta cheese
1 cup grated Greek *kefalotíri* or parmesan cheese
1 tbs. dried spearmint leaves
½ cup chopped parsley - optional
5 eggs beaten
1 cup milk

Generously butter a medium sized, oblong baking dish. Spread a sheet of phyllo in it and brush it with butter. Lay another sheet of phyllo over it and again, brush it with butter. Continue this for 5 to 6 sheets. Mix all the filling ingredients together and spread it over the buttered phyllo layers. Top it off with more phyllo and butter layers for 5 to 6 sheets.

Brush the top of your pie with butter and score it into squares. Bake it in a preheated oven at 350ºF for 45 to 50 minutes. The top crust will brown easily so if you think it's cooking too fast, cover it loosely with a sheet of aluminum foil. Remove the foil to brown the top just before it's ready.

Plain Cheese Pie / *Tirópita Aplí*

This version of the traditional cheese pie is made with plain cheese and no herbs are added so young children will enjoy this treat. It gets its creamy texture from the added *Béchamel* sauce. The recipe calls for using phyllo sheets, but you can easily substitute a pastry dough of your choice.

Ingredients:
phyllo pastry sheets
melted butter

Filling:
2 cups feta cheese
1 cup grated Greek *graviéra* or Swiss cheese
3 eggs, beaten
1 cup *Béchamel* sauce - see recipe

Generously butter a medium sized, oblong baking dish. Spread a sheet of phyllo in it and brush it with butter. Lay another sheet of phyllo over it and again, brush it with butter. Continue this for 5 to 6 sheets. Mix all the filling ingredients together and spread it over the buttered phyllo layers. Top it off with more phyllo and butter layers for 5 to 6 sheets.

Brush the top of your pie with more butter and score it into squares. Bake it in a preheated oven at 350°F. for 45 to 50 minutes. The top crust will brown easily so if you think it's cooking too fast, cover it loosely with a sheet of aluminum foil. Remove the foil to brown the top just before it's ready.

Rich Cheese Pie / *Tirópita Ploúsia*

A variation of the popular cheese pie, this recipe makes for a rich and creamy filling. Although it calls for using phyllo sheets, you can easily substitute a pastry dough of your choice for a denser crust. Made as individual pies, it's excellent.

Ingredients:
phyllo pastry sheets
melted butter

Filling:
2 cups crumbled feta cheese
1 cup grated Greek *kefalotíri* or parmesan cheese
2 cups *Béchamel* Sauce - see recipe
4 eggs, beaten
2 tbs. chopped parsley
dash nutmeg - optional
black pepper to taste

In a mixing bowl, combine all the filling ingredients. Preheat your oven to 350°F. Butter a medium sized baking dish. Spread a pastry sheet into the pan and brush it with butter. Continue to layer pastry and butter for 5 to 6 sheets.

Spread the filling over the pastry. Then resume with pastry sheets brushed with butter for another 5 to 6 layers. Keep folding and tucking in the edges of each sheet so you have a nice smooth top. Brushing butter on the edges helps to hold it down. Brush the final top sheet with butter and score the pie into squares or wedges depending on the pan that you chose. Bake for 30 to 40 minutes until it is golden brown.

Ragged Cheese Pie / *Patsavoúra Tirópita*

The ragged cheese pie gets its name because the phyllo isn't laid out nice and flat. The sheets are bunched up like rags and the filling is poured over them. The original recipe hails from Roumely in continental Greece and is a great way to get rid of damaged phyllo sheets.

Ingredients:
phyllo pastry sheets
melted butter

Filling:
1 cup butter
1 ¼ cups milk
6 eggs
2 cups feta cheese
1 cup Greek *mizíthra* or ricotta cheese
black pepper

In a large bowl, cream the butter and add one cup of the milk. Mix in the eggs and crumble the feta and the ricotta into the mixture, add a sprinkle of black pepper and mix well.

Butter a medium sized baking pan. Line the bottom of it with two sheets of phyllo that have been buttered in between. Crumble lightly like newspaper, a few phyllo sheets and put them on top. Sprinkle them with a bit of melted butter.

Top with a layer of the feta mixture. Then add more crumbled phyllo leaves, butter and filling. Keep layering until you've used up the filling. For the final layer, take two phyllo sheets and layer them flatly, buttering them in between. Score the surface into squares and pour the remaining ¼ cup of milk over the prepared pie. Bake at 350°F for 30 to 45 minutes or until brown.

Simple Chicken Pie / *Kotópita Aplí*

True to its name, this recipe is as simple to make as are its ingredients. By substituting store bought puff pastry or phyllo sheets, it can be put together very quickly and be ready to serve at the dinner table or for company that calls.

Ingredients:
pastry dough - see recipes
melted butter

Filling:
2 cups diced chicken meat
1 cup grated Greek *kefalotíri* or parmesan cheese
2 eggs, beaten
2 tbs. chopped parsley
½ cup chicken stock
salt and pepper to taste

In a mixing bowl combine the filling ingredients. Preheat your oven to 350°F and butter a medium sized baking pan of your preference. You will need to roll out two pieces of pastry dough. One piece will be for the top so roll it out just an inch larger than the surface of the pan. The other piece will be used for the bottom and should be larger because it will need to come up the sides of the pan as well.

Line the pan with pastry and add the filling. Cover the pie with the other piece of pastry, moisten the edges and crimp to seal them. Brush the top of the pie with melted butter and use a fork to make small holes all over it. You can get decorative here and make designs if you wish. Use a small knife and make a small incision in the center of the pie, for more steam to escape. Bake the pie for 45 to 55 minutes.

Chicken Pie / *Ornithópita or Kotópita*

One of my favorite dishes, the *Kotópita* is like a hand held chicken pot pie when made into individual pites. Leftovers from a chicken dinner such as cooked chicken, cooked carrots, potatoes, and peas can be added to this recipe. It's wonderful whether it's served hot or cold.

Ingredients:
pastry dough - see recipes
milk

Filling:
1 cup chopped green onions
3 tbs. butter or olive oil
1 cup sliced mushrooms
2 cups diced, cooked chicken
1 tsp. thyme
1 tbs. chopped parsley
2 tbs. chopped celery
1 minced garlic clove
½ cup chicken Stock
1 cup *Béchamel* Sauce - see recipe
2 eggs, slightly beaten
salt and pepper to taste

In a large skillet, cook the green onions in the butter until they are soft and add the mushrooms, sautéing them together. Add the chicken, thyme, parsley, celery, garlic and chicken stock and simmer it all together for 5 minutes. Set the filling aside to cool.

Preheat your oven to 400°F and butter a medium sized baking pan of your preference. You will need to roll out two pieces of pastry dough. One piece will be for the top so roll it out so it's just an inch larger than the surface of the pan. The other piece will be used for the bottom and should be larger because it will need to come up the sides of the pan as well.

Line the pan with pastry, pushing it into the edges with your fingers. Toss the cooled stuffing with the *Béchamel* and eggs, season it to taste and pour it into the pastry lined dish. Cover the pie with the other piece of pastry, moisten the edges and crimp to seal it. Brush the top of the pie with some milk and use a fork to make small holes all over it for the steam to escape. Bake at 400°F for 15 minutes then reduce the heat to 325°F and bake for another 30 to 40 minutes.

Turkey Pie / *Galópita*

This Turkey Pot Pie has all the taste of the Mediterranean. It's easy to make and it's a good way to get rid of holiday leftovers. If you have cooked carrots, potatoes or peas, go ahead and add them to the recipe. It will taste that much better.

Ingredients:
pastry dough - see recipes

Filling:
1 tbs. corn flour
¾ cup chicken stock, cooled
½ cup chopped onions, slightly browned in 1 tbs. butter
1 cup sliced mushrooms - optional
2 cups diced, cooked turkey
1 cup grated Greek *kefalotíri* or parmesan cheese
1 tsp. powdered thyme
¼ cup chopped parsley
1 minced garlic clove
2 eggs, beaten
salt and pepper
½ cup butter

In a small sauce pan, mix the corn flour and the chicken stock and cook it until it thickens. Set it aside. In a bowl, mix the rest of the filling ingredients, except for the butter. Spoon the thickened chicken stock into the filling ingredients and mix well. If the filling seems too thick to you, add some water. You want it to be creamy and smooth.

Butter a medium sized baking pan and line it with pastry dough. Spoon in the filling and top it with little knobs of butter everywhere. Cover the pie with more pastry dough and crimp the edges, using your fingers or a fork. Cut a cross slit in the center of the top for the steam to escape while cooking. Bake at 350°F for 40 to 55 minutes, or until the pastry is done.

Ham Pie / *Zambonópita*

This pie is an easy take away lunch or snack. You can use any fillings that you prefer to suit your tastes.

Ingredients:
pastry - see recipes
milk
sesame seeds

Filling:
sliced ham
thinly sliced tomatoes
thinly sliced green peppers
grated Greek *graviéra* or cheese of your choice - optional

Preheat your oven to 375°F. Roll out the pastry on a floured surface and cut it into 4 x 8 inch rectangles. On half of the rectangle, arrange the ham, tomato, green pepper and cheese. Brush the edges with a little milk and fold the pastry over, enclosing the filling. Crimp and seal the edges. Brush the pie with a little milk and sprinkle with sesame seeds. Place the pies on a greased cookie sheet and bake them for 20 to 30 minutes.

Sausage Pies / *Loukanópites*

Sausage pies are simply hot dogs in a bun or what some people call Pigs in a Blanket. This Greek recipe uses fresh vegetables in the filling and wraps it all up in flaky pastry. By adding or removing filling ingredients, these pies are easily altered to suit any ones tastes.

Ingredients:
pastry dough - see recipes
milk
sesame seeds

Filling:
spicy sausages of your preference, 5 inches long
tomato, cut into half and thinly sliced
onion, cut into half and thinly sliced
green pepper, cut into thin strips
pepper
crumbled feta cheese or cheese of your choice.
oregano

Preheat your oven to 375°F. Roll out the pastry on a floured surface. Cut 6 x 6 inch squares, so they are one inch wider and longer than your sausages. Lay a sausage link in the center. Add some slices of tomato, onion, and green pepper. Season them with a dash of pepper. Arrange a little crumbled feta over the vegetables and sprinkle with a bit or oregano.

Brush the edges with a little milk and fold the pastry over, enclosing the filling. Crimp and seal the edges. Brush the pie with a little milk and sprinkle with sesame seeds. Place the pies on a greased cookie sheet and bake them for 20 to 30 minutes.

Lamb and Feta Pie / *Píta me Arní ke Féta*

This pie looks as special as it tastes. The lamb, herbs and feta are layered and make for a gorgeous presentation when the pie is cut. Using lamb leftovers is a definite plus and time saver for the preparation of this pita.

Ingredients:
pastry dough - see recipes
1 beaten egg
sesame seeds

Filling:
⅓ cup olive oil
1 cup chopped onions
1 cup sliced green onions
½ cup chopped dill weed
3 cups cooked lamb, cut into small pieces
2 cups crumbled feta cheese
black pepper to taste

Preheat your oven to 350°F. Grease a flat pizza pan or cookie sheet that will fit a pie 12 inches in diameter. You will need to roll out two circular pieces of pastry dough. The first one should be about 13 inches in diameter and the other slightly larger.

In a skillet, heat the oil and add the chopped onions. Fry them until translucent. Mix in the spring onions and dill weed and cook the mixture for 5 minutes longer. Remove the skillet from the heat.

Set the first circle of pastry dough on your cookie sheet. Arrange half of the lamb on the pastry, keeping to one inch away from the edge. Spoon half of the onion mixture over the lamb, sprinkle it with half of the feta cheese and give it a dash of pepper if you like. Repeat the process again, layering lamb, onions and feta, using up the ingredients.

Cover the filling with the second piece of pastry. Wet the edges with a little milk or water and push them together to seal. Wet the edges again and roll the pastry edge over onto itself. Work your way around the pie, sealing it completely. If you like, press a fork against this roll of dough to flatten it slightly and give it a decorative appearance. Use a sharp knife and make small incisions on the top crust for the steam to escape. Brush it with the beaten egg and sprinkle it with sesame seeds. Bake the pie for 45 to 55 minutes or until the pastry is golden.

Lamb Pie from Cephalonia / *Kreatópita Kefalonítiki*

This is a great way to get rid of lamb leftovers as they can easily be substituted here. I don't recommend using phyllo in this particular recipe because of the sauces. Use a pastry dough for a more substantial crust. Because of the high fat content of lamb, make sure that this pie is served hot.

Ingredients:
pastry dough - see recipes
melted butter

Filling:
2½ lbs. lean lamb
2 tbs. olive oil
salt and pepper
2 minced garlic cloves
2 tbs. chopped parsley
½ cup vegetable stock
½ cup white wine
⅓ cup uncooked rice
1 cup diced tomatoes
3 diced hardboiled eggs
1 cup crumbled feta cheese

Cut the lamb into small cubes about one inch thick. Heat the oil in a skillet and sear the lamb. Season it with salt and pepper, add the garlic, parsley, vegetable stock and wine. Simmer it for 30 minutes. If you are using lamb leftovers, cook the mixture over high heat for 10 minutes. Remove the pot from the heat and stir in the rice, tomatoes, eggs and feta.

Preheat your oven to 350°F and butter a medium sized baking pan. This pie is usually served as a round pan pita about 12 inches in diameter, but you can choose the pan of your preference. You will need to roll out two pieces of pastry dough. One piece will be for the top so roll it out so it's just an inch larger than the surface of the pan. The other piece will be used for the bottom and should be larger because it will need to come up the sides of the pan as well.

Line the pan with pastry and add your filling. Cover the pie with the other piece of pastry, moisten the edges and crimp to seal them. Brush the top of the pie with melted butter and use a fork to make small holes all over it. You can get decorative here and make designs if you wish. Use a small knife and make a small incision in the center of the pie as well, for more steam to escape. Bake the pie for one hour.

Cretan Lamb Torte / *Toúrta Krítis me Arní*

This tender lamb filling is surrounded by a flaky pastry which resembles a cake or torte when it's done baking. Like its sister recipe, Lamb and Feta Pie, it's baked on a flat pan so you can slide the pie off of the sheet right onto a serving platter. If you don't have one, just serve the pie as it is, garnishing the pan surrounding it, making it that much more special.

Ingredients:
pastry dough - see recipes
1 egg, beaten
sesame seeds

Filling:
4 cups cooked lamb, cut into small pieces
½ cup cream
2 cups Greek *mizíthra* or ricotta cheese
1 tsp. ground cumin
1 tbs. chopped spearmint

Preheat your oven to 350°F. Grease a flat pizza pan or cookie sheet that will fit a pie 12 inches in diameter. You will need to roll out two circular pieces of pastry dough. The first one should be about 13 inches in diameter and the other slightly larger.

In a mixing bowl, mix together the *mizíthra* with the cream. Set the first circle of pastry dough on your cookie sheet. Arrange half of the lamb on the pastry, keeping to one inch away from the edge. Spoon half of the cheese mixture over the lamb and sprinkle it with half of the cumin and spearmint. Repeat the process again, using up the ingredients.

Cover the filling with the second piece of pastry. Wet the edges with a little milk or water and push them together to seal. Wet the edges again and roll the pastry over the top layer. Work your way around the torte, sealing it completely. If you like, press a fork against this roll of dough to flatten it slightly and give it a decorative appearance. Use a sharp knife and make small incisions on the top crust for the steam to escape. Brush it with the beaten egg and sprinkle it with sesame seeds. Bake the torte for 45 to 55 minutes or until the pastry is done.

Leek and Beef Pie / *Prasópita me Kréas*

Ingredients:
phyllo pastry sheets
butter

Filling:
1 cup olive oil or butter
4 cups chopped leek bulbs
1 lb. ground beef
½ cup dry white wine
dash white pepper
dash nutmeg - optional
salt and pepper to taste
6 eggs, beaten
1 cup grated Greek *kefalotíri* or parmesan cheese
4 cups *Béchamel* Sauce - see recipe

In a skillet, heat the olive oil and sauté the leeks until they are tender and slightly gold in color. Add the ground beef and sauté it for 10 minutes, stirring so it becomes crumbly. Pour in the wine and season with the spices. Simmer it for 20 minutes or until the moisture has evaporated. Set it aside to cool.

Preheat your oven to 350ºF. Butter a medium sized baking dish. Spread a pastry sheet into the pan and brush it with butter. Continue to layer pastry and butter for 8 to 10 sheets.

Mix the remaining filling ingredients with the cooled leek mixture and spread it in the pastry lined pan. Resume with pastry sheets brushed with butter for another 8 to 10 layers. Fold and tuck in the edges of your top layers so you have a nice smooth surface. Brushing butter on the edges will help to hold it down. Brush the final top sheet with butter and score the pie into squares or wedges depending on the pan that you have chosen. Bake for 35 to 45 minutes until it is golden brown.

Leek and Egg Pie / *Prasavgópita*

This multi-leveled pita is a little extra work, but it looks as wonderful as it tastes. Serve it as a *mezé* or as an entree with sliced fresh tomatoes on the side.

Ingredients:
Pastry:
4 cups of flour
1 tsp. salt
3 tbs. olive oil
1 tbs. vinegar
water

Filling:
1 cup olive oil or butter
4 cups chopped leek bulbs
1 cup rice, boiled for 10 minutes then drained.
1 cup milk
1 cup strained yogurt
6 eggs, beaten
2 cups mixed cheeses such as feta and kefalotíri or parmesan
salt and pepper to taste

Heat the oil in a skillet and add the leeks. Sauté them until they are tender and there is very little moisture. Stir in the rice and remove the skillet from the heat. Set it aside to cool

To make the pastry, sift the flour into a bowl with the salt. Using your fingers, incorporate the olive oil and vinegar. Add water a little at a time, working it through until you get a stiff dough. Take ⅓ of the dough and form it into a ball and separate the rest of the dough into three equal balls of smaller size.

Preheat your oven to 375°F and grease a medium baking pan. Flour your work surface and roll out the largest ball of dough. This will become the bottom crust. Line the prepared pan with it, pushing the dough into the edges with your fingers. Roll out the remaining three balls of pastry large enough so they will lay flat in the pan. These will become the layers in between. Set them aside.

Mix the rest of the filling ingredients with the leek mixture. Spread ⅓ of the filling in the pastry lined pan and lay a piece of pastry over it. Continue with filling and pastry until you get to the last piece of pastry which will become the top crust. If you need to, roll out this last piece a little more so it's large enough to cover the top.

Trim away any edges that overhang. Dip your finger into milk or water and wet the edges. Push them together so they seal . Crimp the edges using your fingers or a fork. Brush olive oil over the surface of the pie and using a fork or knife, make holes or incisions to vent the steam. Bake it for 30 minutes then reduce the heat to 325°F and bake it for 30 minutes longer.

Basic Meat Pie / *Kreatópita Aplí*

Many variations exist for the *Kreatópita* because of regional differences and preferences of ingredients through out Greece. Some recipes use slices of meat as their fillings where this one uses ground beef and others have cheeses mixed in where as this recipe doesn't.

Here are some variations on the theme for *Kreatópita*:

> Instead of using ground meat, slice the meat into small pieces.
>
> Use pork, lamb, or beef or a mixture of different meats.
>
> Add 2 chopped hard boiled eggs to the cooled meat mixture.
>
> Add 1½ cup crumbled feta cheese to the cooled meat mixture.
>
> Add 1½ cups grated cheese of your choice.
>
> Use fresh spring onions instead of dried.
>
> Add 1 tbsp. crumbled, dry spearmint to the mixture.
>
> Add 1 cup of chopped fresh tomato to the meat as you are simmering it down.

The great thing about *Kreatópita* is that you can use your imagination and also add cooked vegetables or rice to the filling to suit your tastes. This traditional recipe is for a pan style pita, but there is no reason why you couldn't fold up the mixture into individual pies. Just remember to simmer the mixture longer so it thickens and is more manageable.

Ingredients:
phyllo pastry sheets
melted butter

Filling:
½ cup olive oil
1 onion, minced
1 minced garlic clove
1 lb. ground Beef
salt and pepper
1 tbs. dill weed
1 cup dry red wine
3 eggs, beaten

In a heavy saucepan, heat the oil. Add the onions and garlic and fry until translucent. Stir in the ground beef, bit by bit, keeping it crumbly. Add the salt and pepper, dill and the wine. Reduce heat and simmer for

20 minutes, or until the moisture has evaporated. Set it aside to cool.

Preheat your oven to 350°F. Butter a medium sized baking dish. Spread a pastry sheet into the pan and brush it with butter. Continue to layer pastry and butter for 6 to 8 sheets. Take the cooled meat mixture and combine it with the beaten eggs and turn the mixture into the pastry-lined pan.

Resume with pastry sheets brushed with butter for another 6 to 8 layers. Fold and tuck in the edges of your top layers so you have a nice smooth surface. Brushing butter on the edges will help to hold it down. Brush the final top sheet with butter and score the pie into wedges or squares depending on the pan of choice. Bake for 25 to 35 minutes until it is golden brown.

Beef and Cheese Pie / *Kreatópita me Tirí*

Ingredients:
phyllo pastry sheets
olive oil

Filling:
½ cup olive oil
1 cup chopped onions
2 lbs. ground beef
salt and pepper to taste
3 eggs, beaten
½ cup bread crumbs
1 cup grated Greek *kefalotíri* or parmesan cheese
2 tbs. chopped parsley

Heat the oil in a skillet. Add the onions and fry them until translucent. Add the ground beef and sauté together until done. Remove from the heat and let it cool down.

Preheat your oven to 350°F. Butter a medium sized baking dish. Spread a pastry sheet into the pan and brush it with olive oil. Continue to layer pastry and oil for 7 to 8 sheets.

Mix the rest of the filling ingredients with the beef mixture and spread it in the pastry lined pan. Resume with pastry sheets brushed with oil for another 7 to 8 layers. Keep folding and tucking in the edges of your top layers so you have a nice smooth surface. Brushing oil on the edges will help to hold it down. Brush the final top sheet well with oil and score it into squares. Bake for 30 to 40 minutes until it is golden brown.

Fried Sweet Meat Pies / *Pitákia me Kimá*

The spices that are used to season the meat in this recipe give these *pítes* a sweet taste. This Cypriot recipe calls for the pies to be fried in oil and not baked, making them crispier and more flavorful.

Ingredients:
Pastry:
2 cups flour
1 tsp. salt
4 tbs. olive oil
1 tbs. fresh lemon zest
6 tbs. water

Filling:
1 chopped onion
¼ cup olive oil
1½ lb. ground beef
½ cup vegetable stock
½ tsp. cinnamon
½ tsp. cloves
½ tsp. nutmeg
2 tbs. chopped parsley
salt and pepper to taste

oil for frying

In a mixing bowl, stir together the flour and salt. Using your fingers, work in the olive oil, lemon zest and water until it is a dough that can be rolled out. Add a bit of water, if the dough seems dry or add some flour if the dough seems too moist. Set the dough aside to rest.
To prepare the filling, heat the olive oil in a skillet. Add the onions and fry until translucent. Add the beef and the rest of the stuffing ingredients and cook the mixture until the beef is done and there is little moisture left. Set it aside to cool
Flour your work surface and roll out the dough to about 1/6 inch thick. Using cookie cutters or a wide mouthed jar, cut out rounds that are from 4 to 6 inches in diameter. Place two tablespoons of stuffing into the center of a round. Wet the edge with your finger that's been dipped in water or milk, and fold it over making a crescent. Use a fork to crimp the edges and seal in the stuffing. Continue the process until you've used up the pastry and the stuffing. Heat an inch or two of oil. Drop the pies into it and fry on both sides until the pastry is golden. Remove them to paper towels to drain before serving.

Rice Pie / *Rizópita*

This triple layered pie is easily made and looks and tastes like you fussed. It's simple ingredients make it an easy entree to serve with any kind of salad or vegetable dish.

Ingredients:
phyllo pastry sheets
olive oil

Filling:
2 cups of rice
10 eggs, beaten
2 tbs. butter
2 cups crumbled feta
black pepper

Boil the rice for 10 minutes, drain it and rinse it with cold water. Let it drain thoroughly and cool down. Mix together the rice, eggs, butter, and feta. Season with a touch of black pepper.

Preheat the oven to 375°F. Oil a medium sized baking dish. Spread a pastry sheet into the pan and brush it with oil. Continue to layer pastry and oil for 3 to 4 sheets. Spread half the filling over the pastry. Make another layer of pastry sheets brushed with oil, using another 3 to 4 sheets. Spread the rest of the filling over this and continue to finish the pie by layering phyllo and oil again for another 3 to 4 sheets.

Keep folding and tucking in the edges of your top layers so you have a nice smooth surface. Brushing oil on the edges will help to hold it down. Brush the final top sheet with oil and score the pie into squares. Bake it for 30 to 40 minutes until it's golden brown.

Eggplant Pie / *Melintzanópita*

Another of the summer time pies, *Melintzanópita* is a specialty that comes from Thessaly which is in Northern Greece and home to the famous Metéora mountain monasteries. Although the pie is not a local recipe, it is still enjoyed in the islands as well. Serve it as a *mezé* or as an entree, accompanied with a juicy tomato salad and cold wine.

Ingredients:
phyllo pastry sheets
olive oil

Filling:
1 cup olive oil
½ cup butter
4 cups chopped eggplant
1 lb. ground beef
1 cup chopped onions
4 eggs, beaten
1 cup grated Greek *kefalotíri* or parmesan cheese
salt and pepper
dash cinnamon - optional

In a skillet, heat the olive oil with the butter. Fry the eggplant with the onions and ground beef until little moisture is left. Set the mixture aside to cool.

Preheat your oven to 375°F. Oil a medium sized baking dish. Spread a pastry sheet into the pan and brush it with oil. Continue to layer pastry and oil for 3 to 4 sheets.

Combine the cooled eggplant mixture with the eggs, cheese and cinnamon if you're using it. Spread half the filling over the pastry. Then resume with pastry sheets brushed with oil for another 3 to 4 layers. Spread the rest of the filling over the pastry sheets and continue to finish the pie by layering phyllo and oil for another 3 to 4 sheets.

Keep folding and tucking in the edges of your top layers so you have a nice smooth surface. Brushing oil on the edges helps to hold it down. Brush the final top sheet well with oil and score into wedges or squares, depending on the pan that you've chosen. Bake for 30 to 40 minutes until it's golden brown.

Spinach Pie / *Spanakópita*

The Greek Spinach Pie enjoys a great popularity amongst the tourists and locals of the islands. Kids who don't eat spinach on it's own, will eat Spinach Pie. Maybe it's the crust or the mixture of feta and herbs, but whatever the reason, it's delicious. Make your Spinach Pie in a pan or as individual pies for a snack. Keep in mind that the feta cheese will add some saltiness to the spinach, so taste it before you use more salt. Also, frozen spinach works just as well in this recipe. Just make sure that it is well drained before you add it to the onions. Other than the oil, you want the filling to be as dry as possible.

Ingredients:
phyllo pastry sheets
melted butter

Filling:
1 cup olive oil or butter
1 cup chopped onions
¼ cup fresh chopped dill weed
1 lb. fresh spinach, washed and trimmed
1 cup crumbled feta cheese
salt and white pepper to taste

In a large sauce pan, heat the olive oil. Add the onions and fry until translucent. Stir in the dill. Add the spinach and toss together. Keep tossing and cooking the spinach until it is fully wilted. Remove the mixture from the heat and fold in the feta.

Preheat your oven to 350°F. Butter a medium sized baking dish. Spread a pastry sheet into the pan and brush it with butter. Continue to layer pastry and butter for 4 to 5 sheets. Spread the filling over the pastry. Then resume with pastry sheets brushed with butter for another 4 to 5 layers. Fold and tuck in the edges of your top layers so you have a nice smooth surface. Brushing butter on the edges will help to hold it down. Brush the final top sheet well with butter and score it into squares or wedges, depending on the chosen pan. Bake for 20 to 30 minutes until it is golden brown.

Wild Greens Pie / *Hortópita*

A sister to the spinach pie, *hortópita* is a mixture of wild greens as well as garden grown spinach, kale and watercress. Since this recipe also calls for feta as an ingredient, don't add more salt until you've tasted the filling.

Ingredients:
phyllo pastry sheets
melted butter

Filling:
1 cup olive oil or butter
1 cup chopped green onions
¼ cup chopped fresh dill weed
2 tbs. chopped parsley
1 lb. fresh assorted greens such as dandelion, kale, spinach, watercress.
1 cup crumbled feta cheese
salt and white pepper to taste

Wash and trim the greens then chop them into small pieces and set them aside to drain. In a large sauce pan, heat the olive oil. Add the onions and fry until they soften. Stir in the dill and the parsley. Add the greens and toss it all together. Keep tossing and cooking them until they are fully wilted. Remove the mixture from the heat and fold in the feta.

Preheat your oven to 350°F. Butter a medium sized baking dish. Spread a pastry sheet into the pan and brush it with butter. Continue to layer pastry and butter for 4 to 5 sheets. Spread the filling over the pastry. Then resume with pastry sheets brushed with butter for another 4 to 5 layers. Keep folding and tucking in the edges of your top layers so you have a nice smooth surface. Brushing butter on the edges will help to hold it down. Brush the final top sheet with butter and score the pie into wedges or squares depending on the pan of choice. Bake for 25 to 35 minutes until it is golden brown.

Zucchini Pie / *Kolokithópita*

Kolokithópita is one way we prepare zucchinis which are abundant in the islands during the summer months. The recipe uses pastry dough as the crust but Zucchini Pie can be made using phyllo sheets as well. The choice is yours.

Ingredients:
pastry dough - see recipes

Filling:
4 cups diced zucchinis
1½ cups grated onion
¼ cup olive oil
2 ½ cups grated Greek *graviéra* or Swiss cheese
4 eggs, beaten
3 tbs. parsley
salt and pepper to taste

Place the diced zucchini into a sauce pan and cover it with water. Bring it to a boil and cook until it's tender. Pour the zucchini into a strainer and add the onions to it so both ingredients can drain. Heat a skillet and toss in the drained zucchinis and onions. Cook them until the moisture has evaporated. When the skillet seems dry, add the olive oil and sauté the vegetables together for 10 minutes. Remove it from the heat and allow it to cool down for 20 minutes or longer.

Preheat your oven to 350°F and butter a medium sized baking pan. This pie is usually served as a round pan pita about 12 inches in diameter, but you can choose the pan of your preference. You will need to roll out two pieces of pastry dough. One piece will be for the top so roll it out so it's just an inch larger than the surface of the pan. The other piece will be used for the bottom and should be larger because it will need to come up the sides of the pan as well.

Line the pan with pastry. Mix together the cooled zucchinis with the cheese, eggs and parsley and season it with salt and pepper. Pour the filling into your pastry lined pan. Cover the pie with the other piece of pastry, moisten the edges and crimp or seal them. Brush the top of the pie with melted butter and use a fork to make small holes to vent the steam. Bake the pie for 40 to 50 minutes.

Stuffed Vegetables
Gemistá and *Dolmáthes*

Village Secrets of *Dolmáthes*

My mother-in-law has never set a pan of *Gemistá*—Stuffed Vegetables in the oven. In fact when I asked her to share her secrets for baking the vegetable and rice dish, she looked at me bewildered. It wasn't until after a long, confusing conversation, that I finally realized that what I have been eating all these years was not baked at all. The delicious vegetables, were just simmered on stove top along with the *Dolmáthes*.

Perhaps this is another example of how the Greek villagers don't waste anything—not even the extra space inside a pot. Or, perhaps they just know a secret or two that we don't.

According to her ways, she will roll enough *Dolmáthes* to use up half the stuffing mixture. The rest is spooned into prepared vegetables and they are set right on top or squeezed in between rolls of *Dolmáthes* in the pot. The vegetables are fitted snugly together and weighed down just as plain *Dolmáthes* would be.

The vegetables simmer slowly with the *Dolmáthes*, releasing their own juices into the pot. Since the cooking rice absorbs these tastes, I now know why her *Dolmáthes* are absolutely the best that I have ever tasted.

Another little secret that she let me in on, is to add a bone to *Dolmáthes* to give them some richness. Living in the mountains, she chooses wild hare when available, as her "bone." The meat is cut into small pieces and is arranged as the top layer of the *Dolmáthes* pot. As the game meat steams in the juices, the drippings will again be absorbed by the rice and give it a very rich flavor.

I do realize that most of us don't have wild hare available to do this, so for a substitution you can use chicken or any game birds as well as pork or beef pieces. Lamb can be used also, but be sure that you are a lamb lover because it will give the dish a distinct flavor. Of course, there is the solution of just using a plain bone. Beef or pork bones will work nicely. Set the bone over the last layer of *Dolmáthes* and let it steam in the cooking juices.

The next time you make *Dolmáthes*, try one of these village secrets in your recipe. Toss in a bone or add a few tomatoes, green peppers, and zucchinis as stuffed vegetables to your *Dolmáthes* pot. Let it all simmer together and you'll have a wonderful dish, village style.

Making Stuffed Vegetables / *Gemistá*

Gemistá or Stuffed Vegetables, is a popular dish that is enjoyed in all parts of Greece. It's simple to prepare and makes a beautiful presentation at the table. Any selection of vegetables can be used or only a certain one, so it's easily adaptable to individual preferences.

This dish can be prepared hours in advance of a special meal. The stuffed vegetables can be refrigerated without adding the stock or oil that is called for and baked when you're ready. It's very convenient if you're having company that's calling later in the day.

Vegetable Preparation for *Gemistá*

Green Peppers:
Use medium sized green peppers that are 3 to 5 inches in length. Slice the tops of the peppers, remove seeds, and wash them inside and out. Set them aside with their caps to drain.

Zucchinis:
Use small sized zucchinis no longer than 6 inches. Wash the zucchini, rubbing the fuzz off under running water. Cut off the stem end. Using an apple corer or a small knife hollow out the center, being careful not to cut through the skin. For an easier method, you can cut them length wise in half, and scoop out the centers. The zucchini halves can be reassembled after they are stuffed.

Potatoes:
Use medium sized, round potatoes. Peel the potatoes and rinse them under running water. Using an apple corer or a small knife, hollow out the center so you have a casing ½ to ¾ inch thick. Keep the potatoes submerged in salt water so they don't blacken. Prior to use, par boil the hollowed potatoes in stock or water for 5 minutes. Let them drain before stuffing.

Onions:
Use medium sized, yellow or red onions. Cut off the root and stem ends. Peel the onions and rinse them under running water. Using an apple corer or a small knife, hollow out the center so you have a casing ½ to ¾ inch thick, being careful not to cut through the root end. You can use the cut out onion in the stuffing ingredients. Prior to use, par boil the hollowed onions in stock or water for 5 minutes. Let them drain before stuffing.

Tomatoes:
Wash the tomatoes and slice the tops only ¾ off, so they remain hinged to serve as covers. Using a small knife or spoon, scoop out the pulp. The pulp can be used in the stuffing. Set the tomatoes aside to drain.

Eggplants:
Use small sized eggplants that are oblong and narrow in shape, no longer than 6 inches. Cut off the stem end and rinse the eggplant under running water. Using an apple corer or a small knife hollow out the center, being careful not to cut through the skin. For an easier method, you can cut them length wise in half, and scoop out the centers. The eggplant halves can be reassembled after they are stuffed. Keep the eggplant submerged in salt water so they don't blacken. Drain them before stuffing.

Zucchini Blossoms:

The fresh yellow blossoms of the zucchini plant are often used as a vegetable casing for stuffing. If you have your own zucchini plants, pick the blossoms when they are almost open. Rinse them in cold water and par boil them for 3 to 5 minutes. Set them aside to drain. Stuff the blossoms and fold over the petals so they enclose the mixture. They are cooked following the same directions as *Dolmáthes* and *Gemistá*.

Arranging Stuffed Vegetables for Baking

When setting your vegetables into the pan, follow these basic guide lines. Tomatoes, onions, potatoes and round green peppers should be arranged stuffing side up. Long vegetables, such as zucchini, eggplant, and long green peppers, should lay on their sides. Zucchini blooms should sit so that the folded petals are against the side of the pot or another vegetable, helping to hold in the stuffing.

Make sure that you always have a snug fit for your vegetables. A good way to choose a pan is to fit the vegetables in it before they get stuffed so you know if the pan is too big or too small.

Working with Fresh Grape Vine Leaves

Spring time in the islands brings with it the fresh grape vine leaves that are used for our traditional dish—*Dolmáthes*. You can easily purchase preserved leaves in brine, but the fresh leaves are truly delicious. If you are lucky enough to have grapes growing near your home, pick some of the tender young leaves and give yourself a treat.

The best time to pick the fresh leaves is May and June. Start by holding up the tip of the vine and count down it. The third or fourth leaf are usually a good size to pick. Another gauge to use is the palm of your hand. The tender leaves should be about palm size. Leaves past the 4th 'eye' are usually tough and won't make good *Dolmáthes*. Remember, that for most recipes, you'll need 50-60 leaves, so make sure you pick enough. After you get the leaves home, snip off the stem part from each leaf and drop them into a large basin full of soapy water. Just a bit of dish detergent will do. Wash the leaves well to get rid of dust and pesticides, rinse them and set them aside to drain. Pile them into small stacks of ten.

Vine leaf preparation methods depend on how long you want to store them and when you'll be planning to use them so choose the method that best suits you.

To use Fresh Vine Leaves immediately: Drop enough stacks of leaves for your recipe into a pot of boiling water. Boil them for 5 - 10 minutes, submerging them often until they have become tender. Remove them with a slotted spoon and set them aside to drain and cool down.

To use Fresh Vine Leaves within a few days: Wrap the amount of leaves that you want to use in a clean, cloth towel and set them aside. Check on them after two days. Usually, they have wilted enough to be used on the 4th or 5th day.

To Freeze Fresh Vine Leaves: Put the amount of stacks that you need for one recipe in a zip lock bag. Pour in ¼ cup of water and seal the bag. They can be kept for long periods in the freezer.

To preserve Fresh Vine Leaves in Brine: Wash and sterilize wide mouthed jars. Pile in the stacks of vine leaves, packing them tightly together. Using the recipe for Olive Brine, make enough to cover the contents of each jar. Cap the jars and set them in a cool, dark place. The leaves will keep for months.

Step by Step *Dolmáthes* Making

Dolmáthes are a very popular Greek *mezé* as well as a main course dish. The recipes call for a bit of special technique in preparing and rolling up the delicate packages of stuffing and some people think that they are a lot of work and just not worth the effort to make. I won't lie to you, they are a lot of work. But I have found that if you are prepared, it can be much easier and relatively stress free.

The best grape leaves to use are the tender, fresh ones that grow on the vines in spring months before the vines begin to bear fruit. Here in the Islands, the village women will harvest the small leaves and preserve them in brine. Since most of us don't have grape vines growing in our yard, you can check out a Greek specialty shop or market that will have the preserved leaves.

Cabbage leaves are often used to make *Dolmáthes* especially when grape leaves are out of season. Choose fresh heads that are very tender and almost lettuce like when you squeeze them. The hard types of cabbage that are used for slaws will be very difficult if not impossible to roll.

Preparing The Leaves

Fresh Grape Vine Leaves

For fresh leaves, you will need to par boil them in plain water for 5 to 10 minutes until they become tender. Let them drain before using.

Preserved Grape Vine Leaves

For leaves that have been preserved in brine, you will have to use your judgment. Leaves that have been sitting in brine for a while will be soft and all you will have to do is rinse them off. Other preserved leaves may be a fresher batch and are tough. In this case, par boil them in plain water for 2 to 3 minutes. Let them drain before using.

Cabbage Leaves

Using a sharp knife, cut out the core from the cabbage head. Rinse the cabbage under cold running water, using your fingers to spread the leaves apart, gently. Separate each leaf and set them aside to drain. In a large pot, bring plain water to a boil. Add the cabbage leaves and simmer them for for 2 to 5 minutes, just enough to get them tender. Using a slotted spoon, remove them to a strainer and let them drain before using.

Preparing The Stuffing

You'll notice as you read over the recipes, that the stuffings are very easy to make and it's only a matter of throwing ingredients together. In some cases, you can make the stuffing the day before you take on the task of rolling up the *Dolmáthes*. Keep the meat and rice separate, but mix everything else together. By doing this, you can simply sit at your kitchen table the next day and roll up the parcels.

Preparing The Cooking Pot

Whenever making *Dolmáthes*, always choose a pot that has a flat bottom and a good fitting lid. The opening of the pot should be wide enough so that an oven proof plate or dish can be set into it.

Prepare the pot by lining the bottom with two or three layers of prepared grape or cabbage leaves. Use damaged and torn leaves as well as any that seem too big or too small to roll up. Since you can't stir *Dolmáthes*, by lining the bottom, you will save them from scorching during their cooking time.

Stuffing the Leaves

Begin by placing a grape leaf in the palm of your hand 'veins up'. Put a tablespoon of the stuffing mixture into the center of the leaf. Fold in each side over the stuffing, then fold up the bottom so it resembles an envelope, and roll it up into a parcel.

For some people, its easier if they fold up the bottom of the leaf first and then fold in the sides, proceeding to roll them up. Use which ever technique is easiest for you and be patient, as it takes time and practice to learn how to roll these babies up.

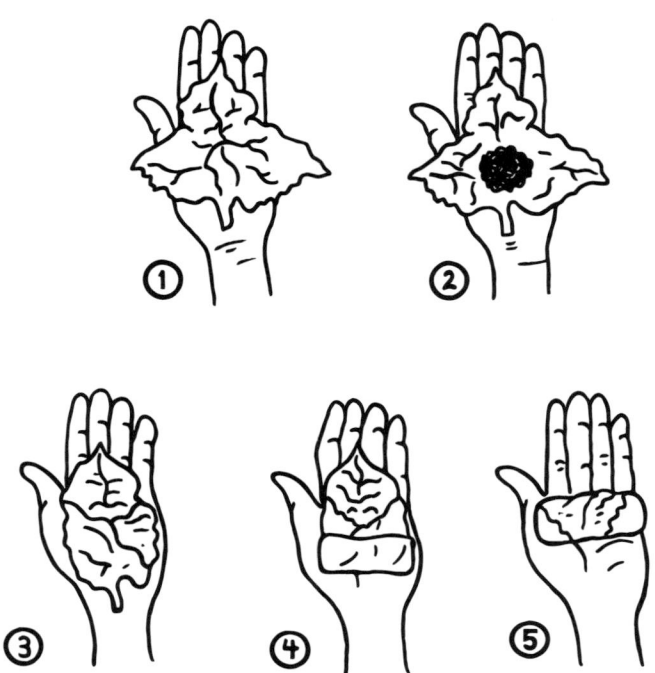

The rolled leaf should be small in size, 1 to 2½ inches in width and maybe ½ to ¾ inches thick. Place the finished roll, seam side down in your prepared pot.

Rolling the Cabbage Leaves

Cabbage *Dolmáthes* are rolled up in the same manner as those made from grape leaves. But parts of the cabbage leaves, especially near the core may be tough. Use a knife to cut away any hard stem parts to make the rolling easier for you. The finished rolls will be 2 to 3 inches in width and up to an inch in thickness, making them a little larger then when using grape leaves.

Cooking the *Dolmáthes*

The *Dolmáthes* should be arranged side by side in the prepared pot. You want a tight fit so that they don't unravel when cooking. Once a layer of rolls has been formed, begin a new layer right on top of them. For odd corners and spaces, you can do as my mother-in-law and add a stuffed tomato or green pepper.

When you have rolled up and arranged all the rolls, you will need to place an inverted oven proof dish over the rolls to weight them down. Again, this is done so that they don't unravel while cooking.

Dolmáthes are always simmered and never boiled. The force of a heated boil will tear apart the leaves and give you a pot of vine leaf and pilaf goo instead of delicate little rolls. Use a low heat setting and simmer the rolls until the rice is cooked.

I must tell you that the village women will simmer *Dolmáthes* up to an hour or more, making the rice very over cooked. Since these rolls are served at almost room temperature, the rice cools down again and becomes firmer. Because the leaves and stuffing ingredients have basically been stewed together, the taste is fantastic.

Remember to check on the *Dolmáthes* and the amount of liquid that is in the pot periodically during the cooking time. Even though the layer of leaves is on the bottom, protecting the rolls, they can still burn and give the *Dolmáthes* a terrible taste. If the stock has been absorbed or evaporated, then you'll have to add more. Don't soak them in liquid, just add a cup or two of stock at a time. Let them simmer again until the juice is absorbed before adding any more.

Serving *Dolmáthes*

Let the *Dolmáthes* cool down considerably before serving them. Remember to be gentle when removing them from the pot, as the rolls will tear rather easily. I use a tablespoon instead of a fork because it keeps the leaves from breaking.

Any sauce can be used as an accompaniment, but some of the more popular are the Egg-Lemon Sauce, *Tzatzíki* and Sesame Sauce.

Stuffed Grape Leaves with Meat / *Dolmáthes* or *Giaprákia me Kréas*

This recipe for Stuffed Grape Leaves includes the ground meat of your preference. Serve them with a Greek Village Salad, and a yogurt sauce such as *Tzatzíki*.

Ingredients:
40 to 50 grape vine leaves plus extra to line the pot.
salt and pepper
½ cup olive oil
chicken, beef or vegetable stock

Stuffing:
⅓ cup olive oil
1 onion, minced
1 lb. ground beef, pork, or lamb
1 cup uncooked rice
2 tbs. tomato paste
½ cup chopped fresh dill weed
salt and pepper

Prepare your leaves and set them aside to drain. Mix all the filling ingredients in a bowl and set it aside. Prepare the cooking pot by layering a few vine leaves on the bottom. Use the large or torn leaves for this.

Follow the directions for Stuffing Leaves and proceed to roll them up. Place the roll seam side down in your leaf-lined pot. Continue rolling up the leaves and arranging them side by side in the pot until all the stuffing is used.

When you have rolled up and arranged all the rolls, pour ½ cup of olive oil over them. Use a small inverted plate to weight down the rolls. Add enough stock to fill the pot to one inch below the top layer. Cover your pot with the lid and simmer over low heat for 40 to 60 minutes or until the rice is done to your preference.

Vegetarian Stuffed Grape Leaves / *Dolmáthes Pseútiki* or *Giaprákia Pseútika*

For religious fasting days or for people who prefer their diets without meat, there is the variation of this recipe know as *Dolmáthes Pseútiki* or Fake *Dolmáthes*. The method is the same, simply omit the meat and increase the rice to 2½ to 3 cups.

Stuffed Vegetables with Meat / *Gemistá*

Ingredients:
12 to 15 prepared vegetables of your choice.
1½ cup chicken or beef stock
olive oil

Stuffing:

⅓ cup olive oil
1 chopped onion
1½ lb. ground beef
½ cup chopped parsley
1 cup rice
1 tbs. tomato paste
½ cup chopped tomatoes or scooped out pulp
½ cup chopped fresh dill
½ cup pine nuts - optional
salt and pepper

Heat the oil in a skillet over moderate heat and fry the onion until translucent. Add the ground beef and cook it until crumbly. Stir in the rest of the stuffing ingredients. Simmer the mixture over medium heat, stirring it so the rice doesn't stick, for 5 minutes or until the water is absorbed. Set it aside to cool slightly.

Preheat the oven to 350°F. Using a spoon, stuff the vegetables and cap them. Arrange them in a shallow pan.

Pour the vegetable stock into the bottom and drizzle olive oil over the vegetables. Cover them loosely with a piece of aluminum foil and bake them for 40 to 50 minutes. Remove the foil and bake them for an additional 10 to 15 minutes.

Stuffed Vegetables Vegetarian Style / *Gemistá Pseútika*

For religious fasting days or for people who prefer their diets without meat, there is the variation of this recipe know as *Gemistá Pseútika* or Fake *Gemistá*. The method is the same, simply omit the meat and increase the rice to 2½ cups.

Stuffed Cabbage Rolls with Meat / *Lahanodolmáthes*

This recipe comes from the village of *Sálakos*, here in Rhodes.

Ingredients:
prepared cabbage leaves from 2 medium sized heads
1½ cups olive oil
2 cups chicken or beef stock

Stuffing:
3 cups rice
1 lb. ground beef, pork or lamb
2 tbs. butter
1 cup chopped parsley
3 cups chopped tomatoes
1 cup chopped dill weed
1½ tbs. crumbled dry spearmint
1 tsp. ground cumin
salt and pepper

> **Menu Idea**
> Stuffed Cabbage Rolls with Meat
> Egg-Lemon Sauce
> Lamb Pie from Cephalonia
> Fried Fresh Potatoes
> Tomato and Herb salad
> Greek Vinaigrette
> Feta Cheese
> Olives
> Fresh Bread

Add all the stuffing ingredients into a large bowl and mix together well. Prepare the cooking pot by layering a few cabbage leaves on the bottom.

Following the directions for Stuffing Leaves, proceed to roll them up. Try to keep them small, about 2 or 3 inches in width. It may take some practice, but the finished results will be worth it.

Set the rolls on the bottom of the pot, seam side down and continue until you've used up all the stuffing. Once you have filled up the pot, pour the oil over the *Lahanodolmáthes*. Use a small inverted plate to weight down the cabbage rolls. Add the vegetable broth to the pot and cover it with a lid. Simmer on low heat for 40 to 50 minutes or until the rice is done to your preference.

Stuffed Cabbage Rolls - Vegetarian Style / *Lahanodolmáthes Pseútiki*

For religious fasting days or for people who prefer their diets without meat, there is the variation of this recipe know as *Lahanodolmáthes Pseútiki* or Fake *Lahanodolmáthes*. The method is the same, simply omit the meat and increase the rice to 4 cups.

Tomato-Onion *Dolmáthes* / *Dolmáthes Nistísimi*

This stuffing can be used for *Dolmáthes*, *Gemistá*, or *Lahaodolmáthes*. This is the traditional dish served after mass on Holy Thursday Night when the Twelve Gospels are read.

Ingredients:
5 onions, grated
1½ cup olive oil - optional
3 grated tomatoes
1 cup chopped parsley
1 cup chopped dill
3 cups rice
salt and pepper
vegetable stock

Heat a skillet and fry the onions until dry. Add the oil, tomato, parsley, dill, and rice. Season it with salt and pepper and simmer it together until the juice is absorbed. Remove the stuffing from the heat, and following the directions, stuff the vegetables or leaves of your choice. Add some vegetable stock to your pot, depending on the method that you've chosen, cover it and simmer or bake until the rice is done.

Bulgur Wheat Dolmáthes / *Dolmáthes me Pligoúri*

Another variation to the delicious *Dolmáthes*. This recipe uses bulgur wheat in place of the rice and is a simple mix-it-all-together recipe to follow. It's a wonderful change in taste and texture from other *Dolmáthes* recipes.

Ingredients:
1 lb. ground pork
1 cup bulgur wheat
1 cup chopped fresh tomatoes
1 onion, minced
½ cup melted butter
¼ cup chopped parsley
½ tsp. ground cumin
salt and pepper

Simply mix together all the stuffing ingredients. Follow the directions for stuffing grape or cabbage leaves or the vegetables of your choice. Add some chicken stock to the pot and depending on the method that you have chosen, cover it and simmer or bake, until the wheat is done.

Pine Nut Stuffing / *Gémisi me Koukounária*

This versatile stuffing can be used for an assortment of recipes other than *Dolmáthes* or *Gemistá*. It is delicious when used as a holiday stuffing for turkey, chicken, duck, and other poultry dishes.

Ingredients:
1 cup olive oil
1 cup chopped onions
2 cups rice
1 cup pine nuts
½ cup seedless raisins - optional
½ cup chopped parsley
½ cup chopped dill weed
2 cups chopped tomatoes
½ cup chicken or vegetable stock
1 tsp. ground cumin
salt and pepper

Heat the oil in a skillet and fry the onions with the rice. Add the pine nuts, raisins, parsley and dill and sauté it together for a moment or two. Add the rest of the ingredients and cook the stuffing just until the juice has evaporated. Remove it from the heat.

Following your chosen recipe, fill the vegetables, leaves, or poultry with the stuffing. Continue to cook according to the instructions and enjoy.

Pilafs and Pastas
Piláfia Ke Makarónia

Aegean Pilaf / *Piláfi tou Aegéou*

A very simple and inexpensive dish that is as colorful as it is good. This rice accompaniment is great for roasts or for just eating on its own when you want something light. This is great with Shish Kebabs or just as a side dish for a good steak.

Ingredients:
2 cups long grain rice
1 clove garlic, minced
½ cup chopped green pepper
1 cup olive oil
½ cup chopped red pepper
chicken or vegetable stock
½ cup chopped onion
salt and pepper
¼ cup chopped celery
dash oregano, thyme and cumin
2 tbs. minced parsley

In a large pot, heat the olive oil. Add the peppers, onions, celery, parsley and garlic. Fry lightly then add the rice and fry it all together for a few minutes, stirring constantly so the rice doesn't stick to the bottom. Add your spices then pour in just enough stock to cover it all.

Bring it to a boil then reduce the heat and cover the pot. Simmer the pilaf until it's done. You will have to keep your eye on it in case you need to add more liquid. You want the finished product to be moist and somewhat fluffy, but not dry, so when the rice is almost done, take the pot off the heat and cover tightly, letting the rice absorb the liquid.

Lemon Pilaf / *Piláfi Lemonáto*

Use this pilaf recipe as a bed for shish kebabs and roasts. It can also be served as a side dish for stewed vegetables and meats.

Ingredients:
½ cup olive oil
1 quartered onion
1 garlic clove
2 stems parsley
1 rib celery
1 carrot
5 cups vegetable or chicken stock
2 cups rice
juice of 2 lemons
grated peel of 2 lemons
1 tsp. oregano
salt and pepper

Bring the stock to a boil and add the onion, garlic, parsley, celery, carrot and olive oil. Boil the vegetables for 15 minutes then remove them from the stock. Bring it back to a boil, and add the rice, lemon juice, peel, oregano and season it with salt and pepper. Cover the pot and simmer the pilaf, stirring occasionally so it doesn't stick. If needed, add little bits of water or stock as you go along. When the pilaf is almost done, remove the pot from the heat and keep it covered so the rice will absorb the juice.

The Bride's Pilaf / *To Piláfi tis Nífis*

A specialty dish from *Ikónio*, this sweet pilaf is served on the wedding day at the reception.

Ingredients:
4 cups vegetable stock or water
1 cup rice
½ cup dark raisins
1 cup cooked chick peas
¼ cup butter
½ tsp. sugar
salt and pepper

Bring the stock to a boil and add the rice, raisins, and chickpeas and season it with salt and pepper. When the rice is done, strain the mixture. Toss the pilaf with the butter and sugar and serve.

Lentils with Rice and Onions / *Fakórizo me Sívrasi*

Though this dish may have once been considered a poor mans meal, today it is an Island favorite and very easy to prepare. In Rhodes, we serve raw onions—spring or dried, olives and *Rénka* or smoked herring as an accompaniment to this dish. Some grated parmesan or Greek *kefalotíri* is a delicious accent.

Ingredients:
1 lb. dried lentils
vegetable or chicken stock
1 cup rice
1 bay leaf
salt and pepper
1 cup olive oil
3 onions, chopped

In a large pot, simmer the lentils in enough stock to cover them twice. When they are almost done, add the rice, bay leaf and the salt and pepper to taste. Simmer the mixture for 15 to 20 minutes. You want the mixture to be thick, so stir it occasionally to keep it from scorching and add small amounts of stock if needed.
Once the rice is done, remove it from the heat and set aside.
In a skillet, heat the olive oil. Add the onions and sauté until golden brown. Pour the oil and onions into the lentils and stir through.

Bulgur Wheat Pilaf / *Pligoúri Piláfi*

Ingredients:
2 tbs. butter
1 grated onion
1 med. potato diced
2 tbs. grated cheese
2 tomatoes grated
vegetable or chicken stock
1 cup bulgur wheat
1 cup rice
salt and pepper

Brown the butter and the onions together. Stir in the cheese and the potatoes and fry lightly. Add the tomato and stock. When the potato is half done, stir in the wheat and rice. Season it with salt and pepper, and simmer the mixture until the pilaf is cooked.

Orzo in Tomato Sauce / *Kritharáki*

Orzo is simply a pasta and some people refer to it as *manéstra*. Some traditional recipes for the small noodle use barley and others use wheat flour. The dough is shaped into thick, rice-like grains and let to dry just like any other pasta would be. It cooks up like spaghetti, using salted water or a flavored sauce, but is more prone to sticking to the pot because of it's shape and size. This traditional dish uses orzo, but if you can't get it, any small pasta or long grain rice can be substituted.

Ingredients:
1 lb. orzo macaroni available in Greek specialty shops.
½ cup olive oil
1 cup chopped onions
2 cups fresh chopped tomatoes
1 cup dry white wine
salt and pepper to taste
vegetable or chicken stock

In a large pot, fry the onion in the oil until translucent. Stir in the wine and the tomatoes. Season with salt and pepper and sauté the sauce for 5 minutes. Add two quarts of stock and bring it to a boil, letting it cook for 15 minutes.

Add the orzo and simmer it for 15 minutes, stirring often so it doesn't stick or scorch. More stock can be added if needed, but remember that you want this dish to be on the dry side, without much moisture. Remove from the heat, cover it and let it stand until the juice has been absorbed. Serve with grated cheese as a side dish or as an entree.

Pasta Imam / *Makarónia Imám*

Serve your favorite pasta in this delicious vegetable sauce with a Mediterranean flair. This is great with lots of parmesan cheese, a Lettuce Salad, a hot crusty loaf of bread, and a good bottle of red wine.

Ingredients:
2 eggplants
3 zucchinis
oil for frying
1 lb. cooked pasta of your choice

Sauce:
½ cup olive oil
1 cup chopped onions
3 minced garlic cloves
2 cups chopped fresh tomatoes
1 tsp. thyme
1 bay leaf
1 vegetable or chicken bouillon cube
1 tsp. oregano
½ tsp. sugar
salt and pepper

Wash the eggplants and zucchinis, removing the purple peel from the eggplants if you prefer. Quarter and cut the vegetables into one inch chunks. Heat enough oil in a skillet to cover the bottom and fry the vegetables until browned. Remove them to paper towels to drain.

In a saucepan, heat the olive oil and fry the onions and garlic until translucent. Add the browned vegetables and toss together. When heated through, add the tomato and spices. Cook over low heat for 20 minutes until the sauce is thick. Don't over stir, you want the vegetables chunky. Serve the sauce over pasta or rice.

Pepper Pilaf / *Piláfi me Piperiés*

This colorful dish is very easy to make and is as delicious as it looks. If you like spicy foods, add the pepper flakes for a bit of zip. It can be served as a side dish for a variety of roasts or for making a "bed" for stewed meats and vegetables. It's also wonderful on it's own as a light lunch. When serving it hot, use *Tzatzíki* or one of its sister yogurt sauces as an accompaniment. It can also be served cold as a rice salad, using Greek Vinaigrette as a dressing.

Ingredients:
½ cup olive oil
1 onion, chopped
2 garlic cloves, minced
1 green pepper, chopped
1 red pepper, chopped
1 yellow pepper, chopped
1 stalk celery, chopped
½ cup dry white wine
4 cups chicken stock
2 stems parsley, chopped
2 cups long grain rice
½ tsp. dry red pepper flakes - optional
½ cup toasted pine nuts - optional

Heat the oil in a deep sauce pan. Add the onions and garlic and fry until translucent. Stir in the peppers and celery and sauté the vegetables together for 5 minutes. Add the wine, chicken stock, parsley and pepper flakes. Bring it to a boil and add the rice. Cover the pot and simmer the mixture over low heat for 15 minutes, stirring it occasionally as you don't want the rice to stick. Give it one final stir and remove the pot from the heat. Stir in the pine nuts and cover it for an additional 5 minutes for the moisture to be absorbed by the rice. Serve it hot or cold.

Spinach Rice / *Spanakórizo*

A tasty light meal that goes great with a Greek Village Salad. Obviously, fresh spinach is preferred, but frozen can be used without much sacrifice of taste.

Ingredients:
½ cup olive oil
1 cup chopped onions
1 cup uncooked rice
4 cups vegetable or chicken stock
salt and pepper to taste
2 lbs. fresh or frozen spinach
grated Greek *kefalotíri* or parmesan cheese

Wash the spinach well, removing the hard stems and set it aside to drain. In a large pot, sauté the onions in the oil until they are tender. Stir in the rice and the stock and season with salt and pepper. Reduce heat and simmer for 10 minutes, being careful to add more stock as needed. Add the washed spinach and carefully stir it together with the rice. Cover the pot and cook for another 5 to 10 minutes until it is done, stirring occasionally so it doesn't stick. Serve with a sprinkling of cheese.

Tomato Rice with Garlic / *Tomatórizo me Skórdo*

From *Ípiros*, a side dish that is not only easy to make but is a fantastic accompaniment to roasts and chops—especially lamb. This meatless pilaf is also served as an entree on fasting days in the Greek religious calendar.

Ingredients:
1 cup olive oil
1 cup chopped onions
4 cloves minced garlic
2 cups chopped fresh tomatoes
1 bay leaf
salt and pepper
5 cups vegetable or chicken stock
2 cups uncooked rice

In a medium size pot, heat the olive oil and fry the onions and garlic until translucent. Add the tomato, bay leaf and season with salt and pepper. Sauté the mixture for 5 minutes.

Pour in the stock. When the mixture begins to boil, add the rice and let it simmer for 15 to 20 minutes or until its done. Remember to stir it occasionally so the rice doesn't stick to the pot. Remove the pot from the heat and cover it, so the moisture can be absorbed.

Lenten Spaghetti / *Makarónia Nistísima*

The Greek version of Napolitan Sauce. Not only is this easy to prepare but it also makes a nice change even for those who like meat. Using the cinnamon will give your sauce a sweet taste where as for a more savory and spicier version, you can add the spices liberally as well a bit of dry hot peppers.

Ingredients:
Sauce:
1 cup olive oil
1 chopped onion
1 clove mashed garlic
3 cups chopped tomatoes
1 cup vegetable broth
1 bay leaf
1 tsp. dry thyme
1 tsp. dry oregano
½ tsp. sugar
salt and pepper
cinnamon stick – optional

1 lb. cooked pasta of your choice

Heat the oil in a large saucepan. Sauté the onions and garlic until translucent. Pour in the tomatoes and broth and once it comes to a boil, lower the heat. Add your spices and simmer for 30 minutes, stirring occasionally, until the sauce is thick. That's it. Simple and quick. Pour the sauce over your favorite pasta and you have a wonderful meatless dish.

Spaghetti from Hálki / *Halkítika Makarónia*

Just across from the north western coast of Rhodes you'll find my dad's home island, *Hálki*. It is an isolated small fishing island that is very dry and barren because it's nothing more than what I like to call a big rock in the Aegean. Other than the winter rains, fresh water has never been readily available to the islanders because of the impossibility of digging through so much rock in hopes of finding it.

Another commodity that the island lacks is dirt. Yes, plain old dirt is very hard to come by on the island and the *Halkítes* themselves were known to sail to the shores of Rhodes just to dig some up and take home with them so they could pot a plant. The island of *Hálki* is so mountainous and rocky that gardening is unheard of.

More than likely, this recipe came to be, due to the lack of fresh vegetables available to the islanders. Dry onions could be purchased and stored for a long time until another boat would sail into the harbor with fresh cargo. The *Halkítes* found a way to team the dry vegetable with some olive oil to give us a very easy and quick recipe for a delicious pasta dish. It's great for when you need a last minute meal or as a side dish to chops and steaks.

Ingredients:
1 cup olive oil
2 cups chopped onions
drained boiled spaghetti
salt and pepper
grated cheese

Heat the oil in a skillet and fry the onions until they begin to brown. Toss the onions and oil with the spaghetti and season it with salt and pepper. Serve it with lots of grated cheese.

For more great Pilaf and Pasta Dishes see the following recipes:

Rice Pie / *Rizópita*
Beef with Orzo Macaroni / *Moscári Yiouvétsi*
Easter Stuffed Lamb / *Lambriátiko Arní Gemistó*
Pastítsio
Greek Beef Soup / *Kréas me Kritharáki Soúpa*
Island Chicken with Orzo / *Kotópoulo me Kritharáki*
Stewed Chicken and Macaroni/ *Kotópoulo me Makarónia*
Goat Stuffed with Rice / *Katsíki Kapamá*
Partridge Pilaf / *Pérdika Piláfi*
Partridges Stuffed with Wheat / *Pérdikes Gemistés*
Stuffed Pigeon / *Peristéria Gemistá*
Mussels with Rice / *Mídia Piláfi*
Octopus with Macaroni / *Htapódi me Makaronáki*
Shrimp with Rice / *Garídes Piláfi*
Heart and Kidney Pilaf / *Piláfi me Nefrá ke Kardiés*
Stuffed Vegetables / *Gemistá Ke Dolmáthes*

Vegetables
Lahaniká

Greek Seasons and the Vegetable - *Lahaniká*

Greek cooking is very seasonally oriented and the average household menu changes as fast as the temperatures do. Some vegetable recipes may use only one main ingredient where as others use lots of different kinds. These are differences that the seasons brought about. For example, in mid-July when the tomatoes are dropping off the vines, tomato omelets, tomato sauces, tomato salads as well as pickled and sun dried tomatoes were the recipes that the village home would use. Of course any soup or stew that included other summer vegetables, almost always included tomato as well.

For the winter months, recipes took on a lighter, greener coloring. Lemons would be used to make sauces that would replace the tomato and greens such as cabbage, broccoli, spinach and kale would replace the eggplants and zucchinis.

A very good example of this would be for *Dolmáthes*. In the spring, fresh grape vine leaves would be picked to preserve for the making of this traditional dish. But by the time winter set in, the household stock of preserved leaves may have been depleted. This is where the tender leaves of the cabbage would be used, making the variation *Lahanodolmáthes* so the same delicious recipe could be enjoyed year round.

Even today, although ships come into port everyday carrying their cargos of fresh produce, we are still used to our ways. A tomato omelet just doesn't taste as good as it does in the summer months and spinach rice is for those cold winter days.

Boiled Vegetables

On a Greek dinner table you'll often find plain boiled vegetables. Broccoli, cauliflower, spinach and green beans, just to name a few, are boiled in salted water, drained and served with Lemon-Oil Dressing. Although it may seem like a simple dish, these fresh vegetables are really good when served this way and make a great accompaniment to meats, roasts or *mezédes*.

Many times you'll find that leafy vegetables such as spinach, Swiss chard, kale and wild mountain greens are boiled with potatoes for a more substantial side dish. This method is also great for when you only have a small quantity of ingredients. For instance, a handful of green beans and zucchinis boiled with some small potatoes will make enough to feed a family.

Boil the vegetables of your choice in plain salted water until they are as tender as you prefer. Drain them and serve them with a good dousing of Lemon Oil Dressing. These vegetables can be served hot or cold, and can be considered as salads and *mezédes* as well.

Sívrasi

Another island secret is to dress plain boiled vegetables with olive oil and fried onions. It can be used with leafy green vegetables or for vegetable dishes such as lentils and rice or spinach rice.

Ingredients:
1 cup oil
2 cups chopped onions
salt and pepper

Heat the oil in a skillet and fry the onions until they are golden brown. Toss the onion-oil mixture with the boiled vegetables, season with salt and pepper and serve.

Artichokes with Egg Lemon Sauce / *Agináres Avgolémono*

This vegetable dish is great in the winter and the Egg-Lemon Sauce gives it a refreshing tang. Serve this as an entree with an accompanying green salad and a slice of one of the many savory pites.

Ingredients:
2 - 1 lb. cans or 12 fresh artichoke hearts
¼ cup olive oil
1 large onion, chopped
1 lb. potatoes, peeled and cut into 1" chunks
1 lb. peas, frozen or fresh
1 cup chopped dill weed
vegetable or chicken stock
salt and pepper to taste
Egg-Lemon Sauce - see recipe

Rinse and drain the artichokes. See the section in "Kitchen Techniques" for tips on how to clean and prepare fresh artichokes. If you are using canned, simply put them in a strainer to drain.

Heat the oil in a deep saucepan and fry the onions until translucent. Add the fresh artichokes, potatoes, peas and dill weed with enough stock to cover it all and season with salt and pepper. Simmer for 25 minutes.

If you are using canned artichokes, simmer the vegetables for 15 minutes or until the potatoes just start to get tender before adding them. Continue to simmer the mixture for 10 minutes longer.

Remove the pot from the heat. Spoon out one or two cups of broth and set it aside to cool. Once it's cooled, use it to make the Egg-Lemon Sauce following the recipe directions. Pour the sauce over the artichokes and serve.

Artichokes with Tomatoes / *Agináres me Tomáta*

This side dish can easily be served as a vegetable sauce over a bed of rice. Simply cut the fried artichokes into quarters before adding them to the final sauce and you have the makings for a delicious vegetarian meal.

Ingredients:
8 artichoke hearts, canned or fresh
⅓ cup olive oil
½ cup chopped onions
2 cups fresh chopped tomatoes
¼ cup fresh chopped dill weed
salt and pepper

Rinse and drain the artichokes. See the section in "Kitchen Techniques" for tips on how to clean and prepare fresh artichokes. If you are using canned, simply put them in a strainer to drain.

Heat the oil in a skillet. Add the artichokes and fry them until they brown on all sides. Using a slotted spoon, remove them from the skillet.

Re-heat the skillet, making sure you have enough oil to cover the bottom - add more if needed. Fry the onions until translucent. Add the tomatoes, dill weed and season with salt and pepper. Simmer the sauce for 10 minutes. Add the fried fresh artichokes and cover the skillet. Simmer them for 20 minutes, checking on them occasionally so they don't scorch and basting them with sauce.

For canned artichokes, simmer the sauce for 15 to 20 minutes before adding them. Continue to simmer them together for an additional 10 minutes.

Baked Beans in Tomato / *Fasoláda tou Foúrnou* or *Lópia*

This is the dish that was made every Saturday by my dear, departed Aunt Leukothéa. This is wonderful when baked in the village wood ovens, but it can be delicious when made at home as well. When using a modern oven, the secret is to bake the beans for a long time, without using too much stock at once. Let them bake and absorb the liquid, then stir in a little more and let them absorb that. Continue doing this and your beans will be tender and the sauce very thick. If you have trouble cooking beans, see the Mysterious Bean in the "Kitchen Techniques" section for tips on how to get great results.

Ingredients:
1 lb. dry white beans that have been soaked over night and drained.
1 cup chopped onions
2 cups chopped tomatoes
3 tbs. tomato paste
1 cup chopped celery or dill weed
1 carrot, sliced
1 cup olive oil
1 tbs. cumin
salt and pepper to taste
chicken or vegetable stock

Put your beans in a soup pot and cover them with plain water. Bring them to a boil and cook them until the surface gets frothy - about 5 minutes. Pour the beans into a colander and rinse them.

Preheat your oven to 325°F. In a roasting pan, mix together all the ingredients and add enough stock so the beans are just covered. Cover the pan with a lid or aluminum foil and bake for 2 to 4 hours, depending on how well done you like your beans. Check on the beans every half hour, stirring them and adding enough stock so they are juicy but not swimming in liquid. When the beans are almost done to your preference, remove the lid and let them bake for 20 to 30 minutes longer.

Baked Eggplant with Cheese / *Melintzánes Foúnou me Tirí*

Dating back to 1899, this recipe comes from *Trípoli* in Arcadia and her surrounding villages. Serve the dish as a lunch with a green salad or as a side dish for a roast. Use crumbled feta instead of the grated cheeses for a flavorful variation.

Ingredients:
2 lbs. eggplant, the smaller the better
3 cups chicken broth
1 cup olive oil
3 garlic cloves, crushed
3 onions, chopped
4 cups fresh chopped tomatoes
1 cup chopped parsley
1 bay leaf
pinch thyme
pinch oregano
salt and pepper
grated Greek *kefalotíri* or parmesan cheese

Wash the eggplant, cut off the tops and make a lengthwise slit down one side on each. In a large pot, bring the chicken stock to a boil, and add the eggplant. Boil them until tender 5 to 15 minutes, depending on their size. Remove them to a strainer to drain.

Heat the oil in a medium saucepan. Add the garlic and onions and fry until translucent. Add the tomato, parsley, bay leaf, thyme, oregano and salt and pepper. Cook the sauce over medium heat for 20 minutes until it thickens.

Take an eggplant and open it like an envelope. Sprinkle the insides generously with cheese. Spoon some tomato sauce over it and press the eggplant together again. Lay it in an ovenproof pan. Continue for the rest of the eggplants. When you're finished stuffing them, pour the unused sauce over the eggplants and sprinkle with more cheese. Bake in the oven at 350°F for 25 to 35 minutes.

Fried Vegetables / *Tiganitá*

This dish is quite commonly found on the islands as an entree and as a *mezé*. Fresh vegetables are lightly fried in olive oil and then covered in a sauce. The traditional garlic sauces or S*kordaliés* are usually used as an accompaniment, but often you'll find tomato sauces used as well. Try it both ways and see what suits your taste. Have lots of crusty bread around when serving this dish. A Greek Village Salad and a cold bottle of Retsina will complete the meal.

Ingredients:
4 potatoes peeled and cut into ¼ inch slices
2 eggplant cut into ½ inch slices
2 zucchinis cut into ¼ inch slices
2 green peppers seeded and quartered
salt and pepper
olive oil for frying

Garlic Sauce - see recipe
or
Cold Tomato Sauce - see recipe

Wash and slice your vegetables. Salt them and set them in strainers to drain. Heat the oil in a skillet. Starting with the potatoes, fry the slices until brown then turn them over and brown the other side. Proceed with the zucchini, eggplants and green peppers in the same way. Removing the vegetables from the skillet to paper towels to drain. Once the excess oil has been removed, arrange them on a platter.

Prepare the Garlic Sauce, using your preference for a thin or thick version. Other garlic sauces such as Walnut-Garlic or Almond-Garlic can be used as well. You can simply pour the sauce over the fried vegetables or serve it on the side, so everyone can use the amount they prefer.

If your preference is for a tomato topping, prepare the Cold Tomato Sauce and serve it on the side or poured over the vegetables. Other tomato sauces can be easily substituted and will give different flavors to the dish. Try Tomato-Dill or Tomato-Pepper for delicious variations.

Greek Green Beans / *Fasolákia Giahnistá*

Our restaurant in Baltimore would constantly run out of the popular side dish, Greek Green Beans. My dad had a very special way of stewing the simple vegetable so all the flavors would accent each other. He never used parsley in his version; instead he topped off the servings with a generous amount of grated parmesan cheese. Try the traditional recipe and then try it my dad's way and see what suits your taste.

Ingredients:
½ cup olive oil
1 cup chopped onions
1 minced garlic clove
1½ cups fresh chopped tomatoes
1 cup vegetable or chicken stock
⅓ cup chopped parsley – optional
salt and pepper
oregano to taste
thyme to taste
dash cumin
1½ lb. fresh or frozen green beans

In a saucepan, heat the oil and sauté the onions and garlic until translucent. Add your tomatoes, stock, parsley and spices and cook it for 5 minutes, stirring occasionally so it doesn't stick. Add the green beans. Reduce the heat and let it simmer together until the beans are tender and the sauce is thick. If you're using frozen green beans, cook the sauce for 15 minutes before adding them.

Spinach with Onions / *Spanáki Sívrasi*

Ingredients:
1 cup olive oil
2 chopped onions
½ cup chopped red peppers or pimento - optional
1 lb. chopped cooked spinach, drained
¼ cup chopped dill weed
salt and pepper

Heat the oil in a skillet and fry the onions with the peppers until they begin to brown slightly. Toss in the spinach and the dill and season it with salt and pepper. Cook it together for 10 minutes, stirring occasionally.

Zucchini Stew / *Kolokithákia Giahnistá*

This vegetarian stew can be used as a side dish or a sauce as well. Serve this vegetable dish over a bed of rice or pasta as an accompaniment to roasted meats or chops.

Ingredients:
½ cup olive oil
1 cup chopped onions
2 cups fresh chopped tomatoes
½ cup chopped dill weed
salt and pepper
4 cups zucchinis, cut into one inch slices .

Heat the oil in a saucepan and fry the onions until translucent. Add the tomatoes, dill weed, salt and pepper. Cook the sauce for 10 minutes. Stir in the zucchini. Cook for 20 minutes, covered over low heat. Don't stir it again or you might squish the cooking zucchini, just gently shake the pan occasionally. For a thicker sauce, remove the lid and let it cook until the liquid is reduced.

Green Beans with Zucchini and Feta / *Fasolákia me Kolokitháki ke Féta*

A green bean stew that's wonderful as a side dish or on its own. It's easy and can be a one-pot meal when you serve it with lots of fresh bread. For a more elaborate entree, you can serve this vegetable stew over a bed of pilaf.

Ingredients:
1 cup olive oil
1 celery stalk, chopped
1 onion, chopped
1 cup crushed tomatoes
salt and pepper
2 cups vegetable or chicken broth
1 lb. fresh or frozen green beans
1 lb. zucchini, cut into 1 inch slices
1 cup crumbled feta cheese

Heat the oil in a stew pot and fry the celery and onions until translucent. Add the tomato and vegetable broth, season with salt and pepper. Simmer the sauce for 5 minutes. Add the green beans first. If you're using fresh, cook them for 15 minutes before adding the zucchini. If you are using frozen green beans, add both in at the same time. Cook the vegetables in the sauce until tender, taking care that it doesn't scorch. If the sauce is too thick, add more broth. When the vegetables are done, fold in the feta and serve.

Okra with Potatoes/ *Mbámies me Patátes*

A fantastic vegetarian dish that has all the flavor of the Greek islands. This dish can be served with a Tomato and Feta Salad and a generous portion of Greek Village Bread.

Ingredients:
2 lbs. fresh or frozen okra - If using fresh okra, see the "Kitchen Techniques" section for tips on how to clean and prepare this vegetable.
vinegar
1 cup olive oil
3 onions, chopped
6 cloves garlic, chopped
2 cups chopped tomatoes
salt and pepper
1 bay leaf
2 lbs. potatoes, pared and cut into large chunks
chicken or vegetable stock

For fresh okra, sprinkle them with a bit of salt and vinegar and toss. After a few minutes, rinse them and spread on a tray to air dry.

Pour the oil into a large pot, add the onions and garlic and fry until translucent. Add the tomatoes, salt, pepper, and bay leaf and simmer together for 5 minutes, stirring occasionally. Add the okra and potatoes, and enough stock to cover it. Bring the mixture to a boil then reduce the heat and simmer for 30 to 45 minutes.

Sponge with Lettuce and Onions / *Sfouggáto me Maroúli ke Kremídi*

The recipe for this village quiche comes from the island of *Lésvos* and her capital city *Mytinlíni*. It's a wonderful baked omelet full of flavor. Serve it with a tomato salad, fresh bread and a cold bottle of Retsína wine.

Ingredients:
olive oil
2 heads romaine lettuce, finely chopped
10 spring onions finely chopped
1 cup chicken or vegetable stock
salt and pepper
2 tbs. dried spearmint
1 cup chopped fresh dill weed
12 eggs

In a large pot, heat enough oil to cover the bottom. Add the lettuce and onions and stir-fry for 1 or 2 minutes. Add the stock and some salt and pepper and continue to cook until the liquid has evaporated. Remove from the heat and add the mint and dill weed. Toss it together and set it aside to cool completely.

Heat the oven to 450°F and generously butter a large baking dish. In a large bowl beat the eggs until frothy. Gently fold in the cooled lettuce mixture. Pour it into the buttered dish and bake until the center is firm.

Tomato-Egg Omelet / *Tomáta me Avgó*

Every village has its own version of this easy omelet. Serve it as a lunch or as a midnight snack.

Ingredients:
½ cup olive oil
1 chopped onion
1 garlic clove
1 cup chopped tomatoes
1 bay leaf
salt and pepper
6 eggs, beaten

Heat the oil in a non stick pan and fry the onions with the garlic until they are translucent. Add the tomatoes and the bay leaf, season it with salt and pepper and simmer them for 15 minutes. Stir in the eggs and cook it until its set.

Village Omelet / *Omeléta Horiátiki*

A wonderful vegetarian dish that is served quite often in the Mediterranean islands. If you prefer, the purple skin can be peeled from the eggplants before frying as this tends to soften the taste.

Ingredients:
olive oil
2 large potatoes, peeled and cut into thin strips
2 cups chopped eggplants
½ cup chopped onion
1 minced garlic clove
1 cup chopped tomatoes
1 bay leaf
3 eggs
salt and pepper

Fry the potatoes in a bit of oil until tender and brown then remove them to paper towels to drain. Fry the eggplant until brown and remove them to drain also.
In a non-stick sauce pan, heat enough oil to cover the bottom and fry the garlic and onions until translucent. Add the tomato and bay leaf and simmer for 15 minutes, stirring occasionally. Return the eggplants and potatoes to the pan and toss with the sauce and season it with salt and pepper.
In a small bowl, whisk the eggs with a bit of salt and pepper. Pour them over the vegetables, and cook until the omelet is set.

Peas with Dill Sauce / *Mbizélia me Ánitho*

The light dill sauce gives plain peas a wonderful, summer flavor. Serve them as a side dish for roasts and steaks accompanied with mashed potatoes.

Ingredients:
1 lb. frozen peas
½ cup olive oil
1 cup chopped onions
2 tbs. flour
1½ cups chicken stock
1 tbs. lemon juice
¼ cup chopped dill weed
salt and white pepper to taste

Heat the oil in a skillet and fry the onions until translucent. Whisk in the flour and fry until it turns light tan in color. Pour in the chicken stock, stirring constantly to remove any lumps. Add the lemon juice and dill weed and season with salt and pepper. Stir in the peas and simmer until they are tender and the sauce has thickened.

Thessalonian Peas / *Arakás Thessalías*

I know I may be straying a bit from Greek cooking by saying this, but personally, I think this dish is great with fast-food fried chicken. It's so versatile that it can be served with all sorts of roasts, steaks and chops or simply eaten on its own.

Ingredients:
½ cup butter
3 cups vegetable broth
4 cups frozen peas
1 medium head romaine lettuce, chopped
½ cup olive oil
6 green onions, chopped
3 carrots, chopped
¼ cup dill weed, chopped
2 cups diced potatoes
salt and pepper

In a medium saucepan, boil together the butter, broth and peas for 5 minutes. Add the lettuce and stir it through so it wilts then set it aside.
In a medium saucepan, heat the olive oil and stir-fry the green onions, carrots, and dill. Pour this mixture into the pea-lettuce pot. Add the diced potatoes and season with salt and pepper. Bring it to a boil and cook it until the potatoes are done and the juice is thick.

Lemon Roasted Potatoes / *Patátes tou Foúrnou Lemonátes*

Lemon potatoes are a popular dish in the islands, particularly in the winter months when the lemons are abundant. For a quick short cut, par-boil the potatoes for 10 minutes in plain water with a cube or two of chicken base. After they drain and cool down a bit, toss them with the ingredients and then bake, uncovered, using just enough stock to cover the bottom of the pan. Thirty minutes later and the dish is ready to serve.

Ingredients:
2 lbs. potatoes, peeled and cut lengthwise into quarters or sixths, depending on their size.
½ cup olive oil
¼ cup fresh lemon juice
salt and pepper
2 tbs. oregano
1 crushed garlic clove
chicken or vegetable stock

In a roasting pan, toss the potatoes with all the ingredients - except the stock. I prefer to set them aside for a little bit to marinade them so the flavors get absorbed but if you're in a hurry, don't worry about it. They'll still be delicious.

Add enough stock to the pan so that they are half covered. Cover the pan with aluminum foil and bake them for 30 to 40 minutes at 350°F. Check that they are tender. If they're still hard, bake for another 20 minutes and if you need more liquid, add more stock but just enough to cover the bottom so they don't stick to the pan. When they are almost done, increase the oven temperature to 400°F. Remove the foil and bake them uncovered for another 10 to 15 minutes so they get a nice red-brown color.

Mint Roasted Potatoes / *Patátes me Diósmo*

The fresh taste of mint makes this a great side dish for roasts and holiday meals. Accompany it with a tomato salad for a wonderful combination.

Ingredients:
2 lbs. small new potatoes
¼ cup butter or olive oil
¼ cup fresh chopped mint or use 2 tbs. dried
salt and pepper

Wash and scrub the potatoes with their skins on. Bring a pot of salted water to a boil and cook the whole potatoes until they are almost tender. Drain the potatoes and let them cool enough so you can handle them.

Cut the potatoes into wedges or slices, again, leaving the skins on. Toss them with the butter or oil and sprinkle them with the mint, salt and pepper. Arrange them in a baking dish. Roast the potatoes at 400°F until they get golden brown.

Potatoes with Rosemary / *Patátes me Dendrolívano*

This aromatic way of preparing potatoes gives them a gourmet touch. Serve the potatoes as a side dish for roasted or grilled meats, especially lamb chops.

Ingredients:
2 lb. potatoes, peeled and washed
3 tbs. chopped fresh rosemary or 1 tbs. crushed dried
salt and pepper
½ cup olive oil

Cook the potatoes in salted water until they are almost tender. Drain and let them cool down enough so you can handle them. Cut the potatoes into wedges or slices and toss them with the rosemary, olive oil, salt and pepper. Arrange them in a baking dish. Bake at 400°F until they are golden brown.

Tomato Roasted Potatoes / *Patátes toú Foúrnou Kokkinistés*

Tomato roasted potatoes are served with poultry and meats and are often an accompaniment for game. For a quick short cut, par-boil the potatoes for 10 minutes in plain water with a cube or two of chicken base. After they drain and cool down a bit, toss them with the ingredients and then bake, uncovered, using just enough stock to cover the bottom of the pan.

Ingredients:
2 lbs. potatoes, peeled and cut lengthwise into quarters or sixths, depending on their size.
½ cup olive oil
1 cup fresh crushed tomatoes or puree
salt and pepper
2 tbs. oregano
1 tbs. thyme
1 crushed garlic clove
chicken or vegetable stock

In a roasting pan, toss the potatoes with all the ingredients except for the stock. I prefer to set them aside for a little bit to marinade them so the flavors get absorbed but if you're in a hurry, don't worry about it. They'll still be delicious.
Add enough stock to the pan so that they are half covered. Cover the pan with aluminum foil and bake them for 40 minutes at 350°F. Check that they are tender. If they're still hard, bake for another 20 minutes. If you need more liquid, add more stock but just enough to cover the bottom so they don't stick to the pan. When they are almost done, increase the oven temperature to 400°F. Remove the foil and bake them uncovered for another 10 to 15 minutes so they get a nice red-brown color.

Vegetables Imam Baildi / *Imám Baildí*

When given this recipe, I was told that its name actually means "swooning *Imám*." From Middle Eastern origins, this dish is supposedly named after the Imám who after eating too much of it, passed out.

When looking at the ingredients for this recipe, it's no wonder that the poor *Imám* couldn't handle it. This is a very rich and heavy dish, using lots of oil, although this does not stop people from enjoying it. This is a delicious vegetable dish that should be served with lots of bread and a green salad. For a special meal or as a side dish, you could also serve it over pasta or rice.

Ingredients:
olive oil for frying
2 cups cubed eggplants
2 cups cubed zucchini
2 cups cubed potatoes
1 cup chopped green peppers
1 cup sliced carrots - optional
1 cup cut green beans - optional
1 cup sliced fresh mushrooms - optional
½ cup olive oil
2 onions, chopped
3 minced garlic cloves
4 cups fresh chopped tomatoes
1 cup vegetable or chicken stock
½ cup chopped parsley - optional
salt and pepper
1 tsp. oregano
1 tsp. thyme
1 bay leaf
½ cup crumbled feta, grated Greek *kefalotíri* or parmesan cheese

Begin by sprinkling the eggplant and zucchini cubes with salt. Keeping them separate, set them into colanders to drain for 2 hours or more. Using your hands, squeeze out any excess moisture.

Cover the bottom of a skillet with olive oil and fry the eggplant. Remove it to paper towels to drain. Heat more oil and fry the zucchini, again, removing it to paper towels to drain. Continue frying the potatoes, green peppers, carrots, green beans and mushrooms, setting them all aside to drain.

Heat ½ cup of olive oil in a skillet and sauté the onions and garlic. Add the tomatoes, stock, parsley and seasonings. Simmer the sauce for 10 minutes.

Preheat your oven to 350ºF. Toss all the fried vegetables together and arrange them in a deep casserole dish. Pour the sauce over the vegetables and bake the casserole covered for 30 to 40 minutes. You can check to see if it's done by piercing a potato with a fork. Once the casserole is almost finished, top it with the cheese and bake it uncovered for another 10 minutes so the cheese can melt and brown.

Oven-Baked Imam / *Imám tou Foúrnou*

A lighter version of *Imám Baildí*, this recipe skips the frying of the vegetables and simply bakes it in the oven as a casserole. As with the original recipe, serve this dish with fresh bread and a green salad.

Ingredients:
2 eggplants
2 zucchinis
3 potatoes, peeled
1 onion, chopped
3 cloves garlic, crushed
2 cups crushed tomatoes
2 cups vegetable stock
1 cup olive oil
1 bay leaf, crushed
1 tsp. oregano
1 tsp. thyme
1 tbs. chopped parsley - optional
salt and pepper

Wash the vegetables and cut them into cubes or slices as to your preference. If you choose to cube the eggplant, the rest of the veggies should also be in cubes. Vegetable cubes should be one inch thick or if your slicing, keep the slices to ¼ inch thick. In a bowl, mix together the onions, garlic, tomatoes, stock, oil and your spices.

For cubed vegetables, toss the veggies with salt and pepper and put them into a casserole dish. Pour the tomato mixture over them and mix thoroughly.

Although sliced vegetables can be tossed together as above, they can also be arranged in layers. Start with potatoes, then zucchini and eggplant. Spoon some of the tomato mixture over the vegetables then repeat the steps starting with potatoes. Continue until you have used up the veggies and sauce. Remember to salt and pepper each layer as you go along.

Heat your oven to 375°F. Cover the casserole and bake it for 50-60 minutes. Remove the cover and bake for another 30 minutes or until the potatoes are tender.

For more great vegetable dishes see the following recipes:

Tomato Balls / *Tomatokeftédes*
Stuffed Cucumbers / *Agourákia Gemistá*
Fried Stuffed Olives / *Tiganités Gemistés Eliés*
Peppers Stuffed with Feta / *Piperiés me Féta Tiganités*
Ptolemies' Tomatoes / *Tomátes tis Ptolemaídas*
Batter fried Broccoli & Cauliflower / *Tiganitó Mbrókolo ke Kounoupídi*
Fried Pumpkin / *Kolokítha Tiganití*
Savory Pumpkin Pancakes / *Kolokithópites*
Spicy Pickled Eggplant / *Pikántikes Melintzánes*
Zucchini Blossoms / *Anthoús Kolokithiás*
Stuffed Zucchini Blossoms / *Anthoús Kolokithiás Gemistí*
Zucchini Pancakes / *Kolokithokeftédes*
Spinach and Lentil Soup / *Spanáki me Fakí*

Soups
Soúpes

The Perfect Soup - *Soúpes*

Soup making is an easy process and usually doesn't take much thought. Throw a bunch of ingredients into a pot, bring them to a boil and you have soup. Yet when you do think about it, a soup can range between a light snack or a hearty meal.

The soup recipes include the standard directions for making each of them. Though in some cases, you have a choice as to how you would like to serve them and the texture that they should take on. By taking an extra step, you can customize these recipes so you and your family will enjoy them that much more.

The basic difference for the making of a different style of soup will be in the vegetable preparation. Should you dice your veggies or cut them into quarters and large pieces? Depending on what you want the finished product to look like and the style of soup you prefer, you will use your preference to make the decision.

The Hearty Soup

My definition of a hearty soup is a dish of broth that has chunks of vegetables or meats. Every time your spoon goes into the bowl, it comes up with an assortment of goodies. And as you chew slightly, the different textures are a delight to the palate. A hearty soup is filling to the stomach as well as to the eye.

To get this effect, simply make your broth according to the recipe directions using the meats, poultry or seafood that are called for. Your vegetables should be diced into spoon sized pieces and are thrown into the soup pot to cook after any straining of the broth is called for, at the same time as the rice or pasta. When the rice has finished cooking, so have the vegetables. Follow the recipe directions for making any sauces that may be needed to finish off the soup and serve.

The Smooth Soup

Another way of making a soup would be to puree the vegetables and then return them to the pot, mixing them in so they are not seen. This is a great way to get kids who "don't like the weeds" to eat some vegetables with out their making a fuss. Other than the meat and the rice or pasta, nothing else is visible.

Cut the soup vegetables into large pieces so they can easily be removed later. Boil them in the initial stock with the meat to cook. Strain the cooked veggies from the soup and put them in a blender or food processor. Follow the recipe directions and after the rice or pasta has been cooked, stir the puree back into the soup. You'll find that your soup becomes much thicker and creamier at the same time. Follow the recipe directions for making any sauces that may be needed to finish it off and serve.

The Soup and The Entree

Some soups can be made using the boiled meat or seafood as a separate entree once it's cooked. You'll find that many Greek dishes consist of boiled meats that are served on platters with an accompanying mayonnaise or sauce.

In these instances, the vegetables can be quartered or cut up into large chunks to cook in the initial stage of broth making with the meat. The meats and veggies are strained from the broth and set aside. The meat or seafood would be arranged on a platter, garnishing it with the boiled vegetables and kept warm until the soup is finished. Of course, you could choose to only use the meat as an entree, in which case, pureeing the vegetables and adding them back to the stock would be a good idea.

Fish and Seafood Soups

When cooking fish or shellfish, remember to always strain your broth through a fine sieve or cheese cloth into another pot before adding the rice to finish it off. Many times there are stray scales or pieces of shells and bones in the broth so this step is very important.

When picking through fish and vegetables that will be pureed or returned to the finished soup, be just as careful. Make sure that the ingredients are bone free before you put them into the finished product.

The strained fish and shell fish can be arranged on a platter to serve along side the soup for everyone to take what they want. Or, you can take the extra step of picking through the cooled fish, removing any skin and bones and returning the clean flesh to the soup after it's done.

The Soup Stocks

Almost every recipe that calls for a liquid uses a stock made from chicken, beef, vegetable or fish. This is simply plain water that is boiled with meats, vegetables, herbs and spices that results in a flavorful broth. By using this broth in your recipes, you'll add an extra taste or richness to the flavor of the finished product as opposed to just using plain water.

Store-bought bases, granulated bouillon and canned broths can easily be substituted, especially for convenience sake. Being a working mom, I completely understand that often there just isn't time to boil a stock for 2 or 3 hours before even beginning to cook for the dinner table. And I, too, will use a teaspoon or two of ready made, granulated base as a replacement, with great results.

The difference is that home made stocks have the advantage of being easily adjusted to suit your taste preferences. To begin with, you can control the amount of salt that is used. Most store bought broths are very salty. You can dilute them but by doing this, the flavor gets diluted and lost as well. When you make the broth yourself, you can also control the richness of it. By adding more meat, bones and vegetables to the boiling water, you'll get a richer or stronger flavor, something that just can't be found in ready made stocks.

You may not want to be bothered by taking the time to make your own stock, but at some time, the opportunity may present itself. Perhaps you'll decide to make a boiled meat or vegetable dinner. Instead of discarding the water, turn it into stock. It only takes an added step or two of adding some vegetables and seasonings and you'll have homemade broth to use for your cooking. Freeze the fresh stock in zip-lock bags by one or two cupfuls, depending on the quantities that you cook for. It keeps great in the freezer and you'll have some ready when a recipe calls for it.

Some traditional stock recipes call for the use of very pungent herbs and spices such as cloves and garlic to be used in their making. Personally, I think that these aromatic flavorings are best left to add into the individual dishes and recipes themselves, as they are called for. By including these strong flavored ingredients, the stock would take on a distinct taste and may not be useable in some recipes. Instead, I have chosen to share with you recipes for simple basic stocks that can be used in any recipe that calls for a liquid.

Beef Stock / *Zomós Vodinoú*

Ingredients:
2 lbs. beef trimmings and bones - the more bones, the richer the stock
1 onion, quartered
1 carrot, coarsely cut
1 celery stem, coarsely cut
2 stems of parsley
salt and pepper to taste
1 bay leaf

Put the beef into a large soup pot and cover it with water. Bring it to a boil and remove any froth that collects on top. Add the vegetables and lower the heat. Simmer it together for 2 to 3 hours. Strain the broth through a sieve and let it cool. Skim the fat off the top. This can be done easily by refrigerating the broth overnight. Once completely cold, the fat will be wax like and you'll be able to skim it off easily. The broth is ready to freeze or use in any recipe that calls for it.

Chicken Stock / *Zomós Kótas*

Ingredients:
2 lbs. chicken backs, necks, wings or any parts of your choice. Or, use a whole chicken to make the stock. The cooked meat can be used in another recipe such as Chicken Pie.
1 onion, quartered
1 carrot, coarsely cut
1 celery stem, coarsely cut
2 stems of parsley
salt and pepper to taste
1 bay leaf

Put the chicken into a large soup pot and cover it with water. Bring it to a boil and remove any froth that collects on top. Add the vegetables and lower the heat. Simmer it all together for two hours. Strain the broth through a sieve and let it cool. Skim the fat off the top. This can be done easily by refrigerating the broth overnight. Once completely cold, the fat will be wax like and you'll be able to skim it off easily. The broth is ready to freeze or use in any recipe that calls for it.

Fish Stock / *Zomós Psarioú*

Ingredients:
2 lbs. fish trimmings such as bones, heads, tails and fins
1 onion, quartered
1 carrot, coarsely cut
1 celery stem, coarsely cut
2 stems of parsley
salt and pepper to taste
1 bay leaf
1 cup dry white wine - optional

Put all the ingredients into a large soup pot and cover it with water. Bring it to a boil then reduce the heat so it simmers. Cook the stock for 1 hour. Strain the broth through a sieve into another pot and boil it for another 30 minutes to reduce and the flavor to get stronger. Remove the stock from the heat and let it cool.

Vegetable Stock / *Zomós Lahanikón*

Ingredients:
2 onions, quartered
2 carrots, coarsely cut
2 celery stems, coarsely cut
1 cup chopped fresh tomatoes
1 cup chopped cabbage - optional
2 stems of parsley
salt and pepper to taste
1 bay leaf

Put all the ingredients into a large soup pot and cover it with water. Bring it to a boil then reduce the heat so it simmers. Cook the stock for 1 hour. Strain the broth through a sieve into another pot and boil it for another 30 minutes to reduce and the flavor to get stronger. Remove the stock from the heat and let it cool.

Bean Soup / *Fasoláda* or *Lópia*

Bean soup is a traditional favorite amongst the islanders. It's made at least once a week in the village homes and is often served on fasting days when meat is not allowed. Some of the very religious Greeks, will also omit the oil from this recipe, to suit their beliefs. If you have trouble cooking beans, see the Mysterious Bean in the "Kitchen Techniques" section for tips on how to get great results.

Ingredients:
1 lb. dry white beans that have been soaked over night and drained.
1 cup chopped onions
2 cups chopped tomatoes
1 cup chopped celery
1 carrot, sliced
1 cup olive oil
2 tbs. cumin
1 dry chili pepper - optional
salt and pepper to taste
chicken or vegetable stock

Put your beans in a soup pot and cover them with plain water. Bring them to a boil and cook them until the surface gets frothy - about 5 minutes. Pour the beans into a colander and rinse them.

Return the beans to the soup pot with the rest of the ingredients and add enough stock to cover them twice. Bring it to a boil and reduce the heat. Partially cover the pot with a lid and simmer the beans for 1 to 2 hours or until they are done. Stir the soup occasionally and add more stock as needed.

For a faster method, use a pressure cooker and cook at medium heat for 15-20 minutes.

Lentil Soup / *Fakés*

This vegetarian dish is a great one pot meal for when you don't want to fuss about dinner. Make it up ahead of time as it tastes even better the next day.

Ingredients:
1 lb. dry lentils
1 cup crushed tomatoes
1 onion, finely chopped
1 bay leaf
2 cloves of garlic, chopped
salt and pepper
½ cup celery, chopped
½ cup olive oil
½ cup carrots, sliced
chicken or vegetable stock
vinegar - optional

Pick through the lentils and make sure all stones, bad lentils and anything else that is not edible is removed and rinse them. Put the lentils into a large pot with all the ingredients, except the vinegar. Add enough stock to cover it twice. Bring it to a boil then reduce the heat and simmer until the lentils are tender, 1½ to 2 hours. Add more stock as necessary. To save time, use a pressure cooker and cook at medium pressure for 15 minutes.

Serve the lentil soup with some vinegar on the side as some people like a bit sprinkled in their soup.

Greek Chickpea Chili / *Revíthia*

The Greeks are very fond of beans and I must say that this particular recipe is my favorite. The chickpeas are cooked until very tender and the savory sauce goes well with fresh, crusty bread, feta cheese and a glass of wine. It's a one pot meal that is easy to make, is a great warmer-upper and you can serve it on the Greek fasting days too.

Ingredients:
1 lb. dry chick peas, soaked overnight
⅓ cup olive oil
1 large onion, chopped
2 tbs. ground cumin
2 cups crushed tomatoes
salt and pepper
2 large carrots, sliced
2 whole chili peppers
vegetable or chicken stock

First, boil the chick peas in plain water for 10 minutes and then drain, throwing away the frothy water. Put all the ingredients into a large pot, cover with stock and bring to a boil. Reduce the heat and cover the pot. Simmer the chick peas for 1½ to 2½ hours until they are tender, adding more stock as needed.

For a much faster method, use a pressure cooker on medium pressure and cook the beans for 20 minutes.

Spinach and Lentil Soup / *Spanáki me Fakí*

This is a great combination of tastes that is served on a chilly Spring Day. You can make this soup as thick or as thin that you prefer by adding more or less stock. I like a thick version with lots of crusty bread.

Ingredients:
1 lb. fresh or frozen spinach
1 cup dried lentils
chicken or vegetable stock
½ cup olive oil
1 chopped onion
1 clove garlic, mashed
½ tsp. ground cumin
salt and pepper

Wash and drain your spinach and cut any large leaves in half. In a large pot, cook the lentils in enough stock to cover them, until they soften. In a separate pan, heat the olive oil. Sauté the onions and garlic until translucent and pour the mixture into the lentils. Add the cumin, spinach, salt and pepper and simmer it all together until the spinach settles and the lentils are very tender. If the soups is too thin, simply boil it down. If it's too thick, add a bit more stock.

Village Vegetable Soup / *Soúpa Horiátiki*

This soup recipe is a Serbian specialty from *Kozáni* in northern Greece. Originally intended as a "poor man's" soup, this hearty recipe is very easy to make and a great warmer-upper for cold wintry days. Serve this simple soup with feta cheese, green olives and fresh, crusty bread.

Ingredients:
3 potatoes, cut into bite sized pieces
3 onions, chopped
2 cups chopped fresh tomatoes
1 carrot, chopped
1 celery stalk, chopped
2 zucchini, cut into bite sized pieces
1 tbs. chopped parsley
1 cup olive oil
salt and pepper
chicken or vegetable stock
1 cup rice

Prepare all your vegetables, cutting them into small pieces so they cook faster. In a large soup pot, add everything but the rice and cover it with chicken or vegetable stock. Let the vegetables cook for 10 minutes, then add the rice. Cook for another 20 minutes and you have Village Soup. You can easily make the broth thicker by boiling it for a few minutes after adding a bit of flour diluted in cold water.

Tomato Soup / *Tomatósoupa*

This recipe is so fast and easy that you'll just love it. A do-ahead short cut that you can take is to chop up all your vegetables the night before and keep them refrigerated, covered in the stock. The next day bring the stock and vegetables to a boil and cook the rice.

Ingredients:
2 chopped onions
2 cups chopped fresh tomatoes
1 chopped celery rib
2 chopped zucchinis
vegetable or chicken stock
1 cup rice
1 cup olive oil
salt and pepper

Put all the chopped vegetables into a pot and add enough stock to cover them. Bring the mixture to a boil and add the rice and the olive oil. Simmer the soup until the rice is done. Season it with salt and pepper and serve.

Chicken-Vermicelli Soup / *Soúpa Fidés*

Just as chicken soup is considered a cure-all for westerners, the Greeks use this simple mixture as an aid for a bad stomach or for a cold. Serve this light soup to anyone who isn't feeling well or an elder who can't handle a heavy meal.

Ingredients:
chicken stock
vermicelli noodles

Bring the stock to a boil and add the vermicelli noodles. Cook it together until the noodles are done. For a thicker version, add a bit of flour thickener or boil some fresh vegetables in the stock before the vermicelli is cooked. The vegetables can be pureed and returned to the pot after the noodles are done.

Chicken Egg Lemon Soup / *Soúpa Avgolémono*

This traditional Greek chicken soup is topped with a fluffy Egg-Lemon Sauce. Serve this up as a winter warmer with lots of crusty bread. For a heartier version, add the vegetables with the rice instead of pureeing them.

Ingredients:
2 lbs. chicken, whole or in pieces.
1 chopped onion
3 ribs chopped celery
2 potatoes, peeled and chopped
2 carrots, peeled and chopped
salt and pepper to taste
1 cup rice
Egg-Lemon Sauce - see recipe

Rinse the chicken and set it in a soup pot. Add the onions, celery, potatoes, carrots and season it with salt and pepper. Add enough water to cover the ingredients and bring it to a boil. Simmer until the chicken is tender. Remove the chicken to the side and strain the broth. Return the broth to the pot, add the rice, and cook until it's done. Remove the pot from the heat, spoon out two cups of liquid and allow it to cool.
  Puree the cooked vegetables and stir them into the soup. Remove the chicken skins and bones, cut up the meat into small pieces and return it to the pot.
  Make the Egg-Lemon Sauce following the recipe directions, using the cooled stock. Pour the sauce over the soup and serve.

Rooster Soup / *Soúpa Petinoú*

This recipe uses the rooster to make a soup and entree dinner but it's delicious when served as a hearty soup too. Simply cut the veggies into smaller pieces and return the de-boned meat to the soup.

Ingredients:
one 2 lb. rooster or stewing chicken, cut into pieces.
1 quartered onion
3 ribs celery, quartered
2 carrots, halved
salt and pepper to taste
chicken or vegetable stock
1 cup rice
1 cup cream
flour
1 cup olive oil

Rinse the rooster pieces and set it in a soup pot. Add the onions, celery, carrots and season it with salt and pepper. Add enough stock to cover the ingredients and bring it to a boil. Reduce the heat and partially cover the pot. Simmer the rooster for 1 to 2 hours, until its tender. Strain the soup stock through a sieve into another pot. Return the stock to the heat, add the rice, and cook until done.

Separate the rooster pieces from the vegetables and set it aside to drain. Put the cooked vegetables through a blender and puree them. Stir them back into the soup pot. If the soup seems very thin, mix a little flour with water and stir it in. Bring the soup to a boil to thicken it and remove it from the heat. Add the cream and stir it through. The soup is ready.

Heat the olive oil in a skillet. Lightly flour the cooked rooster pieces and fry them in the hot oil until they get brown on both sides. Remove the rooster to a platter and serve.

Greek Beef Soup / *Kréas me Kritharáki Soúpa*

Years ago in our Baltimore restaurant, my dad had the best Greek Beef Soup offered on the menu every day. Although it's made with simple ingredients, it was one of our best sellers.

Ingredients:
2 lbs. beef, preferably shin, cut into one inch chunks and a bone or two for a rich stock
2 cups orzo or an other small macaroni of your choice
1 bay leaf
2 cups fresh chopped tomatoes
salt and pepper

In a large soup pot, cover the meat with water. Add the bay leaf, tomatoes and season with salt and pepper. Stew the meat gently for an hour. You want the meat to be tender, so cook it longer if needed, adding more liquid as it evaporates. If you're in a hurry, try using a pressure cooker to make the stock. Use medium pressure for 20 minutes and your meat should be tender.

When the meat is almost done remove the bone and add the orzo, stirring occasionally so that it doesn't stick to the bottom and scorch. When the orzo is done so is the soup. Serve it hot with some grated parmesan cheese on the side, for those who want a sprinkle of it.

Poached Meatball Soup / *Youvarlákia Soúpa*

These easy to make meatballs are the main ingredient for this hearty *Youvarlákia* Soup. Just as for the sister recipe Poached Meat Balls, the soup is also served with the Egg-Lemon Sauce to give it a tangy edge.

Ingredients:
1 chopped onion
1 cup chopped celery
1 cup sliced carrots
1 cup diced potatoes
1 cup rice - optional
chicken, vegetable or beef stock
flour
Egg-Lemon Sauce - see recipe

Meat Balls:
1 ½ lbs. ground beef, pork or lamb
½ cup uncooked rice
1 chopped onion
3 tbs. chopped parsley
1 tsp. cumin - optional
1 egg
salt and pepper to taste

In a soup pot, add the onions, celery, carrots and potatoes and add enough stock to cover them twice. Bring the mixture to a boil then reduce the heat and simmer it.

Mix together all the ingredients for the meatballs, kneading it with your hands. Form the mixture into balls 1½ to 2 inches in diameter. Roll the meat balls in flour and drop them gently into the boiling stock. For a heartier soup, add a cup of rice into the soup pot. Simmer the soup for 20 minutes or until the rice is cooked, adding more stock as is needed.

Follow the recipe directions for making the Egg-Lemon Sauce, and finish off your soup and serve.

Traditional Easter Soup / *Magirítsa*

This soup is only made once a year and is traditionally eaten after the Midnight Mass of the Greek Orthodox Easter. I have to tell you, that at first I couldn't bear the idea of eating this soup. Growing up on America's East Coast, we didn't have many dishes with lamb innards. When I finally got up my courage to try it, I was impressed. It really is a delicious soup. So be adventurous, you may be pleasantly surprised too.

Ingredients:
1 lamb's head, halved
1 lamb's heart
1 lamb's lung
1 lamb's liver
½ lb. lamb's intestines
juice of 3 lemons
3 bunches spring onions, chopped
½ cup fresh dill weed, chopped
2 sprigs fresh parsley, chopped
1 cup celery leaves, chopped
3 tbs. butter
½ cup long grain rice
salt and pepper to taste
Egg-Lemon Sauce - see recipe

Prepare and clean the lamb organs. See the "Kitchen Techniques" section for tips and details on how to do this. Soak the cleaned head and all the organs in enough water to cover them mixed with the lemon juice for at least one hour, then drain.

Place all the lamb parts into a large pot and cover with cold water. Add salt and pepper and bring to a boil. Remove any foam that collects on top and let it boil over medium heat 40 minutes or until the meat is tender.

Remove the lamb parts from the pot and set them aside so they can cool down a bit for you to handle them. Strain the broth through a fine sieve and return it to the pot, setting aside 2 cups of broth for the Egg-Lemon Sauce.

With a heavy knife, finely chop the intestines and brains and return them to the broth. Chop the heart, liver and lung finely, discarding any cartilage or thick membranes and return them to the broth as well. Pick over the head and return any meat to the broth. If it's your preference the eyes can also be included.

Add the onions, dill, parsley and celery with the butter into the soup pot and bring it all to a boil, cooking over medium heat for one hour. Add the rice and boil gently until it's done, about 15 minutes more and then remove the pot from the heat.

Following the recipe directions, make the Egg-Lemon Sauce using the reserved liquid. Pour it over the soup and serve it immediately.

Tripe Soup / *Patsás*

A common found specialty of the Greek islands, *Patsás* has long been thought of as a cure for too much drinking. There are tavernas that stay open all night for the late night clubber who will stop by to have a bowl of this soup. It's said that *Patsás* coats the stomach and is a preventative for a hangover.

Ingredients:
1 lb. tripe - the stomach of a lamb or baby goat
1 quartered onion
2 celery stalks
salt and pepper
chicken, vegetable, or beef stock
Egg-Lemon Sauce - see recipe

Follow the directions for cleaning tripe in the Kitchen Techniques section and prepare the meat, cutting it into small pieces. Put the tripe, onions, and celery into a soup pot and add enough broth to cover it. Season it with salt and pepper. Simmer the soup for 2 to 3 hours, until the tripe is tender. Make the *Avgolémono* Sauce following the recipe directions. Serve the soup with fresh lemon wedges.

Greek Bouillabaisse / *Kakaviá*

Any variety of fish and shellfish can be used for this soup. Clams and mussels make a nice presentation if left in their shells but they are messy for your guests to handle. Preferably, remove the shells after cooking, returning the meat to the pot.

Ingredients:
2 lbs. various fish – rockfish, sea perch, scorpion etc.
1 lb. various shell fish – mussels, oysters, clams, crab legs etc.
2 carrots, cut into chunks
2 cups fresh crushed tomatoes
1 stalk celery, quartered
1 onion, quartered
½ cup olive oil
lemon juice
salt and pepper

Clean the fish and shellfish and rinse thoroughly. Cut the fish into pieces and sprinkle with salt and pepper. In a deep soup pot, heat the oil and gently brown the fish, onion, celery, and carrot. Add the tomatoes and enough water to cover it by two inches. Simmer it all together for one hour.
Strain the soup through a fine sieve into another pot. Clean the fish from the skins and bones and return the flesh to the soup. Puree the vegetables and return them to the pot. Add the shellfish and simmer it together for 20 minutes. Add more salt and pepper according to your taste. Serve the finished soup with fresh lemon wedges.

Island Fish Soup / *Psarósoupa*

For this traditional soup, the Greeks use a red rockfish which is called *Scorpiós* or scorpion. It's given the name because its fins are poisonous and will cause a painful wound if you get stabbed with them.

Although this hearty recipe serves the fish separately on a platter, you may choose to serve the soup "ready" so it won't be as messy for your guests. Simply pick through the fish and remove any bones and skin. Return the flesh to the finished soup before serving.

Ingredients:
one 2 to 5 lb. Ocean Perch - Although almost any fish can be used to make this soup.
½ cup olive oil
1 cup chopped onions
2 cups diced potatoes
¼ cup chopped parsley
½ cup chopped celery
½ cup sliced carrots
1 cup rice
salt and pepper
Egg Lemon Sauce - see recipe

Cut your fish into large pieces and salt and pepper it. Put it into a soup pot, pour the olive oil over it, and cover it with water. Bring it to a boil, then reduce your heat to simmer and cook it for 20 to 30 minutes, until the meat is flaky but not falling apart.

Strain the broth into another soup pot. Always remember to strain fish from its broth using a fine sieve to make sure that there are no stray bones or scales in your soup. Arrange the strained fish on a platter and cover it with aluminum foil. Keep it warm until the soup is ready to be served. Bring the broth back to a boil. Add in the vegetables and rice. If needed, add more water and season again with salt and pepper.

Once the rice is cooked, remove the soup from the heat and set it aside. Remove two cups of broth so it can cool down. Follow the recipe directions for Egg-Lemon Sauce, using the reserved stock. Pour the sauce into the soup and serve it immediately. Place the platter of fish on the table so everyone can get the serving of fish that they want.

Cheese Soup Santorini Style/ *Tirávgoulo Santorinítiko*

The volcanic island of *Santoríni*, also known as *Thíra* is said to keep many secrets. Some researchers even believe that the solution to the mystery of lost Atlantis may lie within her surrounding waters.

Although we may never find out about that myth, the island does share with us one of her local dishes. This recipe combines fresh vegetables with cheese for a light lunch or as a starter for a more elaborate meal. For a creamy version, puree the cooked vegetables in the soup stock.

Ingredients:
2 cups zucchini, cubed
2 cups potatoes, cubed
1 egg
½ cup grated Greek *kefalotíri* cheese
1 tbs. tomato paste
2 tbs. butter
salt and pepper
2 cups chicken or vegetable broth

In a soup pot, melt the butter. Stir in the tomato paste and cook it until it's bubbly. Add the chicken broth and bring it to a boil. Add the zucchini and potatoes, season it with salt and pepper and boil the soup until the vegetables are done. Remove it from the heat.

In a small mixing bowl, beat the egg with the cheese. Spoon a little broth from the hot soup into the mixing bowl while stirring constantly so the egg doesn't cook and separate. Pour the egg-cheese mixture into the soup, again stirring the soup constantly to incorporate the egg and melt the cheese.

Yogurt Soup / *Yiaourtósoupa*

All through the Mediterranean you'll find many variations for Yogurt Soup. This one uses hot peppers for a spicy version.

Ingredients:
3 tbs. olive oil
1½ cup chopped onions
1 tbs. flaked hot peppers
½ cup white wine - optional
5 cups chicken stock
⅓ cup bulgur wheat
3 tbs. semolina flour
2 cups plain yogurt
2 tbs. dry spearmint
salt and pepper

In a large skillet, heat the oil and fry the onion until translucent. Stir in the hot peppers, wine - if you're using it - and the chicken stock. When the mixture comes to a boil, add the wheat and the semolina. Mixing it occasionally, so it doesn't stick, let it cook for 15 minutes then remove it from the heat.

Put the yogurt into a bowl. In a slow, steady stream, whisk in one cup of hot broth mixture. Return the yogurt mixture to the pot, stirring constantly. Add the spearmint and season with salt and pepper. Serve immediately.

Sesame Soup / *Tahinósoupa*

Also know as the island of Mastic, *Chios* serves up this great soup that combines fresh vegetables with the nutty taste of sesame seeds. Serve this velvety soup as s mid day meal with a green salad, crusty bread, and nice wine

Ingredients:
2 chopped potatoes
2 chopped carrots
2 chopped onions
2 chopped tomatoes
2 chopped zucchinis
1 chopped celery rib
vegetable or chicken stock
 juice of 1 lemon
1 lb. orzo
⅓ cup *tahini**

Put all your vegetables into a soup pot and add enough stock to cover. Bring them to a boil and cook until they are soft and tender. Strain the vegetables from the broth and puree them with a food processor or blender.
Bring the stock back to a boil and add the orzo. When it's cooked, remove the pot from the heat and stir in the vegetable puree. Whisk the *tahíni* with the lemon juice and add little bits of hot broth while stirring constantly so it doesn't curdle. Pour the heated *tahíni* mixture into the rest of the soup and serve.

*A paste made from ground sesame seeds that can be bought at a Greek or Middle Eastern specialty shop.

Meats
Kréata

Meats - *Kréata*

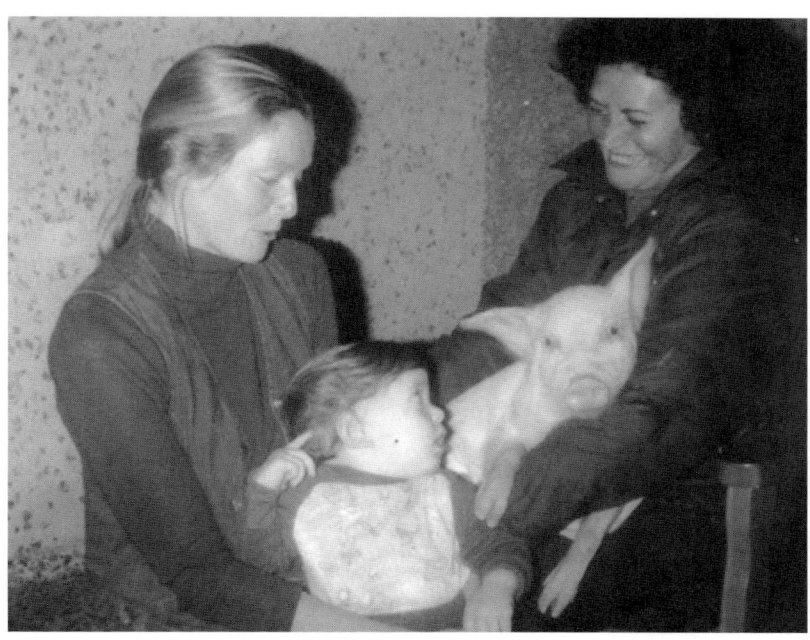

Just as the vegetables are seasonal for the islanders, so are the meats. The spring time will bring with it baby lambs and goats that will be slaughtered for the Easter and summer celebrations such as weddings and festivals, and the young pigs that are born will be fattened up for the winter months and the Christmas holidays.

In days of old, beef was not as plentiful for the islanders as it is today. In northern Greece where there are grazing lands, young calves could be found, but in the mountainous islands, beef was a sparse commodity. Although some of the farming villagers kept animals such as oxen for tilling the lands and an occasional cow for milk and butter, these animals were few because in the dry summer months, grazing lands were hard to come by and the expense of growing or buying feed was a luxury that most villagers couldn't afford.

The sheep and goat were the principle sources of meat for the islanders—the goat in particular, since it could climb almost any rocky crag to find food.

Almost every island village home kept chickens, pigs, and goat herds as their *Zóa* or animals. These animals would be cared for by the families and fed on basically anything that could be found. Mainly table scraps and the wild grasses of the mountains would be used as sustenance for these animals.

Even today in the islands, the village pigs and chickens are raised almost entirely on table scraps. Since there are many restaurants and hotels, some villagers that have large farms, strike up deals with the owners. They are allowed to keep their buckets in the kitchen area, getting lots of scraps for their pigs, and in return the owner has a choice of a pig for slaughter when they are grown-about Christmas time.

In times of no refrigeration, larger animals such as pigs, lambs and goats would only be slaughtered for special occasions. The fresh meat from a slaughtered animal would have to be eaten, used to barter with or preserved in some way, before it would go bad.

Take for instance the pig. Since pork was the meat available for winter, it became traditional to serve it at Christmas time. A pig would be slaughtered four or five days before the holiday. The carcass itself would be suspended from the rafters of the *esóspito* or inner house, and the men of the family would skin it and remove the internal organs. The outer flesh would be rubbed down with sea salt and covered with a piece of tulle to protect it from insects. It would remain hanging for two to three days, for the blood to drain from the meat, tenderizing it.

The organ meats would be the first to be prepared in the village home as meals for the family or made into other dishes that would be served later in the holidays. The liver, lungs heart and kidneys would be fried and maybe served up with some *Skorthaliá* sauce. The intestines would be cleaned and soaked then later made into *Kolosafádes* and *Loukánika* which are types of sausages. *Pihtí*, or pork aspic would use up the feet and head, making it a traditional favorite for the Christmas dinner table.

After the carcass itself had drained, it would be cut up and prepared accordingly. A portion of the meat would be used as a roast for the family's Christmas dinner table. Some of the fattier meat would be preserved by frying small pieces of it in it's own fat to make *Kavroumá*, a pork and lard combination that would be stored in clay jars and used in other dishes such as *Dolmáthes*. Any excess fat that would be trimmed off the pork would be fried down and preserved as *Míla*, which is simply pork lard that could be used in other dishes or as a bread spread.

Depending on the size of the family, there may have been too much meat, that simply could not be eaten or preserved. Some village households would take turns choosing animals between their herds and sharing the meat amongst themselves, so there was no waste. Others would use any surplus to barter with, exchanging it for other foods, clothing or shoes. Any piece of meat, fat or skin that could not be used by the family would be cut up and cooked, and given to the hunting dogs and animals.

Other items from a slaughter such as skins and hair were not discarded either. Of course, there is the wool and soft sheep skins that could be sold or made into garments, but did you know that the very coarse hair of the goat had its uses too? The villagers weaved the hairs into thick, heavy blankets called *Tríhenes*. The bible refers to this material as sack cloth. Bags and pouches were also made of the hairs to use on either side of the donkey saddle. The weaved sack cloth was very strong and could hold a good amount of weight.

Today, we don't have to wait for a holiday to enjoy charcoaled lamb chops or a beef stew. Many of the recipes for meats are what I call "special occasion" dishes. This is simply because that is what they were to our ancestors. The abundances available to us in modern times means we don't need to save an open pit barbeque for a wedding celebration. We can have one as a picnic with some good friends, enjoying wine and ouzo, keeping the traditional spirit alive.

BEEF RECIPES

Beef with Orzo Macaroni / *Moscári Giouvétsi*

A traditional meal that is easy to prepare. The few steps involved make it a convenient meal to serve for when company is coming. Serve it with a green salad and Greek red wine.

Ingredients:
½ cup butter
2 lbs. tender beef, cut into chunks
1 onion chopped
½ cup dry white wine
1 cup beef stock
2 cups chopped tomatoes
salt and pepper
1 lb. orzo macaroni - available at Greek Specialty Shops

In a large pot, heat the butter and brown the meat with the onions until translucent. Add the wine, stock, tomatoes, salt and pepper and simmer it for one hour, or until the meat is tender. If needed, add more stock accordingly.

In salted, boiling water cook the orzo for 15 minutes, stirring occasionally so it doesn't stick and scorch. Drain it and toss it with 2 tbs. of butter. Mix the orzo with the beef together in a large roasting pan. Bake covered at 350°F for 20 minutes or until the orzo is done and the juice has been absorbed.

Beef Stew with Peas / *Moscári me Mbizélia*

A delicious stew that is an easy one-pot meal or make ahead dinner. Any meat can be used in this stew, including poultry.

Ingredients:
2 lbs. stewing beef, cubed
1 cup olive oil
1 large chopped onion
2 garlic cloves, crushed
2 cups crushed tomatoes
1 cup beef stock
1 large bay leaf
1 tsp. thyme
1 tsp. oregano
salt and pepper to taste
2 lbs. potatoes, peeled and cut into 1 inch cubes
1 lb. peas, fresh or frozen

Salt and pepper the beef chunks. In a large pot, heat the olive oil and add the beef, browning it on all sides. Add the onions and garlic and continue to fry until the onions are translucent. Add the tomatoes, stock and spices and stir through. Reduce the heat and simmer the beef, covered from 1 to 1½ hours. If needed, add more stock accordingly.

When the meat is tender, add the potatoes and peas. Simmer it together for 20 minutes or until the potatoes are done.

Beef Stewed with Potatoes / *Moscári me Patátes Giahní*

This is a traditional winter favorite that is usually made with baby goat, but beef is just as good. When the potatoes are almost done, you may want to remove the lid and cook down the sauce for a thicker stew.
Serve this with lots of fresh bread, feta and olives.

Ingredients:
2 lbs. stewing beef, cut into 1 inch cubes.
1 cup olive oil
1 large onion, chopped
4 cups beef broth
2 cups chopped tomatoes
2 bay leaves
salt and pepper
2 lbs. potatoes, peeled and cut into large chunks

Salt and pepper the beef cubes. Heat the oil in a large pot, add the beef chunks and fry them until browned. Add the onions and sauté them until translucent. Pour in the broth, tomatoes, bay leaves and salt and pepper and bring it to a boil. Reduce the heat and cover lightly. Simmer the stew until the meat is tender, adding more stock if needed. Add the potato chunks and simmer for another 30 minutes or until the potatoes are done.

Stuffed Beef Rolls / *Skartotséta apó Moscári*

The islanders of *Zákinthos* in the Ionian Sea, enjoy this dish throughout the year. It involves a bit of work and coordination in tying up the rolls, but the presentation is not only delicious, it's gorgeous as well. Serve this dish with spaghetti, fried potatoes or a bed of pilaf. Add a green salad and you have a wonderful meal.

Ingredients:
2 lbs. boneless beef sliced thinly-about ½ inch thick. Flank steak or rump will work, but have your butcher tenderize it first.

Stuffing:
½ lb. feta cheese, crumbled
½ lb. Swiss cheese, grated
½ cup bread crumbs
2 hardboiled egg yolks, crumbled
1 chopped onion
1 tbs. parsley, finely chopped
3 tbs. olive oil
salt and pepper
pinch nutmeg-optional

Sauce:
¼ cup olive oil
2 cups fresh chopped tomatoes
1 bay leaf
½ cup dry white wine
1 cup beef stock

Salt and pepper your beef slices and set aside. In a mixing bowl, combine all the stuffing ingredients. Take a slice of meat and spoon some stuffing into the center. Roll it up and tie it with some butchers cord. It may be easier to use a metal skewer first, to hold the roll together as you tie it. Repeat the procedure until all your meat has been rolled up and tied.

In a large pot, heat the ¼ cup olive oil and add the beef rolls, gently turning them so they brown on all sides. Add the tomatoes, bay leaf, wine, stock and season with salt and pepper. Reduce your heat and simmer the rolls in the sauce for 1 to 1½ hours. Checking occasionally to add more stock if it's needed.

When the rolls are done, using a slotted spoon, place them on a platter. Carefully remove the strings and pour the sauce over them.

Veal Roll with Feta / *Moscári Tiliktó me Féta*

The tangy flavors of feta and spices make this a special dish that is easy to prepare but tastes like you fussed for hours.

Ingredients:
one 2 lb piece of veal shoulder, using a mallet, pound it out thinly.
salt and pepper
oregano
1 cup crumbled feta cheese
½ cup parsley, chopped finely
1 cup butter
2 cups beef or vegetable stock
1 cup red wine
thyme

Spread the meat flat and sprinkle salt, pepper and oregano on both sides. Spread the crumbled feta in the center of it and sprinkle with the parsley. Roll up the meat lengthwise and secure tightly with string all around. To simplify this step, try using metal skewers to hold the roll together while you tie the butchers cord.

In a deep skillet, heat the butter and brown the meat on all sides. Add the stock, wine and thyme to the pan and cover. Allow it to stew for 1½ to 2 hours or until tender, adding more stock as needed.

Put the veal roll on a platter and carefully remove the string. Let it stand for at least 20 minutes to set before you slice it. The remaining juices and stock can easily be made into a gravy to serve with the roll. Simply mix a bit of flour with some cold water and stir it into the drippings. Bring them to a boil and cook it until the sauce thickens.

Boiled Beef and Vegetables / *Vrastó Moscári me Lahaniká*

This easy to make entree can be made extra special by accompanying it with one of many sauces such as a mayonnaise, gravy or a white sauce.

Ingredients:
one 4 lb. cut of beef such as a chuck or rump roast
½ cup white wine
2 bay leaves
beef or vegetable stock
3 quartered potatoes
3 carrots, cut into 2 inch pieces
3 celery ribs, cut into 2 inch pieces
2 onions, quartered
2 sprigs fresh parsley
salt and pepper

Rinse the meat under cold running water. Put it into a soup pot and add the wine, bay leaves and enough stock to cover it. Heat the stock to simmering, and skim off the froth that collects on the top. Continue to simmer for 2 to 3 hours or until the meat is tender, adding more stock as necessary.

Add the vegetables to the soup pot and continue simmering it until they are done. Using a slotted spoon and a large fork, carefully remove the meat to a serving platter. Remove the vegetables and arrange them around the meat.

Don't discard the remaining stock as it can be used in any recipe or can be made into a soup. A gravy for this entree is easy to prepare by boiling down some of the stock and simply adding some basic thickener.

Pastitsáda from Kerkyra / *Kerkiráiki Pastitsáda*

Although the name may sound like the popular *Pastítsio* and it uses the same noodles, this recipe from the island of Corfu is very different from the casserole dish. The pasta is served on a platter and is covered in a sweet, chunky meat sauce. Serve it with plenty of grated cheese and a green salad.

Ingredients:
1 lb. pastítsio noodles, also know as macaroni #3 that can be found in Greek or Middle Eastern specialty shops. Penne macaroni can also be substituted.
grated Greek *kefalotíri*

Sauce:
1½ cup olive oil
2 chopped onions
2 minced garlic cloves
2 lbs. beef, cut into one inch chunks
1 cup dry, white wine
2 cups beef stock
2 cups chopped tomatoes
1 tsp. red pepper
1 bay leaf
1 cinnamon stick
4 whole cloves
1 tsp. sugar
salt

Heat the oil in a skillet and fry the onions, garlic and meat together. Add the wine and stock and cover the skillet. Let the meat simmer for one hour so it becomes tender. Stir in the rest of the sauce ingredients and simmer it for 40 minutes, adding more stock as needed. Once the sauce is finished, remove the cinnamon stick, bay leaf, and cloves.

Cook your pasta and drain it. Toss the hot pasta with some sauce and put it on your serving platter. Sprinkle it generously with grated cheese. Top it off with the meat and the remaining sauce and serve.

PORK RECIPES

Baked Pork with Lima Beans / *Hirinó me Gígantes*

A special party dish that is easy to prepare so you have time to join in the festivities. This winter dish is great when served with a lettuce salad topped with Greek Vinaigrette.

Ingredients:
1 lb. dried lima beans
4 to 6 lb. pork leg, with bone
yellow mustard
salt and pepper
3 tbs. ground cumin
1 large chopped onion
3 cups chopped tomatoes
2 large chopped carrots
3 ribs celery, chopped
½ cup olive oil
chicken or vegetable stock

Soak the lima beans overnight in water. Wash and dry the pork leg. Cover the meat in yellow mustard, salt and pepper and cumin. Cover well and refrigerate. Let the leg marinate for at least 3 hours or better yet, overnight.

In a large cooking pot, add the drained lima beans, onions, tomatoes, carrots, celery and season with salt and pepper. Pour in the olive oil and enough stock to cover the beans. Bring them to a boil then reduce the heat and simmer them covered for 30 minutes. Preheat your oven to 325°F.

Pour the hot lima mixture into a deep baking pan. Set the meat in the center and cover it with a lid. Bake it for 3 to 4 hours or until the meat is tender and the beans are cooked, adding more stock as needed.

Pork Aspic / *Pihtí*

A traditional Christmas centerpiece for the dinner table, *Pihtí* can also be enjoyed as a *mezé* on other days of the year and they don't have to be holidays.

Ingredients:
6 lbs. pork meat with bones such as knuckles, feet, and head.
3 small onions
3 carrots
1 rib celery
4 sprigs of parsley
3 bay leaves
5 garlic cloves
10 pepper corns
peel of half a lemon
2 tbs. capers - optional
¼ cup chopped dill pickles - optional
salt to taste
⅓ cup vinegar

If you're using a pig's head, have a butcher chop it into several pieces and discard the brain and eyes. Wash the pieces of feet, knuckles and head well and place in the refrigerator in lightly salted water to remove all traces of blood - about 2 hours, changing the water once or twice.

Drain and rinse the pork, put it in a large pot and cover it with water. Add the spices, vegetables and lemon peel and heat it to boiling, skimming the froth that collects on top. Boil it for 10 to 15 minutes until the stock is clear. Cover the pot and reduce the heat so it simmers for about 4 hours or until the meat falls off the bones easily.

Strain the meat and bones from the stock and return it to the heat. Pick the meat from the bones, discarding any skins and return the bones to the stock so it boils together, reducing to about 5 cups. Skim off any fat that collects on top.

Chop the meat into small pieces. Slice the carrots and celery and toss it in a bowl with the capers and pickles if you're using them, and the meat pieces. Arrange the mixture in a mold of your choice and refrigerate.

Once the stock has reduced, add the vinegar and boil it for another 5 minutes. Pour the stock through a strainer that has been lined with cheese cloth to remove any little bits of bone.

To test your stock for the gel stage, spoon a small amount of stock on a plate and refrigerate it. It should thicken to a gelatin consistency. If not, boil and reduce your stock another 15 minutes, checking again for the gel stage. For a thicker aspic, unflavored gelatin can be added. Once it's ready and gels easily, set the entire pot of stock aside to cool. Let it cool down enough so that it begins to thicken and then spoon it over the meat - veggie mixture that's in the mold. Refrigerate the mold until it's set. Invert the mold onto a platter and serve.

Pork Roast / *Hirinó sto Foúrno*

For a very tender way of baking pork, try this recipe. It's easy because it can be made in advance of a special meal and all you have to do is shove the pan in the oven. This recipe also works great with whole, suckling pigs.

Ingredients:
one pork roast, such as leg or shoulder with the bone in. Quantity doesn't matter so choose a roast that suits your families appetites.
salt and pepper
ground cumin
oregano
thyme
yellow mustard
1 minced onion
1 cup white or red dry wine
1 cup olive oil
3 fresh lemons
bay leaves

Get yourself a bowl or pan that will fit the roast so it will be at least half covered in marinade. Rinse the roast under running water and pat it dry with paper towels. Sprinkle the roast with salt, pepper, cumin, oregano, and thyme and rub the spices into the meat. Using some plain yellow mustard, spread it over the entire surface of the roast, coating it. Place the roast into the bowl. In a separate bowl, mix together the minced onion, wine, oil and juice of three lemons. Crumble in the bay leafs and pour it over your roast. Let the roast marinade at least over night. If only half of the roast is covered in the marinade, turn it over every few hours so the other side can soak too.

Take the roast out of the refrigerator and let it set at room temperature for 1 or 2 hours. Preheat your oven to 325°F. Arrange the roast in a pan and pour the marinade over it. Cover it tightly with a lid or some aluminum foil and bake.

Depending on the size of the meat cut, the cooking time can take anywhere from 2 to 6 hours. Don't increase the temperature because you want it to cook slowly and become tender. You'll know it's ready when a fork can be used to cut the meat. Do check on it occasionally and if one side is getting too crisp, turn it over.

Depending on the cut, you may have a pan full of juices as well. Carefully remove them from the pan using a ladle, but don't discard them. Pour any drippings through a strainer and skim off the fat. Add some basic thickener and you have a delicious, smooth gravy to serve with your roast.

Stuffed Suckling Pig / *Gourounópoulo Gemistó*

The very fancy dish, Stuffed Piglet can be served whole for any holiday dinner table. The ingredients may seem like a lot, but the preparation is not at all difficult and you can show off your talents as a Greek Chef. For spicier pork, see the recipe for Pork Roast and use the mustard coating for the piglet.

Ingredients:
one 10 to 15 lb. whole piglet. Ask your butcher to remove the internal organs but to leave the head and feet intact as the presentation of the piglet is an important part for an extra pat on the back for the cook. Remember to ask him to give you the liver, as you will need it for the stuffing.
lemons
salt and pepper
cumin
softened butter
preserved grape leaves in brine, rinsed
a red apple

Stuffing:
½ cup olive oil
½ cup butter
1 piglet liver, chopped
2 cups chopped onions
1 cup white wine
1 cup seedless raisins
½ cup pine nuts
1 cup rice
1 cup chestnuts, blanched and chopped
1 cup chopped, pitted green olives
1 cup bread crumbs
1 tsp. rosemary
½ tsp. ground cinnamon
½ tsp. ground nutmeg
salt and pepper

Soak the piglet for one hour in salted water then let it drain thoroughly. Using fresh lemon halves, rub the pig inside and out, squeezing out the juice of the lemon as you go along. Set the piglet aside to absorb the juice.

Heat the oil and butter in a skillet. Fry the liver with the onions until the meat is cooked. Pour in the wine, raisins, and pine nuts and let the mixture simmer for 5 minutes. Remove the skillet from the heat. Stir in the rice, chestnuts, olives, bread crumbs, rosemary, cinnamon, nutmeg, and season it with salt and pepper.

Sprinkle the entire piglet with salt, pepper and cumin, inside and out. Take the butter and smear it all over to coat the meat. Fill the body cavity with the stuffing and using bamboo skewers or a poultry needle, close it up.

Preheat your oven to 325°F. Lay the stuffed pig on its stomach on your work surface. Pull the fore legs forward and tie them together with some butchers cord. Pull the hind legs so that the pig will sit nicely without tumbling over. Tie them in the direction which is easiest for you, forward or back. Set the pig in your roasting pan.

To keep the mouth open, so you can insert an apple later, use a piece of wood, or some bunched up foil in the opening. Pull the mouth open wide, and insert the wedge.

Wrap the ears with aluminum foil so they don't burn, then cover the whole pot with a lid or some foil. The pig will take 3 to 4 hours to roast and during this time, you should check on it occasionally basting it so you have juicy, tender meat. For the last half hour of cooking, remove the foil and let the pig brown.

Once the pig is done, remove it from the oven and let it cool off for a few minutes to set. A gravy can easily be prepared by using the drippings and some basic thickener.

Prepare a large platter by spreading preserved grape vine leaves on the bottom, so they hang over the edges. Carefully tumble the pig and remove the string from the cavity and spoon the stuffing around the outside edges of your platter.

Carefully scoop up the pig by using two large spatulas and set it in the center of the platter. For this part, it may help to have a friend or spouse handy to use another set of spatulas. Once the pig is situated, cut away the strings from the legs, remove the foil from its mouth, and gently insert a red apple. Be prepared for the oohs and ahhs of your guests as you enter the dining room.

LAMB RECIPES

Charcoal Grilled Lamb Chops / *Arnáki sta Kárvouna*

A truly delicious way to serve lamb, even for the most discerning taste. For those of you that have a fireplace, these chops can be done right in there if you carefully arrange the wood coals. It's also fun to do when you have company over, but again, be careful of flare-ups.

Ingredients:
2 lbs. lamb chops, rinsed and drained
salt and pepper
ground cumin
1 tbs. minced parsley
2 minced garlic cloves
Marinade:
2 cups olive oil
1 cup lemon juice

> **Menu Idea**
> Charcoal Grilled Lamb Chops
> Potatoes with Rosemary
> Yogurt and Pimento Sauce
> Roasted Eggplant Salad
> Garden Salad
> Greek Vinaigrette
> Fresh Lemon Wedges
> Feta Cheese
> Olives
> Fresh Bread

Lay your chops out on a work surface or cutting board. Sprinkle them generously with the salt, pepper and cumin on both sides. Put them into a large bowl and pour the oil and lemon juice over them. Add the parsley and garlic, tossing it all together with your hands and arranging them so that they are sitting in the marinade. Cover tightly and marinade for a few hours or refrigerated overnight.

Drain the chops from the marinade and barbecue over an open pit. You want the coals hot, but be careful that it's not too intense and you burn the chops. You want to cook them slowly and serve them medium done. Lamb has a lot of fat and the oil of the marinade will drip into the coals as well, so watch out for flare-ups. Serve them sizzling hot with fresh lemons to squeeze over the meat.

Easter Lamb on a Spit / *Arní Soúvlas*

This is the traditional Easter Sunday favorite for the Greeks as well as the main course for a celebration feast such as a wedding.

Ingredients:
1 whole spring baby lamb, 16 to 30 lbs, depending on the quantity needed. Have the butcher remove the head and internal organs. You can use them in the recipe for *Magirítsa* Soup.
lemon halves
salt and pepper
olive oil
ground cumin
ground oregano
ground rosemary

Open Pit Marinade for Lamb:
1 cup olive oil
1 cup butter
1 tbs. chopped rosemary
1 tbs. cumin
1 tbs. oregano
Lemon or Herbal Brush using fresh basil or fresh rosemary stems - see "Kitchen Techniques" for more details and tips on how to make these wonderful accessories.

To begin with, you're going to need a large table or counter top to work on, so get an area ready that you won't mind if it gets a bit messy. Wash the lamb carcass inside and out with running water and set it aside to drain. Set the carcass on your work surface and using paper towels, remove any excess moisture that is left on the meat.

Rub it inside and out, with the lemon halves, squeezing out the juice as you go along. Sprinkle it, inside and out with salt, pepper, cumin, oregano and rosemary. At this point, I recommend wrapping it up and refrigerating it over night for the meat to absorb the spices or at least let it stand at room temperature for a few hours.

Follow the directions in the "Kitchen Techniques" section to attach the carcass to the spit. Pouring some oil into your hands, rub the entire lamb so it's coated. This will help seal in the juices as well as give you a crispy outer crust.

Place the spit over the coals. You want to roast it slowly over low heat, for 3 to 5 hours, depending on the size. Remember lamb is best when it's medium cooked. In a bowl, mix together the marinade ingredients. Using the Lemon or Herbal brush, or just a plain one, brush this oil-marinade over the meat as it's turning and roasting. Obviously, the more you do this, the better the meat. Check on the thickest part of the meat for doneness – I pierce the thigh. When it's cooked, remove it from the spit. Remove all the wire and cut into serving size pieces, using a heavy knife. Serve it immediately.

Easter Stuffed Lamb / *Lambriátiko Arní Gemistó*

The traditional *Lambriótis* is baked in a *foúrno* or village wood oven. It is placed inside the heated oven on Holy Saturday and the oven door is sealed with a dough made from plain flour and water which keeps the heat from escaping. The *Lambriótis* is left inside over night and is taken out on Easter Sunday with the finished result being that the meat literally falls off the bone.

Ingredients:
1 large cut of lamb such as the front half or chest.
1 or 2 lemons, halved
½ cup olive oil
salt and pepper
ground oregano
ground cumin
3 cups beef or chicken broth

Stuffing:
1 lamb's liver, cleaned and chopped into very fine, small pieces.
1 cup olive oil
1 cup onions, chopped
3 cups long grain rice
2 cups chopped tomatoes
½ cup fresh chopped dill weed
dash of ground cumin
salt and pepper
3 cups broth
½ cup raisins - optional
½ tsp. cinnamon - optional
½ cup pine nuts - optional

Wash the meat thoroughly under running water and let it drain. Rub it all over with lemon halves, inside and out, squeezing the juice against the meat. Drizzle the oil over the carcass and rub it in. This will seal the meat for a tender roast and will give it color too. Sprinkle with the salt, pepper, oregano and cumin and set it in a roasting pan.

Heat the oil in a large skillet and lightly fry the onions. Add the liver and cook it until the red color has disappeared then add the rice and sauté it until it's slightly golden. Add the rest of the ingredients and cook for 5 to 10 minutes, stirring constantly until the liquid has been absorbed and remove the stuffing from the heat.

Fill the cavity of the lamb loosely with the stuffing. Sew it up with a heavy needle and cord, or use skewers to secure it. If you have extra stuffing left over, you can bake it separately, or add it to the pan the last half-hour or so before you take it out.

Pour the broth into the pan and cover it tightly. Bake in a preheated oven at 325°F for 2 to 3 hours. If you have time to cook it slower, use a heat setting of 300°F and bake the lamb for 4 to 5 hours which will result in making the meat very tender. The actual cooking time will depend on the size of your lamb cut. Check on it occasionally and add more water or broth if necessary. For the last 20 to 30 minutes of baking, remove the cover and let the outer layer brown and crisp.

Lamb with Lettuce Fricassee / *Arní Frikasé*

During the winter months, lettuce is found growing in every village garden. This stew is a great way to use the popular salad vegetable in a different way. For a heartier version, add cubed potatoes to the stew for the last 20 minutes of cooking time.

Ingredients:
2 lbs. lamb with bone, cut into stew size chunks
salt and pepper
½ cup olive oil
1 large chopped onion
4 cups chicken stock
4 heads romaine lettuce, the leaves separated and washed. Chop any large leaves up coarsely.

Wash and dry the lamb and salt and pepper it. Heat the oil in a large pot. Brown the meat with the onions. Add the chicken stock and bring it to a boil. Reduce the heat and simmer the broth until the lamb is tender.

Add the lettuce to the stew, and cook until it has wilted. It will only take a few minutes. For a thicker stew, add some flour that has been diluted in water and simmer for an additional 5 minutes.

Lamb In Paper - *Kleftiko* Style / *Arní Kléftiko se Hartí*

The lamb is marinated overnight and then wrapped tightly in wax paper, sealing the juices and herbs together. Truly magnificent and delicious, this is a wonderful special occasion meal.

Ingredients:
1 medium leg of lamb - boneless pieces can be used too.
4 garlic cloves - optional
salt and pepper
oregano
cumin
rosemary
2 tbs. chopped parsley
5 tbs. olive oil
juice of 1 lemon
½ lb. cheese - feta or Greek *kefalotíri*, sliced thickly

> **Menu Idea**
> Lamb In Paper - *Kleftiko* Style
> Tomato Rice with Garlic
> Lettuce Salad
> Greek Vinaigrette
> Onion Fritters
> Yogurt Sauce
> Grated Cheese
> Feta Cheese
> Olives
> Fresh Bread

Wash and dry the lamb. If you prefer a garlic taste, make small slits in the thickest parts of the leg and insert the cloves. Salt and pepper it and sprinkle generously with the herbs and spices. Mix the oil and lemon juice together and drizzle it over the meat. Cover and marinate the leg for 3 hours or overnight.

Preheat your oven to 300°F. Spread out a sheet of waxed paper and rub it with oil. Take the marinated leg and lay it on the paper. Arrange the cheese slices over the top. Wrap the leg up tightly in the paper, making sure that the juices won't seep out. Wrap the entire parcel once more in aluminum foil. Place in a shallow pan and bake for 2 to 3 hours, depending on the how well done you like your meat.

Lamb In Pastry Country Style / *Arní Exohikó*

Though the recipe calls for phyllo sheets, you can easily substitute a pastry dough which will give you a thicker crust.

Ingredients:
2 lbs. boneless lamb cut into ½ inch slices
salt and pepper
oregano
phyllo pastry sheets
melted butter
½ lb. feta cheese
2 tbs. olive oil

Heat your oven to 325°F. Rinse the lamb under running water, pat it dry and sprinkle it with salt, pepper and oregano. Spread out a sheet of phyllo and brush it with melted butter. Lay another sheet over this and again, brush with butter. Continue until you have 4 to 6 sheets of pastry.

Arrange the lamb over the pastry sheets, allowing yourself two inches of room from the edges to fold it over. Top the meat with the feta cheese and drizzle it with olive oil. Fold the sides over and then roll the whole thing up lengthwise so you have a nice package. Use butter at the edge of the phyllo roll to seal it down.

Move the roll to a buttered, shallow baking pan, seam side down. Be careful, you don't want the phyllo to split while you're transferring it. If it does, just use strips of phyllo and butter as "glue" to patch up any holes. Place it in the oven and bake for one hour or until the meat is cooked to your preference. You will have to keep an eye on the pastry, as phyllo tends to brown easily. If this happens and the meat is not done, cover the pan with a sheet of aluminum foil and remove it during the last 10 to 15 minutes of cooking time.

Lamb Kleftiko - Traditional / *Arní Kléftiko Paradosiakó*

Traditionally, this is made in a ceramic casserole dish. A dough is made from flour and water and is used to seal the cover to the pot. Its then baked in a *foúrno* or village wood-oven overnight. The results are absolutely fabulous. This is only one of many versions of Lamb *Kléftiko*. Any recipe for *Kléftiko* includes some way that the meat is sealed so that the juices remain inside, steaming with the meat. For a very tender bake, try the recipe and you'll find that the meat just falls off the bones.

Ingredients:
2 lbs. lamb, cut into pieces
salt and pepper
3 potatoes, cut into wedges
3 green peppers, cut into wedges
2 carrots, sliced thickly
1 onion, cut into wedges
1 lemon, cut into slices
½ cup olive oil

Rinse the lamb pieces and drain. Put the lamb in an ovenproof casserole dish and sprinkle it with salt and pepper. Add the cut vegetables and lemon and toss together. Drizzle the olive oil over the whole thing and cover tightly. Notice that no liquid is added to this. Everything just steams together. Bake in the oven for 4 hours at 275°F.

Lamb Stew / *Arní Giahní*

The lamb in this recipe is stewed slowly in tomatoes making it very tender and flavorful. The stew can be used as a sauce for a bed of pilaf or pasta. You can also make the stew a one pot meal by adding a few vegetables such as okra, peas or potatoes the last thirty minutes of cooking time.

Ingredients:
2 lbs. lamb cut into chunks
salt and pepper
2 tbs. flour
½ cup olive oil
1 cup chopped onions
1 crushed garlic clove
2 cups chopped tomatoes
chicken or beef stock

Rinse and drain the lamb. Toss it with the salt, pepper and flour. Heat the oil in a deep skillet and brown the meat on all sides. Add the onions and garlic and fry until translucent. Pour in the tomatoes and two cups of stock. Simmer the meat, partially covered for one hour or until tender, adding more stock as needed.

Lamb with Green Beans / *Arní me Fasolákia*

For the lamb lover, this dish cooks in one pot and makes a spectacular meal. Serve it with a green salad, feta cheese and of course, fresh crusty bread.

Ingredients:
2 lbs. lamb, cut into stewing chunks
salt and pepper
oregano
cumin
½ cup olive oil
1 clove garlic
1 onion, finely chopped
2 cups fresh, chopped tomatoes
2 cups chicken or beef stock
2 bay leaves
2 lbs. fresh or frozen green beans

Rinse the lamb under running water and pat it dry. Salt and pepper it and sprinkle with cumin and oregano. In a deep pot, heat the olive oil. Add the lamb, garlic and onions and fry it together until the onions become translucent. Pour in the tomatoes, stock and the bay leafs. Reduce the heat and simmer the lamb for 30 to 45 minutes, stirring occasionally and adding more stock if it's needed.

When the lamb is almost tender, add the green beans and simmer it together for another 20 minutes. If you're using frozen, add them only at the last 10 or 15 minutes before the lamb is done.

Roasted Leg of Lamb / *Arní tou Foúrnou*

An elegant meal that has the convenience of being one pot and is perfect for entertaining or for the working mom or dad. The lamb leg can be prepared the night before, marinating with the spices. Keep the potatoes separate, soaked in water and add them just before it goes into the oven.

Ingredients:
one 3 to 6 lb. leg of lamb
salt and pepper to taste
2 to 4 garlic cloves
6 medium potatoes, peeled and quartered
2 tbs. dried rosemary
½ cup crushed tomatoes
½ cup olive oil
1 cup chicken or beef stock

Preheat your oven to 350°F. To prepare the lamb leg, remove any visible fat with a sharp knife. Cut 2 to 4 deep gashes on opposite sides of the leg all the way to the bone. Tuck in the garlic cloves and a little of the rosemary. Place the lamb leg in a roasting pan and drizzle with some of the oil and rub it all over with your hands. Salt and pepper it and sprinkle with the remaining rosemary.

Arrange the potatoes around the leg and top it all off with the tomatoes. Pour in the stock and drizzle a bit more olive oil over the potatoes. Cover the pan with aluminum foil and bake for 40-60 minutes, depending on how well you like your meat cooked. Remove the foil and bake it for an additional 15 minutes to crisp the potatoes, adding more stock if needed.

GROUND MEAT RECIPES

Eggplant-Potato Casserole / *Mousaká*

One of the most popular Greek dishes. This casserole may seem complicated, but if done in stages, it's fairly simple and definitely worth the extra effort. *Mousaká* can easily be made as a vegetarian dish by substituting a different sauce. Try the recipes for Tomato-Onion Sauce or Tomato-Vegetable Sauce for a meatless variation. Fantastic with a green salad and fresh bread.

Ingredients:
4 lbs. large eggplant
4 lbs. potatoes
oil for frying
Basic Meat Sauce for Casseroles-see recipe
Béchamel sauce-see recipe

Peel and cut the potatoes into thin ¼ inch slices. Weight them down in a bowl of salted water with an inverted plate until you're ready to use them. Cut the eggplants into thin ¼ inch slices. I don't remove the purple peel, but you can if you prefer. Sprinkle them with salt and set them aside to drain.

Drain the potato slices. Heat oil in a skillet and fry the potatoes until they are golden on each side. Remove the slices to paper towels to drain. Continue by frying the eggplant slices, one side and then on the other so they are evenly browned. Remove them to paper towels to drain off as much oil as possible.

While the veggies are draining, follow the recipe directions and prepare the meat sauce.

To assemble the casserole, use a large baking pan that is 3 inches deep. Line the bottom of it with a layer of potatoes. Next, add a layer of eggplant, and top it with half of the sauce. Begin a new layer of potatoes, continuing with eggplant and the remaining sauce. Preheat your oven to 350°F.

Follow the recipe directions and make the *Béchamel* Sauce. Pour the sauce over the casserole and sprinkle it with grated cheese. Bake it for 30 to 40 minutes or until the crust has browned. Let the casserole cool down for 20 minutes or longer to set before you serve it.

Mousaká with Yogurt / *Mousakás me Yiaoúrti*

Even the traditional dish *Mousaká* has its variations. This recipe uses hot peppers and sweet raisins in the meat sauce as well as green peppers layered through the vegetables. The yogurt topping is much easier to make than the traditional *Béchamel* and is very flavorful.

Ingredients:
4 lbs. large eggplant
4 lbs. potatoes
½ lb. green peppers
oil for frying

Meat Sauce:
¼ cup olive oil
2 lbs. ground beef or lamb
1 large onion, chopped
2 crushed garlic cloves
1 tsp. hot pepper flakes
⅓ cup red wine
½ cup raisins - optional
pinch nutmeg - optional
2 cups crushed tomatoes
salt and pepper
bay leaf

Topping Ingredients:
3 cups strained yogurt
3 egg yokes

Peel and cut the potatoes into thin ¼ inch slices. Weight them down in a bowl of salted water with an inverted plate until you're ready to use them. Cut the eggplants into thin ¼ inch slices. I don't remove the purple peel, but you can if you prefer. Sprinkle them with salt and set them aside to drain. Remove seeds from the green peppers, rinse them, and cut them in half. Set aside to drain.

Drain the potato slices. Heat oil in a skillet and fry the potatoes until they are golden on each side. Remove the slices to paper towels to drain. Continue by frying the eggplant slices, one side and then on the other so they are evenly browned and lastly, fry the green peppers. Remove them to paper towels to drain off as much oil as possible.

While the veggies are draining, make the sauce. Heat the oil in a pot. Brown your ground beef with the garlic and onions. Add the rest of the ingredients and simmer the mixture for 20 minutes.

To assemble the casserole, use a large baking pan that is 3 inches deep. Line the bottom of it with a layer of potatoes. Next, add a layer of eggplant, some green peppers, and top it with half of the sauce. Begin a new layer of potatoes, continuing with eggplant, peppers and the remaining sauce. Preheat your oven to 350ºF.

In a mixing bowl, whisk the eggs until frothy. Add the yogurt and combine well. Pour the yogurt sauce over the finished casserole and bake it for 30 to 40 minutes or until the top has set and browned. Let the casserole cool down for 20 minutes or longer to set before you serve it.

Macaroni Casserole / *Pastítsio*

Another traditional casserole dish that is simple to prepare but tastes like you've fussed. *Pastítsio* can easily be made as a vegetarian dish by substituting a different sauce. Try the recipes for Tomato-Onion Sauce or Tomato-Vegetable Sauce for a meatless variation.

Ingredients:
1 lb. *Pastíitsio* noodles #3- Try a Greek specialty shop or substitute Penne macaroni
1 egg, beaten
½ cup grated Greek *keflotíri* or parmesan cheese
Basic Meat Sauce for Casseroles - see recipe
Béchamel Sauce - see recipe

In a large pot, boil your noodles in salted water until al-dente. Drain and let cool.
Follow the recipe directions and make the meat sauce.
Butter a large casserole pan and put the noodles into it. Add the beaten egg, and toss the noodles. Pat them down into the pan. Pour the sauce over the noodle layer, smoothing it out and set it aside. Pre heat your oven to 350°F.
Follow the recipe directions and make the *Béchamel* Sauce. Pour it over the casserole and sprinkle it with the grated cheese. Bake the casserole for 20 to 30 minutes until the top has browned. Let the casserole cool down for 20 minutes or longer to set before you serve it.

Goat Herder's Pie / *Pastítsio me Pouré*

This casserole dish comes to us from the Island of Crete. It is an easy meal to prepare and can be made a day or two in advance. Servings are easily microwaveable which makes it convenient for the working mom or dad.

Ingredients:
1½ lb. ground beef, pork, lamb, or goat as to your preference.
1 cup olive oil
1 cup chopped onions
1 cup chopped fresh tomatoes
½ cup chopped parsley
 salt and pepper
2 eggs, beaten
2 sheets of phyllo pastry
½ cup melted butter
½ cup grated Greek *kefalotíri* or parmesan cheese

Potato Topping:
4 lbs. potatoes cleaned and cubed.
4 eggs, beaten
1 cup chopped fresh dill weed
½ cup grated Greek *kefalotíri* or parmesan cheese

Begin by making the topping. Boil the potatoes in salted water until done. Drain them, mash them thoroughly and set them aside. Once they have cooled, add the rest of the topping ingredients and mix well.

In a large skillet, heat the oil and brown the ground beef with the onions. Add the tomatoes, parsley and salt and pepper. Cook the mixture for 15 minutes then set it aside. Once it has cooled, add the beaten eggs and mix it all together.

Butter a large baking dish and lay the sheet of phyllo pastry in the bottom. Brush it with some butter and place the other sheet on top. Smooth half of the potato mixture over the pastry, then smooth the beef mixture over it. Top it off with the remaining potatoes. Pour the remaining melted butter over the casserole and sprinkle with cheese. Bake it for 40 minutes at 350°F. Let the casserole stand for 15 minutes or longer before serving.

Beef Rolls from *Smýrni* / *Souzoukákia Smyrnéika*

These little rolls are simple to make and very convieneient. They can be made well in advance and re-heated at meal time. Serve them over a bed of pilaf, pasta or mashed potatoes.

Ingredients:
1½ lb. ground beef
½ cup bread crumbs, moistened slightly
1 egg
3 cloves crushed garlic
1 onion, minced
salt and pepper
1 cup chopped parsley
1 cup olive oil
flour for rolling
2 cups chopped tomatoes
½ cup dry white wine - optional
1 tsp. sugar

> **Menu Idea**
> Beef Rolls from *Smýrni*
> Mashed Potatoes
> Peas with Dill Sauce
> Cabbage Salad
> Greek Vinaigrette
> Feta Cheese
> Olives
> Fresh Bread

In a mixing bowl add the ground beef, bread crumbs, egg, garlic, onions, salt and pepper and parsley. Knead the mixture and form it into little log shapes about the size of half a cigar.

Heat the oil in a skillet. Roll the logs in flour and fry them in the oil. Remove and place them on paper towels to drain.

In the same oil, add the tomatoes, wine and sugar. Cook the tomatoes for 25 minutes then add the beef rolls. Baste the rolls with the sauce and let them simmer for another 10 minutes.

Poached Meat Balls / *Youvarlákia*

Youvarlákia are simply boiled meatballs. They take almost no time at all to make and can be served with any side dish that you like. These little bundles are so popular that there is also a recipe for Poached Meatball Soup.

Ingredients:
2 cups chicken stock
flour
Egg-Lemon Sauce - see recipe

Meat Balls:
1 ½ lbs. ground beef, pork or lamb
½ cup uncooked rice
1 chopped onion
3 tbs. chopped parsley
1 tsp. cumin - optional
1 egg
salt and pepper to taste

Mix together all the ingredients for the meatballs, kneading it with your hands. Form the mixture into balls 1½ to 2 inches in diameter. In a sauce pan, bring the stock to a boil. Roll the meat balls in flour and drop them gently into the boiling stock. Simmer them for 20 minutes or until the rice is cooked.

Using a slotted spoon, remove the meatballs from the stock and set them on a platter. Follow the recipe directions for making the Egg-Lemon Sauce, using the stock that the meatballs were cooked in. Spoon the sauce over the meatballs and serve.

Greek Hamburgers / *Mpiftéki*

Mpiftéki is a common menu item that exists in every restaurant in Greece. There are many variations for this dish, but I chose the most popular one to share with you. The best tasting *Mpiftékia* are always cooked over charcoals so next time you barbeque, add some of these tidbits to your menu.

Ingredients:
1 lb. ground beef - beef, pork or lamb can be used
1 egg
½ cup fine bread crumbs
2 cloves garlic, crushed
1 onion, finely chopped
2 tbs. finely chopped parsley - optional
2 tbs. olive oil
1 tsp. cumin
salt and pepper to taste

Simply mix all the ingredients together in a big bowl and form into patties. You can fry, bake, or broil them. Charcoal really brings out the taste of these burgers, so if you can, use a barbeque. Make a simple marinade using Lemon-Oil Dressing and follow the directions in the "Kitchen Techniques" section to make an herbal brush. Baste the burgers using the brush and the marinade as they cook. The finished product is fantastic.

For more great recipes using meats, be sure to see the following sections:

The Marinade Recipes
The Art of *Souvláki* Making
The Infamous *Gýro*
The Game Meats
The Organ Meats
Stuffed Vegetables / *Gemistá* and *Dolmáthes*

Individual Recipes to see:

Ham Pie / *Zambonópita*
Lamb and Feta Pie / *Píta me Arní ke Féta*
Cretan Lamb Torte / *Toúrta Krítis me Arní*
Leek and Beef Pie / *Prasópita*
Meat and Cheese Pie / *Kreatópita me Tirí*
Basic Meat Pie / *Kreatópita Aplí*
Sweet Meat Pies / *Bourekákia me Kimá*
Lamb Pie from Cephalonia / *Kreatópita Kefalonítiki*
Greek Meat Balls / *Keftédes*
Greek Beef Soup / *Kréas me Kritharáki Soúpa*
Poached Meatball Soup / *Youvarlákia Soúpa*

The Infamous *Gýro*

In the Islands, our *Gýro*-pronounced yee-ro, is made from pork slices that are stacked and cooked on a vertical, rotating spit. If you've ever had the chance to see the real thing then you would have noticed that these huge revolving spits of meat really do resemble gyros or "tops."

The meat is grilled slowly with aromatic herbs and spices and then sliced thinly into a pita. Variations for this favorite include the use of ground pork and lamb as well as poultry.

Gýro Making from Ground Meats

Choose the pork, lamb or poultry recipe as to your preference. Mix all the ingredients together in a large bowl. Form the meat into thin, oblong patties. You can fry, bake, broil or charcoal grill them, depending on your taste preference.

Gýro from Pork - Ground Version
2 lbs. ground pork with fat
2 tbs. minced onion
3 tbs. ground cumin
1 tbs. oregano
1 tsp. paprika - optional
1 crushed garlic clove
salt and pepper

Gýro from Lamb - Ground Version
1 lb. ground lamb
1 lb. ground beef
2 tbs. minced onion
2 tbs. oregano
1 tsp. spearmint
1 crushed garlic clove
salt and pepper

Gýro from Poultry - Ground Version
2 lbs. ground chicken or turkey
2 tbs. minced onion
2 tbs. ground thyme
1 tbs. oregano
1 crushed garlic clove
salt and pepper

Traditional Spit *Gýro* From Pork

Ingredients:
boneless pork with fat
salt & pepper
ground cumin
granulated garlic
oregano
sweet or hot Paprika

I'll leave the quantity up to you, but you should have enough meat to stack up at least 10 inches. We use pork shoulder that has been cut into steak like slices, not thicker than ½ inch and 8 to 10 inches in diameter. For home use, I recommend a smaller cut, maybe 4 to 6 inches in diameter so it cooks quicker.

Arrange the pork slices on a cutting board. Generously sprinkle with all the spices on both sides. Skewer the slices onto your spit, packing them very tightly against each other. You want it to resemble a roast. *Gýro* is cooked vertically, on a rotating electric spit. Though I've never tried a horizontal spit, I would think that you would lose too much juice that way and you would have a dry *gýro* where as vertically, the meat bastes itself.

Begin by rotating your *gýro* on medium heat setting for one or two hours. You do not have to wait for it to cook completely through in order to serve. You slice the crisp outer layer of gýro as it gets done and let it continue to rotate and cook, slice again, cook again, etc. To serve, use a very sharp knife and run it down the length of the *gýro* as it rotates, slicing off the cooked layer. You want the slices to be thin and bite sized.

If you are entertaining and want the entire *gýro* to be eaten rather quickly, there is a short cut. You can arrange your pork slices into a roast and tie it together with butcher's cord. Bake it in the oven for an hour or two, depending on its size. Then skewer the whole thing and set it in the spit to grill and crisp the outer layers. You won't have to wait as long in between slicing for the pork to cook.

Pork *gýro* is one of the easiest recipes that I know. The trick is in the meat cuts and the equipment that you use to cook it. The higher the fat content, the crispier and juicier your *gýro* will turn out.

Assembling The Sandwich

Sandwich Ingredients:
cooked pork, lamb or poultry
Greek *píta* bread - see recipe
Tzatzíki - see recipe
sliced onions
sliced tomatoes
chopped parsley

Fry a *píta* in a hot skillet with a dash of olive oil, just until golden on each side. Spread the *píta* with *Tzatzíki* and add the meat to the center. Top it with sliced tomato, onions and a sprinkle of parsley. Roll the *píta* up, and you have *gýro*.

These are messy sandwiches, so if you'd like to keep it neat, wrap a piece of waxed paper over the bottom half of the sandwich and crimp the edges to keep the juices from running down your hands.

***Gýro* as a Dinner Entrée**

Gýro can be served as a main entrée for dinner. Platters of meat should be accompanied by dishes of *Tzatzíki*, fried potatoes, Greek Village Salad, and of course Greek *píta* bread.

> **Menu Idea**
> Traditional Pork *Gýro*
> Pepper Pilaf
> Fried Fresh Potatoes
> Greek Village Salad
> *Tzatzíki*
> Grated Cheese
> Feta Cheese
> Olives
> Greek Pita Bread

The Art of *Souvláki* Making
Shish Kebob

During the summer festivals, charcoaled S*ouvlákis* can be found all through the streets of the village squares. They are served on a stick with a wedge of fresh village bread and are eaten as you stand by the road side.

Making *Souvláki* is not a difficult task and the dish itself can be easily altered to suit anyone tastes. The meats that are used can be pork, lamb, beef, poultry or fish. The meat is skewered with or without vegetables and then marinated. The marinade makes the meat very flavorful and tender.

Souvlakis can be fried, baked, grilled in an oven or set over hot coals of a barbeque. It can be served over a bed of pilaf which will catch the juices from the meat or simply with fried potatoes and *Tzatzíki*.

Vegetables for *Souvláki* Making:
Any vegetable that you like can be used for skewering with the meats. Some of the more popular are:

Quartered onions separated into pieces
Green peppers cut into one inch pieces
Whole Cherry Tomatoes
Whole Mushrooms
Zucchinis cut into one inch slices

Souvláki Marinades

Beef Shish Kebobs / *Moscarísio Souvláki*
2 lbs. tender beef cut into 1-inch cubes

Marinade:
2 cups olive oil
1 cup fresh lemon juice
1 crushed garlic clove
1 tbs. oregano
1 tbs. thyme
1 tsp. dry spearmint
salt and pepper

Pork Shish Kebobs / *Hirinó Souvláki*
2 lbs. tender pork cut into 1-inch cubes

Marinade:
2 cups olive oil
1 cup fresh lemon juice
1 crushed garlic clove
2 tbs. cumin
1 tbs. oregano
1 tbs. grated onion
salt and pepper

Lamb Shish Kebobs / *Arní Souvláki*
2 lbs. tender lamb cut into 1-inch cubes

Marinade:
2 cups olive oil
1 cup fresh lemon juice
2 crushed garlic cloves
2 tbs. rosemary
1 tbs. grated onion
1 tsp. oregano
salt and pepper

Chicken Kebobs / *Kotópoulo Souvláki*
2 lbs. boned chicken breasts cut into 1-inch pieces

Marinade:
2 cups olive oil
1 cup fresh lemon juice
2 crushed garlic cloves
1 tbs. oregano
1 tbs. ground cumin
1 tbs. thyme
salt and pepper

Swordfish Kebobs / *Xifías Souvláki*
2 lbs. swordfish cut into 1-inch cubes

Marinade:
2 cups olive oil
1 cup fresh lemon juice
2 tbs. minced parsley
1 tbs. oregano
salt and pepper

Preparing the *Souvláki*

Using wooden or metal skewers, alternate the meat with a vegetable, keeping it tightly packed on the skewer. Use your imagination, and make colorful Shish Kebobs until you have a nice serving size portion. Repeat with the rest of the meat until you use it up. Depending on your vegetables, you should have 4 to 6 skewers filled.

Salt and pepper the finished skewers and lay them in a shallow pan or plastic container. Make the marinade in bowl, mixing together all the ingredients for the type of meat which you are using. Pour the marinade over the skewered meat and cover them with cling film. Let them marinade for at least 2 hours or preferably overnight.

Cooking the *Souvláki*

To cook the shish kebobs, remove them from the marinade and let them drain. Make sure that you reserve the marinade as it can be used to baste the baking or charcoal grilled kebobs. The shish kebobs can also be fried on stove top. Use a non stick pan with a lid and fry the kebobs on each side, keeping the pan partially covered.

To bake the shish kebobs, lay them in a pan or on a grill rack and bake them at 375°F for 30 to 40 minutes or until the meat is done to your preference. Use the reserved marinade to baste them during their cooking time. To charcoal the kebobs, lay them on your grill and cook each side over the hot coals. Again, use the reserved marinade for basting the kebobs as they cook.

Souvláki as a Sandwich

Souvláki is often served in a pita just as the *Gýro*. The meats are cut into smaller cubes that are threaded onto a skewer and grilled. For sandwich *Souvlákis*, only marinated meat is used, leaving any vegetables to be added to the pita later.

Sandwich Ingredients:
cooked *Souvláki* of your choice
Greek *Píta* Bread - see recipe
Tzatzíki - see recipe
sliced onions and tomatoes
chopped parsley

Fry a pita in a hot skillet with a dash of olive oil, just until golden on each side. Hold the fried pita in one hand, and put the skewered *Souvláki* in the center. Squeeze the pita around the *souvláki*, holding down the meat as you pull out the skewer. Top the meat with *Tzatzíki*, onions, tomatoes and parsley and roll it up just as you would a *Gýro*.

Menu Idea
Pork Shish Kebob
Aegean Pilaf
Tomato and Herb Salad
Fresh Fried Potatoes
Tzatzíki
Fresh Lemon Wedges
Grated Cheese
Feta Cheese
Olives
Fresh Bread

Poultry
Pouleriká

The Village Chicken - *Pouleriká*

I paliá i kóta éhi to zoumí
or
It's the older chickens that are the juiciest.

    This old village proverb holds a lot of truth. Because of the stewing techniques involved, it really is the "older chickens" that are the juiciest. Sometimes, the villagers use this proverb in reference to women as well, but I'll save that discussion for another time.
    Almost every village home of old, in the Greek islands kept chicken coups and many of them still do today. The villagers consider chickens as natural "weed killers" for the areas that they are left to roam in because they pick at any small growing greens. In the islands, they are sometimes kept in orchards, where they fertilize the land and keep it clean from tall grasses. The best part about keeping chickens is that a household has a way to get rid of scraps so they won't be wasted and provides fresh eggs and poultry for their family at the same time.
    Commercially raised chickens and roasters that are available in your local supermarket are slaughtered at a young age and before the hens begin to lay their eggs. They are kept in small areas so they don't build much muscle, keeping their meat tender so they can be made into any poultry dish without a second thought.
    Village home-kept chickens are a different story. They are raised primarily to supply a home with eggs. Once a hen has aged and stops laying them, she's considered not worth keeping and soon will become the main course for dinner. The hen is slaughtered, plucked and cleaned and left to drain for a day or two, so the meat becomes more tender. Not that this helps much. Older hens are bigger birds and much tougher to cook so they are made into stews and soups, simmering slowly, sometimes for hours.

The same goes for roosters. A household coup will only keep one rooster. Any extra are slaughtered when young and become a main course. Roosters are much tougher than hens to begin with so stewing is necessary to get the meat to soften and tenderize.

In considering the preparation and cooking time involved, I'm sure your asking yourself why would you possibly want to try a fresh chicken when a store bought one cooks up in less than an hour.

The simple answer is... because of the taste. A fresh chicken makes the best stock and the meat tastes, well... like chicken. When a fresh chicken is available from a small farm or homestead, it is usually fed with less additives and the modern super feeds that commercial poultry raisers use. Home kept chickens are allowed to roam around, foraging for food and eating what God intended them to eat. This is absolutely evident when you take the first bite.

If you have a chance to get fresh chicken, use one of the recipes for a stew and give it a try. There are detailed instructions in the Kitchen Techniques section on how to clean and prepare fresh birds, if you need any help. Or, you could simply ask an elder or village woman to give you a hand with the cleaning and preparation. Although, if you do choose to do this, I should give you a few words of advise about their ways.

When I first moved to the islands, I was given a fresh slaughtered chicken by my mother-in-law. Being the wonderful woman that she is, she had plucked and cleaned it and cut it up into serving sized pieces for me. Not knowing when she would see me to give me this gift, she had frozen the chicken pieces into a small bundle.

Happily, I took the the frozen parcel home. I had heard much about the difference between having fresh poultry as opposed to store bought, so I couldn't wait to find out for myself just how delicious a stew would be when made with fresh chicken.

Knowing that the chicken was cleaned and cut up, I simply threw the frozen lump into the pressure cooker to defrost and cook at the same time. I closed the lid and went about my business. A half hour or so later, I opened the pot. Horrified, I stared at the broth as two small eyes bobbed up at me and what I think had to be feet, were floating in my stew.

After a long deep breath and not a small amount of reassurance from my husband, I realized just how frugal these village women are. Literally, nothing that is edible is thrown away. And although this realization did calm me down a bit, I couldn't help but have my husband remove the chicken head and feet from the stew before I could continue. I guess I'm just not a true village woman.

Chicken in Tomato / *Kotópoulo Kokkinistó*

This elaborate recipe makes a stove top version of stuffed chicken. The stuffing can be made sweet or savory, depending if you choose to use the raisins or not. Since the recipe also use vegetables, you can offer a wonderful selection of tastes to your dinner guests. Serve this dish with a green salad, feta cheese and some nice wine.

Ingredients:
one 4 or 5 lb. roaster
½ lemon
½ cup olive oil
2 ribs celery, cut into 1 inch chunks
2 carrots cut into ½ inch slices
4 potatoes, peeled and cut into wedges
½ cup chicken stock
1 cup chopped tomatoes
2 garlic cloves, chopped
1 bay leaf
salt and pepper

Stuffing:
¼ cup olive oil
1 onion, chopped
chopped chicken giblets - optional
½ lb. ground beef - optional
1 cup chicken stock
½ cup uncooked rice
2 tbs. parsley chopped
1 tbs. tomato paste
1 tsp. powdered thyme
salt and pepper
½ cup pine nuts - optional
½ cup raisins - optional

Wash the chicken inside and out, rub it with the lemon and set it aside.
 To make the stuffing, heat the oil in a skillet. Add the onions and fry them until translucent. Stir in the giblets and the beef and toss them with the onions, cooking them until all the red color has gone. Add the rest of the stuffing ingredients and simmer it together until the liquid is absorbed.
 Fill the chicken with the stuffing and sew up the cavity. Sprinkle it with salt and pepper and fold back the wings. Heat ½ cup olive oil in a large, deep pot and brown the chicken on all sides. Turn the chicken so it's laying on it's back and arrange the celery, carrots and potatoes around the chicken. In a small bowl, mix together the tomatoes, stock and garlic. Pour it over the chicken and vegetables and tuck in the bay leaf. Partially cover the pot and simmer for 40 minutes, or until the chicken is done. Add more stock if it's needed during the cooking time.
 Carefully set the chicken on a platter and remove the string from the cavity. Arrange the vegetables around it and serve. Any extra sauce that remains can be served separately in a gravy boat or poured right over the arranged chicken and vegetables.

Chicken Baked with Vegetables / *Kotópoulo sto Foúrnou*

A wonderful, uncomplicated meal that you don't have to spend all day in the kitchen with. Almost any vegetable can be used in this oven stew recipe.

Ingredients:
one 3 to 4 lb. roaster
3 tbs. olive oil
1 tsp. thyme
6 medium potatoes cut into wedges
3 stalks celery, cut into 1 inch pieces
2 peeled carrots, sliced into chunks
1 chopped onion
1 cup crushed tomatoes
1 tbs. chopped parsley
2 cups chicken or vegetable stock
salt and pepper to taste

Preheat your oven to 375°F. Wash the chicken inside and out, rub it with oil, salt, pepper, and thyme. Set the chicken in a large roasting pan. Toss all the vegetables together with salt and pepper and arrange them in the pan, around the chicken. Dribble some oil over the vegetables and add the stock to the pan. Cover it with aluminum foil and bake for 30 minutes. Uncover it and cook for another 30 minutes, adding more stock if necessary.

Lemon Baked Chicken / *Kotópoulo Lemonáto*

Lemonáto is served often in the winter months when the lemons are dropping off the trees. This zesty marinated chicken dish can be served with the traditional potatoes, but for a nice variation try a pilaf or plain, white pasta. Make the sauce thicker by using a bit of flour and you have a gravy that is just fabulous.

Ingredients:
one 2 to 3 lb. chicken
2 lbs. potatoes
chicken stock

Marinade:
½ cup olive oil
½ cup fresh lemon juice
5 crushed garlic cloves
3 tbs. oregano
salt and pepper

Clean and wash the chicken and cut it up into serving pieces. Mix the marinade, and toss the chicken with it to coat all the pieces. Chill, covered in the refrigerator over night.
Peel and slice the potatoes into wedges and put into a large casserole pan. Arrange the chicken over the potatoes, and add the marinade and enough chicken stock so the potatoes are half covered. Bake at 350°F for 50 to 60 minutes. If needed, add more stock to the pan until the potatoes become tender.

Chicken with Lentils / *Kotópoulo me Fakés*

From Byzantine origins, this dish uses lots of black, white and cayenne peppers as its seasoning. Use your own taste preference to make it spicier by adding more peppers or blander by not using as much.

Ingredients:
2 cups lentils
olive oil
one 2 lb chicken, quartered
salt and pepper
flour
½ cup red wine vinegar
1 tsp. corn flour mixed with 4 tbs. cold chicken stock
pinch white pepper
pinch cayenne
pinch. black pepper
½ tsp. ground cumin
1 cup chopped onions
chopped parsley

Bring a small pot of water or chicken stock to a boil and add the lentils. Cook until they are tender but not mushy. Set them in a strainer to drain.

Heat enough olive oil to cover the bottom of a skillet. Salt and pepper the chicken pieces and coat them with flour. Sear the meat on each side until light golden. Remove the chicken. Add the vinegar, corn flour mixture, peppers and cumin to the skillet. Stir it all together and return the chicken pieces to simmer until they are done and the sauce thickens.

Put the drained lentils in a casserole dish. In separate skillet, heat enough oil to cover the bottom. Fry the onions until they are golden then mix them into the lentils. Pour some of the sauce from the chicken into the lentils and mix it through. Arrange the chicken over the lentils and pour the rest of the sauce over it. Sprinkle with parsley and serve.

Chicken with Quince / *Kotópoulo me Kidónia*

Though this could possibly be the Greek version of Sweet & Sour, the quince cooks tender and just slightly sweetens this dish. Mind your hands when cleaning the quince as it is a very hard fruit. Use a cutting board and keep your fingers out of the way. Serve this dish with a pilaf and green salad.

Ingredients:
1 chicken, cut into serving pieces.
2 lbs. quince, cleaned and sliced into thin wedges
1 onion, chopped
1 cup butter
1 tbs. sugar
2 cups chopped tomatoes
4 cups chicken stock
salt and pepper

> **Menu Idea**
> Chicken with Quince
> Plain Buttered Rice
> Green Bean Salad
> Cheese *Saghakanáki*
> Fresh Stuffed Olives
> Grated Cheese
> Feta Cheese
> Fresh Bread

Salt and pepper the chicken pieces. In a large saucepan, heat the butter and sauté the onions. Add the chicken and toss it with the frying onions. Stir in the tomatoes, the quince and the sugar, adding enough stock to barely cover it all. Bring it to a boil, then reduce the heat and simmer for 40 to 50 minutes, or until the chicken is done and the quince is tender.

Herbed Chicken Breasts / *Kotópoulo Riganáto*

The wine in this dish gives the chicken an extra zing. This wonderfully easy dish is served best with buttered noodles and a Greek Village Salad.

Ingredients:
6 boned chicken breasts, with the skin
1 lemon, halved
½ cup olive oil
¼ cup chopped parsley
2 tbs. oregano
1 garlic clove, minced
½ cup white wine
salt and pepper
½ cup chicken stock

> **Menu Idea**
> Herbed Chicken Breasts
> Buttered Noodles
> Beets in Garlic Sauce
> Zucchini Pancakes
> Greek Village Salad
> Fresh Lemon Wedges
> Grated Cheese
> Feta Cheese
> Olives
> Fresh Bread

Rub the chicken breasts with the lemon halves, squeezing out the juice, and set them aside to absorb it. Heat the oil in a deep skillet over moderate heat and put the breasts in skin side down to fry until lightly golden, then turn them over and fry them a few minutes on the other side. Pour the wine and chicken stock over the chicken. Add the herbs, garlic, salt and pepper, then reduce the heat to low and simmer the chicken uncovered until its tender. For a thicker sauce, mix a little flour with some water and stir it into the simmering pot.

Island Chicken with Orzo / *Kotópoulo me Kritharáki*

Another easy, one pot meal with a taste of the Greek Isles. Serve this poultry dish with a green salad and a nice bottle of Greek wine.

Ingredients:
one 2 to 3 lb. roaster
salt and pepper
1 large onion, minced
2 cup chicken stock
2 cups crushed tomatoes
2 tbs. oregano
2 cups orzo macaroni available from a Greek Specialty shop. Another small macaroni, or rice can be substituted.

Rub the chicken with salt, pepper, oregano, and the minced onion, inside and out. Set it in a bowl and pour the tomatoes over it. Cover it and refrigerate overnight.

Preheat your oven to 350°F. Put the chicken in a roasting pan. Add the stock and bake covered for 20 minutes. Add the orzo and stir it through, mixing it well with the juices. Cover the pan again and bake for another 20 minutes. If the dish seems dry, add a bit more stock as the orzo absorbs the liquid. Not too much though, because you want the orzo fluffy, not dripping in juice.

Marinated Chicken / *Kotópoulo Marinátha*

Excellent for a barbeques, use this marinade recipe for any poultry of your choice. Turkey breasts are exceptional when soaked in the marinade overnight then put over hot coals to broil. If it's wintry where you live and you've got a fireplace - use it!

Ingredients:
1 chicken, cut into serving pieces

Marinade:
¼ cup chopped parsley
¼ cup chopped dill
1 tbs. oregano
1 tbs. thyme
1 tbs. paprika
1 tsp. basil
2 cups olive oil
3 cloves crushed garlic
²/₃ cups fresh lemon juice
salt and pepper

> **Menu Idea**
> Marinated Chicken
> Greek Green Beans
> Mashed Potatoes
> Tomato and Feta Salad
> Cheese *Saghanáki*
> Zucchini Pancakes
> Fresh Lemon Wedges
> Fresh Bread

Lay the chicken out on a cutting board and sprinkle with salt, pepper and the herbs. Toss the pieces together then arrange them in a bowl or plastic container. Mix the olive oil with the lemon juice and garlic and pour this over the chicken. Cover the container or bowl tightly and refrigerate over night.

Let the marinated chicken stand at room temperature for an hour. Drain the chicken from the marinade and bake, broil or grill the chicken as to your preference, using the excess marinade as a basting liquid.

Sesame Fried Chicken / *Kóta Tiganití me Sisámi*

This is Grandmom's recipe for the ultimate fried chicken, Greek style. This recipe is great to use when you're planning an outing such as a picnic or for a great meal at home. Team the chicken with other finger foods and *mezédes* and you have the making for a great party buffet.

Ingredients:
1 whole chicken, cut up into frying pieces
salt and pepper
thyme
oregano
whole sesame seeds
flour
oil for frying

Batter:
2 eggs
2 tbs. *tahini**
1 cup flour

> **Menu Idea**
> Sesame Fried Chicken
> Thessalonian Peas
> Mashed Potatoes
> Cabbage Salad
> Stuffed Cucumbers
> Feta Cheese
> Olives
> Fresh Bread

Rinse the chicken under running water and pat it dry. Sprinkle it with salt, pepper, thyme, and oregano. Mix together the batter ingredients, adding water or more flour to get a thin cake batter like consistency.

Prepare a bowl with some plain flour in it and another with the sesame seeds and set them both next to your work area. Dip the chicken into the batter and tap it gently to remove any excess. Sprinkle some sesame seeds onto the chicken and then roll it in the plain flour. Continue with all the chicken parts.

Heat a half inch of oil in a heavy skillet. Add the chicken pieces and fry them until the meat is cooked and they are golden brown.

*A paste made from sesame seeds that can be purchased at a Greek or Middle Eastern specialty shop.

Stewed Chicken and Macaroni/ *Kotópoulo me Makarónia*

Right from the villages of Rhodes, this simple stew recipe can turn any tough chicken into a tender one. Try the Poor Man's Cabbage Salad with this. It's a great combination.

Ingredients:
1 cup olive oil
2 lbs. chicken pieces
1 large chopped onion
2 cloves garlic, chopped
2 cups chopped tomatoes
2 cups chicken stock
2 bay leaves
pinch oregano
pinch basil
salt and pepper
1 lb. cooked Pasta
grated Greek *kefalotíri* or parmesan cheese

Wash and dry the chicken pieces and sprinkle them with salt and pepper. Heat the oil in a large skillet and brown the chicken, onions and garlic together. Add the tomatoes, chicken stock, bay leaves and spices. Lower the heat and simmer the stew until the chicken is tender - about 1 hour. If needed, add a bit more stock during the cooking time to keep the chicken and sauce juicy. Serve over the pasta of your choice with lots of grated cheese.

Stuffed Chicken / *Kotópoulo Gemistó*

Ingredients:
one 3 lb. chicken or roaster
lemon halves
salt and pepper
olive oil
2 cups chicken stock mixed with 1 tbs. tomato paste

Stuffing:
olive oil
½ cup chopped onions
¼ lb. ground pork
1 cup chopped tomatoes
½ cup rice
¼ cup pine nuts - optional
¼ cup seedless dark raisins - optional
¼ cup chopped parsley or celery
2 tsp. dry sage
salt and pepper
1 cup chicken stock

Wash and dry the chicken and rub it with lemon halves, inside and out, squeezing out the juice as you go along. Sprinkle it with salt and pepper and set it aside.

To make the stuffing, heat enough olive oil to cover the bottom of a skillet. Fry the onions until translucent and then add the pork. Toss and cook the mixture until the meat is done. Add the rest of the ingredients and simmer the mixture just until the juices are absorbed.

Preheat your oven to 350°F. Stuff the chicken cavity sew it closed using a poultry needle and thread. Fold the wings under the back and tie the legs together. Set the chicken in a roasting pan, drizzle it with olive oil, using your fingers, rub it in. Pour the tomato-chicken stock over the chicken.

Wrap the pan in aluminum foil and bake it for one hour. Remove the foil and bake it for another 30 minutes, basting it often so the meat is tender.

Duck with Olive Stuffing / *Pápies me Eliés*

Even on the islands, we no longer have to wait for the men to come home from hunting to cook dinner. Duck is available year through and makes a beautiful and delicious entree. Because duck is an oily bird, you may want to set them on a rack in the pan so the fats can drip away. But don't discard the drippings. After skimming the fat, use them to make a wonderful sauce to serve along side.

Ingredients:
2 ducks, cleaned and gutted

Stuffing:
1 cup minced bacon
1 cup dry breadcrumbs
1 cup chicken stock
1 cup green and black olives, pitted and sliced
3 tbs. cognac
1 large onion, chopped
½ cup olive oil
salt and pepper to taste

Preheat your oven to 425°F. Salt and pepper the ducks and rub with a bit of olive oil. Set them aside in a shallow pan.

In a skillet, heat the olive oil. Add the onions and bacon and sauté lightly. In a mixing bowl, add the bread crumbs, olives, cognac, half the stock and the onion-bacon mixture. Toss it together thoroughly.

Stuff the birds with the mixture and sew or skewer the openings. Add the remaining stock to the bottom of the pan and bake for 30 minutes. Reduce the heat to 325°F and bake for one hour longer or until they are done.

Turkey with Potatoes and Onions / *Galopoúla me Patátes Stifádo*

Turkey doesn't have to be just for the holidays. This recipe makes a fantastic Sunday dinner or party entree. Add a Greek Village Salad and maybe a few appetizers and you have the makings for a great feast.

Ingredients:
one 10 to 12 lb. turkey, cleaned and cut into serving sized pieces.
6 lbs. potatoes, peeled and cut into medium sized pieces.
5 large onions, quartered
5 bay leaves
3 cloves garlic, crushed
2 cups chopped fresh tomatoes
olive oil
salt and pepper
chicken or vegetable stock

Salt and pepper the turkey pieces and rub them with olive oil. Place them in a large, deep casserole pot and toss the turkey pieces with the onions and garlic. Mix the tomatoes with the stock and pour it over the ingredients and tuck in the bay leaves. Heat your oven to 325°F. Cover the casserole and cook for 2 to 3 hours or until the turkey starts to get tender.

Add the potatoes to the turkey. If needed, add more stock and return the pot covered to the oven again. Continue cooking for 40 minutes or until the potatoes are done.

Holiday Stuffed Turkey / *Galopoúla Gemistí*

Ingredients:
one 12 lb. turkey
lemon halves
salt and pepper
olive oil
4 cups chicken stock

Stuffing:
olive oil
1 cup chopped onions
chopped turkey giblets
½ lb. ground pork
1 cup rice
½ cup pine nuts - optional
½ cup seedless dark raisins
½ cup chopped parsley
2 tsp. dry sage
salt and pepper
1 cup chicken stock
1 cinnamon stick - optional

> **Menu Idea**
> Holiday Stuffed Turkey
> Village Gravy
> Stuffed Beets
> Mashed Potatoes
> Tomato-Green Bean Salad
> Russian Salad
> Crab Salad
> Feta Cheese
> Olives
> Fresh Bread

Wash and dry the turkey and rub it with lemon halves, inside and out, squeezing out the juice as you go along. Sprinkle the turkey with salt and pepper and set it aside.

To make the stuffing, heat enough olive oil to cover the bottom of a skillet. Fry the onions until translucent and then add the pork and giblets. Toss and cook the mixture until the meats are done. Add the rest of the ingredients and simmer the mixture just until the juices are absorbed. Remove the cinnamon stick.

Preheat your oven to 425°F. Stuff the turkey cavity and neck areas and sew them closed using a poultry needle and thread. Fold the wings under the back and tie the legs together. Pour a little olive oil on the bottom of the pan and set the turkey on it, breast up. Drizzle more oil over the bird and using your fingers, rub it in. Pour the chicken stock into the bottom of the pan.

Bake the turkey for ½ hour then remove it from the oven. Reduce the heat to 325°F and wrap the turkey pan in aluminum foil. Return the bird to the oven and bake it for 3 to 4 hours longer, basting every so often so the meat is tender.

See these other great recipes for poultry:

Simple Chicken Pie / *Kotópita Aplí*
Chicken Pie / *Ornothópita - Kotópita*
Turkey Pie / *Galópita*
Chicken Vermicelli Soup / *Soúpa Fidé*
Chicken Egg Lemon Soup / *Soúpa Avgolémono*
Rooster Soup / *Soúpa Petinoú*
Partridge Pilaf / *Pérdika Piláfi*
Partridges Stuffed with Wheat / *Pérdikes Gemistés*
Partridges in Vine Leaves / *Pérdikes se Ambelófila*
Stuffed Pigeon / *Peristéria Gemistá*
Eggplants Stuffed with Quails / *Melintzánes Gemistés me Ortíkia*
Quails in Tomato and Wine / *Ortíkia me Tomáta ke Krasí*

Game Meats
Kinígi

Game Meats - *Kinígi*

The Windmills of *Mandráki* Harbour, Rhodes.

The island of Rhodes, being the largest of the Dodecanese or twelve island group of Greece has always been considered rich hunting ground and in her thickly forested mountains, an array of wild creatures could be found. By far, the most popular of these game animals was the wild deer but to hunt it down, meant risking a heavy penalty.

In ancient times, the island of Rhodes was know as *Ophioússa* or island of vipers because of the abundance of snakes. The deer, being their natural predator, were guarded animals since they helped to make the island safe. The deer was so revered that it became the symbol of the island and you will find it depicted in statues in our harbor as well as carved into jewelry and pottery.

In times of hunger and less abundances, the villagers resorted to whatever means they could in order to feed their family and many times, this meant facing a jail sentence for getting dinner on the table. A villager that had the good fortune of catching a deer would see to it's preparation in extreme secrecy. He would share his prize only with his closest friends, and would give them a piece of the meat to feed their family if they were willing to take the risk of getting caught.

To this day, you can still find wild deer in the mountains of Rhodes but unfortunately, these beautiful creatures number far fewer than what they once were. Although most of us don't have to worry about our children going hungry, some villagers will secretly hunt the animals for sport even though they are still considered contraband and the penalty for its slaughter carries with it a ten year jail sentence.

Wild hare and the various birds of the island can be hunted during their seasons, within certain legal limitations. In times ago, I'm sure that our mountains provided much sustenance for the local people, but now, in the age of ecological upheaval and hunting animals to the brink of extinction, the Islanders are also paying the price.

For most of the islanders today, it's a trip to the local butcher shop or small farm that provides any "wild" meats that they want to cook up. While our ancestors used these catches as main courses, we use them as a *mezé* or for a special occasion. If a hunter has the good fortune of catching a wild hare, he will invite his friends for *mezédes* to share it with him, so everyone can get a taste of the rare dish.

Game meats are prepared and cooked with very much care taken. To begin with, the wild meats are much tougher. This means that marinating and stewing is often called for in these recipes to tenderize them. Some of the processes are long ones, but I'm told that the results are delicious.

Pit Roasted Baby Goat / *Katsikáki - Rifáki Soúvla*

Goat turning on a spit, over an open fire is a quite common dish in the Greek islands especially for a holiday dinner. The secret in preparing it is not only the ingredients, but also the slow cooking of the meat. Other than a holiday main course, we've had this as a picnic cookout sort of thing. It's great for a crowd and you can just stand around and eat right off the spit, drinking beer and having a good time.

Ingredients:

1 whole kid or baby goat, 15 to 25 lbs. Have the butcher remove the head and organs. You can freeze the head and save it for soup and fry up the liver, heart and kidneys and serve with some *Skordaliá* Sauce.
salt and pepper
ground cumin
grated Greek *kefalotíri* or parmesan cheese
2 cups melted butter
1 cup olive oil
lemon halves - to use as a brush for the marinade. See the "Kitchen Techniques" section for more details about this home made accessory.

To begin with, you're going to need a large table or counter top to work on, so get an area ready that you won't mind if it gets a bit messy. Wash the carcass under running water and drain well. Lay it out on a large clean surface. Sprinkle it, inside and out with salt, pepper and cumin. At this point, I recommend wrapping it up and refrigerating it over night for the meat to absorb the spices.

Follow the directions in the Kitchen Techniques section to attach the carcass to the spit. When you are finished securing it, sprinkle grated cheese inside the body cavity and out, all over it. Using some wire, sew up the cavity.

Place the spit over the hot coals. You want to roast it slowly over low heat, for 3 to 4 hours.

In a bowl, mix the melted butter and oil with some salt, pepper and cumin. On a long fork, spear the lemon half. You will be using it as a brush for the meat. Dip the lemon in the butter marinade and brush the meat while it is turning over the coals. Obviously, the more you do this, the better the meat. Replace the lemon half with a fresh one as it gets worn.

Check on the thickest part of the meat for doneness – I pierce the thigh. When it's cooked, remove it from the spit. Remove all the wire and cut into serving size pieces. Serve it immediately.

Baby Goat Stuffed with Rice / *Katsikáki - Rifáki Kapamá*

A traditional special occasion dish, this recipe is often made for Sunday dinners or special get-togethers. It may involve a bit of work, but the final result is delicious. Serve this with a green or tomato salad, a yogurt appetizer such as *Tzatzíki* and cold Retsina.

Ingredients:
4 lb. cut of baby goat or kid - the rib section works the best.
salt and pepper
1 cup oil
1 tbs. butter
1 cup chopped onions
2 cups chopped tomatoes
2 tbs. tomato paste
2 tbs. chopped parsley
1 cinnamon stick - optional
1 tsp. ground cumin
2 cups rice

Take your cut of goat and rinse it under cold running water and let it drain. Sprinkle it with salt and pepper and set it aside.

In a medium sized saucepan, heat the oil and butter together. Add the onions and fry until translucent. Add the tomatoes and paste, parsley, cinnamon and cumin. Simmer it for a few minutes and then add the rice, stirring well to mix the stuffing. Remove it from the heat and discard the cinnamon stick.

Stuff the goat cavity loosely with the rice mixture. With a thick needle and thread, sew the cavity shut, or use a skewer as a pin to keep it closed. Any left over rice can be arranged on the bottom of the pan with the meat placed over it. Add a cup of stock or water to the pan and cover it with a lid or with aluminum foil.

Bake at 300°F for 2 to 4 hours, depending on your cut of meat. Check on it occasionally as you may need to add more stock or water.

Spit Barbequed Hare / *Lagós stin Soúvla*

Although this recipe calls for barbequing the meat, it can easily be roasted in an oven for more convenience.

Ingredients:
one 2 to 3 lb. hare
olive oil
5 garlic cloves
1 onion, quartered

Marinade:
3 cups red wine
2 tsp. vinegar
1 tbs. thyme
3 whole cloves
1 cinnamon stick
3 crushed garlic cloves

Sauce:
oregano
salt and pepper
olive oil
5 cups chopped tomatoes
½ cup butter
1 tsp. sugar

Mix together the marinade ingredients and pour it over the hare. Refrigerate it overnight. The next day, drain the hare from the marinade, reserving the liquid.

Rub the entire hare, inside and out with olive oil and sprinkle it with oregano, salt and pepper. Put the garlic cloves and the onion in the stomach cavity and sew it shut. Following the Preparation Tips for Spit Barbeques in the Kitchen Techniques section, attach it to the spit.

Cook it over low heat, basting it with olive oil and oregano every so often.

To make the sauce, boil the reserved liquid from the marinade juice until it reduces to half. Stir in the tomato, butter, sugar and season it with salt and pepper. Pour the sauce over the cooked hare and serve.

Hare in Garlic / *Lagós me Skórda*

From the island of *Kefaloniá*, this savory recipe for hare is delicious when served as a main course with potatoes and a green salad.

Ingredients:
one 3 lb. hare, cleaned and rinsed
1 cup vinegar
15 to 20 cloves garlic, chopped
olive oil
1 cup white wine
1 tbs. tomato paste
1 cup chopped tomatoes
salt and pepper

Cut the hare into small pieces but leave the head whole as it can also be included in the stew. Put the pieces of meat in a bowl and cover them with water. Add the vinegar and set it aside to soak for at least 3 hours. Drain the meat and pat it dry with paper towels.

In a skillet, heat enough oil to cover the bottom. Sear the meat pieces on each side and remove them to a bowl. Add 1 cup olive oil to the skillet and fry the garlic just until it turns gold. Stir in the wine and dilute the tomato paste in it. Add the chopped tomatoes and season it with salt and pepper. Fold in the hare and any juices that may have dripped into the bowl. Stir it all together and lower the heat.

Simmer the stew for 1 to 2 hours or until the hare is tender and the stew is thick. If a liquid is needed, add a little bit of water or vegetable stock during the cooking time.

Hare in Onions / *Lagós Stifádo*

Although this recipe calls for hare, don't think that you are limited to using only game meats for this popular dish. Beef cuts as well as poultry make delicious alternatives - village style!

Ingredients:
one 2 lb. hare
4 lbs. cleaned onions about 1 inch in diameter
4 cups chopped tomatoes
2 cups olive oil
1 cup vinegar
1 cup water
2 cinnamon sticks
3 bay leaves
1 tsp. allspice
3 garlic cloves
salt and pepper

Rinse the hare and cut it into pieces then pat it dry with paper towels. In a pot, layer half of the onions, the hare and then top it with the rest of the onions. Add the rest of the ingredients and cover the pot tightly. Simmer the meat for 1½ to 2 hours until it's tender.

Partridge Pilaf / *Pérdika Piláfi*

And a partridge in a pear tree.... Yes, I know what your thinking, but these birds really are delicious. This recipe is a specialty from the island of Cephalonia and stews the partridges in a light tomato sauce. With the addition of the rice, all you need is a green salad and you have a great meal.

Ingredients:
2 lbs. partridges, cleaned, quartered or halved, depending on the size of them.
½ cup olive oil
1 onion, chopped
2 tbs. tomato paste
4 whole cloves - optional
2 cups chicken stock
1 cup rice
salt and pepper

Sprinkle the partridges with salt and pepper. Heat the oil in a skillet and fry the onions until translucent. Stir in the tomato paste and cook it until it's bubbly. Add the partridge pieces, cloves and chicken stock and give it a good stir. Lower the heat and simmer the partridges, partially covered until they are tender.

Stir in the rice and simmer it over low heat so it absorbs the juices, stirring occasionally to keep it from sticking and scorching. Add more stock if it needs it during the cooking time. You want the rice to be dry and not dripping in juice, so only add a little bit at a time.

Partridges with Wheat Stuffing / *Pérdikes Gemistés*

A wonderful special occasion dish that is a nice change for holidays such as Christmas or Easter. It takes a bit of effort but is truly worth it.

Don't discard the marinade. Strain it and bring it to a boil, adding chicken stock or cream and some corn flour mixed with water. Stir in any drippings and you have a wonderful sauce to accompany this dish.

Ingredients:
6 partridges, depending on their size, this should give you one per serving.
olive oil

Cold Wine Marinade:
⅓ cup olive oil
⅓ cup lemon juice
1 cup dry white wine
1 minced garlic clove
1 tsp. dry thyme
pinch oregano
5 chopped scallions
salt and pepper

Stuffing:
½ cup olive oil
1 chopped onion
1 minced garlic clove
chopped livers from the partridges
1 cup fresh chopped mushrooms
1 cup chopped celery
1 cup cracked wheat
3 cups chicken stock
2 tbs. tomato paste
1 tsp. dry thyme
salt and pepper

> **Menu Idea**
> Partridges with Wheat Stuffing
> Partridge Gravy
> Ptolemies Tomatoes
> Spinach with Onions
> Green Salad
> Olive Salad
> Feta Cheese
> Fresh Bread

Marinade:
Make the marinade by combining all the ingredients together. Pour the marinade over the partridges and cover them. Marinade them refrigerated, overnight.

Stuffing:
Heat the olive oil in a skillet and sauté the onions and garlic. Mix in the livers and cook them until the red color disappears then toss in the mushrooms and celery. Add the wheat, chicken stock and the tomato paste. Stir it in well until the paste dilutes. Add the seasonings and simmer for 25 minutes or until the stuffing is thick. Remove from the heat and let the stuffing cool.

The Birds:
Preheat your oven to 400°F. Stuff the partridges and sew the openings closed or use skewers to secure them. Turn the wings under the birds and tie the legs together. Arrange them in an oiled roasting pan, side

by side with the breasts up. Pour olive oil generously over the birds. Roast them for 10 minutes uncovered. Turn them to one side and baste with the oil, then return the pan to the oven for 15 minutes. Take them out again and turn them on the other side and baste before you return them to roast for another 15 minutes. Ending with the breasts up, baste them often as they finish cooking. The skins should be golden brown and the legs should pull away easily. Carefully remove the strings or skewers and move them to a warm platter and serve.

Partridges in Vine Leaves / *Pérdikes se Ambelófila*

This simple dish is easy to make, yet looks very fussy and unusual. Serve it over a bed of pilaf or plain buttered toast. The partridges can be quartered instead of halved for smaller portions but adjust the other ingredients as well.

Ingredients:
6 partridges, cleaned and cut in half, length wise
½ cup finely chopped dill weed
½ cup finely minced onion
12 strips of pork or beef fat
12 large vine leaves, rinsed and drained
butter
salt and pepper
chicken stock
flour

Wash and drain the partridge halves. Toss them with the dill and onion and season with salt and pepper. Wrap each piece in a strip of fat and then wrap that up in a vine leaf. Tie it with a piece of string to secure it or gently use toothpick or skewers, taking care not to tear the leafs. Rub the packages with butter and lay them in a baking pan. Add enough stock to cover the bottom and seal the pan with aluminum foil. Bake for 1 hour at 350°F, basting occasionally.

When the partridges are done, carefully remove the strings and arrange them on a platter. Pour the drippings into a pot and bring them to a boil. Mix a little flour with some cold stock and stir it into the drippings. Season it with salt and pepper and cook it until it's thick. Pour the sauce over the partridges and serve.

Stuffed Pigeon / *Peristéria Gemistá*

This Macedonian recipe calls for pigeons but if you can't get them, any poultry can be substituted. Although I think that the sweet stuffing tastes exceptional when it's used with game birds.

Ingredients:
4 whole pigeons, cleaned
½ cup rice
½ cup butter
1 small onion, chopped
chopped pigeon livers - if you're able to reserve them
¼ cup walnuts, coarsely chopped
¼ cup raisins
½ cup Greek *kefalotíri* or parmesan cut into small chunks
salt and pepper
2 lemons
chicken stock

Par boil the rice in salt water for 10 minutes and drain. In a skillet, heat the butter and fry the onions with the livers. Add the rice, walnuts, raisins, cheese, and season with salt and pepper. Toss it all together, mixing well. Remove the stuffing from the heat and set it aside.

Preheat your oven to 350ºF. Sprinkle the pigeons with salt and pepper and squeeze lemon juice on them, inside and out. Stuff them with the rice mixture and sew the cavity closed. Arrange them in a pan and drizzle them with olive oil. Pour one cup of chicken stock into the pan and then cover it with aluminum foil. Bake for one hour or until the birds are done. Remove the foil for the final 10 minutes so they brown and the skins crisp.

Eggplants Stuffed with Quails / *Melintzánes Gemistés me Ortíkia*

This unusual dish makes a beautiful presentation at the table. Serve the eggplants with pilaf or mashed potatoes.

Ingredients:
8 medium sized eggplants
8 quails, cleaned and rinsed
4 cups fresh chopped tomatoes
1 cup chopped onions
2 cups fine bread crumbs
salt and pepper
butter
bay leaves
chicken stock

Wash and rinse the eggplants and cut off the stem ends. Using a knife and a spoon, hollow out as much of the insides as you can so that a quail will fit inside each one. Set each hollowed eggplant in salted water to soak as you continue with the rest of them. When done, prick each eggplant several times all over with a fork and set it upside down to drain.

Heat the butter in a skillet and sauté the quails so they brown on each side. Use a slotted spoon to remove them from the butter and drop them into the bread crumbs. Roll them around so they are fully coated and set them aside.

To the hot skillet and butter, add the onions and fry until translucent. Stir in the tomatoes and the bay leaves, and simmer the mixture for 15 minutes.

Stuff each eggplant with a spoonful of sauce, push in the quail and top it off with more sauce. Lay the finished eggplant in a shallow baking pan. Continue until all the eggplants are stuffed. Pour the left over sauce over them and add enough stock to cover the bottom of the pan. Seal the pan with aluminum foil and bake the eggplants at 350°F for 1 hour. Remove the foil, baste the eggplants with the juices and bake uncovered for 20 to 30 minutes.

Quails in Tomato and Wine / *Ortíka me Tomáta ke Krasí*

The wine in the recipe give the sauce a delicious edge. Chicken can easily be substituted for the quail, just cut it into small pieces. Serve the dish over buttered noodles with lots of grated cheese on the side.

Ingredients:
6 quails, cleaned
½ cup olive oil
1 cup chopped onions
1 cup red wine
4 cups pureed tomatoes
1 bay leaf
1 tbs. thyme
salt and pepper
chicken stock

Rinse the quails and set them aside to drain. In a deep skillet, heat the olive oil and fry the onions until translucent. Salt and pepper the quails and stir them into the onions, frying them on both sides. Stir in the wine, tomatoes, bay leaf, and thyme. Season it with salt and pepper and add a little stock if more liquid is needed. Lower the heat and simmer the mixture for 40 minutes, stirring occasionally and basting the quails with sauce.

Rabbit in Yogurt / *Kounéli me Yiaoúrti*

The gravy and yogurt in this recipe make it an exceptional dish to be served with a pilaf or simply a bed of boiled rice or bulgur wheat.

Ingredients:
one 2 lb. whole rabbit, cleaned and washed
1 cup lemon juice
1 lb. strained yogurt - see "Concoctions for the Greek Kitchen"
½ cup butter
salt and pepper
vegetable stock
flour

Put the rabbit in a bowl with enough water to cover it and mix in the lemon juice. Let it soak for 2 hours. Drain the rabbit and pat it dry with paper towels. Sprinkle it with salt and pepper, inside and out. Fill the stomach cavity with the yogurt and sew it shut. Place the rabbit in a baking pan with only enough stock to cover the bottom. Add the butter and seal the pan with aluminum foil.

Bake the rabbit at 325°F for 40 minutes. Remove the pan from the oven and very gently, turn the rabbit over. Seal the pan again with aluminum foil and bake the other side for another 40 minutes. There should be a good amount of drippings in the pan, but if it looks dry to you, add a bit more stock.

When done, put the rabbit on a platter and carefully remove the thread from the cavity. Strain the drippings into a sauce pan and bring them to a boil. Mix a little flour with some stock and stir it into the drippings, cooking it until it's a thick gravy. Pour it over the rabbit and serve.

Rabbit with Walnut Stuffing / *Kounéli Gemistó me Karídia*

From Crete, this recipe for stuffed rabbit is easy to make right on your stove top. It's a delicious meal that can be served as a holiday or Sunday dinner.

Ingredients:
one 2 to 3 lb. rabbit
butter
olive oil
vegetable stock
½ cup lemon juice
1 tbs. oregano

Stuffing:
½ lb. chopped calf's and rabbit liver
½ cup crumbled feta cheese
1 cup chopped walnuts
1 cup rice
¼ cup chopped parsley
2 minced garlic cloves
salt and pepper

Heat a skillet with 2 tbs. of butter and sauté the liver. Put the liver into a mixing bowl and toss in the rest of the stuffing ingredients.

Rinse and drain the rabbit and pat it dry with paper towels. Rub butter all over it, inside and out and season it with salt and pepper. Fill the stomach cavity with the stuffing and sew it shut. In a large skillet, heat enough oil to cover the bottom and sear the rabbit on both sides. Add one inch of stock, cover the skillet and lower the heat. Simmer the rabbit for 1 to 2 hours, basting it every so often. If more liquid is needed, add little bits of stock.

When the meat is tender, beat the lemon juice with the oregano and pour it over the rabbit. Simmer it uncovered for 5 to 10 minutes. Place the rabbit on a platter and carefully remove the string from the stomach cavity. Pour the sauce over the rabbit and serve.

Wild Boar in Wine / *Agriogoúrouno Krasáto*

Wild boars are native to the northern regions and not found in Rhodes. Yet on some occasions, the delicacy can be found at a butcher shop. The wild boar is prepared very carefully because it is a very tough meat to cook. When a home does have it for a meal, friends and family are invited to share it along with other *mezédes* and wine.

Ingredients:
4 lbs. wild boar
½ cup butter
2 cups chopped tomatoes
vegetable stock
1 cup cognac

Marinade:
2½ cup red wine
1 carrot, sliced
2 onions, sliced
1 rib celery, sliced
1 bay leaf
1 tbs. rosemary
1 tbs. thyme
salt and pepper

> *Mezé* **Menu Idea**
> Wild Boar in Wine
> Tomato Roasted Potatoes
> *Tzatzíki*
> Fried Mussels
> Savory Pumpkin Pancakes
> Spicy Pickled Eggplants
> Lettuce Salad
> Greek Vinaigrette
> Greek Village Salad
> Yogurt and Pimento Sauce
> Feta Cheese
> Olives
> Fresh Bread

Rinse the meat and cut it into small pieces and set it in a large bowl. Add all the marinade ingredients and let it stand refrigerated for 6 hours or over night.

Drain the ingredients from the wine marinade, reserving the liquid. Heat the butter in a skillet and sauté the meat with the strained ingredients. Pour in half of the reserved liquid, the tomatoes, salt and pepper and if needed, add a bit of vegetable stock. Cover the skillet and simmer the mixture for 1 to 2 hours or until the meat is tender and the sauce is thick. Pour in the cognac and simmer it for 15 minutes longer.

Baked Venison / *Eláfi sto Foúrno*

Although a villager could get arrested for slaughtering a deer, in times of hunger, many men took that chance simply so they could feed their families. This recipe comes from some very old ladies in the mountain village of Embona, here in Rhodes. This recipe uses a roast, but you can also cube the meat and follow the same process for a much more tender entree.

Ingredients:
5 lbs. venison roast
olive oil
2 cups chopped onions
4 cups chopped tomatoes

Marinade:
1 cup olive oil
2 cups dry red wine
1 cup cognac
salt and pepper
bay leaves
rosemary sprigs

Rinse the roast under running water and set it aside to drain. Make the marinade by mixing together all the ingredients. Put the roast into a deep bowl and cover it with the marinade. Refrigerate it for 24 to 48 hours.

Drain the roast from the marinade, reserving the liquid. Heat oil in a large skillet and sear the roast on all sides. Set the roast in a deep casserole or baking dish. Preheat your oven to 325°F.

Reheat the skillet and add enough oil to cover the bottom. Fry the onions until translucent and stir in the tomatoes. Add the reserved marinade and let it boil together for 5 minutes. Pour the sauce over the roast and cover the pot. Bake the roast for 3 to 4 hours, basting it occasionally.

Stewed Land Snails / *Karavóli Giahní*

When the first rains come in the fall season, the villagers go to the mountains and collect *karavóli* or land snails. This recipe is for snails in a simple tomato sauce that can be served with a pilaf or plain, with lots of crusty bread. A variation to this recipe is to add one pound of fresh chopped spinach to the stew the last ten minutes of cooking time.

Ingredients:
1 cup olive oil
3 cups chopped onions
2 cups chopped tomatoes
2 bay leaves
1 tsp. ground cumin
salt and pepper
1 lb. land snails - see "Kitchen Techniques" for tips on preparing land snails

Heat the oil in a skillet and fry the onions until translucent. Stir in the tomatoes, bay leaves, cumin and season it with salt and pepper. Simmer the mixture for 10 minutes, then stir in the prepared snails. Cook the stew over low heat until most of the juice is evaporated and the sauce is thick.

Organ Meats
Entóstia

Organ Meats - *Entóstia*

    Who would have believed that one day we would be told that eating liver could be bad for us? Surely not my mother, as I have many childhood memories of her chasing me with a forkful of the stuff. Never having been a big liver eater, I'd sit at the dinner table and watch my older brothers devour the meal with much enthusiasm while smiling at me and humming "mmm......good."

    The seventies adage "Try it, you'll like it" was heard often during a liver dinner at my house as was the common argument "....it's good for your blood, and you'll grow up big and strong...." Of course, none of these techniques managed to sway me into eating the meat and unlike my mother, I offer it on my own dinner table only when its requested by guests or family.

    Organ meats in general may not be eaten much at all these days. Modern times has brought with it animal ailments that are the high prices that we pay for progress. Even the local Islanders are weary about enjoying these types of meats. They will choose local animals that have been bred on small farms for a fresh cut of liver or intestines for sausage making, and somehow feel more at ease that it's safe to eat.

    On more than one occasion, I've felt like telling my mother, "See, I told you so..." but then I think about how my parents grew up. For most of the poor villagers, having any kind of meat on the dinner table was considered a blessing. A village mom would cook up a pot of food and set it in the center of the table. For the family members, this meant either eat it or go hungry until the next meal. The village home was not full of snacks that they could eat to tide them over nor was there a local McDonald's on the donkey trail for the kids that preferred a Happy Meal over fried liver.

    When I first began collecting these recipes, I was very surprised at our ancestors' ingenuity. Even if you never cook up these recipes, glance over them to get an insight on how things were done in our grandmothers' days.

    They had ways of preparing all of the organ meats to make them pleasing to the eye as well as the to the pallet, leading me to believe that perhaps I wasn't the only Greek child that didn't want to eat liver.

Beef Tongue with Olives / *Glósa Moscarísia me Eliés*

This old recipe goes to show you how our ancestors thought up wonderful ways to get rid of every edible part of an animal. Serve the stew over pilaf or fried fresh potatoes.

Ingredients:
1 cup pitted green olives
2 tbs. capers
1 beef tongue
lemon halves
½ cup vinegar
1 cup chopped onions
3 chopped garlic cloves
2 cups chopped fresh tomatoes
¼ cup olive oil
1 tbs. melted butter
2 bay leaves
salt and pepper

Put the olives and capers in a bowl with enough water to cover them. Set them aside to soak.

Rinse the tongue under running water. Sprinkle it generously with salt and rub it in with the lemon halves. Rinse it again and set it in a pot. Cover the tongue with water and add the vinegar. Simmer it until its tender and then drain it, reserving 1 cup of the liquid. Let it cool down enough so you can handle it and peel off the membrane. Slice the tongue into small pieces.

Put the onions in a pot with the garlic then layer the tongue slices and the tomato over them. Add the oil, butter, bay leafs and the reserved liquid. Season it with salt and pepper and simmer the mixture for 30 minutes.

Drain the olives and capers and add them to the cooking stew. Simmer it for another 10 to 15 minutes.

Heart and Kidney Pilaf / *Piláfi me Nefrá ke Kardiés*

Ingredients:
2 calf kidneys
1 calf's heart
½ cup olive oil
flour
2 minced garlic cloves
2 cups chopped onions
¼ cup chopped parsley
1 cup dry white wine
1 cup water
¼ cup butter
1 lb. rice, cooked and drained
grated cheese
salt and pepper

Prepare the kidneys and heart by cutting away any excess fat and tough membranes. Slice the organs into small pieces, rinse them and set them aside to drain.

Heat the olive oil in a skillet. Sprinkle the organ meat with salt and pepper and lightly flour it. Fry it in the olive oil until brown. Add the garlic, onions and parsley and fry it together for 5 minutes. Stir in the wine and water and season it with more salt and pepper. Let it simmer for 15 minutes over low heat.

Melt the butter in a skillet and toss the rice with it. Turn the rice out onto a serving platter and sprinkle it with grated cheese. Pour the heart-kidney sauce over the rice and serve.

Chicken Livers in Vinegar / *Sikotákia tis Kótas Xitháta*

Ingredients:
1 lb. chicken livers
flour for rolling
½ cup olive oil
½ cup chopped onions
1 tbs. flour diluted in 1 cup cold chicken stock
¼ cup red wine vinegar
1 tbs. chopped fresh thyme
salt and pepper

Cut the livers in half and discard any pieces of tough membrane. Rinse them under cold water and set them aside to drain for half an hour.

Heat a skillet with the olive oil. Put a bit of flour in a dish or bowl and roll the livers in it. Fry the livers in the oil, a few at a time, until they are brown on all sides. Remove the livers to a platter and keep them warm.

In the same skillet and remaining oil, add the onions and fry them until they're translucent. Add the rest of the ingredients and simmer the sauce, stirring constantly. When it thickens, pour the sauce over the livers and serve. Sprinkle with a bit of chopped parsley for a garnish.

Liver Roúmelis in Paper / *Sikóti se Hartí*

Similar to Lamb *Kléftiko* in Paper, this recipe is an alternative to plain fried liver. Serve it as a *mezé* or as a main course with a vegetable or salad side dish.

Ingredients:
2 lbs. calf liver
4 garlic cloves, crushed
oregano
salt and pepper
grated Greek *kefalotíri* or parmesan
2 onions, sliced thinly
1 cup crumbled feta cheese
3 tbs. olive oil
½ cup lemon juice

Rinse the liver under running water and pat it dry. Cut a large piece of wax paper and rub it with oil on one side. Put the liver in the center of it, arranging it in a log shape. Sprinkle it with the garlic, oregano, salt, pepper and a bit of grated cheese. Top it with the onions and the feta and drizzle the oil and lemon juice over it. Roll the whole thing up into a nice package, being careful not to let any of the juice escape. Bake at 325°F for 2 hours or until the liver is done to your preference.

Remove the roll from the oven and set it aside to cool enough so you can handle it. Place the wrapped roll on a platter and carefully begin to unwrap it. The juices will pour out so take care not to burn your fingers. Cut the roll into slices from 1 to 2 inches thick. Serve with fresh lemon wedges.

Liver with Leeks / *Sikotariá me Prása*

From the island of *Kérkyra* or Corfu, this sweet liver stew can be served as a main course or as a *mezé*. Although the recipe calls for a pig liver, any liver of your choice can be substituted.

Ingredients:
1 whole pig liver
1 cup olive oil
3 chopped onions
1 cinnamon stick
¼ tsp. ground nutmeg
¼ tsp. ground cloves
salt and pepper
2 lbs. leeks, cleaned and sliced thinly
4 cups vegetable stock

Wash the liver under running water and set it aside to drain. Cut away any tough membranes and cut it into small pieces.
Heat the oil in a skillet and sauté the onions with the liver. Add the spices and season it with salt and pepper. Stir in the leeks and stock. Let the mixture simmer until the leeks are done and the juice is thick.

Liver with Rosemary / *Sikotákia me Dendrolívano*

If you're tired of plain old fried liver or liver with onions, try this recipe. The rosemary gives it a wonderful Mediterranean taste and the sauce is great to dip fresh bread into - or so I'm told.

Ingredients:
2 lbs. calf liver, cleaned and the tough membranes removed
1 cup olive oil for frying
flour for rolling
2 tbs. flour
2 tbs. vinegar
4 bay leaves
2 large sprigs fresh rosemary or 3 tbs. dried
salt and pepper

Slice the liver into one inch pieces and sprinkle it with salt and pepper. Heat the oil in a skillet. Roll the liver in the flour, shaking off any excess and gently drop it into the hot oil. Fry it on both sides and when done, remove the liver to a platter.
To the oil in the skillet, stir in 2 tbs. flour and the vinegar with a little water so you have a creamy mixture. Add the bay leaves and the rosemary and let it bubble together for 10 minutes. If needed, add more water to keep it smooth. When ready, pour the sauce over the liver and serve.

Roasted Pig's Head / *Kefáli Gourounioú Psitó*

Here on the islands this dish is considered a delicacy especially over the Christmas holidays. It wasn't until I was given a pig's head as a pre-holiday present that I realized the only existing recipes for this were safely guarded secrets in the minds of the old village women. I thought to share it with you so the tradition can live on. This dish is often served as a *mezé*. So have lots of chilled ouzo or *raki* on hand as well as an array of other appetizers.

Ingredients:
1 pig's head, with 2 to 4 inches of neck attached.
2 to 4 whole garlic cloves, or more for a larger head
ground cumin
salt and pepper

Marinade:
2 cups olive oil
1 cup freshly squeezed lemon juice

The pig's head must be cleaned. The snout, mouth and ears will have to be cleaned but I think you can get a good butcher to do it for you. He will also have to skin it to remove the tough skin and the hairs, but leave the fat intact. If you want to do this yourself, see the "Kitchen Techniques" section for a detailed description.

Wash the pigs head under running water and let it drain. Set the head on your cutting board and make a few slits in the fleshier parts and insert the garlic cloves. I put them towards the back of the head, near the neck and in the cheeks. Sprinkle the whole thing with lots of salt and pepper and a generous amount of cumin. Set it in a large bowl and pour the marinade over it. Let it stand over night, covered, in the refrigerator to absorb the spices.

The next day, preheat your oven to 325°F. Set the head in a shallow pan on it's neck, so it's sitting up and basically, staring at you. Add an inch of water, and sprinkle the whole thing with more salt, pepper and cumin.

To keep the mouth open so you can insert an apple later, use a piece of wood or some bunched up aluminum foil in the opening. Pull the mouth open wide and insert the wedge. Cover the pan with aluminum foil, taking care that it's loose over the head, but that you have a tight seal around the pan. Roast the head for 2 to 3 hours, depending on the size. Larger heads will take up to 6 hours to cook. You can check if it's done by piercing the fleshiest part, at the neck or at the cheek, it should cut easily and almost fall off the bone. For the last half hour of cooking, remove the foil and increase the temperature to 375°F so that the outside can brown.

Remove the head from the oven and set it aside to cool enough so you can handle it. You will have to split the cranium with a heavy knife in order to serve it. I let the men do this part because sometimes you need a lot of strength behind the cleaver to cut through the bone cleanly and not crush them. Pigs don't have a large brain cavity, so most of it will be meat. Arrange the portions on a platter and garnish with fresh lemon wedges.

Baked Beef Head / *Kefáli Moscarísia sto Foúrno*

Another of our grandfathers' *mezédes*, this dish is said to go wonderfully with cold Retsina, a Greek Village Salad, and Fried Vegetables with Garlic Sauce.

Ingredients:
one beef head, cleaned and skinned by your butcher.
salt and pepper
oregano
thyme
cumin
fresh lemon juice
softened butter

Clean and prepare the head by following the directions in the "Kitchen Techniques" section. Soak the head for one hour in enough water to cover it with the juice of 2 or 3 lemons mixed in. Remove the head and let it drain. Sprinkle it all over with lemon juice and then with the spices and inside the mouth too. Using your fingers, coat the head with butter.

Preheat your oven to 350°F. Wrap the head in 3 or 4 layers of waxed paper and tie it shut with butchers cord. Bake it for 4 to 5 hours or longer if its a big head. When it's done, use a cleaver and crack open the skull. Separate the brains and eyes and arrange them on a platter. Cut out the tongue and remove and discard the membrane. Slice the tongue into pieces and put it on your serving platter. Using your fingers or a fork and knife, remove any cooked flesh from the neck and cheeks, adding them to the platter and serve.

Village Mountain Oysters / *Amelétita*

Some of the old villagers hold this recipe as a traditional delicacy. When a young male animal is slaughtered or when young male pigs are castrated so they can be fattened up, the testicles of these animals are fried and served up as a *mezé*.

Ingredients:
pig, goat, or lamb testicles
salt and pepper
oil for frying
chopped parsley
fresh lemon wedges

Rinse the testicles under running water and set them aside to drain. The testicles of baby goats or lambs can be left whole, but for larger animals such as pig, they can be sliced in half. Heat some oil in a skillet. Salt and pepper the testicles and fry them in the hot oil. Serve them with a sprinkling of parsley and fresh lemon wedges.

Fried Brains / *Mialá Tiganitá*

Ingredients:
2 calves brains
1 tbs. salt
2 tbs. vinegar
salt and pepper
pinch cumin
pinch oregano
oil for frying
1 beaten egg
flour
lemon wedges

Prepare the brains by putting them into a bowl with enough water to cover them and let them soak for one hour. Drain them and remove the thin membrane by peeling it off with your fingers and using a knife, cut away any dark spots.

Set them in a pan and cover them with water. Add the salt and vinegar and bring them to a simmer, removing any foam that collects on top. Cook them for 10 to 15 minutes, drain them and set them aside to cool.

Slice the brains into ½ inch slices and season them with salt, pepper, cumin, and oregano. Heat enough oil in a skillet to cover the bottom. Dip the slices into the beaten egg and then in the flour. Fry them until golden on both sides and serve with fresh lemon wedges.

Stewed Lung / *Pnevmóni Giahní*

Not wanting to waste any edible part of their animals, the villagers use this stew as a *mezé* or served over a bed of pilaf.

Ingredients:
1 lung from goat or lamb
½ cup oil
2 onions, sliced
1 cup chopped tomatoes
1 cup red wine
4 garlic cloves
1 tsp. ground cumin
2 bay leafs
salt and pepper

Rinse and drain the lung and chop it into small pieces. In a skillet, heat the oil and fry the onions and the lung together. Add the rest of the ingredients, reduce the heat and let it simmer until the lung is tender.

Pork and Rice Sausages / *Kolousafádes*

This treat is very popular here in Rhodes. Traditionally, the sausages were made over the Christmas holidays when the fresh pork was available in the villages. Today they are served as a *mezé* at most tavernas and cafés.

Ingredients:
pig intestines
½ cup butter
beef stock

Stuffing:
2 lbs. finely ground pork or beef
2 cups rice
1 cup chopped tomatoes
1 tbs. cumin
salt and pepper
butter
beef stock

Follow the directions for "Cleaning Intestines" in the "Kitchen Techniques" section.

In a bowl mix together the pork, rice, tomatoes, and cumin and season it with salt and pepper. Mix it all together and add a little bit of water so you have a smooth mixture.

Take a piece of prepared intestine and tie a knot in one end. Hold the other end open and spoon the mixture into it, pressing it down with your fingers to pack it tightly. Some village women use a funnel to help hold the end open. Pack the sausages with enough mixture to give you a sausage that is 3 to 4 inches in length. Twist the filled sausage enough times so it is kept separate from the rest of the intestine and use more filling to make another one. Continue tying off and stuffing until the ingredients are used up.

Lay the finished sausage lengths into a pan, being careful that the twists don't unravel. Add the butter and enough stock to cover them. Bring them to a boil then reduce the heat and simmer them for 1 to 1½ hours. Serve as you would any sausage.

Garlic Rice Sausages / *Kolousafádes Skordáti*

A variation of the Traditional Rice Sausage, this recipe gives you an aromatic and spicy sausage with the rich flavor of garlic. After the sausages have been boiled, give them extra flavor by laying them on hot coals for a few minutes to grill.

Ingredients:
prepared pig intestines
½ cup butter
beef broth

Stuffing:
1½ lb. ground pork
2 cups rice
½ cup chopped parsley
6 minced garlic cloves
2 tbs. ground cumin
1 tbs. oregano
1 tbs. thyme
2 eggs
salt and pepper

Follow the directions for "Cleaning Intestines" in the "Kitchen Techniques" section.

In a bowl mix together the stuffing ingredients and season it with salt and pepper. Add a little bit of water so you have a smooth mixture.

Take a piece of prepared intestine and tie a knot in one end. Hold the other end open and spoon the mixture into it, pressing it down with your fingers to pack it tightly. Some village women use a funnel to help hold the end open. Pack the sausages with enough mixture to give you a sausage that is 3 to 4 inches in length. Twist the filled sausage enough times so it is kept separate from the rest of the intestine or tie it off and use more filling to make another one. Continue tying off and stuffing until the ingredients are used up.

Lay the finished sausage lengths into a pan, being careful that the twists don't unravel. Add the butter and enough stock to cover them. Bring them to a boil then reduce the heat and simmer them for 1 to 1½ hours. Serve as you would any sausage.

See the following recipes for more organ meat dishes:

Traditional Easter Soup / *Magirítsa*
Tripe Soup / *Patsás*

Seafood
Thalassiná

Seafood - *Thalassiná*

Geographically, Greece is almost entirely wrapped by not one, but three seas. The Mediterranean, Ionian, and Aegean all grace the her coast lines as well as surround her islands which number well over 3,000.

It's no surprise that with so much water around us, the Greeks would be very much into seafood. The fish in our seas are sometimes referred to as the best in the world. Because of our abundances of reefs and rocks, the creatures that inhabit them are know only as strange delicacies to many parts of the world.

For the islanders, these seafoods are commonly served on the dinner table. Many of our island natives are known for their abilities as sponge divers and as being seasoned fishermen both with a spear and a net. From a very young age, boys will spend hours and hours on the beaches watching and learning from the older men, trying to get a catch of their own that they can proudly take home for dinner.

Fishing has always been done pretty much the same way through the ages in Greece. The rocky bottoms and reefs of our seas make it difficult to fish with large commercial boats or to dredge the bottoms. Many island fishermen stick with the tried and true method of floating nets and baiting long lines of hooks. Sure, there is sonar and radar and the mechanical devices that haul in a full net as opposed to a team of fishermen using their hands, but on some islands you will still find fishermen that prefer the old way, even if it's just for fun of the sport.

Here in Rhodes, we often have what I like to call fishing parties on the shore lines.

Well after dark, the local fishermen will take out their boats and throw bait into the water. This bait is an old village secret formula that consists of stale bread and stinky fish parts. Once the water is baited, the fishermen will sail around the area, forming a huge semi-circle as they lower their nets into the water.

On shore, the families and friends of the fishermen hold ropes that are connected to one end of the nets. When the fishermen return, they bring with them the other end, and the people all form into one team and haul them in. The fishermen always give some of the fresh catch to the the helpers and the rest is taken to the market at day break to sell.

This type of fishing is done for small catches such as white bait. I remember as a little girl, we forgot to take plastic bags or containers with us. For lack of a better place to put the things, my very practical Aunt Leukothéa, just filled her jacket pockets with the fresh, jumping fish. Although, now that I think about it, I believe that it was my uncle's jacket that she was wearing that night.

Stewed Cuttlefish / *Soupiés Giahní*

This is a nice variation for cuttlefish and an appropriate dish for the Lent season. This dish can be eaten alone with just a loaf of crusty bread to dip in the sauce or you can use it as a topping for your favorite pasta or rice.

Ingredients:
2 lb. cuttlefish, cleaned. For tips and instructions on this, see the "Kitchen Techniques" section.
1 cup olive oil
1 chopped onion
1 cup dry white wine
1½ cups chopped tomatoes
1 sprig parsley, chopped
salt and pepper

Wash the cuttlefish, cut them into small pieces and set them aside to drain. Heat the oil in a skillet and add the onions. When they turn translucent, add the cuttlefish and fry them together. Add the wine, tomatoes, parsley and salt and pepper. Reduce the heat and let them simmer for 30 minutes until the cuttlefish are tender. If the sauce gets too thick, add a bit of water.

Cuttlefish in Wine and Sepia / *Soupiés Krasátes me Meláni*

Ingredients:
1 lb. fresh cuttlefish, serving sized
1 cup green olives, pitted
1 cup red wine
1 cup pearl onions
½ tbs. whole black pepper
olive oil

Follow the directions in the "Kitchen Techniques" section for cleaning the fresh cuttlefish. Reserve one ink or sepia sac.
In a skillet, heat enough oil to cover the bottom. Sauté the onions and the olives together until they wilt. Add the cuttlefish and simmer them for 15 minutes. Stir in the wine and pepper corns and break the inc sac so the sepia is added in. Mix it together and let it simmer until the cuttlefish are done. Add some water if more liquid is needed.

Baked Grouper / *Orfós sto Foúrno*

There was a time when large Grouper were commonly caught in our seas. These days, this prime catch has become more and more scarce so when one is caught, it is prepared with utmost care for a truly special meal.

In my family, it's the head of the fish that is the most sought after portion. Though I've never been brave enough to try it, they tell me that it truly is the best part. It sort of snaps apart like a softer version of steamed crabs and is eaten pretty much the same way. So if you're daring enough, give it a go!

Ingredients:

one 8 to 12 lb grouper. Though any fish or fillet will work well with this recipe if you adjust the quantities. Your fish must be scaled, de-gilled, gutted and rinsed. It is also preferable and makes a much more dramatic presentation if the head, tail, and fins are left on. For do-it-your-self instructions, see the "Kitchen Techniques" section.

olive oil

10 cloves garlic

salt and pepper

Salt and pepper your fish inside and out. Lay it out in a large pan and arrange the garlic cloves around and over the fish. Don't forget the slit where the fish has been gutted. Tuck a few pieces in there too as well as giving it a sprinkle of salt and pepper. Pour a generous amount of olive oil over the fish and add only enough water to cover the bottom of the pan. You want the fish to steam in its own juices.

Preheat your oven to 300°F. Cover the pan with aluminum foil, sealing all the edges well and put into the oven to bake. Depending on the size of your fish, you will bake it from 1 to 2 hours total. It is done when the meat is flaky.

Let the fish stand at room temperature a few minutes before serving. This will make it easier to portion out. Beginning at the neck or tail end and using a spatula or a large flat spoon gently cut into the fish just half way deep so that the utensil runs against the spine. This will give you beautiful portions with minimal bones. Remember to spoon some of the broth from the pan over each portion and to serve lemon halves for those that would like a squeeze or two. When the top half of the fish has been served, discard the spine and serve the bottom half.

Simple Poached Fish / *Psári Vrastó*

Poached fish is a simple dish to make and can easily be dressed up with a variety of cold sauces and mayonnaises that are served as an accompaniment. I use Herbal Mayonnaise for this recipe, but you can choose another topping, according to your taste.

The fish will need to be whole after the poaching, so if you have a poaching pan, use it. If you don't have one, wrap the fish in a piece of cheese cloth so you can easily pick it up it in one piece.

Ingredients:
- one 3 to 6 lb. salmon, pike, bass, or any large fish of your choice, scaled, cleaned, and gutted but with the head and tail left on. See the "Kitchen Techniques" section for tips and detailed instructions.

Poaching Stock:
1 cup dry white wine
3 whole garlic cloves
1 coarsely cut carrot
2 ribs celery, cut in half
4 sprigs parsley
1 onion, quartered
1 bay leaf
1 lemon cut into slices
salt and pepper
water

Herb Mayonnaise - see recipe

> **Menu Idea**
> Simple Poached Fish
> Herb Mayonnaise
> Island Potato Salad
> Plain Boiled Greens
> Lemon Oil Dressing
> Tomato Wedges
> Fresh Lemon Wedges
> Feta Cheese
> Olives
> Fresh Bread

Rinse the fish under cold running water and let it drain. Sprinkle it with salt and pepper, inside and out and set it into the poacher. Combine the stock ingredients and pour them into the poaching pan. Add enough water so the fish is covered. Simmer the fish gently for 30 minutes or until it's done. Do not bring it to a boil because the fish will break apart. Gently lift the cooked fish out of the pan and set it on a platter. Serve it with the herbed mayonnaise either spread right onto the fish or served on the side.

Fish in Rosemary and Garlic / *Psária Skordaliá me Dendrolívano*

The rosemary in this recipe adds a very special Mediterranean flavor to the fish, which can be fresh or frozen. The longer the fish stand covered in the sauce, the more pronounced the flavors. Serve this hot or cold.

Ingredients:
3 lbs. small fish such as smelts or whitebait, cleaned and gutted, but with the heads on. See the "Kitchen Techniques" section for tips and detailed instructions.
salt and pepper
oil for frying
flour for rolling plus 3 tablespoons
3 cloves minced garlic
1 cup water
½ cup vinegar
1 tsp. dried rosemary

Wash the fish well under running water and let them drain. Season the fish with salt and pepper and dip them into the flour, shaking off the excess. Heat ½ inch of oil in a skillet and fry the fish until they are golden on both sides. Remove them to a deep pan or platter.

Strain some of the used oil into a saucepan, enough to cover the bottom of it and sauté the garlic until it is light gold. Add 3 tbs. flour and stir constantly until the flour is absorbed by the oil. Slowly add the water, vinegar and the rosemary. Season with salt and pepper to taste. Simmer for a few minutes and pour the sauce over the fish.

Spicy Fish in Tomato Sauce / *Pikántiko Psári me Tomáta*

Baked fish is a favorite in the islands. This recipe can be altered to make an easy one pan meal. Just add some small cubes of potatoes, carrots, and zucchini to the pan to bake along with the fish.

Ingredients:
2 lbs. fresh fish fillets such as flounder, cod, salmon, or swordfish
Spicy Fish Marinade - see recipe
½ cup tomato puree
2 tbs. chopped parsley
½ tsp. black pepper

Preheat your oven to 350°. Salt and pepper the fillets and place them in an oven proof dish. Pour the marinade over the fillets and let them stand for one hour at room temperature. Bake the fish for 15 to 20 minutes or longer, depending on the thickness of your fillets.

Remove the pan from the oven and cover the fillets with the tomato puree. Sprinkle them with parsley and black pepper. Increase the oven temperature to 400°F and bake until the tomato has browned.

Tuna in Tomato Sauce / *Sáltsa me Tóno*

This simple to make seafood sauce uses canned tuna, so it's very convenient as well as very delicious. It can be served with rice, pasta, or anything that takes your fancy.

Ingredients:
1 cup olive oil
2 tbs. butter
2 onions, chopped
2 green peppers, chopped
2 cups mushrooms, sliced
5 garlic cloves, chopped
1 cup chopped parsley
3 hot peppers, chopped
1 cup dry white wine
2 cups chopped tomatoes
salt and pepper
oregano
tabasco sauce
1½ lb. canned tuna fish, drained
1 tbs. corn flour

In a large pot, heat the oil and butter together. Add the onions, green peppers, mushrooms, garlic, parsley and hot peppers and sauté until tender and translucent.

Pour in the wine and tomatoes and 1 cup of water. Add salt and pepper, a good sprinkle of oregano and a few dashes of tabasco and simmer for 30 minutes.

Mix the corn flour with ½ cup of cold water and pour into the sauce to thicken it. Add the drained tuna and cook just long enough to heat through, stirring gently.

Mussels and Feta in Tomato Sauce / *Sáltsa Mídia ke Féta*

Although this recipe has been slightly westernized, it is truly an awesome way of cooking mussels. Serve with rice or pasta, and Greek bread of course.

Ingredients:
2 to 3 lbs. fresh mussels
⅓ cup olive oil
6 medium sized onions sliced thinly
8 medium sized tomatoes chopped
6 garlic cloves minced
1½ cups ketchup
1 cup water
3 heaped tbs. granulated chicken stock
4 tbs. worcestershire sauce
juice of 3 lemons
⅓ cup chopped parsley
1 tbs. seasoned salt
4 dashes hot sauce to taste
1 small can smoked mussels
1 cup crumbled feta cheese

Heat the oil in a large heavy pot or skillet. Sauté the onions until translucent. Add the tomatoes and garlic and simmer for 15 to 20 minutes. Add all the ingredients except for the feta. Simmer the sauce for 15 minutes or until the mussels open. Crumble the feta into the pot and simmer it just until the feta begins to soften.

Mussels with Rice / *Mídia Piláfi*

This pilaf can be served on it's own or as a special side dish. The shells give it a beautiful and exotic touch but they are messy. Share this dish with your family and good friends who don't care if they get their hands dirty.

Ingredients:
4 lbs. fresh mussels
½ cup olive oil
2 large chopped onions
3 cloves crushed garlic
2 large chopped green peppers
6 cups chicken broth
2 cups long grain rice
salt and pepper

Clean the mussels, using a wire brush and a small knife to scrape them and remove their beards. Wash them in cold water, drain and rinse. Discard any opened mussels.
In a deep saucepan, fry the onions, garlic and green peppers in the oil until tender. Add the broth, rice and season it with salt and pepper. Boil it for 10 minutes then reduce the heat and add the cleaned mussels. Simmer it for another 10 - 15 minutes until the mussels open and the rice is done.

Octopus with Macaroni / *Htapódi me Makaronáki*

All kinds of seafood are enjoyed during the season of Lent and many creative recipes exist to spruce things up a bit. This is one of them.

Ingredients:
2 lbs. octopus cleaned and cut into medium pieces. See the "Kitchen Techniques" section for details.
1 bay leaf
1½ cups olive oil
1 chopped onion
2 cups chopped tomatoes
1 cup white wine
pepper
1 lb. elbow macaroni, uncooked

In a large saucepan, add one cup of water, the bay leaf and the octopus. Cover it and cook it for 20 minutes. Remove the cover and let the water evaporate. Add the oil and onion and sauté. Pour in the wine, tomatoes and sprinkle with a bit of pepper. Bring it to a boil then reduce your heat and simmer the sauce for 1 to 1½ hours.

Since it will take some time before the octopus becomes tender, add water accordingly and stir occasionally. When the octopus has softened, add the macaroni and let it cook in the sauce over medium heat. Again, add water if needed but only a little bit at a time so the macaroni won't be dripping in sauce.

Steamed Crayfish / *Karavída*

Very similar to lobster, *Karavída* is a delicacy in the islands. When the fishermen have a catch of this delicious shell fish, its steamed and served as soon as possible. From the sea to the pot... you can't get much fresher than that.

Ingredients:
one 2 to 4 lb. crayfish
2 cups dry white wine or beer
2 bay leaves
1 lemon, sliced
1 garlic clove
1 tbs. black pepper corns
2 sprigs parsley

Rinse the crayfish under running water and set it into a steaming pot. Add the rest of the ingredients. Cover the pot and bring it to a boil, steaming the crayfish for 15 to 20 minutes or until its done. The shell will turn to an orange color and the flesh will be white, not translucent.

Remove the crayfish to a cutting board and use a heavy knife to split it in half length wise, from the head to the tail. Place the halves on a serving platter and accompany it with fresh lemon wedges, a mayonnaise or sauce of your choice.

Baked Shellfish Casserole / *Thalassiná tou Foúrnou*

When preparing for this dish, don't limit yourself to the choices of seafood below. Mussels, clams, oysters, shrimp, and lobster are delicious alternatives as well as simply using only cod or sole fillets.

Ingredients:
1½ lb. assorted seafood such as flounder fillets, scallops, and crab meat.
½ cup olive oil
1 chopped onion
½ cup chopped green and red peppers
1 tbs. chopped parsley
2 tbs. chopped celery tops
salt and pepper
1 cup *Béchamel* Sauce - see recipe
fine bread crumbs
grated Greek *kefalotíri* or parmesan cheese

Preheat your oven to 375°F. Cut the flounder fillets into ½ inch cubes. Wash and drain the scallops. If the scallops are large, cut them in half as you want all the pieces of seafood to be uniform in size. Pick through the crab meat and remove any shells. Make sure all your seafood is free from any bones or shells before you proceed with the recipe.

In a medium sauce pan, heat the olive oil. Sauté the onion with the peppers and add the fish and scallops. Cook them until they are done and toss in the parsley and the celery. Season with salt and pepper and fold in the *Béchamel* Sauce.

Spoon the mixture into individual serving dishes or for a real spectacular treat, use clean, flat sea shells such as large oyster, scallop or clam shells. Sprinkle each serving with bread crumbs and grated cheese. Set the serving dishes or shells on a cookie sheet to catch any drippings and bake them in the oven for 15 to 20 minutes until the tops are brown.

Shrimp with Rice / *Garídes Piláfi*

A wonderful one-pot meal which is easy and extravagant at the same time. You can choose to peel the shrimp before cooking, or leave them with their shells on to be removed when you are actually eating this dish. I personally prefer the latter, as I have found that the shells add that much more flavor to this recipe. Keep a supply of napkins handy because it does get messy.

Ingredients:
2 lbs. shrimp, rinsed and cleaned
½ cup olive oil
1 cup chopped onions
2 garlic cloves, crushed
1 cup celery, chopped
1 cup red pepper or pimento, chopped
1 cup mushrooms, sliced
1 cup crushed tomatoes
salt and pepper
1 tsp. oregano
2 cups long grain rice
1 cup crumbled feta cheese

In a large saucepan, heat the oil. Brown the onions and garlic until translucent. Add the celery, red pepper and mushrooms and cook it all together until the vegetables have softened. Pour in the tomatoes and spices and cook for 10 minutes then add the rice and the shrimp. Give it all a good stir, and let it simmer for 15 minutes. You will have to keep an eye on it, and add water as necessary until it is absorbed and the rice is cooked to your preference. A few minutes before it's done, fold in the feta cheese.

Shrimp Saghanaki / *Garídes Saghanáki*

Also known as Shrimp Athenian or Shrimp with Feta Casserole on some restaurant menus, this favorite dish is served in the Greek Islands and mainland too. You'll often see this specialty offered as a *mezé* as well as an entree. This is a very pretty casserole and can be served with a pilaf or potatoes and a nice salad.

Ingredients:
2 lbs. shrimp, shelled and de-veined
¼ cup olive oil
2 tbs. lemon juice
2 peeled tomatoes, sliced thinly
¼ lb. thinly sliced feta cheese

Sauce:
¼ cup olive oil
1 onion, chopped
1 garlic clove, minced
2 cups fresh chopped tomatoes
⅓ cup dry white wine
½ cup chopped parsley
salt and pepper

In a skillet, heat the oil, and cook the onions until translucent. Add the rest of the sauce ingredients and cook, stirring occasionally, until the sauce thickens. Pre-heat your oven to 450°F.

In another skillet, heat the oil and sear the shrimp for one minute. When they turn pink, remove them to a bowl and toss them with the lemon juice.

In a baking dish, pour some sauce into the bottom. Arrange the shrimp in a layer over it and top it with the rest of the sauce. Arrange the tomato slices over this and top it off with the feta. Bake it for 15 minutes, until the feta begins to melt.

Stuffed Squid / *Kalamarákia Gemistá*

You'll find a variation of this dish in every village, especially during the Lenten season. Serve this with pasta or rice—or just plain fried potatoes. It's delicious.

Ingredients:
12 medium sized squid

Stuffing:
½ cup olive oil
1 dry onion, finely chopped
4 green onions, finely chopped
1 tbs. fresh dill
1½ cups rice
3 tbs. raisins - optional
1 oz. cognac
salt and pepper

Sauce:
½ cup olive oil
2 tbs. tomato paste diluted in 1 cup water
2 tbs. fresh lemon juice
salt and pepper

Remove the heads from the squid. Open the hood part and carefully pull out the innards and the bone without splitting the hood. Rinse thoroughly under running water and set aside to drain. Cut the tentacles from the heads and chop finely.

In a saucepan heat ½ cup oil. Fry the the onions, dill and chopped tentacles. Add the rice and brown it slightly, stirring constantly so it doesn't stick and toss in the raisins, if you're using them and the cognac. Season it with salt and pepper and give it a good stir. Remove it from the heat.

Fill the squid with the stuffing mixture. You will have to secure the hoods shut. I think that using skewers or toothpicks are difficult because squid is so tough, so I use a poultry needle and thick thread. When all the squid have been stuffed, arrange them in a large pan and drizzle ½ cup olive oil over them.

Pour in the tomato paste, lemon juice and sprinkle it all with salt and pepper. The liquid should be enough to cover the squid but if you need more, add some water. Simmer the squid over medium heat for 1 hour, being careful not to burn them. They are done when a fork easily pierces them. To serve, remove the strings and place on a platter. Pour the sauce over them.

Moray Eel in Tomatoes / *Smírna Plakí*

The moray eel can be used in any fish recipe because it's meat, although slightly oilier, is similar in taste and texture. The same hold true vise-versa as fish can be used in any moray eel recipe too. So, if you're corner supermarket just ran out of fresh morays, don't despair...frozen fish fillets work just as well.

Ingredients:
2 lbs. moray eels slices
juice of ½ lemon
½ cup olive oil
2 cups chopped tomatoes
1 cup chopped onions
2 minced garlic cloves
½ cup chopped parsley
½ cup chopped celery
¼ cup white wine
salt and pepper

See the "Kitchen Techniques" section for instructions on cleaning and preparing a fresh moray.
Preheat your oven to 350°F. Salt and pepper the eel and set it in a baking pan. Drizzle the slices with the lemon and oil and toss them so they get coated. Arrange the slices in the pan.
In a mixing bowl, toss together the rest of the ingredients and pour them over the eel. Bake the casserole for 45 to 55 minutes or until the eel is tender and flaky.

For more great Seafood recipes see:

Tarama (Roe) Salad / *Taramosaláta*
Fish Roe Fritters / *Taramokeftédes*
Charcoal Grilled Eel / *Souvlomoutariá*
Eel with Eggs in Vinegar / *Héli me Avyá ke Xíthi*
Fried Mussels / *Mídia Tiganitá*
Charcoal Grilled Octopus / *Htapódi sta Kárvouna*
Octopus in Wine / *Htapódi Krasáto*
Sun Dried Octopus in Garlic Sauce / *Htapódi Xiró Skordaliá*
Grilled Sun Dried Fish / *Psária Heliókafta*
Salt Cod with Garlic Sauce / *Bakaliéros Skordaliá*
Salt Cod Croquettes / *Bakliéros Krokétes*
"Singing" Sardines / *Sardéla pou Keladái*
Fried Whitebait / *Marídes Tiganités*
Shrimp Cocktail - Greek style / *Garídes me Kókkini Sáltsa*
Shrimp in Wine / *Garídes Krasátes*
Squid Rings / *Kalamári Tiganitó*
Squid in Spicy Batter / *Kalamári Tiganitó Pikántiko*
Greek Bouillabaisse / *Kakaviá*
Island Fish Soup / *Psarósoupa*
The Art of *Souvláki* Making

Bread Making

The Village Foúrno

Almost everyone has seen or heard of the Greek village ovens. The tourist books available will show pictures of the big structures and often refer to them as "beehives" because they really do resemble them.

Made from pieces of baked terracotta, clay bricks, mud and cement, a *foúrno* was not an easy thing to build and only the experienced men of the village were called upon to undertake the project. Today, it's a rarity that someone will order a *foúrno* built for their home. Modern times has brought with it electric and gas powered ovens that have taken the place of the traditional *foúrno* in the Greek villages too. Sadly, as the years pass, these *foúrno* specialists are dying out with their secrets and it's only their sons that may perhaps, have a small recollection of how one was built.

You may notice that some of these ovens are built into round beehive shapes while others are built into squares and sometimes are built right onto an outside wall of a house. No matter what a *foúrno* looks like on the outside, they are all the same on the inside. Although some may be bigger or smaller, the inside area that gets heated is built into a dome shape that allows the heat to circulate around the food without burning it.

All of the ovens are built with a large, level stone floor which is "the baking rack" and the breads and pans of food are placed directly onto this. The floor was made by crushing baked terracotta clay into the size of small gravel and mixing it with sand and builders lime. Some "modern models" of village ovens have a small gully or pit dug into the left side of the baking floor for the hot coals to be pushed into, while the older ones don't.

A door is made from a simple sheet of metal. It is completely removable and is made to fit the opening of the oven. For certain holiday dishes such as Easter *Lambriótis*, the oven is converted into a giant crock pot. This is done by making a dough from flour and water. This dough is pushed into the crack between the door and heated *foúrno*, sealing in the pan of food completely. The heat of the oven will diminish slowly and the food is removed 12 to 15 hours later, very, very tender.

Foúrno Accessories

A village home *foúrno* has its own line of baking accessories too. These are usually home made by the men and serve the purpose of reaching deep into the oven where your hands can't get.

The *fournístra* is a large wooden spatula on the end of a long handle. This tool is very much like the wooden paddle that pizza makers use. Its wide paddle is used to slide raw breads into the oven. The *sfahtári* has a round, metallic paddle. This tool is used for picking up baked breads and cookies as well as moving heavy items such as pots and pans. The *difoúrki* or *dihaloúra* resembles a double pronged pitch fork on a long stick. It is used to stoke the fire and move the wood and coals around.

Whenever bread is baked in a village oven it has to be misted with water. To do this the village way, sea sponges are tied onto the end of a bamboo cane, making what's called a *rodistíri*. The sponge end of the *rodistíri* is dipped into water and used to brush the hot baking loaves.

The *skálathro* is a name given to the plain wooden canes that are used to attach things onto the ends of them. Some of these canes may have metallic rings or hooks on the ends of them for this purpose. For example, when ever a *foúrno* is lit, there will be a need for a *sfógios* or sweeping cane. This is made by tying big bunches of pine needles, fresh oregano, thyme, or rose geranium onto the end of the *skálathro*. The herbs used must be fresh and not dry, because it will be used to sweep the inside of the hot oven.

In the spirit of keeping our traditions remembered, here are the instructions for heating and using a Greek village *foúrno*.

The *Foúrno* Tutorial

To begin with, plan on when you want to bake. Traditionally, bread baking day in the villages is on Saturdays, but the actual time of day will have to planned on as well. If it's winter and the weather is cold, then the heat of the oven won't be bothersome. But in the hot summer months, it's best to heat the oven and have finished with baking before the morning sun is too high in the sky and the heat generated from the oven will be almost unbearable. This would mean starting the process of preheating at about 4 or 5 a.m.

Make a pile of twigs and small branches in the center of the *foúrno*, using dry wood such as hickory, pine and olive. Light the twigs and keep feeding the fire with more branches for 1 to 2 hours. As ashes build up, brush them to the side so it's the hot coals that have the most contact with the floor of the oven.

Keep in mind that the actual preheating time has many variables. You will have to take into consideration if its been cold and rainy weather, what kind of wood you're using and if its dry enough to produce an intense heat. Use your judgment and preheat the oven longer if necessary.

The initial fire and addition of wood will produce big flames and lots of smoke. Don't close the door of the oven during this time. Once the fire dies down, you can partially place the door over the opening so more heat is kept inside, but remember that fire needs air, so don't shut it completely.

The terracotta and clay bricks that the oven is built with will absorb the heat and in some ovens you can actually see the interior terracotta turn to an off red or ash color, meaning that its hot. In others, you'll have to give it the 'hand test'. Since there is no temperature gauge on the wall of the *foúrno*, you will have to test for the heat by inserting your hand into the oven itself. The heat inside the oven should feel very hot, and give your skin a "crinkle" feeling. If it doesn't feel right, add more wood and keep preheating it.

When you think that you have the right temperature, let all flames die down. Closing the door at this point for a few minutes will help to extinguish them. The remaining hot coals and the heat absorbed by the oven itself will do all the baking. Any remaining fire or flames will only smoke your breads and blacken them.

The inside of the *foúrno* that you are using may have a small gully or pit to catch the coals, if so, use your tool and slide them into it. If not, simply arrange the coals off to the side of the floor. Dip the cane with the herbs attached into a bucket of water and use the wet leaves to sweep the center of the baking floor clean, getting rid of any small coals and ashes off to the side. Repeat this step as often as necessary so you get a nice clean floor. This is important, or else the breads may sit on ashes or get a chunk of coal baked into the bottom crust, breaking someone's tooth when they take a bite.

Using the wooden paddle, slide your breads onto the clean oven floor. Close the door and let it bake. Although the entire oven has been heated, the coals that are pushed off to the side will generate more heat so anything placed close to them can be considered baking at a high heat setting. The center of the oven is more moderate and the opposite side of the interior would be a low heat setting.

For your breads to cook evenly and to keep them from burning, you will have to exchange their places and turn them around. Do this every 15 minutes of baking time and close the door. Remember that the power of the oven is in the heat that has been absorbed by the structure so don't leave the door off for long periods of time and always work quickly or else you'll lose that heat.

Once the breads have begun getting some color, use the sponge cane, dipped in water to brush the tops of the baking breads. This process is called *na rodízoume* the breads. The water keeps the breads from burning and helps the crusts thicken.

After approximately one hour of baking time, depending on the type and size of your loaves, the breads should be ready. You can check for doneness by knocking on a loaf's under side. Use the metal spatula tool and retrieve a loaf of bread. Pick it up using a thick towel because it's going to be very hot. Using your knuckles, tap on the bottom crust. It should give you a hollow sound, indicating that it's baked. Once you are certain that the bread is done, remove all the loaves to an old blanket and wrap them up. Let them stay there until they cool off.

The burnt ashes that remain inside the oven are hot and still have some cooking power left in them. Use them to cook dinner by having a pot of stew or beans prepared and bury it in the ashes and shut the door. Depending on what you're cooking, this can be left in the oven all day and will give you a delicious meal as a reward for braving the heat of the oven.

Once the oven is completely cold, sweep out the burnt ashes and put them in the ash-water barrel, in the preserving bin or just throw them into the garden to be tilled with the soil. Your *foúrno* is now clean and ready for another days use.

The Praxis of *Prozími*

Prozími is what we would call Sour Dough Starter or a yeast that is used in bread making. It's a piece of dough, about the size of an orange, that is reserved from a bread making session before the dough is kneaded. It is kept until the next baking day, when it will be refreshed and used as yeast in the recipe. Again, another piece of dough will be reserved from that session, keeping the chain going.

Traditionally, the village women make their *prozími* on the 14th of September. This is the celebration or festival of the Holy Cross or *Tou Stavroú*. On this day, church services are held and water is blessed during the ceremony. The village women take some home and use it to make their starter. The starter is used for their weekly bread making and always, a small piece of bread dough is reserved for making the next weeks starter. This continues every week, for the entire year so there is always Holy Water in their breads. It's only at the next years festival, that they will again take home Holy Water and make a fresh, new batch.

Almost all village women today still use sour dough starter in their bread recipes. If they don't have some of their own, they borrow a bit of dough from a neighbor. Aside from the wonderful smell and taste, I'm told that by using this starter it acts as a preservative, keeping their home made breads fresh for the week.

As if bread making in itself wasn't enough, this may seem like an unnecessary and time-consuming step. But sour dough starter is very basic to Greek bread making and gives the recipes much more flavor and aroma than using plain yeast. The breads have a much firmer texture than the yeast breads and the heavy village breads are always made with it.

If you bake bread often, it's easy to have a batch of sour dough starter always on hand. All you have to do is reserve a small portion of raw bread dough – about ½ lb. or the size of an orange, from your next bread making session. Wrap it in cling film or put it in a covered container. Some ladies say to refrigerate it and other say to let it sit out. Try it both ways and see what works best for you. *Prozími* will keep up to two weeks, but for best results, use it within one week. Take out the dough the day before you bake your next batch of bread and using the directions, refresh the starter.

A basic rule for using the starter would be to use one part of starter for every 4 to 5 parts of flour called for. In other words, if your recipe is using 4 to 5 lbs. of flour, you will need 1 lb. of starter instead of the yeast. This means that by using an orange sized ball of reserved dough and refreshing it with 2 or 3 cups of flour and an equal amount of water, you'll have enough *prozími* to make up to 5lbs. of flour into bread dough.

Don't be overly concerned about using too much or too little *prozimi* in a recipe. If you do incorporate more than is called for, you'll get a deeper aroma and a heavier textured bread. For using too little, you'll simply have to wait longer for the dough to rise.

Until you get the method down, take notes on what you did and the amounts that you used. It may take a few trys to get the flavor and texture that you are looking for, but even the mistakes will be delicious. You can always use a recipe from the *Paximádia* section to turn your mistakes into other wonderful Greek snacks.

Beginning the Chain of *Prozími*

You will have to start some where to make the *prozimí*. You can ask a friend that bakes bread for a small amount of dough or you can make the starter yourself.

For the modern method, after the initial 24 hours fermentation period, the mixture will appear bubbly and is ready to use in any bread recipe. Some village women will let it ferment for one or two days more, which will give a much stronger Sour Dough flavor to their bread. You can also choose to refrigerate the starter for use on another day, but make sure that you refresh it before beginning your recipe.

Village Sour Dough Starter / *Prozími Horiátiko*

Modern Method
Ingredients:
½ oz. fresh yeast or 1 tbs. dry yeast
2 cups tepid water
½ lb. whole wheat flour or any flour of your choice can be substituted

Using Fresh Yeast:
Put a little water into a medium sized mixing bowl and add in the yeast. Mix it together until it's a smooth paste. Add the remaining water to the yeast mixture and stir it together. Slowly mix in the flour. The consistency will be like a thick batter. Cover the bowl and set it aside in a warm place to ferment for 24 hours.

Using Dry Yeast:
Pour ½ cup of warm water into a medium sized mixing bowl and whisk the yeast granules into it. Set it aside for 20 minutes to ferment. Add the remaining water to the yeast mixture and stir it together. Slowly mix in the flour so it resembles thick batter. Cover the bowl and set it aside in a warm place to ferment for 24 hours.

Old Way's Method
Take two *hoúftes* or handfuls of flour and put them in a bowl. Add a little salt and enough water to make it into a very soft dough. Cover it with a towel and set it aside to ferment over night. The next day, feed the *prozími* by adding another two *hoúftes* or handfuls of flour and just enough water to make it into a soft dough. Cover it with a towel and again, set it aside to ferment over night.
Continue to feed the *prozími* in the same manner for three more days. At the end of this time, the dough will have small bubbles forming in it. Don't add anymore flour or water. Keep the *prozími* covered with a towel and let it ripen for 4 days. After this time, it's ready to use in any bread recipe that calls for yeast.

Refreshing Sour Dough Starter
Take the reserved dough or starter out of the refrigerator and let it come to room temperature. Put it into a bowl and add equal amounts of flour and water to make it into a thick batter once again. Cover it with cling film and set it aside in a warm place to ferment for 24 hours or more. Keep note of the amount of flour that you have incorporated into the *prozími* and subtract it from your recipe.
Another alternative is to sift all the flour that is called for in the bread recipe that you will be using into a large bowl. Make a well in the center. Dilute the *prozími* in some warm water and pour this into the well. Taking some flour from the sides, incorporate the *prozími* with only enough flour until you have a thick batter, leaving the unused flour around the mixture. Wrap the whole thing up in a towel and an old blanket and set it aside to ferment overnight. The next day, you can continue to incorporate the rest of the flour and the other ingredients that are called for.

Step by Step Village Bread Making

The *psomothíki* or bread keeper was hung from the rafters of the house. The families bread supply would be wrapped in a blanket or linen and suspended high, out of the way.

Preparing the Dough

One or two days before you bake bread, prepare the sour dough starter by refreshing it according to the method that you prefer.

Bread Making Day:

Begin by sifting the flour, salt and any dry spices that are called for in your recipe into a large bowl. If you are using fresh or dry yeast, dilute it according to your recipe.

Make a well in the center of the dry ingredients and add the liquid yeast mixture to the flour or the sour dough starter. If your recipe calls for other liquids such as milk or honey, add it now with a little warm water to help you incorporate it. Don't add any oils yet unless the recipe that you are using calls for it at this stage.

If the recipe doesn't call for other liquids, begin adding warm water to make your dough. Do this very sparingly. You want the dough to be moist but not not wet. All you may need is to dip your hands into water and knead it in. If your using a bread machine, add it by teaspoonfuls.

At the first stages of bread making the dough will look like paste. It will stick to your hands and to the sides of the bowl. As you knead the dough it will release the gluten in the flour and the dough will become elastic. Bread dough can be turned onto a floured work surface so you can knead it easier. If you like using sour dough starter, remove a ball the size of an orange from the dough and save it for the next bread making session.

To make sure that you have kneaded the dough enough, wet your fingers with warm water and brush them over the dough. If it's kneaded enough, the water on your fingers will have a milky color. If it's clear, the dough isn't ready and you should knead it some more.

Rye flours will give you a heavy dough, wheat flours will be some what lighter and white flours are the lightest. What you should check for is elasticity. Pull the dough apart slightly and see if it comes back. The dough should not be overly wet, so don't add a lot of water to begin with. If you do have a very wet dough, knead in little bits of flour very well until the dough comes around and stiffens.

If your recipe calls for raisins, nuts, dry fruits, sesame or poppy seeds to be mixed in, add them now and knead it again so they are fully incorporated.

At the end, add any oil that is called for in your recipe. The white oils such as sunflower, corn and cotton are light and have very little taste. Olive oil, on the other hand will give it a rich aroma and flavor. Knead the dough again so the oil is completely incorporated. You should have a very smooth and airy dough at this stage.

The First Rising

Spread olive oil on the inside surface of a bowl that is at least twice the size of your dough. Place the kneaded dough in the bowl and cover it with a cloth kitchen towel. Wrap it once more in an old blanket and set it aside in a warm place to rest and rise.

Light doughs that are made with white flour and don't use nuts or seeds can rise within 30 to 50 minutes. The heavier doughs that are made with wheat or rye flours may take from 60 to 90 minutes to rise. When using sour dough starter, fruits, nuts or seeds in a recipe, the doughs are the heaviest and can take from 1 to 3 hours to rise.

Always remember that light, white flour doughs will rise to almost doubled in bulk, where as heavier doughs may rise only one third or half in size. Make sure that you have given the dough a warm place and sufficient time to rise, and don't worry if a dough such as whole wheat has not doubled. It's natural.

Preparing the Loaves

Punch the dough back down and knead it again as per your recipe directions. Separate the dough into portions that will become the individual loaves. Remember that the dough will double again in size, so when looking at a portion, you can imagine the finished size and estimate the amount of dough that you prefer for each loaf. Roll the potions of dough into balls, being careful that they have no cracks in the surface.

To Use Baking Pans or Forms:
Grease baking pans or forms and spread out a ball of dough in the bottom, using your fingers to press it down. Use just enough dough so that the pans will be half full, allowing room for them to rise.

To Make Free-Hand Loaves:
Form the balls of dough into loaves. They can be round, oblong or any shape that you prefer. Knead them into shape on your work surface and place them on greased cookie sheets. Make sure that you keep a good distance between the loaves to allow for rising and circulation of heat when they are baking.

To Use Bowls or Baskets as Forms:
Take medium sized bowl or baskets and line them with clean kitchen towels. Sprinkle the towels with a good amount of flour. Press the ball of dough into the bottom of the bowl and spread it out.

Note, that If you are making a Church bread, such *Prósforo* or *Ártos*, press the *Tipári* or wooden stamp into the breads now.

The Second Rising

Set the breads on a level surface to rise and begin to preheat your oven according to recipe directions at this stage. The time that it takes for the breads to rise will again depend on the recipe and the flours that you are using. Once you see that the breads have risen again to almost double in bulk, gently push the dough with your finger tips. Don't poke your fingers into it, just give it a light press. It should return to its shape and it's ready to bake.

Do any last minute preparation of the loaves now. Cut the surfaces with a small knife if its called for. Brush the tops with a glaze and sprinkle with any seeds or herbs.

Baking The Loaves

Bake in the preheated oven according to the recipe directions. Remember that depending on the size and types of loaves that you have chosen to make, some will bake faster than others. Most breads will need 1 to 1½ hours baking time, depending on individual oven temperatures.

You can test for doneness by picking up a hot loaf with a towel and knocking on its bottom crust with your knuckles. If the bread is ready, the sound will be dry and hollow.

Cooling The Loaves

Prepare an area for the breads to sit and cool down. Use old blankets or towels and if you prefer, a baking rack in the center. When the breads come out of the oven, place them on the blankets and wrap them up. Leave them wrapped until they cool down completely. For hard crusts on your bread, brush the hot loaves with plain water just as they come out of the oven. Set them aside, wrapped in blankets to cool down.

Village Bread Making Tips

Helping Dough to Rise:
All of your ingredients should be at room temperature or tepid-warm. Don't use milk, eggs, oil or other ingredients called for in your recipe cold, from the refrigerator because it will slow down the process.

To keep doughs warm during the rising time, wrap the bowls or pans of dough in a clean kitchen towel. Use a blanket to wrap them again, over the towel and set them in a warm place or out of the way of drafts. The added padding of the blanket will help keep them warmer so they rise faster.

The doors and windows in your bread making area shouldn't be left open because you'll cause drafts. Most modern homes have air conditioning that may pose a problem when you need the dough to keep warm and rise. If your home is kept air conditioned, wrap the bowl of dough up as directed above, and set it an area that is kept warmer. Closets, an unheated oven or even the back seat of your car will work.

Sour dough breads and recipes that use heavy rye or wheat flours will take longer to rise, so don't be discouraged. Make sure that the dough is kept warm and make yourself a cup of Greek coffee, while you wait.

For Thick Bread Crusts:
If you like thick crusts on your bread, you can use a sharp knife and make ½ inch deep slashes at one or two inch intervals across the top of the loaves before you glaze and bake them. Although the village women don't do this for every variety of bread, it does give you a thicker crunchier crust and make the loaves look prettier at the same time.

For Lighter and Airier Bread:

Many modern day ovens have steam available as a setting. If your oven doesn't have this control, simply place a pan of water in the bottom of the oven when you begin to bake. Let it steam for 15 minutes then remove it. The steam that will be released will help the dough rise more.

Burning Bread Crusts:

To begin with, don't use a convection oven. It will burn the breads before they are done. Use the bake setting and the temperature that your recipe calls for.

When you're baking the loaves, if they seem that they are getting too brown too fast, loosely cover them with a sheet of aluminum foil. Remove the foil for the last 5 or 10 minutes of baking time.

The Bread Glazes

Often you'll see beautiful loaves of bread decorated with crushed herbs, whole seeds or simply a shiny surface. These effects can easily be given to your home made breads. Use the ideas below to dress up plain loaves of bread or add a special touch to an old recipe.

Brush the glazes on the loaves before they are baked. You can use the glaze alone, or add a sprinkling of herbs, seeds or anything that your imagination can think of.

Plain Glaze:
Plain water or milk can be used to get small pieces of herbs or seeds to stick to the surface of your breads. Brush the tops with the water and sprinkle with flour, dried herbs, sesame or poppy seeds.

Clear Glaze:
For a shiny, clear surface, brush the tops with beaten eggs or sugar water.

Brown Glaze:
This mixture will give you a brown, dark glaze. Beat two egg yolks with a little milk and brush the glaze over the loaves.

Glaze for Heavy Seeds:
The following recipe uses sea salt as the "seeds" but this glaze is thick enough to hold sunflower seeds, chopped nuts, and other heavier ingredients on the surface of the loaves.

Mpouloumasí / Serbian Bread Glaze

Mix ½ cup of flour with enough warm water so its very thick and honey like. If you like, you can add to this any herbs or spices that may be included in your recipe. Brush the glaze over the loaves and sprinkle with crushed sea salt.

Breads
Psomiá

The Bread Stamp - *Tipári or Sfragítha*

A bread for home use stamped with the small side of the *tipári*.

When you see the recipes for Church Breads such as the *Pentárti* —The Five Church Breads or *Prósforo*—Holy Communion Bread, you will read in the instructions that at a certain point during the bread making preparation, the loaves must be stamped with the *tipári*.

The *tipári* is a round piece of wood which has been carved on either side of it with crosses and the initials IC XC NIKA which means, Jesus Christ Conquers. The use of the *tipári* is to seal the breads in Christ's name. Since these breads will be used by the church to "feed" the congregation, the whole process is seen as symbolizing the Sermon on the Mount bible story, when Christ fed the thousands in the desert with only five loaves of bread.

The *tipári* has two sides, large and small. The large side is used for marking the church breads such as the *Pentárti* and the *Prósforo*. During the church service, the priest will cut out the center square portion of this stamped area on the loaf and use it in the Holy Communion. The squares on either side of the center square are cut out as well and are used in the service to memorialize the Saints and the Virgin Mary.

The wide side of the *tipári* used for Church breads.

The small side of the *tipári* is carved only with the center square. Since it lacks the carvings for the Saints and the Virgin Mary, it is generally used by the house wives to mark their own, home made breads with the symbol of Christ.

Since I'm a clutzy sort of gal, I asked what would happen if a mistake would be made? Would the housewife have to re-bake more breads or miss her Sunday service because she used the wrong side? I was assured that as long as the Church breads carried the stamp, a priest would not make a fuss if the wrong sides of the *tipári* was used by accident.

Because bread is symbolic of Christ's body and is considered a gift from God, a housewife will always make the sign of the cross over a new loaf of bread before she cuts into it. If a piece of bread falls on the floor, it is picked up and kissed before anyone steps over it as this would be a sin. No bread is ever thrown away. If it is not eaten in some way or another, it is fed to the animals—chickens or pigs, and even dogs, as it would be a sin for it to end up in the garbage and has to be consumed by some living creature.

Greek Pita Bread / *Pítas*

Traditional Greek *pítes* are made using one recipe for either the pocket or flat versions of the bread. The difference is how you cook the dough. If you choose to bake it longer, you will have a pita bread which is also sliceable and can be used as a pocket. Or, you can fry a pre-baked pita, on a grill or shallow skillet, which will give you the flat pita bread that we use to roll up our *Souvlaki* and *Gýros* sandwiches.

Ingredients:
1 envelope dry granular yeast
1 tbs. sugar
1½ cups warm water
2 tsp. salt
4 cups white all purpose flour
1 tbs. olive oil

Combine the yeast and sugar in a small bowl, add ½ cup of the warm water and let it stand for 10 minutes to ferment. Dissolve the salt in the remaining warm water. Put the flour in a large mixing bowl, making a well in the middle and put the dissolved yeast and salt water into it.

With your hands, blend it into a dough. You may need a bit more or less water depending on your flour. Knead the dough in the bowl with your fists for 10 to 15 minutes or until it is smooth. Pour the oil over the dough and knead it again until the oil is absorbed. Cover the dough in the bowl with a towel and set it in a warm place to rise to double its bulk - 1 to 2 hours. Punch it down and knead it again for 5 minutes.

Preheat your oven to 350°F. Cut pieces of dough, the size of eggs and roll them into balls on a floured surface. Using your hands or a rolling pin, flatten the balls to ¼ inch thick rounds. Set 2 or 3 *pites* on a lightly oiled cookie sheet and bake them on the lower rack 2 to 3 minutes. Flip them over and bake the other side for another 2 to 3 minutes.

Pítes should be white and soft. Wrap the baked *pítes* in a clean towel until they are cool, then store them in plastic bags to prevent them from drying out. When you are ready to use them, heat a bit of oil in a shallow skillet and fry them a minute or so on each side, or until golden brown. Use them immediately, because they get hard when they dry out.

For pita pocket bread: Follow all the directions as above but bake the *pítes* 5 to 10 minutes. Pita pockets will puff and separate when they are fried. Remove them from the grill and carefully slice into the centers.

Greek Village Bread / *Psomí Horiátiko*

Here in the islands, fresh bread is baked in the village homes on a weekly basis. Every Saturday, the *foúrno* or village beehive oven gets fired up and the air fills with the wonderful aroma of thick and crusty, fresh bread.

Ingredients:
1 oz. fresh yeast or 1 tbs. dry yeast or ½ lb. Sour Dough Starter - see recipe
2 ½ lbs. whole wheat flour but any flour can be substituted
1 tbs. salt
2 ½ to 3 cups warm water
2 tbs. olive oil
2 tbs. milk
2 tbs. honey - optional

Although it's preferable to use the sour dough starter, you can use yeast for a quicker version of this bread. It won't give you the heavy flavor, but it will still be delicious. If you're using fresh or dry yeast, dilute it in 1 cup of warm water. Into a large mixing bowl, mix the flour with the salt and make a well in the center of it. Pour in the yeast mixture or sour dough starter, oil, milk, honey and the remaining water.

Using you hands, incorporate the flour from the sides of the bowl into the mixture. Keep mixing it until it's soft and sticky. Flour a work surface and turn the dough out onto it, kneading it until it becomes elastic—10 to 15 minutes.

Add a bit of olive oil to the empty mixing bowl and using your fingers, coat the sides with it. Put the dough back into this bowl. Cover it with a clean, cloth kitchen towel and set it aside in a warm place to rise. Let it rise until it's double in bulk—1 ½ to 2 hours.

After it's risen, punch the dough back down and turn it out onto the floured work surface. Knead it for another 5 minutes. Divide the dough into 3 loaves and shape them. Round or cylindrical, …the choice is up to you. Place them on un-greased baking sheets, allowing for room between them when they rise. Cover the breads with clean towels and let them rise again in a warm place—about 1 hour.

After they have risen for the second time, bake them in a hot oven at 450°F. If they seem that they are getting too brown too fast, loosely cover them with a sheet of aluminum foil. Also, don't use a convection oven because it will burn them. Just good old fashion bake them. After 20 minutes, reduce the temperature to 400°F and bake them for another 20 to 25 minutes until browned.

Bread from *Kárpathos* / *Karpáthika Glykanálata Psomiá*

This is a very basic, heavy white bread with a thick crust. The name *Glykanálata* means sweet and unsalted. It may take a few tries to get the exact quantity of water right, but even the mistakes are delicious.

In *Kárpathos*, the village women use mixing bowls as bread forms. They line the bowls with cloth towels and sprinkle them with flour. Then they add the dough to the lined bowls for the dough to rise the second time. The risen dough is then turned out onto greased sheets, the towels are peeled away and the bread is baked. I'm told that this makes it much more crustier.

Ingredients:
4 lbs. flour
3 envelopes dry yeast
1 tsp. salt - optional
water
½ cup olive oil

Dilute the yeast in ½ cup warm water. Put the flour in a large bowl and make a well in the center. Add the salt and the yeast. Mix in enough water until you have the consistency of very thick cake batter. Put the mixture in a greased bowl and cover it with a clean towel or blanket. Set it aside in a warm place to rise until double in bulk - from 1 to 2 hours. After it has risen, punch it down and knead in the olive oil.

Grease the bread forms that you are going to use and spread in enough dough to fill them almost half way up. Cover the filled forms and set them aside in a warm place to rise once again. Bake the loaves at 350°F for 1 hour. If you see that they are getting too brown too quick, cover them with a sheet of aluminum foil.

Stuffed Olive Bread / *Eliópsomo Gemistó*

This bread is often made in late fall and the winter months when families are picking their olive trees. The breads are formed into small, round loaves and whole olives are folded into the dough, baking right along with it. Not only delicious, they are very handy as a take along meal for the long hours that are spent tending the lands.

Ingredients:
3 envelopes dry yeast
½ cup warm water
5 lbs. white flour
1 lb. whole wheat flour
1 tsp. salt
2 tbs. dried spearmint
1 cup minced raw onions
4 cups olive oil
drained black olives, pitted if you prefer

Dilute the yeast in the warm water and set it aside. In a large bowl, add the flours and mix them with the salt and spearmint. Toss the onions with the dry ingredients. Make a well in the center of the flours and add the yeast. With your hands, incorporate the mixture, using only enough warm water to make it a dough. Knead the mixture until it's smooth and elastic. Add the oil and knead again until it's all incorporated. Cover the dough with a towel and set it aside in a warm place to rise—about 1 hour.

Rub olive oil on cookie sheets and set them aside. Punch down the dough and form it into balls about the size of grapefruits. Roll each ball flat with a rolling pin to about one inch thickness. Place a handful of black olives in the center and bunch up the edges of the circle over them, crimping them together.

Flip the round loaf over, onto the cookie sheet so the seam is on the bottom and the top is smooth. Continue for the rest of the dough balls. Wrap the cookie sheets in towels and set them aside for the second rising. Preheat your oven to 375°F. When the loaves have almost doubled, bake them for approximately one hour depending on your oven.

Ground Sesame Bread / *Tahinópsomo*

As the *Lagána* is today's traditional favorite for Clean Monday, at one time *Tahinópsomo* had the same distinction. This sweet bread was enjoyed on many of the fasting days and is seldom found today.

Ingredients:
3 envelopes dry yeast
½ cup warm water
8 lbs. flour
2 lbs. sugar
½ tsp salt
1 tbs. ground mastic - see "Mystic Mastic"
1 tbs. cinnamon
1 tbs. nutmeg
1 tsp. cloves
2 lbs. *tahíni**
sesame seeds

Dilute the yeast in the warm water. In a large bowl, mix together the flour, sugar and spices and make a well in the center. Add the yeast and the tahíni and incorporate the flour. Knead the dough until it's smooth and elastic. Separate and shape the dough into loaves, depending on your preference. Roll each loaf in sesame seeds and set it on a greased cookie sheet. Put the loaves in a warm place to rise until almost doubled. Bake the loaves at 375°F for approximately one hour depending on your oven and the size of the loaves.

*A paste made from ground sesame seeds available at a Greek or Middle Eastern specialty shop.

Sesame Breads for Fasting / *Sisamotá Psomiá Nistísima*

For the many fasting periods throughout the year, the Greeks have ingeniously come up with recipes that taste good and still keep within their religious beliefs. These sweet sesame breads need only to rise once so they are faster to make than other breads and can be eaten as a snack, with a nice cup of tea or coffee any time of day. Since the recipe does not use dairy products or oil, these breads can be eaten by those who are following a rigid fast.

Ingredients:
3 envelopes granular yeast
1 cup warm water
10 lbs. flour
2 cups sugar
1 tbs. ground cloves
1 tbs. ground cinnamon
1 tsp. salt
sesame seeds for rolling

Dissolve the yeast in the warm water. Mix the flour in a large bowl with the sugar, cloves, cinnamon and salt. Make a well in the center and pour in the yeast. Begin to incorporate the yeast mixture into the flour, adding warm water as you go along. Work the dough until it's smooth and elastic.

The dough can be shaped into small loaves or buns, rolled in sesame seeds and placed on non-stick cookie sheets. For larger loaves, prepare mixing bowls or baskets by lining them with clean cloth kitchen towels. Sprinkle the towels generously with flour. Separate the dough into balls and roll them in sesame seeds. Press the dough into the floured form. Wrap up the cookie sheets or bowls with clean towels and a blanket and set them aside to rise in a warm place.

Preheat your oven to 380°F. Overturn the bowls of large loaves onto non-stick baking sheets. Bake the breads for 30 minutes to one hour, depending on the size of your loaves.

Seven Seed Bread / *Eptásporo Psomí*

This multi-textured bread is a favorite on the islands. It's served for breakfast with butter and jam as well as an accompaniment to any Greek meal.

Ingredients:
1 envelope granulated yeast
½ cup warm water
1 lb. whole wheat flour
1 lb. white flour
1 tsp. sugar
2 tsp. salt
3 tbs. whole oats
3 tbs. white sesame seeds
3 tbs. sun flower seeds
3 tbs. wheat germ
2 tbs. linseeds
1 tbs. black sesame seeds
1 tbs. poppy seeds
1 cup butter milk
¼ cup olive oil

Dilute the yeast in the warm water. Put the flours in a large bowl and mix in the sugar, salt, and oats. In a separate bowl, toss together all the seeds. Make a well in the center of the flour and pour in the yeast and the butter milk. With your hands, incorporate the mixture, using only enough warm water to make it a soft dough. Knead the mixture until it's smooth and elastic. Sprinkle in the seeds and add the oil. Knead the dough again until it's all incorporated. Cover the dough with a towel and set it aside in a warm place to rise.

Punch down the dough and form it into a large round or oblong loaf or smaller loaves and buns. Grease cookie sheets and lay the loaves on them. Wrap the cookie sheets in towels and set them aside for the second rising.

Preheat your oven to 375°F. When the loaves have almost doubled, bake them for 30 minutes to one hour, depending on the size of your loaves.

Herbal Bread / *Áspro Psomí me Vótana*

The versatile herbal bread can be made into dinner buns or large loaves to be enjoyed throughout the day. This particular bread is a nice addition for lunches when serving light soups and salads and is exceptional when baked as a loaf to be sliced for sandwich making.

Ingredients:
1 envelope granulated yeast
½ cup warm water
2 lbs. white flour
2 tsp. salt
1 tsp. sugar
1 tsp. black pepper
1 tsp. ground sage
1 tbs. dry tarragon
1 tsp. thyme
¼ cup minced parsley
¼ cup minced dill weed
¼ cup olive oil

Dilute the yeast in the warm water. Put the flour in a large bowl and mix in the salt, sugar, pepper, sage, tarragon and thyme. Make a well in the center of the flour and pour in the yeast. With your hands, incorporate the mixture, using only enough warm water to make it a soft dough. Knead the mixture until it's smooth and elastic. Sprinkle in the parsley and dill and add the oil. Knead the dough again until it's all incorporated. Cover the dough with a towel and set it aside in a warm place to rise.

Punch down the dough and form it into a large round or oblong loaf or smaller loaves and buns. Grease cookie sheets and lay the loaves on them. Wrap the cookie sheets in towels and set them aside for the second rising.

Preheat your oven to 375°F. When the loaves have almost doubled, bake them for 30 minutes to one hour, depending on the size of your loaves.

Black Garlic Bread / *Mávro Skordópsomo*

This spicy garlic bread is a delicious addition to a cocktail buffet table or simply to be enjoyed at dinner time. If you would rather have a milder version, reduce the amounts of pepper to little pinches so you still have a rich flavor.

Ingredients:
1 envelope granulated yeast
½ cup warm water
2 cups whole wheat flour
1 cup rye flour
1½ cup white flour
1 ½ tsp. salt
1 tsp. oregano
1 tsp. thyme
1 tsp. black pepper
1 tsp. green pepper
1 tsp. red pepper
1 to 2 tbs. crushed garlic
1 tsp. honey mixed with ½ cup olive oil

Dilute the yeast in the warm water. Put the flours in a large bowl and add the salt, oregano. thyme, peppers, and garlic, mixing it all together. Make a well in the center and pour in the yeast. With your hands, incorporate the mixture, using only enough warm water to make it a soft dough. Knead the mixture until it's smooth and elastic. Add the honey-oil mixture and knead again until it's all incorporated. Cover the dough with a towel and set it aside in a warm place to rise.

Punch down the dough and form it into a large round or oblong loaf or smaller loaves and buns. Grease cookie sheets and lay the loaves on them. Wrap the cookie sheets in towels and set them aside for the second rising.

Preheat your oven to 375°F. When the loaves have almost doubled, bake them for 30 minutes to one hour, depending on the size of your loaves. If you see that they are getting too brown too quick, cover them with a sheet of aluminum foil.

HOLIDAY AND CELEBRATION BREADS

St. Basil's Bread / *Vasilópita*

For the traditional New Year's bread, a foil wrapped coin should be mixed into the dough, so it bakes inside. The tradition is that after the stroke of midnight, the *Vasilópita* is cut into the number of pieces as there are family members and friends present in the home and each one chooses a piece for themselves. The person that finds the coin in his piece is deemed the luckiest for the year.

In the days of old, the *Vasilópita* was divided amongst the household members and four extra pieces were reserved. These pieces of bread were meant for Jesus, The Virgin Mary, the house and the poor. If the coin was found in the pieces that were dedicated to Jesus or the Virgin Mary then the coin would be given to the Church. If the coin was found in the piece for the poor, then it would be gifted to the first poor man, woman or child to knock on the family's door. Of course, if the coin was found in the house's piece, it meant that the family could share it.

In our home, we have New Year's Eve parties that usually include a guest list of over 50 people so our *Vasilópita* is a large one, doubling or tripling the recipe. For added fun, we insert different sized coins such as a dime, nickel, and quarter. The pita is shared amongst all present for the party and the winners of the coins each get a small gift, such as 1st, 2nd, and 3rd prize. The first prize is always a collection of cash that we have made on the same evening by passing around a "hat." For the 2nd and 3rd place winners, we give them small gifts such as charms or keepsakes that are reminiscent of the day.

The enjoyment of *Vasilópita* is not limited to just a bread as there is a wonderful recipe for a cake version in the Desserts section. Follow the tradition and serve a cake on New Year's day that is fun to cut up and delicious to eat.

Ingredients:
2 packets granular yeast
½ cup warm water
4 lbs. white flour
2 cups sugar
1 tbs. baking soda
1 tbs. mastic - see "Mystic Mastc"- grated orange rind can be substituted
1 tsp. ground cloves
1 tsp. ground cinnamon
½ tsp. ground nutmeg
½ tsp salt
½ cup oil
½ cup cognac
3 cups softened butter
rose or orange blossom water - *anthónero* - optional
1 coin wrapped in aluminum foil and coated with flour
blanched almonds
1 beaten egg

Dissolve the yeast in the warm water. Mix the flour in a large bowl with the sugar, soda, mastic, cloves, cinnamon, nutmeg and salt. Make a well in the center and pour in the yeast, oil, cognac, butter and rose water.

Begin to incorporate the yeast mixture into the flour, adding warm water only as needed, as you go along. Work the dough until it's smooth and elastic and knead in the coin.

Generously grease a large, round baking pan. Arrange the dough in the pan, gently pushing it into the edges. Push the almonds onto the surface, arranging them into the digits of the new year coming. Wrap the pan up with towels and set it aside to rise until almost doubled.

Preheat your oven to 375°F. Brush the top of the loaf with the beaten egg and bake for 45 to 60 minutes.

Christmas Bread from Constantinople / *Christópsomo Constantinoúpolis*

The different parts of Greece have their own traditional recipes that are used though out the Holidays too. This recipe comes from Constantinople or what would be modern day Istanbul. It makes a wonderful sweet bread that doesn't have to be just for the Christmas holidays. Keep it on hand for a snack or toast the bread slices and serve them as breakfast with butter and marmalade.

Ingredients:
2 oz. fresh yeast or 2 tbs. dry yeast
⅓ cup warm water
1 lb. flour
½ tsp. baking powder
½ tsp. salt
½ tsp. ground mastic - see the "Mystic Mastic"
⅓ cup melted unsalted butter
1 cup sugar
⅓ cup warm evaporated milk
2 eggs and 2 egg yolks, slightly beaten
2 tsp. vanilla
1 tbs. ground *mahlépi* - see "What Is Mahlep?"
1 egg yolk beaten with 1 tsp. water
blanched almonds for decoration - any nut can be substituted

Dissolve the yeast in the warm water. Add 2 tbs. of flour and mix it together. Cover and set it aside to ferment for 10 minutes. Sift together the flour, baking powder, salt, and mastic into a large bowl.

In a separate bowl, mix together the butter, sugar, milk, eggs, vanilla, *mahlépi* and yeast mixture. Make a well in the center of the flour and pour this mixture into it. Using your hands, fold it together until it's all incorporated and forms a dough. If the dough is stiff, add more warm milk to soften it or, if it's too thin and it sticks to your fingers, add more flour. Knead the dough just until its smooth. Cover the bowl with a clean towel and set it aside in a warm place to rise until almost double in bulk—from 1 to 2 hours. Punch it down and knead it again lightly.

Butter the baking pan or sheet that you want to use and spread the dough in the bottom. These breads can be simple rounds or formed into wreaths. You can also roll out the dough into a rope and coil it up, so it takes on a decorative round appearance. Of course, there is no reason why you can't use some other form if you wish.   Arrange the nuts in the dough into a pattern of your choice. Cover it and set it aside once more for the last rising—about 30 minutes.

When the bread has risen sufficiently, brush the top of the loaf with the beaten egg. Bake at 400°F for 30 minutes until it's golden brown.

Sweet Christmas Yeast Bread / *Christópsomo*

This variation for the *Christópsomo*, the traditional bread that is baked on the days before Christmas, is made by forming the dough into a wreath and small pieces of it are used to make decorative crosses on the surface. Walnuts, almonds and raisins are pushed in, giving the loaf a very festive look.

Ingredients:
6 to 8 cups of flour
2 cups warm milk
2 oz. fresh yeast or 2 tbs. dry
1 lb. butter
1 lb. sugar
½ tsp. salt
½ oz. crushed mastic - see "Mystic Mastic"
anise flavoring or 1 tbs. ouzo - optional
5 eggs
1 beaten egg for glaze
sesame seeds, walnuts, raisins, and almonds

Sift 6 cups of the flour into a large bowl. Dilute the yeast in the warm milk. In a separate bowl, cream the butter, sugar, salt, mastic and anise flavoring. Add the eggs one by one and beat just until it's mixed. Stir in the milk and yeast.

Make a well in the center of the flour and pour the butter mixture into it. Using your hands, fold it together until it's incorporated and forms a dough. If the dough is stiff, add more warm milk to soften it or, if it's too thin and it sticks to your fingers add more flour. Knead the dough just until smooth. Cover the bowl with a clean towel and set it aside in a warm area to rise until about double in bulk.

When it's ready, punch it down and knead again lightly. Butter a cookie sheet or baking pan. To make the traditional decorative crosses, reserve a good handful of dough. Roll the remaining dough into a rope and form it into a doughnut or wreath shape on the greased pan. Push in the walnuts, raisins and almonds to decorate it. With a rolling pin, roll out the reserved dough and use a sharp knife to cut strips. Form them into "X" shapes all around the top of the loaf. Although not traditional, you can use some of the wonderful holiday cookie cutters and cut out other festive shapes too.

Cover it and set it aside once more for it to rise—about half in bulk. When the bread has risen sufficiently, brush the top of the loaf with the beaten egg and sprinkle it with sesame seeds if desired. Bake at 400°F for 10 minutes or until it begins to brown. Reduce the temperature to 350°F and bake for 40 to 50 minutes until its done.

Easter Bread / *Lambrópsomo*

The traditional bread for the Easter holidays is sweet smelling and rich in texture. You can make this bread in any design that you like and add a decorative appearance by inserting dyed, hard boiled eggs or nuts into the surface of the dough before the final rising.

Ingredients:
3 envelopes granular yeast
½ tbs. sugar
½ cup warm water
2 eggs
¾ cup sugar
½ cup butter, melted
½ cup milk, scalded and set aside
½ tsp. salt
1 tsp. vanilla extract
2 tbs. ground *mahlépi* - see "What Is Mahlep?"
6 cups flour
2 egg yolks
3 tbs. milk
sesame seeds

Prepare the yeast by sprinkling it into a small bowl with the sugar. Stir in the warm water to dissolve the yeast and cover it and set it aside to ferment.

In a small bowl, beat the eggs on medium speed until they are thick and creamy - about 5 minutes. Increase the speed to high and add the sugar gradually, using a spatula to make sure that all the sugar is dissolved. Still on high speed, drizzle in the melted butter and continue to beat for 5 minutes longer.

Pour the egg mixture into a large mixing bowl. Add the milk, salt, vanilla and *mahlépi* and stir it all together. Stir in the yeast mixture.

Start adding flour, 1 cup at a time by using your hand to incorporate it. Keep adding flour until all but 1 cup has been mixed in. Begin kneading the dough with both fists. You will notice that the dough may be spongy but is sticking to the sides of the bowl. Toss a bit of the reserved flour under the dough, between the bowl surface and dough, and continue to knead, flipping the dough over in the bowl. Again, toss more flour between the surfaces and continue to knead. Keep doing this until all the flour has been incorporated and the dough leaves the sides of the bowl. At this point you can use an electric mixer with a bread hook attachment and knead the dough for 5 minutes longer. If kneading by hand, remove the dough to a floured work surface and knead continuously for 15 minutes. Return the dough to the bowl, cover it with a clean cloth and set it aside to rise in a warm place until doubled in size. This could take from 1 to 3 hours.

Once the dough has risen, punch it down and knead it again vigorously for 1 minute. Again, cover it and set it aside to rise once more—up to 2 hours.

After it has risen a second time, you can now form the dough into the design of your choice. Some people make plain loaves, others roll out coils and braid them *Tsouréki* style, or you can just form wreaths. The choice is yours. You can insert dyed hard boiled eggs into the breads to make them more festive looking. Place the loaves on a foil lined baking sheet. You will have to cover them again and set them aside for the final rising which will take up to 1½ hours.

Pre-heat the oven to 350°F. In a small bowl, mix the egg yolks and milk together. Brush the loaves with this mixture and sprinkle with sesame seeds. Don't glaze hard boiled eggs if you're using them as decoration in the loaves. Bake the breads for 30 to 40 minutes, depending on the size of the loaves. They will look golden brown and will have a hollow sound when you tap them on their bottoms. Let them cool for 30 minutes before you remove them from the sheets. Set them aside to cool down for 4 to 6 hours before slicing them.

Lenten Flat Bread / *Lagána*

The traditional Clean Monday bread

Ingredients:
Yeast mixture:
1oz. fresh yeast or 1 tbs. granular yeast
1 cup warm water
flour

Bread Ingredients:
2 - 2½ lbs. flour
1 tbs. salt
2 to 2½ cups warm water
4 tbs. olive oil
1 tbs. sugar
sesame seeds

Mix the yeast with the warm water in a bowl, stirring well to dissolve it. Add enough flour to this mixture so that it becomes a paste. Cover it with some plastic wrap and set it aside in a warm place to ferment over night.

The next day, add 2 lbs. of flour to a large bowl. Mix it with the salt and make a well in the center of it. Add the yeast mixture, water, oil and sugar. Begin by incorporating the flour into the liquids, kneading gradually until you get a dough. Keep kneading the mixture until it's soft and elastic.

Divide the dough into 4 to 6 balls and place them on a greased sheet. Cover them with a damp towel and set them aside to rise until double in bulk.

Place a risen dough ball on a floured work surface. Using a rolling pin, roll out the dough ball into a flat, oblong oval. Keep flattening the form until it's almost to ½ inch thick. Continue for all the dough balls and then place them on greased sheets, covering them once again and setting them aside to rise until doubled.

Preheat your oven to 400°F. Dust the risen forms with a bit of flour and gently use your fingers to poke the risen dough flat again. Your fingers will leave indentations in the dough so it looks bumpy. Brush the bumpy dough with a bit of water and sprinkle it with sesame seeds. Bake in the oven for 15 to 20 minutes.

Sweet Easter Bread / *Tsouréki*

This braided, sweet bread is found in all Greek shops and homes during the Easter Holiday. For a little variation, you can add pieces of dried orange peel and mix it into the dough. If you would like to get more decorative with your *Tsourékia*, you can braid hard-boiled, dyed eggs right into the loaf.

Ingredients:
2 envelopes granular yeast
½ cup warm water
½ lb. unsalted butter, softened
1¼ cups sugar, plus 1 tbs.
5 eggs
2 cups warm milk
10 cups all purpose flour
½ tsp. ground mastic - see "Mystic Mastic"

Dissolve the yeast in the warm water with 1 tbs. sugar, set it aside to ferment for 10 minutes. Cream the butter and sugar in a large bowl until its light and fluffy. Beat in four of the eggs, one at a time, beating with each addition. On low speed, slowly pour in the warm milk. Add 1 cup of the flour and the mastic and mix into the other ingredients. Add the dissolved yeast and slowly start adding the remaining flour.

When the mixture gets too thick to stir, remove it from the mixer. Dip both your hands into flour so they don't get sticky, and start kneading the dough by hand, until all the flour is incorporated. It should be pliable and smooth, not stiff. Cover the dough with a towel and set it in a warm place to rise for 1 hour or until its double in bulk. Knead it again for one minute and then set it aside to rise once more.

Punch the dough down and then divide it into 12 orange sized balls. This will give you 4 finished loaves. Roll each ball on a floured board into a rope 1½ to 2 inches thick and 15 to 20 inches long.

Take three ropes, and press the edges of the ropes together and fold the end under the loaf. Braid the length of the ropes and when finished, press the other end together and fold under the loaf. If you would like to use the hard boiled eggs as a decoration, use them now, braiding them into the dough as you go along. Set each braided loaf on a well-greased sheet and cover them so they rise again until doubled.

Preheat your oven to 275°F. Beat the last egg lightly and brush the tops of the braided loaves with it. Bake the loaves for 15 minutes then lower the heat to 250F and continue baking until they are golden brown—about 30 minutes. They can be stored in airtight bags or wrapped in cling film and frozen to enjoy on another day.

Bread of Seven Fermentations / *Eptázima*

This religious bread is made in the villages for the Festival of the Cross or *Toú Stavroú* on the 14th of September. The house wives will awaken seven times through the night for the ritualistic preparation of this bread.

Ingredients:
1 lb. dry chickpeas that have been soaked overnight
1 envelope granular yeast
12 lbs. wheat flour
2 lbs. sugar
1 tsp. of salt

Spice Water:
4 bay leaves
½ tsp. ground cloves
1 cinnamon stick
½ tsp. ground cinnamon
½ tsp. aniseed
one gallon of water

In a pot, mix together the ingredients for the spice water and boil it for 15 minutes. Remove it from the heat and set it aside to cool down. The spice water will have to kept tepid warm throughout its use in this recipe.

Grind the chick peas and put them in a bowl with the yeast. Mix in some warm spice water so the yeast and chick pea mixture becomes a thick batter. Wrap it up in a towel and let it ferment in a warm place overnight.

Throughout the night, you will need to stir in some spice water to the fermenting chick-pea mixture. This is done seven times through the night, every 45 minutes to an hour and is why the recipe gets it's name. The chick pea mixture will get frothy and foamy as it ferments.

In the morning, skim the froth off of the chick pea mixture and mix it with enough flour to form a soft dough. Set the dough aside to rise for 1½ to 2 hours.

Mix together the remaining flour, sugar and salt and make a well in the center. Put the risen dough in the center and begin to incorporate it into the flour, adding in enough spice water so you have a smooth and elastic dough. Form the dough into small buns and loaves and set them on greased cookie sheets or bread pans. Any larger loaves can be stamped with the bread tipári by sprinkling it with some flour and pressing it firmly into the center. Wrap up the sheets and set the breads aside, in a warm place to rise. Bake the breads at 380°F for 30 to 60 minutes, depending on the size of your loaves.

Church Bread from Crete / *Ártos Kritikós*

This sweet church bread is made in Crete as the *Pentárti* or The Five Church Breads which are cut up, and the slices given as gifts to the church and congregation. Since this recipe includes oil, it is not used during the fasting periods.

Ingredients:
3 envelopes granular yeast
1 cup warm water
5 lbs. flour
1 cup honey
1 cup dry white wine
1 cup olive oil
1½ cup sugar
½ tsp. ground mastic - see "Mystic Mastic"
pinch salt
sesame seeds

Dissolve the yeast in the warm water. Put the flour into a large mixing bowl and make a well in the center. Pour in the yeast with the rest of the ingredients, except for the sesame seeds. Incorporate the flour into the liquids, kneading the dough until it's smooth and elastic. If more liquid is needed, add little bits of warm water.

Once the dough is ready, separate it into five round loaves, one of which to be slightly larger than the other four. Coat baking sheets or pans with oil and set the loaves on them, allowing space between them to rise. Dust the wide end of the wooden church stamp or *tipári* with flour and firmly press it into the center of the loaves so the indentations are prominent. Wrap the loaves in towels and a blanket and set them in a warm place to rise.

Preheat your oven to 380°F. Brush the tops of the prepared loaves with water and sprinkle them with sesame seeds. Bake the loaves for 45 to 60 minutes.

Holy Communion Bread / *Prósforo* or *Liturgiá*

The Holy Communion bread that is used in the Orthodox church is known as *Prósforo* which means offering and is sometimes called *Liturgiá* by the villagers, which means liturgy.

The housewives that make this single round loaf of offering and take it to the church, can include a list of their family deceased. As the priest blesses the bread, he reads out their names in memorial.

The wide end of the wooden *tipári* stamp is used for marking the center of this leavened bread. After he blesses it, the priest will cut out the stamped part from the center and use it in his cup of wine which is symbolic as Christ's blood, for the Holy Communion. The remaining bread will be given to the congregation as *Antídoro* or the anti-gift of the Holy Communion itself which is symbolic of Christ's body.

The *Prósforo* can be made for any Sunday service as well as special ceremonies, but it must always accompany a *Pentárti* or the Five Church Breads in the ritual know as an *Artoklasía*.

Ingredients:
1 envelope granular yeast
½ cup warm water
6 to 7 cups flour
1 tsp. salt
2 to 2½ cups warm water

Dissolve the yeast in the warm water. Mix the flour in a large bowl with the salt and make a well in the center. Pour in the yeast and begin to incorporate the yeast mixture into the flour, adding warm water as you go along. Turn the dough out onto a floured work surface and knead it until it is smooth and elastic.

Set the dough on a non-stick cookie sheet and form it into a round loaf, using your hands to make the top smooth and even. Dust the large end of the *tipári* stamp with some flour and firmly press it into the center, so the indentations are prominent.

Wrap up the cookie sheet with clean towels and a blanket and set it aside to rise in a warm place. Preheat your oven to 380°F. Bake the bread for 15 minutes then reduce the heat to 350°F and bake it for 40 minutes longer.

The Five Church Breads / *Pentárti*

For a celebration of happiness such as a name day, the Greek Orthodox make what's called a *Pentárti*. This is a batch of five breads which are taken to the church and the priest will bless them and say prayers for the living or what's called *Paráklisi yá toús zontanoús*.

The ritual of the *Pentárti* is called an *Artoplasía* or *Artoklasía*, which in Ancient Greek means bread and cut. It is symbolic of the bible story when Christ was in the desert and blessed the five breads, feeding the thousands of people amongst him.

Each of the five breads is stamped with the wide end of the wooden stamp or bread *tipári*. They are arranged on the church table three in a line and one on either side, so they form a cross. It's also said that it is traditional that the priest giving the liturgy service may take one home with him, if he pleases.

The *Pentárti* is not given as *Antídoro* or the anti-gift of Holy Communion. It is simply passed out to the congregation at the end of the service. The people will walk up to the maker of the Pentárti and their family to wish them *Chrónia Polá* or many years and a happy name day.

The *Pentárti* is always accompanied by another Church bread called the *Prósforo* which the house wives must include.

Ingredients:
3 envelopes granular yeast
1 cup warm water
12 lbs. flour
1 cup sugar - optional
1 tbs. ground cinnamon
1 tbs. ground cloves
1 tbs. nutmeg
1 tbs. ground mastic - see "Mystic Mastic"
3 tsp. salt
sesame seeds

Dissolve the yeast in the warm water. Mix the flour in a large bowl with the sugar, cinnamon, cloves, nutmeg, mastic and salt. Make a well in the center and pour in the yeast. Begin to incorporate the yeast mixture into the flour, adding warm water as you go along. Work the dough until it's smooth and elastic.

Separate the dough into five round loaves, one being slightly larger than the other four. Roll the loaves in sesame seeds and place them on non-stick cookie sheets. Using your hands, gently form them so they are nice and smooth. Dust the wide end of the *tipári* stamp with some flour and firmly press it into the center, so the indentations are prominent.

Wrap up the cookie sheets with clean towels and a blanket and set them aside to rise in a warm place. Preheat your oven to 380°F. Bake the breads for 15 minutes then reduce the heat to 350 and bake them for 40 to 60 minutes longer, depending on the size of your loaves and the oven.

Lazarus Bread Cookies / *Lazarákia*

These cookies are actually made from bread dough and are traditionally served on the Feast Day of Lazarus. This is the Saturday before or the eve of Palm Sunday. The cookies are twisted and formed into little people, using nuts and raisins to decorate them. Since this feast day falls within the Lenten season, these cookies are *nistísima* or proper for a fast because they contain no oil or dairy products.

Ingredients:
2 envelopes granular yeast
½ cup warm water
5 lbs. flour
1 cups sugar
½ tbs. ground cloves
½ tbs. ground cinnamon
½ tsp. salt
sesame seeds for rolling
raisins, almonds, and walnut halves for decoration

Dissolve the yeast in the warm water. Mix the flour in a large bowl with the sugar, cloves, cinnamon and salt. Make a well in the center and pour in the yeast. Begin to incorporate the yeast mixture into the flour, adding warm water as you go along. Work the dough until it's smooth and elastic.

Take an egg sized piece of dough and roll it into a rope about 6 inches long. Fold the rope in half and then twist it two times. Lay it on a non stick baking sheet and proceed with the rest of the dough. If you like, you can make an extra rope of dough and press it over the twist, forming arms.

As you fill up each sheet sprinkle the cookies with sesame seeds and use raisins, almonds and walnuts to decorate the cookies by making little faces or simply sticking them into the cookie all over. Wrap up the cookie sheets with clean towels and a blanket and set them aside to rise in a warm place.

Preheat your oven to 380°F. Bake the cookies for 30 to 40 minutes, depending on their size. The best way to check if they are done, is to simply have a cup of coffee and taste one.

Wedding Breads / *Kouloúres tou Gámou*

These huge bread-cookies are made in the village of *Archángellos* in Rhodes. They are given by the bride's family to the groom's family on the Thursday before the wedding. A special cookie is made for the groom which is the largest and most elaborately decorated.

Ingredients:
3 envelopes granulated yeast
½ cup warm water
10 lbs. flour
1 lb. melted butter
1 lb. olive oil
1½ lb. sugar
2 tbs. ground cinnamon
1 tbs. ground cloves
1 tbs. nutmeg
1 tbs. ground mastic - see "Mystic Mastic"
dyed hard boiled eggs - optional
Jordan almonds

Dissolve the yeast in the warm water. Put the flour in a bowl and make a well in the center. Add all the ingredients and incorporate the flour. Knead it together so you have a stiff dough and roll the dough into ropes about ½ inch thick. Grease cookie sheets or pans. They can be any size that choose, round or square. Take a rope of dough and make a border all around the edge of the sheet. Take another rope and make a cross in the center of it, connecting the edges. Fill in the rest of the design with more ropes that can be arranged straight, twirled, coiled or any way that you like, always connecting the edges to each other so the design forms one big cookie.

Press an egg into each intersection of dough. Make sure that you use an odd number of eggs in your cookies because even numbers are considered bad luck. Bake the pans of cookies at 375°F for 20 to 30 minutes, until they are golden. Let the cookies cool in the pans and then sprinkle Jordan almonds around the eggs to further decorate it.

Notes on Making Zwieback or Rusks / *Paximádia*

Paximádia are simply pieces or slices of very hard and dry bread that are often served with hot coffees and teas to be dunked into them as a snack. Other people wet the dry *Paximádia* with water and use them as a fresh bread substitute.

According to many village women, *Paximádia* are made from a basic bread recipe. The small loaves are baked then they are sliced and re-baked until all the moisture is gone. Other women, as per the ladies from *Kárpathos*, say that bread dough should be formed into small doughnut shapes instead of loaves and baked that way, so the *Paximádia* are whole little wreaths.

There are many recipes for *Paximádia* as well as many variations on the basic theme. Below you'll find alternative spices that you can add or substitute in the basic recipes if you would like to try a different taste.

Optional Flavorings for *Paximádia*:
Vanilla Extract
Whole Corriander Seeds
Whole Cumin Seeds
Anise Seeds
Ground Cinnamon

Use any of theses spices in place of a flavoring or as an addition to a recipe that you like. The art of *paximádia* making doesn't stop here. Use your imagination and add other spices that you like.

Another alternative to making *Paximádia* is to simply use bread that you already have on hand. Cut it into slices and bake them until they are dry and hard. The *Paximádia* are stored in covered containers or plastic bags and keep a long time.

Lenten Zwieback or Rusks / *Paximádia Nistísima*

The loaves of dough are baked and then sliced and toasted for this village treat. This recipe excludes eggs and milk so these *Paximádia* can be enjoyed while fasting. Fresh baked, crunchy and sweet, they are delicious as a snack, dunked into hot coffee and tea.

Ingredients:
2 tbs. fresh yeast or 2 envelopes granular yeast
1 cup warm water
1 lb. white flour
6 oz. whole wheat flour or a mixture of flours as to your preference
½ tsp. salt
¾ cup sugar
warm water
3 tbs. olive oil
black and white sesame seeds - optional

Dilute the yeast in the warm water. Into a large mixing bowl, mix the flours with the salt and sugar and make a well in the center of it. Pour in the yeast mixture and the oil. Using you hands, incorporate the flour from the sides of the bowl into the mixture, adding more warm water slowly, a little bit at a time. Keep mixing it until it's soft and sticky adding just enough water so the dough sticks to your hands. Flour a work surface and turn the dough out onto it. Keep kneading it until it becomes more elastic.

Add a bit of olive oil to the empty mixing bowl and using your fingers, coat the sides with it. Put the dough back into this bowl. Cover it with a clean, cloth kitchen towel and set it aside in a warm place to rise. Let it rise until it's double in bulk – 1½ to 2 hours.

Punch the dough back down and turn it out onto the floured work surface. Knead it for 5 minutes. Divide the dough into balls about the size of an orange and form them into oblong loaves or wreath shapes. Place them on un-greased baking sheets, allowing for room between them when they rise. Cover the breads and sheets with clean towels and let them rise again in a warm place – about 1 hour.

After they have risen for the second time, brush the loaves with water and sprinkle sesame seeds over them. Bake at 350°F for 30 to 40 minutes. Let them cool down completely.

Cut the loaves into slices one inch thick and arrange them on cookie sheets. Return them to the oven and bake until they are toasted, dry and crisp then turn them on the other side to crisp as well.

Riganáda
A *Paximádi* Snack

Having a stock of *Paximádia* is useful especially when company calls unexpectedly. These crisp bread slices can be made into a delicious snack, quickly and easily.

Ingredients:
dry *paximádia*
oregano
black pepper - optional
chopped fresh tomato
crumbled feta
olive oil

Wet the *paximádia* by passing them under running water. Arrange them on a cookie sheet. Sprinkle each slice with some oregano and pepper. Spoon a little tomato on them and top it off with crumbled feta cheese. Sprinkle them once again with oregano and pepper. Drizzle each slice with olive oil.

Place the prepared *paximádia* in the oven and use a high heat to grill them. The feta will melt slightly and begin to brown. Serve the *paximádia* as a snack or as an accompaniment to *mezédes*.

Raisin Filled Rusks / *Paximádia me Stafídes*

Dough Ingredients:
3 cups oil
2 cups sugar
1 cup ash water - *alisíva* - see "Concoctions for the Greek Kitchen"
1 cup orange juice
1 tbs. baking powder
white flour

Filling:
2 lbs. chopped raisins
1 cup nuts
1 cup sugar
3 tbs. toasted sesame seeds
1 tbs. grated lemon peel
½ tsp. ground nutmeg
½ tsp. cinnamon
⅛ tsp. cloves

Mix together all the filling ingredients and set them aside.

In a bowl, mix together the oil, sugar, ash water and orange juice. Add the baking powder and enough flour so you have a stiff dough that you will be able to roll out. Knead the dough until it's smooth and then flour your work surface. Separate the dough into four balls. Using a rolling pin, flatten one ball and roll it out so it's less than ¼ inch thick.

Spoon one quarter of the filling over the dough and beginning at one end, roll it up tightly, Swiss roll style. Set the finished roll on a greased cookie sheet and continue the same procedure for the rest of the dough and filling.

Bake the rolls at 375°F for 35 to 40 minutes. Remove them from the oven and let them cool down completely. Using a sharp knife, cut the rolls into slices about one inch thick. If you prefer a drier rusk, you can set the slices on a cookie sheet and return them to the oven to toast and dry out.

Sesame Rusks / *Sisamotá Paximádia*

Ingredients:
3 envelopes granular yeast
1 cup warm water
10 lbs. white or wheat flour
2 cups sugar
2 tbs. ground mastic - see "Mystic Mastic"
1 tsp. salt
2 cups oil
sesame seeds

Dissolve the yeast in the warm water. Mix the flour in a large bowl with the sugar, mastic and salt. Make a well in the center and pour in the yeast. Begin to incorporate the yeast mixture into the flour, adding warm water as you go along. Work the dough until it's smooth and elastic.

Put the mixture in a greased bowl and cover it with a clean towel or blanket. Set it aside in a warm place to rise until double in bulk - from 1 to 2 hours. After it has risen, punch it down and knead in the olive oil.

Form the dough into oblong loaves, roll them in sesame seeds then place them on a greased cookie sheet. Cover the loaves and set them aside in a warm place to rise once again. Bake the loaves at 350°F for 40 to 60 minutes, depending on the size of your loaves.

Cut the baked loaves into slices one inch thick and arrange them on cookie sheets. Return them to the oven and bake them until they are toasted, dry and crisp then turn them on the other side to crisp as well.

Oil Rusks from Smýrni / *Smyrnéika Paximádia me Ládi*

Ingredients:
3 envelopes granulated yeast
1 cup warm milk
1 cup flour
2 cups milk
4 lbs. flour
2 cups oil
2 cups sugar
7 eggs
½ cup aniseed
juice and peel from 3 oranges
beaten egg for glazing

    Dissolve the yeast in the milk. Mix it with one cup of flour and set it in a warm place to rise over night. In the morning, warm up the milk to tepid and stir it into the yeast mixture.

    Put the flour into a large bowl and make a well in the center. Add the yeast mixture, oil, sugar, eggs, anise seed, orange juice and peel. Knead the dough with your hands until it is smooth and elastic.

    Cover it with a blanket and let it rise in a warm place for 2 to 3 hours. Punch down the dough and form it into oblong loaf shapes, setting the loaves on greased sheets. Cover them again and set them in a warm place to rise.

    Preheat your oven to 375°F. Brush the loaves with the beaten egg and bake them for 30 minutes to one hour, depending on the size of your loaves.

    Cut the baked loaves into slices one inch thick and arrange them on cookie sheets. Return them to the oven and bake them until they are toasted, dry and crisp then turn them on the other side to crisp as well.

Barley Bread Wreaths / *Kritharénies Kouloúres*

Barley wreaths are popular in the islands because they can be dried out like *Paximádia* and preserved for a long time.

Ingredients:
1 packet dry granular yeast
½ cup warm water
1 lb. barley flour
1 lb. white flour
2 tsp. salt
2 tsp. ground mastic - see "Mystic Mastic"
2 tbs. honey mixed with ½ cup olive oil

Dilute the yeast in the warm water. Put the flours in a large bowl and mix in the salt and mastic. Make a well in the center of the flour and pour in the yeast. With your hands, incorporate the mixture, using only enough warm water to make it a soft dough. Knead the mixture until it's smooth and elastic. Pour in the honey-oil mixture and knead the dough.

Form the dough into two large wreaths or into smaller wreaths about 3 inches in diameter. Grease cookie sheets and lay the loaves on them. Wrap the cookie sheets in towels and set them aside to rise.

Preheat your oven to 375°F. When the loaves have risen, bake them for 30 minutes to one hour, depending on the size of your loaves.

Using Left-over Breads and Mistakes

You've been baking your little heart out and have managed to spoil your family with fresh bread every few days or so. What do you do with the left over breads?

Make *Paximádia*:
One of the easiest ways to get rid of left over breads and mistakes is to simply toast them until they are dry and hard. Follow the directions in the *Paximádia* section and you'll give your breads another delicious chance of getting eaten or try the recipes for *Riganáda* for a fast treat.

Make Croutons:
Croutons are a delicious addition to salads and soups and are a good way to get rid of breads that have a heavy taste such as onions and garlic. Don't wait for your bread to get very stale. Crouton making bread should only be a few days old and still be a little moist. Cut the bread into slices and then cut them again into strips. Hold a handful of strips in one hand and use your knife to cut them once again into small cubes. The cubes can be frozen and used at your leisure, frying them up fresh on another day or you can use them to make a western bread stuffing.

For making croutons right away, simply heat an inch or two of light oil such as soy or corn. Let it get hot and then drop in a handful of bread cubes. Let them fry until brown and remove them to paper towels. Continue until you've made the amount of croutons that you want.

For a low fat version of croutons, simply arrange the bread crumbs on a cookie sheet and bake them until they are toasty brown.

Make Bread Pudding:
Follow the recipe directions for Greek Bread Pudding or *Poutínga* in the dessert section for a sweet alternative to getting rid of bread.

Make Bread Crumbs:
Cut your breads into slices and toast them in the oven until they are dry. Using a food processor or a cheese grater, grind the toast and you have wonderful, fine bread crumbs that can be used for any recipe that calls for them.

Make Salt or Sweet Fried Bread:
These fast and easy recipes for old bread will have you cutting into your fresh loaves so you can make more. Follow the simple directions for these great snacks that can be enjoyed all through the day.

Salted Fried Bread / *Tiganópsomo Almyró*

This is a wonderful snack for just lounging around on the couch as well as a way to use up left over, stale bread. Try the salted fried bread as an appetizer with one of the cold Greek sauces or just enjoy it as is.

Ingredients:
1 loaf of 2 or 3 day old Greek Village Bread or any whole wheat bread of your choice. The bread should be slightly moist. Don't use very stale and dry bread.
olive oil
salt

Cut the loaf into ½ inch slices. In a skillet, heat enough oil to cover the bottom. Add the bread slices and fry them until they are golden on each side. Remove the bread to paper towels to drain. Continue with the rest of the slices, adding more oil if needed. While still warm, sprinkle the slices with salt and enjoy!

Sweet Fried Bread / *Tiganópsomo Glykó*

The Greek version of French Toast but without the mess. Use good quality olive oil and a good brand of honey if you can't get fresh.

Ingredients:
1 loaf of 2 or 3 day old Greek Village Bread or any whole wheat bread of your choice. The bread should still be slightly moist. Don't use very stale and dry bread.
olive oil
powdered cinnamon
honey

Cut the loaf into ½ inch slices. In a skillet, heat enough oil to cover the bottom. Add the bread slices and fry until golden on each side. Remove the bread to paper towels to drain. Continue with the rest of the slices, adding more oil if needed. While still warm, sprinkle the slices with cinnamon and top with honey.

PASTRY DOUGHS

Rich Short Crust Pastry

This pastry can be used with any sweet recipe. It can be formed into tart casings, pie crusts or pastry sheets and pre-baked to fill with any sweet custards and creams.

Ingredients:
3 cups all purpose flour
1 tsp. baking powder
1 cup unsalted butter
⅓ cup sugar
2 egg yolks
2 tbs. brandy
1 tbs. grated lemon rind or 1 tsp. vanilla extract

Sift together the flour and the baking powder and set aside. In the bowl of an electric mixer, cream the butter. Add the sugar and keep beating until its light and fluffy, scraping the sides of the bowl occasionally. Add the egg yolks, brandy and rind or flavoring.

On low speed, fold in the flour mixture little by little, continuing until it becomes a stiff dough. When it becomes too stiff to use the mixer, start kneading it by hand. Work the dough only until its smooth and light. Don't over do it or else it will become tough. Bake at 380°F for 15 to 20 minutes to make a pie crust or use it in your favorite recipe.

Home Made Phyllo Pastry Sheets / *Phýllo Spitísio*

Although I preach fresh is best, this is one case where I would recommend buying ready made Phyllo pastry sheets. It's very difficult to make your own sheets and usually left to the expert ladies of the villages because they are so thin and tear easily. I have tried and failed many times, but you may be more adept to making them, so here is the recipe:

Ingredients:
1 lb. white flour
1 tsp. salt
3 tbs. olive oil mixed with 1 cup water
flour for rolling

Sift your flour and salt together in a mixing bowl. Using your fingers, incorporate the oil mixture, working it until you get a dough. Flour a work surface and begin kneading the dough until it's smooth and elastic. If it's too moist, add a bit more flour. Cover it with a clean kitchen towel and let it rest for 30 minutes.

Divide the dough into 8 to 10 balls. Flatten a ball on your floured work surface with a rolling pin and keep rolling it out until its less than $1/8$ inch thick. Sprinkle flour on the sheet and on your work surface to keep the phyllo from sticking. Carefully put the sheet aside and cover it with a clean towel to keep it from drying out and begin to roll out the next ball.

When you have finished rolling out the sheets, they can be used immediately in your favorite recipe. Phyllo dries out very easily so make sure that you keep it covered when it's not in use.

Home Made Phyllo Pastry Sheets with Egg / *Phýllo Spitísio me Avgó*

A variation to the plain phyllo pastry, this recipe uses the same procedure but eggs are called for, making it a denser pastry sheet. You can use this pastry when making individual pies because it won't be as flaky as the plain phyllo and will hold saucy fillings better.

Ingredients:
1 lb. white flour
1 tsp. salt
2 beaten eggs mixed with ½ cup water
flour for rolling

Sift your flour and salt together in a mixing bowl. Using your fingers, incorporate the egg mixture, working it until you get a dough. Flour a work surface and begin kneading the dough until it's smooth and elastic. If it's too moist, add a bit more flour. Cover it with a clean kitchen towel and let it rest for 30 minutes.

Divide the dough into 8 to 10 balls. Flatten a ball on your floured work surface with a rolling pin and keep rolling it out until its less than $1/8$ inch thick. Sprinkle flour on the sheet and on your work surface to keep the phyllo from sticking. Carefully put the sheet aside and cover it with a clean towel to keep it from drying out and begin to roll out the next ball.

When you have finished rolling out the sheets, they can be used immediately in your favorite recipe. Phyllo dries out very easily so make sure that you keep it covered when it's not in use.

Butter Pastry for Pies / *Zími Voutírou yia Pítes*

This pastry dough uses a lot of butter which gives it a wonderful, flaky texture. There is more work involved in this particular recipe, but the rich results are worth it. Use this pastry with one of the many savory pita recipes.

Ingredients:
4 cups flour
1 tsp. salt
1 tsp. cream of tartar
1½ cups butter or shortening at room temperature
chilled soda water
melted butter
flour

Sift the flour with the salt and cream of tartar. Using a pastry blender, two knives or a hand held mixer, cut in the butter so the flour resembles coarse meal. Sprinkle the soda water over the mixture one tablespoon at a time and use your fingers to mix the dough. Add only enough soda until it holds together. Wrap it up in saran wrap and refrigerate it for 30 minutes.

Flour your work surface and roll out the chilled dough into an oblong shape until it's about 1/8 inch thick. Brush the entire surface of the dough with melted butter and sprinkle it with flour. Begin at one end of the oblong shape and roll it up Swiss roll style so that the butter and flour are enclosed.

Using your rolling pin, flatten out the dough again into an oblong shape. Roll it up once more—don't use more butter or flour, and again, roll it out into an oblong shape. Repeat this step two more times so the butter and flour will become very thin, light layers in the pastry itself. The pastry can be used immediately or you can wrap it up in cling film and keep it chilled until you're ready for it.

Pastry Dough - Savory Style

This is a general purpose pastry and can be used for many of the Greek recipes. The vinegar that is called for will give the pastry a bit of a tang, so use it for one of the many Greek savory pies, such as Cheese Pie, Spinach Pie, and Meat Pie.

Ingredients:
5 cups plain white flour
5 tbs. oil
pinch salt
2 tbs. vinegar
2 ½ cups water

Mix the flour, oil, salt and vinegar together. Using your fingers to make a dough, add the water a little at a time until the pastry holds together.
Knead it and form it into a ball. Allow to stand for 1 hour in a cool place. On a floured surface, roll out the dough into a flat sheet as thin as desired. Use as your recipe directs.

Lemon Pastry / *Zími me Lemóni*

The lemon rind in this pastry gives it a very fresh and delicate flavor.

Ingredients:
2 cups flour
1 tsp. salt
4 tbs. olive oil
1 tbs. fresh lemon zest
6 tbs. cold water

In a mixing bowl, stir together the flour and salt. Using your fingers, work in the olive oil, lemon zest and water until it is a dough. If you need more water, add a little bit or if the dough seems too moist, add some flour. Set the dough aside to rest for 30 minutes before using it for your recipe.

Desserts
Glyká

The Greek Sweet Tooth

Standing over six feet tall, the old village wax press or *mángano*, was a massive structure. The honey combs would be placed on the small wooden platform and the heavy central column would be screwed down, pressing every bit of honey out of the combs. The remaining wax could then be used for candle making.

If you're anything like me, you would understand when I say that life just wouldn't be complete with out the sweet taste of a dessert or pastry. I admit that I must be one of the worlds biggest sugar addicts and as if that wasn't enough, I'm a chocoholic too. Although I may not be single handedly responsible for the popularity of companies such as Hershey's and Nestle being the giants of the industry that they are today, I know deep in my heart that I did have something to do with it.

Pastry making is not a very old science in the Greek islands. The traditional homes of old served yogurt made from goat's milk with a bit of honey or a rice pudding, again from goat's milk as a dessert or a sweet snack. Sugar was scarce if not impossible to come by, especially during the war years.

In the northern areas of Greece, where cows were kept, the desserts of the villages used creams and butters as ingredients. Sugar beets, which are also grown in the north made that rare commodity available to the village folk to use in recipes that the islanders just couldn't duplicate.

Instead, the island folk used nuts, seeds, fruits, and simple doughs to make their desserts. Honey, which is abundant in the mountainous islands, was the source of sweetening power used. They came up with wonderful combinations that have become traditional favorites not only for the Greeks, but internationally known as well.

For example, a simple pastry using flour and water could become a spectacular dessert when nuts and a mild honey syrup were added to it. Perhaps this became the basis for our traditional *Baklavá*. Fresh fruits that would be gathered during their season could be canned and preserved, to make spoon sweets, a dessert that is found in every Greek home today.

Since Greeks always strive to use fresh ingredients, these differences of availability has to this day elected what is traditional for the different parts of Greece as well as the islands and villages themselves. As modern times has brought with it abundances of sugar and different ingredients, the Greek pastry kitchen has evolved and become the unique delight that it is today.

The Legend of St. Fanourios' Cake - *Fanourópita*

Commonly followed here in Rhodes is the ritual of the *Fanourópita*. It is said that when you have a problem or a question you can ask for St. Fanourios for help and to *Fanérose* or to show you the answer. It is generally used in cases when you need to see or find something. For instance finding lost keys, seeing a good report from a doctor or having a lost love come to redeem him or herself.

I've tried to get more information about St. Fanourios himself, but not much is know about him other than that he was the patron Saint of the Island in Byzantine times. His Icon was found in Rhodes in the 14th century and he was dressed in military clothing and carrying a cross. I can only assume that he was one of the Crusaders of the era that protected the Mediterranean. His Name Day is celebrated on August 27th.

According to Greek lore, he will show you the answer to your problem or question if in return you offer him a cake and ask God to forgive his mother and rest her soul in peace. It is unclear as to why we ask for his mother's forgiveness. Some stories say that she was a prostitute or sinner of some sort, others say that it's only spoken out of respect as Greeks always ask God to forgive and rest a soul in peace when they refer to the dead.

The *Fanourópita* is not just any cake. Other than the oil, It is made completely out of fasting ingredients and contains no dairy products. While you're making this cake you keep in mind the problem at hand or the question that you wish an answer to.

After it is baked, the cake must be given to at least seven different houses. In other words, people from at least seven different families have to eat it. Of course, after meeting the seven-house requirement, you and your family can have some too. None of this cake can be thrown away, all of it has to be consumed.

When you have given your seven different friends a slice of this, each individual has to say these words out loud before taking the first bite:

"O Theós na sihorési toú Ágiou Fanoúri tin mána"
or
"May God forgive St. Fanouris' mother."

This is the only prayer that has to be said, and after those words are spoken, you can enjoy the cake. You will get an answer to your problem or question within time.

I have also been told that some villages have a variation to this superstition. The seven different houses have to be women by the name of Mary or a derivative of it. I've always just kept the seven house standard, but if you do know seven different Mary's, it couldn't hurt.

It is also said that the ingredients for this cake should number seven as well. A few detail minded ladies have pointed out that in my recipe, when you omit the raisins, which are optional, they number nine. To explain and put your minds at ease, the original recipe calls for "the juice and peel of two oranges," in essence, omitting the lemon peel and making the use of the orange one ingredient. If you take into consideration the changes this detail makes, and recount your ingredients, you will end up with the proper number of seven ingredients for the *Fanourópita*.

Since I always consider taste as playing an important part in any of the foods I make regardless if they are for traditional, superstitious or religious reasons, I have altered the recipe to include lemon as well as orange peel, simply because the fresh aroma of lemons gives it a wonderful flavor and I'll be able to get seven persons to happily eat my cake. If you are a stickler for details, remember that the peels and juice are considered as one ingredient and don't be afraid to enjoy the cake yourself.

St. Fanourios Cake / *Fanourópita*

The tasty, moist cake is very simple to make. You'll notice that it doesn't contain any dairy products so it can be eaten during the Lent season. If you are not observing a fast, I recommend substituting one cup of milk for the wine. I think it gives it much better texture. I also prefer to use the raisins for some added sweetness and zip.

Ingredients:
1 cup light oil - soy or corn oil works well
1 cup sugar
1 cup fresh orange juice
1 tbs. baking powder
3 cups flour
1 cup white sweet wine
1 tbs. grated lemon peel
1 tbs. grated orange peel
1 cup raisins – optional, toss with some flour if you're using them
sesame seeds

Oil and flour a baking pan of your choice. The usual is a sheet cake pan but I use a bundt pan instead and after I have oiled it well, I sprinkle the sesame seeds onto the oil instead of using flour - it makes a beautiful cake when it's turned out of the pan. Add all the ingredients into a large mixer bowl, except for the sesame and beat well. Pour the batter into your pan and sprinkle with the sesame seeds. Bake in a preheated oven at 350°F for almost an hour for a bundt form. Use a toothpick to check if it's done with other cake forms as it may take less baking time.

St. Basil's Cake / *Vasilópita Glýkisma*

St. Basil enjoys much popularity as he has cakes as well as breads named after him. This traditional cake takes it's place on the New Year's table and if you want to partake in the tradition, simply wrap a small coin in aluminum foil and drop it into the unbaked cake batter. When serving the cake, who ever finds the coin is said to have good luck through out the year. Be sure to see the recipe for St. Basil's Bread to read more about the folklore as well as get a delicious variation for this traditional favorite.

Ingredients:
6 eggs - separated
½ cup butter
2 cups sugar
3 cups flour
1 cup fresh orange juice
I cup cognac
1 tsp. soda
1 tsp. mastic - see "Mystic Mastic"
1 tsp. ground nutmeg
½ cup finely chopped blanched almonds
whole blanched almonds for decoration

Preheat your oven to 375°F and generously butter a medium sized, round baking pan. Beat the egg whites until stiff. In a separate bowl, cream the butter with the sugar and add the egg yolks. Add the flour, orange juice, cognac, soda, mastic, nutmeg and chopped almonds. Add the foil wrapped coin at this point if you are using it and fold in the egg whites. Turn the mixture into the prepared pan. Use the almonds to decorate the top of the cake, writing the digits of the New Year. Bake the cake for 40 minutes.

Custard Pies / *Mpougátsa*

Ingredients:
3 eggs
1½ cup sugar
¾ cups fine semolina
6 cups milk
grated rind of 1 lemon - optional
1 tsp. vanilla
phyllo pastry sheets
½ cup melted butter
confectioners sugar
cinnamon

Beat the eggs in a bowl with the sugar until creamy. Mix in the semolina. Slowly add the milk while beating continuously. Pour the mixture into a medium sized pot and add the lemon rind and the vanilla. Over medium heat, bring the mixture to a boil, stirring constantly with a wooden spoon. Be careful that the mixture doesn't stick to the bottom of the pot and burn. When it has thickened, remove the pot from the heat, set aside and cover with a lid so skin doesn't form over it.

Take 4 phyllo sheets and lay them out on a counter on top of each other. Cut the pastry into 4 quarters cross wise so you have 16 equal pieces. Brush each phyllo square with butter and again, stack them up on the side. Take one whole phyllo sheet and lay it out. Brush it over with butter. Stack 2 of the cut squares in the center of the right half of the sheet. Spoon 2 or 3 tablespoons of the cream filling over the squares, in the center. Now you will have to fold up the sides and fold up the center trying to keep a square shape. You are trying to make a package for the cream filling, making it as big or small as you would like. Use butter, brushed on the pastry sides as a glue to hold the phyllo down. Repeat this procedure to make more *Mpougátses* until the cream and phyllo are used up.

Arrange the finished *Mpougátses* on a buttered cookie sheet, and brush them with more butter. Bake at 350°F for 35 minutes or until the pastry is flaky and golden. When done, remove them from the oven and sprinkle them with powdered sugar and cinnamon.

Cretan Almond Torte / *Amygdalópita Krítis*

From the island of Crete, this flavorful cake recipe traditionally uses fresh almonds. But don't worry if you don't have an almond tree in your yard. Store bought almonds work too. This recipe is very similar to Almond-Brandy Cake which is a syrup cake. Why not give both a try.

Ingredients:
1 cup butter
2 cups sugar
8 eggs, separated
1 tsp. cream of tartar
1 tsp. soda
1 cup milk
3 cups flour
1 cup ground almonds

Preheat your oven to 375°F. Butter and flour a 9" x 13" pan. Beat the butter with the sugar until its light and fluffy. Add the egg yolks and mix well. Dilute the cream of tartar and the soda in the milk and add it to the mixture. On low speed, add the flour and the almonds.

In a separate bowl, beat the egg whites until stiff peaks form. Fold the egg whites into the yolk mixture gently as to not let the whipped in air escape. Turn the mixture out into your prepared pan and bake for 45 minutes, or until a toothpick inserted in the middle comes out clean.

Byzantine Rice Cake / *Vizantiní Rizópita*

Although this recipe is old, it is still enjoyed today. It makes a great breakfast cake or a snack that is not too sweet.

Ingredients:
1 cup butter
5 eggs, separated
1 cup sugar
1 cup rice flour
1 cup blanched almonds, ground
½ cup sweet white wine such as Greek *Moscáto*

Preheat your oven to 375°F. Butter and flour a 9" x 13" pan. Whip the butter until light and fluffy. In a separate bowl, cream the egg yolks with the sugar then beat in the whipped butter. Add the rice flour, almonds and the wine.

In a separate bowl, beat the egg whites until stiff peaks form. Fold this into the yolk mixture, gently as not to lose the air that has been incorporated. Turn the batter out into your pan and bake for 30 to 40 minutes or until a tooth pick inserted into the center comes out clean. Sprinkle the finished cake with powdered sugar.

Lemon Cake / *Lemonópita*

Lemons are abundant through out the islands during the winter months and this is one delicious way that the islanders have found to use them up. You can cut the warm cake into serving size squares and arrange them on a platter, ready for when company calls.

Ingredients:
½ cup butter
¾ cups sugar
2 eggs
½ cup warm milk
1½ cups flour
1½ tsp. baking powder
¼ tsp. salt
1½ tbs. grated lemon peel

Topping:
½ cup fresh lemon juice
1 cup sugar

Preheat your oven to 350°F. Cream the butter thoroughly in a bowl and gradually add the sugar while beating. Beat the eggs until light and creamy and with a spoon fold them into the butter and sugar. Stir in the milk with a wooden spoon, then slowly add the flour, baking powder, salt and lemon peel.

Pour the batter into a well-greased 9" x 12" pan and bake for 25 minutes.

Mix the topping ingredients together in a bowl. Remove the cake from the oven and spoon the mixture evenly over the hot cake and return it to the oven to bake for another 5 to 10 minutes. The juice will penetrate into the cake and the sugar will crust over the top.

Ouzo-Coconut Cake / *Revaní me Oúzo ke Karída*

Ingredients:
2 cups flour
1 tbs. baking powder
1 oz. (or 1 shot glass) Ouzo
1 tsp. baking soda
1 tsp. vanilla extract
8 eggs, separated
1 cup butter
1 cup sugar
1 cup milk
1 cup flaked coconut

Syrup:
3 cups sugar
3 ½ cups water
½ cup ouzo
1 tsp. lemon juice

Heat your oven to 350°F. Butter and flour a medium sheet cake pan. Mix the flour with the baking powder and set aside. Mix the ouzo with the baking soda and vanilla and set aside. In a separate bowl, beat the egg whites until stiff but not dry.

In large bowl, at high speed, cream the butter. Gradually add the sugar, mixing well and add the egg yolks, beating until it's light and fluffy. At low speed, add the milk, the ouzo mixture, and the coconut. When it is mixed together, add some flour, then some beaten egg white, again flour and then egg white, continuing until it all incorporated. Don't over mix it, as you want the egg whites to keep the air that has been beaten into them. Pour the mixture into your pan and spread evenly. Bake for an hour or until a toothpick inserted in the center comes out clean.

When it is done, set it aside to cool and make the syrup. In a saucepan, combine all of the ingredients for the syrup, except the lemon. Boil it for 5 minutes, then add the lemon juice. Pour the syrup over the cake and let it cool before serving.

Raisin Cake / *Stafidópita*

Since grapes are abundant during the fall season, this cake is very popular in the islands during the winter, when the sun-dried raisins are fresh.

Ingredients:
4 cups flour
4 tsp. baking powder
1 tsp. salt
1 cup butter
1 cup sugar
2 eggs
dash cinnamon
dash ground ginger
2 cups white raisins, tossed with a bit of flour
grated rind of 1 orange
1½ cup milk
½ cup chopped almonds
powdered sugar

Preheat your oven to 375F. Butter a 13" x 15" pan. Mix the flour, baking powder and salt together. In a medium bowl, cream the butter. Mix in the sugar and add the eggs and beat until fluffy. On low speed, mix in the flour alternating with the milk. Add the cinnamon, ginger and orange peel. Stir in the raisins.

Turn the mixture out into your prepared pan, spreading it out evenly. Sprinkle with the chopped almonds. Bake for 1 hour or until a toothpick inserted into the center comes out clean. Remove from the oven and let the cake cool. Sprinkle the top with powdered sugar.

Island Cheese and Honey Pie / *Melópita Nisiótiki*

The Greek version of cheesecake. This pie can be eaten hot, while it is still light and fluffy or when it's cold and more the consistency of a western cheesecake. Either way, it's wonderful.

Ingredients:
Crust:
1 cup all purpose flour
1 tbs. sugar
5 tbs. butter
2 tbs. ice water

Filling:
1 lb. Greek *mizíthra* or ricotta cheese
½ cup sugar
½ cup honey
3 eggs, beaten
1 tsp. grated lemon peel

Make the crust by sifting the flour into a bowl and adding the sugar and the butter. Work it together with your fingers until you have small beads of dough. Add the ice water and work it into a dough, picking up all the small particles. Form it into a ball, wrap it tightly and refrigerate it for 30 minutes.

Preheat your oven to 350°F. Roll out the dough on a lightly floured board until it is about 1 inch bigger on each side than a 9-inch pan. Fold it in half and gently move it to your baking pan. Fold the edges under, and press against the sides to make a fluted rim ½ inch higher than the pan to hold the filling when it rises. Line the crust with a sheet of aluminum foil and add some dry beans to weight it down (baking blind). Partially bake the crust for 15 minutes, until it is slightly golden. Let it cool before you remove the beans and foil.

Put the cheese, sugar and honey in a bowl and mix well. Add the eggs and lemon peel and mix again. Pour the mixture into the cooled shell and bake for 45 minutes or until the surface is golden brown and cracks appear on it.

Sweet Cheese Tart / *Tárta me Mizíthra*

The ancient Greeks were very fond of dried fruits and nuts for their desserts and modern day Greeks are no different. When teamed with the sweet *Mizíthra* cheese of the islands, fruits and nuts make for an exceptional dessert. Any nut or dried fruit on hand can be used for this recipe so feel free to use your imagination.

Tart Casing Ingredients:
1 cup flour
¼ tsp. cinnamon
¼ tsp. salt
3 tbs. powdered sugar
1 tsp. vanilla extract
3 tbs. olive oil
1 egg, beaten

Filling:
½ cup raisins
½ cup chopped dry fruits such as figs, apricots, pineapple, dates or a mixture.
½ cup sweet red wine such as Greek *Mavrodáphne*
1½ cup Greek *Mizíthra* or ricotta cheese
½ cup sugar
2 eggs
1 tbs. grated orange rind

Topping:
¼ cup coarsely chopped nuts or a mixture such as almonds, walnuts or hazelnuts.
2 tbs. sugar
ground cinnamon

Put the raisins and the dried fruits for the filling into a small bowl and cover them with the wine. Set it aside.

Make the Casing: In a large mixing bowl stir together the flour, cinnamon, salt, powdered sugar and vanilla. Pour in the olive oil and using a fork with a cutting motion or a pastry cutter, work the ingredients until they resemble coarse corn meal. Add the egg and work it some more until it's been fully incorporated.

Generously butter a 9-inch spring form pan. Put the dough on a floured work surface and roll it out until it's the shape and size of the pan making sure that you have enough to come up the sides of the pan. Line the buttered pan with the pastry dough. It would be nice if there were no tears in the casing, but if it happens, don't worry. Just use small pieces of dough to patch up the tears and holes. Wrap it with saran wrap and refrigerate for 1 hour.

Preheat your oven to 375°F. Prick the entire surface of the dough with a fork. Since we have to bake blind the pastry dough, line the entire surface of the dough with aluminum foil. Pour into it bakers beans, rice, or plain old dry beans to use to weight it down so it keeps it's form and doesn't puff up.

Bake for 15 minutes then remove it from the oven and let it set for another 5 minutes. Remove the weight and the aluminum foil and return it to the oven for another 15 minutes baking time. Set the baked tart case aside to cool down.

Lower the oven temperature to 350°F. Mix together the cheese, sugar, eggs, and the orange rind until it's creamy. Strain the fruits from the wine and stir them into the cheese mixture. Pour it into the cooled tart casing and bake it for 20 minutes or until the cheese mixture begins to set.

Sprinkle the surface of the tart with sugar, cinnamon and nuts. If the surface has set too much, gently push the nuts down into it. Return the tart to the oven and bake it for another 20 minutes or until the center is set. Let it cool completely before serving.

Apricots and Cream / *Chrisómila Poltós*

This fruit dessert is an elegant end to any meal and the puree is also great on a thick slice of pound cake. Instead of the whipped cream, pour sweetened cream over it. It's like an apricot short cake.

Ingredients:
1 lb. dried apricots
½ cup split, blanched almonds
sugar to taste
whipped cream

Cover the apricots with cold water and let them soak overnight. Transfer the apricots and the water to a pot and simmer gently, stirring occasionally until they are soft. Put the apricots into a food processor and puree. Add the water from the pot as needed to make a smooth paste. Add sugar to taste. Stir in the almonds. Put the mixture into serving dishes and refrigerate. Top off with whipped cream just before serving.

Rice Pudding - Traditional Style / *Rizógalo Paradosiakó*

A favorite of mine, this dessert is great hot or cold. I prefer this with the raisins in it. They get plump as they cook and add an extra sweetness to the pudding.

Ingredients:
⅓ cup short grain rice
1 quart milk
½ cup sugar
1 tbs. finely grated lemon peel
½ cup raisins – optional
powdered cinnamon

Cover the rice with ½ cup of water and set it aside for 5 minutes. Combine the milk and the sugar in a saucepan and bring them to a boil over moderate heat. Add the rice with the water to the hot milk and bring it to a boil, while stirring constantly. Add the grated lemon peel and raisins. Reduce the heat and gently simmer the mixture until it is thick and creamy. If the liquid has evaporated before the rice is cooked, add a little more hot water to it. Pour the pudding into small serving bowls and sprinkle with cinnamon.

Custard Style Rice Pudding / *Rizógalo*

This recipe makes a thick and sweet style of rice pudding. I use the raisins and the lemon peel in it as it gives it so much more flavor. Rice pudding makes skin on the surface as it cools. To avoid this, wrap each bowl with a piece of cling film while it's warm and let it cool while covered.

Ingredients:
1 cup rice
2 cups water
3½ cups milk
1½ cup sugar
2 tbs. corn flour diluted in ½ cup milk
2 egg yolks beaten with 2 tsp. vanilla
½ cup raisins soaked in warm water overnight - optional
grated rind of 1 lemon - optional
powdered cinnamon

In a medium saucepan bring the rice and the water to a boil. Reduce the heat and add the milk. Simmer and stir the mixture until it begins to thicken, being careful that it doesn't scorch. Add the sugar, the milk and corn flour mixture and quickly stir in the eggs and vanilla. Cook the mixture for another two minutes while stirring constantly. Remove from heat. Stir in the raisins and lemon rind - if you're using them. Fill small bowls with the rice pudding, sprinkling cinnamon over the top. Let them cool then refrigerate.

Pasta Pudding / *Matsógalo*

Very much like rice pudding, this dessert is traditionally served on the early spring days of *apokriés* or carnival for the cheese fasts when the fresh milks are available from the animals. It used to be that during these days, the herders would not use the milk to make cheeses, instead they shared it with their fellow villagers to make *Matsógalo*. Fresh *Mátsi* noodles that are thinly cut are the traditional pasta used in this recipe but vermicelli makes a nice substitute.

Ingredients:
4 cups milk
3 tbs. sugar
1 cup vermicelli pasta
cinnamon

Heat the milk with the sugar and stir in the vermicelli. Simmer it until the pasta cooks and the pudding thickens. If you prefer a thicker pudding, stir in a bit of corn flour that has been diluted with some milk. Spoon the pudding into bowls, and sprinkle it with cinnamon.

Grape Pudding / *Moustoaleuriá*

This may sound a little weird, but for ages I never ate this stuff because I assumed that grape "must" was a mold or fermented ingredient. Quite to the contrary, grape must is the freshest of all grape juices that comes right out of the pressed grapes.

Easy Recipe

Ingredients:
3 cups unsweetened, store bought grape juice
4 tbs. corn starch
4 tbs. sugar or more if you prefer it sweet
chopped walnuts and almonds
ground cinnamon

Dilute the corn flour in one cup of grape juice. Bring to a boil the remaining grape juice and stir in the sugar to dissolve it. Stir in the corn flour mixture and cook it until it gets thick. Spoon the pudding into bowls or cups and sprinkle the tops with cinnamon and chopped nuts.

Village Recipe

Ingredients:
7 cups fresh pressed grape juice or must
3 tbs. sifted wood ashes
1 cup flour
walnuts and almonds
cinnamon

Put the ashes in a fine cheese cloth. Bring the wine to a boil with the ashes and remove any foam that collects on top. Remove the ashes and let the grape juice settle for a bit. Pour the juice through a fine sieve that has been lined with a few layers of cheese cloth and remove one cup for it to cool down completely.

Whisk together the flour with the cooled juice. Bring the rest of the juice to a boil and stir in the flour mixture, heating it until it thickens. Spoon the pudding into bowls or cups and sprinkle the tops with cinnamon and chopped nuts.

Bread Pudding / *Poutínga*

It wasn't until I received a request for this recipe from one of my readers, that I realized how elusive it really was. This recipe comes from the northern mainland of Greece and is a great way to use up stale breads and make a delicious dessert at the same time.

Ingredients:
½ lb. stale white bread cut into cubes.
½ cup melted butter
3½ cups milk
½ cup sugar
5 eggs
1 tsp. vanilla
1 tsp. grated orange or lemon peel
½ tsp. ground nutmeg
½ tsp. white pepper - optional
1 cup seedless raisins
strawberry or blueberry marmalade - optional
sweet Greek wine such as *Mavrodáphne* - optional

Preheat your oven to 380°F. You will need to use two pans for this recipe, one will be the baking dish for the pudding and the other will be used as a bain marie or water bath. Make sure that a medium sized baking dish fits inside of the second pan and that it's deep enough to hold enough water that will come at least half way up the side of the baking dish.

Generously butter your baking dish and arrange the bread chunks in it. Pour the melted butter over the bread. Warm the milk and sugar together, stirring it so the sugar dissolves then set it aside. Beat together the eggs, vanilla, peel, nutmeg and pepper. Slowly incorporate the warm milk into the egg mixture, whisking constantly so the egg doesn't curdle.

Pour the mixture over the bread and sprinkle the raisins over the pudding. Let the pudding rest for 10 minutes so the bread can absorb the custard mixture. Set the baking dish into the bain marie and set it in the oven. Pour enough hot water into the bain marie so the level is at least half way up the side of the baking dish. Bake the pudding for 45 to 55 minutes or until the center is set.

After it's baked, set the pudding aside to cool completely. The wine and marmalade can be used as a topping for the pudding. Spoon servings of the pudding onto a dish and pour a bit of sweet wine over it. Heat the marmalade and spoon it over the finished pudding.

Figs Stuffed with Nuts / *Síka Gemistá me Xiroús Karpoús*

Figs are a common fruit found in all parts of Greece as well as the countries of the Mediterranean. Almost everyone has a *Sikiá*—fig tree growing in their yard. Use this recipe to make a delicious dessert that is quick and easy and has a taste of the exotic.

Ingredients:
1 cup sweet red wine such as Greek *Mavrodáphne*
12 to 16 dried figs
1 cup blanched almonds or nut of your choice
1 cup almond or hazelnut liqueur
¼ tsp. ground cinnamon
⅛ tsp. ground cloves
¼ tsp. ground nutmeg
¼ cup brown sugar
3 tbs. butter

Pour the wine with one cup of water into a medium sized pot. Add the figs and bring them to a boil. Reduce the heat and simmer for 30 minutes to soften them. Remove them from the pan with a slotted spoon and set them aside to drain and cool down. Reserve the liquid that they cooked in.

Fill each fig with some nuts and place them in an oven proof dish, side by side. Mix the cooking liquid with the liqueur, cinnamon, cloves, and nutmeg. Pour the mixture over the figs and sprinkle them with the brown sugar and dot with the butter. Grill them in the oven at 400°F for a few minutes, basting the tops occasionally so they caramelize.

Remove the dish from the oven and cover it with aluminum foil. Set them aside to cool and soak up the liquids and spices for at least 6 hours. Overnight is better. To serve, place two figs on a dessert dish and top it with a dollop of whipped cream or sweetened plain yogurt.

Stuffed Melon / *Piponáki Gemistó*

Casaba, cantaloupes and honeydew melons are available throughout the summer months on the islands. This recipe is not only a "dress me up" for plain fruit, but makes a beautiful presentation as well. This is an easy summer dessert that is light and kids love as a snack too. If you like, top off the servings with a dollop of sweetened fresh whipped cream.

Ingredients:
1 whole melon - cantaloupe or honey dew
1 package gelatin - your choice of flavor
assorted chopped fruits or drained, canned fruit cocktail

Wash the melon well under cold running water. Carefully, cut off one end - just enough so you can de-seed it using a spoon. In a small bowl, make the gelatin as per package instructions. Stuff the melon with the fruits and pour the gelatin into the cavity and put the "lid" back on. If you need help keeping it upright, set it in a bowl and stuff kitchen towels around it. Refrigerate overnight.

To serve the melon, just slice it crosswise into rounds. The gelatin center will be a pretty contrast to the fresh fruit.

Mastic Ice Cream / *Pagotó Mastíhas*

It may seem a bit fussy to make your own Ice Cream, but the taste of *Mastíha* is very unique. I doubt that you'll find this flavor in your neighborhood ice cream shop. Make sure that you have a home ice cream machine before you start this recipe. The exotic spice of the Mastic tree is the flavoring for this dessert and since there are no substitutions for it, make sure that you have some on hand as well.

Ingredients:
6 egg yolks
1 cup sugar
2 cups full fat milk
4 tsp. corn flour
1 tsp. ground Mastic - see "Mystic Mastic"
1 cup strained yogurt or fresh cream

In a mixing bowl, beat the egg yolks with the sugar until they have turned a pale yellow color.
Mix the milk with the corn flour in a pot and heat it on medium, stirring constantly until it thickens. Remove the pot from the heat and add a bit of the hot milk mixture to the yokes, whisking constantly. Add some more and whisk again. You want to raise the temperature of the yokes enough so that you can add it to the milk mixture without worrying about scrambling the eggs. When you think that the yokes are warm enough, pour the mixture into the milk, again, whisking constantly.
Heat the mixture over medium while stirring constantly until it's creamy. Pour it into a bowl that has been set over another bowl full of ice. If the milk mixture has formed lumps, pour it through a sieve first. Stir in the mastic and the yogurt or cream. Let it cool down, stirring it occasionally to help it along. Using the cooled mixture, follow the directions for your ice cream maker to finish off the treat.

The Fried Doughs and Desserts

This section is home to the very popular recipe, *Díples*. Time and time again, I have been asked to disclose the secrets of making this dessert from commercial restaurateurs as well as plain folk who would just like to enjoy the dessert at home.

There is no great secret behind making *Díples* or any of the Greek fried dough desserts. Since I can't find out what exactly the history behind them is, I can only speculate that these desserts began as excess dough from the preparation of another dish. Our grandmothers being the frugal women that they were decided to fry it up instead of discarding it. Some how, by mistake or intended, honey got poured over these bits of dough, making them the sought after recipes that they are today.

There are variations on the theme, as you will see when going over the recipes. And you can use your imagination to add other spices or toppings to the finished products. The fried doughs keep very well and don't need refrigeration. Keep them covered on a counter in your kitchen at room temperature.

I've also found that the fried desserts soak up the honey syrups and flavorings when left to sit. So make sure that you pour a little more honey over them when you want to serve them again and maybe a bit more of the spices.

Deep Fried Apple Rings / *Tiganítes me Míla*

A Greek version of apple dumplings, these are very easy to make and taste delicious. For more of an apple pie flavor, add some spices to the apples before you dip them into the batter.

Ingredients:
2 lbs. apples, pared and cored and sliced into ½ inch rings
1 cup sugar
juice of 1 lemon mixed with 1 cup cognac or brandy
1 egg
1¼ cup milk
flour
1 tsp. vanilla
pinch salt
oil for frying
powdered cinnamon
powdered sugar

In a bowl, sprinkle the apple rings with the sugar and pour in the lemon-cognac. Toss them well and set aside. In a mixing bowl add the egg, milk, vanilla and salt. Add enough flour so you have a thick batter-like consistency.

Heat oil in a deep skillet. Take an apple ring and dip it in the batter then drop it into the oil. Fry on one side, then the other until golden. Remove to paper towels to drain. Arrange the cooked apple slices on a platter and sprinkle with powdered sugar and cinnamon.

Díples

The traditional fried dough of the Greeks, *Díples* are very popular with tourists as well. These crispy pieces of pastry are smothered in honey and topped with chopped nuts. The recipe may seem complicated, but in fact, they are very easy to make.

You want to fry these up until they begin to form blisters and are golden brown. Since it's pastry, you want the oil hot because it will soak up too much of it if it fries a long time. And if you've had *Díples* before, then you know that they shouldn't taste greasy. I always remove the *Díples* to paper towels to let them drain a little more and then I arrange them on a platter and coat them with all the toppings and goodies.

Ingredients:
5 eggs
½ cup fresh orange juice
2 tbs. sugar
pinch salt
2 tsp. baking powder
flour
oil for frying
honey for topping
powdered sugar - optional
cinnamon
chopped walnuts

In a large mixing bowl, beat the eggs, orange juice, sugar and salt together until its well combined. Mix in the baking powder and begin to add flour, a little at a time. You will continue to add flour until you have a thick consistency. Using your hands add enough flour so you have a dough that you can roll out. Set it aside to rest for 30 minutes.

When you're ready, knead the dough once more, then turn it out onto a floured surface. Take balls of dough, about the size of an orange, and roll them out thinly. Now you will cut out shapes from this pastry. The shape depends on your preference. Some people cut plain squares, others cut long strips that are later twirled in the hot oil to form flowers, or then again... as a personal thought ... cookie cutters might make neat and interesting shapes. The choice is yours.

After you have cut out your pastry shapes, heat oil in a deep skillet—2 to 3 inches of oil should do it. Carefully drop a piece of pastry into it and brown gently on one side, then flip it over to brown the other. The *Díples* should float and make the oil foam or bubble when it hits it. If it just sinks to the bottom, then the oil is not hot enough. When both sides are golden brown, remove it to drain on paper towels and fry another one.

If you want to get imaginative, you can form the dough into other shapes as it fries. You will have to pierce one side of the dough with a fork so you can hold it and work with it, BEFORE you drop it into the oil, or else it will be too crispy to pierce. Squares can be folded one side over the other making "cannelloni" shapes, or strips of dough can be swirled around in the oil forming rosettes. It will probably be easier to have a spatula or another fork in the other hand so you can work. Just be careful as hot oil really causes nasty burns.

When you're done frying up all the pastry, sprinkle them with cinnamon and powdered sugar—if you like. Arrange them on a platter and drizzle honey over them all. Finally, sprinkle the *Díples* with the chopped walnuts and serve.

Fried Almond Fingers / *Amygdalotá Tiganitá*

Ingredients:
½ cup ground almonds
1 cup sugar
4 eggs
½ cup melted butter
1 cup cognac
flour
oil for frying
confectioners sugar mixed with cinnamon

In a bowl, mix together the almonds, sugar, eggs, butter and cognac. Add enough flour so you get a stiff dough. Roll out logs and cut them into 3 inch fingers. Heat an inch of oil in a skillet and fry the fingers until they are golden.

Sprinkle a sheet of aluminum foil with the powdered sugar and cinnamon mixture. Using a slotted spoon, remove the fried dough to the aluminum foil, sprinkle the fingers with more powdered sugar mixture and close the foil. The hot cookies will steam and absorb the sugar while they cool down. Once cooled, arrange them on a platter and sprinkle with more powdered sugar and cinnamon.

Fried Dough Balls / *Loukoumádes*

This island favorite is served as a dessert or for just a snack. They are especially good on a cold wintry afternoon with a nice cup of Greek coffee. I have found that *Loukoumádes* are tastier the longer that they sit as they have been soaking up the honey and cinnamon.

Ingredients:
6 cups all purpose flour
½ tsp. salt
2 cups evaporated milk, undiluted
4 eggs
2 tbs. baking powder
1 cup sugar
1 tsp. vanilla
2 envelopes dry yeast, dissolved in ½ cup warm water
soy or corn oil for frying
honey
ground cinnamon
chopped walnuts - optional

In a large mixing bowl, mix the flour, salt, milk, eggs, baking powder, sugar and vanilla. Stir in the yeast and water. Your mixture should be a smooth batter like consistency. Cover the bowl with a clean cloth and set it aside to rise in a warm area until doubled in bulk.

Heat two inches of oil in a deep skillet or pot. Using a tablespoon, drop the mixture into the oil. Roll them around gently so they fry to a golden brown on all sides. Using a slotted spoon, remove the fried balls to paper towels to drain.

To serve the *Loukoumádes*, arrange the fried balls on a platter or individual serving dishes. Sprinkle them with cinnamon and pour a generous amount of honey over them. If you like, you can top it off with a sprinkling of chopped walnuts.

Fried Cheese Pies / *Mizithrópites*

Ingredients:
4 cups flour
1 cup water
pinch salt
1 lb. Greek *mizíthra* or ricotta cheese
1 egg
½ cup sugar
butter
sugar or honey
ground cinnamon

Mix together the flour, salt and water to make a stiff dough. Separate it into 8 balls. Flour your work surface and roll out the balls so they are flat and round about the size of a dinner plate. In a bowl, mix together the cheese, egg and the sugar.

Take one piece of dough and put $1/8$th of the cheese mixture into the center. Wet the edges of the pastry and bunch it up, enclosing the filling. Lightly roll down the seam so the pie is flat again, taking care that the pie filling remains enclosed. Continue with the rest of the pies.

Heat the butter in a skillet and fry each pie until its golden on each side. Remove the pies to a platter and sprinkle with cinnamon and powdered sugar or pour honey over them.

Cheese Filled Crescents from Crete / *Kaltsounákia Kritiká*

The island of Crete is rich in tradition and folklore, being the home of myths and legends such as King Minos, the Minotaur and the famous painter El Greco. It's no wonder that they would have a fabulous traditional dessert as well.

This variation of the local recipe fries the cheese filled pies instead of baking them. The sweet crescents can be served as a dessert, with coffee or kept on hand as a great snack.

Ingredients:
2 lbs. flour
2 eggs
⅓ cup olive oil
1 tbs. lemon juice
½ tsp. baking soda
1 cup milk
pinch salt
oil for frying
confectioners sugar or honey

Filling:
2 lbs. Greek *mizíthra* or ricotta cheese
3 eggs
1 cup sugar
1 tbs. cinnamon

Mix together the oil, lemon juice, eggs, soda, and milk. Add the flour and begin kneading it until it becomes a stiff dough. Set it aside. Mix together all the filling ingredients.

Flour your work surface and roll out the dough so it's a thin sheet - ⅛ to ¼ inch thick. Using a cookie cutter, cut out circles about three inches in diameter. Put a spoonful of stuffing into each circle, wet the edges and fold over into crescent shapes. Use your fingers or a fork to crimp the edges.

Heat an inch of oil in a skillet and fry the *Kaltsounákia* until golden on each side. Remove them to paper towels to drain and then arrange them on a platter. Sprinkle them with powdered sugar or pour honey over them before serving.

Fried Phyllo from Thrace / *Kourkoumpínia Thrákis*

In northern Greece, you will find Thrace which has a mixture of Greek and Turkish influences not only in her architecture and languages, but in her cooking as well. This simple recipe is easy to make and because the pastry is cut into small pieces, it's a great idea for a cocktail party dessert.

Ingredients:
1 lb. phyllo pastry sheets
flour
melted butter
1½ lb. sugar
1 tsp. vanilla
oil for frying
ground cinnamon
ground walnuts for sprinkling
1 cup water

You will need a wooden dowel longer than the length of the phyllo and the thickness of a finger -about ½ inch thick.

Lay 2 sheets of phyllo on the counter. Using your fingers, spread a bit of flour on the dowel and lay it on the long end of the phyllo pastry. Wrap the long side around the dowel and continue rolling it up until you are 1 or 2 inches from the edge. Brush some butter on the edges to help keep the phyllo from unraveling and finish rolling up the pastry into a tube around the dowel. Carefully remove the dowel and lay a towel over the finished tube to keep it from drying out. Continue rolling up all the phyllo, and placing the tubes under the towel.

Prepare the syrup by mixing the sugar and water in a pot. Bring it to a boil and simmer it for 2 minutes. Add the vanilla and set it next to your stove.

Heat one inch of oil in a skillet. Cut the phyllo tubes into 1 inch lengths. Drop the pieces into the hot oil, frying them until brown. Using a slotted spoon, let them drain a second over the skillet and then dip them into the syrup. Again, remove them with the slotted spoon and let them drain for a second over the syrup, then put them in a pan or platter. Sprinkle the fried pastry with cinnamon and walnuts. Continue until all the pastry is fried, dipped and sprinkled. Spoon some extra syrup over the finished pastry.

Crispy Pastry in Syrup / *Xirotígana*

The village of *Afántou* in Rhodes holds the tradition that the bride's family gives these pastries to wedding guests along with their printed invitations with trays of the goodies sent to the groom's family as well. It is also customary that these crispy sweets are served on November 30th, which is the name day for St. Andréas.

Ingredients:
oil for frying
sesame
chopped almonds or walnuts

Pastry:
2 cups oil such as corn or soy
1 lb. oranges, juiced
½ tbs. cinnamon
½ tbs. nutmeg
flour

Syrup:
1 cup honey
1 cup sugar
1 cup water
a few drops of rose water - optional

Make the pastry by mixing together the oil and orange juice in a large bowl with the spices. Add enough flour to form it into a stiff dough. Roll it out on a floured surface and cut it into strips 2 to 3 inches wide. Twist a strip of dough so you get a decorative curl and then coil the dough around itself, forming a rosette. Continue with all the dough.

To make your syrup, boil together all the ingredients for 10 minutes and set it next to your work surface. Heat two to three inches of oil in a pot. Drop the pastry into the hot oil and let it fry until golden. Remove the pastry with a slotted spoon and dip it into the syrup. Set the pastry on a platter and sprinkle them with sesame seeds and nuts.

Fried Rice Balls / *Akoúmia*

On the island of *Sími*, this specialty is made on New Year's Eve. Instead of the traditional *Vasilópita*, the *Sími* residence will put a gold coin into one of the *Akoúmia* for the lucky person of the New Year to find.

Ingredients:
oil for frying
powdered sugar
ground cinnamon

Batter:
1 cup rice
4 envelopes yeast
1 cup warm water
2 lbs. flour
1 cup orange juice
1 cup ouzo
½ tsp. salt

Put the rice into a pot and cook it in plain water until it is very soft and over done. Drain it and put it through a blender. Dissolve the yeast in the warm water. Put the flour into a large bowl and add in the rest of the batter ingredients. Mix it well, adding a little water so you have a very thick batter. Wrap it up in a clean kitchen towel and set it aside to rise until doubled. You'll know it's ready when you see bubbles that have popped on the surface.

Heat two inches of oil in a deep skillet. Drop the batter by tablespoonful into the hot oil. Fry them until golden brown and remove them to a platter. Sprinkle the fried *Akoúmia* with powdered sugar and cinnamon or with a good dousing of honey.

The Syrup Pastries and Cakes

Baklavá, Kataífi, Ekmék Kataífi, Amygdalópita..., just to name a few, are what the Greeks refer to as *Siropiastá* or syrup desserts. Each recipe calls for a syrup to be made and poured over the prepared dessert for it to soak in.

Many people believe that the syrups used are made simply with diluted honey and they probably were at one time or another in our history. Today, we often use sugar and water with a few spices to make a light syrup that is not overpowering to the rest of the dessert. For the syrup recipes that do call for it, make sure that you use a very good quality honey so the taste and aroma are not too strong for the delicate flavors of the pastries to come through.

Almond Cake in Syrup / *Amygdalópita Ípirou Siropiastí*

This specialty of *Ípiros* is especially delicious if served with a scoop of ice cream on top.

Ingredients:
8 eggs, separated
1¼ cup sugar
1½ tsp. baking powder
¼ cup good cognac or brandy
1½ cup ground almonds
½ cup very fine bread crumbs
grated rind of 1 lemon
pinch salt

Syrup:
1½ cup sugar
2 cups water
juice of ½ lemon

Preheat your oven to 375°F. Generously butter and flour a 9" x 13" pan. Beat the egg yolks with the sugar until they are a light yellow color. Dilute the baking powder in the cognac and pour into the egg mixture and stir in the almonds, breadcrumbs, and the lemon rind.

In a separate bowl, beat the egg whites with a pinch of salt until stiff peaks form. Fold the egg whites into the yolk mixture gently as to not let the whipped in air escape. Turn the mixture out into your prepared pan and bake for 40 minutes, or until a toothpick inserted in the middle comes out clean.

To make the syrup, boil together the sugar and the water until it reduces to almost half. Be careful as to not let it burn or caramelize. Remove it from the heat and add the lemon juice. Pour the hot syrup over the baked cake. When the cake is completely cooled, run a knife along the inside edge of the pan and serve.

Almond - Brandy Cake / *Amygdalópita Siropiastí*

Although delicious on its own, *Amygdalópita* can be served with whipped cream, and some restaurants have adapted the recipe to include a chocolate or vanilla frosting. Use your imagination, frosted or not, *Amygdalópita* is a wonderful dessert.

There are many fine nut flavored liqueurs on the market. Perhaps something like a hazelnut or almond liqueur would make an interesting variation instead of the brandy.

Cake Ingredients:
8 eggs, separated
1¼ cup sugar
2 tsp. baking powder
¼ cup good quality brandy
2 cups ground almonds
½ cup very fine bread crumbs
1 cup flour
grated rind of 1 lemon or ½ tsp. almond extract
pinch salt

Syrup Ingredients:
1½ cup sugar
1½ cups water
juice of ½ a lemon
¼ to ½ cup Metaxa or good quality brandy

Preheat your oven to 375°F. Generously butter and flour a medium sized sheet cake pan. Beat the egg yolks with the sugar until they are a light yellow color. Dilute the baking powder in the cognac and pour into the egg mixture. Add the almonds, breadcrumbs, flour and the lemon rind.

In a separate bowl, beat the egg whites with a pinch of salt until stiff peaks form. Fold the egg whites into the yolk mixture gently as to not let the whipped in air escape. Turn the mixture out into your prepared pan and bake for 40 minutes, or until a toothpick inserted in the middle comes out clean.

To make the syrup, boil together the sugar and the water until it reduces to about half. Be careful as to not let it burn or caramelize. Remove it from the heat and add the lemon juice and brandy. Pour the hot syrup over the cake and set it aside. Make sure its completely cooled before serving.

Baklavá

The innumerable requests that I have received for this recipe hold as testament to its international popularity. *Baklavá* has always been a timeless, special treat for the Greeks. You can use any kind of nuts or mixture of nuts for this. Almonds, raw peanuts, hazelnuts—use your imagination.

Ingredients:
2 lbs. ready made sheets of phyllo pastry
2 lbs. walnut meats, chopped finely
2 tbs. cinnamon
1 tsp. ground cloves
1 lb. butter

Syrup:
2 lbs. sugar
6 cups of water
vanilla extract
the juice of 1 lemon

Mix the walnuts with the cinnamon and cloves. Butter a baking pan and melt the remaining butter. Spread a pastry sheet into the pan, and brush it with butter. Continue to layer pastry and butter for 3 to 4 sheets. Sprinkle with a layer of walnut mixture. Then resume with pastry sheets, then with nuts, etc. To finish off, layer the last 4 pastry sheets and coat the top sheet with butter. Score with a knife into diamond shapes. Bake at 350°F for 40 to 60 minutes.

To prepare the syrup, mix all the ingredients together and bring to a boil. Cook for 20 minutes, until thick, but not hard. When the *Baklavá* has cooled pour the syrup over it. Let it cool down and serve. *Baklavá* should be kept and served at room temperature.

Kataífi

Like phyllo sheets, *Kataífi* is a very delicate pastry. It resembles angels hair pasta or vermicelli and is made by pouring thin strands of dough batter onto a hot grill that is quickly wiped off. The *Kataífi* rolls are traditionally eaten during the *Apokriés* or Carnival - Mardi Gras weeks before Lent. Other than the pastry itself, *Kataífi* is almost the same as *Baklavá*, so any nut filling recipe can be used amongst the two desserts.

Ingredients:
1 lb. *kataífi* pastry - available from Greek or Middle Eastern specialty shops
½ lb. melted butter

Filling:
1¼ cup ground walnuts
¼ cup sugar
1 tbs. cinnamon
1 beaten egg

Syrup:
3 cups sugar
2¾ cups water
1 tbs. fresh lemon juice
1 tbs. rose or orange blossom water - *anthónero* - optional

Mix together all the filling ingredients and set it aside. Mix together all the syrup ingredients and bring it to a boil, simmering it for 10 minutes. Set the syrup aside to cool. Preheat your oven to 350°F.

Take a small handful of the pastry strands and fluff it up, making a square shaped nest. Spoon some filling in a two inch line in the center of the nest. Fold over the side strands and roll up the nest so you have a nice package that encloses the filling completely.

Place the rolls side by side in a medium sized pan and brush them with the melted butter. Bake them for 35 to 45 minutes until they are golden brown. When the rolls are done, pour the syrup over them and cover the pan with a piece of aluminum foil. Let them cool while covered to soften and absorb the syrup. *Kataífi* is served and stored like *Baklavá* - at room temperature.

Ekmék Kataífi

This dessert is the result of a mixture of the two cultures of Greece and Turkey that probably dates way back into the days of the Turkish occupation. It is enjoyed through out Greece and although it's made with variations, it can be found in almost any Greek restaurant in Europe as well as the United States.

Traditionally, the dessert *Ekmék* is made with a base of *Kataífi* pastry. This pastry resembles angel's hair pasta or vermicelli because its in thin strands. It's raw pastry dough that you can buy in a Greek Specialty shop, but if you can't find it, you can alter the pastry base.

Use a firm cake as the base so it will hold up in the syrup. As a personal thought, I would recommend making Walnut Cake - *Karidópita* or Almond Cake - *Amygdalópita*, right in the pan that you will be using. These are syrup cakes too and will hold up well for you.

Pastry Base Ingredients:
1lb. *kataífi* pastry dough - available from Greek or Middle Eastern specialty shops
½ cup melted unsalted butter

Syrup Ingredients:
½ cup sugar
¼ cup water
1 cinnamon stick
1 tsp. fresh lemon juice

Custard Ingredients:
1½ cup sugar
7 egg yolks
7 tbs. fine semolina flour
6 cups milk
2 tbs. corn flour
1 tsp. vanilla
grated rind of 1 lemon

Topping Ingredients:
2 cups sweetened whipping cream
1 tsp. vanilla

Heat your oven to 375°F. Butter a 9" x 13" pan. Make sure it's deep enough to accommodate the layers of pastry, custard and cream.

Make the base. Take the *Kataífi* pastry and pull the strands apart so it lays light and fluffy on the bottom of the pan. Brush the pastry with the melted butter then put it in the oven to toast. Just a few minutes should be enough, as you want it golden brown.

Make the syrup. In a small saucepan, boil the sugar with the water and cinnamon stick. You only need to boil it until it thickens a bit, but if you prefer thicker syrup, just keep boiling off the water. Be careful though, you don't want the syrup to burn or caramelize. When it's thick enough for your preference, remove from the heat and stir in the lemon juice. Pour the hot syrup over the toasted pastry base. Make the custard. In a medium saucepan, beat the sugar and the egg yolks together. Slowly add the semolina flour, milk, and the corn flour, alternating them until all are incorporated. Move the pan to medium heat and cook this custard, stirring constantly. Again, be careful, you don't want to scorch it, so keep right over it and stir continuously. When the custard thickens, remove from the heat. Beat in the vanilla and the lemon rind then pour the custard over the syrup/pastry base. Let it cool completely before you add the final topping. If you like, you can refrigerate it overnight and make the topping the next day.

Make the Topping. Beat the whipping cream with the vanilla until it's stiff. Spread this over the cooled custard/pastry and there you have it.... *Ekmék*!! You can garnish the *Ekmék* with maraschino cherries, chopped almonds, whole pitted dates, or whatever takes your fancy.

Milk Custard Pie / *Galaktomboúriko*

This recipe hails from the village of *Kalithiés* in Rhodes. This traditional dessert can be made up as a pan pie or small, individual pies can be folded up, using the filling. The individual pies are soaked with the syrup, just as the pan recipe version. If you'd like to try your hand at making the individual pies, see "Using Phyllo Pastry" for details and tips on the technique.

Ingredients:
2 lbs. ready made phyllo sheets
1 cup melted butter

Filling:
10 cups milk
7 tbs. rice flour
5 tbs. corn flour
1 cup sugar
1 tsp. vanilla

Syrup:
2½ cups water
3½ cups sugar
1 cinnamon stick
1 peel from a lemon

In a medium sauce pan mix the cold milk with the flours. Put over medium heat and, stirring constantly, add the sugar and vanilla. Keep stirring until the mixture thickens. Set aside.

Butter a baking pan. Melt the remaining butter. Spread a pastry sheet into the pan, and brush it with butter. Continue to layer pastry and butter for 7 to 8 sheets. Pour the filling over the pastry leaves, and continue to layer another 7 to 8 leaves again. Tuck in any edges of phyllo by folding them under the last layers with a generous brush of butter. Finish off the top layer by brushing with butter and scoring diamond shapes or squares into the phyllo with a sharp knife.

Bake at 350°F for 30 to 40 minutes. While the *Galaktomboúriko* is baking, make the syrup. In a medium sauce pan combine all the ingredients and simmer for 10 minutes, or until it's as thick as you prefer. When you remove the pie from the oven, pour the syrup over it. Let it cool and Enjoy !!

Macedonian Semolina Halva / *Makedonikós Halvás apó Simigdáli*

This recipe uses semolina flour to make a delicious syrup cake that can be eaten on fasting days too. The name may confuse you into thinking store bought, ground sesame seed *halvá*, but they are two entirely different recipes, each delicious in their own way.

Ingredients:
2 cups olive oil
2 lbs. coarse semolina flour
5 cups sugar or 2 cups honey
1 cup chopped blanched almonds
8 cups water
ground cinnamon

Prepare a medium size bundt form by lining it with butter and wax paper.
Heat the oil in a deep skillet. Add the semolina and fry it until it begins to turn golden brown.
In a separate pot, heat the water with the sugar or honey. Boil it until it begins to get syrupy. Using a ladle, spoon the hot liquid into the semolina mixture while whisking all the time. Keep stirring until all the syrup has been incorporated and add the almonds. Pour the *halvá* into the prepared form and set it aside to cool. Turn the *halvá* out onto a platter and peel away the wax paper. Sprinkle it with cinnamon and serve.

Walnut Cake / *Karidópita*

A traditional Greek dessert that is simple to make. This is excellent with fresh whipped cream.

Ingredients:
2 cups chopped walnuts
1 tsp. cinnamon
¼ tsp. ground cloves
1½ cups dry bread crumbs
1½ cups flour
3 tsp. baking powder
1 tsp. soda
2 tbs. cognac
½ cup butter
1 cup sugar
5 eggs
1 cup milk

Syrup:
2 cups of sugar
1 cups of water
2 tbs. cognac
1 tbs. orange juice
1 cinnamon stick
1 tbs. lemon juice

Preheat the oven to 350°F. Butter and flour a 9" x 13" baking pan. In a bowl combine the walnuts, cinnamon, cloves, breadcrumbs, flour, and baking powder. In a small glass, dilute the soda with the cognac. In a large mixer bowl, cream the butter with the sugar and then add the eggs. Mix in the soda with cognac, and add the milk and the walnut mixture, beating until well combined. Spread into the prepared baking pan. Bake for 45 to 60 minutes, or until the center is firm.

Prepare the syrup by mixing all the ingredients together, except for the lemon juice, in a medium sauce pan. Bring it to a boil and let it thicken until it's to your preference and stir in the lemon juice. Pour it over the baked cake. Let the cake cool completely before serving.

Yogurt Pie / *Yiaourtópita*

From Attica, this recipe has roots that date back to the days of the Classical Greeks in Egypt. It's a simple recipe but absolutely delicious.

Ingredients:
1 cup butter
1 cup sugar
3 cups, strained yogurt - see "Concoctions for the Greek Kitchen"
1 tbs. flour
3 tsp. baking powder
1 lb. semolina flour
whole blanched almonds

Syrup:
2 cups sugar
2 cups water
1 cinnamon stick - optional
juice of ½ lemon

Preheat oven to 375°F. Butter a 9" x 13" pan. Cream the butter. Add the sugar, yogurt, flour, baking powder and the semolina. Your batter will look like a thick puree. Pour the mixture into your prepared pan. Arrange the blanched almonds on the surface in any design that you like. Bake for 40 minutes or until the center is firm. Remove from the oven and set aside.

Make the syrup. Boil together the sugar, water and the cinnamon until the liquid reduces to about half. Be careful as to not let it burn or caramelize. Remove it from the heat and add the lemon juice. Pour the hot syrup over the cake and set it aside to cool.

Cookies, Sweet Biscuits, and Bars

Greek cookies and biscuits are often eaten for breakfast dunked into coffee as well as eaten as a midnight snack, just like the western milk and cookies combination.

For holidays such as Christmas and Easter, baskets of cookies are made to be given to mother-in-laws, *Koumpári*—see "Greek Weddings & Baptisms," as well as kept on hand in the home to share with company when they come calling.

Chocolate Chestnut Bars / *Glykó me Kástana Attikís*

Chestnuts are abundant during the winter season in Greece. The recipe for these chocolaty and delicious bars comes from Attica.

Ingredients:
3 cups shelled chestnuts
1 cup sweetened chocolate, grated
½ cup butter
½ cup sugar
1 tsp. vanilla

Preheat your oven to 375°F. Butter a 9" x 9" pan, line it with waxed paper and then butter the paper. In a medium saucepan, boil the chestnuts in plain water. When they are tender, remove them from the heat, drain them and peel off the loose skins. Using a food processor, puree the cooked chestnuts. While still warm, add the chocolate, butter, sugar and vanilla to the puree.

Turn the mixture out into your prepared pan and bake in the oven until the top is golden brown. Let it cool completely, then turn it out of the pan. Remove the wax paper and slice into bars.

Easter Cookies / *Koulourákia Pascaliná*

These traditional sweet cookies are found in every home at Easter time and they are also given to friends and relatives as part of their Easter Baskets.

Get creative using your Easter eggs too. Wrap a rope of dough around them so they can be baked into the cookie itself these are called *Avgoúles*. My mom used to coil dough around an egg and left a small piece straight so it resembled a flat snail and had two whole cloves pushed in for eyes.

The most famous of all *Avgoúles* is the *Ófios* or viper. Again, a rope of dough is coiled, forming the shape of a snake. The front of the coil is cut and a dyed egg is inserted into its mouth.

Ingredients:
2 cups butter
1½ cup sugar
4 egg yolks
½ cup milk or fresh orange juice
8 cups flour
2 tsp. baking powder
1 tsp. vanilla
1 tsp. grated orange rind – optional
1 egg - beaten

Cream the butter and the sugar. Add the egg yolks one at a time, beating well after each addition. Stir in the milk, vanilla, orange rind, 2 cups of the flour and the baking powder. Mix it all together. Gradually add the rest of the flour. You will have to work with your hands as the dough will get rather stiff.

Break off small portions – about the size of walnuts or golf balls and roll them into ropes about the size of a pencil. These can be arranged into circles or coiled length wise, resembling an "N" shape. Place your cookies on an un-greased baking sheet and brush the tops with the beaten egg. Bake at 350°F for 20 minutes.

For larger cookies such as *Avgoúles*, use bigger pieces of dough to roll out for the coils. Get as decorative as you like, using a knife to cut small details into the dough and spices to dress it up.

Short Bread Biscuits / *Kourambiédes*

Traditional at Christmas time, these crumbly cookies can be shaped into rounds, diamonds, or crescents or even cut out with large cookie cutters. They are served covered in powdered sugar and offered to guests and relatives that come for coffee over the holidays. You'll often find these cookies given as gifts as well.

You can layer the *Kourambiédes* on top of each other pyramid style to fill your platter up, just dust each layer with more powdered sugar before you start the next or they can be set into muffin papers which keeps them much neater. Store the *Kourambiédes* covered in a cookie tin and they'll keep for up to a month.

Ingredients:
2 cups unsalted butter, softened
½ cup confectioners sugar
1 egg yolk
3 tsp. vanilla, ouzo or brandy
1 cup chopped almonds
4 to 5 cups flour
confectioners sugar - for dusting
orange or rose water for spritzing - optional

Preheat your oven to 350°F. In a mixing bowl, cream the butter. Mix in the sugar, egg yolk and flavoring and beat until creamy. Slowly stir in by hand the almonds and 2 cups of flour. When adding the rest of the flour, the dough will begin to stiffen but will still be on the soft side. Use your hands to knead it just until smooth and add only enough flour so that it doesn't stick to your fingers.

Divide the dough in half and roll out each half into ropes about 12 inches long. Use a knife and cut the snake into 1-inch pieces. Form the pieces into the desired shapes, rounds or crescents, or slice it diagonally for diamond shapes. You can also flatten out a ball of dough and use a floured cookie cutter to cut out shapes. Arrange the cookies on an un-greased cookie sheet about 2 inches apart as they tend to spread. Bake for 20 to 25 minutes or until they've turned slightly golden in color. Note that these cookies shouldn't brown and should stay almost dough colored.

Take a sheet of wax paper or a large flat pan and sprinkle it generously with powdered sugar. Remove the hot cookies from the cookie sheet right onto the powdered sugar. Spritz the cookies with flavored or plain water and sift lots of confectioners' sugar over them. Allow them to cool. Remove the cooled cookies onto a platter or place them into muffin papers. Sprinkle them with more powdered sugar if needed.

Sesame Honey Bars / *Melekoúni*

These toasted sesame bars are traditionally made for celebrations such as Greek weddings and baptisms. It is symbolic of a sweet life with many children. Blanched almonds can be pressed into the warm bars for a bit of zip. The *Melekoúni* is cut into diamond shapes and the bars are wrapped in colorful cellophane.

Ingredients:
1½ cup sesame seeds
1 cup thick honey

Preheat the oven to 350°F. Spread the sesame seeds in a shallow roasting pan and toast them in the oven for 5 minutes, stirring occasionally. Put the honey in a sauce pan and boil it over moderate heat until it foams. Remove it from the heat and add the sesame seeds. Cook it for 2 to 3 minutes longer, stirring constantly.

Lightly oil a marble or formica surface. Pour the hot sesame mixture on it and pat down with a damp spatula. Wet the edge of a large knife and cut the *Melekoúni* into bars. When it has cooled, remove the bars to a plate and store in a cool, dry place or wrap up each piece individually in cellophane. This does get messy. To help you along, keep a bowl of water near by and dip your knife and hands into it occasionally.

Phoenician Stuffed Biscuits / *Finíkia*

These delicate syrup drenched cookies are traditional for Christmas time. Platters of *Finíkia* are given to friends and relatives as holiday gifts. For a more elaborate presentation, set each finished cookie into a muffin paper and stack them up, pyramid style on your platter.

An unstuffed version of this cookie is known as Honey Macaroons or *Melomakárouna*.

Ingredients:
Filling:
1 ½ cups chopped walnuts, almonds or hazelnuts
⅓ cup sugar
1 tsp. cinnamon
½ tsp. ground cloves
½ tsp. ground nutmeg
1 tsp. rose or orange blossom water - *anthónero*

Cookies:
1 cup oil
1 cup butter
2 cups sugar
1 cup orange juice
3 tsp. baking powder
1 tbs. cinnamon
1 tbs. nutmeg
½ tsp. baking soda
grated rind of 2 oranges
3 to 4 lbs. flour

Syrup:
2 cups honey
1 cup water
1 cinnamon stick

Extra chopped nuts or sesame seeds for garnish

In a small bowl, mix together the filling ingredients and set it aside.

Heat the butter with the oil until it melts. Let it cool slightly and stir in the sugar. Stir in the rest of the cookie ingredients and mix in enough flour so you have a soft cookie dough that you can handle.

Preheat your oven to 350°F. Take a walnut sized piece of dough and flatten it into a circle. Some ladies flatten the dough over an upside down dish that has cut-glass designs for a more elaborate surface. Place a spoonful of walnuts in the center and enclose the dough around it, forming it into an oval cylinder or log shape. Put the cookie onto a greased cookie sheet, seam side down and pat it down slightly. Proceed with the rest of the dough and the filling.

Bake the cookies 10 to 15 minutes, until they are golden brown. While the cookies are baking, make your syrup. Mix together the syrup ingredients in a sauce pan and boil it for 10 minutes. Remove the pot from the heat and set it close to your work area along with a platter or pan for the cookies to go into.

As the cookies finish baking, using a spatula or slotted spoon, dip the cookies into the syrup for 30 seconds and then set them in your pan or platter and sprinkle them with chopped nuts. Continue with all the cookies. When the bottom of one pan has been completely filled with cookies, start another pan so the cookies remain in single layers. Once the cookies have cooled off completely, they can be arranged in muffin papers and sprinkled with extra chopped nuts if desired.

Honey Macaroons / *Melomakárouna*

Melomakárouna are very similar to Phoenician Stuffed Biscuits except that these treats are not stuffed. Instead, the nuts are incorporated right into the dough. The crumbly cookies are soaked in syrup and served in muffin papers with a sprinkling of chopped nuts. They are traditional for the Christmas holidays too, so make up a batch of each recipe for a great holiday treat.

Ingredients:
Cookies:
2 cups oil
1 cup sugar
1 cup orange juice
½ cup water
1 tbs. honey
1 cup chopped walnuts
3 tsp. baking powder
1 tsp. soda
1 tbs. nutmeg
½ tsp. cinnamon
½ tsp. ground cloves
grated rind of one orange
3 to 4 lbs. flour

Syrup:
1 cup honey
1 cup water
1 cup sugar
1 cinnamon stick

Extra chopped nuts or sesame seeds for garnish

Mix the oil with the sugar in a large mixing bowl and add all the ingredients except for the flour. Mix it well and begin adding in the flour, a cup full at a time, working it with your hands until you have a soft cookie dough that you can handle.

Preheat your oven to 350°F. Take a walnut sized piece of dough and shape it into an oblong oval. Some ladies press the cookie on an upside down dish that has cut-glass designs for a more elaborate surface. Put the cookie onto a greased cookie sheet. Proceed with the rest of the dough.

Bake the cookies 10 to 15 minutes, until they are golden brown. While the cookies are baking, make your syrup. Mix together the syrup ingredients in a sauce pan and boil it for 10 minutes. Remove the pot from the heat and set it close to your work area along with a platter or pan for the cookies to go into.

As the cookies finish baking, using a spatula or slotted spoon, dip the cookies into the syrup for 30 seconds and then set them in your pan or platter and sprinkle them with chopped nuts. Continue with all the cookies. When the bottom of one pan has been completely filled with cookies, start another pan so the cookies remain in single layers. Once the cookies have cooled off completely, they can be arranged in muffin papers, sprinkling them with more nuts if desired.

Almond Meringue Biscuits / *Amigdalotá*

For a melt in your mouth treat, this is the recipe to use. *Amigdalotá* can be found in every pastry shop in Greece. The delicate biscuits are often given as gifts when visiting friends and family, to be shared over coffee and good conversation.

Ingredients:
4 cups finely chopped almonds
3 cups sugar
1½ tsp. baking powder
½ cup fine bread crumbs.
10 egg whites

Mix together the almonds, baking powder and bread crumbs with half the sugar. Beat the egg whites until stiff peaks form and beat in the remaining sugar a little at a time until it's all incorporated. Fold the mixture into the dry ingredients.

Preheat your oven to 375°F. Grease a cookie sheet and using a pastry bag with a wide tip, make swirls about 2 inches in diameter. Press an almond into the center and bake until they are golden. Let them cool down a few minutes before you remove them from the cookie sheet with a spatula.

Oil cookies / *Koulourákia Ladioú*

These cookies contain no dairy products and are often served during a religious fast such as the Lenten season.

Ingredients:
3 lbs. flour
1 tbs. baking powder
1½ cup oil
½ cup ash water - *alisíva* - see "Concoctions for the Greek Kitchen"
½ cup fresh orange juice
2½ cups sugar
1 tbs. grated lemon peel
1 cup cognac
1 tsp. cinnamon
1 tsp. ground cloves
1 tsp. soda
sesame seeds

Sift together the flour with the baking powder. In a bowl, mix together the the oil, ash water, sugar, and orange juice until the sugar dissolves. Stir in the lemon peel, cognac, cinnamon, cloves, and soda.

Add the flour into the mixture, a little at a time, mixing well after each addition. When the dough becomes stiff, knead the dough using your hands until it's smooth and can be rolled out. If the dough is too soft, add a bit of flour or for a hard, dry dough, add a bit of water.

Preheat your oven to 350°F. Take egg sized pieces of dough and roll them into ropes, forming them into twists or wreath cookies. Place the cookies on a greased cookie sheet and use a mixture of sugar and water to glaze them. Sprinkle them with sesame seeds and bake for 15 to 20 minutes.

Moonshine Cookies / *Kouloúria me Rakí*

Although this recipe hails from *Chíos*, the island of mastic, the choice of using this spice is optional. No water is used for making the dough, only the Greek home-made spirit, *rakí*. If you would like to experiment, try substituting a nut flavored extract along with a nut flavored liqueur to replace the moon shine.

Ingredients:
5 lbs. white flour
½ lb. softened butter
½ lb. sugar
3 tbs. baking powder
1 tbs. ground mastic - see "Mystic Mastic"
rakí or strong vodka

In a large bowl, mix together the flour, butter, sugar, baking powder and mastic. Add little bits of *rakí* or vodka, kneading the dough as you go along so you get a consistency that is easy to roll. Flour your work surface and roll out the dough into 6 or 7 inch ropes. Fold them in half, then twist them once or twice. Lay the finished cookie on a greased sheet and continue with the rest of the dough. Bake the cookies at 375°F for 15 to 20 minutes.

Loukoúmia

Although these sweet jelly-like candies are also known as Turkish Delight, some old villagers argue that they definitely come from Greek origin and became misnamed during the centuries of the Turkish occupation. Whatever the roots of this sweet may be, they are a delicious treat to have around the house.

Ingredients:
4 cups sugar
½ cup corn syrup
6 cups water
2 pkgs. unflavored gelatin
1 cup corn flour
1 tbs. rose or orange blossom water - *anthónero*
½ cup chopped almonds - optional
1 tsp. vanilla
½ tsp. ground mastic - see "Mystic Mastic"
red or green food coloring - optional
powdered sugar

Prepare a medium sized sheet pan by greasing it generously and lining it with wax paper.

In a pot, stir together the sugar, corn syrup, water, gelatin, corn flour, and almonds. Simmer the mixture until it's thick and stir in the vanilla and mastic. If you would like some color to your *Loukoúmia*, add a few drops of food coloring just so you get a light, pastel color. Pour the mixture into the prepared pan and set it aside to cool completely.

Sprinkle powdered sugar on a flat work surface and over turn the pan onto it. Remove the wax paper and sprinkle the entire block with powdered sugar, so it's less sticky to work with. Using a sharp knife, cut the block into narrow strips and then cross wise again, so you have small cubes about 1 x 1 inch. Roll each cube in powdered sugar and set them an a platter to finish setting. The *Loukoúmia* are ready to enjoy.

The Spoon Sweets - *Glyká Koutalioú*

Under the structure of the *apokrévato* or the bed of a village home, you'll find a storage area such as this. The huge clay jugs are for holding the olive oil supply where as the smaller pots and jugs are used for a diverse assortment of purposes.

With the summer months come high abundances of tomatoes, cucumbers, baby eggplants as well as the summer fruits. The Greeks use a bit of sugar and turn these fresh vegetables and fruits into Spoon Sweets that preserve the taste of the summer months, the whole year round.

Spoon Sweets are often served to guests that come to visit a family home. These home made preserves are served on a small dessert plate to be eaten with a spoon. Hence the name "Spoon Sweets."

There are many varieties of these fresh preserves, using all kinds of fruits and vegetables as well. They are simmered in sugar and spices until the preserves are thick and are kept in simple glass jars. They keep wonderfully and are an excellent substitute for store bought preserves and jams.

I've looked through volumes and volumes written about Greek preserve making and I have to say that personally, I don't think that there is any great mystique about making spoon sweets. True, each fruit and vegetable has it's own preparation method that should be followed and some recipes are very time consuming and take days to finish. But for most of these Greek preserves, it's a simple process of simmering sugar and water with spices and the main ingredient for a delicious dessert.

Whole Apricot Preserves / *Chrisómila Glykó*

The Greeks call this delicious fruit *Veríkoka*, *Kaísia*, and *Chrisómila* or golden apples. They grow in almost every yard in the islands and the markets are full with them in the summer months. This spoon sweet is one of the more popular recipes that is used to preserve the fresh summer taste, all year round.

When cleaning the apricots in days gone by, the pits were not thrown away. Other than being used in liqueur making, and as toys by the children, the apricot pits were cracked open like almonds and the tender meats would be mashed in a mortar and pestle with a little sugar. This paste mixture was known as *Matzoúni* and the village children would eat it with a spoon, right out of the mortar.

Ingredients:
2 lbs. whole firm apricots
lime water - optional - see "Concoctions for the Greek Kitchen"
whole blanched almonds - optional
2 lbs. sugar
2 cups water
¼ cup lemon juice
1 tsp. vanilla - optional

Wash the apricots in soap and water to remove any traces of dust and pesticides. Set them aside to drain. Take an apricot in your hand, holding the stem end up and using a clean screw driver or small knife, dig out the pit. If this is too difficult for you, try to push the pit out the other end, but be careful that you don't stick your hand with the knife. Continue to remove the pits of all the apricots.

You can peel off the thin skins of the apricots, or leave them in tact as I do, for a simpler version. If you do choose to leave the skins on, wipe the fuzz off with a kitchen towel after you have washed them. Fill each apricot with a blanched almond. To simplify again, if you don't feel like taking the time to stuff each fruit, you can just throw a handful of almonds into the cooking preserves later.

By using the lime water, you'll have a firmer fruit preserve. Personally, I don't use the lime water because I like the fruit in my preserve to be softer. If you do choose to use it, put the apricots into a glass or enamel bowl and cover them with the lime water. Let them sit submerged for 2 hours. Drain them and rinse them very well under running water, setting them aside in a colander.

In a pot, combine the sugar with the water and bring it to a boil. Add the apricots and almonds, if you didn't stuff the fruit with them, and boil the mixture together. Foam and froth will collect on the surface of the cooking apricots, remove this with a spoon and discard. Keep boiling the fruit until they soften—30 minutes. Stir in the lemon juice and cover the pot with a cloth towel. Let the apricots cool down in the syrup for 5 to 6 hours or over night. This is done because they will release more liquid during this time and make the syrup thin again.

After they have cooled, bring the mixture back to a boil, and simmer it until the syrup is as thick as you prefer then stir in the vanilla. Some ladies say that a temperature of 200°F to 210°F on a candy thermometer is good for this spoon sweet, but I always let my own preference decide. Let the sweet cool down and pack it into clean, sterile jars.

Bergamot Spoon Sweet / *Pergamónto Glykó*

The sweet smell of bergamot is used to make home made perfumes and home air fresheners. This aromatic fruit is also used to make a delicious spoon sweet. The process is long and a bit complicated because of the bitterness in the fruit peel, but the finished product is great.

Ingredients:
14 medium sized bergamot
4 lbs. sugar
2 cups water
¼ cup fresh lemon juice
1 cup bergamot juice

Wash the bergamot to get rid of any dust and pesticides. Gently grate the peel just enough for it to release the alcohol aroma. Cut the bergamot into quarters and discard the inner flesh, reserving the peel. Remember to juice one of the fruits so it can be added to the preserve.

Cut the peel into strips less than ½ inch wide. Rinse the peels and set them in a pot with enough water to cover them. Bring it to a boil and simmer them until they soften. Drain the peels and return them to the pot. Cover them again with water and set them aside to soak over night.

The next day, drain the peels and set them in the sun, on a cloth covered tray to dry for 6 to 8 hours. Return the peels to the pot and cover them with the sugar. Let them stand for 1 hour. Add the water and bring it to a boil, simmering the peels until the syrup is thick. Stir in the juices and cook for 1 minute longer. Remove the pot from the heat and let it cool. Pack the sweet into clean, sterile jars.

Bitter Orange Spoon Sweet / *Nerantzáki Glykó*

Bitter oranges are used in Greek preserving and the peels lend their aroma to other preserves too. This "old ways" village recipe will take 10 days to complete, which may seem very long, but it's necessary because the soaking time will get rid of the bitterness in the orange peel.

Ingredients:
50 small, hard, green bitter oranges, also called Seville Oranges
3 lbs. sugar
½ cup bitter orange juice
2 tbs. lemon juice

Wash the oranges with soap and water to remove any dust and pesticides. Set them in a pot and boil them with clean water for 1 hour. Drain and rinse them thoroughly and set them aside to cool. Using an apple corer, push through the stem end to the opposite side, removing the seeds. Put the oranges into a pot and cover them with water. Let them soak for eight (8) days, changing the water 2 or 3 times each day. During this time, taste an orange and see if the bitterness has gone, in which case, proceed with the recipe.

Put the sugar in a pot and add 2½ cups of water. Bring it to a boil and then set it aside. Add the drained oranges to the syrup and let them soak for 24 hours. The next day, bring the pot to a boil and simmer the sweet until the oranges are tender and the syrup is as thick as you prefer. Stir in the juices and cook for one minute longer. Remove from the heat and let it cool. Put the sweet into clean, sterile jars.

Cherry Spoon Sweet / *Kerási Glykó*

This simple preserve is very easy to make and cooks up very quickly. The most time consuming part of the whole recipe is pitting the cherries but once this step is done, it only takes about half an hour to get a delicious homemade fresh spoon sweet.

Ingredients:
3 lbs. cherries
3 lbs. sugar
1 cup water
2 tbs. fresh lemon juice
2 tsp. vanilla - optional

Wash the cherries to remove any dust and pesticides. Remove the stems and pits using a knife or pitter gadget. In a pot, add the sugar and the water and bring it to a boil, stirring it so the sugar dilutes and it begins to thicken. Add the cherries and simmer the mixture until the cherries are done and the syrup is thick. Stir in the lemon juice, simmer it for 1 minute longer and remove it from the heat to cool. Pack the sweet into clean, sterile jars.

Dry Fruit Sweet / *Glykó apó Xirá Froúta*

This recipe uses ready dry fruits as the main ingredient. You can leave the fruits whole or halved, or you can cut them into smaller pieces. Served over plain yogurt or ice cream, this makes for a fast and easy dessert.

Ingredients:
1 lb. dry fruits such as apricots, figs, plums, pineapple
1 cup sugar
¼ cup raisins
1 tbs. grated lemon peel
½ cup orange juice

Put the dry fruits into a pot and soak them for 24 hours in just enough water to cover them. The next day, bring them to a boil, adding the rest of the ingredients, simmer it for 20 to 30 minutes until the syrup is thick. Remove it from the heat to cool. Pack the sweet into clean, sterile jars.

Eggplant Spoon Sweet / *Melintzanáki Glykó*

Ingredients:
60 baby eggplants
lime water - optional - see "Concoctions for the Greek Kitchen"
½ cup lemon juice
60 blanched almonds
3 lbs. sugar
2 cups water
2 tsp. vanilla
1 cinnamon stick
whole cloves - optional
2 tbs. lemon juice

Wash the eggplants to remove any dust and pesticides and peel them. Make a small incision on the side of each eggplant. Soak the eggplants in a bowl with ½ cup lemon juice and enough water to cover them. An inverted plate helps to keep them submerged while they soak for 1 to 2 hours. The lime water will cause a firmer fruit preserve. My preference is for softer fruit in my preserves, so I don't use the lime water. If you choose to use it, put the eggplants into a glass or enamel bowl and cover them with the lime water. Let them sit submerged for two hours. Drain them and rinse very well under running water.

Drain the eggplants from the lemon water and put them in a pot with enough water to cover them. Bring them to a boil and simmer them for 10 minutes. Drain the eggplants and return them to the bowl, covering them again with water. Let them soak for 2 to 3 hours, changing the water every hour.

Drain the eggplant and push an almond into each of the incisions that you made. Put the sugar in the pot with 2 cups of water, bring it to a boil and let it simmer until the syrup just begins to thicken. Add the eggplants and soak them overnight in the syrup. The next day, add the vanilla, cinnamon and cloves and simmer the eggplants until the syrup is thick. Remove it from the heat and stir in the lemon juice and let it cool. Use a slotted spoon to put the eggplants into clean, sterile jars then pour the syrup over them.

Fig Spoon Sweet / *Síko Gkykó*

Ingredients:
2 lbs. very firm figs
lime water - optiona l- see "Concoctions for the Greek Kitchen"
2 lbs. sugar
2 cups water
1 cup plus 2 tbs. fresh lemon juice

Wash the figs to remove any dirt and pesticides. The lime water will cause a firmer fruit preserve. My preference is for softer fruit in my preserves, so I don't use the lime water. If you choose to use it, put the eggplants into a glass or enamel bowl and cover them with the lime water. Let them sit submerged for two hours. Drain them and rinse very well under running water. Using a small knife, cut the stem and cut out the bottom "eye," inspecting each fig for worms and other pests. Discard any that you think may be infected. Put the figs into a pot and bring them to a boil for 5 to 10 minutes. Strain the figs and discard the water. Repeat this process two more times to get rid of any bitterness in the skins and to soften them. Pierce a fig with a fork, it should fall off easily, this means that they are soft enough to continue.

Drain the figs and set them in a bowl. Add 1 cup of lemon juice and enough cold water to cover them. Let them set in the lemon water for 3 hours.

In a pot, dilute the sugar with the water. Bring the syrup to a boil and remove it from the heat. Drain the figs from the lemon water and add them to the syrup. Cover the pot with a towel and let them sit for 24 hours.

The next day, bring the figs to a boil and simmer them until the syrup is thick. Gently stir in the 2 tbs. lemon juice, simmer it for 1 minute longer and remove it from the heat to cool. Pack the sweet into clean, sterile jars.

Grape Spoon Sweet / *Stafíli Glykó*

A traditional sweet made at the end of summer when there are literally tons of grapes. It is served plain, spooned in a dish, with a cup of thick Greek coffee when company calls. This is great with peanut butter as a sandwich.

Ingredients:
2 pounds seedless white grapes
2 cinnamon sticks
1½ pounds sugar
1 tbs. lemon juice

Remove the stems from the grapes and wash under cold running water. Drain well in a colander. In a deep pot, put the grapes, sugar, and ¾ cup cold water. Cook at medium heat, stirring occasionally until the sugar dissolves. Add the cinnamon and increase heat to moderate, and remove any froth that collects on top. Cook until the syrup is thick. Stir in the lemon juice and remove from the heat. Cool and put into sterilized jars.

Pear Spoon Sweet / *Ahládi Glykó*

The pear spoon sweets make for a very pretty presentation because the small fruits sit beautifully on the dish. Serve it with yogurt or ice cream as well as a plain vanilla custard for an elaborate dessert.

Cinnamon is called for as an optional flavoring, but using it will turn the fruits a little brown in color. If this doesn't matter to you, I would suggest using it because the tastes go together wonderfully.

Ingredients:
2 lbs. small green pears
2 lbs. sugar
1 cinnamon stick - optional
½ cup. lemon juice
2 tsp. vanilla - optional

Wash the pears and set them aside to drain. In a large bowl, mix two quarts or so of water with half of the lemon juice. Peel the skins from the pears and use an apple corer to remove the core and seeds. Put the pears into the lemon water and let them sit for 2 hours.

Drain the pears and set them in a pot. Add the sugar and one cup of water with the cinnamon stick, if you're using it. As the water heats, the sugar will dilute and the pears will also begin to release their liquid. If needed, add little bits of water in stages, until all the sugar has diluted and you have the beginnings of a syrup. Simmer the fruit for 40 minutes, skimming any froth that may collect on the surface. Add the rest of the lemon juice and simmer it until the syrup is as thick as you like. Remove it from the heat and stir in the vanilla. Let it cool and put the sweet into clean, sterile jars.

Quince Spoon Sweet / *Kithóni Glykó*

In my family, this is a favorite dessert that always has to be kept on hand. Peanut butter and jelly takes on a new meaning when this preserve is used and it's also a great topping for plain yogurt and pancakes.

Ingredients:
4 lbs. quince
4 lbs. sugar
rose geranium stem or cinnamon stick
water
½ cup fresh lemon juice

Wash the quince to remove any dust and pesticides. Remove the tough peel and any dark spots on the fruit. The fruit can be grated or can be sliced thinly into wedges. Quince is a very hard fruit, so I prefer to slice it, saving my hands from the grater. Put the prepared fruit into a bowl with lemon juice mixed with water until you are ready to cook it, so it doesn't turn brown.

Drain the quince and put it in a pot. Cover it with the sugar and add the cinnamon or geranium. As it simmers, the quince will release it's own liquid, but if needed, add more water, a little bit at a time until the sugar is diluted. Simmer the mixture until the quince is done and the syrup is as thick as you prefer. Stir in the lemon juice and remove it from the heat. Let it cool down. Have some clean, sterile jars ready and pack your spoon sweet into them.

Strawberry Spoon Sweet / *Glykó Fráoulas*

This has to be the fastest of all the spoon sweet recipes. Strawberries are a soft fruit so their cooking time is minimal. The finished preserve can be used as a dessert or topping as well as a bread spread.

Ingredients:
2 lbs. fresh strawberries
1 lb. sugar
1 cup water
2 tbs. fresh lemon juice

Wash and hull the strawberries and set them in a pot. Cover the strawberries with the sugar and add the water. Simmer the mixture for 3 minutes.

Using a slotted spoon, remove the strawberries to clean and sterile jars. Return the syrup to the heat and continue to cook it until it's thick. Stir in the lemon juice, simmer it for 1 minute longer and remove it from the heat to cool. Pour it over the strawberries.

Green Walnut Spoon Sweet / *Karidáki Glykó*

Making this preserve definitely requires some work and lots of planning ahead. The whole process of this "old ways" village recipe takes sixteen days to finish. Although I've never had the sweet myself, I'm told that it's absolutely worth the effort.

The recipe says to keep the walnuts covered during cooking and hot soaking. This is so that the skins don't wrinkle like a raisin so make sure that you do this. But then again, even if they do crinkle a little bit, I'm sure that they will still taste good.

In the Greek islands, we use fresh walnuts that are available in early May that have not formed their hard shells. Check if the walnuts are tender by sticking an upholstery needle through them. If they pierce with little effort, then they are alright to use in this recipe. During the soaking phase of this process, taste a walnut to see if the bitterness is gone, in which case, proceed with the recipe.

Ingredients:
4 lbs. green whole walnuts
8 lbs. sugar
water
2 cinnamon sticks
½ tbs. whole cloves
1 tsp. vanilla extract
juice of 2 lemons

Begin by washing the walnuts in soapy water and rinsing them well to get rid of any pesticides and dirt. Set them in a colander to drain. Using your upholstery needle, pierce through each walnut twice. From top to bottom and then from side to side, so you've made a cross. You might also like to wear a pair of rubber gloves when you do this as the moisture from the skins will turn your hands a dirt color.

Put the walnuts in large pail or bowl and cover them with water. Let them soak for seven (7) days, changing the water each day. On the 8th day, put them into a large pot with a lid and cover them with clean water. Boil them covered for 30 minutes and let them remain in the covered pot over night.

The next day, drain the walnuts from the old water and again, cover them with clean water. Let them soak for five (5) more days, changing the water every day. On the 6th day, boil them covered for 30 minutes and then let them sit again in the covered pot.

On the next day, rinse the walnuts under running water and drain them in a colander. To a large pot add the walnuts, sugar, enough water to cover them, the cinnamon, cloves and vanilla. Cover the pot and bring it to a simmer. Cook them for 30 minutes and then set them aside, covered until the next day.

Finally, you will uncover the pot and bring the mixture to a boil, paying close attention that it doesn't boil over as it gets to be a sticky mess to clean up. Cook the walnuts until the syrup is the consistency that you like. Stir in the lemon juice and let it cook for 5 minutes more. Remove the pot from the heat and let it all cool down. Have some clean, sterile jars ready and pack your spoon sweet into them.

Walnut Meats in Syrup / *Karídia Glykó*

This recipe is a sister version of the Green Walnut Spoon Sweet but is much easier and less time consuming to make. True, you will have to sit down and shell the walnuts before they are used, but the actual recipe process takes just two days. You can use the finished spoon sweet as a dessert or a topping on any cake or pudding. And don't forget the prospect of using it with ice cream.

Ingredients:
1½ lbs walnut meats
4 lbs. sugar
4 cups water
1 cinnamon stick
½ tbs. whole cloves
1 tsp. vanilla extract.
juice of 1 lemon

Rinse the walnut meats under running water making sure that there are no hard shells in them. In a large pot, bring the walnuts to a boil with enough water to cover them. Reduce the heat and simmer them until they are tender. You can check for tenderness by using a needle or some other sharp tool to pierce them. If this is done easily, they're ready. Drain the walnuts in a sieve and then lay them out on a thick cloth towel for the moisture to be absorbed.

In a large pot, bring the sugar and water to a boil. Add the cinnamon, cloves and vanilla and cook it for 10 minutes then remove it from the heat to cool down. When the syrup is just warm to the touch, stir in the walnuts and let them rest in the syrup for 24 hours.

The next day, bring the mixture to a boil. Reduce your heat so it simmers, being careful that the syrup doesn't boil over. When the syrup is to the consistency that you prefer, stir in the lemon juice. Let it cook and thicken for 5 minutes longer, then remove from the heat. Let it cool down for a few hours then pack your spoon sweet into clean, sterile jars.

Preserving and Pickling
Toursés

The Greek Olive

Greeks preserve many good foods, but perhaps the most famous are the Greek olives. When visiting my home town Baltimore, I've been asked on every single journey that I've made to bring preserved olives for my American friends. Although they can purchase canned Greek olives in any supermarket, they prefer the island variety.

The difference is that the olives that we preserve here in the islands are hand picked and preserved in small batches, enough to last for only one season. They are crisp and flavorful where as many commercially packed olives are bruised by machinery as they are picked and will become mushy and very salty as they sit in the brine for long periods of time. Many commercial packers will also heat the olives and brine during the canning process to sterilize and seal the containers, something that is just not done to island olives.

Olive picking season begins about the end of October in the islands when the rains have started. Since there is no precipitation during the summer months, the olives are very small and rock hard. After the first few rains fall, the olives begin to fatten up and ripen.

In our grandmothers days, the entire family would get prepared for the olive season. Since many islanders' orchards were miles away from their home village, it would be impractical to "drive" the donkey back and forth these great distances. So the house hold would have to be moved to a second house. This second home, was nothing more than a stable or barn in the orchard itself that the family could live in for a few weeks, or months depending on the amount of olive trees that they owned.

Caravans of donkeys would set out at night as the villagers made their way to the lands. Various families that had adjacent plots would travel together, telling stories and helping each other on the long walk to the orchards. When asking some of my friends about their childhood experiences on these trails, they laughingly added that although the dirt roads were cleared and made for vehicles, the most worn and torn areas were the sides, where the high traffic of donkeys had grooved their paths.

The caravans would reach the orchards by day light and the families would begin to settle in and prepare for the very hard work of olive harvesting. Some families had old blankets and sheets that could be laid under the olive trees for the olives to drop onto while others didn't have this luxury and would have to pick them off the ground.

The men would climb the trees and using their long canes or *vítses*, they would whack the olive branches in an expert way so as to not break the tender tips yet have the olives drop off, down to the ground. The women and children would gather the fallen olives and collect them into Kofínia or large baskets.

Since some varieties of olives are used for preserving while others are grown only for their oil, the women would also take care that the olives of each tree harvested would be separated for this purpose. The very black, over ripened olives would be picked off the ground and collected separately to make *Zoúpes* or wrinkled black olives.

Working in the olive orchards would bring many families together as they worked side by side in adjacent plots. Often, meal times were shared with each other as the families would set under the shade of the trees and offer each other what food they had brought with them. These picnics consisted of simple things such as savory *pítes*, olives, salted sardines, wild greens, tomatoes, and cheeses. Jugs of water as well as bread completed the meal.

When the meal was finished, they would resume with the olive picking, stopping only when it got dark. Of course all this hard work meant a guaranteed good night's sleep until the next morning, when the olive picking would begin again.

Once enough olives were picked, the *kofínia* would be placed on the donkeys and task of transporting them to the mills would begin. This meant many long trips back and forth from the orchard before the olives could be pressed into oil.

Today, the commercial growers in the north that have thousands of olive trees, use special machines to harvest their crop. But here in the islands, the modern methods we use are not much different than those of our ancestors. Nets are used in place of old fabrics to line the ground under the trees so the fallen olives can be collected easier and safer than picking through the grasses and rocks.

And although pick up trucks have replaced the donkeys, it's still a lot of hard work and I often comment how much easier it is to just buy a bottle of oil or a jar of olives instead of all this back breaking work. The answer that I always get from the local Greeks is that the olives on their trees are considered gifts from God and should not be left to go to waste. Humbled, I get back on the ground and collect the olives.

Green Olives in Vinegar / *Eliés Xithátes*

Ingredients:
1 bucket of green olives
water
5 lemons, washed and sliced
vinegar
olive oil

Brine / *Salamoúra - Álmi*:
water
coarse salt (fine salt will work too)
1 raw egg, washed thoroughly

Wash the olives in soap and water to remove any dust and pesticides and rinse well. Get a bucket that is large enough to hold the olives, half fill it with clean water and set it next to your work space. Get comfortable, because this step is time consuming. Take a hand full of olives, and using a sharp knife, make a slit down the length of each one. Throw the cut olives into the water. Continue until all the olives have been cut. While you are doing this step your hands will turn a dirt brown color because of the oils that are released from the olives. Make sure that you wear old clothes too, because the juice from the olives makes terrible stains on clothing.

When you have finished with all your olives, rinse and drain them. Return the olives to the bucket and fill it up with fresh, clean water. The olives will need to be soaked for 10 to 14 days to get rid of the bitterness in them. Some people prefer a little bitter taste, so only soak them for 10 days. For those that prefer a sweeter olive, soak them the full 14 days. The soaking water will have to be changed 1 to 2 times per day during this period.

When the olives have finished soaking, rinse and drain them. Pack them into large, wide mouth jars or a big container, adding lemon slices as you go along. Leave 2 inches of head space in your jar.

Make the Brine: You will need enough brine to cover the olives completely so put an adequate amount of water into a pot and bring it to a boil. Boil it for 5 minutes, then remove it from the heat. Add some salt to the water. You will be using the egg as a gauge for the salinity of your brine. Float the egg in the brine. Some of the shell should float above water level, if not, remove the egg and add more salt to the brine. Put the egg back in to test it again. You want 1 to 2cm of shell to be exposed at the water level. The more shell that floats, the saltier the brine. Keep floating the egg and adding salt until you get the salinity that you want. Cover the brine and set it aside to cool down completely.

You will need to use one cup of vinegar for every quart jar of olives so in other words, if you are using gallon sized jars, pour in 4 cups of vinegar. Add the cooled brine into the olives, just enough to cover them and pour olive oil over the brine. This will float over the whole lot, sealing the olives and the brine from contact with the air.

The olives should be completely submerged because they will darken. If you would like, you can set a small inverted dish over them, inside the jar or container to weight them down.

The olives will be ready in 4 to 6 days but the longer they sit, the more pronounced the vinegar flavor. Always use a slotted spoon to remove the olives and not your hands. Rinse them under running water, drain them and serve. Green olives should be very firm and crisp. If the stored olives ever soften or become mushy, they should not be eaten. Discard them right away.

Green Cracked Olives / *Eliés Tsakistés*

The method and recipe is exactly the same as for Green Olives in Vinegar but you will use only brine, omitting the vinegar that is called for. The difference is in the preparation. Where Green Olives in Vinegar are sliced with a small knife, cracked olives, will have to be...well, cracked. Make sure that you use very green olives that have been picked right off the tree. They are the crispiest and will crack open easier.

Begin by finding your self a good rock. It has to be smooth on one side and fit easily into the palm of your hand so it can be used as a mallet to crack the olives. The weight of the rock is also a consideration as you want it heavy enough that the olives will crack with one blow.

Prepare a work area that has a hard surface such as cement and a garden hose near by for clean up. Here in the islands, we often sit in the drive way or on the steps of the front porch. Mind you that the actual cement surface will become stained will olive oil, so don't choose an elaborate stone path to do this. Also, as you are cracking the olives, you as well as any surroundings will get spattered by the oil too. Wear old clothes and again, make sure that your work area is suitable.

Assuming that you have one bucket full of green olives, you will need an empty bucket the same size or larger. Half fill this with water. Set the water bucket on one side of you and the olive bucket on the other. Take an olive and set it on the pavement. Give it one solid whack with the rock that you have chosen and it should split. If you just can't get the hang of it, it could mean that the rock is not the best. Choose another one, maybe heavier, and try it again

It does take a bit of practice to do this, so don't despair. You want the olive to crack right away instead of having to hit it multiple times because it will bruise and you will need to use the right amount of force because you don't want to smash the olive either. Keep practicing one olive at a time. Eventually, you will get to the point where you can take a whole handful of olives and whack them open in one swing.

Pick up the olives that have cracked and put them right into the bucket of water. Keep cracking all the olives until you are finished. Use the garden hose to rinse the olives with fresh water and clean the area that you have worked on. Follow the recipe directions for Green Olives and start with the soaking process.

Oh, and don't discard the rock that you have used. Save it on top of the refrigerator for another olive cracking session, because according to the village ways, a good rock is hard to find.

Olives in Bitter Orange / *Eliés Nerantzátes*

The bitter-citrus flavoring of Bitter Oranges or Seville Oranges gives these olives a bit of tang, which personally, I don't think tastes like oranges at all.

Every good village house wife makes at least one small jar of *Nerantzátes* Olives that can be served on the *mezé* table. They are easily made, especially if you're already making another variation of olive.

Slice the olives and soak them for 14 days as per the directions for Olives in Vinegar. Pack the finished olives into jars or containers, leaving a few inches of headroom.

Squeeze bitter oranges and strain the fresh juice into the jars, filling them $2/3$ full. Use a dish and a stone as a weight or wedge a few stems of herbs such as thyme or oregano inside the neck of the jar to keep the olives down. Fill the rest of the space with olive oil and close the lid. The olives are ready within a few days.

Black Wrinkled Olives / *Eliés Zoúpes*

The very ripe, black olives are used for making *Zoúpes*. Wash and rinse the olives and set them in a basket or strainer. Shake the basket every so often so the olives get tossed, exposing their surfaces to air so they don't turn moldy. Let them remain in the basket for two days to drain, tossing them every so often.

Sprinkle the olives with rock salt, toss them and again let them drain for a few more days. The olives will be releasing their juice and the skins will begin to wrinkle during this time. Toss the olives every day until they don't release anymore red juice. The *Zoúpes* are ready and can be stored in the refrigerator in a covered container. Remember to give the refrigerated container a shake every so often, again, because they mold easily.

Here in the islands, we will often package small bundles of *Zoúpes* in plastic bags and freeze them. A bag can be taken out and eaten, without worrying about the whole lot getting moldy. If you make a large quantity of these olives, give it a try. They taste just as good with little change in texture or flavor and can keep almost forever if they are frozen in plastic bags.

Spicy Olive Oil / *Pikántiko Eleólado*

This recipe makes about a quart of spicy olive oil. Use it in place of plain olive oil when you want to add a bit of zip. It is especially nice when used with spaghetti sauces and meat stews. The ornamental peppers are used for just that—ornament. But they will give off some of their hot properties the longer that they sit, so don't add more than just two unless you want a very hot, spicy taste.

Ingredients:
⅓ cup olive oil
4 tbs. hot pepper flakes
2 to 3 whole ornamental peppers
olive oil - enough to fill the bottle you're using

Wash and dry a bottle of your choice—approximately quart size. I use old wine bottles with cork stoppers, but you can get fancy and use an ornamental one if you wish.

Heat ⅓ cup olive oil in a small skillet. Add the pepper flakes and sauté them for 2 minutes, being careful that the peppers don't burn. Strain the oil through a fine sieve into the bottle. Add the ornamental peppers and fill the bottle up with more olive oil. Cork the bottle and keep it with your spices in the kitchen.

Sun Dried Tomatoes / *Tomátes Xerés*

If you're lucky enough to have fresh tomatoes growing in your yard, you can preserve this summer goodie by drying it. Use the dried tomatoes in your cooking or you can have them as a *mezé*. Refresh the tomatoes first, then fry them up in some batter. Serve them with garlic sauce.

Ingredients:
2 lbs. tomatoes
salt

Use very ripe tomatoes that about the same in size. Wash them to remove any dirt or pesticides. Remove the stems and then cut them in two halves. Sprinkle them with salt.

Place the tomato halves on a large board or tray and cover them with a piece of tulle. Set the board or tray in the sun to dry until they have dehydrated completely. This can take from 2 to 5 days, depending on the weather. Turn them over every day so they don't get moldy. Once they are dry, use an upholstery needle and thick thread to pass through them so they can be hung up. To refresh the dry tomatoes, soak them in water for one hour and then drain them.

Sun Dried Octopus

In Rhodes, we dry the fresh caught octopus in the hot summer sun. Many tourists to the islands have walked down the beach and seen a taverna with a washing line strung up and fresh caught octopus drying in the summer breeze. This is taken as a a signal that the taverna will have fresh dried octopus on the menu that evening.

To sun dry octopus, begin by tenderizing and cleaning it. If you're not sure how to do this, see the Kitchen Techniques section for instructions and tips. Once this is done, cut down the back of the center of the hood so it lays flat. Hang the octopus on a line or use clothes pins for a secure hold. To aid in the drying process, you can clip the left most tentacle to the line and then proceed to clip the right most tentacle up, so the octopus is spread out. Some folk will use bamboo skewers as a wedge to keep the legs apart for the dry air to circulate better.

I suggest that you cover the octopus with a piece of tulle to keep the flies and insects off of it while it's drying. In the hot sun of Rhodes, it only takes 8 to 12 hours or so before the octopus is fairly dried out as you don't want it leathery.

Once dried, it can be kept indefinitely in the refrigerator, but the islanders usually prepare it right away. So, I guess you're wondering what's the sense of sun-drying octopus if you're going to cook it immediately? Sun-drying octopus lets the water evaporate so the full taste of the sea remains in the flesh and it is absolutely delicious when cooked over an open flame. To enjoy the delicacy, the island way, see the recipe for Charcoal Grilled Octopus and have a chilled bottle of ouzo or *Súma* on hand.

If you'd prefer to store and cook your octopus on another day or in a different recipe, keep it in the refrigerator until you're ready to use it. Soak it in plain water for 4 to 8 hours, depending on it's size, and then it can be used in place of fresh octopus in recipes such as Octopus in Wine or Octopus with Macaroni.

Peppers Stuffed with Anchovies / *Piperiés Gemistés me Antzoúgies*

This wonderful *mezé* is easy to make and can be kept for a long time in the refrigerator so you'll always have something good to serve with ouzo. Make sure that you save the oil once you've eaten up all the peppers as it can be used in any recipe that calls for olive oil, such as spaghetti sauces or salad dressings.

Ingredients:
12 small green peppers about 4 inches in length
12, 24, or 36 anchovy fillets depending on how many you want to use
whole parsley stems
3 bay leaves
2 cloves garlic
1 tsp. oregano
olive oil

Slice off the caps of the peppers and remove the seeds. Stuff each pepper with anchovy fillets and one stem of parsley. Fill a clean and sterile jar with the peppers, packing them tightly together. Add the bay leaves, garlic and the oregano and fill the jar with olive oil. Cap the jar tightly and refrigerate for 6 weeks.

To serve, remove from the jar the desired amount of peppers and let them stand at room temperature 2 to 3 hours before serving. Chop the stuffed peppers into fork size pieces and top with a sprinkle of vinegar if you wish.

Pickled Peppers / *Piperiés se Salamoúra*

Ingredients:
2 lbs. small, fresh green peppers
fresh dill weed stems
garlic cloves
thyme stems
Basic Brine - see "Concoctions for the Greek Kitchen"
vinegar

With a small knife, slice down the length of the peppers on one side. Wash them to remove any dirt and pesticides and let them sit out at room temperature to wilt for two days. Pack the peppers into clean and sterile jars so they are ⅔ full. Add the dill and the garlic if you prefer. Push the thyme stem into the jar, so it acts as a stopper, keeping the peppers from floating. Fill the jar ⅔ with olive brine and top off with vinegar. They are ready to serve in 2 to 3 days.

Sinking Sauce for Fish / *Sáltsa Savoúro*

This is an old recipe that I thought to include to give you a bit of insight to our ancestors ingenuity. I wouldn't try this recipe myself, simply because of the modern conveniences such as refrigeration and freezing available today, make food preserving so much safer. None the less, this recipe is an interesting part of our heritage. A days catch of fresh fish could be preserved with this method and kept up to 10 days without refrigeration. For longer periods—up to two months, you would have to check on the fish and add more vinegar and oil, making sure that the fish remained entirely submerged in the liquid.

Ingredients:
4 heads garlic, cleaned
2 cups dark raisins
1 cup chopped fresh rosemary
2 cups vinegar
2 cups olive oil
2 tbs. salt

Begin by cleaning and frying your choice of fish. They can be any variety, but the smaller ones work better. Make sure that they fit into the crock that you will be using.

Add all the sauce ingredients to a pot and let it simmer for 30 minutes. Strain the sauce and let it cool. In a clay enamel pot, layer fried fish on the bottom. Pour some cooled sauce over them. Add another layer of fish and add more sauce. You will need to have enough sauce to cover the fish completely. If you find that you don't have enough sauce, add equal amounts of olive oil and vinegar until you get the desired level. Cover tightly and keep in a cool dark place.

Home-made Feta Cheese / *Tirí Féta Spitísia*

This is the recipe for home-made Feta cheese as it's made here in our villages. It isn't a difficult recipe to follow—actually it's rather easy, but you will need to master the quantities of salt and *pitiá* or starter that will give you the consistency and saltiness that you prefer.

Fresh cow's or sheep's milk can be substituted for the cheese but it will give you a different flavor and consistency. *Pitiá* is a lactose starter that is used in cheese making to get the milk to separate into whey (liquid) and curd (solids). Cultured buttermilk or some other lactic culture, such as milk that is in the process of turning sour can be substituted. You'll need a larger quantity—perhaps ½ cup to 2 liters of milk or you can use commercial coagulants that are available.

Ingredients:
2 to 3 liters fresh goats' milk
½ to 1 tbs. *pitiá* or lactose starter
½ cup warm water
½ to 1 tbs. salt

Brine / *Salamoúra - Álmi*:
water
coarse salt (fine salt will work too)
1 raw egg, washed thoroughly

Extra Supplies:
cheese cloth or fine tulle/netting
fine weaved basket or strainer
clean and sterilized wide mouth jar or container
a dish that will fit inside the jar
a heavy rock that will fit into the jar

Begin by making sure that all your utensils, pots and supplies are very clean. Put the milk into a pot over medium heat. Heat it to a low boil, but keep careful that it doesn't scorch. Cook it for 5 minutes then set it aside to cool down until warm to the touch. Dilute the *pitiá* in the water and stir it into the warm milk. Stir in the salt and cover the pot with a clean, cloth towel and set it aside to thicken and curdle in a warm place. This can take anywhere from 6 to 12 hours.

Pour the thickened milk into a basket or strainer that has been lined with cheese cloth or fine tulle/netting. Cover the basket with another piece of net to keep the insects off and hang it over a sink, or outside so it can drain thoroughly. Check on the draining cheese. If it seems that the chunks of curd are too big, you can slice through them with a knife to break them up so more of the water will drain out. It takes about a full day for the cheese to drain to feta consistency, but if you prefer a harder, dryer cheese, you can let it drain longer. You can also weight down the draining cheese with a dish and a heavy rock placed over it to aid in squeezing out more water and will also give you a thicker cheese.

Make the Brine: You will need enough brine to cover the cheese completely so put an adequate amount of water into a pot and bring it to a boil. Boil it for 5 minutes, then remove it from the heat. Add some salt to the water. You will be using the egg as a gauge for the salinity of your brine. Float the egg in the brine. Some of the shell should float above water level, if not, remove the egg and add more salt to the brine. Put the egg back in to test it again. You want 1-2cm of shell to be exposed at the water level. The more shell that floats, the saltier the brine. Keep floating the egg and adding salt until you get the salinity that you want. Cover the brine and set it aside to cool down completely.

Invert the basket with the drained cheese onto a clean work surface and remove the cheese cloth. Cut the cheese into large blocks and put them into a clean and sterile container. Pour the cooled brine over the cheese. Keep in mind that feta has to be completely submerged in the brine or else it will go bad. Use an inverted plate with a heavy rock placed on it to keep the feta under the brine level.

Village Raisins / *Stafídes*

Ingredients:
4 handfuls sifted wood ashes from olive or pine
basket of seedless grapes of your preference
olive oil

Bring a large pot of water mixed with the ashes to a boil and remove it from the heat to cool completely. Pick through the grape stems and discard any moldy or bruised grapes. Rinse the grapes under running water and drain.

Pour a little olive oil into the ash water, dip each stem of grapes into it and set the stem in a *Kofíni* or basket to drain. Continue with all the grapes. Once they have drained, lay them on a clean sheet in the sun to dry for 6 days. Every day you should sprinkle them with clean ash water, using your fingers to flick it over the drying grapes.

When the raisins have dried, pull them off the stems and rinse them in clean water. Lay the raisins out to dry once more. They are ready to use at this point or you can store them for later use. For long term storage, seal the raisins in plastic bags and keep them in a cool dark place or in the freezer.

Preserved Pork Fats / *Míla and Tsirígia*

Míla and *tsirígia* were traditionally made during the Christmas holidays with the bits of left over pork fats and meats from a fresh slaughtered pig. It is still made in village homes today whenever fresh pork is available. *Míla* is used to replace butter and oil in pasta and pilaf recipes as well as used to simply fry eggs. It can also be eaten as a bread spread with a sprinkling of sugar or salt. Use pork fat that also has bits of meat on it and heat it in a large pot slowly. The fat will melt and you can strain it through a sieve into jars. This is the *míla*. The remaining bits of fats, rinds and meat that are in the strainer are called the *tsirígia*. These bits can also be packed into jars and covered with *míla* to be preserved for later use in a recipe.

Preserved Pork in Lard / *Kavroumás*

Just as *míla* and *tsirígia*, *kavroumá* was also a traditional Christmas recipe. *Kavroumá* is made with lean bits of pork fried in fats and is then packed into jars to be preserved. It is used in place of ground meats in recipes such as *Dolmáthes*, *Gemistá* and spaghetti sauces. My fondest memory of the stuff is plain fried in a skillet with two beaten eggs added in.

Use lean pork that has been chopped into very small cubes and pork fat. Heat a little of the fat in a pot to melt it and then fry the pork meat. Once the meat is browned, remove it to a clean jar. To the hot skillet, add more of the fat to keep melting it down. You will need enough fat that can cover the meat entirely. Once the fat is melted, pour it over the lean meat in your jar, making sure that you cover it completely. The *kavroumá* will keep a very long time in the refrigerator. To use it, simply spoon out some of the *kavroumá* and heat it. The lard will melt and separate and you'll be left with lean meat.

Wheat Baby Cream / *Kréma gia Morá*

I understand completely that you will not run to the kitchen and make up this recipe for your baby especially since there are so many ready, fortified creams and baby foods on the market shelves.

I only thought to include this recipe, maybe because I'm a romantic, and the thought that my mom and dad were fed this stuff is so much like a "fun fact" that I wanted to share it.

Ingredients:
2 lbs. wheat flour
1 cup good olive oil
pinch grated nutmeg

Sift the flour twice and add the nutmeg. Stream in the oil while rubbing the mixture between your fingers, getting rid of the lumps. Put it into a pan and bake it, stirring every so often until it turns golden brown. Let it cool and put the wheat into a jar and cap it tight.

To make baby cream, stir together 1 or 2 tbs. of wheat with some cold milk and heat it over low heat while stirring constantly, until it thickens into a smooth cream.

Home-Made Pasta / *Mátsi*

The simple village pasta recipe can take on many shapes and forms. You can cut it into small squares and rectangles or if you have the patience, you can pinch off little bits and make home made orzo noodles by rubbing it between your fingers.

Mátsi noodles are added to lentils, beans and when very thinly cut, made into *Matsógalo* - or *mátsi* in milk which is very similar to rice pudding. It can also be cooked up as any pasta and served with a tomato sauce.

Ingredients:
3 cups flour - white, wheat, or barley
½ tsp. salt
1 egg yolk - optional
water
extra flour

Mix together the flour and salt and make a well in the center. Add the yolk, if you're using it and enough water to make a stiff dough that you can roll out. Separate the dough into 3 balls.

Take one ball and begin to roll it out into a round, very thin sheet. Sprinkle flour on your work surface and rolling pin as you go along to help keep it from sticking. Once the dough is as thin as you can get it, use a sharp knife and slice it in length about the width of a noodle. Set the cut lengths on a table or tray to dry. Continue with the rest of the dough.

The *mátsi* can be used right away by sifting it in a strainer to remove any loose flour or it can be dried over a few days for later use. If you do use fresh *mátsi*, remember that it will cook up much quicker than any dry noodle.

Beverages and Bottling
Potá

Súma, Rakí, and *Tsípouro*

All these terms, as well as too many to mention, are the names given to the Greek, home-made moonshine by the different islands and parts of Greece. In the fall season, when the grapes are collected many village men will pull out their home *kazánia* or stills and ferment, with utmost care this special kind of village spirit.

It is enjoyed at the dinner table instead of ouzo, with an assortment of *mezédes*. Other, more heroic drinkers will simply sit down with their friends and enjoy shots of it in a party atmosphere and although I am considered a good drinker that can hold her own, I do not partake in *súma*.

I'm told that the actual moonshine is taken from the top layer of fermenting alcohol which will be used to make ouzo by adding sugar and anise. In other words, it's the cream of the crop.

The alcohol content is high, so be forewarned when a villager offers you a shot of the stuff. 50% alcohol or 100 proof, is considered a medium strength for *súma* here on the islands, and many villagers consider the drink to be worthless unless it ignites when cold.

Because it's so strong, *súma* is often used for medicinal purposes too. It can be used as an antiseptic or a gargle for sore throats. But perhaps the best know use for the stuff is for when you have a cold. Nothing beats a *súma* rub down administered by an "old ways" village woman. Just remember not to go near an open flame.

Village Wine Making

I was once given an American volume of a wine making book and after reading the first few pages I became discouraged, and gave up any attempt at doing it myself. Other than not understanding the mile long list of procedures, the recipes called for all kinds of supplies and chemical ingredients that I had never heard of before.

The Greek villagers make their home-made wines simply and easily. When invited to a dinner at a villagers home, you will often be asked to taste test their newest batch of the fermented crop.

Not one villager that I spoke to uses any type of preservative or additive in their wine so you know that what you are drinking is naturally delicious. True, they only make small batches of the stuff and any long term storage will probably sour the lot, but vinegar has it's uses too.

Not all varieties of grapes are used by the villagers to make their house wines, so the folk that grow grapes for the fruit, have a few vines of wine grapes growing in their vineyards just for this purpose.

Village Style Home-made Wine

Wash the grapes to get rid of any pesticides and dirt and spread them on sheets or linens in the sun to dry. The time involved for drying depends on the flavor you want the wine. Grapes for dry wine or *broúsko*, will need 5 days in the sun, where as for a sweet wine or *glykó*, the grapes should sun from 9 to 11 days.

Once the grapes have been sunned, take them to the *linó* or *patíri* which is the pressing vat, built like a small reservoir or trough. Set a small barrel or ceramic pot at the spout of the *patíri* so the juice can be collected.

Wash your feet, be happy and jump on in. This part is important because it's said that a bad disposition or mood will sour the wine. Children are often used to do this task and it's traditional that the house wives bake them cookies and sweets to keep them happy through out the duration of the grape pressing.

The juice that runs out is called the *moústo* or must. After you have stepped on all the grapes and are sure that most of the juice has been pressed out, the remaining skins and seeds are collected and put through a *mágkano* which is a generic name for a hand cranked press, so any remaining juice can be extracted.

Bring a large pot of water to a boil with fresh *athroúmba* and *pevkovelónes* - thyme and pine needles. The wine barrels are washed with this mixture and left to sit and soak it up for one hour before they are over turned to drain.

Strain all the juices or *moústo* from the *linó* and *mágkano* through fine cheese cloth. Pour the *moústo* into the barrels and let it sit for 10 to 15 days for it to *vrási* and *zimósi* - heat and ferment. Keep the barrel open and covered with a cheese cloth during this time. After the days have passed, and the fermentation stops, close the barrel with its cap. Wooden barrels are rubbed on their exterior with builders lime and ash to seal them. The wine is allowed to sit for 40 days, after which it is ready to enjoy.

Do note that clay or plastic barrels can be used for village wine making. If you will be using wooden barrels make sure that you don't use barrels made from fresh pine wood or else your wine may get a distinct pine resin flavor similar to *Retsína*.

Greek Coffee / *Kafés Ellinikós*

Greek coffee is made in what's called a *mbríki* that can be found in Greek or Middle Eastern specialty shops. It's a wide bottomed pot that tapers towards the top with a long handle. To the point of the narrow neck is as far as you should fill it with water and coffee. The area above the neck is needed for the foam that will cook and bubble up.

Using your serving cups, measure out ⅔ cups of water per serving. Remember that the maximum amount for filling a *mbríki* is to the neck, so if it doesn't hold it, just make another batch for more servings.

Use the table below to select the kind of coffee you would like and stir in the appropriate amount of coffee and sugar. Place it on high heat, stirring occasionally and let the coffee foam up to the top. Remove the *mbríki* from the heat and stir it down. Again, reheat it and let the foam form. Don't boil it. You can't walk away when making Greek coffee as it will foam up very fast and run over, so keep an eye on it. The foam that's on top should be in every Greek coffee, so pour a little into each cup and then finish off with the rest of it so there is foam in every serving. Always serve Greek coffee accompanied with a glass of cold water.

Quantities:
The general rule is one heaping teaspoon of Greek coffee and one teaspoon of sugar per demitasse cup. This will make a *métrios* or medium sweet coffee. But since there are different strokes for different folks, you'll find some of the more common variations below:

Black plain coffee	*Skétos*	1 heaping tsp. coffee
Medium sweet coffee	*Métrios*	1 heaping tsp. coffee & 1 tsp. sugar
Sweet coffee	*Glykós*	1 heaping tsp. coffee & 2 tsp. sugar
Strong and sweet	*Varís Glykós*	1½ heaping tsp. coffee & 2 tsp. sugar

Apricot Pit Liqueur / *Likér apó Koukoútsia Veríkoko*

Ingredients:
140-200 apricot pits
1 quart good quality cognac
2 cups sugar
3 cups water

Crack the pits open with a nut cracker and remove the soft insides. Put them into a large glass bottle and pour in the cognac. Let the mixture sit on a sunny window sill for 2 months in which time it will turn yellow.

Once the cognac mixture has aged, pour it through a strainer into another bottle. In a small pot, combine the sugar and the water and bring it to a boil. Cook it until it thickens and becomes a syrup. Let it cool and strain it into the bottle with the apricot-cognac. Give it a shake and your liqueur is ready to serve.

Blueberry or Raspberry Liqueur / *Likér apó Vatómoura*

Ingredients:
2 lbs. blueberries or raspberries
1 quart ouzo
1½ lb. sugar
4 whole cloves
1 cinnamon stick

Wash and drain the berries and put them into a large, glass jar. Add all the ingredients, cap it tightly and allow it to sit for 40 days. When the blueberry mixture has aged, pour it through a fine sieve into clean bottles and enjoy!

Mandarin Liqueur / *Likér apó Mandaríni*

Ingredients:
2 cups mandarin peel - wash the mandarins before peeling them
3 cups pure grain alcohol
1 cup cognac
5 cups sugar
8 cups water
2 cinnamon sticks
4 whole cloves

Put the peel into a wide mouthed, large jar. Pour in the alcohol and the cognac and let it sit for 2 weeks. Once it has aged, boil together the sugar, water, and spices for 5 minutes and then let it cool. Pour the syrup mixture into the jar with the mandarin peels and let it age for another week on a sunny window sill. Strain the liqueur and pour it into bottles. It's ready to enjoy whenever you wish.

Morello Cherry Liqueur / *Likér apó Víssino*

Ingredients:
2 lbs. black cherries
3 lbs. sugar
2 sticks cinnamon
4 cloves
2 whole nutmegs
1 quart brandy or cognac

Remove the stems and wash the cherries with soap and water. Rinse them well and set aside to drain. Wash and rinse a large mouth, screw top jar. Add the drained cherries, sugar, cinnamon, cloves and nutmegs. Cover tightly and give the jar a shake. Place the jar on a sunny windowsill for 1 month. Don't open the jar during this time, just shake it occasionally. After one month, open the jar and add the cognac. Close the lid tightly and again, set it on the windowsill for another 10 days.

The liqueur will be ready. Using cheesecloth, strain the liqueur into bottles. Personally, I prefer to keep it as is with the fruit and spices. I think it ages that much better. And the cherries really pack a punch!.

Walnut Liqueur / *Likér apó Karídia*

Ingredients:
15 small green walnuts, harvested before they make their hard shells
2 lbs. sugar
1 quart ouzo
5 cloves
2 cinnamon sticks

Wash the nuts in soap and water and put them in a wide mouth jar. Add the rest of the ingredients. Let it set for 40 days on a sunny windowsill, shaking the jar on occasion. When ready, pour the mixture through a fine strainer and then into bottles. Your liqueur is now ready to be enjoyed.

Orange Liqueur / *Likér apó Portokáli*

Ingredients:
2 orange peels - wash the oranges before you peel them
1 mandarin peel - wash the mandarin before you peel it
2 cinnamon sticks
3 cloves
1 quart cognac
2 cups sugar
1 cup water

Chop the peels into small pieces and place them in a wide mouthed jar. Add all the ingredients except for the sugar and the water, cap it and let it rest on a sunny window sill for 20 days. Once it has aged, boil together the sugar and the water for 5 minutes then set it aside to cool. Strain the orange peel mixture through a sieve into a clean bottle and add the sugar syrup. Give it a shake and your liqueur is ready for serving.

Spearmint Liqueur / *Likér apó Diósmo*

Ingredients:
4 bunches of fresh spearmint
5 cinnamon sticks
15 whole cloves
2 whole nutmegs
½ quart of *tsípouro* or strong vodka
½ quart ouzo
sugar

Wash and rinse the spearmint. Place it in a large, wide mouth jar so it sets on the bottom. If you need to, chop the sprigs. Put the spices over the spearmint and add enough sugar into the jar so the spearmint is completely covered. Let the mixture rest for 10 days, giving it a shake every so often to help the sugar dissolve. After it's aged, pour in the tsípouro and ouzo and set it on a sunny window sill for one month. Strain the liquid through a sieve into bottles and enjoy the refreshing taste.

Village Hangover Cure / *Stomahikó*

I just had to include this recipe for the village hangover cure, simply so you can see what our forefathers had to go through after a night of partying. The village wives would quickly whip up a glass of the stuff and serve it to their husbands who had a bad stomach or headache the next day. Perhaps, in their own way, these ladies knew that pay backs were hell and if the drinking itself, the night before didn't do their husbands in, this hang-over cure was sure to.

Ingredients:
1½ quarts village *rakí* or strong vodka
1 inch piece of horseradish
1 tbs. whole cloves
1 whole nutmeg
2 cinnamon sticks
1 tbs. coriander seed
1 tbs. whole black pepper
1 lb. sugar
1 cup water
fresh egg

Put the horseradish, cloves, nutmeg, cinnamon, coriander and black pepper in a cheese cloth and tie it up. Put the *rakí* into a large, clean jar and add the spice bundle. Let it set in a cool place for 40 days.
Once the *rakí* has aged, remove the spice bundle. Prepare the syrup by boiling together the sugar with the water for 2 to 3 minutes then set it aside to cool. Mix the syrup with the *rakí* and keep it stored in a cool, dark place.
To administer the hangover cure, beat one egg in a glass with ½ cup of the *rakí* mixture and smilingly, hand it to the ailing person.

Greek Cooking for Children

Greek Cooking for Children

I've been asked on numerous occasions to suggest recipes that children can make by themselves for a school project. Cooking Greek food does not have to be difficult or time consuming in order for it to be Greek. Maybe it strays from the traditional way of doing it, but I think that if our grandmothers had ready made pastry and canned tomatoes available, there would have been more than one occasion on which they would have used them.

As I've said before, we're living in the age of conveniences and there are many short cuts that we can take to simplify the recipes so our children can learn about the Greek culture through its food. Perhaps one day, when they are grown, they'll really care about the true way that it was done or learn the lesson that "fresh is best" and at that time, Greek cooking will take on a new meaning.

Grown ups may want to use these tips and short cuts as well, especially since they simplify many dishes. Go ahead and do it, especially if you are pressed for time.

Greek village children on a school trip, sharing their lunch under the pine trees, mid 1960s

Pies / *Pítes*

There are many different true recipes for *Pítes* in the Savory Pies and the Desserts section, which are really easy in themselves. To further simplify, I've given you some suggestions and shortcuts that can be used by children so they can make their own variations of the traditional Greek goodies.

Ready Made Pastry Suggestions:
Get yourself some store bought ready made pastry dough or sheets. Make the fillings following the recipe of your choice.

For individual pies, you may be able to find pastry dough that is already cut into nice shapes, if not, roll out the dough and cut pieces with a knife or large cookie cutters. Drop a spoonful of filling in the center. Wrap them up and bake at 350°F to 375°F until brown.

You can also make a pan version of all the pies which is easier and faster. Just line a buttered pan with some pastry, add the filling and top it off with more pastry and bake.

Short Cut Savory Pítes

Short Cut Cheese Pies / *Tirópites*
Make the filling as the recipe directions for the Cheese Pie of your choice. Substitute a mixture of different cheese such as ricotta, parmesan, and Swiss if you can't get Feta. Follow the pastry suggestions above.

Short Cut Spinach Pies / *Spanakópites*
Follow the directions for spinach pie and make the filling. Substitute frozen or canned spinach, making sure that you drain it well. Follow the pastry suggestions above.

Short Cut Chicken Pies / *Kotópites*
1 can cooked chicken, drained
1 can mixed vegetables, drained
1 can Cream of Chicken soup or gravy - optional
salt and pepper

Mix together all the ingredients and season with salt and pepper. Follow the pastry suggestions above.

Short Cut Sausage Pies / *Loukanópites*
1 lb. small cocktail hot dogs or sausages
1 jar ready made spaghetti sauce or mild salsa

Lay a sausage on your pastry and spoon some ready sauce over it. Follow the pastry suggestions above.

Short Cut Ham Pies / *Zambonópites*
1 lb. sliced ham
½ lb. sliced cheese, such as edam - optional
1 jar ready made salsa

Layer a piece of ham with some cheese or a spoonful of mild salsa, on your pastry. Follow the pastry suggestions above.

Short Cut Turkey Pies / *Galópites*
1 can cooked turkey, drained
1 can mixed vegetables, drained
1 can turkey gravy
½ cup grated parmesan cheese
salt and pepper

Mix together all the ingredients and season with salt and pepper. Follow the pastry suggestions above.

Beef and Cheese Pie / *Kreatópita me Tirí*
Substitute small, ready made cooked beef patties or meatballs for the meat. If needed, cut it to size and set it on the pastry. Top it with some grated cheddar or Swiss cheese. Follow the pastry suggestions above.

Short Cut Sweet Pies

Custard Pies / *Mbougátsa*
Substitute vanilla or lemon flavor pudding for the stuffing. Wrap them up and bake them at 375°F to 400°F until the pastry turns golden brown. Sprinkle them with powdered sugar and cinnamon. Follow the pastry suggestions above.

Island Cheese and Honey Pie / *Melópita Nissiótiki*
Make the filling following the recipe directions and use the pastry suggestions above.

Short Cut Syrup Cakes

In the Dessert section you'll find the recipe for Almond Brandy Cake. The following directions and variations are for much simplified versions and omitting the brandy. The syrups are made using honey instead of the cooked syrups which can be dangerous for children to make.

Almond Cake in Syrup / *Amygdalópita Siropiastí*
Use your favorite vanilla flavored ready-cake mix and add one cup of ground almonds and an extra egg to the mix. Bake as per directions as a sheet cake in a flat, rectangular pan. When the cake is done, set it aside to cool in it's pan. Dilute ½ cup of honey with a bit of hot water. Not too much water though, as you want it to remain thick, but pour-able, so that the cake will soak it up. Pour it over the cake and let it all cool down and set.

Using a knife, slice the cake on a diagonal, left to right and then vice versa, to form diamond-shaped pieces. You can serve the pieces right from the pan or put them into muffin papers - which I personally think makes it much neater and prettier. If you would like to get fancy, you can insert one whole almond into the center of each of the diamonds.

Chocolate Almond Cake / *Amigdalópita Siropiastí me Sokoláta*
Follow the directions as for the above Almond Cake and frost the cooled cake with a ready made chocolate or fudge frosting before you cut it into diamonds.

Walnut Cake / *Karidópita*
Follow the directions as for the above Almond Cake but substitute 1 cup ground walnuts for the almonds. Use walnut halves inserted in the diamonds as decoration.

Milk Pie in Syrup / *Galópita Siropiastí*
Follow the directions as for the above Almond Cake using the nut of your choice in the cake mix. Make a vanilla flavored pudding mix and top the cooled cake with it. Cut this into squares and serve right out of the pan.

Ekmék
A very fancy dessert! The original version is known as *Ekmék Kataífi* and can be found in the dessert section. Follow the directions as for the above Almond Cake but don't add any nuts. Add ½ teaspoon of cinnamon to the honey syrup. After the cake has cooled and set, make a vanilla or lemon flavored pudding mix and top the cooled cake with it. Then top off the whole thing with some ready made whipped cream topping. Serve the *Ekmék* cut into squares, right out of the pan.

Short Cut Cakes

Lemon Cake / *Lemonópita*
Make any ready lemon or vanilla flavored cake mix and add to the batter 1½ tbs. grated lemon peel. Bake it according to directions. Make the topping following the recipe for Lemon Cake.

Raisin Cake / *Stafidópita*
Make any ready vanilla flavored cake mix. To the batter add: ½ tsp. cinnamon, ½ tsp ginger, 1 tsp. grated orange rind and 2 cups of raisins that have been tossed with a bit of flour. Spread the batter into a sheet cake pan and sprinkle it with ½ cup chopped almonds. Bake it as per directed. When the cake is done, let it cool and sprinkle it with powdered sugar. Cut it into pieces and serve right from the pan or set them into muffin papers.

St. Fanourios Cake / *Fanourópita*
Follow the recipe directions for St. Fanourios Cake in the dessert section. The recipe is very easy and you put it all together in one bowl. Make sure that you read the folklore about the *Fanourópita*. It'll give you an interesting story to tell as people are enjoying the cake.

Kitchen Techniques

Working with Pastry Dough

Using Pastry dough for Pan Style Pies:

Pastry dough for savory pies should be rolled out thinly but you can use your preference. A thickness of 1/8 inch will give you a thin crust where as 1/4 inch will give you a thick crust but don't use a crust thicker than this as it may be tough to cut and difficult to eat.

Pan versions of every savory pie recipe will need two pieces of rolled out pastry dough. Divide 1/3 of your dough for the top crust and use the rest for the bottom.

Roll out the larger portion of dough first as this will line your pan and become the bottom crust. Gently lay your pan over the rolled out dough to check for size. You should have enough dough on every side that is enough to line the entire inside surface of your pan, including the sides. If it seems small, roll it out some more and then check it again. Once it's the correct size, lay the pastry gently in the pan and use your fingers to smooth it into the corners. If there are odd bits hanging over the rim of the pan, trim them away with a knife, but don't cut away too much as you'll need some extra to crimp with when the top crust has been added.

Tears and holes in your pastry should be patched up because the sauces and juices of the fillings will seep out, making the pie rather messy. To do this, simply roll out a small piece of dough that you have cut off from the overhanging edges. Wet the area of the tear slightly with water or milk and press the dough over the tear, patching it up.

Roll out the top crust the same way as you did for the bottom, using the pan as a size gauge. The top crust needs to be only about 1/2 inch larger on all sides of the pan.

Once you've added your filling and have laid the top crust in place, you will need to seal the pie. Begin by checking the top crust for fit against the sides. Trim away anything more than 1/2 inch of excess dough. Dip your finger into milk or water and brush the edges, wetting them slightly. This works like a glue and will help keep the pastry together while you're working. Press the edges together and then begin crimping them. You can crimp by using your fingers and just pinching the dough edges together, or you can use a fork pressed into the edges which also makes a nicer appearance. There are also pie crimping gadgets available that make beautiful edges, so if you have one, use it.

After you have sealed your pie, be sure to make some kind of holes on the surface for the steam to escape. You can do this in a number of imaginative ways, adding decoration to a plain crust at the same time. A fork can be used to poke holes or a knife can make small incisions in the crust. Start in the center and poke holes to make a starburst or geometrical design. Use your imagination and have fun.

The unbaked surface of your pie will need to be coated with milk, melted butter or beaten egg. This will protect the surface from the heat as well as give your crust a gorgeous appearance. Milk and butter will turn the crust golden, where as egg will give it a shiny coating as well. Most recipes will tell you what to use, but there is no rule that says that you can't substitute one for the other, especially if you've just run out of eggs.

Using Pastry Dough for Individual Pies:

Pastry dough is basically used in the same manner as above for making individual pies, but you will have to choose what shape you want your finished pies to be so you can cut the pastry. Some shapes can be made by cutting two piece of dough and layering filling in between, or another way is to cut one piece of dough and fold it over the filling, onto itself.

Some Pastry cutting choices:
Two squares cut 3" x 3" ...will give you one square pita.
two rectangles cut 3" x 6" ...will give you one rectangular pita.
Two circles cut 4" to 6" in diameter... will give you one round pita.
One square cut 5" x 5"... will give you one triangular pita when folded over.
One circle cut 4" to 6" in diameter... will give you one crescent pita when folded.
One rectangle 3" x 6" ...will give you one square pita when folded over.
One strip 3" x 12" ...will give you one rectangle when folded over

You are in no way limited to these shapes or dimensions. There are many nice cookie cutters and holiday molds that could easily be used for cutting out shapes. When I can't find a particular cutter, I often use the rims of drinking glasses or jars as cutters. Some expert pastry making ladies that I know, just use a sharp knife and in no time, they have a stack of pastry shapes ready for filling.

Now that you know what shape you want your pitas, proceed to cut them out. Dip the cutter into flour and press it into the rolled out pastry. And that's it. Set it aside and keep cutting out shapes until you've used up your pastry. Cover the cut pastry with a clean cloth towel until you're ready to use it.

To fill these little beauties, just scoop some filling onto the pastry. The exact quantity depends entirely on the size of the pastry shape. Small shapes will take less stuffing and larger shapes will obviously use more. I recommend keeping away from the edge of the pastry shape ½ to 1 inch. This way you'll have enough pastry to crimp and seal the pita properly.

Use the filling, depending on the method that you chose. If you chose to use the two piece method, count up your shapes and divide them by two. Scoop filling into the center of half the shapes and save the other half for the top.

The method for folding over pastry requires a bit more thinking. Set a shape in front of you and fold it over, empty so you can see what it will look like finished. This will help you to imagine where the center of the finished pita will be and therefore, the area to place the stuffing. Spread filling on all the pastry pieces at the appropriate spot.

Once the filling is done, get yourself a small bowl of water or milk and set it by your side on your work surface. You'll be using this as sort of a glue to get the edges of the pastry to attach themselves to each other. I use my finger and just dip it in the milk and then run it over the ½ inch of pastry edge. You can use a brush, but I think that it's much more time consuming and messier.

Wet the edges slightly and press the top pastry into place or fold the pastry over the filling onto itself. Begin to crimp the edges as you would for a pan style pita, using your fingers, a fork or a gadget of some kind. Once the pita is sealed, place it on your cookie sheet and brush the top with milk, butter or egg just as the pan versions. Bake as per your recipe directions.

Working with Phyllo Pastry Sheets

Using Phyllo for Pan Version Pies:

Some of you may choose to roll out your own phyllo, in which case you should remember a rule of thumb. When using home-made phyllo sheets, use one sheet of home made for every 2 to 3 sheets of store bought that is called for because home made phyllo is much thicker. Read through your recipe and estimate your needs accordingly.

Store bought phyllo is one of the best short cuts that I know. The ready made, paper thin pastry sheets are a true time saver as opposed to rolling your own. Frozen phyllo can be defrosted by letting it sit at room temperature for a few hours. Don't use a microwave as it will ruin it. At room temperature, the phyllo is easier to work with and less rigid, so even if it's in the refrigerator, let it warm up a while before you begin a recipe.

Because phyllo is so thin, it dries out very quickly. Upon opening a package of the sheets (or when using home made), lay them flat and cover them with a slightly moistened kitchen towel until you're ready to use them.

Phyllo is known for its flaky and crispy characteristics. The layered sheets have to be brushed with an oil of some kind so that each sheet layer cooks individually. Although some recipes call for olive oil, butter is the most commonly used.

Layering phyllo is very simple. Spread a sheet of phyllo into your prepared pan. Use your fingers to gently press it into the corners and brush the entire surface and sides with melted butter. Lay another sheet of phyllo over this, again pressing the edges down and brushing it with more butter. Continue to layer the phyllo and butter for 4 to 6 sheets for a thin crust or 7 to 8 sheets for a thicker crust.

You'll notice that you have all sorts of corners and edges hanging out over your pan, but don't cut them away. Put your filling into the pie and then fold the edges over it, using more butter brushed on the edges to keep them down.

Lay a sheet of phyllo over the top of the filling and brush it with butter. You can get an exact fit by folding the edges under or tucking them down, into the sides between the pan and the bottom crust. I use a stiff pastry brush and tap on the edges gently to get them to tuck into the pan. Continue layering the top sheets as you did for the bottom. When you have added the last phyllo sheet, brush the entire surface with butter.

Most phyllo pan pie recipes call for you to score the top before you bake it. To do this, look at your prepared pie for a moment and imagine how you will serve it. Squares, wedges or as for Baklavá, diamonds. Whatever design you choose, remember that it will cook right into the crust, so there's no changing your mind after it's baked. Although you could slice it another way to serve, it won't look so nice.

Once you've decided how you want the servings to be, get yourself a small bowl of water and place it on your work surface. Dip your knife into the water and gently run it along the phyllo to indent the layer. Don't worry about water dripping on the surface of the pie, it will quickly evaporate when it's in the oven. Dip your knife again and make another indent. Keep doing this until the surface of the pie is finished. Personally, I try not to actually slice through the layer because when the pastry bakes, it flakes up at the cuts so I use the non cutting edge of my knife. But others prefer to get the cuts so that they have the added crispiness. The choice is yours.

Once you've finished scoring the top, your pie is ready to be baked as per your recipe directions. During the baking time, I have sometimes found that my phyllo is browning much too fast for the filling to be cooked. My first response is to check that the oven is on Bake and not Convection. A convection setting will crisp the thin phyllo way too fast. After I check the setting, and I see that the pie is still in danger of getting the phyllo burnt before it's done, I lower the oven temperature by 25°F and loosely lay a sheet of aluminum foil over the pie. The foil is removed at the last 10 minutes of baking time for the crust to finish browning.

Using Phyllo for Individual Pies:

Phyllo sheets are commonly used for an assortment of individual savory as well as sweet pies. Any filling can be wrapped up in the thin flaky pastry sheets and they can take on any size or shape. Always remember that phyllo is a delicate pastry and shouldn't be filled with soggy ingredients. When making indiviual pies especially, make sure that you cook down the filling more so than for a pastry dough crust, so it's dryer and easier to manage.

If you'd like to get creative with phyllo, practice first. Take a cloth kitchen towel and lay it out, pretending that it's a sheet of phyllo. Fold it and wrap it up, imagining what shape your pie would take. This is also a good way to figure out exactly where the filling should go so it's centered.

Folding Phyllo Triangles:

Lay a stack of phyllo sheets on a cutting board and cut them into 3" x 10" strips for small triangles. For larger triangles, slice the phyllo sheets into half or thirds length wise. Phyllo dries out very quickly, so keep it covered with a slightly dampened cloth until you're ready to use it.

Take a strip of phyllo and brush it with butter and lay another strip over it. Scoop a tablespoon of filling about 2 inches away from the bottom edge. Fold the bottom corner, forming a right angle, over the filling. Continue to fold up the pastry and filling into right angles - or "flag style" until it is a neat little wrapped package.

Following recipe instructions, place the triangles on a greased cookie sheet, seam side down and brush them with butter, or olive oil. The actual size of the triangles can be altered to accommodate more filling if you wish. Just cut the strips into bigger pieces.

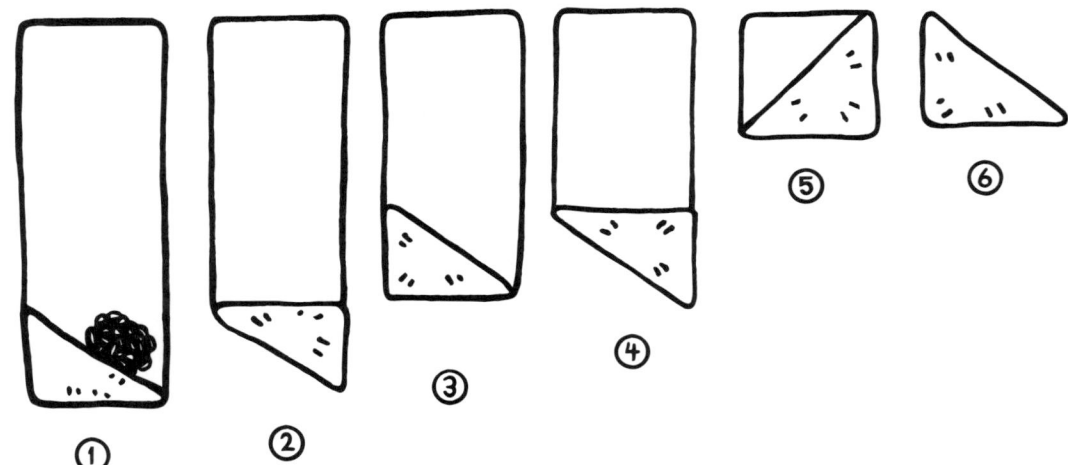

Folding Phyllo Rectangles:

Taking four phyllo sheets, lay them out on a counter on top of each other. Cut the pastry into 4 quarters cross wise so you have 16 equal pieces (enough for 8 pites). Brush each phyllo square with butter and set them aside, covered with a towel.

Take one whole phyllo sheet, lay it out and brush it with butter. Take two of the cut squares and place them on top of each other in the center of the right half of the full sheet. Spoon filling in the center of the squares.

Fold in the sides, lengthwise, over the filling and brush the edges with butter. Begin at one end of the rectangle and begin to fold it up. You are simply making a package for the filling, so fold it as big or as small as you would like. Repeat the steps using up the phyllo and the filling. Place the squares on a greased cookie sheet, seam side down and brush them with butter, or olive oil. Repeat the steps until you've used up the filling and pastry sheets. Bake as per your recipe directions.

Folding Phyllo Tubes or Cigars:

Lay your stack of phyllo on the counter and cut them into four quarters by making a cross. Set them aside, covered with a towel.

Lay one square in front of you and brush it with butter and lay another square over it. Take one spoonful of filling and place it in a line like fashion keeping two inches away from the bottom and side edges of the phyllo square.

Fold in the side edges lengthwise, over the filling and brush them with butter. Take the bottom edge of the phyllo and fold it over so the filling is at the fold. Gently take the filling end and begin to roll it up like a cigar. Place the rolls on a greased cookie sheet, seam side down and brush them with butter, or olive oil. Repeat the steps until you've used up the filling and pastry sheets. Bake as per your recipe directions.

Folding Phyllo Coils and Wreaths:

Simply follow the directions for the phyllo tubes, using a little less stuffing and rolling the tubes looser so they are more pliable. For a wreath, place the tube on the cookie sheet and gently pull it around so the ends meet.

For a coil, simply wrap the tube around on it's self, being careful that the phyllo doesn't break or tear. Large coils make nice Holiday centerpieces and desserts.

Basic Seed and Nut Knowledge

Village style almond shelling.

Some recipes call for roasting, toasting or blanching fresh seeds and nuts. By taking this extra step, you will give these ingredients a rich flavor and aroma.

Roasting:
Spread the seeds or nuts out on a cookie sheet, into a single layer. Bake them at 350°F for 20 to 30 minutes, shaking or stirring them occasionally. The seeds and nuts will turn a slight golden color and the actual time involved will depend on the size of the nut or seed that you are using. Let them cool down completely and store the unused seeds and nuts in zip-lock bags or glass jars.

Stove top Toasting:
Heat a heavy skillet and dry-fry the seeds and nuts, stirring them constantly. They will turn a rich color and are ready to be used for any recipe.

Blanching:
To blanch nuts such as chestnuts and almonds, bring some water to a boil. Boil the nuts for 2 to 3 minutes, drain them and let them cool down a bit so you can handle them. Use your fingers to slide off the skins.

Salting:
To make salted peanuts or chickpeas, spritz the hot roasted nuts with water. Sprinkle them with salt and return them to the oven for a few minutes to dry them out again.

Whitening Sesame Seeds

Plain sesame seeds are whitened because they hold up better in baking and cooking recipes as well as give a nicer appearance.

Ingredients:
2 lbs. sesame seeds
2 cups sifted wood ashes from olive and pine
water

In a cooking pot, mix together the sesame and the ashes with enough water to cover them. Bring it to a boil and cook for 15 minutes. Pour the mixture into a fine strainer and rinse it under the running water, stirring it with your hands to get rid of any ashes. Let the sesame drain and then spread it out on kitchen towels to dry.

Toasted Chickpeas / *Stragália*

Dried chickpeas can be made into a delicious cocktail snack. Old ways or modern method are two ways of making these nutty tasting tidbits.

Modern Method
Bring some water to a boil and add the chick peas. Let them cook for 5 minutes and then drain them. Spread the chickpeas on a cookie sheet and bake them at 400°F for 30 minutes.

Old Ways Method
On your next trip to the beach, get a bucketful of fine sand. When you get it home, rinse it many times under running water, getting rid of any dirt and particles. Spread it out on a piece of linen and set it out in the sun to dry completely.

Rinse a pound of dry chick peas in water and then drain them. To a cooking pot, add enough clean sand so it comes up to about the middle of it. Heat the sand so it gets hot and stir in the chickpeas. Toss and mix them as they toast. You'll know when they're done by tasting one. It should be crisp yet chewed easily. Pour the contents of the pot a little at a time into a mesh sifter and shake it so the sand falls through and you are left with clean chickpeas.

Preparing Fresh Vegetables

For common sense vegetables such as potatoes, tomatoes, cucumbers, carrots, green peppers, mushrooms and so on....I'll spare you the list of instructions simply because most people can handle cutting up a salad. Do make sure that you wash all your vegetables very well. Because of the amount of poisons and pesticides used today, always begin your vegetable preparation by making up a basin of soapy water, using a mild dish detergent. Use your hands to wash the vegetables and leafy greens and then rinse them in running water.

Cleaning Fresh Artichokes:

Fill a large bowl half full with water - about 2 quarts. Squeeze the juice of two lemons into it and give it a slight stir to mix. You will be using this mixture to keep the cleaned artichokes from turning brown until you're ready to use them in your recipe. Wash the whole artichokes in soapy water and rinse well to remove any dust, pesticides and insects. Let them drain.

Lay an artichoke on a cutting board and cut off the bottom. Begin removing the leaves until you get to the tender heart. You will have to remove quite a few leaves and the heart will only be about $1/3$ or $1/4$ the size of the whole artichoke. You'll also notice a change in texture and color. The outer leaves are very tough and dark where as the heart will be much more pliable and lighter in color. The first time I tried to clean a fresh artichoke, I ended up pulling off all the leaves because I couldn't tell the difference between them. If this happens to you, don't despair. Just think of the first one as a practice run.

Once you've gotten to the heart, cut off the pointy tips of the leaves. Use your fingers to spread them apart so you can get to the center of it. You'll find that the center is fuzzy and has spiky leaves in there. Cut away the fuzz and the prickly leaves then use a spoon to scoop out any more fuzz that remains in the center. Drop the cleaned artichoke into the lemon-water and proceed with the next one.

Cleaning Fresh Broccoli and Cauliflower:

I have found on occasion, small caterpillars in my unprepared broccoli and cauliflower, so I am very careful when I clean it. Begin by washing it in soap and water, letting the heads soak for 5 minutes. Rinse them off and then return them to the basin to soak for another 5 minutes in clean water. If there are any critters in the heads, they will begin to emerge, so check them out and then set them aside to drain. Fill your basin up with water and mix in some vinegar, just incase there are any stubborn visitors remaining. Take a head of the vegetables and begin cutting off the clusters. If they are large, slice them in half so you have uniform pieces. Drop the clusters into the water to soak until all the vegetables have been cut up. Swish the cut pieces through the water and rinse them off. Set them aside to drain and use as per your recipe directions.

Cleaning Fresh Eggplant:

Many people think that eggplants have to be soaked for a long time to remove any bitterness in the peel. Personally, I don't think this is true, but since many people are set in their ways, I won't argue. Make yourself a basin of fresh, salted water. Cut off the green, stem end from the washed eggplants. Depending on the recipe you are making, the eggplants will be sliced, cubed, hollowed out or halved. Proceed with the preparation as per your recipe requirements. Once the eggplants have been cut, put them in the salted water and use a dish to keep them submerged. I only do this to keep them from oxidizing or turning brown until I'm ready to use them. If you would prefer to soak them for a sweeter taste, 30 minutes to an hour should be ample time to get rid of any bitterness. Drain the eggplants and proceed with the recipe.

Cleaning Fresh Green Beans:

Choose firm beans that are crisp and don't look wilted or brown. Pick up a green bean and using your fingers, snap off an end. Some beans will snap apart nicely and other will need to have the strings removed. You can tell if the string is tough and will need to be pulled off because they will come up at the veins as the bean snaps. If this happens, pull the string down lengthwise on the bean and then snap off the other end and pull that string down. Depending on the length of your beans, you can snap them in half or quarters so they are easier to cook and serve, removing any strings that come up as you go along. Continue until all the beans are done.

Cleaning Fresh Leafy Greens:

For vegetables such as spinach, kale, lettuce and Swiss chard, begin by picking through the stems and discarding any browning or very wilted leaves. Cut off any hard stems so the tender leaves and stalks are left and put them into a basin with soapy water. Wash the leaves well, swishing them through the soap. Drain them and place them under running water, rinsing them well then setting them aside to drain thoroughly.

Cleaning Fresh Okra:

Okra can be a tricky vegetable. Personally, I get itchy whenever I handle the hairy little pods, so I wear plastic gloves to prepare them. You have to be very gentle when you handle okra. If you break the pods and any seeds come out, when you cook them, they will turn your soup or stew "glutinous" or, in layman's terms—slimy.

Fill a large bowl, half full with water - about 2 quarts, and pour in 1 cup of plain vinegar. Begin by rinsing them. I prefer to use a bit of dish detergent in a small basin for a good wash because of all the pesticides out there, before I rinse them off. But if you're leery about handling them too much, skip this and just rinse them under running water in a colander. Lay out a large kitchen towel, and spread the rinsed okra on it to dry as you're working.

Take an okra in one hand and a paring knife in the other. You want to "peel" off the outer layer of the cap. Don't cut straight across or you'll cut into the pod. Cut it on a diagonal, round and round, so it looks like the okra has a little pointed hat. Use a few okra as practice pieces, it really isn't difficult at all. Put the cleaned okra into the vinegar water and proceed with the next one. When you're done with all the okra, strain them from the vinegar water. You can use them right away in a recipe or put them into zip-lock bags and freeze them for later use.

Roasting Vegetables

Some Greek recipes call for roasted vegetables as ingredients. This is the easiest way that I have found to prepare them with as little hassle possible. Use only firm, fresh vegetables. Green peppers for example are much easier to clean if the skins are smooth and unwrinkled. Wash the whole vegetables well with soap and water and set aside to drain. Take each vegetable individually and wrap it completely in a piece of aluminum foil. Make sure that you have a good seal as the vegetable will roast in it's own juices and you don't want the steam to escape.

Heat the oven to 400°F and place the wrapped vegetables on the center rack. Bake them until tender. You'll know that they're done by giving them a squeeze (wear an oven mitt as the veggies will be hot). Eggplants, for example will be very soft and squishy when they're done.

Remove the roasted vegetables from the oven and let them cool down, while still wrapped. When they are manageable, carefully remove the foil - watch out as it may have liquid in it condensed from the steam. Personally, I reserve this vegetable liquid and use it in the recipe.

Roasted eggplants can be sliced down the middle and the pulp scooped out with a spoon. Peppers are a bit trickier. If you took my suggestion and used fresh, smooth peppers, you'll see that the skins have almost separated by themselves. Using a spoon, scrape off the pepper pulp, discarding the skins, seeds and stems.

The Mysterious Bean

Greeks are very fond of legumes and use them in an infinite way throughout their cooking. There was a time that legumes were depended on as the major source of protein for a growing family - especially during the war years. Back then, a hot dish of plain boiled lentils served with a dousing of olive oil and some bread was considered a very good meal that you were lucky to have. Although today, you may hear them referred to as a Poor Man's meal by some folk, legumes are still enjoyed very much in Greece. Other than being good for you, they fit in beautifully with the Greek Orthodox weekly and Lenten fasting days.

I've often been asked questions concerning the preparation and cooking of beans and legumes. It seems that to a lot of people, beans are a mysterious ingredient and they are hesitant to enjoy these goodies, simply because they don't know how to prepare them or they have tried to cook them but they came out tough.

Beans are economical, a wonderful source of protein and a very popular ingredient in Greek cooking. So don't get discouraged, you just have to find the method that suits the beans that are available to you. Here you'll find some tips and pointers that will help you prepare the perfect bean.

Where do I begin ?...

The easiest way to begin a recipe with dried beans is to soak them overnight. Just put the dry beans of your choice into a large bowl or pot and add enough water to cover them twice. Let them set out at room temperature until the next day or at least for 6 hours. Drain them and then begin your recipe.

I forgot to soak the beans...

If you have forgotten to soak your beans the night before, there is still hope. Put the dry beans in a pot with enough water to cover them twice. Bring them to a boil and let them cook for 15 minutes. Remove the pot from the heat, cover it tight and let them soak in the hot liquid for 2 hours. This should soften them enough to use in the recipe of your choice. Drain them and then begin your recipe.

Beans give me gas...

I have found that by pre-boiling beans before beginning a recipe reduces the amount of gas that they produce. The process is very simple. Drain the beans that have been soaking overnight and put them in a pot with fresh water. Bring them to a boil and cook them for 5 to 10 minutes. You will notice that all sorts of foam and froth collects on the surface of the water. Strain the beans and rinse them under cold running water, removing any foam residue. They are ready to use in the recipe of your choice.

I can't get my lima beans to cook...

Some larger beans may need more preparation before beginning a recipe to insure that they will cook up tender. After the beans have been soaked overnight, drain them and stick them in a pot with plain water and boil them for an hour or two, until they are more than half done. Drain them from the hot liquid and begin your recipe.

The chickpeas were tough....

Chick peas can be tricky to cook up. Although they look small, they are a very tough bean. One way to tenderize them is to soak the chickpeas overnight in plain water. The next day, after you have drained them, toss them with 1 tbs. of baking soda and let them sit for about an hour. Rinse them with lots of running water then use as per your recipe directions.

There's too much olive oil in the recipe...

Yes, I know that some of the legume recipes call for quite a bit of olive oil to be poured into them. There is a Greek saying on the islands that goes.....

"I fakí éfaye to ládi" ... or... "The lentils ate the oil"

And that is exactly what happens. Legumes absorb the oil in the recipes. Bean and lentil soups especially, so much so that you won't see any oil in the finished product. Other than giving your stew a wonderful taste, the olive oil will also thicken it. In recipes that include meat cuts such as "Pork and Limas," it's preferable that you remove as much fat from the meat as possible, but go ahead and use the olive oil that's called for. Not only will you have a flavorful meal, it's healthier too.

The Glorious Pressure Cooker

The pressure cooker has become an indispensable modern convenience for me, especially when cooking legumes. I always use a medium pressure setting and watch the clock carefully. Lentil soup can be cooked in 15 minutes, white and navy beans need about 20 minutes and fat beans, such as limas can be done in 25 to 30 minutes. As you can see, it drastically reduces cooking time so you're not stuck in the kitchen all day. Just make sure that you have enough liquid in the pot so the beans don't scorch.

Plucking, Cleaning & Preparing Fresh Birds

Begin the preparation process by getting yourself a pot or pan, larger than the bird that you want to clean and fill it ²/₃ with plain water. Bring the water to a boil them set the pot into a large sink, or even outside on your porch, depending on where you want to work. Note that this does get messy, so have a large work- space available. Lay the bird into the hot water and let it soak for a few minutes, using a wooden spoon or dowel to submerge it.

Now lift the bird out of the water and begin to pull the feathers off with your hands. It will be hot, so be careful. Though slightly uncomfortable, you may want to try wearing plastic gloves for this. Continue to dip the bird into the hot water and pulling off the feathers until they are all gone. Some birds have very fine feathers that are almost impossible to get off. Don't worry about them as they can be burned off later with a flame from a candle or fire.

Set the plucked bird down on a cutting board. Cut off the neck, head and feet. Feel for the bottom of the breastbone and cut from there all the way down and to the back. Remove the organs from the inside cavity, taking care not to rupture the small green sac of bile because it will make the meat taste bitter. Rinse the bird inside and out and pat it dry.

Depending on your choice of bird and the size of it, you should let a fresh bird sit in the refrigerator for a day or two to drain the blood from the meat which will also help make it more tender. After this time, it's ready to be used in your favorite recipe.

Cleaning and Preparing Heads for Soups and Roasts

Beef, Lamb and Goat Heads:
The mouth, nose and ears of the head have to be cleaned. The easiest way to do this is to simply remove the nose and ears completely. Use a sharp knife to cut a hole into the ear cavity and scoop out the cartilage and unwanted debris. The mouth should be pulled open and rinsed out under running water, very well. If you have a hard time doing this, make incisions on either side of the cheeks, next to the jaw bones so it's easier. Scrape off the tongue and if parts of the neck and throat are intact, you should rinse that out too.

For making soup, if possible, have your butcher do as much of the cleaning as possible and split the cranium in half. It will make cooking and serving much easier for you. If the head you are preparing is from a fresh slaughter then you should let it sit in the refrigerator for the blood to drain from the flesh. A large beef head should be kept for 3 to 4 days where as smaller lamb or goat heads would only need to drain for 1 or 2 days. After this time, soak the cleaned head in enough water to cover it with the juice of 2 or 3 lemons squeezed into it. Keep the head submerged for one hour then drain and use in your recipe.

Pig Heads:
Many times, the pigs head will still have a few stray hairs as well as the hard rind on it. You can easily get rid of the hairs by burning them off with a flame from a candle. Another solution is to put the head in your kitchen sink and pour boiling hot water over it. This will get the rind to come up and you can peel it off, hairs and all or use a knife and scrape it away. The village ladies of old, used to set the pig's head over an open fire, turning it often to get the rind to come up. This is an option for you if you have a fire place or a barbeque grill.

The snout, mouth and ears will have to be cleaned out and rinsed thoroughly as well as any inner throat area. Again, get a good butcher to do this for you or follow the directions above and do it yourself. If the head you are preparing is from a fresh slaughter then you should let it sit in the refrigerator for 2 to 3 days, depending on the size of the animal, for the blood to drain from the flesh. After this time, soak the cleaned head in enough water to cover it with the juice of 2 or 3 lemons squeezed into it. Keep the head submerged for one hour then drain and use in your recipe.

Cleaning Intestines

If you are a seasoned sausage maker, you may have one of those attachments for a food processor that packs the intestines with stuffing and you can use any length of intestines that you prefer. When stuffing sausages by hand, it's much easier to have the intestines cut into smaller, manageable pieces that are about 20 to 30 inches in length.

Since it's the large intestine that is used, it should be cleaned out very well. Begin by running clean water through each intestine piece by attaching it to the tap, very much like a garden hose. Press the intestine between your fingers, rubbing it to clean away any brown or gray particles. Continue with each intestine piece and set them aside.

Using a wooden dowel or stick, push the one end of the intestine into itself to turn it inside out and again, wash them very thoroughly. The intestines should look very white and clean, with no traces of gray or brown matter.

Set the clean intestines in a large bowl and cover them with water. Add the juice of 4 or 5 lemons and mix it in. Let the intestines soak for at least one hour. Drain them well and they are ready to use for sausage making or for your favorite recipe.

Cleaning and Preparing Tripe

Tripe, the stomach of animals such as goats and lambs is used to make into soup and other strange, Greek delicacies. To prepare fresh tripe, you should begin by rinsing the stomach under running water. Turn it inside out and rinse it some more. If needed, cut it into smaller, manageable pieces. You'll notice that the interior lining is similar to a brown-gray, carpeting sort of stuff, let the tripe drain with this lining on the outside.

Bring a pot of water to a boil and set it next to your sink. Dip the tripe into it for a few minutes. Remove the tripe from the hot water and using a knife, scrape off the gray, rough lining so the meat remains clean and white. Rinse the tripe and let it drain.

Cut the clean tripe into pieces one to two inches square. Put the tripe into a bowl and cover it with water. Add one or two tablespoons of salt and the juice of 4 or 5 lemons. Let the tripe soak for one or two hours. Rinse the meat and set it aside to drain. It's ready to use in your favorite recipe.

Preparation tips for Open Pit Barbeques - *Soúvles*

Many Greek celebration and holiday menus include open pit barbeques. Whether the main course is lamb, goat or pig, it roasts slowly as it turns over the hot coals, making every bite tender and juicy. Today, this type of cookout is often had just for fun as a picnic or as a party for good friends. The crowd gathers having drinks and *mezédes* for the hours it takes for the meat to cook. Many times, the soúvla doesn't make it to the table because everyone just picks off the spit as it roasts.

Many villagers use old barrels or water heating tanks that have been cut in half as their home barbeque pit. For larger celebrations, when many animals will be roasted, they will actually dig an area of their yard and convert it for this purpose. No matter what type of pit or grill you are using, remember to position it away from any wind. Aside from losing heat from the coals, you don't want your meat covered in ashes that may be stirred up by a sudden gust.

Villagers light their charcoal 1 to 2 hours before they begin roasting the meats. This is because our charcoal is made from burned olive and pine woods and need to be fired longer in order to get coals. The kind of briquettes that you can buy in a store, will be easier and faster to light but they won't last as long as real wood charcoal. Read the directions on the type of charcoal that you're using and estimate how much you'll need for the hours that it will take to roast the meat.

For *soúvles*, use small animals. Baby goat or kid, should be from 16 to 30lbs. for best results. Lamb and pork are heavier, so choose an animal that is from 20 to 35lbs.

You're going to need a large work surface so clear an area that you don't mind getting messy. Have your butcher remove the head and internal organs. The heads can be saved for soup or roasts and the livers and kidneys from goat and lamb can be fried up as a *mezé* to serve to your guests while they are waiting for the meat to cook.

Wash the carcass under running water and drain well. Lay it out on a large clean surface. Rub it down with the seasonings that your recipe calls for, inside and out. At this point, I recommend wrapping it up and refrigerating it over night for the meat to absorb the spices. If you don't have a refrigerator that will fit it, at least let it stand at room temperature for a few hours before you begin the barbeque.

Attach the carcass to the spit. You will have to spear through its rear end and come up through the neck, so the length of it is stretched out along the spit. Tie the legs, neck and forearms down tight. We use a fine grade aluminum wire that is available at hardware stores and pliers. You have to get the meat secured on the spit so that it turns evenly, without slipping while cooking.

Also pass some wire through the body cavity and out the back of the meat at the spine and tie it to the spit from there as well. This will make it that much more secure. Make it tight – remember as it cooks, it will shrink. When you are finished securing it, follow your recipe directions and if no other ingredients are called for, use more wire and "sew" up the cavity.

Pour some oil into your hands, rub the entire carcass so it is coated. This will help seal in the juices as well as give you a crispy outer crust.

Arrange the hot coals so there will be more at the breast and hind area, which is the thickest part of the animal. Place the spit over the coals at a high position for the first hour. Once the heat of the coals has died down a bit, lower the spit and continue cooking. You want to roast it slowly over low heat, for 3 to 6 hours, depending on the size and type of the animal. A 22 lb. goat will take 4 hours cooking time where as a 22 lb. lamb will need 5 hours. If you have an electric spit, great. If you have a hand turned one, make sure that you keep the cook in plenty of Ouzo for the duration! You can check if the meat is done by piercing the thickest part, such as the thigh area with a fork.

Remember to baste the roast with marinade every so often. See the section about Herbal Basting Brushes and concoct one of your own. By using it, you'll really add so much more flavor.

For an added treat, wrap some eggplants and green peppers in aluminum foil and put them in the coals to roast when you begin the barbequing. Take them out an hour later and make Roasted Eggplant Salad, to go along with your meal. Potatoes are also delicious when roasted in coals. Wrap them up in some aluminum foil and roast them for the last hour of cooking time. They'll be ready and hot just as the meat comes off the spit.

To serve a spit roast, simply take the cooked meat on the spit back to your work surface. Using wire cutters or pliers, remove all the wire that was used. Have a friend hold down the meat using forks or rags and pull the spit out. With a heavy knife or cleaver, cut the meat into portions and serve.

Herbal Basting Brushes

It wasn't until a few years after I moved to the Islands that I actually witnessed what would forever stay in my mind. We were entertaining a few friends for a garden party and my brother-in-law offered to take over as "chef" of the barbequing. Grateful for the offer, I passed him the tray of luscious marinated pork chops and chicken pieces with a small bowl of extra marinade and a long handled basting brush. He looked at the brush as though he had never seen one before and handed it back to me saying that he had no use for it.

Now, we all know, good basting is the secret to tender, juicy meats so as I reached for the brush, I'm sure that I looked horrified. All I could imagine was my hard work dripping away with the juices of the meats into the burning coals. Taking a deep breath, I quickly walked away.

A few moments later, after I practiced a short speech about how we were going to have "shoe soles" for dinner, I went back outside but stopped in my tracks. There he stood, over the hot coals, basically whacking the sizzling meat with a small piece of greenery dipped in the marinade. Dip and whack, dip and whack, he continued right across the grill. Coming to his side, I just stared at the implement, trying to figure out what exactly the greenery was. He smiled knowingly as he explained that it was simply a few sprigs of fresh basil cut from a plant that I had growing right there in the yard. He also promised that I was in for a treat.

And he was right. I can't explain just how delicious the pork and chicken was. You could taste only a hint of the fresh herb, but that was all that was needed. It was heavenly. From that day on, no barbequing of ours has been done without an herbal brush of some kind.

Any fresh herbs can be used for the brush so use your imagination and experiment. Try using some fresh rosemary sprigs the next time that you're barbequing lamb and you'll be pleasantly surprised, as I was, as to how something so simple can make such a big difference.

The brush is very simple to make. Cut off a large branch or some stems at least 6 inches long as you want a nice bunch. You can tie them together as they are or for barbequing safety, tie them securely to a long barbecue fork using butchers cord or wire. Dip the sprigs into some marinade and brush them over the meat that's grilling or roasting. Very easy and absolutely delicious.

For seafood and fish you may want to try the Lemon Brush. Use a long fork as a handle and poke it through a lemon half. Dip the lemon in the marinade and gently spread it over your grilling meats. The lemon brush is also used quite often when open-pit barbequing meats such as whole lamb and baby goat.

Don't limit the use of herbal brushes to just barbequing. Fantastic gourmet results can be obtained when you're roasting meats, fish, chops or poultry right in your kitchen oven. If you're lucky enough to have a selection of herbs growing close to home, try using a mixture of them. Just a sprig or two of rosemary, basil, marjoram, sage and oregano can turn plain roasted chicken into a delight.

The Do's and Don'ts of Fish Preparation

The Greek islands are famous for their fresh fish and seafood. On many occasion, you'll witness the surprised look on a tourist's face when he gets a fish entree. Expecting to see a filleted portion, they are rather taken aback when they get the whole thing from head to tail. Not knowing where to begin, they usually start by hacking off the head, much to our despair because as most Greeks know, the head is the best part!

Shopping for Fresh Fish:
Lets begin with a fresh fish of your choice. Although most fish can be used in an array of different recipes, some varieties are exceptional when used in specific recipes. Take a look at the end of this section to help you choose what variety you are looking for and for what purpose. More of a guide line than a rule is that large fish are usually for baking, grilling and making soups where as medium and small sized fish are used for pan frying.

Checking for Freshness:
The easiest way to tell if fish is fresh is to look at it's eyes. A fresh fish has clear eyes so the color shows through where as an older fish will have cloudy eyes. Check out the gills as well as they should be red in color. If the gills look dark, then it's been at the fish market for a while. Another test you can do is to poke the fish with your finger. Fresh fish has firm meat where as an older fish will be soft.

Cleaning Fresh Fish:
Cleaning the fish is the first part of the preparation process. You may want to wear gloves for this. Some fish have very sharp fins and may prick you, so be careful. Depending on the variety, some fish have very large fins and long tails. You can shorten them if you choose to by cutting them with a knife or a pair of poultry cutters. This is especially useful if you need your fish to fit into a frying pan. For baked fish, I would just let the fins be. I think that they make a much nicer presentation.

Begin by taking off the scales. You can do this by using a knife, fork, or a fishermen's scaler. Hold the fish by it's tail and run the tool up towards the head. You'll notice that you're going against the grain of the scales and they will probably spatter everywhere, so I do suggest that you do this outside or in an area that is easily cleaned up. Once the scales have been removed from the entire fish, rinse it off and lay it on your cutting board.

Place the fish so its belly is facing you. Make a cut just below the head all the way back to the tail. Remove and discard all the innards and guts. If you choose to leave the head on - Greek style, just poke your fingers into the gills and pull them out and discard. If you have decided to remove the head (tisk, tisk!), then just cut it off at the neck. Rinse the fish, inside and out under running water and set it aside to drain.

Filleting Fresh Fish:
The thought of having to deal with fish bones, fins or heads may be a little too much for some people and they prefer that their fish be filleted. It's not a difficult process, but it may take you a few practice runs to get the knack of it. Don't discard the head, tail and fins. Use them to make *Psarósoupa* - Island Fish soup.

Lay the cleaned fish on a cutting board. Cut off the head and tail fin as well as all other fins on the fish, depending on the variety. It's easier to cut off a little bit of meat along with the fin when doing this. Now look at the neck, where you have cut off the head. The thick spine bone should be very visible. Use a sharp knife and run the knife along the bones, cutting down the belly and around the back so you end up on the neck side again. It helps if your other hand is gently pulling up on the fillet while your doing this so you can see exactly where the bones are. After the top fillet has been removed, you can pull up the spine bone and using you knife, cut under it to get the second fillet.

Seasoning Fresh Whole Fish:
Always season your fish with salt and pepper or any herbs that your recipe calls for, inside and out. Do this at the start of a recipe so the fish has time to soak up the spices before you cook it.

Tips for Fried Fish:
Make sure that when frying fish your oil is hot before the fish is placed in the skillet. This will help to keep the fish from sticking to your pan as well as giving you a wonderful crusty skin. Don't overly heat the oil though, as you want the fish to cook, not burn while it's frying. To test heating oil, sprinkle a pinch of flour into it. If it foams up when it touches the surface, then it's ready.

There should be enough hot oil in the pan so that the fish is half submerged. The first side will cook evenly and then when you flip it over, so will the other.

Test fried fish for doneness by gently piercing it with a fork. The meat should be flaky and there should be no traces of translucent color left. A medium sized fish may take between 3 to 5 minutes to fry on each side.

Serving Large Fish:
Let the fish stand at room temperature a few minutes before serving. This will make it easier to portion out. Beginning at the neck or tail end and using a spatula or a large flat spoon gently cut into the fish just half way deep so that the utensils run against the spine. This will give you beautiful portions with minimal bones. Remember to spoon some of the broth from the pan over each portion and to serve lemon halves for those that would like a squeeze or two. When the top half of the fish has been served, discard the spine and serve the bottom half.

Tips for Charcoaled Fish:
Take care when charcoaling fish because it's very easy to burn the skin and you'll get a burnt taste. The grill of your barbeque should be positioned about 4-6 inches over medium hot charcoal.

The best kind of grill to use is a double sided one that encloses the entire fish. It's easy to flip over and your fish will keep it's shape beautifully. Rub oil or marinade on the cold grill before you lay the fish on it to help keep it from sticking.

If your fish is very large, you can choose to score it or cut small incisions diagonally in the thickest parts of the meat. Although I believe that you lose a lot of natural juices this way, some folks insist that it's the best way for the perfect grill.

Use a marinade freely, basting the fish as often as possible to keep the meat succulent. Use an Herbal Brush or poke a long handled fork through a lemon half and use the juicy side dipped in marinade as the brush. Baste one side then flip the grill over for a minute or two while you baste the other side, then flip it over again. Continue the process and you'll have a great meal. A medium sized fish cooked over charcoal may take from 25 to 35 minutes until it's done. Test the fish for doneness by gently piercing it with a fork. The meat should be flaky and there should be no traces of translucent color left. Serve charcoal grilled fish immediately as the meat tends to dry out if you wait too long.

Defrosting Fish:
Fish should not be defrosted at room temperature because they will lose moisture from the meat and will become dry when you cook them. You can defrost the fish in the refrigerator for a day or two or for a

faster method, you can put the frozen fish in a basin of water to defrost.

Removing Fish Odors:

After cooking fish, bring a small pot of water to a boil with some lemon peels and let the steam go through the kitchen. Potpourri works nicely too.

Cooking utensils and pans may have a fish smell long after the meal has been eaten and the dishes have been done. When cleaning up after a fish dinner, rinse your utensils and pans in vinegar water or some baking soda mixed with water. Then proceed to use dish detergent or stick them in the dish washer.

Fingers and hands can get very smelly too. To get rid of the fishy odors just rub your hands with lemon juice or vinegar and then give them a good wash with soap. This also works if you're out to dinner. Take a lemon wedge with you to the restroom and wash up.

Fish Variety List

Use the following list to get an idea of what fish can be used for what purpose. It is not a rule book, so simply use it as a guide that can help you out when you're at the fish market. When making fish soup or fried fish, remember that almost any variety can be used. Use the economical fish for soups and fries and save the expensive varieties for grills and bakes.

Varieties of Fish to Broil or Charcoal Grill:

Turbot, Red Bream or Pandora, Large Pickerel, Red Mullet, Swordfish, Sea Bass, Whiting, Gilt head, Red Snapper, Grouper, Porgies, and Sea Bream.

Varieties of Fish for Soups:

Red Rockfish or Scorpion, Grouper, Striped Grey Mullet, Sea Pike, and Snapper.

Varieties of Fish for Oven Stews:

Gurnard, Pike, Striped Bass, Ocean Perch, Haddock, Halibut, and Snapper.

Varieties of Fish for Baking:

Flounder or Sole, Sea Bass, Sardines, Grouper, and Red Snapper.

Varieties of Fish for Frying:

Cod, Flounder or Sole, Red Mullet, White Bait, Pickerel and Smelt, Perch, Trout, and Red Snapper.

Preparing Fresh Squid and Cuttlefish

Today, many supermarkets carry frozen squid that has already been cleaned and cut into rings, saving you a lot of time and effort. But there may be an occasion, that you do decide to try some fresh squid for a certain recipe and that's when you'll find out just what the difference is. Taste wise, there is no comparing fresh seafood to frozen. The only draw back is that you're going to have to clean them before you can cook them up.

To clean a squid, you must first remove the elastic, gray skin. Its easily done by using a paring knife and just scraping down the sides of it. The skin will come up and then using your fingers peel it off and discard.

Cut the head away from the body just above the eyes. Cut off the tentacles from the rest of the head, just under the eyes so they remain in a cluster. The tentacles are completely edible, so don't throw them away. Do toss out the eyes because they will pop and spatter if they are cooked up. There is a small bony beak in the center of the tentacles - the mouth, which can be squeezed out easily using your fingers.

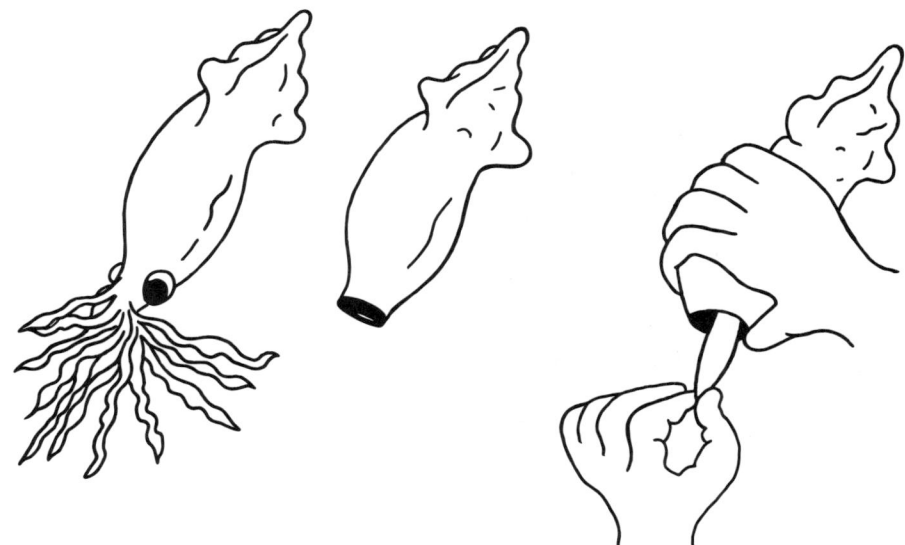

The body cavity contains a quill like cartilage. Pull this out and then squeeze out any jelly like insides. If you break the ink sac while you're cleaning the squid, don't worry. Just rinse it under cold running water while discarding the head and innards. You don't want sepia residue left on your squid as it's rather bitter tasting. Also, take care not to get ink on your clothing. It's a terrible stain to remove. Rinse the cleaned squid under cold running water, inside and out and let it drain. It's ready to be used in any recipe that you like.

Preparing Fresh Octopus

This fisherman sports a belt full of fresh caught octopus.

Many tourists to the Greek islands have caught glimpses of men at the beaches with mask and snorkel at their feet, beating a fresh caught octopus against the rocks of the shoreline. The process tenderizes the flesh of the octopus, making it that much nicer for cooking.

When an octopus is caught and taken out of the water, the fisherman will first turn its hood inside out. This will kill it. He then will begin the ritual of throwing it, full force against the jagged rocks, stopping on occasion to rub it against the rough surface. The octopus meat becomes foamy as this is done and is dipped into the sea to rinse off, before throwing it against the rocks again. This is continued for 40-50 times or until the flesh takes on a purplish gray color.

So now, your man has brought home his prize catch, and proudly, he hands it you fully expecting that you'll be able to clean it as well as cook the thing up. I do understand if by looking at the sac like body and the eight tentacles with the suckers discourages you. I wasn't too happy the first time that I was handed one. But really, it isn't difficult to clean them. In fact, I think that they are much easier to clean than fish - and less messier.

Start by turning the hood inside out and removing any traces of jelly like stuff. If your octopus has the ink sac and innards still in the hood, remove them. If the ink sac breaks, don't worry, just rinse the octopus under cold running water to get rid of it because it has a bitter taste and take care not to get it on your clothes because it stains.

Rinse the octopus well. Where the tentacles cluster together, you will find a thick beak. This is the mouth and should be removed as well as the eyes, because they pop and spatter when they cook. If you want to keep the whole octopus intact, for presentation purposes, make a small cut at the back of the head and remove any insides. Personally, I find it easier to cut away the clean flesh of the hood, just above the eyes. Then cut away the leg cluster, just below the eyes, and discard the eyes and all that's in-between.

Since most people don't have the luxury of having their octopus tenderized the island way, you may want to do it yourself. All you have to do is pound it against a sturdy surface or smack it with a mallet. Rinse the flesh under running water and set aside to drain. The octopus is ready to be used in your favorite recipe.

Preparing Fresh Moray Eels

When the fishermen tenderize their fresh caught octopus, special care is taken as moray eels can inhabit the surrounding reefs of the rocks that the octopus are thrown against. They are attracted to the smell of the foam and it's not unusual to have one swim up - too close for comfort.

This is when it's handy to have a spear gun and a talented friend nearby. Morays are dangerous creatures and very mean looking to the average person, like myself. Their bodies are much thicker than fresh water or smaller salt-water eels and their teeth are razor sharp. I am told that when a moray bites, his needle like teeth sink into the flesh and his strong jaws shut down, not letting go of the victim.

When hunting for morays, fishermen in the Islands always use a triple pronged spear - like Poseidon's. The single arrow like spears are not used because it's said that a wounded moray could slide up the spear and bite you. The fishermen always aim for the neck and once it's speared, they hold it against a rock so the moray doesn't slip off. Wounded morays thrash around violently but eventually they will tire and give in.

Once again the proud fisherman of the family appears at the door, but now the question is... What to do with the three foot "baby" moray that he's holding?... My first suggestion is to have a shot or two of Ouzo so you can get up the courage to approach the thing. Of course don't tell this to the fisherman. Tell him that you're toasting his good fortune. They really are ferocious looking creatures and extremely, absolutely slimy too. I still have a hard time getting near one much less handling it as well. But lets suppose that you are of thicker hide than I am and are willing to prepare this delicacy.

Begin the cleaning process by hanging up the moray from a sturdy structure. Insert thick fishing hooks into it's mouth and hang it up. You will need two rods from wooden dowels or pieces of bamboo reed. Don't use your hands as you may get stuck with a broken piece of spine. Take the rods in one hand and arrange them front and back around the moray. With your other hand, clamp the rods together, so you are forming a vice around the neck of the eel. Now, holding firmly, pull the rods down the length of the body. Move the rods back to the neck and again, pull down the length.

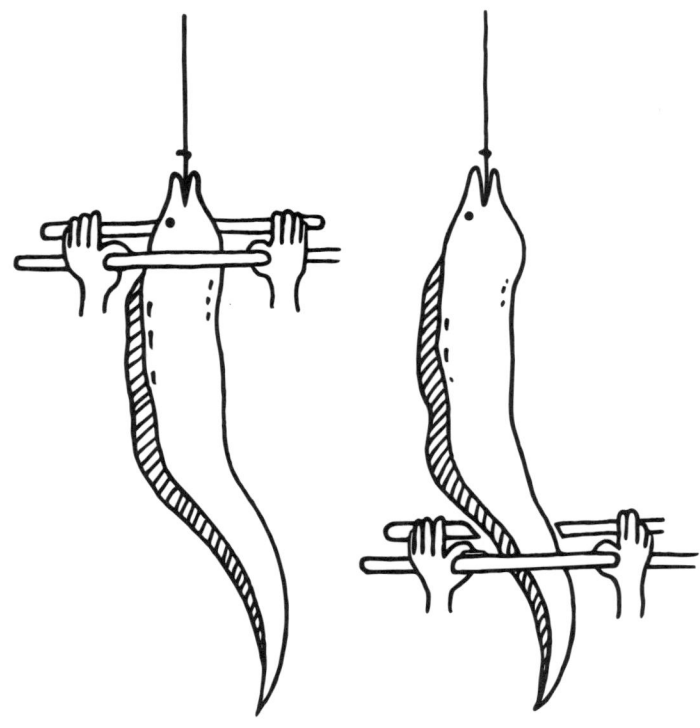

Continue doing this until a clump of bone forms at the tail. This clump is composed of the finer bones along the spine so by doing this, your meat will be that much cleaner. While the eel is still hanging, make an incision all around the neck, just below the head. The thick filmy skin will separate. Grip the skin on both sides of the body with pliers, and pull it down the length of the eel to the tail.

Lay the moray down on a sturdy work surface and use a cloth towel to hold it down while you're working. Cut off the peeled skin and the knob of bones at the tail. Slice down the stomach of the eel and remove the innards then cut off the head at the neck. Rinse the eel under cold running water, inside and out. Return it to your work surface and slice the body into pieces, about 1 inch thick. The slices can be used in any fish recipe of your choice.

Preparing Other Fruits Of The Sea

Fresh or Salt Water Eels - *Hélia*
Although fresh and salt water eels are not as dangerous looking as the moray, they are still very slimy and slippery too. You'll need to hold it down by the head on a solid work surface with a towel. Take a sharp knife and make an incision around the neck, just below the head. The thick filmy skin will separate. Grip the skin with a pair of pliers, and pull it down the length of the eel to the tail and cut it off. Make a slit down the length of the stomach and pull out the innards. Rinse the eel inside and out under cold running water. Cut off the head and slice the body into pieces.

Mussels - *Mídia*
This wonderful shell fish can be used in pilafs, stews and sauces or simply steamed. Mussels can be cleaned from any dirt or mud and added to a dish as they are with their shells on. They make a beautiful appearance and I think that by stewing the shell, it also adds more flavor. Although, it does get messy and sometimes it would be preferable to serve a dish with the small tidbits out of their shell.

To do this, begin by scrubbing them under running water. Discard any mussels that have already opened. Fill a pot with about an inch of water or use a steamer. Add the washed mussels and bring the water to a boil. Let them steam for 3 to 5 minutes, just until their shells open. Remove the pot from the heat and let the mussels cool down enough so you can handle them.

The shells can be pried open with your fingers or by using a blunt knife or oyster shucker. Use a knife and cut scoop out the flesh. Remove the hairy beards, and they are ready to use in your favorite recipe.

Sea Urchins - *Ahinioús*
Sea urchins are a delicacy on the islands that are found growing on the rocky reefs of the shallows during the summer months. Many times tourists will walk along these rocks and accidentally step on one, getting a painful thorn or spine embedded in their foot. These little balls of thorns resemble a chestnut casing but with much longer spines. Not all varieties of sea urchins are eaten and only the females, at that. You can tell apart the good ones from the color as the edible urchins are blue to brown and the completely black ones should not be eaten at all.

Unless you are a seasoned expert with sea urchins, you should wear heavy gloves to prepare them or else you take the risk of getting stuck with a spine. Pick up one of the thorny balls and examine it, looking for the 'eye'. Using a knife, grate away some of the thorns around the area and carefully break away the shell surrounding it so you have a good opening. Run your knife around the inside to get any eggs or membrane loose and pour the contents into a bowl. Some people prefer to grate away a much larger area of thorns so they can eat the contents "on the half shell."

Sea urchins have very little food inside them and are in no way as substantial a bite as an oyster, clam or mussel. I would say that eating the things is more like taking a drink of sea water. Serve sea urchins with fresh lemon wedges or if you pour the contents into a bowl, give it a sprinkle of olive oil as well.

Preparing Land Snails

Wild mountain or land snails are used for the recipes that call for them and not your ordinary garden variety. Often commercial grocers will import crates of the little critters in supermarkets of the islands. We don't eat garden snails because of the fact that they are considered unclean because of pesticides and weed killers.

When you are contemplating making a recipe that calls for land snails, remember that they have to be left in a covered crate or basket for 5 days with out food prior to their use so they can empty their intestines.

When preparing land snails, the *mánes* or females won't come out of their shells, so a small piece of the shell itself is cut away during the preparation stage. Although they are served whole in their shells, you can simply suck out the contents when they've been properly prepared. The males or *mounouhária* are smaller and usually, you can pull them right out, discarding the shells before you cook your meal.

Begin by setting your snails in a covered pan or basket in a corner for 5 days. After this time, rinse the snails in plenty of salted water, as many times as it takes to get rid of the slime. After they have been rinsed, fill a bowl with water and let them soak for one hour so they will come out of their shells.

Bring a pot of salted water to a boil and working quickly so they don't have time to retreat, drain the snails and throw them into the hot water. Let them boil for a moment or two and then drain them. Here you will see the difference of the males and females as the males should be almost completely out of their shells. Pick the meat and discard the empty shells. For the full, female shells, you will have to cut away a portion of the shell. Look at the side and how it coils around. Slice off the shell at the inner most 2 or 3 coils. By doing this, you are releasing the vacuum and the snail can be sucked out at dinner time by your guest.

Rinse them once or twice again, to remove any bits of shell and they are ready to use in your recipe of choice.

The Greek Pantry

The Greek Pantry

Contrary to popular belief, Greek cooking does not mean that you need a lot of special, unheard of ingredients. Let me remind you of the fact that no supermarkets were available to our ancestors. The staples of their daily meals consisted of very basic, simple items. Fresh produce, home-made cheeses, olives and olive oil, and wheat. On occasion there would be a catch of fish or a cut of meat that could be prepared for an evening meal or preserved for another day.

If anything, because of the conveniences available to us in our modern times, Greek cooking is simpler than ever. Today, you can buy a packet of phyllo pastry sheets at the supermarket where as our grandmothers had to make them from scratch. We can enjoy something as simple as a tomato salad throughout the year, but our ancestors had to wait for the summer season. Olive oil is another common item that is available on every supermarket shelf, and the best part is that you don't have to pick the olives yourself nor take them by donkey express to the mill. Ah! ... the joys of modern times!

To give you an idea of just how simple Greek cooking is, I've made a list of some basic items that should be in-stock in the Greek kitchen. Some are necessary for every day cooking, but others are for special occasion dishes. Take a look at the lists and see for yourself how simple our cuisine really is.

Fresh Produce:
Tomatoes
Cucumbers
Green Peppers
Carrots
Onions
Potatoes
Celery
Parsley
Dill Weed
Garlic
Eggplant
Zucchini
Mushrooms
Broccoli
Cauliflower
Spinach
Green Beans
Peas
Artichokes
Lemons

Dairy Products:
Eggs
Butter
Milk
Cream
Plain Yogurt

Feta Cheese
Greek *Kefalotíri* or Parmesan
Greek *Mizíthra* or Ricotta

Condiments & Garnishes:
Olive Oil
Vinegar
Mustard
Capers
Olives
Pickled Vegetables

Meats:
Pork - cuts of your choice
Beef - cuts of your choice
Lamb - cuts of your choice
Ground beef, pork or lamb
Liver

Poultry:
Chicken
Turkey
Duck

Game:
Use your preference

Seafood:
Fish of your choice
Shellfish of your choice

Specialties such as octopus and squid

Staples:
Flour, white and wheat
Corn Flour
Rice
Pastas of your choice
Legumes of all kinds

Bakery Items:
Ready Phyllo Pastry Sheets
Sugar
Baking Powder
Baking Soda
Granulated Yeast
Vanilla Extract
Raisins
Nuts
Sesame Seeds
Honey

Spices:
Basil
Rosemary
Bay Leaves / Laurel
Oregano
Spearmint
Salt
Pepper
Thyme
Cumin
Cinnamon
Nutmeg
Cloves

Greek Specialty Shop:
Vine Leaves
Taramá - Fish Roe
Salted Anchovies or Sardines
Smoked Herring - *Rénka*
Tahíni
Orzo Noodles
Mastic Spice
Mahlépi

Liquor Store:
Ouzo
Brandy
Wine

Have you noticed how most of the listed items are already in your home kitchen? As I said earlier, it doesn't take exotic ingredients to make Greek food. Since most of us are struggling to juggle families, jobs and homes, I know that there is often not enough time for the working mom or dad to make tomato sauce from scratch or clean fresh green beans for a stew.

Go ahead and use canned tomatoes or frozen green beans in your cooking as well as any other short cuts that are available to you. Although I'm a very adamant believer that "Fresh is Best," I do understand the need for some simplicity in our lives too. If you want to make Cheese pies, go ahead and use store bought, ready-made pastry. You'll have a delicious Greek snack and still have time to play with the kids.

Perhaps on a Sunday afternoon, or on a leisurely day you'll have a chance to get into Greek cooking in more detail. Or maybe it'll be a special occasion such as your Greek mother-in-law coming for a visit. Take the extra step of grinding up fresh tomatoes for a stew. Use the food processor to speed you along, and you'll see how something so simple can make such a big difference in taste.

Herbs and Spices for the Greek Kitchen

If you ever get a chance to walk through the mountains or even just the road sides of the Greek Islands, ... literally, "stop and smell the herbs." When I first came to the Islands, I couldn't tell one herb apart from another unless they were in small, clearly marked boxes on the supermarket shelf. One day, a walk with a local cousin gave me a lesson that I've remembered ever since.

You'll see all sorts of small bushes, about knee high as you walk around. Stop and take a good look at it. We do have many thorny plants so at first make sure that it is devoid of thorns as well as any "critters" such as snakes or scorpions that may be using it for shade.

Once you've taken a good look, rub a few leaves between your fingers and then smell them. You may be pleasantly surprised to find wild oregano, thyme and sage growing right on the roadside or where you least expect it, as happened to me, right next to my home. This also works with citrus trees such as lemons and oranges. The fragrance is beautiful.

The villagers will pick large bunches of wild herbs and teas in the spring time. After they are rinsed to remove dust and dirt, they are hung up to dry in the *esóspito*. A year's supply of the sweet smelling stems hang from the rafters readily available for any use.

Harvesting Fresh Herbs

Cut stems of fresh herbs about 6 to 12 inches in length. When you get the stems home, make some sudsy water using a plain dish detergent and swish the stems through it to get rid of any dust, pesticides and insects. Rinse them thoroughly and put them on a kitchen towel to drain.

Bunch together the herb stems and using some yarn or butchers cord, wrap the stems together. Remember that as they dry, they will shrink so make sure that it's tight. Make a loop at the end of the cord and hang them up to dry in a shady area. You don't have to wait to use the herbs. Cut off bits of the stems and use them, finely chopped in your favorite recipes. Once the herb has dried out completely, you'll notice that it will break up easily and at this time you can crumble it into a screw top jar.

Allspice / *Báhari* - Allspice is used in Greek cooking very much as in western recipes. Often you'll also find it used in tomato sauces and savory recipes to add a bit of sweetness.
Anise Seed / *Glykániso* - This aromatic little seed really packs a punch. Its distinct flavor lends itself to bread and sweet making as well as giving Ouzo it's black licorice taste.
Basil / *Vasilikó* - Every home in the Islands has a basil plant outside its door. Other than its use in recipes for sauces, salads and meats, it's said that the basil plant is a wonderful pest repellant and keeps mosquitoes away.
Bay Leaves or Laurel / *Dáphni* - Bay laurel trees grow wild in Greece. It's large leaves are used in recipes where tomatoes are used and is often an ingredient used when preserving or pickling.
Black Pepper / *Mávro Pipéri* - Both ground and whole black pepper is an often used ingredient in Greek recipes. Always have some on hand.
Capers / *Kápari* - Another herb that is found growing wild in Greece. Its small flower buds alone can be pickled or, as the islanders do it, the entire tender stalks are pickled in brine and served in salads.
Cayenne Pepper / *Kokkinopípero* - Red hot pepper made from dried seeds of the pepper plants. You can use ground up seeds or use the small pods whole in your soups and stews for a milder flavor.
Celery / *Sélino* - Although the islands don't have the stalky variety of this wonderful vegetable - instead we have a very leafy version, it's use remains the same. Soups, stews, salads and roasts can all be dressed up with *sélino*.
Chamomile / *Hamomíli* - Chamomile is a time honored herb. It is picked fresh from the mountains and dried out. It is used for making a tea which is said to have a calming effect and is given often to new

born babies and toddlers. It is also said to have medicinal purposes and is used especially for eye infections. Another use that chamomile has, is as a hair bleach. Blond hair can be rinsed with chamomile tea to "catch the suns rays."

Cinnamon / *Kannéla* - The aromatic bark from East India is used in all kinds of pastry and bread making as well as flavoring sauces and stews.

Citric Acid / *Xinó* or *Lemóntouzo* - Citric acid is used primarily for pickling and preserving because it keeps the fruits and vegetables from discoloring or turning brown. The juice from fresh lemons can be used in place of citric acid, although you'll need a much larger quantity.

Cloves / *Garífalo* - Whole or ground cloves are used in flavoring sweets and breads as well as some roasts.

Cumin / *Kímino* - A small plant of the parsley family, its seed can be used whole or ground up. Its uses include soups and stews as well as meat barbeques, sausages and roasts.

Curry / *Kárri* - The spice of India is not used very much in traditional Greek food. Today, there are modern Greek recipes that use the spice, but again, these recipes are few.

Dill / *Ánitho* - Fresh dill is used often in Greek cooking. Most every home garden has the herb available to use in salads, rice dishes and sauces.

Eucalyptus / *Eukáliptos* - Like the Bay laurel, the eucalyptus tree can be found growing wild in Greece. The oil from its pressed leaves are used as a rub for aches and pains. It is also steeped and made into a "steam" for small children to breath in and open their sinuses.

Fennel / *Máratho* - This plant tastes very much like dill and is used the same way. In salads, sauces as well as vegetable and meat dishes.

Garlic / *Skórdo* - This strong flavored little root is used very much in Island cooking. It not only is a delicious addition to Greek dishes but it also has a lot of folklore associated with it. It's medicinal value is also something that the Greeks believe in and some villagers faithfully swallow one whole clove everyday, swearing that it keeps their blood pressure in check.

Linden Tree Flowers / *Tílio* - The flowers of the Linden Tree are dried and used for making hot teas.

Marjoram / *Matzouránti* - This sweet and savory herb is used to flavor sauces and certain specialty dishes.

Spearmint / *Diósmos* - Spearmint is a spring time herb that grows just about anywhere in the Islands. It is picked and boiled for tea, chopped fresh and used in salads, or dried out for later use.

Mustard / *Moustárda* - This spice is fairly new to Greek cooking. You'll find it called for in some of the recipes that hail from the northern parts of Greece, but until recently, it was rarely used in Island cooking.

Nutmeg / *Moskokárido* - Nutmeg is not only used in sweets and puddings, it is also called for in more savory recipes such as Tomato and *Béchamel* sauce.

Oregan / *Rígani* - Oregano is found wild in the mountains of the Greek Islands. I for one, have never bought it in a shop here because it's so abundant and easy to find by just taking a short walk. The taste and aroma of fresh oregano is much more pungent than the dried, so if it's available to you, use less fresh in your cooking or else it may give your recipe a bitter taste.

Paprika / *Páprika* - Sweet or hot, paprika is used to flavor foods just as western recipes call for it. Sometimes, we're lucky enough to get the native Hungarian paprika which really gives any recipe an added lift.

Parsley / *Maitanó* - Parsley is used in so many Greek dishes, I'll skip making you a listing. Its flavor is crisp and fresh and turns something like plain meatballs into something delicious.

Pine Nuts / *Koukounária* - Pine nuts are found through out Greece and are used quite often in pilafs and stuffing's for an extra special touch.

Purslane / *Glistrída* - What most westerners would consider a troublesome garden weed, the Greeks think of as a great addition to salads. Bunches of fresh purslane are gathered and chopped up to be added to any fresh vegetable salad. It's said that glistrída "loosens the tongue" so if someone talks too much, they've been eating lots of this herb.

Rose Geranium / *Rodostamiá* - The aromatic leaves of the Rose Geranium have a very distinct taste and are used to flavor fruit preserves.

Rosemary / *Dendrolívano* - No village home is complete without this little evergreen growing in its yard. It's true that lamb or fish just wouldn't be the same without a sprig of fresh rosemary added to the recipe, but other than the kitchen, the rosemary bush has many uses in island life. Other than its cooking and superstitious qualities, it is also thought of as a medicinal plant. Our grandmothers used this fragrant herb as a hair rinse. A handful of rosemary was steeped in some water and then was used as a final rinse for dark hair. Other than smelling great, it helped keep pests such as lice away.

Sage / *Faskómilo - Lesfakiá* - Another herb that is found plentiful in the mountains of the Greek Islands. Sage is collected and used for tea that is delicious on cold wintry nights. The oil from the pressed leaves is thought to have medicinal qualities and is used often as a rub for aches and pains. Cold sage tea can also be used as a hair rinse.

Sesame / *Sisámi* - These little seeds are used in a lot of Greek pastry and sweet making. Sesame oil is not used as much as the whole ground sesame seed, which is what *halvá* and *tahíni* are made of. In some cases their use symbolizes a plentiful life with many children, such as the making of *Melekoúni* at Greek weddings.

Thyme / *Thimári - Athroúmba* - Spring is when the wild thyme comes into bloom. Thyme has long been used as a tea or as a spice in tomato sauces and stews. Some villagers believe that tomato "needs" thyme, and it must be added to every sauce.

Mystic Mastic

Mastic is a special spice that is used in Greek breads and pastries. It is the gum resin of the Mastic Tree which is native to the island of *Chíos*. The tree bark is slashed in certain places and the amber resin drips out and hardens into small, crystal like pebbles that very much resemble rock candy. The pebbles can be ground up to use as a flavoring or they can be used as chewing gum - although, believe me, you need some strong teeth to chew *Mastíha*.

According to the island lore of *Chíos*, the spice came to be when St. Isídoros was led to his execution by the Romans. Because he was in so much pain along the trail, he wept and his tears became this mysterious spice.

Since mastic has a very distinct taste, there are no substitutions for this ingredient that I know of. Check out your local Greek or Middle Eastern grocer to see if they have it in stock. If not, you may want to use vanilla or anise in its place in a recipe. Although you won't get the traditional taste, it would flavor the bread or pastry towards the sweet side.

Whole pebbles of mastic will need to be ground up before you can use it in a recipe. The villagers use a mortar and pestle to do this. I found the whole process to be much easier if the mastic is kept frozen. Put a few pebbles of frozen mastic into your mortar with a teaspoon of sugar and then work it with the pestle. It grinds up beautifully. Also note, that if you do choose to use this method, make sure that you use a marble or metal mortar and pestle because the mastic will get stuck to the sides of the wooden ones.

What is Mahlep or Muhlep / *Mahlépi*?

Some traditional recipes include the use of a spice known as *Mahlépi*. It is the kernel from the Mahaleb or St. Lucy's Cherry. The spice resembles small seeds, a little larger than pepper corns that are light brown in color and are ground up before using. You may be able to find it in a Middle Eastern or Greek Specialty shop. It has a very unique taste so again, there are no ready substitutes that I know of. I have come across a recipe for a liquid substitute that seems to work just as well.

Liquid *Mahlépi* Substitute
1 tbs. whole cloves
3 bay leaves
1 cinnamon stick
1 cup water

Simmer all the ingredients together until it reduces to about ½ cup. Strain the spices from the liquid. To substitute the liquid, use 2 tbs. of liquid for every 1 tbs. dry *Mahlépi* that is called for in the recipe.

Concoctions For The Greek Kitchen

Ash Water / *Alisíva - Alousiá - Stahtónero*

Ash water is often called for in cookie and biscuit recipes because it helps to make them crunchier. To make *Alisíva*, boil together 2 tbs. of wood ashes (use pine or olive wood) with 2 cups of water for 5 minutes. Set it aside for the ashes to settle, then carefully scoop out the water without disturbing the ash. Pour this through fine cheese cloth and use as per your recipe directions. You can substitute ash water by mixing one tablespoon of baking soda with one cup of water or cognac.

Basic Brine / *Salamoúra - Álmi*

Brine is often used in Greek recipes to preserve vegetables and cheeses such as feta and olives. A simple recipe for a general purpose brine is as follows:

Ingredients:
water
coarse salt (fine salt will work too)
1 raw egg, washed thoroughly

Put the amount of water that you would like to make into brine into a pot and bring it to a boil. Boil it for 5 minutes, then remove it from the heat. Add some salt to the water. You will be using the egg as a gauge for the salinity of your brine. Float the egg in the brine. Some of the shell should float above water level, if not, remove the egg and add more salt to the brine. Put the egg back in to test it again. You want 1 to 2cm of shell to be exposed at the water level. The more shell that floats, the saltier the brine. Keep floating and adding salt until you get the salinity that you want. Cover the brine and set it aside to cool down completely.

Lime Water / *Asvestónero*

Lime water is a mixture of hydrated lime and water. It's used often for preserving because the fruits and vegetables that are soaked in this stay harder and firmer after they have been cooked. I don't use lime water in any of my preserve making, simply because I don't like using chemicals in my food. I like the soft texture of the cooked fruit and harder rind fruits such as oranges and walnuts will be firmer anyway. The choice is yours as to using lime water or not, but if you do, be sure that you rinse the soaked fruit extremely well, 3 or 4 times in plenty of running water before you proceed with your recipe.

Western Recipe
2 tbs. hydrated lime
2 quarts of water

Mix the ingredients together and strain it through a cheese cloth. Use as per your recipe directions.

Modern Village Recipe
1 tbs. lime paste
6 cups of water

Whisk the lime in the water and use per the recipe directions.

Old Ways Recipe
Take a few lime stones and wash them. Set them in a bucket and fill it up with clean water. Cover the bucket with a towel and let it sit for 2 to 3 days. The lime water is ready to be used.

Blossom Water - *Anthónero*

Many Greek recipes for breads, desserts and pastries call for the ingredient *Anthónero* which means blossom or pure water. It is made using blossoms such as jasmine, lemon, orange or roses and can be purchased in a shop or pharmacy here in the islands.

Although only a small amount is called for in the recipes, by using this extract or flavoring in your recipe, you will get a unique flavor and aroma. I have found that often, *anthónero* is the missing ingredient for many of my readers that have been searching for a recipe or trying to duplicate one. To find rose water, I would check out the extract section in a supermarket, ask a pharmacist or a Greek and Middle Eastern specialty shop.

Homemade Village Rose Water

Begin by picking roses, during a sunny afternoon. The flowers that smell the strongest are the best to use. Cut the fresh, whole roses that have no signs of pest infections and that are not drying out. Cut the roses with about 6 inches of stem, and take care of the thorns as you don't want to get stuck with one. Pick enough roses so that the petals would be enough to fill up a quart container or jar.

When you get the roses home, make yourself a bowl of soapy water using a dish detergent. Remove the petals from each stem and swish them through the suds to get rid of pesticides, dirt and insects. Put the petals in a strainer and rinse them off with running water. Turn them into a pot, add 4 cups of water and bring them to a boil. Reduce the heat to simmer and cook them for 10 minutes. Remove the pot from the heat and cover it tightly. Let it rest and cool for 24 hours.

Strain the petals from the water using a piece of cheese cloth and return it to a pot. Bring the water back to a boil for 5 minutes and skim off any froth that collects on top. Remove it from the heat, cover the pot and let it cool down completely. Stir in the strained juice of one lemon. Pour the finished water through a clean piece of cheese cloth into a bottle or jar and keep it refrigerated. It can be used in any recipe that calls for *anthónero*.

Home Made Yogurt / *Yiaoúrti*

The yogurt that is available here in Greece is strained yogurt made from cow's milk. You can get *Provatísio Yiaoúrti* which is made from sheep's or goat's as well, but I would not recommend using it in the cooking recipes unless you really have a fondness for it. Some brands of *Provatísio Yiaoúrti* have a definite gamey taste and aroma to it.

Ingredients:
2 quarts milk - cow, sheep or goat
½ cup store bought plain yogurt

Scald the milk and then let it cool down so it's warm. If the milk is too cold, it won't set and if the milk is too hot, it will curdle. The village ladies suggest that you stick your pinky into the warm milk and count to ten. If your finger feels comfortably warm, then it's at a good temperature.

Mix the yogurt with some of the warm milk in a bowl and stir it into the rest of the milk. Pour the mixture into small bowls or cups and set it in a warm place to set. My mom used to set the cups of yogurt in a pan and then wrap the whole thing up in an old blanket with a heating pad set on low. Once the yogurt sets, refrigerate it.

Strained Yogurt / *Yiaoúrti Stragistó*

When a recipe calls for it, use plain white yogurt made from cow's milk. If you don't have the strained variety available, you can strain it yourself rather easily. By taking this extra step, your sauces will be much thicker and you'll be able to incorporate olive oils or vinegars without the yogurt getting runny.

To strain yogurt, line a mesh sieve with several layers of paper towels or cheese cloth. Spoon the yogurt into the center of it and set it over another bowl to catch the drippings. Refrigerate the whole unit at least 6 hours but preferable overnight. The longer it strains, the thicker it will get. When you're ready to use it, scoop out the yogurt and gently scrape it off the paper towels.

The less you stir strained yogurt, the better. It will get watery if you handle it too much. So when using it in sauces, gently fold it in only to the point where it's been incorporated. Yogurt easily takes the flavors of herbs and spices so when making a yogurt sauce, make it ahead of time and refrigerate it over night for the flavors to meld. Most yogurt sauces can be kept up to a week in a covered container, so if you're planning for a party, these recipes are great for make -ahead.

Greek Cheeses

Young girls from the island of *Kárpathos* wearing their tradional dresses, the *Kabái* and the *Foustáni* (center).

Anthótiro: A variation of *mizíthra* but it's made with a lot of fats so it's very creamy and rich. This cheese is now available in 'low fat' varieties as well.

Féta: By far, the most popular and the most ancient of the Greek cheeses. *Féta* is traditionally made from goat or sheep's milk and is stored in barrels of brine. This white, crumbly, semi-soft cheese is salty and lends its flavor to pies, salads and entrees. *Féta* can be served on its own or with a sprinkling of oregano. With a drizzle of olive oil and fresh lemon juice is also a popular way to serve it.

If you are purchasing a large amount of *féta* and won't be eating it within a few days, ask the shop owner to give you some brine to take home. *Féta* does not keep well and will soon 'turn' if it's not preserved properly.

If the shop owner doesn't give you brine, you can make your own when you get home. Make sure that you have a container large enough to keep the cheese submerged in. If only a small surface area of the cheese is exposed, it will go bad so also find yourself a small weight that fits into the jar or container to keep the cheese down. Inverted dishes and washed rocks work well.

Bring to a boil a sufficient amount of water that will cover the *féta* completely and add one teaspoon of salt for every cup of water. Boil the brine for 10 minutes then remove it from the heat. Let it cool down completely before you pour it over the *féta*. Top the *féta* with an inverted dish and/or a rock for added weight and keep it refrigerated. *Féta* keeps for months when it's in brine.

For the really ambitious cooks, I have included a recipe for homemade *féta* in the Preserves section. Check it out if you'd like to try your hand at some village style cheese making.

Graviéra: Mild in taste, this cheese resembles Swiss in texture and appearance. It is served with meals or used for grating over spaghetti. In Crete, *graviéra* is served as a dessert. The cheese is cubed and accompanied by a dish of honey to be dipped into and eaten.

Haloúmi: Made in Cyprus, this cheese is very much like *féta* in texture but it's often preserved with herbs such as oregano and thyme.

Kaséri: This is a mild to sharp tasting cheese (depending on the variety) with a creamy texture. It is pale yellow in color and usually eaten on its own. *Kaséri* is also the cheese of choice when making recipes such as *Saghanáki*.

Kefalograviéra: A cross between *kefalotíri* and *graviéra*, this cheese is made from cow's milk. Depending on the variety, it's texture can range from medium to a hard cheese. It's pale yellow in color and is often used for grating.

Kefalotíri: This traditional Greek cheese is very hard in texture. It is made with a combination of sheep and goat's milk. Salty and sharp tasting, it's similar to reggato and parmesan and is used for grating over spaghetti or in casseroles.

Kopanistí, Tirokauterí, or Ktipití: All the names that are given to this cheese mean either "beaten" or "spicy hot." True to its name, this cheese is very soft, almost like cream cheese and is very spicy. It's often served with bread as a *mezé* for ouzo. A home made version of this cheese is easy to make by using *féta* cheese and pepperconchinis. See the recipe under the same name for the instructions.

Manoúri: Like *mizíthra*, ricotta and cottage cheese, *manoúri* is soft in texture and unsalted. It is made from full fat sheep's milk and is mostly used for sweet pies. It can also be eaten on it's own with a sprinkling of sugar as a dessert or snack.

Mizíthra: Though it's similar to *féta* in texture, *mizíthra* is unsalted and creamier. It is made with a combination of whey, full fat milks and creams. It is more often used for sweet pies. Many Greeks who want to cut down on sodium intake, choose *mizíthra* over *féta*. A good substitute for *mizíthra* in recipes would be ricotta cheese. *Mizíthra* is sometimes served as a breakfast or a dessert in the islands. Slices of the soft cheese are set on a dish and honey is spooned over it.

Telemés: Is a variation of *féta* cheese. It is crumbly and stored in brine. The difference is that it is made from cow's milk and is off white in color with a drier texture.

Touloumotíri: Made by the ancient Greeks, this cheese is similar to *féta* in texture. It is sweeter, not as salty and is stored by hanging in goatskin or sheepskin bags. Not many villagers make it now a days, so finding this rare cheese would be a delicacy to enjoy.

The Greek Menu Planner

Menu Suggestions

As in any cuisine, some foods go with others, but this is not to say that you can't use your own preferences to make meal times pleasurable for all your family members. Use the menus in this section simply as suggestions to guide you in the right direction. Greek food is so versatile, especially when having a *mezédes* dinner, that there is almost no way that you can make a mistake when serving a Greek meal.

The subject of bread is a very important one and is a must for any Greek meal. Many Greeks will often say that they "can't eat" without bread so make sure that you always have some on hand.

Another suggestion is that unless you are having *mezédes*, lemons and tomatoes don't mix. In other words, don't serve a tomato salad with a dish that is soaking in *Avgolémono*. The tastes just don't blend. Serve any heavily lemon flavored dishes with a green salad and choose a vegetable or side dish that doesn't have heavy tomato sauces. This does not mean that you shouldn't serve meats or seafood with fresh lemon wedges and a tomato salad. To the Greek palette, this is definite exception to the rule.

Fresh fried potatoes are a very common side dish for Greek foods. Even though a dish may be a starch such as a pilaf or *Dolmáthes*, potatoes are also served along side of it.

The Staples of a Village Meal
No matter what you serve, these staples of a Greek meal can be included on the table for all to share.

Feta Cheese
Green or Black Olives
Salted Sardines, Mackerel or Herring
Fresh Bread

A *Mezé* Style Dinner Party

The *mezé* dinner is a wonderful way to dine and drink as well as enjoy the good company of friends and family. The meal is very long and drawn out, nibbling on food as you drink and talk. The main principle is variation, meaning that anything can be served from raw vegetables and little bits of left over food to large roasts or special entrees.

Mezédes are an informal affair so set your place setting simply. A small appetizer or salad plate with a fork and knife is all that is really needed. You want to leave room on the table for the dishes of food instead of filling it up with china.

Serve your *mezédes* on small plates by setting them in the center of the table. Each guest will take what he wants at what ever time he chooses during the course of the meal. If dishes empty and you have more of the goody, take away the plate, fill it up and return it to the table. Don't remove any plates unless they are empty and you don't have more to replenish it.

A Greek *mezé* dinner is accompanied by wine, ouzo or the Greek equivalent to moonshine which is known as *Rakí*, *Tsípouro*, or *Súma*, depending on what island you're on. This doesn't mean that you can't serve your guests their favorite drink. In fact, I like good old Kentucky Bourbon when I'm having *mezédes* and some of my village friends prefer Scotch.

For a party of eight, I prepared the following menu for a *mezé* dinner. At first glance it may seem like a lot and you may think that I spent an entire day and night in the kitchen. The truth is that I made or prepared most of my dishes one or two days in advance. On the day of the party, I fried the meat balls, seafood and vegetables for the recipes, set my roast in the oven and cut up the salad. The barbequing was taken care of by the guests themselves when they arrived.

Menu Suggestions:
Tzatzíki
Feta and Hot Pepper Dip
Greek Village Salad
Taramá Salad
Octopus in Wine
Greek Meat Balls
Fried Vegetables with Garlic Sauce
Dolmáthes
Roasted Pig's Head
Meat Pie
Fried Squid Rings
Mussels and Feta in Tomato Sauce
Salt Cod with Garlic Sauce
Shrimp *Saghanáki*
Fried Whitebait
Barbequed Marinated Pork Chops

You can see the variety of meats, seafoods and vegetables that were offered at my dinner party. I should tell you that the roasted pig's head was not my choice, but since it was given to me as a gift for the *mezé* table, I had to cook it.

Along with the above mentioned foods, there was plenty of fresh bread, a small arrangement of olives, sardines and anchovies, feta cheese and a dish of raw green onions. The dinner lasted for almost 6 hours and I had very few leftovers to worry about.

I also prepared sweet cheese pies as a dessert but no one was interested except me. According to the islanders, sweets don't go with drinking. So if you'd like to serve a dessert, go ahead and offer it, but don't think that you should make up a whole buffet—unless of course you know that your guests are big sweet eaters such as myself.

The Greek Barbeque

When barbequing Greek style, the process itself gives the meal a fun, party kind of atmosphere. Since many people like being asked to join in the preparation process of a barbeque, give your guests a beer or some ouzo and have them help you with the grilling. Have your meats ready in their marinade and if possible, make yourself an herbal brush to use for the cooking.

Menu Suggestions:
Pork and Chicken *Souvláki*
Pilaf or Buttered Noodles
Dolmáthes or *Gemistá*
Coal Roasted Potatoes
Roasted Eggplant Salad
Greek Village Salad
Onion Fritters
Tzatzíki
Feta Cheese
Olives
Fresh Breads

Clean Monday Picnic

Clean Monday is a day of fasting and marks the beginning of Lent. The Greeks celebrate it as a picnic style family outing and the foods served are very much in the *mezédes* fashion. Although the use of meats and dairy products is not allowed, olive oil, mollusks and shellfish are eaten. When going to a Clean Monday picnic, the Greeks take along a portable hibachi and grill their foods right in the country. Make sure to take along blankets and balls for the children to play and don't forget the kites, since it's traditional to fly them on this day.

Menu Suggestion:
Grilled Octopus
Grilled Shrimp
Grilled Crabs
Stuffed Squid
Vegetarian *Dolmáthes*
Taramosaláta
Lima Bean Salad
Greek Village Salad - omit Feta cheese
Island Potato Salad
Boiled Greens
Fresh Green Onions
Fresh Radishes
Olives
Pickled Vegetables
Store Bought *Halvá*
Lagána Bread
Macedonian Semolina Halva
Fresh Fruits

Holy Saturday Night

It is traditional that after the Mass of Holy Saturday Night, the light of the resurrection is taken home. The family will sit down for a light midnight meal and since this ends the great Lenten fast, it is a simple one, consisting of *Magirítsa* Soup and some bread or *Tsouréki*. The *Magirítsa* is made from the innards of the lamb that traditionally will be served for Easter Sunday Dinner. It is also traditional on this night that the family *Tsoungrísoune* or crack their eggs with each other to see who has the strongest egg and is the winner.

Easter Dinner

For the great feast of Easter Sunday, many Greeks will traditionally serve lamb or baby goat. For some people, the tastes of these meats does not fall into their preferences, so alternatives must be used. What ever your choice is for an entree, it really won't matter. You can serve Stuffed Ducks or simply have grilled steaks.

The preparation process of the Easter meal itself is what makes it special. Remember, that Easter is the end of a long fasting period so a lot of foods have been missed. The Greek housewives will take great care in preparing the specialties that they and their families have been deprived of for so long.

Menu Suggestions:
Easter Stuffed Lamb
Basic Meat Pie
Pastítsio
Dolmáthes
Greek Meatballs
Fried Potatoes
Shrimp and Artichoke Salad
Greek Village Salad
Assorted Cheeses
Ekmék Kataífi
Easter Bread - *Tsourékia*
Easter Bread - *Lambrópsomo*
Easter Cookies
Dyed Eggs

Christmas Dinner

Just as for Easter, the Christmas feast marks the end of a long fasting period and the village women will fuss over their preparations for this holiday too. The seasons play a big role in the foods that are served so the traditional entrees are usually from pork. Many modern Greeks will serve stuffed turkeys or chickens as well, and the stuffings almost always include raisins and pine nuts, making them very festive dishes.

Menu Suggestions:
Stuffed Suckling Pig
Mousaká
Mashed Potatoes
Greek Green Beans
Stuffed Cabbage Rolls
Pork Aspic
Green Salad
Tzatzíki
Cranberry Sauce
Kourambiédes
Phoenician Stuffed Biscuits
Sweet Christmas Bread

New Year's Eve Party - *Revegión*

New Year's Eve is usually spent at the homes of friends and families, playing cards and cutting up *Vasilópites* to find out who the lucky one will be for the year. The foods offered for a New Year's get together are *mezé* like and usually a buffet is laid out so people can nibble on the foods all through the night.

Since we entertain for quite a crowd on New Year's Eve, some of my closer friends volunteer to bring a pot of a Greek specialty to the party. This works out great as by the time all the guests have arrived, we have a feast laid out that is fit for Zeus himself.

Buffet Menu Suggestions:
Baked Pork With Lima Beans
Stuffed Chickens
Shrimp *Saghanáki*
Rabbit in Onions
Octopus in Wine
Spicy Tomato Salad
Green Salad
Colorful Slaw
Island Potato Salad
Luncheon Meat Platter
Raw Vegetable Platter
Salted Sardines, Mackerel and Herring
Assorted Cheese
Assorted Pickled Vegetables
Assorted Dips
Assorted Breads and Pites
Vasilópita
Kourambiédes
Phoenician Stuffed Biscuits
Honey Macaroons
Akoúmia

Children's Name Day or Birthday Celebrations

Depending on what kind of party you're having you can choose to make it a simple one or go for the more elaborate get together. Personally, I like joining in on the fun with the kids, so I go for the easy style. Although I do serve a special dessert, such as *Ekmék Kataífi* for the adults to have with coffee, I make up foods that I know the kids like and are easy to eat on paper plates. And since I'm a working mom, I always order the birthday or name day cake from the baker, saving me the hassle of doing it myself.

Menu Suggestions:
Pastítsio
Plain Fried Chicken
Greek Meat Balls
Dolmáthes
Small Individual Sandwiches
Individual Sausage Pies
Individual Cheese Pie
Individual Spinach Pies
Individual *Mpougátsa*
Fried Phyllo from Thrace
Almond Meringue Biscuits
Birthday Cake

The Greek Orthodox Fasting Periods

The religious Orthodox observer adheres to the rules of fasting and deprivation through out the calendar year. Our religion states that every Wednesday and Friday are days of almost complete deprival and the rigid fast of no meat, fish, dairy products or oil is followed. This is observed because Wednesday is seen as the day that Christ was arrested and Friday as the day that he was crucified.

Some fasting periods specify that if they fall on Saturdays or Sundays, then eating oil is allowed. This is because Saturday is seen as the day that Christ was resurrected so these two days are considered as happy and celebratory.

Other fasting periods allow the eating of fish but any other food that may come from a blood animal such as dairy products is forbidden.

Modern times has brought with it different ways of thinking and many of the Greek Orthodox villagers have slightly altered the religious laws of fasting. Though, don't tell this to any of the local village priests as they are very strict in their beliefs.

Some villagers will not eat meat, yet will eat dairy products and consider that they have made their sacrifice and can receive Holy Communion. The most observed fasting period for all the Greeks is for the 40 days of Lent. Although some people will use a lenient fast for the majority of the Lenten period, Holy Week or *Megaló Evdomáda* is observed as a very rigid fast by almost everyone.

Fasting from food is not the only form of deprival that the Greeks follow to cleanse their souls. The deprival of foods is to simply help the body deal with the more spiritual sacrifices that have to be made. During the fasting periods, no spiritual pleasure is allowed. This means that celebrations, drinking and sex are out of the question and is the reason that wedding ceremonies can not take place during a fasting period.

For many of us, refraining from physical contact every Wednesday and Friday or holding out for the 40 days of Lent may seem like a long time to go without a little bit of love making. Some modern Greeks have had the same thought and have once more altered this religious tradition to be more lenient. But again, for the period of Holy Week or *Megaló Evdomáda*, even the younger generations will refrain from the spiritual and bodily pleasures.

To get an idea of the religious beliefs involved, here are a few of the fasting periods that are followed by the rigid Greek Orthodox observers:

Fasting periods that eating fish is allowed:

The 40 Days before Christmas
This fasting period begins on the 14th of November which is the Feast Day for St. Phillip, and ends on the 25th of December which is Christmas Day. This means no Thanksgiving or Christmas Eve parties and remember that Wednesdays and Fridays are days of rigid fasting.

The *Eortí Ton Vagión* - Palm Sunday
Although Palm Sunday is during the rigid fasting period of Lent, we are allowed to eat fish on this day.

***Kimíseos tis Theotókou* - The Assumption (Sleep) of the Virgin Mary**
The fasting period begins on August 1st and continues through the 15th. On the 15th of August, anything is allowed including meat unless the holiday falls on a Wednesday or Friday in which case, eating fish is allowed.

The days of *Télia Nistía* or Perfect - Rigid Fasting:
Every Wednesday and Friday throughout the calendar year, unless specified by the holiday itself.

Katharí Deutéra* to *Megálo Sávato
From Clean Monday to Holy Saturday which is the entire Lenten period. On Saturdays and Sundays during this time, oil and wine is allowed.

***Paramoní ton Theofaníon* - The Eve of the Epiphany**
The 5th of January which is the eve of the Epiphany or *Ton Fotón*, is a rigid fasting day unless it falls on a Saturday or Sunday in which case we can eat oil.

As you can see, there are many days that the Greek Orthodox refrain from their pleasures. There are more fasting periods in the religious calendar such as The Annunciation of the Virgin Mary or *Toú Evangelismoú*, The Feast of the Apostles or the *Eortí ton Agíon Apostólon*, and still others that I won't list for you simply because I think you get the idea. In fact, it would probably be easier to list the days on which we CAN eat.

If you are interested in adhering to the Greek Orthodox religious fasting periods, or learning more about them, talk to your local Greek Orthodox priest. Many of our churches offer small books which explain the fasting periods and the different details involved.

Fasting Menus - *Nistísima*

Many Greeks *nistévoun* or fast for the religious holidays and some will observe every Wednesday and Friday as days of no meat. While some Orthodox observers are very strict in their beliefs, others can be more lenient. Since there are different degrees of fasting, when having Greek guests for a meal on these days or during a fast such as the Lenten season, always ask if they are fasting from meat, fish, shellfish or dairy products and ask them if their fast includes oil as well.

This will help you decide what foods to cook and if you should omit the oil from a recipe or not. Don't think that you can pass a dish by. Greeks are very serious about their fasting and will consider themselves "unclean" to take Holy Communion if they break it. It's best to be honest than to offend them by thinking that a little chicken stock or oil in a recipe doesn't matter. Your guests will appreciate your honesty and that you respected their religious beliefs.

To give you an idea of what we eat during our fasting days, I've put together some sample menus that would cater to the different degrees or levels of Greek fasting. These are simply suggestions. Use the guide lines and substitute recipes and make other choices for your own special meal. Your guests will be pleased that you took into consideration their religious beliefs and cooked up a delicious meal that they can enjoy.

Staples of a *Nistísmo* Meal
Offer these staples on the table during any fasting period.

Tahíni
Fresh Bread
Green or Black Olives
Fresh Tomato Wedges
Pickled Vegetables
Raw Vegetables such as Green Onions and Radishes

The Lenient Fast:
This lenient fast omits all types of meats and fish that contain blood in the flesh. It does allow eating mollusks and shellfish as well as the use of dairy products and olive oil in recipes.

Serve any recipe that is vegetarian oriented. Don't use chicken or beef stocks in your recipes, substitute vegetable stock. Seafood such as shrimp, crab, octopus and squid are allowed but fish are not. Using butter, cheese, milk and eggs is also considered alright because no blood was shed in order to obtain the ingredient.

Sauces and Dressings: made by substituting vegetable stock when called for.
Appetizers: that don't contain meat or fish can be served.
Salads: that don't use meat or fish as an ingredient can be served.
Savory Pies: that don't contain meat can be served.
Soups: any recipe that does not use meats or fish. Greek Bouillabaisse can be served if it's made entirely with shellfish.
Pilaf or Pasta: can be served omitting meats and using vegetable sauces.
Vegetables: any entree can be served.
Seafood: serve any mollusk or shell fish recipe.
Greek Specialties: such as *Mousaká*, *Pastítsio*, *Dolmáthes* and *Gemistá* can be served when made without meat, vegetarian style.
Desserts: are allowed as well as Spoon Sweets, Dried Fruits and Nuts.

Sample Menu for a Lenient Fast:
Mussels and Feta in Tomato Sauce
Plain Rice Pilaf tossed with Butter
Grated Cheese
Spinach and Onions
Colorful Salad with Greek Vinaigrette
The Staples of a *Nistísimo* Meal
Sweet Cheese Pies
Fresh Fruit

The Semi-Rigid Fast:

This semi-rigid fast allows olive oil but does not allow meats or seafoods of any kind and dairy products are omitted completely. Choose vegetarian oriented recipes that call for no cheeses, butter, milk or eggs.

Alter your recipes so only vegetable stock is used and olive oil replaces any butter called for. Omit the use of any cheeses in the recipes - this includes the use of feta. Since grated cheese can not be used, serve pilafs and pastas only if you know that your guests can enjoy something like spaghetti without it.

Sauces and Dressings: don't use recipes that include yogurt or other dairy products. Substitute vegetable stock when called for.

Appetizers: that don't contain dairy products, meat, fish, mollusks or shellfish can be served.

Salads: that don't use meat, fish, mollusks or shellfish as an ingredient can be served. Omit the use of feta and any other dairy products.

Savory Pies: that don't contain meat or dairy products can be served. Use olive oil in place of butter in your pastry or phyllo layers.

Pilaf or Pasta: can be served omitting meats, fish and dairy products. Substitute vegetable sauces and serve them without grated cheese.

Vegetables: can be served as long as the recipe doesn't use dairy products.

Greek Specialties: *Dolmáthes* and *Gemistá* can be served when made with out meat, vegetarian style.

Soups: that don't use meats, fish or dairy products.

Desserts: that don't use dairy products such as St. Fanoúrios Cake, Fried Phyllo from Thrace and Macedonian Semolina *Halvá*. Spoon Sweets, Dried Fruits and Nuts can be served.

Sample Menu for a Semi-Rigid Fast:
Tomato - Onion *Dolmáthes*
Fried Vegetables
Garlic Sauce
Greek Village Salad - omitting the feta
The Staples of a *Nistísimo* Meal
Macedonian Semolina *Halvá*
Fresh Fruits
Note: Be sure that the bread you serve is not made with dairy products.

The Rigid Fast:
The most difficult of all fasts to cater for is the rigid fast. No meats, seafoods, dairy products or oil of any type can be used in the foods. Choose simple vegetable entrees such as hearty soups, that can be made without the use of oil and will still taste good.

Salads: All the raw vegetable salads can be served. Sprinkle the herbs and spices that a dressing calls for right into the salad and use plain lemon juice or vinegar.

Vegetables: Serve plain boiled vegetables such as potatoes, green beans, broccoli, or cauliflower. Use fresh herbs such as chopped parsley or dill to liven them up and serve them with fresh lemon wedges.

Soups: Prepare any vegetable soup such as Lentil Soup, Greek Chili, Bean Soup, Spinach and Lentil Soup, or Village vegetable soup without using any oil that is called for in the recipe.

Desserts: Fresh fruits, Spoon Sweets, Dried Fruits and Nuts.

Sample Menu for a Rigid Fast:
Bean Soup - omitting the oil
Island Potato Salad - omitting the oil
Fresh Tomato Wedges
Lettuce Salad - using fresh lemon juice
The Staples of a *Nistísimo* Meal
Pear Spoon Sweets
Note: Be sure that the bread you serve is not made with dairy products or oil.

Superstitions, Traditions, and Legends

Superstitions, Traditions, and Legends

When I first moved to the Greek islands, I simply assumed that the Greeks were a very superstitious breed of people and followed the traditions and customs just because "that was how it is done." Through the years, while collecting the pieces of this book, I came to realize that much of what I had deemed as Greek superstitions, were in fact religious beliefs and teachings of the Greek Orthodox Church.

Sure, there are stories of the quirks and village ways of doing things, but I was very surprised to find out, for instance, the evil eye and the custom of spitting also referred to in Orthodox prayers and ceremonies.

Many traditions and customs date back to ancient times and some are just tall tales, and yet others referred to in Greek Mythology. What ever the source for these tidbits of Greek lore, I have to say that this is my favorite part of the book.

The Story of O.K.

As a bit of trivia or as a debate to bring up at your next discussion of Greek Generations with your friends, here is the story of O.K., supposedly another feather in the hat of our forefathers.

According to some of the old Greeks that have returned to the motherland after working in the United States, it is said that the very common phrase "O.K." came into being because of the Greek immigrants living and working in America.

Since the turn of the 20th century, many Greeks had immigrated to the United States in hopes of a better future and opportunities that Greece just wasn't able to give them at that time. Unfortunately for these forefathers, the language was a problem and many had to settle for jobs doing physical labor such as loading and unloading of cargo for shipping and transportation companies.

Sometimes, they had to mark cargo crates and boxes, signifying that it was all right to proceed with the transportation. The Greek term *Óla Kalá* means "everything is all right" and they used the letters O and K to signify this. If the story holds true, it was our Greek forefathers that gave us the phrase that is still internationally used today to say that "all is well" or O.K.

The Evil Eye - *To Máti*

The most commonly talked about ancient superstition in the Greek Isles, the evil eye can strike at any given moment. More than likely, you've had it happen to you, but you've just never realized what did it.

Take a moment and think about it. Perhaps there was an occasion that you were dressed up and someone told you how nice you look. A few minutes later you spilled coffee down the front of you or split your pants. Or maybe someone told you how beautiful your new vase was and a while later it fell to the ground shattering into a thousand pieces. That's the evil eye.

To ward it off, there are a few different things you can do. They sell "eyes" here that are like charms, blue in color with an eye painted on them to reflect the evil and you wear them on a necklace or on a bracelet. You can also purchase a plain blue bead to wear instead of an eye, which will have the same effect. I have been told by some villagers that in order for these charms to work, they must be given as gifts to the wearer, which complicates the matter but it does explain why many of the jewelry shops on the Island give small blue beads as gifts to their customers.

Although blue is considered the color that wards off the evil eye, it is said that blue eyed people are exceptional givers of the evil vibes themselves. So beware when a blue eyed person pays you a compliment, according to the superstition, it could be disastrous.

Another way to ward off the evil eye is with garlic. There are rare instances when a single clove will grow into the shape of a small head of garlic. If you're lucky enough to come across one, guard it well as it is the best thing to keep away the evil eye. You can carry it in your pocket, or as I do, keep it in a hanky in your bra. I know what you're thinking, but believe me, as long as the skin is left on, it doesn't smell at all.

If you can't brave the garlic, there is an alternative. When you get a compliment remember to say *Skórda* or garlic, under your breath and spit three times on your own person. If you know the individual that is complimenting you, tell them to spit on you too.

Through out Greece and her villages, you will find certain individuals that are known for being able to remove the evil eye from your person or *na se xematiásoune*. These persons can be male or female that will ritualistically whisper a prayer over you. According to the custom, a person that is infected with the evil eye will make the prayer giver yawn terribly and make their eyes water. If the person does not have the evil eye, nothing at all will happen to the prayer giver.

Some of the prayer givers also use a dish of water and olive oil. As they speak the prayer, the oil is dripped into the water and for an infected person, the oil will spread into very large circles or "eyes." When a person is not infected, the oil that is dripped into the water miraculously dissolves and there is no trace of it.

For either method used, once the person has been rid of the evil eye, the prayer giver will spit on him three times and the person must move from the place that he was standing or sitting, stepping away from the evil.

The prayer that is said is kept as a very big secret. According to lore, it is only the men who can pass down the words of the prayer to women, so unfortunately, my friend, who is a woman and knows this prayer, cannot tell it to me. I must wait to find a man that knows the words and ask for it myself.

The Greek Orthodox Church also believes in the evil eye, and they refer to it as *Vaskanía*. The village priests will often be called on to read a prayer over a person who is thought to be infected with it. My mom, a very religious woman gave me a copy of this prayer but unfortunately, I'm not a professional translator so it's in Greek. Perhaps you can get an elder or Greek friend to read it and translate it for you if you're interested in the words spoken.

Ευχή επί βασκανίαν

Κύριε ο Θεός ημών ο Βασιλεύς των αιώνων, ο παντοκράτωρ και παντοδύναμος, ο ποιών πάντα και μετασκευάζων μόνω τω βούλεσθαι ο την επταπλάσιον κάμινον και την φλόγαν την εν Βαβυλώνι εις δρόσον μεταβαλών και τους αγίους σου τρείς Παίδας σώους διαφυλάξας ο ιατρός και θεραπευτής των ψυχών ημών η ασφάλεια των εις σέ ελπιζόντων σου δεόμεθα και σε παρακαλούμεν, απόστησον, φυγάδευσον και απέλασον πάσαν διαβολικήν ενέργειαν, πάσαν σατανικήν έφοδον και πάσαν επιβουλήν, περιέργειαν τε πονηράν και βλάβην και οφθαλμών βασκανίαν των κακοποιών και πονηρών ανθρώπων από του δούλου σου (τούδε) και η υπό ωραιότητος ή ανδρείας ή ευτυχίας ή ζήλου και φθόνου ή βασκανίας συνέβη, αυτός, φιλάνθρωπε Δέσποτα, έκτεινον την κραταιάν σου χείρα και τον βραχίονα σου τον ισχυρόν και ύψιστον, και επισκοπών επισκόπησον το πλάσμα σου τούτο, και καταπέμψον αυτώ Αγγελον ειρηνικόν, κραταιόν, ψυχής και σώματος φύλακα, ος επιτιμήσει και απελάσει απ'αυτού πάσαν πονηράν βουλήν, πάσαν φαρμακείαν και βασκανίαν των φθοροποιών και φθονερών ανθρώπων, ίνα υπό σου ο σος ικέτης φρουρούμενος, μετ'ευχαριστίας ψάλλη σοι «Κύριος εμοί βοηθός, και ού φοβηθήσομαι τί ποιήσει μοι άνθρωπος» και πάλιν «Ού φοβηθήσομαι κακά, ότι σύ μετ'εμού εί ότι σύ εί ο Θεός, κραταίωμα μου ισχυρός εξουσιαστής, άρχων ειρήνης, πατήρ του μέλλοντος αιώνος». Ναί, Κύριε ο Θεός ημών, φείσαι του πλάσματός σου, και σώσον τον δούλον σου από πάσης βλάβης και επηρείας της εκ βασκανίας γινομένης, και ανώτερον αυτόν παντός κακού διαφύλαξον πρεσβείαις της υπερευλογημένης, ενδόξου Δεσποίνης ημών Θεοτόκου και αειπαρθένου Μαρίας, των φωτοειδών Αρχαγγέλων, και πάντων σου των Αγίων, Αμήν.

Knot Ropes - *Komboskínia*

The *komboskínia* bracelets, pictured above, are made by the local nuns in Rhodes.

The monks and nuns of the small monasteries make what are called *komboskínia*. These are rosary like ropes, made from black cord that is tied into knots. The ropes are tied off into belts, bracelets, or necklaces and are worn by the faithful.

Although some *komboskínia* can have over 100 knots, most of the bracelets and necklaces are made with 33 knots, symbolic of the years of Christ's life. Seven prayers are said by the nuns and monks as they tie each knot so the ropes are considered a very religious charm to have. The *komboskínia* have become very fashionable here in the islands and often the plain, knotted black ropes will also have small charms such as crosses or blue beads incorporated into them.

When purchasing a *komboskíni*, do be sure to get it from a monastery or from a church-going individual who is helping the nuns and monks. This way your money will go to the people who deserve it and not to the tourist industry.

Talismans - *Filahtá*

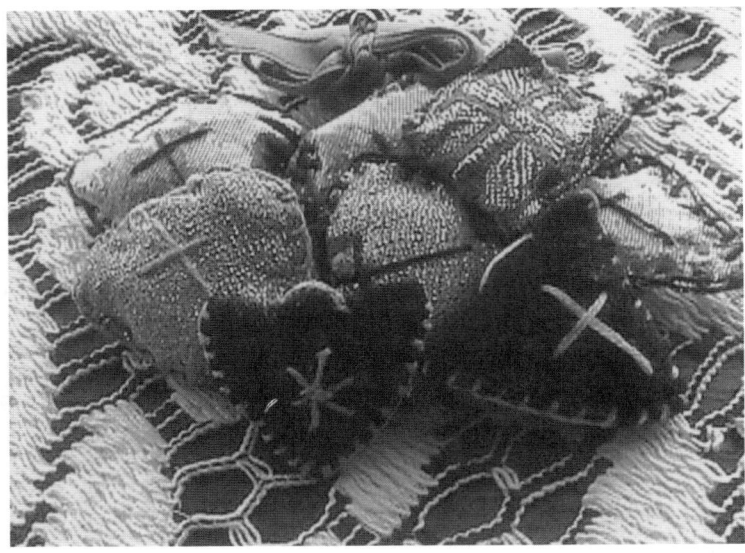

Assorted *filahtá* that are used to keep away evil spirits.

Talismans or *filahtá* are regularly used in Greece. Most commonly you will see these charms pinned to the backs of small children's and infant's clothing. But you will also find that many of the older people carry them in their pockets and purses or have them discretely pinned to their clothing too.

There are numerous items that are used for *filahtá* that are thought to guard you from the evil eye or what the Greek Orthodox Church calls *Vaskanía*. Of course, there are the simple gold crosses or medals of Saints, and evil eyes and beads, but there are also small pieces of cloth sewn into sachets, holding an array of mysterious contents.

These sachets can be filled with pieces of olive branch or basil that have been used by a priest in some ceremony, dirt from the grave of a Saint or maybe burnt candle shavings from a Church altar. Anything can be used for these charms, but the rule is that it has to be something from holy ground or something that has been blessed. Any one item, or a combination is sewn into a very small, triangular or square sachet and sometimes adorned with beads in the sign of the cross.

The Nuns and Monks of Jerusalem make beautiful *Filahtá* that are filled with dirt or stones of the Holy Land. Perhaps the most famous of all *filahtá* is the *Constantináto*. These are gold medallions that St. Helena had commissioned and named after her son Constantine. The legend says that these medallions contained wood shavings from the Holy Cross itself, mixed in with the gold. But that is another story.

Breaking Plates

One of the most commonly know customs associated with the Greeks is plate breaking. It seems that many people, regardless of which corner of the world they come from, have been to a Greek wedding or to a party at a Greek club and have seen dinnerware flying through the air and heard the roar of the crowd cheering when it breaks at the feet of the entertainer. Others perhaps, have just seen this strange occurrence in a Greek movie but never in real life.

Plate breaking supposedly started in the Greek night clubs called *Ta Bouzoúkia*. It's a generic name given to these establishments after the sitar-like Greek instrument *Bouzoúki*.

It's not an old tradition. Some say that it began at the early part of the 20th century - or in the 30s but didn't become fashionable until the movie *Zorba the Greek* and the 50s when Aristotle Onassis would visit Greece. Not worrying about money or the cost of damage, and basically showing off, he would break stacks of plates for female singers or dancers.

A symbol of giving-my-all-for-you is what it came to as the domestic Greeks also followed suit. When a particular song's lyrics or music would raise their enthusiasm to a climax, they would order stacks of plates to be broken on the dance floor in front of the entertainer, expressing their pleasure. The object of this affection could be a singer that was wonderful and moved them or a friend that was dancing solo to a tune.

These plates were not quality china pieces, they were specially made from cheap clays and enamels solely for this purpose - to be bought and broken. (Just as a bit of trivia: It's been rumored that Jackie Onassis, while at her own wedding reception, grabbed a stack of fine porcelain plates to break, but they were swiftly removed from her hands by Ari). Although their cost was low, you were charged heavily by the night clubs for these plates. So the extravagance of breaking plates for someone had the same meaning as "throwing money at their feet."

Although it's been a symbol of appreciation for the past years here in Greece, it is no longer done. Entertainers often got hit by flying plates from enthusiastic audiences and many establishments got more than just their plates broken. Nowadays, at the *Bouzoúkia*, you can purchase baskets of flowers and throw them at singers, or husbands and wives dancing. I've seen basket after basket poured over the heads of girlfriends and wives that have gotten up to belly dance.

Of course, none of this is free. You pay quite a bit of money for the basket of flowers, therefore literally "giving your all" when the bill arrives.

Incense Burning - *Thimíama* or *Thímiasma*

The *thimiató* with coals, frankincense, and dried olive leaves can be found in every village home.

A visit to a Greek church will show you the use of a Greek *thimiató* or incense burner as well as the ritual of *thimíama* as well. At various points during a ceremony a priest will use an elaborate, gold incense burner hung from a series of four gold chains which symbolize the Four Evangelists. Holding the burner, he will swing it to and from the congregation, directing the smoke to them. As this is done, a light ringing or jingle is heard from the twelve bells that are attached to it. These bells are symbolic of the Twelve Apostles.

The church incense burner as a whole symbolizes heaven and earth. The dish in which the incense burns in and hangs at the end of the chains is seen as earth and the long lengths of chains meeting at the handle would be the heavens.

That is why it is said that incense burning raises your prayers to God. The smoke rises from the dish or earth, up the chains to heaven.

The burning of incense is done not only in the Greek church, but at homes as well. Many village women will light their incense in the morning and walk through the house with the burner as they are saying their prayers. The burner is moved in the air, making the sign of the cross and often, the women will burn the incense under and around children or elders, enveloping them in the sweet smoke. Prayers are said during this time and each individual will make the sign of the Cross over himself, sending his prayers to God.

The home incense burners are not as elaborate as the church's. They are usually made from brass or pottery and can be as simple as an old small dish. Some brass burners also have a hinged cap that can be used to cover the incense, smothering the coals when the prayers are finished.

Small round coals are sold through out the markets in Greece that are used for this purpose. They are ½ to 1 inch in diameter and about ½ inch thick. One coal is lighted and set into the incense burner. Over the burning coal, the village women sprinkle *moscolívano* or frankincense and many times, blessed, dried olive leaves that have been collected from a Holy tree or brought home from Jerusalem. Some westerners, such as myself think that the sweet aroma is wonderful, but to others, it is very overpowering and they leave the house whenever the incense is lit.

Holy Water - *Agiasmós*

Holy water is known as *Agiasmós* and is symbolic of St. John the Baptist and the rite of baptism. In the Greek Orthodox religion, we also have a short ceremony that is called an *Agiasmós*. This rite is performed for new homes, businesses or just when a family would like their homes or families blessed.

The priest is invited to a home and water is put into a bowl and set on a table. A short ceremony is said and the water is blessed. The family that requested the *Agiasmó* will go to the priest who is holding a gold cross. They will kiss the cross and in turn, the priest will sprinkle water over their heads using fresh basil sprigs dipped in the water. He will continue to sprinkle water throughout the house, blessing it.

In the islands, an *Agiasmós* ceremony is always done for the opening of a new business. It is considered part of the "Grand Opening" and food and drinks are served to the attending guests afterwards.

The 14th of September is the day of the Festival of the Cross or *Toú Stavroú*. On this day, the village women will take small bottles of *Agiasmós* home from church and prepare their sour dough starter for making their home baked breads throughout the year.

Some village people believe that Holy water has many healing powers and will often drink it themselves or give it to persons who are sick.

Buildings, New Homes, and Businesses

Building a structure on the Greek islands or villages does not go without its traditions and customs. Since Greece is prone to earthquakes, any modern building columns, frames and foundations are built from solid concrete with steel bars interlaced throughout following anti-seismic regulations.

According to ancient folklore, for a building to stand strong and steadfast, a sacrifice must be entombed within the foundations. It is said to have been done to remind us that it takes sacrifices to have successful endeavors.

The poetic story of the Bridge of *Árta* on the river of *Árahtho* tells the tale of how this particular bridge was built during the day but it would crumble down at night. To appease the Gods, the master builder's wife was buried within its foundations and the structure was then able to be completed.

Even today, when a plot of land is excavated for the cement foundations to be poured, many people still deem it customary that a symbolic sacrifice of blood be made to insure a steadfast building. A rooster is sacrificed and the blood spilled into the footing foundation itself. Other villages hold that the right shoe from each of the owning family members should be buried into the foundation concrete so the structure will stand well. And yet other villages will throw thin gold coins or *flouriá*, into the cement foundation so the structure will attract money and have a rich future.

Once the house or building is finished, it is traditional to bring icons, the light of the resurrection and holy water into it before the owners move in or a business is begun. A priest is called to perform an *Agiasmó* to get rid of all evil sprits and to bless the building as well as the people who will live or work in it. An *Agiasmó* for a business is considered its grand opening and invited guests will bring plants, flowers and wall decorations such as evil eyes as gifts to the owners. In the islands, catered buffets and open bars make these occasions elaborate cocktail parties.

When entering a new building or home, it is customary to step into the door with your right foot for good luck. And remember to always leave a home or structure by the same door as you entered or else bad luck may follow you.

Worry Beads - *Kombológia*

The name *kombológia* literally means knotted words. If you've ever visited Greece and have had a chance to go into a village cafë, then you've probably have seen the old men holding a string of kombológia or worry beads. Worry beads are used as sort of a meditation prop to "count your worries" by the old men, but they are also used to simply have something in your hands to fidget with. Some people may jingle loose change, others twirl their hair and Greeks play with worry beads, very much resembling *kehrinbári*.

The true worry beads were made from *kehrinbári* or amber. The ingenious villagers of old used the yolks of left over Easter eggs. In time, the yolks would dry up and harden and they were passed onto string to make the beads.

In every tourist shop in Greece, you will see brightly colored strings of beads that can be made from simple plastic to sterling silver or even gold. Although old men hold the beads "for company" most modern uses are for decorating a home or hanging them in a car.

Promise to a Saint - *Táma* or *Táximo*

The icon of *Profítis Amónis* adorned with the *támata*.

One way the Greek Orthodox show their love and belief is by making a promise to God, Christ, the Virgin Mary or one of the many Saints. The believer promises gifts such as large candles or *lampádes*, elaborate Church decorations such as chandeliers as well as gifts of gold and jewelry. In exchange, they ask for the help and wisdom of God and the Saints in order to get through a problem, sickness or hardship.

You can see many glass enclosed icons in our churches throughout the islands that have elaborate jewelry, rings of diamonds and emeralds as well as gold chains hanging on them. These gifts to the particular Saints of the churches have been made by the faithful because of a vision that they may have seen or as an exchange for having their prayers answered.

Many times you will also find small gold plaques that have engravings of bodies, eyes or limbs on them and are hung on the icons of a Greek church or monastery. These too are gifts from the believers that have made a promise that in exchange for this gift, the Saint of the icon will heal the ailment.

If a young couple can not conceive or if a woman is pregnant and there is trouble with the pregnancy or with the baby's well being, often villagers will promise a Saint that the baby shall have their name if all goes well. To make this promise, the people will seek out the Saint's monastery which many times is not only on another island but also situated on the top of a mountain. They will make the journey and climb to the monastery and as they light their candles, they promise their Saint the unborn child's name in exchange for it's well being.

The Village Cures

Even in these days of modern medicine, you can still find a few village women that strongly believe in the old ways to cure many different ailments. When told about these home cures, I compared some of these village methods to the use of leeches in the middle ages. Yet many of the older villagers have sworn to me that these practices really made them feel better when they were sick.

Bee and Wasp Stings - *Tsimpímata Mélissas*
For a simple wasp or bee sting, this village mixture was known for bringing quick relief to those who had no other allergic reaction to such a bite. A simple blend of urine with plain dirt would be made into a paste and rubbed over the sting. As this mud pack would dry up, the pain of the sting would subside. This remedy may hold some truth to it as urine has a high ammonia content.

Boils - *Mávres*
Many of us have had to suffer with a large, infected pimples or boils. The village ladies say that boils need "to be sweetened" so they open up and discharge their infected contents. The way to do this is to grind up raisins, dry figs or Greek *Loukoúmia* into a paste. Put a bit of this paste onto the infected area and cover it with a bandage. The boil will open in a day or two and then go away.

Breasts - *Stíthos*
For the village woman who wants to keep herself firm and supple, this popular breast cream can be used. Take one cup of pork lard and mix it with some vinegar. Spread the cream over your breasts at night, once a week.

For the young girl who would like large breasts, the solution is found in sage. Boil a few handfuls of sage in plain water and let it steep for a few hours so you have a strong tea. Fill up your tub with just warm water and put half of the tea in it. Soak in the tub for one hour. When you're done bathing, rub some of the remaining sage tea on your breasts and then drink the rest of it. Follow this regimen for a few weeks and you'll have bigger curves than Mount Olympus.

Colds and Flu - *Kriologímata*
Even the warm temperatures of Greece don't stop us from getting the flu. When you are feeling a cold coming on, the village cure of a pure petroleum or kerosene oil rub down will work wonders for you. Of course this rub down is administered by a large village woman who will make sure that you are completely covered in the stuff and look like an ecological disaster.

If you don't have pure petroleum handy, you can substitute the Greek moonshine of *Súma*, *Rakí* or *Tsípouro*, using the highest proof you can find. Don't light a match and remember to keep your eyes closed because the fumes will make your eyes water terribly. If this healing wisdom does not do the trick, you can use finely grated onions as the ultimate mustard plaster on the chest area.

Another "old ways" cure was what is known as *vendoúzes* or suction cups. The very sick individual would lay in bed on his stomach with his shirt pulled over his head. Cotton that was sprinkled with some pure petroleum or alcohol would be wound around a fork and set on fire. The burning cotton would be inserted into a thick glass for a second or two. The glass would then be placed on the sick individual's back. The flame from the cotton would use up the oxygen so the glass worked like a suction cup, "sucking out the cold" from the body.

The most medieval type of home cure that I've heard about was the *koftés vendoúzes*. The process of this suction method was the same as above, except that a razor blade was used to slice into the flesh on the back so that the sick blood could be sucked out of the ailing victim.

Constipation - *Diskiliótita*

The village remedies are many for this common ailment, but the more popular cures that are for "guaranteed results" are the simple ones. For small children or babies that have constipation, give them a sweet tea made from chamomile and a bit of sugar. Give them the tea often and in a few days, they should be all right.

For older people, a meal of figs, dates, spinach and greens with lots of olive oil does the trick. Of course there is the preventative to this ailment which is simply to have a tablespoon of olive oil, every day upon awakening.

Corns and Calluses - *Kálous*

To the villagers of old, corns and calluses were common ailments. If shoes did not fit properly, few people could afford new ones and the long distances that had to be walked in them, didn't help either. To ease the pain of a corn or to soften calluses, the villagers would slice up tomatoes, garlic, and onions and strap them to their feet.

Strips of rags would be wound around the vegetables to hold them in place and a thick sock would be placed over it all. This veggie-sock would be worn for a few hours or overnight. The treatment would continue for a couple of days at which time a razor blade could be used to scrape and cut away as much of the painful hardened area as possible.

Diarrhea - *Efkiliótita*

To cure diarrhea, simply make the ailing person a strong tea of sage and bay leaves and feed them bananas and apples. Have them drink this every so often and eat the fruit. They should be alright within a day or so.

Eye Infections - *Krithária*

For sties or irritated eyes and infections, use compresses of chamomile tea. Boil a few handfuls of chamomile in plain water and let it steep until it's a strong tea. Strain it and let it cool down. Compresses are made with cotton soaked in the tea and they are pressed over the eye area. After a few treatments, the infection would subside.

Headaches - *Ponokéfali*

The village women swear by the use of willow bark for getting rid of headaches. Small pieces of the bark are cut up and are given to the ailing person to suck on and chew. Come to find out, this village wisdom holds true because willow bark contains natural aspirin.

Hemorrhoids - *Emoróides*

These varicose veins of the butt were troublesome for our ancestors too. The village ladies concocted a special salve made from mountain herbs and plants to use for the relief of piles. Some brave and daring ladies would help the sufferer by winding plain thread around the growths, cutting off the circulation. After a while, the hemorrhoids would dry up and fall off naturally.

Skin Rashes and Burns - *Erethismoús ke Kapsímata*

To soften skin after a long hard day in the fields, mashed potatoes could be mixed with milk and used as a salve. For very dry skin, make up a hand cream with pork lard and some lemon juice mixed in.

To sooth a skin rash, make a pot of strong tea by boiling whole acorns in plain water. Strain the tea into a bath and soak in it for half an hour. The remaining acorns and shells can be grinded up and used as a salve over the rash.

For a bad sunburn, the ever popular yogurt is used by many people as a soothing cream and some times you'll see a tourist being chased by an old village woman holding a cup of a sheep's milk blend. This is done with good intentions and as I've been told by the sufferers after they've been doused in the stuff, this remedy really works.

Sprains and Swelling - *Stravopátima ke Bríximo*
Onions seem to be popular cure ingredients and their healing powers go way back in village folklore not only for colds, but for sprains and swellings too. To ease the swelling from a bad sprain, grate onions and mix them with a bit of ouzo. Apply the paste to the swollen area and bandage it up. Leave it on over night and by morning, the swelling should be gone.

Sweat - *Idrótas*
If you are the type of person that sweats a lot, don't despair. Make yourself a strong tea using sage and strain it into a tub. Add some warm water and soak in it for a half hour. The sage will help you not sweat so much. Another batch of sage tea can be made and used all through the day as a lotion. Rub the sage water over yourself from your armpits to your feet, and you'll be just fine.

If this remedy doesn't appeal to you, then you can try this homemade cologne.

Village Eau de Toilette
1 quart vinegar
Grated rind of 5 oranges, Lemons or Bergamots
2 cups water

Put the vinegar and rind in a clean, glass jar. Let them steep for two weeks and then using fine cheese cloth, strain the liquid into a bottle. Add the water. Your cologne is ready for use.

Whooping Cough - *Kokítis*
In the days before vaccinations, Greeks held that donkey's milk should be given to a child infected with whooping cough. According to the old wives tales, there is some kind of substance in the milk that cures the illness. As strange as it might sound, I know a man who hunted high and low for a nursing donkey and managed to get the milk. It was given to his son for a few days and after that he was cured. I don't know if it was just coincidence, but I won't argue with the village ways either.

Other Greek Superstitions and Religious Beliefs

Basil - *Vasilikós*
Basil is used by the church in services such as an *Agiasmó* because it is seen as a holy plant. According to religious lore, when St. Helena found the Holy Cross, the area in which it was buried was covered in basil plants. That is why the herb is used for religious purposes and most villagers keep basil plants growing near their homes.

Bat Bones - *Kókala Nihterídas*
I have found that many of these Greek superstitions vary not only from island to island, but in between the villages as well. Bat bones are a good example. For some island folk, bat bones are considered to be very lucky. These people carry a small bit of the bone in their pockets or purses with them wherever they go. The only problem is getting the bone as it is supposed to be very bad luck to kill a bat. Other islanders believe quite the opposite. They think that bats are unholy creatures and should be avoided at all costs, and would never dream of carrying a piece of one as a talisman.

Brooms - *Skoúpes*
Before a village home is swept, the housewife will take into consideration if a husband or family member has just walked out the door or if they are traveling on a journey. To use a broom and sweep at this time would be as though she was trying to get rid of them and could bring very bad luck onto the family member.

Cactus - *Káktos*
No Greek home would be complete with out at least one cactus positioned somewhere near the front entrance. In a big feta can or garden pot, a cactus with its thorny spikes, takes its place proudly warding off the evil eye from the property.

Children - *Pediá*
Whenever your children crawl on their hands and knees in your home, take it as an omen that company will soon be calling on you. Never step over a child that is laying on the floor as it's said to be bad luck and the child won't grow taller.

Church Altar - *Agía Trápeza*
Any visitor to Greece will see many monasteries and churches through out the villages, islands and mainland. Each and every one of these churches is different and can range from a poor, simple mountain monastery to a very elaborate cathedral. No matter how these places of worship look on the outside or in which direction the structures are built, they all have one thing in common. The altars of the Greek Orthodox Churches and monasteries are always built facing east because this is symbolic as the Kingdom of Christ.

Crows - *Korákia*
Crows are considered omens of bad news, misfortune and death. When you see or hear a crow cawing, you say "*Sto Kaló… Sto kaló…. Kalá néa na me féris*" which loosely translated means, "go well into the day and bring me good news."

Fish - *Psária*
In ancient times, religious symbols such as icons and crosses couldn't be used by the faithful because of the fear of prosecution by the Romans. Many of the ancients used the fish as a symbol of their Christianity

amongst themselves.

Blessed by Christ himself, fish are believed to be wise and knowledgeable and the Church also sees the fish as a revered symbol of silence because they don't speak or make noise. Perhaps some of you have seen the sign of the fish in your own church, as many non-Orthodox religions also use its symbolism with the Greek letters ΙΧΘΥΣ.

ΙΧΘΥΣ - *Ichthís* - Translated means fish and is the Greek name for the zodiac sign of Pisces. But it also has a deeper meaning. If each letter is taken individually, you will see it's religious significance.

Ι	ΙΗΣΟΥΣ	*Isoús*	Jesus
Χ	ΧΡΙΣΤΟΣ	*Christós*	Christ
Θ	ΘΕΟΥ	*Theoú*	Gods
Υ	ΥΙΟΣ	*Yiós*	Son
Σ	ΣΩΤΗΡΑΣ	*Sotíras*	Savior

Garlic - *Skórdo*

The evil repelling powers of garlic is not just for vampires. Greeks believe very much in its power to keep evil away. You will usually find beautiful braids of garlic, or some huge, one of a kind heads, dangling in the entrances of shops, restaurants and homes. It is thought that garlic not only wards off the evil eye but also keeps away evil spirits and demons. It is also common for some folk to carry a clove of it on their persons or in their pocket books. A single clove, head of garlic is the best, but very hard to find.

Hands - *Héria*

Like many cultures, the Greek superstition for itchy hands holds that if the right one is itching, you will receive money and if it's the left, you will be giving it away.

Jordan Almonds - *Kouféta*

Jordan almonds are used in ceremonies of the church and the *bounbouniéres* or favors that are given out at baptisms and weddings. They are symbolic of a sweet life that is *karperó* or bearing many children and families.

In a church wedding, a tray is placed on the altar that is filled with rice and Jordan almonds. This is where the *stefánia* are laid until the priest places them on the heads of the bride and groom. The Jordan almonds on this tray are blessed and considered special.

According to superstition, when the wedding guest pass the newly married couple, young unmarried girls should take one of the Jordan almonds from this tray. When they go to sleep at night, they are to place the almond under their pillow and they will see dreams of the man that they will marry.

Knives - *Mahéria*

Never hand some one a knife. Set it down and let them pick it up, or else you will get into a fight with that person. Knives are never used to cut breads that are served at weddings as they are thought of as bad luck and could sever a relationship.

Knock on Wood - *Htúpa Xýlo*

In ancient times, the Greeks had the custom of knocking on the wooden door of their home before walking through it. It's said that when you leave your home empty, you are tempting evil spirits to come in and "play while you're away." The ancient Greeks knocked on the door to wake up the *Neráides* or nymphs and good fairies that live in the wood. These nymphs were thought to protect their home while they were away and would ward off any evil spirits that may want to enter.

It was also thought that if they were taking a long journey away from their home, by knocking on the wood and awakening the nymphs, some would follow, keeping evil away and bringing good luck and fortune on their trip. Take for example an ancient warrior. When leaving for battle, he would knock on the door and then step out of it so good luck and safety would follow him and insure a safe return to his home.

Menstruation - *Períodos*
During their menses, women are considered unclean and can not kiss the Icons in a church nor take Holy Communion. The same holds true for a woman who has just delivered a baby. Again, it is said that she is unclean and must wait for 40 days. Once the time has elapsed, a special ceremony is given to new mothers which "cleanses" them and they can attend church once more.

Mirrors - *Kathréftes*
After midnight it is bad luck to look into a mirror as an evil spirit can take your reflection.

Money - *Chrímata*
Greeks believe that money attracts money, so never leave your pockets, purses, or wallets completely empty and never completely empty your bank account. Always leave at least a coin or two. It is also considered good luck that when you give a gift of a wallet or a purse, that you put a coin or two in it before giving it to the recipient.

Peacock - *Pagóni*
The peacock was considered a Holy bird in ancient times and was kept roaming free around monasteries and churches. It was said that the only creature that should be proud is a peacock, so they were reminders of humility. Today, you can still see the beautiful birds in some areas and the monks and nuns as well as villagers, will often tend to them, feeding them old breads. The village housewives consider that having peacock feathers in your home is bad luck, so they never collect the fallen feathers from the monastery areas.

Plants and Cuttings - *Phytá*
If you have tried to take a cutting and root it without success, maybe you are doing something wrong. Greeks believe that in order for a cutting to root, it has to be stolen. You have to nonchalantly cut off a piece of the desired plant and take it home without telling the owner. According to superstition, it will root easily.

Pregnancy - *Egimosíni*
Pregnant women when walking down the street are often offered *mirodiá* from the village house wives. *Mirodiá* literally means a smell but it's actually a taste of food that is offered to these women. It's thought that if a pregnant woman smells a food cooking she should have at least a taste of it. If she doesn't have a taste and touches herself, the baby will have a mole or mark in the shape of that food. For instance, smelling frying fish could lead to a mole in the shape of a fish on the baby. For the same reason, it's believed that a pregnant women must have whatever she is craving as well so you'll often find village men hunting down strange delicacies in the middle of the night.

The old village women also had ways of predicting the sex of the baby. It is thought that if a pregnant woman is craving for sugar or sweet foods, then the baby will be a girl. If the cravings are for salty foods, then the baby will be a boy.

Another way to predict the baby's gender is said to be by looking at the woman's stomach. If the baby is carried high and very prominent, then it's a boy but if the baby is carried low and the added padding of pregnancy seems to be all over, then it's a girl. Of course today, there are tests and sonograms available to tell you for sure, if you really want to know.

Priests - *Papádes*
Greek Orthodox priests are very revered. When greeting one, it is customary to kiss his hand or ring in respect. But it's considered a bad omen to see one walking in the street, and most folk whisper *Skórda* or garlic under their breath.

Salt - *Aláti*
We are all familiar with the superstition of throwing salt over our left shoulder to repel evil or a demon. In Greek folklore, salt can be used to get rid of an unwanted human presence as well. If you have an unwanted guest in your home and you want them to leave. All you have to do is sprinkle salt behind them. The powers of the salt will chase him out. It is also customary to sprinkle salt in a new home before you occupy it, as the salt will drive any evil out and away from you and your family.

Shoes - *Papoútsia*
Overturned shoes (soles up) are considered very bad luck and even omens of death. Never let your shoes lay upside down. If you accidentally take them off and they land soles up, turn them over immediately and say *Skórda* or garlic and a spit or two won't hurt either.

Sneezing - *Ftárnisma*
In Greek superstition, if you sneeze, it means that someone is talking about you. If you want to know who it is, there is a way you can find out. Ask someone around you to give you a three-digit number. Count each digit together and then count down the alphabet. Whatever letter it falls on, is the initial of the person that is talking about you. For example, 534 is the number given. Add it together 5+3+4=12 . Count down the alphabet to 'L', which is the twelfth letter. That is the first initial of the person that is talking about you. Because you never know if what they are saying about you is good or bad, it wouldn't hurt to whisper *Skórda* or garlic under your breath, just to be on the safe side.

Spitting - *Ftísimo*
Often you will see Greeks spitting on themselves or others, particularly the old ladies. It is believed that by spitting, you keep evil away from you. At the beginning of a baptism ceremony, the priest will read the passage that denounces Satan and will turn his head and make a blowing gesture, three times towards the west. This is symbolic of spitting on Satan, keeping the evil away.

Other superstitious beliefs include when hearing of misfortune or bad news. If you fear the same thing happening to you, you would spit three times on your own person. Greeks say "*Ftíse Ston Kórfo Sou*" or loosely translated, spit on yourself. It wards off the evil from coming to you. Now I'm not talking about drawing from the depths of your throat… a simple little spray will do. Spit three times and remember …Ptew not Phtewwey.

Spitting is also commonly used to avoid misfortune, so you don't give the evil eye to yourself and jinx some endeavor. Take for example Greek fishermen. They will spit in their nets before lowering them into the sea so they ward off evil and get good day's catch. Likewise, a student may feel that he wrote a wonderful report and spit on it before handing it in for grading. The spit will chase the bad spirits away and avoid the jinx.

Touch Red - *Piáse Kókkino*

It might be considered a form of ESP or maybe just coincidence, but sometimes two people have the same thought and speak the same words at the same time. Take for example two girlfriends going out shopping together and stopping to admire a dress in a window. They both say "That's beautiful" simultaneously. Greeks believe this to be an omen that those two persons will get into a fight and they say to *Piáse Kókkino* or to touch red to avoid the argument. Both persons have to touch something that's red, right then and there. Any item will do, clothing, food – anything.

Tuesday the 13th - *Tríti Dekatrís*

Different from western cultures, it is Tuesday the 13th of the month that is considered unlucky in Greece and not Friday the 13th.

Holiday Celebrations

The Name Days

Often it seems that there is confusion as to what exactly a name day is and what its role is when compared to a birthday. The Greek Orthodox observe many holidays through the year that although, they may not be bank or school holidays, they are celebrated in the Church with special liturgies given. Each of these holidays commemorates a different saint.

Since the Orthodox are very religious people, through out the centuries, they have given their offspring religious and saintly names. The tradition of naming a child follows a long line of ancestral blood, so these names remain within a family and often children have the names of their grandparents and forefathers.

When it is a Saint's day, the person that also has the same name, celebrates along with the saint. In days of long ago, during occupations and wars, perhaps it was easier to remember the holiday of the Saint as opposed to a birthday because of the lack of writing and document keeping. Today, the Greeks celebrate their birthdays right along with the rest of the world and as an added plus, they keep the tradition of the name day too.

A name day celebration is very much like a birthday party, although there is no cake and candles nor invitations. For instance, when the Greeks realize that today is St. Peter's name day, they will phone or visit the people they know with the name Pétros, Peter or Petra - the female derivative.

They will take with them a gift of flowers, sweets, whiskey or toys, depending on the age of the celebrator. In turn, all the Peter's or Petra's are prepared for company and have sweets or *mezédes* ready to to serve to the well wishers.

On these Saint days, special breads such as the *Pentárti* are baked and taken to Church services by the name day celebrator. Sometimes *kóliva* are made on these days too, for the deceased that shared the same name as the celebrating Saint, commemorating their memorial.

Although I did give it a go, I found that trying to put together a full list of Saint's days rather difficult. The list is almost endless because many saints share days amongst themselves as well as celebrate two or three times in one calendar year.

The no-where-near-complete list that follows is of some of the more prominent Saint or Name days that we celebrate. The best way to find out your own Saint day is to ask your local Orthodox priest. Other than telling you the day, he can fill you in on other Saints that celebrate along with you.

Keep in mind that a name day is not an exact science. For instance, although January 1st. is St. Basil's Day, not only do the men with the name of Basil or Vasíli celebrate but also the ladies with the name of *Vasilikí*, so any derivatives of the saint's name is also celebrated on that particular day.

Saint	Date	Names
St. Basil	January 1	Vasíli, Vasilikí, Bill or William
The Epiphany - *Ton Fotón*	January 6	Fótis or Fotiní
St John the Baptist	January 7	John, Joanne, Iánnis, Ian
Annunciation of the Virgin Mary	March 25	Mary, Mariánthi, Despiná,
St. George	April 23	George, Georgia
St. Irene	May 5	Irene or Iríni
St. John the Evangelist	May 8	John, Joanne, Iánnis, Ian
St. Constantine	May 21	Constantine, Kóstas, Gus
St. Helena	May 21	Helen, Eléni
St. Peter	June 28	Pétros, Peter, Petra
St. Paul	June 28	Paul, Pávlos, Pauline, Paula
St. Elías the Prophet	July 20	Elías, Eli
Assumption of the Virgin Mary	August 15	Mary, Mariánthi, Déspina,
St. John the Baptist	August 29	John, Joanne, Iánnis, Ian

The Festival of the Cross	September 14	Stávros, Stavroúla
St. Dimítrios	October 26	Dimítri, Dímitra, James, Jim
Archangel Michael	November 8	Michael, Michele
Archangel Gabriel	November 8	Gabriel, Panormítis
St. Phillip	November 14	Phillip, Phílipos
St. Andrew	November 30	Andrew, Andréa
St. Varvára	December 4	Barbara
St. Samuel	December 5	Samuel, Sávvas, Sam, Samantha
St. Nicholas	December 6	Nicholas, Nick, Nicole
St. Spirídonas	December 12	Spíros
St. Eleutherios	December 17	Eleuthéris, Eleuthería
St. Anastasia	December 21	Anne, Anna, Anastasía
Christmas	December 25	Christopher, Christina, Emmanuella

Spring and Easter Traditions and Celebrations

March Bracelet - *Mártis*

On March 1st, it is customary for mothers to braid bracelets for their children. These bracelets are called *Mártis*. They are made of red and white string and are tied onto the wrists of the children.

The superstition is that the children wear these bracelets so that the sun of early spring doesn't burn their cheeks. The bracelet is red and white, symbolic of rosy cheeks yet a white complexion.

The bracelets are worn until the Midnight Mass of the Greek Orthodox Easter. When the traditional bonfires are lit, the bracelets are removed and thrown into the fires.

Saturday of the Souls - *Psihosávato*

The Saturday before Pentecost is one of the *Psihosávata* or Saturdays of the Souls. There are others through the Orthodox calendar year. On the *Psihosávata*, the dead are remembered in Church services and memorials. Families will give the priest lists of names of the deceased and he will read them out loud in church as part of the service. During the special services *Kóliva* are handed out to all those in attendance.

On this evening, people will dress up in their masquerade costumes and go from house to house as this also marks the eve of the *Apokriés* or Carnival.

Carnival - *Apokriés*

Before the season of Lent, there are the *Apokriés*. For the duration of Lent through Holy Week, weddings, parties, festivals and celebrations come to a stop. Because there are many days of deprival through the fasting season, and Greeks being the party people that they are, they use the three weeks prior to lent to "lift up" their spirits.

The three-week period of *Apokriá* consists of three feasts that are most celebrated on the Sunday of the week. The first one is called *Protofoní* or first voice. It's given the name because some one in Greek Lore kept saying or voicing that the *Apokriés* are here. The only day of fasting this week is Friday since it precedes *Psihosávato* – All Souls Day and Lenten dishes are prepared. The second feast is *Kreatiní* or meat filled because during this week, it is allowed to eat meat on Wednesday and Friday.

The Third feast is called *Tiriní* or cheese filled. As the name suggests, cheeses are eaten throughout this week and in most villages, lots of pasta too. On the Sunday of this week – the last day before Clean Monday, we fast from meats but can still enjoy the cheeses and dairy products. Through the entire *Apokriés*, people go to visit each other at their homes, playing games, singing songs and telling jokes. Prudity and modesty are put aside and good fun with good company prevails. Balloons and streamers are decorated everywhere and it's not uncommon to walk down the street and get a face full of paper confetti. It's a time of happiness and celebration. Adults and children alike, dress up in costumes of one kind or another. You will even find old women that will hang veils over their faces or smear themselves with ashes from the fireplace just to spook the younger children. At night, the maskers take to the streets, singing, playing practical jokes and just plain having fun. The bars, clubs and restaurants this time of year, are full of people in costumes and quite often you won't recognize who you're talking to. The last night of *Apokriá* is the most celebrated and bonfires are lit in the streets. The maskers sing songs and dance around them. When the flames die down, some of the braver folk will jump over the fire to "burn the fleas off."

Some villages hold the tradition that the man of the house secure a boiled egg on the end of a string and rhythmically swing it into the open mouths of the family members. This is done so that "with the egg we close our mouths and with the egg we open them again"—the coming of Easter and Easter eggs. It is also said that on this last night of *Apokriá*, the younger members of the family should genuflect before the elders and ask for forgiveness for whatever sins they might have committed. This leaves their hearts 'Clean' to celebrate the next day, which is Clean Monday. All areas of Greece hold parades that are lavish extravaganzas. Perhaps the most famous is the Carnival of *Pátra* on the mainland. Some people say that the rituals of *Apokriés* or Carnival have Pagan roots. I don't know about that, but I will say that *Apokriés* in Greece are a wonderful, magical time for the young and old.

Burnt Thursday - *Tsiknopémpti*

The Thursday of the second week of *Apokriés* is known as *Tsiknopémpti* or Burnt Thursday. It is traditional on this day to cook foods and let them char or burn so that the smell is carried out through the village. Charcoal pits burn bright on this day as most homes have barbecues and maskers of all ages visit each other. It is also a night filled with laughter and practical jokes.

Clean Monday - *Katharí Deutéra*

Clean Monday is the first day of *Sarakostí* or the season of Lent. For a Greek Orthodox observer, it marks the beginning of the great fast. On this day, families will picnic in the country or beaches. The picnics are simple affairs with everyday utensils and colorful tablecloths laid next to pits that have been dug to house hot charcoals to cook over.

The foods for this day are *Nistísima* or Lenten and contain no blood. Fresh and pickled vegetables, salads of all kinds, *Lagánes* - a bread, shellfish, octopus and squid as well as *Halvá* make up the menu. Meat, fish and dairy products are not allowed. Children and adults play games and fly kites, as it is the tradition for Clean Monday.

Feast of Lazarus – *Tou Lazárou*

The day before Palm Sunday is the Feast of Lazarus. It memorializes his resurrection and special church services are said on this day. It is also celebrated as a symbolic day for the coming of spring. In the villages, children will dress as Lazarus in white sheets and wear daisy garlands around their necks and in their hair. They go through the streets singing traditional songs for the day and go house to house with baskets, collecting gifts of Lazarus cookies, cheese, Easter eggs and candy.

This is also the Name Day for all those named Lazarus.

Easter Preparations

The season of Lent and Easter is a time when all village housewives will spring clean their homes and properties. Houses and streets are given new coats of white wash and homes are cleaned from one end to the other. This is also the time of year that the men will begin the chore of tilling their land, pruning their fruit and olive trees as well as sowing their summer vegetables.

In days gone by, Easter was one of the holidays that every member in the family got a new outfit and a new pair of shoes – Christmas being the other. Although we now live in times of abundance, it is still customary for families to buy new outfits and shoes for Easter and wear them to Church for the Resurrection and on Easter Sunday. The godparents of children will also purchase them gifts of clothing and bring them to the house at the end of Holy Week. The mothers will make the godparents or *Koumpári* Easter Baskets filled with home-made Easter cookies, *Tsourékia*, *Avgoúles* and dyed eggs.

Palm Sunday – *To Vagión*

To *Vagión* or Palm Sunday precedes Holy Week and commemorates Jesus Christ's entrance into Jerusalem. After the liturgy, pieces of palm leaves that have been braided and tied into crosses are handed out to all those in attendance. These crosses take their place in the *Iconostásio* when they get home. Palm Sunday is day of fasting from meats and dairy products. Traditionally, fish are eaten. This is also the Name day celebration for all those named *Vagianós*. I've tried to find the English - Latin equivalent and the name "Palmer" seems to have the same meaning as "one bearing palms."

Holy Thursday - *Megáli Pémpti*

Early on this day, the Greek women will begin their Easter preparations by dying their eggs. Traditionally, Greeks dyed only red colored eggs to symbolize Christ's blood, but as modern times have come, we too dye an assortment of colors. On Holy Thursday night the Church will read twelve excerpts of the four gospels relating Christ's Passion in a long and solemn mass. After the first six are read, a large wooden cross with a carved statue of Christ is brought out and placed in front of the altar. With this symbol of Christ's hanging, the next six excerpts are read.

Since this day is symbolic of Christ's death, the village women will mourn all through the night, spending the night in church, in silent prayers until dawn breaks.

Good Friday - *Megáli Paraskeví*

Throughout Greece, Good Friday is known as the day of mourning. It is the only day of the year that the Divine Liturgy will not be celebrated.

During the Lamentation Service, the priest and choir chant Byzantine hymns around the *Epitáphio* or "Tomb of Christ." This is used in the Greek Orthodox Churches to symbolize the bier of Christ and is adorned with a multitude of flowers on this day.

During this service, the priest will remove the symbolic wooden figure of Christ from the wooden cross in front of the altar. This figure is then covered with a sheet and kept in sanctuary for 50 days when it will be taken out for the Pentecost and returned to it's original position.

The *Epitáphio* is taken out of the church and carried by men through the village to the cemetery and back, with a slow procession of priests and altar boys carrying gold crosses and icons. The church congregation follows, holding lit candles symbolizing the mourners. The chants are sad and solemn and the Church bells will ring slow and rhythmically as they do when signaling a funeral.

After the procession returns to the church, the followers walk past and under the *Epitáphio*, kissing the image of Christ which is laid upon it.

Holy Saturday - *Megálo Sávato*

If you watch Greek television on Holy Saturday afternoon, it is most likely that you will see the arrival of a Greek military jet carrying the "Eternal Flame" from Jerusalem. Multitudes of priests wait with their lanterns at the airport for its arrival to take this flame or the light of God to their churches.

Everyone in Greece, young and old, attend the Resurrection service for Easter. Shortly before midnight, the churches are filled to overflowing and most of the congregations stand outside in the courtyards. Facing the altar, they silently pray while holding unlit candles.

Just before midnight, the church will turn off all it's lights - except for the Eternal Flame that is inside the Altar. Everything is dark and the congregation is silent, symbolizing the darkness and silence of the tomb.

When the clock strikes midnight, the priest lights his candle from the Eternal Flame and sings out *Christós Anésti* meaning Christ is risen. Holding his lit candle out, he offers the flame to the congregation that is closest to him. After lighting their own candle, they pass the flame back to the others so in a few minutes the entire church and courtyards are filled with flickering candle light. While doing this, the Byzantine Chant *"Christós Anésti"* is sung by all in attendance.

At midnight, everything around comes alive. Buildings are floodlit, sirens wail from the ships and the church bells begin to ring continuously. Villagers fire their shotguns into the air and the more modern city folk set off fireworks. As the congregation leaves the church, with their candles still lighted, the priest gives each one of them a dyed red egg.

Near the church courtyards, huge bonfires are lit, and the people mingle around saying *Christós Anésti*, which the correct reply is *"Alithós Anésti"* meaning "He is truly risen." The children joyously throw their March Bracelets into the fires as the adults talk and cheer. And it's common to be challenged to *Tsoungrísoume* or crack the Easter egg that you got from church. It is one fantastic celebration. The candles are handled carefully so they stay lit until the people get home. Before entering their homes, the Greeks make the sign of the cross with the lit candle over the doorframe. The smoke will leave the mark of the cross. This is symbolic of the bible story of Moses, where the doors were marked in sheep's blood. This sign stays there all year through and means that the spirit of the Resurrection has been brought into the house.

The burning candles are then used to light the lantern at the *Iconostásio* and set on the table to enjoy with the late dinner. The Resurrection Meal traditionally consists of *Magerítsa* soup, *Tsourékia* and Easter cookies.

Easter Sunday – *Lambrí* or *Pásca*
Easter Sunday is a holiday that is spent with family, relatives and friends. The meal is usually a communal affair with roasting lamb turning over open pits. Some women will bring pots of *Lambriótis*. This is a dish of stuffed goat or lamb that has been cooking overnight in the village *Foúrno* or wood coal ovens.

Tables are decorated with colorful cloths and fresh spring flowers as well as baskets of dyed eggs for *Tsoúngrisma*. Since this is the biggest celebration of the year for the Greeks, there is lots of ouzo, Retsina and village *Súma* or *Rakí* - the Greek "Moonshines" to drink. Of course, no Greek party would be complete without the traditional *Bouzoúki* music and the Greek dancing. Greeks celebrate life to its fullest and Easter is a very good example of that. It would not be uncommon for a tourist couple or passers by to be invited to join in the meal and festivities, as this culture is very generous and open hearted. And even though she probably doesn't speak your language, you would find some old Greek village woman motioning for you to come and enjoy a glass of ouzo with her.

Memorial Wheat - *Kóliva*
The Greeks honor their dead with memorial services throughout the year, but Easter is a time when all the dead are remembered. Cemeteries are visited and the names of the deceased are read out loud in church. When a memorial service takes place, *Kóliva* are blessed by the priest and given out to the congregation in memory of the deceased.

Easter Eggs – *Pascaliná Auyá*
On Holy Thursday, eggs are traditionally dyed a deep red color. They are used for decorating the Easter breads and a bowl is kept for the house. I have been told that beets were used in the old days to boil with the eggs to get the red color. In some of the more creative villages, onions and dandelions were used for yellow, and grasses were used for greens, though that strayed somewhat from tradition. In our modern times, most of the Greeks use the packets of store bought dyes and don't stick to just red anymore. During Easter week, housewives make their Greek Easter baskets, which consist of dyed eggs, traditional cookies and maybe a few candies. These are given to friends, relatives, Godparents and neighbors.

After the Resurrection Mass and on Easter Sunday, children and adults will challenge you with the question *"Na Tsoungrísoume?"* meaning "Shall we crack them?" This tradition is still very much enjoyed throughout Greece. You can use the egg that you got from the Church service or you can choose one from the basket of dyed eggs that is left for the house. You hold the egg in your fist with one end exposed. The other person does the same, and then you tap them together. Who ever ends up with the cracked egg is the loser.

I have seen families go through dozens of eggs in a matter of minutes, smashing one end and then the other. Greeks are always hunting for the "hardest" egg to *Tsoungrísoune* with each other and it's not uncommon to end up with a basket of cracked and smashed eggs.

Tomb of Christ - *Epitáphios*

The *Epitáphios* is used to symbolize the bier or coffin of Christ during the Holy Week services of the Greek Orthodox Church. It resembles a large table with a domed canopy built over it and it is adorned with intricate filigree that carpenters have painstakingly carved out by hand. In each of its four corners, wooden handles extend so that it can be carried.

On *Megáli Paraskeví* or Good Friday, the *Epitáphios* is decorated with hundreds, if not thousands of flowers, usually carnations. Their stems are pushed through the filigree, inside and out and they are secured next to each other so no wood is seen. It really is a beautiful sight and the fragrance is unbelievable.

Laid in the center of the *Epitáphio* is a special cloth that has been elaborately embroidered with the image of Christ, symbolizing his dead body. The parishioners file past the symbolic tomb and kiss this cloth.

You may also see some young and maybe some not so young, children and folk crawling under the *Epitáphio* to the other side. This is done because it is considered a blessing to pass under it.

Fasting - *Nistía*

There are different kinds of fasts for the Greeks. Some are days of no meat while others strictly prohibit eating dairy products as well. There is also some confusion when it comes to fasting. Villagers have told me that it's all right to eat olives but you shouldn't eat olive oil. Also, as in Clean Monday, you can eat shellfish and molluscs and fish roe, but you can't eat fish.

The Greek Orthodox Church prescribes fasting for the entire duration of Lent. Most of the newer generation Greeks fast only during the last two weeks before Easter, Holy Week being the most severe.

Fridays and Wednesdays are the exceptions. Most Greeks will fast on those days year through not eating meat and sometimes not even fish or oil.

Icon Station - *Iconostásio*

In every Greek home, you will find a corner – most likely in the master bedroom, with an *Iconostásio*. This is a shelf that houses icons, various holy items and an oil burning candle, which is never left to go out. The icons are usually of the saints whose names are in the family and of Christ and the Virgin Mary. You will find sprigs of dried basil, olive, or rosemary, burnt candles, vials of holy water and holy oil as well as

The *iconostásio* of a traditional village home in Rhodes.

wedding *Stefánia*—the "wreaths" from the owner's wedding. Any item that is considered blessed and holy takes its place here.

The *Kantíli* or lantern is usually nothing more than a glass filled with water and olive oil with a *fitíli* or wick floating on the surface of it. The *Kantíli* is lit with the Light of the Resurrection from Good Saturday, and is never left to go out. The Greek housewives diligently check the oil level and refill it as needed.

In the more modern houses, the *Iconostásio* as a shelf is non existent, but you will find that there is a wall somewhere in the house that is dedicated to this purpose and has the icons hanging on it.

Annunciation of the Virgin Mary – *O Evagelismós*

March 25th marks the celebration of the Annunciation of the Virgin Mary or *O Evangelismós*. Special church services are performed in tribute of the Virgin Mary and the Archangel Gabriel. It's also the name day for those named *Evangéli* or *Evangeliá*.

March 25th - Greek Independence Day

March 25th is also Greek Independence Day. After the liturgy, special prayers are said to God for liberating the Greeks from the Ottoman Turks in 1821. Although this day falls within the Lenten period, the church allows fish and seafood to be eaten because of the celebration of Liberty.

May Day - *Protomagiá*

The 1st of May is traditionally seen as a celebration of spring and fertility. Greek families will take their picnics out to the country where the children will play and pick wild flowers—the first spring blooms. The flowers are then braided carefully into wreaths of all sorts of sizes to be taken home and adorn their front doors. Some islanders, particularly taxi drivers even hang them on the grills of their cars. The wreaths remain in place until the Feast of St. John on August 29th, when they are burned in the great bonfires of the festival.

O Koukoumás - A *Sími* Tradition

On the Island of *Sími*, there is the custom know as the *Koukoumás*. On May 2nd, the day after May Day, groups of young unmarried men and women get together at an elder's home. The elder takes out a special tray or pan on which a large pot sits, this is the *Koukoumá*. The youngest girl members must go to seven different springs or wells with their *stámnes* or water jugs and bring fresh water back to the house.

The *Koukoumá* is set in the middle of the living room and the water is poured into the pot. Each of the unmarried men and women take off their gold rings and throw them into the pot as the elder begins to sing the song for the *Koukoumá*.

Using the water from this pot, the elder will make a pita or pie, which is seasoned heavily with salt. After the pita is cooked, it is shared amongst the young people who have put their rings in the water. They eat their piece of salty pita before they go to sleep and it is said that who's ever house they dream of drinking water in, is the person that they will marry.

Cemeteries

Easter is a time that all the dead are memorialized. From the time of Carnival and All Soul's Day through Good Saturday and the Resurrection, all Greeks go to the cemeteries to visit their deceased loved ones. It is customary to take flowers and light the lanterns on the memorials of the dead. You will find that the Greek village cemeteries are filled with pine trees. Pine is considered a holy tree for its beauty and respect to the sleeping dead. It stands straight and its leaves or foliage makes no noise.

Easter Monday - *Deutéra tou Pásca*
The entire week of Easter Monday through Friday is a holiday. Each day a different monastery is visited honoring a different Saint. Friends and families gather together for dinners and dances. The celebration of the Resurrection continues until the Holiday of the Virgin Mary on Friday night, when the biggest parties are held.

Christmas - New Year - The Epiphany

The Fast of Christmas - *Nistía*

The 40 days prior to Christmas is another fasting period for the Greek Orthodox. It begins on November 14th, which is the Name Day of St. Phillip and lasts until Christmas morning when the Church liturgy is finished.

Christmas Preparations - *Protimasíes*

As for any great holiday, the preparations for Christmas always begin by cleaning out the home. The housewives will busy themselves with taking down curtains, beating rugs and general house cleaning so the New Year will find their homes clean and organized.

The village homes are full of sweet smelling cookies and biscuits baking. Christmas day marks the end of the 40 day fast, so the house wives will once again, prepare all the goodies and traditional foods that have been missed during this time. *Christópsomo*, *Kourambiédes*, *Finíkia*, and *Melomakárouna* are only a few of the traditional sweets that are prepared for this day.

In some villages and islands such as *Símí*, tree branches or large hooks are suspended from the rafters of the homes. Cookies are baked into wreaths and the neighborhood children are called to toss the small baked shapes onto the prongs. Each child is assigned a certain branch or hook and is allowed to take home the cookies that he successfully passes onto it. The hooks remain in place, suspended over the living room or kitchen, and are used to store the homes supply of the sweet smelling wreath cookies.

Christmas decorations were not as popular as they are today in the islands. Small pine trees would be cut down from the properties and forests and decorated in a simple fashion on Christmas Eve. Today, there is an abundance of lights and various decorations available for any one who wishes to festively liven up their home.

Christmas - December 25th - *Christoúgena*

Christmas day begins in the islands at the break of dawn with the very early church liturgy. After receiving Holy Communion, the islanders will go to their homes and prepare for a great feast. The fasting period is over and the day is spent enjoying traditional foods and celebrating with drinking, dancing and song.

Until recent years, Christmas day was not considered a time of gift giving for any of the village Greeks. Presents are traditionally given on New Year's day or St. Basil's day. As modern times have come about, some of the villagers will exchange gifts on Christmas or let the children open up a box or two, but others will wait for St. Basil to bring them on New Year's Day.

New Year's Preparations - *Protohroniátikes Protimasíes*

The preparation for New Year's day is very similar to Christmas. Depending if the home will be hosting a party or get together, the house wives will prepare a special dinner or an extravagant buffet of *mezédes*. Of course the traditional St. Basil's Bread or *Vasilópita* is made and in some homes, *Akoúmia* are fried up. Make sure that you see these recipes for more tidbits of lore about them.

New Year's Eve - *Paramoní Protohroniá*

In the islands, there is seldom big New Year's Eve parties such as we have in the United States. New Year's get-togethers consist of friends and family meeting at a home, eating, drinking, dancing and playing games of chance such as cards. Since it's thought that the luck of the entire year rests on this night, many die-hard poker players will stay up until dawn to make sure that they have won at least a few hands.

In the past few years, great fire work displays can be seen in the Island harbors at the stroke of midnight. Many of the locals will go to watch the display and wish each other Happy New Year in the open air atmosphere, again retreating to some ones home for a further celebration of the evening.

New Year's - St. Basil's Day - *Protohroniá - Toú Agíoy Vasíli*

The day begins much like the fashion of a western Christmas with the children waking up early to open their presents that St. Basil has brought them. Since most of the adults have been up all night partying, it's spent very sublimed for the early part of the day. In the afternoon, most people will go out and visit with friends that are named William, Bill, Basil, or *Vasíli* and *Vasilikí* since this is their name day.

This is also the day that the traditional *Vasilópita* is cut up. A gold coin is baked right into the cake or bread and the person who finds it, is deemed the luckiest for the New Year. For more details on this tradition, see the recipe for the traditional St. Basil's Bread.

Podarikó

The custom of the *podarikó* says that the first person to come into your home in the New Year, after the stroke of midnight, has to step in with his right foot, to bring the house luck. Businesses will often ask their best customers to do the *podarikó*, so they will have a fruitful business year. Some villagers hold that a pomegranate must be stepped on and broken by this person for the good luck to be valid.

The Epiphany - *To Fotón* – January 6th

One of the most looked forward to days of the Greek calendar year is the Epiphany or *Ton Fotón* or "The Lights." After the morning Church liturgy, the priests and congregation will go to the harbor piers or beaches. The priests give a small ceremony, blessing the water. Since the Epiphany is the day that Christ was baptized, it is done to symbolize the Jordan river and the time of St. John the Baptist. It is said that this is when "Light" was shed on the people and is why the holiday has that name.

Once the water has been blessed, the priests will throw a cross into the harbor. The waiting men will dive into the cold water to retrieve the cross. It is said that the man who comes up with the cross is the luckiest for the entire year as he is already blessed by having been able to retrieve it from the depths. Although this custom has been a man's thing for centuries, in our modern times there are occasions that the village priests will allow women or young girls to dive in for the cross as well.

The Summer Festivals

Throughout Greece and her islands, the warm summer days often bring with them the celebration of the Saint or name days. When the name day of a Saint approaches, the churches and monasteries that have his name, prepare for a celebratory festival. Many villagers and islanders will seek out the church or monastery that is celebrating so they can make a symbolic pilgrimage and light a candle for themselves and their family.

The areas surrounding these monasteries fill up with street side vendors that offer keepsakes, toys and foods to the visiting faithful and at some festivals, there are elaborate, carnival like rides set up for the children to play.

Most of the festivals begin two or three days prior to the Saint day, and end on the Name day itself. The last day of the festival is very party like because it usually means the end of some type of fasting period. There is an abundance of foods offered as well as music and dancing on this day. If you have a chance to visit Greece, these festivals are wonderful celebrations and these village parties shouldn't be missed.

October 28th - *Ohi* Day - "No" Day
All through Greece, October 28th is celebrated as a patriotic day with elaborate parades and marches. It is commemorative of General John Metaxas, who in 1940 said Ohi or "No" to the demands of the Italians for Greece to open her northern Greek-Albanian borders to them. By giving this reply, Greece was brought into World War II.

Men and Women

Village Babies

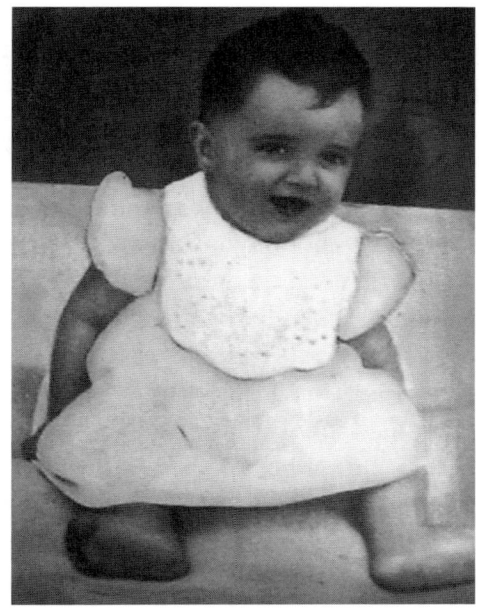 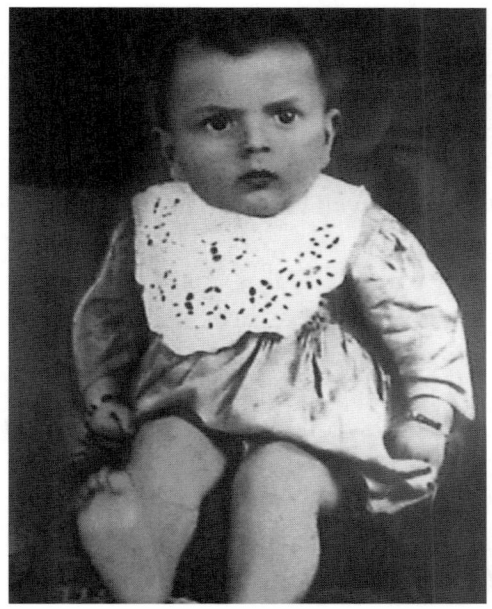

In days of old, village babies were kept tightly swaddled or *faskioména* in a neat little bundle. It was said that by doing this, the baby would grow straight and tall. As the years passed, the practice ceased and modern baby clothes replaced the bandage like wrappings. Although, the distinction of wearing a dress was not only for girls. It was fashionable for boys to wear cute frocks, too.

When a baby is born, friends and family are expected to give presents to the newborn. This tradition is rooted from the bible story of the Three Wise Men visiting the baby Jesus and bringing him gifts.

Hand made linens with intricate designs are often given and used to adorn the babies crib as well as gifts of clothing. Very close friends and family members such as the grandparents, aunts and uncles of the newborn present the baby with a gift of gold. Necklaces, bracelets, charms and crosses are given as well as medallions or family heirlooms. These presents of gold are pinned to a small pillow which is kept inside the crib, at the corner so that visitors to the baby can see is "riches."

The mother can wear these gifts of gold if she chooses to until the child grows up. Sometimes a child, as young as two will wear one of the small gold gifts that it received, where as the larger heirloom pieces will be worn at ceremonies such as their wedding.

A talisman or *filahtó* is kept pinned on the shoulder of the babies clothing. The talisman can be a gold cross, a small sachet of Holy items, an evil eye or a blue bead or all of these combined on a big safety pin. The talisman is said to keep the child safe from evil spirits and is worn every day until the baby is baptized. Although, I do know of mothers that keep the talisman on their child for much longer.

After the initial few days of visiting the new born and presenting the gifts, the baby and its mother are to have no more visitors nor are they allowed to leave their home for forty days. Attending church is not allowed for the mother either as it is said that she is "unclean" during this time. The mother should stay indoors to get her rest and so that the child can *mestósi* or ripen.

When I had one of my own babies here in the islands, I asked a pediatrician about this custom, since I knew that in the States, where I had grown up, there were no such restrictions. I found that he was very adamant about keeping the baby from further visitors for this time period. His argument was that many of the older women keep to the Greek custom of spitting to chase evil spirits away. A new born baby has enough problems with out the added germs spit onto it. Once he explained this to me, I agreed completely and stayed in the house for the full forty days.

According to lore, during these forty days no one is allowed to enter or leave the house after midnight. It's thought that evil spirits roam during this time and could enter your home if the door is opened. So if you're superstitious and your husband is on the night shift, he should change his schedule for a while. Personally, I think that this was a nice way of telling family helpers like your mother or mother-in-law that they couldn't stay late so you could get some added peace and quiet.

It is also believed that when a babies' laundry is hung out to dry, it has to be brought indoors before the moon can shine its beams on it. The moon is thought to invoke mystical and maybe evil spirits that would come to the baby through its clothing.

For the religious mothers, staying away from church for this time would be very difficult. Many times, particularly if the baby had colic or was just plain cranky, the mother would believe that some evil was trying to get to her unbaptized child. There are small ceremonies that can be performed by the Greek neighborhood priest. They are simple blessings that are done when the baby is one, nine, and twenty days old. The priest reads some words over the newborn and the mother, putting her mind at ease.

The hair and fingernails of a baby are not to be cut until the baby is baptized. It's said that by cutting hair and nails a demon could find them and use them to perform evil over the unbaptized child. Since it's rather unrealistic to keep a child's nails uncut, I asked a village woman about the custom, and she gave me two solutions to this problem.

When the mother cuts the nails of her baby she should save the cuttings in a small cup or jar at the Icon station or *iconostásio* of her home, where they will be safe from evil. These cuttings would be taken to the church on the day of the baby's baptism and thrown into the blessed water that is used to baptize the child. The other choice is to simply burn any nail cuttings in a fire so they would not be found by evil persons. Hair cuttings can be taken care of in the same manner or as is the fashion today, boys and girls can sport gorgeous pony tails until after their baptism.

The Day of the Fates - *I Iméra ton Mirón*

This is a very old custom that is rarely done today, but in keeping with the tale telling spirit of our folklore, I've included it here. My mom was a midwife in her younger years and as she told me this story, she laughing added that her home never ran out of sugar or bread.

On the seventh day, after a baby is born it is said that the *Míres* or Fates will come to visit the newborn, *na ton mirósoune* or giving him his own fate and destiny. On this day, the midwife that delivered the baby is invited to the mothers house and other female members of the family are present as well.

The midwife is given a loaf of bread, a bowl of sugar, a lit candle, an incense burner, and the baby to hold. I was very curious how the midwife managed to juggle all these items and still hold the baby, so in asking, I found out that they had it all figured out. The loaf of bread was placed under the midwifes arm. In those days, the women wore scarves, so the bowl of sugar would be wrapped in the scarf and set on her head. The baby would be laid in one of her arms and the lit candle and incense burner was held by the opposite hand.

The midwife would step out the door with the baby, so it could "see the light of day" and then step back into the house. The elder female relations would call to the midwife, "*Kalósti, Kalósti, Apó Poú Eíse?*" or "Welcome, welcome, where are you from?"

The midwife would reply, "I am from the Virgin Mary and Christ. *Kalορίζικο, kalorίziko na éhi kalí míra* or well rooted, well rooted, may the baby have good fate."

The midwife would walk out the door again, then step back in repeating the same words and yet once again, until the entire process was done three times. The baby would be given back to it's mother and the women would treat the midwife to coffee and sweets. The bread and sugar was her gift for delivering the baby and helping with its fate.

Forty Days after the Birth - *Sarántoma*

On the fortieth day after the birth of the baby, the mother and child visit with the local priest at the church to receive a blessing. The process only takes a few minutes and is done any time after the normal church service. He reads a few words over them, basically blessing them both for good health and well being. The mother can tell the priest the name that has been chosen for the baby and he will bless the name as well. After this blessing, the mother is considered 'clean' again and can go to church regularly and receive Holy communion.

Baby Names

A baby's name is not just picked in Greece. It comes from a long line of ancestry and is fully expected to live on and keep going. Mother-in-laws and fathers alike, often mention to a new bride that they are waiting to "hear their name." This is a gentle hint to get pregnant because they want a baby, which according to tradition, will be named after them.

Every area of Greece has a different system of priority for giving names to their children. Some places, particularly in Northern Greece, say that the husbands' family 'has the names' for the first two children born. Other places, such as Rhodes, share the priority between both families. The possibility of arguments begin when say, an Islander marries into a family that has different customs concerning the names. It's not a misunderstanding between the married couple, in fact they usually stick together wondering what all the fuss is about. It's a fierce, argument that can become almost feudal between the in-laws as to who will have their name passed on to the child.

One example of the severity of the arguments over names concerns some friends of mine. A very nice young couple, in their late twenties wanted to baptize their first born girl. The wife is from Rhodes, but her husband is from *Halkída* in the north. According to her custom, the baby should be named after her mother, but according to the customs of *Halkída*, the baby should be named after the father's mother. Sadly, The only way they found to have a civilized baptism was to go to a small mountain monastery with a handful of friends and baptize the baby without their parents knowing. To this day, the in-laws still don't speak to each other. Just as a note, they chose to stick to the mother's local custom and named the baby after her mother.

Because this tradition varies greatly within the regions and villages of Greece, I'm giving you the priority for naming children here in Rhodes. That's not to say that you won't find more differences between the villages of the island itself, but this will give you an idea of what the tradition is.

<u>First Born Sons</u>: First born sons are named after the father's father. Put another way, the first baby son gets its paternal grandfather's name.

<u>First Born Daughters</u>: If your first born child is a girl, it is named after the mother's mother. Put another way, the first baby daughter gets its maternal grandmother's name.

<u>Second Born Sons</u>: The second born boy to a family is named after the mother's father. Put another way, the second baby son gets its maternal grandfather's name.

<u>Second Born Daughters</u>: The second born girl to a family, is named after the father's mother. Put another way, the second baby daughter gets its paternal grandmother's name.

What happens if you have triplet girls or boys? Most Greek names have a feminine and a masculine version. It is not uncommon for a family of all girl children to name a few after the grandfathers, using the derivatives. Note that this is only after the priority of first born and second born has been met. The first two daughters are named after the grandmothers and vice versa for boy or sons. After the priority has been met, then the derivatives can be used.

There are occasions when you are allowed to give a child another name. One of these times is when the name has already been given to other children within the family. For instance, the brothers or sisters of the parents may have already named a girl child after the grandmother. In a case like this, you can ask if it would be alright to skip over her and name the child after the other grandmother since she hasn't a grandchild with her name.

Another exemption is when a mother, father or family has made a *táma* or *táximo* - a promise to a saint or church. These promises are made when there is trouble with the pregnancy or with the well being of the mother or child. The Saint is promised that the baby will have his name in exchange for making everything go well. Family members understand completely and there is no resistance when a *táximo* is the reason for naming a child.

What to Say?
When greeting a couple, grandparents, or family of a new born child, it is proper to use the Greek phrase "*Kalorízico*" which means "may it be well rooted" or "*Na Sas Zísi*" which means "may it live (long and happy)."

The traditional dress of the islet of *Kastelórizo*.

The Village Woman

A young girl from the village of *Émbona*, Rhodes in the traditional dress in the 1940s.

As I begin to write on this topic I can imagine the cringing faces of many western feminist ladies who are very much into equality and what their reactions will be as they go through the next few pages of text. Perhaps its just better to get it over with by saying that the traditional role of women in Greek villages has always been very defined and in a lot of older men's opinions, we were meant to cook, clean and have babies.

Many Greek men of old time were very strict with their wives and their children. Often, the women had to ask their permission to go out of the house to visit with friends or neighbors and to make purchases. "Where did you go?...Who were you talking to?... Who did you see?..." were very common questions that were asked by any husband. Women were expected to have dinner on the table at a certain time, men's clothes laid out and ready for wear, shoes shined and any men's necessities as maybe a bath, would have to be drawn and prepared at his desire.

Other men were more lenient. I never met my grandfather Dimítri because he passed away before I was born, but I'm told that he was an exceptional individual. My mom's memories of her father are loving ones as she remembers him sitting around the fire with his seven children, telling them jokes and stories to make them laugh in order to pass the time. He was very gentle and kind to his wife as well as understanding the needs and differences of character amongst his kids.

Men did not fuss with anything in the kitchen so something as simple as getting a glass of water would be the wife's responsibility. Even today, you will see older couples, where the 80 year old wife will still get up from her chair to fetch her husband a cup of coffee. My mom, who has been a mid-wife in the Greek villages of old and a successful restaurateur in the United States for 25 years, will still shell my dad's hardboiled eggs for him. Yes, we are in very modern times, but simply, some habits are hard to break.

Many of our traditional customs that we follow today still reflect this way of old thinking. One of which being the wedding custom and the grooms dowry of cooking utensils and bed linens. I've often said to my American friends that this tradition clearly states that we were only thought of as good for those two things. Even though this way of thinking has us deemed as house hold care takers and mothers, this does not give you a true understanding of the responsibilities of our female ancestors. Simply stated, these women had a very hard life.

To begin with, girls were seldom sent to school. Although the village schools of the time consisted of a priest in a small room of the church with a few shared books amongst the children, it was still considered an education. Unfortunately, for most villages, the old traditional roles of the time considered that girls should learn house keeping where as the boys would be best suited to use the schooling for their lands or business practices that would be inherited when they got older.

The girls at the School for Mid-wives in Rhodes, 1940.

The School of Carpet Weaving Class *Kalithiés*, **Rhodes -1937**

This does not mean that there were no exceptions. Households that had many daughters did send one or two of the younger ones to school. Having many girls in the family meant having to give each of them some kind of dowry, something that most parents of the time just couldn't afford. Some of these girls would be sent to school, and their education itself would be considered as part of their wedding dowry. Other young women, such as my mom, became professionals. They worked to help feed the many mouths of the family as well as providing their own assets for their marriages.

But for most village girls, their household roles were defined almost at birth. To say that these girls began to learn house keeping at a very young age would be an understatement, they were born into the village life. After their first steps were taken, they began as apprentices at their mothers side. Their areas of responsibility would be learned by watching their mother or other sisters as well as grandmothers or aunts. Depending on their age and the number of siblings, many, by the age of twelve were experienced enough to hold down the complete responsibility of a household, freeing the adults to work in the *horáfia* or fields.

When the crops were in season and it was harvest time, all of the family members would go to the fields to help. Women, and children no matter how young would be packed up to take the long walks to the orchards and vineyards in order to get the crop harvested in time. During other seasons, the men would mainly be responsible for tending the lands and the women and children would remain at home, taking care of other, lighter chores.

When the roosters would begin their serenade of "cock a doodle do," the women of the house would already be awake and busy with their daily preparations. Fires would have to be lit for heating water, milk and any other necessities for the breakfast table and family members. For a bread making day, the doughs would be kneaded well before dawn and the heating of the *foúrno* would also begin at a very early hour so it could be used before the hot sun would make the chore unbearable.

Once everyone was up and around, they would share a simple breakfast and get on with their daily work. Depending on the family's lands, the seasons and the chores at hand, the mother would help an older daughter with as much preparation as she could, before she would leave with the rest of the family to work in the fields. The daughter would remain at home to prepare the meals and take care of the household chores.

Cooking and cleaning was only a small part of the daily routine for these amazing girl-women. Something as simple as having fresh water on tap, which many of us take for granted, was not available in those days. Whether it was summer or winter, water had to be carried from a near by well, spring or the village fountain. After filling the *stámnes* or home water jugs, the remaining water could be used for the house hold duties. If it wasn't enough, then it meant another trip to the well.

Once the household chores were done, the garden or *kípo* as well as any livestock that was kept near the house such as chickens or goats had to be tended to. This meant carrying more water or feed or moving a herd of goats to a greener grazing area.

Any younger siblings would be left at home by the mother so she could help in the fields, resting fully assured that the baby would be cared for by its older sister. Keep in mind that there were no disposable diapers back then and jars of baby food with the easy screw off caps were nothing more than a wishful dream. Yet these girl-women managed to raise their brothers or sisters with absolutely none of the conveniences that we have today.

The table would have to be set and the meal ready by the time the family would return from the fields. The mother would assume her place as chief caretaker and help the daughter with serving the meal and pouring water from the jugs as the family ate. The men have always been taken care of first therefore, grandfathers, fathers, uncles and brothers were always the first to be served. Only when no one had need of anything else, the women would take their place and eat their own dinner.

After the meal, if there were no other heavy chores to be tended to, the men could relax or nap by sitting around the *soufá* or fire place area. *Kafenía* or coffee houses were a big hit in those days and often the men would go to these cafés to meet with friends, play cards or for a round of *távli* - backgammon.

The women, on the other hand were left with a houseful of chores that would have to be done. The table would have to be cleared and water would have to be heated in order to get the dishes washed up. Once the task was finished, they would busy themselves by laying out the men's clothes and shoes for the next day, taking care of sewing, and preparing for the next day's work. If there was any bathing to be done, water would have to be heated and the women would prepare the bath area by laying out floor cloths and toweling. Any meal preparation for the next day would also have to be done at this time, before the light of day was gone.

After an exhausting typical days routine, if there was any free time to spare, it was spent by candle light or gas lamp, doing crochet and needle point work that could be sold or used to barter with or take its place in the dowry of the girl or one of her brothers' or sisters'.

For most village girls, their typical home life would continue until they reached puberty and would get married. This meant anywhere between the ages of 12 to 16 although some girls would remain unmarried until their early twenties simply because the family needed them to help in the fields. At that time, she would move into her own household and again, be caretaker but also help her new husband in the fields at crop time. Even an event such as pregnancy would not pre-empt this work and it wasn't unheard of for a pregnant village woman to go to the fields in the morning only to come home later with her newborn child in her arms.

The babies' *náka* hanging on a tripod.
The most popular use for the *náka* was for transporting babies as it could easily be swung over the mother's shoulder or hung from a tree branch when she had work to do.

The mother would remain at home with the newborn for forty days as is our custom. After this time, she would take the baby with her to the fields, keeping it near by so she could nurse it, when it was hungry. Some village women used a *náka* or sling type sack to keep their babies in. The *náka* could be hung up on a tree branch while the mother worked and could be used to swing the baby to sleep.

Since mothers' milk was the only available formula for feedings, leaving a nursing baby with a sitter, was more than a little difficult. Yet, some very dynamic women did figure out a way to do this. Because of the fact that girls got married at a very young age, you would hear of instances where mother and daughter would both had new born babies at the same time. One such instance concerns my own great grandmother

Déspina and my grandmother Anastasía who were mother and daughter and who both had baby girls named Mariétta and Stamatoúla, respectively. To help with the baby, so her mother could work in the fields, Anastasía would stay home and take care of the household chores and nurse both her own child as well as her baby sister. The nursing-sitter relationship did not have to be solely mother and daughter as sisters would often help each other, too.

The child would continue to accompany its mother to the fields or stay home with her when there were other household duties to be done until it had grown. As other siblings were born, depending on the sex of the older child, the training for their responsibilities would once again begin the traditional chain.

When I see an old, frail village woman I can't help but admire her because I've come to understand the difficulties and obstacles that she has had to over come in order to survive and raise a family. The deep creases carved in her face from the hours of working in the sun, tending the fields and household animals are a testimony to the fact that she was not simply stirring a pot of beans or having a good time in bed.

The next time you meet with an old Greek lady or elder, take a good look at her hands as well as her face and try to imagine her as a young village girl. You'll see the creases and wrinkles in a different way and realize that although she doesn't hold a scholastic degree, she's lived through an experience that many of us just can't imagine. In times of no electricity, plumbing, telephones, central heating or any conveniences, these little girls, in essence, raised a nation of Greeks.

The Village Launderette

Laundry days for the village ladies of old were quite an experience. Because of the lack of plumbing and simple tap water and regardless if it was summer or winter, the family laundry had to be done by hand.

If a family was fortunate enough to have a river or spring running through their property, then the household laundry could be done close to home with minimal concern over towing the many tools and supplies needed. But for most of the village folk, a laundry day meant traveling a great distance with small children in order to get the task accomplished.

In a village, each housewife would designate a stream and an area where their family laundry would be done. Many of the women would also choose their laundry days as well so that each family knew for instance that on Wednesdays, the Atsaides family would be doing their laundry on the south river bank. These arrangements were made between the women themselves so that each family would get a fair turn as well as the ample time needed to get their clothes clean and dry.

My mother-in-law recalls that her family would wake up at 3 a.m. on a laundry day. Once the supplies and the *kofínia* or baskets of clothes were packed up on the donkeys and mules, they would begin the long trip to the nearest stream, which at the time, was almost ten kilometers away.

Reaching its banks by daylight, they would set up camp and prepare to do the wash. Fires would be lit to heat the laundry pot and the ash water, which would be used as a final rinse and fabric softener. The "two in one" detergent of the day was *prásino sapoúni* which was a mild bar soap made from the *voúrkos* or muddy residue of olive oil.

The clothes would be dipped in the running stream and rubbed with the bars of green soap. On some of the banks of these launderettes, *plákes* could be found which were age old rocks that had smoothed down flat with use over time. These *plákes* were considered wonderful laundry aids. The clothing could be set on the stones and a *kopáni* or paddle would be used to beat the soap into them. For hard stains or baby whites, the clothing itself would be boiled. The women would sit in front of the fire and use a stick as an agitator, stirring the clothes in hopes that they would come clean.

Once all the clothing had been soaped up and beaten or boiled, they were rinsed in the fresh running water and put into the baskets. The ash water would be strained and poured over the whole lot. The clothes would be left to soak up the ash water before they would be rinsed one final time.

On some banks of the village launderettes, the women could find clothes lines that remained from other lady's laundry doing. If none were available, then make shift lines would be set up between the trees. In winter weather or rain, the wet clothes would be stacked in the baskets and the donkeys would carry the heavy loads home where they would be hung in the *esóspito* or inner house.

Often a stream would be the meeting place of many village girls and women who would tell stories and gossip as they did their own laundry side by side. As a family waited for their laundry to dry, they would eat their packed, picnic lunches and sometimes the women would knit or needlepoint under the shade of a tree to pass the time.

If the men accompanied their wives, they would tend to the donkeys and mules by taking them to the fresh water. Some of the more popular launderettes even had *yoúrnes* or troughs built on their banks just so these animals could easily get a cool drink. The men would usually busy themselves with hunting and maybe fishing or if they owned a property nearby, they would go off and tend to it until the ladies were finished.

Of course, it wasn't very hard in a Greek village to find out what family did their laundry where and on what day, and some very enterprising young men would just happen to be near the river bank when they knew that a young girl of their favor was there. It seems that our forefathers made the village launderettes a common meeting place for young, single people, even in our ancestors times.

The Village Man

Standing over two meters tall, Grandfather Stamátis was affectionately known in the village of *Émbona* as *Stamatouriá* or "Big Stamátis." He got the nickname because he single handedly carried the village church bell up the steps of the church tower.

A traditional Greek man did have his share of hardships and a boy's life was not much easier than a girl child's with their own roles taken on at a very young age. Where women did the cooking, cleaning and lighter jobs, the men had the responsibility of the heavy physical labor such as tending the fields and orchards, any building and irrigation work as well as hunting, slaughtering and collecting fire wood.

Schooling and learning to read and write was usually left to the boys, depending on how well off the family was. For most villagers, the sons attended school only until they were old enough or strong enough to work in the fields and orchards.

You would be surprised to find out how many of our fathers and grandfathers were at the most, educated to the third grade and you would be even more surprised when you actually thought about it and came to realize that what they know today has all been completely self-taught.

Some families could not allow their sons to go to school simply because they could not afford it. Not because they had to pay money for the education itself, but because the children would be needed to help with the chores of the crops and lands so the family could survive.

A young boy would start his day by waking up at the crack of dawn and preparing to assist his father and elders in the fields. After a cup of warm milk and some bread, he would help to saddle up the donkey and make the long walk to the family lands where the demanding, physical labor would begin.

In our grandfathers' days, before ecological upheaval, most of the islands had many springs that overflowed with fresh water all through the year. These springs were irrigated by our ancestors so the flows could be directed into their property as well as their neighbors' and collected into *havoúzes* or *stérnes* which were small reservoirs. If their luck would have it and a spring would be found on their own land, they'd erect small windmills that could draw the well water and fill these reservoirs.

Some groups of enterprising men, directed the flows so the spring water would run to a central fountain in their village or near a church, making fresh water easily available for all. During the Italian occupation of the islands, these flows were captured by using pipes and made permanent by the soldiers. These are the village *vríses* or faucets—fountains and you can still see many of them today, although the flow of water may only be a trickle.

Until after the Second World War, the entire process of digging wells, building trenches, reservoirs and more modernly, laying pipes was done by hand. Men, with their sons at their sides would use shovels and picks to accomplish the tasks. In times of no faucets or garden hoses, more trenches had to be dug in the orchards themselves, so the water could get to the trees instead of being wasted on dirt.

Cultivation of land was also the responsibility of the men. The soil had to be tilled and turned over during the spring seeding season as well as in the fall and winter months after the olive crops had been harvested. Perhaps you may think that this can easily be done by driving a tractor through the plot of land, but at the time of our grandfather, the "John Deere" was at best a tired, old beast of burden such as an ox, mule or donkey. Slings and harnesses would be attached to the animals and they would be 'driven', pulling a homemade wooden or metal tiller. The use of machine tillers didn't begin until after the war years and even then, it was only by the 'rich' families, that could afford the luxury.

Young boys would not be given the task of tilling until they were strong enough to handle the job. Instead, they worked with shovels and picks, to fine tune the areas that their fathers were digging. Any large rocks that would be found and overturned in the dirt would have to be collected and put to the side. Later, they could be built with a simple mud into walls to border property lines.

The early spring and fall months also meant that the tree orchards and vineyards would need to be pruned for a fruitful season. Armed with simple knives and saws, the boys would climb the trees and carefully cut back the outgrowths. When pruning olive trees, the twigs and branches would be collected, bundled and tied to the donkey saddle so they could be taken home. The fresh leaves would be used to feed the *katsíkes* or goats and the branches of twigs themselves would be used in the *foúrno* or for heating the home.

For the boys that were in school, this type of life would begin when they finished the 3rd to the 6th grade. As any parent today, our ancestors too, had the very deep desire that their children would have a better life than what they themselves have had and when given an opportunity, they did make sacrifices to try to help their children.

Some families would send their sons away to apprentice for one skill or another. Young boys between the ages of 13 to 16 would be sent to work along side builders, plumbers or stone masons in hopes that someday the boy would be able to have his own business.

Other children were sent away to work on the cargo ships. Boys as young as 15 would be enlisted by merchant shipping companies to travel the globe. Many, many islanders have at one time or another spent a few years working on these ships because this source of employment meant a steady paycheck and was considered a very good opportunity at the time.

For families that had daughters, the problem of supplying their dowries was a major concern and a thought that seldom left their minds. The sons would be responsible to help the father supply what ever was needed for their sisters' marriages. Sometimes this meant one son tending lands, while another was off apprenticing and yet another was sailing the seas. All the boys would send money home to the father to help him prepare the house and dowry. This is still done today, as the sons of the family will help their father financially or physically with the building and furnishing of their sister's house.

Around the age of 19, all young Greek men are drafted into the military. This draft began in Greece in the late 1800s but for Rhodes and the Dodecanese Islands it began in 1948, when the Italian occupation was over and the islands were re-united with the mother land. It is mandatory and other than postponing it for a few years if the boy is away at school, the time must be served.

For the families of boys, this was yet another issue that had to be planned for and money saved up. Although many parents, saw the draft as an opportunity for their sons to mature into men, it was a difficult time for all involved. The family would lose the help of their son that was much needed for feeding the rest of the family and the boy himself, would be sent very far away - usually to the Greek borders, making any contact with his family almost impossible. The parents would send their sons what little cash they could so the young man could have a cup of coffee or a soft drink on an occasion but for most young soldiers, it was a time of deprivation from such luxuries.

After the military obligation had been met, most men were ready to settle down and begin their own families with their own lands. Some men that returned from the military still were faced with the issues of their sisters' marriages and dowry requirements. Depending on the family's needs, these men would not get married themselves until they were in their 30s or 40s and their sisters' were taken care of.

Following his marriage, the son would be given his own animals and plots of land from his father and sometimes he would also receive land as a dowry from his wife. He would busy himself with tending to these plots and do the best he could with beginning his own family and homestead. Perhaps a year or so later, his own son would be born and once again, the cycle of a Greek boy's life would begin.

After the war years, many married men left home to search for better jobs, leaving their wives and children behind, to tend to lands and animals by themselves. My father-in-law, left behind his wife and four children to work in the re-building of Germany, which at the time offered an abundance of work for anyone who was willing to go. Although my mother-in-law had to take care of the fields and crops with only her children to help, she is thankful because the added money that he sent her from his paycheck, saw them through very hard times.

My mom has the same feelings about her own experiences. My father himself, left behind his young wife and two sons, to work on the cargo and merchant ships. And although he spent five years, alone and away from home, he too considers himself lucky for the opportunity that was given to him.

The village school of *Líndos*, Rhodes - mid 1940s.

The Games They Played

Very unlike our ancestors who didn't have a Toys 'R' Us within their village squares, most of today's parents go home with boxes and bags of toys, computer games and Barbie dolls in hopes of keeping their children educated, happy and quiet, although not necessarily in that order.

If you've read over the section about the traditional roles of men and women and how strict their childhood years were, I'm sure that you've come to the conclusion that the lives of kids were anything but fun. Yet even in those days, time would be found and allowed for the children to play and unwind. True, there were no toy stores with the abundances that we have today nor the means to pay for something as pricey as a bicycle, but this could be seen as an advantage because the children themselves had to use their imaginations to come up with games that were fun to play.

When the mothers were making apricot spoon sweets, sometimes the children would save the pits and set them aside to dry. These oval seeds became the basis for the village game called *koúnes*. By using a stick, a circle was made in the dirt or sand and every player would place an apricot pit into it. One by one, they would toss another pit into the circle. If their pit touched or hit another one, then both pits were theirs, if not, the second pit would remain inside. The game would continue until a winner was declared by having the most pits.

The children of the village of *Ólympos, Kárpathos* - mid 1940s

Another village game was called *dápes* or bottle caps. As the name implies, bottle caps were collected by the children from the village cafés and streets and were used as the playing pieces. One variation of the game was played by using their thumbs and index fingers to flick the caps from a designated distance, to land on a thin, stone wall. The player that landed his *dápa* on the wall could collect the fallen ones as his own.

Other children's games included the international favorite of *kinigitó* which is tag, *mánta*, which was a game similar to stick ball, and *lakoúdia*, which consisted of holes dug in the ground that balls or rocks could be sunk into.

Skatoúlia was a game very much like a carnival ball toss, only that rocks were stacked up instead of tin cans. *Kólasi* or *koutsó* was played with a small broken piece of pottery or rock and would be known as hopscotch today. *Tríliza* is simply tic-tac-toe and *pentóvola* would be jacks, except that there were no jacks or balls so small pebbles were used instead.

One of the oddest of old games that I found out about was known as *vezíris*. The playing piece for this game was a dried knee bone-knuckle from a large animal such as a pig or lamb. The knuckle was assigned four sides, known as *kléftis* or the thief's, *psomás* or the bread eater's, *vasiliás* or the king's and *vezíris'* or the vizier's. The knuckle was tossed, and the children would call out which side they thought it would fall on and the child that called it right was the winner.

Listening to the object of these games, I became curious as to how these children did not become bored, especially since not every game rewarded them with pits, stones or bottle caps. I presented the question to a group of our village friends who laughingly recalled that in most of their childhood games, a small punishment was given to any losers. This could mean a spank on the backside or a slap on the hands by the other players. The object was simply not to get smacked, therefore becoming the winner of the game.

The balls that these children used for their play time were not simply blown up plastic orbs that we can purchase today. The kids of the villages fashioned their own balls by winding up strips of old rags just as we would wind up yarn. After enough rags were wound up, they were covered with another piece of fabric and stitched up, forming a very solid ball.

Bicycles were almost non existent in the old villages. Perhaps one child was lucky enough to get one from a father or uncle who had come to visit from overseas or from a long journey on a cargo ship, but even when a bike was made a gift, the inner tubes where hard to come by and cost money to replace. Once the bicycle tires would be worn, it was usually discarded. To some village children, it didn't matter if the bike had rubber wheels or not and often they would ride it around just as it was, using only the metal rims.

The worn inner tubes of a bicycle were not thrown away, instead they were ingeniously used by the young boys to make sling shots. They would each collect a proper piece of tree branch and trim it down into a 'Y' shape. The inner tube would be cut into strips and attached to the ends of the 'Y'.

Pellets could be made from fruit pits or small stones and some smart boys made their own out of lead. The more modern village boys would scout areas that bathrooms or plumbing fixtures were being installed such as village governmental offices or homes. As the boys knew, plumbers would always discard scraps of lead near their work areas, so building sites were the place to go.

After some lead was collected, it would be melted down in a tin can or discarded pot. The molten lead would then be poured into another tin can that had holes punched into the bottom of it and was suspended over a pot of cold water. As the dripping lead cooled in the water, small pellets were formed that could be used for boy style hunting.

Many times, I'll sit and watch my own children as they fight over who gets to play the Nintendo or I'll listen to complaints about their new stereo system that just doesn't have enough watts and smile to myself, remembering how hard it was for the ancestral children of bygone days.

And after I threaten to fill their Christmas stockings with apricot pits or dry pigs' knuckles, the fuss does die down some what and they too, become a little thoughtful on the subject. I think that in many ways, in our attempt to give our own kids what we never had, we tend to spoil them. But I also believe, that if had given the chance, most of our forefathers would have done the same for us.

The traditional dress of the island of *Sími*.

Grandmom's Dolls

One of the sweetest memories I have from my childhood years is of my mom and my dear departed Aunt Leukothéa, playing dolls with me. Now I don't mean just any kind of dolls that you could purchase in a shop, these where home-made, quick rag dolls that could be made on a whim and keep a child occupied for hours.

Depending on your imagination, the finished dolls can take on any kind of appearance. Although most of our children will not want to play with something like this today, they can be fun projects to make on a rainy day, preserving a small piece of our ancestral history.

Village Rag Dolls

You will need two squares of fabric that measure about 20 to 24 inches on their edge. Begin by folding down two inches of the fabric onto itself and continue until the fabric has been folded into a strip (1). Do the same for the other piece so you have two folded strips that are two inches wide (2). Fold one strip in half and sew together the edges. Arrange the seam in the center of the strip and lay it over the other strip, cross style (3). Fold the other strip over the sewn piece (4). Bunch the fabric together and tie it off with some string or yarn and sew each of the hanging folds closed, making the legs (5).

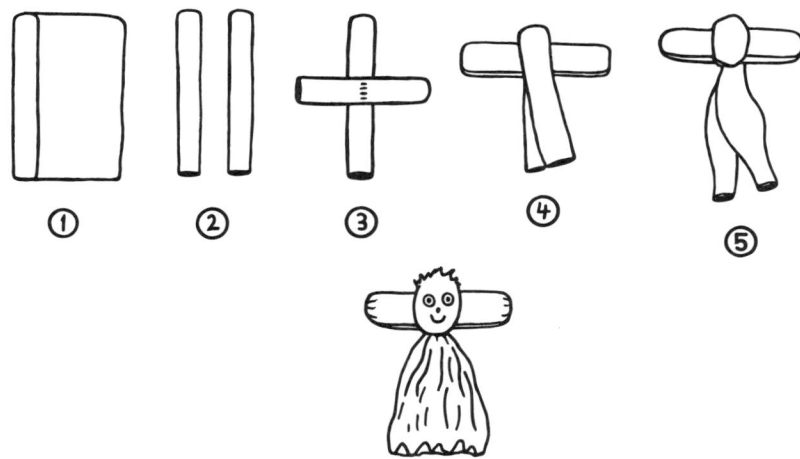

Decorate the face with buttons or markers and use pieces of yarn to make hair. Use other scrap fabrics to make a skirt, underwear, shoes, hats, or purses and any other accessories that you like.

Twin Babies in a Swing

You will need a square piece of fabric that measures about 15 to 20 inches on its edge. Begin by folding the fabric in half so you have a triangle (1). Roll up one side of the triangle until you reach the middle point

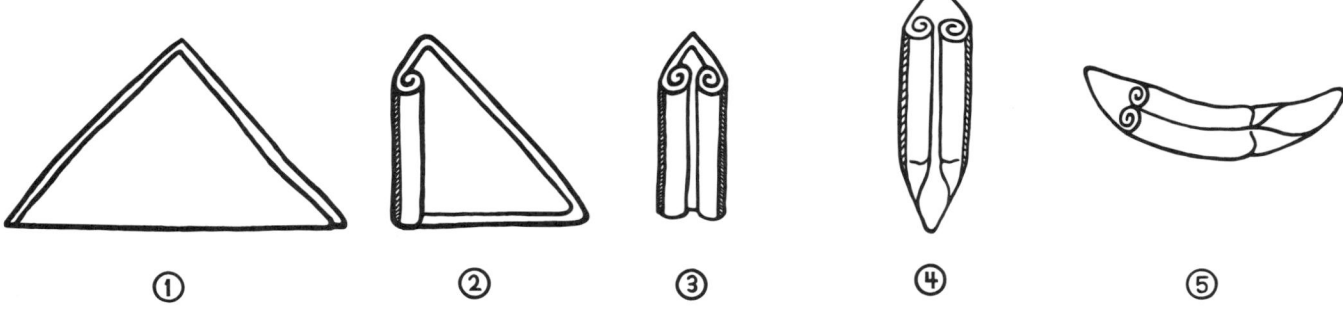

(2). Roll up the other side and you have two babies (3). Carefully pull down the underside of the tip of the triangle, under the babies, holding them in place so they don't unravel, and there you have it— Twin Babies in a swing (4). The swing can easily be attached to the edge of a bed cover or comforter using clothes or safety pins and the child can sit on the floor and play. For a mobile swing, simply tie the ends to a light twig or branch.

Make sure to give the child old socks that can be used as hats and other scraps of fabric that can be folded into pillows and blankets. If the fabric or towel is old, let the child draw the baby faces on it. The twins can also be sewn into place for a more permanent toy and decorated with yarn hair, button eyes, and pink and blue ribbons.

The Elders

Although having daughters in the villages often means that you are financially obligated to supply dowries of homes or lands, the blessed event of having a girl child has been and still is, very much looked forward to. According to the customs of the island, it falls to the grown daughters' realm of responsibility to see after her parents when they get old or if they get sick. This is not to say that a family of all sons won't take care of their parents. Since it's the girls that have been trained as caretakers, the responsibility is shared between daughters and daughter-in-laws as well.

There are nursing homes and hospitals in Greece, but very few families will send their loved ones away from them. Unless there is a very serious physical or mental illness, the elderly are taken care of in their own home.

In some circumstances, the elders have no children of their own to take care of them. In situations like this, the nephews and nieces will look after them and in return, they are made heirs to any property that the elder may have.

If you've ever walked through a Greek village, then I'm sure that you have seen couples or little old women, dressed in black that sit on a chair in front of their homes. These widows live alone, amongst their own belongings, but their daughters look in on them through out the day, bringing them dishes of food or helping them with their chores, baths or any medication.

It is customary in the villages, that when a daughter or daughter-in-law cooks a meal, a dish of food is sent to her mother and mother-in-law. Laundry and shopping days also take into consideration the needs of the elders and the daughters will see that the tasks are taken care of.

In the modern household of today, both husband and wife usually have to work and often there just isn't enough time to look after an aging or sick elder. The daughters can make arrangements with private nurses to help them out or they can ask other brothers or sisters to share in the care taking.

When the children live in the city, sometimes the elders agree to move from the village. The children make arrangements between themselves for an elder to stay one month with one daughter and then be moved to another child's house for one month and then on to another's. This continues for the rest of the elders life, making sure that they are taken care of by his or her own family.

The Greek elders are revered and respected in the islands and if you've read over any parts of "The Village Man" or "The Village Woman" then you too should come to realize that our parents and grandparents deserve our appreciation in many ways, if not only as admiration for what they've been through in life.

Before going to an elderly ladies home, make a stop at the *mbakáliko* or the village grocer. It's customary when visiting old ladies and widows to take a gift of Greek coffee, sugar and some cookies—"*Na teen glykánis*" or to sweeten her. The woman may just say *"Evharistó"* or thank you, or as is the custom, she may give you her blessing. Greeks say that old people are closer to God and to receive a blessing from them is quite an honor. So remember to be nice to the old folks and try to keep them happy, you will receive your rewards from God himself.

Greek Men and Women Today

The individual roles for men and women in Greece are still somewhat traditional. Even as Greece becomes more modernized and there is a need for two incomes in the family, the women are still responsible as caretakers, housewives, babysitters and cooks whether they have careers or not. It's completely un-thought of for a married village man to do a house hold chore such as washing dishes, even today.

More and more women are continuing in school, becoming professionals throughout Greece as well as internationally. They are earning high positions of respect that their women ancestors worked hard for and deserved, but they were never given.

Men also continue in their roles as tenders of any lands and taking care of the heavy work, again, regardless of how physically demanding their paying jobs may be. It is a very rare occasion that a male village land owner will hire anyone to tend his fields for him or that he will buy a truck load of fire wood when his own lands could supply it.

Yet there is a big difference in how modern couples see each other that is quite a contrast to what the relationships of our ancestors were. Equality and mutual respect is very common amongst the younger generations of Greece and often, while the wife works, the husband will sit with his children or go out to the supermarket to do the shopping. A prospect that I'm sure would have made our grandmothers flip over.

The Ceremonies

WEDDINGS
Engagements - *Aravónes*

In Greece, a man does not simply ask a girl to marry him, present her with a diamond ring on bended knee and scoot her off to church. It's a little more complicated than that.

In our grandmother's day many marriages were arranged. Yes, there were some young adults that did have the luxury of choosing a husband or wife for themselves, but this was only after the approval of their families. Some strict parents would choose a husband for their daughter who was nearing puberty or a wife for their son, performing what's called a *proxenió*. If for some reason the daughter or son didn't like the mate that was chosen for them, there was little that could be done about it. Even today, you'll hear the phrase "you'll learn to love him" given as advice to the younger girls by the old village women.

In some of the remote villages of Greece, children were also promised as marital mates to other families when they were as little as babies. When a girl was born to a family, they may of had a friend who already had a son. The families would give a promise to each other that one day they would *simbetheriásoume* or become in-laws. The reasons for a pact like this were many and sometimes it concerned the family's well being as well as the lands. Maybe one family's land was next to another's and by joining their families, they could work together. Or perhaps the brides' family lands were closer to water and would make irrigation easier. Whatever the reason, these children would grow up knowing that one day they would marry each other.

An argument or disagreement between the families would pre-empt any agreement of this kind and make it null and void. Which was alright by the children in some cases. But in others, the children had spent most of their lives together and had really grown to love each other. The circumstances of fighting families would make their marriage an impossibility.

When a son or daughter had chosen a mate on their own, the family would have to approve before any promise of a marriage was given. A mate should optimally come from a good name, or a family that is respected, have lands and the ability to supply the dowry requirements as well as be very likeable by their in-laws. Our forefathers were very picky about these topics.

Once it was assured that the marital mate was deemed in good standing, then the engagement proceeded. And what happened if the family said no? The couple would simply not be allowed to get married. Some of our more courageous ancestors eloped. This meant moving away from their home village as well as leaving behind any assets such as lands or houses that they had. All family ties were severed and they were left completely on their own to take care of themselves and a future growing family. Very brave indeed!

Today, choosing a mate is no where as severe as it was for our ancestors. The Greeks do follow tradition as far as the engagement and wedding process goes, but they no longer arrange the marriages of their children. There are some Greek parents who are very adamant about their children marrying within the village or area that they live and others who put up a terrible argument when non Greeks are chosen as mates. As Greece becomes more modernized, so is their thinking and although the parents may seem very stubborn, eventually, they do come around and accept other nationalities and religions into their homes.

Giving Your Word - *Logodósoume*

In Rhodes, an engagement begins by the groom going to his chosen bride's home "*na tin zitísi*" or to "ask for her." He is accompanied with his parents and with them they take gifts of sweets and drinks. In other villages and islands such as *Sími*, it's the bride's family that has to go to ask for the groom. The bride prepares a basket that's called a *peskési*. This basket is filled with flowers, sweets such as *baklavá*, wine and a few bottles of ouzo and it's covered with a needle pointed cloth that is hand made by the bride to be or her mother. Accompanied by her parents, she gives this gift to her future mother-in-law or *betherá*.

Once the families are together, the parents begin the conversation by saying something like "my son likes your daughter..." or "my daughter likes your son..." The children have very little to say about anything as the parents get into conversation with each other. In our grandmother's day, it would be a long drawn out affair, comparing the details of lands and each others assets. The families would often get into stalemates as to what they were willing to exchange for the hand of the bride or groom. Today, the parents simply get together and have a few drinks toasting each others' health and the happiness of their children.

After the parents approve of each other's families and of the bride or groom, they give their *lógo*, meaning their promised word and their blessing. Once the *lógo* has been given, then the engagement is official and the planning of the wedding can begin.

The Engagement Party

An engagement party is not as big an affair in the Greek Islands as it is in western cultures. It's a simple get together with drinks and food that is usually done at the home of the bride or groom. The immediate families of the couple, a few choice friends and the village or neighborhood priest are invited. If the couple knows who will be the *koumpári* or best men and women to them, they can be invited also.

A small table is placed in the center of the room with an icon of the Virgin Mary or Christ placed on it. The couple's wedding bands or *véres*, rest on the icon waiting to get blessed by the priest. The priest begins the ceremony with a few words from the gospel and he continues to bless the wedding bands and the couple. The bands are then placed on the left fingers of the couple by the priest. They are officially engaged from this moment on.

In some circumstances, a priest is not present during an engagement. When this is the case, it is appropriate for the fathers of the children to put the bands on the fingers of the couple. The groom's father will put the ring onto the bride's finger, and the bride's father will put the ring on his son-in-law to be.

Now comes the *chrísoma*. This is simply, putting gold upon the couple to give them a rich start in life.

Again, you will find variations to this tradition, but in the islands it is customary for the immediate family to put gifts of gold on the couple, meaning jewelry around their necks or hands. This gold will also be worn as part of their wedding trousseau. In some villages and islands, it is customary to pin money on the couples clothing as well, showing their wealth to all in attendance.

The couple stands side by side and the relatives walk past them, pinning their gifts, layering chains around their necks, or fastening bracelets and watches. The parents of the couple purchase gifts of gold for both the bride and groom, where as the rest of the family gives gifts to the new member of their family. After this is done, there is much cheering of *kaloríziki* or "to be well rooted" and the party continues with drinking, eating, and dancing.

Dowries

When speaking of dowries in Greece, we're not just talking about a hope chest filled with family heirlooms or a few suitcases packed with nice sheets and blankets. Dowries are very extensive, supplying the needs for a complete household for the newly married couple. From simple coffee mugs to elaborate furniture, everything is enclosed in the dowry package.

In Greece, you will rarely find a newly wed couple moving into their parents' home. This is simply not done and is the reason that the dowries are so extensive. A home must be supplied either by the bride or the groom and this is where the differences in the custom are found.

Traditions for the dowries can vary from village to village as well as the different regions of Greece. In some parts of the country it is deemed that the groom must supply the complete dowry, where as in other places, the bride takes on the responsibility. This is true for Rhodes. The villages of the island keep the tradition that it's the brides obligation to supply almost all of the newly married couples dowry.

The weddings are simply not planned until the homes and dowry are completed. Many times, you will find that when you ask an engaged couple when they will get married, they answer simply "...when the house is finished." Some couples choose to live in the cities, so they may purchase or rent an apartment. Again, the cost of the apartment will either be paid by the appropriate family or the couple will be given money to help them pay for the rent.

Since there are so many regional differences as to who pays and for what, its impossible to list the traditions of every area. The dowry information that follows is based on the traditions of the villages of Rhodes. Remember, in some other areas or Islands, it may be completely reversed as it would be the groom's responsibility to supply almost, if not everything.

The Bridal Dowry - *Príka tis Nífis*

When a daughter is born, the first thought that comes to the parents' mind is that they will need to build a house for her. This is not an exaggeration as many villages have the custom that it's the bride's responsibility to supply the home for her future husband and although you may have a family of five daughters, you are still expected to give each of them some kind of housing as their dowry.

To this day, even poor families will scrimp and save to be able to afford at least four walls for the girl child. Many families will begin the process when the girl is still a baby. One year they will begin by laying the foundation of the new home. Another year will mean its building and yet another for the tile work and plumbing. This continues until the home is finished and furnished and the girl has grown to marrying age.

The bridal dowry does not stop at the shell of the house alone. It has to be filled as well. Except for one bedroom and the kitchen, all the furniture must be in place. Linens, dishes, wall hangings, rugs - everything that a household needs are collected through the years as part of the girl's dowry.

Mothers will begin to hand-make special, one-of-a-kind linens that will be used to adorn the bridal bed when their daughters are very young. If you've ever had the chance to see some of these elaborate linens, then you'll understand that the reason they start so soon is because the linens take years to complete.

The growing daughters themselves will also use their spare time to hand-make doilies, needle pointed wall hangings as well as fine crocheted curtains and blankets as part of their own dowries that they will present to their future husbands.

On the days preceding her wedding, her entire dowry is carefully arranged throughout the house for all the visitors to see. The hand made linens are hung carefully over the open doors of closets, to show them off as well as allow a glimpse into the closet itself, showing the brides "riches." Privacy is non existent in the bridal home. Guests will look into the closets and kitchen cabinets whether the doors are shut or not, as is the custom.

The groom stands on the left with his bride-to-be next to him in preparation for their engagement ceremony in the village of *Émbona*, Rhodes, 1947.

For the richer families, the bridal home becomes a mark of status and sometimes they compete to have the best house. The finest of marble is used to tile the floors as well as having the best carpenter to hand make the furniture. Today, modern amenities such as Jacuzzis and fully 'packed' kitchens are commonly found in these status houses.

The Groom's Dowry - *Príka tou Gambroú*

You may think that in Rhodes, the grooms really get the best end of the bargain. They get a house that is filled with all the necessities and sometimes luxuries that they have never known as well as a loving, blushing bride. When comparing the groom's dowry to the bride's, it does not seem so much, but it is still a substantial amount that he must present.

Although the bride supplies the furnished house, the kitchen and one bedroom are left untouched by her. This is the groom's responsibility. The groom must supply all the kitchen electrical equipment such as the oven and stove, refrigerator, laundry machine, and in more modern homes, the dishwasher and dryer as well.

All bridal homes have a master bedroom and at least one other bedroom. The second bedroom is known as the *pedikó* or child's room as it will one day be the room that their future children sleep in. The bedroom furnishings for the *pedikó* are bought by the groom who simply takes the bride or his mother-in-law shopping and then pays for the bill.

A groom's dowry does not stop at the furnishings alone. Kitchen supplies such as dishes, pots and pans and other utensils are collected through the years by his mother. She too, will begin when her son is very young to collect the various needs for his future wedding dowry. Bedroom linens and blankets for the master bedroom as well as for the child's room are carefully stored to be used in his future home. If the groom has older sisters, it is more than likely that they have hand needle pointed wall hangings for the bedrooms and kitchen as well as making floor coverings for him.

Traditionally, the groom's dowry was taken to the new couples home on the Thursday before the wedding for the bed making ceremony. His immediate family held the dowry in their arms and walked in the streets on their way to the home, singing wedding songs. Today, his dowry is taken to the home days in advance, so the bride and her family can arrange it properly to be shown off on the night of the beds.

Village Weddings

**Wedding in the village of *Émbona*, Rhodes 1948.
The bride is wearing her traditional dress and boots where as the groom is in
a more modern suit or what is lovingly called a *koustoumiá*. The simple candles they are holding
were the *lampádes* of the times.**

I have been to Americanized Greek weddings held at the Orthodox Churches and Cathedrals of the United States and although they were beautiful, extravagant ceremonies and services, I can't say that they match the traditional Greek experience.

In America, the Greek church wedding ceremony itself is slightly altered, making it more modernized. Bridesmaids, groomsmen, ushers, and flower girls all stand in attendance as the ceremony proceeds in a rather somber fashion. The Dance of Isaiah around the altar, which is traditionally almost riotous in the Island ceremonies, is also performed in a very serious way.

At the reception, the maids are teamed with the groomsmen and are escorted into the hall, in a very organized and practiced way. When the newlyweds walk in, again, their steps are slow and deliberate as they make their way to the head table. Of course, there is the first dance, which is a slow one, for the newlyweds to start and then the family couples join in.

All of this is really beautiful and I'm sure that it takes meticulous planning to get those little flower girls to get their steps right and lots of practice for the groom not to trip over his bride's veil and train while they slow dance. But I can't help but notice that in our attempt to create the perfect wedding, so many of our traditions and customs are becoming lost as the ceremonies become more and more modernized.

Many times, a village or island wedding is far from being perfect, but the feeling of fun and comradarie that is found is unsurpassed. As you read on, you'll see that family and guests are not just bystanders, they play an active role through out the wedding process which lasts for days. And although progress is always thought to be in the better interest of cultures and societies, this is one circumstance that I have to admit to feeling that the old ways are better. Besides... Who would want to miss out on the Dance of Isaiah ?

Wedding Dates

Choosing a wedding date for a Greek wedding means a little planning in advance. A wedding can not take place during the great fast of *sarakostí* or Lent. It is a time of deprival for the Greek Orthodox observers so no parties or celebrations are held during that period. There are also other fasting periods in the Greek calendar year. One of which, is *Tis Panagías* or The Virgin Mary's which is from August 1st through the 15th. Weddings are not allowed to take place during this or any other fasting periods.

It is also believed that the *dísekto* or leap years, are bad luck in which to hold a wedding. It's not uncommon for a superstitious couple to rush their wedding plans or else they will have to wait for twelve months to go by, skipping the leap year. Deaths in a family also put a halt to wedding plans. Depending on the relation of the deceased, weddings are postponed for as much as one year until its considered that the mourning period is over.

Greek Island weddings are traditionally held on Sunday afternoons, after the Divine Liturgy has been given and there has been time to prepare the church. Today, more and more villagers and islanders are choosing to have their wedding on Saturdays. This has made it much easier for the guests who have children that must go to school as well as the night long celebrators that have to make it to work on Monday morning.

Honeymoon Plans - *Ton Mína tou Mélitos*

For our ancestors, there were no such things as honeymoons as we know them. Our grandmothers did not sail the Mediterranean on a Cunard Line cruise or take a trip simply to enjoy the status of being a new wife. After the wedding rituals and ceremonies, life went back to normal and everyday duties, such as goat herding, housekeeping and sowing crops were the priority once again.

Today, things are different for the Greeks. Honeymoons, which are known as the month of honey, are just as extravagant and exotic as any western couple's would be. As the name implies, it is an entire month that is seen as appropriate for the newlywed couple to travel.

Greek honeymoons are planned to begin one to two weeks after the wedding day. The couples rarely take their honeymoons beginning on their wedding night or for the few days after. There is simply so much tradition and family involved in the wedding ritual, that a departure by the couple would be inappropriate. This is not looked at as an inconvenience and most newlywed couples prefer this. The delay in plans gives them a chance to rest after the exhaustive preparations and ceremonies so they can really have a good time when they do go away.

Wedding Invitations - *Prosklitíria*

The modern weddings of today always mean ordering wedding invitations and response cards such as the RSVP. Along with these common invites, the Greek village invitations also include cards with special announcements as to the dates, time and places that special rituals will be held such as the *melekoúnia*, the wedding cookies and the making of the beds.

Few invitations are actually mailed for an island wedding. Having a relative that lives on another island or overseas, would be the only situation where this would be done. Invitations are always personally given out by the couple and their families. The *koumpári* are also given a stack or two of invitations to hand out on their own. It is customary that they can invite whomever they want to witness the ritual.

Our ancestors invited their wedding guests in the same fashion, the only difference being that they had no invitations or cards to hand out. It was done completely by word of mouth. The couple and their families would visit the different homes of their relations and personally invite them to the wedding. If they couldn't find someone, they basically left a message with a neighbor or another family member. Since Sunday was always the chosen day for weddings, the traditional days of pre-wedding rituals were easily remembered.

By giving out the invitation by word of mouth, in essence, the entire village would be invited. Some villages had populations of only a few hundred, where as others numbered in the thousands and everyone was invited.

Best Men or Best Women - *Koumpári*

In a Greek wedding, there is no best man or maid of honor per say, instead we have the *koumpári*. The position is an honored one because the chosen *koumpári* will take an active role in the wedding ceremony itself, by exchanging the *stefánia* or wreaths over the couple as well as the rings on their fingers.

Wedding *koumpári* are usually a mixture of the couple's godparents. If there is a reason that they can't do it personally, then they will elect one of their children in their place or simply tell you to chose someone else. By choosing a *koumpáro*, you are automatically choosing a Godparent for your first born child, as it is customary that the people that will put the *stefánia* on you at your wedding, will also baptize your first baby. As in baptisms, there is no limit as to the number of *koumpári* that you can have. You need at least one, but I have seen weddings that have five and six. This allows you to keep with the tradition yet lets you place a good friend or relative if you wish, as a *koumpáro* also.

It is traditional that the *koumpári* pay for certain wedding expenses. *Bounbouniéres*, *lampádes*, fabric, *stefánia* and the church service itself all fall into the realm, or should I say pocket of the *koumpári*. Depending on the couple that is getting married and just how elaborate the wedding will be, it could mean quite an expenditure. This is when it's best to have more *koumpári* so they can split the bill.

The *koumpári* do not go unrewarded. It is also customary that the newlywed couple present the *koumpári* with gifts at the wedding reception. These gifts are elaborately decorated as large wedding favors and are placed high for all the guests to see. Items such as ceramic vases, silver trays and crystal are often given. In more wealthy services, thick gold necklaces as well as color TV's given as gifts of appreciation to the *koumpári*.

Wedding Favors - *Bounbouniéres*

During the planning of a wedding, the koumpári are responsible for certain preparations beginning with the *bounbouniéres*. These are small favors which are handed out to the wedding guests after the wedding. They are wrapped in tulle, with a few Jordan almonds inside and are tied with a ribbon. Some can be very elaborate and contain silver or ceramic statues and vases while others are made from plain folded tulle with just the almonds. There is always an odd number of Jordan almonds inside a *bounbouniéra* because an even number of almonds is considered to be unlucky.

The Jordan almonds that are used in wedding *bounbouniéres* are said to invoke dreams of a future husband for the unmarried girls. The girl should sleep with the almonds under her pillow to see who she will marry. Some islanders believe that it is the Jordan almonds that are on the priest's tray at the altar that have the dream-invoking power. This is the tray that the *stefánia* or wedding wreaths sit on and since they become blessed, so do the almonds. A superstitious girl can easily get a few almonds from this tray at the end of the ceremony as she is walking past the newlyweds to congratulate them.

Wedding Candles - *Lampádes*

At every Greek wedding ceremony, on either side of the couple there are burning candles. These are known as the *lampádes*. In times ago, the *lampádes* of a wedding were simple candles, that when lit, were to be held by the bride and groom through the ceremony. Today, these candles stand about four feet high and are decorated with fabrics and flowers and are placed on the altar. They can be very elaborate, depending on how much the *koumpári* are spending for the ceremony. They are lit at the beginning of the wedding ceremony, symbolizing the light of God.

Fabric - *Ífasma*

A large piece of fabric is also needed for a Rhodian wedding, as this custom seems to be particular to our island. This will be used during the Dance of Isaiah around the altar. This fabric is placed over the shoulders of the couple, in essence, making them one. This can be a simple fabric or an elaborate brocade or satin, again the elaborateness depending on what the *koumpári* can afford. After the wedding, it was customary that the bride would give this fabric to a seamstress who would make a dress for her.

Wreaths - *Stefánia*

The *stefánia* of a wedding are the most important item that the *koumpári* will buy. Without these wreaths, a Greek wedding can not take place. The wreaths are symbolic as awards of ancient times. In the times of Alexander, over three hundred years before the coming of Christ, wreaths meant wealth and honor. The Greek church uses the symbolism of wreaths to award the couple for being honorable Christians that will go on to create life by making a family. *Stefánia* are made from round metallic bands that sit on your head very much like a crown. They are decorated with imitation pearls, stones or flowers and are always white in color. Imagine a tiara where the sides continue around your head, that is what a *stefáni* looks like. These wreaths are joined together by a three or four foot long piece of white ribbon, so when the bride and groom have the *stefánia* on their heads, they are still joined by the ribbon, symbolizing the unity of the couple in marriage.

The *stefánia* of a wedding are considered to be Holy and blessed and the ribbon joining them must never be cut. After the wedding, the bride will take them to her new home and keep them in the icon station. Some of the older village housewives had elaborate cases made for their *stefánia*. They still hang in the glass enclosed cases today, right along with the icons of the house.

Wedding Bands - *Véres*

Simple gold bands are used for engagements and weddings in Greece. The bands are often blessed at an engagement ceremony and worn by the couple on their left hands. After they are married, they are worn on the right.

Before the wedding ceremony, the couple will give their bands to the priest who will place them on the altar, on the silver tray with the *stefánia* until the appropriate time in the ceremony when he will place the rings on the fingers of the couple. The bands are symbolic of the consistency of the relationship, the trust and mutual giving and seal the union between the couple.

Bridesmaids - *Paránifes*

Greek island weddings don't have groomsmen or ushers and they use very young girls as bridesmaids. Tradition says that the *paránifes* must be unmarried girls. This is a nice way of saying that they must be virgins. Instead of asking her friends or relatives such a personal question, today's island bride chooses children usually between the ages of four and twelve. These children can be relations such as nieces or cousins, but they can also be chosen from the children of close friends or *koumpári*. There is no limit as to the number of *paránifes* that a bride chooses and as is the custom in western cultures, the bride pays for their dresses.

The Bride and Groom's Clothing

In some villages, it is customary that the bride pay not only for her wedding gown, but for the groom's outfit as well. Everything that the groom will wear on his wedding day should be new. This means purchasing new under clothes, new shoes and of course, a new suit.

In our grandmother's day, a bride and groom would dress in the colorful traditional clothes of the village or island. These were not the normal, everyday clothing. An assortment of fabrics for dresses and suits as well as underclothes were embellished by hand with intricate needle worked designs and beads or charms.

The mothers would start working on the fabrics for their daughter's wedding clothes when the child was still young. Often the girl herself as well as her grandmothers, sisters and aunts would help too. The mothers of boys would also begin the tedious process well in advance, often enlisting the help of other family members to prepare what would one day be the groom's trousseau. When the days of the wedding would approach, these fabrics would be sewn into underwear and petticoats as well as skirts, shirts, pants and vests which would be worn by the bride and groom on the big day.

Today, you will rarely find a village wedding in the islands where the bride or groom wear the traditional clothing. Just as western cultures, we too have the various bridal shops that offer an array of white and ivory gowns to be worn by the blushing bride as well as the fashionable boutiques for men's suits.

The Week Before The Wedding

Weddings are just as important and fussy in the islands as they are in western cultures, if not more. The week before a wedding is a time of, well quite honestly, chaos. The bride and groom spend their time finalizing their plans and purchases as well as over seeing the preparations of their new home. The parents of the couple are working to complete the house and the dowry so it's ready to be shown off and the *koumpári* are rushing around preparing their own purchases and plans for the wedding ceremony itself.

There are rituals and parties that are done on almost every day for the week before a wedding, which also means much preparation of food and drinks to serve to guests and helpers. Needless to say, the entire family, including the aunts, cousins, and distant relations of the couple get enlisted to work for the wedding preparations.

The week before the wedding is also the time when the bride's father will prepare the animals that will be slaughtered for the wedding reception. Although some modern couples choose to have their reception catered, others still remain with the tradition, especially if their family has herds of sheep or goats.

Sesame Honey Bars - *Melekoúni*

The family prepares the *melekoúni* for a modern day village wedding.

These are simply candy bars which are made from toasted sesame seeds mixed with honey and are made eight days prior to the wedding. The women will make the *melekoúni* by pressing it out onto large tables and then cut it into diamond shapes. Each diamond is wrapped in colorful cellophane and is given to guests as they visit the homes and at the end of the wedding ceremony along with the *bounbouniéra*. The *melekoúni* is symbolic of a sweet life with many children. In the days before colorful cellophane wrapping was available, our ancestors used the large leaves from citrus trees such as orange or lemons as liners for these sticky sweets.

Wedding Cookies - *Ta Kouloúria*

On the seventh day preceding a wedding, the wedding cookies or *koulouría* are made. This is a day of fun and laughter as it's celebrated as sort of a tame bachelorette party. Female relatives such as the aunts, nieces and cousins as well as good friends, get together at the bride's home. Their purpose is to make wedding cookies.

In the center of the kitchen are large pans or *skáfes* that are filled with flour and other ingredients that are needed. One of the older women will throw a coin into the flour and challenge the young unmarried girls to get it with their mouths. Fully anticipating what is about to happen, the first girl will come to stand in front of the table. Lots of laughter begins the ritual as she bends into the flour to get the coin. Swiftly, the elder will press her face into it, covering her with flour as is customary. Each young girl must take a turn and stand in front of the flour pan before the recipe is started. There are occasions when this turns into an all out "flour battle," but since it's expected, there is much more flour in reserve.

The young village girls making the wedding cookies. The dish of money is collected from well wishers and family for the girls to share.

The long ropes of wedding cookies waiting to be baked.

With their faces covered in flour, they begin making the wedding cookies. The older women help the younger girls with the recipe and sing wedding songs as they knead the dough and roll it out into long ropes. The dough is arranged on cookie sheets and covered with linen. They are left to rest until the next day, when the party continues again.

On the sixth day before the wedding, the young girlfriends and relatives will get together once again at the bride's home. The bee-hive oven or *foúno* is heated up and the cookies are baked. Once they have cooled down, they are broken by hand into pieces about two inches long. They are then mixed with candies, nuts, raisins and Jordan almonds and put into small plastic bags and tied with a ribbon. These bags are given as wedding favors to guests who come to visit the family on the nights preceding the wedding.

Other islands have different traditions. For instance, in *Sími*, they make what's called *mouskopoúgia* for their pre-wedding favors. These are small pies that are stuffed with sugared walnuts, almonds and sesame seeds. After they are baked they are dipped into rose water and then pressed into powdered sugar. Wrapped up in cellophane, they are given to guests and well wishers.

Wedding Breads - *Ta Psomiá tou Gámou*

In some villages and islands it's customary to make wedding breads that will be given out as favors after the ceremony. These breads are always made with sugar so that they are symbolic of a sweet life. Knives are never used to cut these breads as they are thought of as bad luck and could sever a relationship. Instead, the women cut the breads by pulling them apart by hand.

On the island of Crete, loaves of sweet aromatic breads are pulled apart and given out at the pre-wedding rituals as well as the reception.

In areas of Continental Greece, you'll find that the wedding preparations include the making of one huge loaf of sweet, *Lagána* like bread. The massive loaf is set on tables and served by hand, by the unmarried girls to the guests.

Thursday before the Wedding

The Beds - *Ta Krevátia*

The *apokrévato* or bed of a village home is decorated in all its finery to be shown off the days prior to the wedding.

The Thursday before a wedding is know as the day of the *krevátia* or beds. On this day all the wedding guests are invited to the brides new home to witness the making of the beds as well as see her dowry as well as the grooms which has been laid out. Coffee and sweets are served and bags of wedding cookies and *melekoúni* are given out to the guests.

In the master bedroom, the bed is completely bare. The linens or *asprokentímata* that will dress it are on a chair or table to the side. These linens are one of a kind pieces that have been hand made by the brides mother, sometimes with the help from other family members such as the grandmother or aunts. The intricate designs and meticulous attention to detail make them heirloom pieces which will be kept in the family and handed down to other daughters as part of their dowries.

Once the guests begin to arrive, the village orchestra begins to play. Now, I use the term orchestra lovingly here as this is nothing more than two or three of the older village men playing violins, lyres, and mandolins. The older women begin to sing the wedding songs and the young unmarried girls are called to form around the bed.

The young girls are the bride's friends and relatives and again, tradition says that they must be virgins. Their duty is to make up the bridal bed. The sheets, pillows, and blankets are laid out carefully and arranged, so the bed is now covered in all its finery.

Since the first persons to lay on this bed will be the newlywed couple, it is tradition that Jordan almonds and rice be thrown onto it by the guests. Again, this symbolizes a sweet life with many children and to be well rooted.

Taking the tradition one step further, it has become custom to throw money onto the bed, wishing the couple a rich life. This is done mostly by the immediate family and close friends, *koumpári* and Godparents. The fathers of the couple can become very extravagant. Some just throw bank account books onto the bed while others, take the opportunity to have some fun.

The fathers of the couple will exchange an amount of money into small bills and hold the wad over the bed, flipping each bill, one by one onto the covers. At some point they will pretend to put the rest of the money back into their pocket, getting a riotous laugh from the crowd as the bride and groom's expressions are clearly written on their faces. The couple stands next to the bed while this display of well wishing is going on and egg-on their in-laws with jokes for more money. Of course, the guests keep cheering and singing as the wad of money comes back out of the fathers pocket, and again, he dispenses a few bills before putting them away, starting the fun all over.

Before, during and after the ritualistic making of the beds, the bride's house is considered open for all who wish to see it. This means that very nosy village women will be poking their noses into cabinets, closets and drawers. There is nothing that can be done about this because, plain and simple, it's the custom.

Knowing that their dowries will be shown off on this day and for the following days until the wedding, the bride-to-be is fully prepared for the invasion of privacy. The best of her dowry is very prominently showing and the cabinets, shelves and drawers are full with other items that have been neatly folded and carefully arranged.

Wedding Presents

With the exception of monetary gifts, guests and well wishers that come to visit a wedding home will bring with them their wedding present which is much easier than carrying the gift to the church or reception. Today's gift giving is very westernized and can include gifts from a bridal list at a shop or small electrical appliances and household goods.

In the traditional weddings of our grandmother's time, wedding gifts consisted of food and drink. Flasks of ouzo and wine would be given to the families as well as ingredients for cooking. All these items would be used for the wedding preparations as well as what's known as The Bride's Dinner which is the wedding reception itself.

The entire meal to feed all the invited guests was prepared at the bride's home by the families of the couple. Pots, pans and utensils were borrowed from neighbors and family as well as the use of their ovens. Many times, the village bakery would be asked to lend the use of their ovens as well. Guests would give baskets of vegetables, live chickens, cheeses, eggs and other food items as gifts. Basket by basket, these gifts would add up to enough to feed the hundreds and sometimes thousands of guests that would attend the wedding.

Saturday Before The Wedding

The Bride's Bath - *To Loúsimo tis Nífis*

Long, long ago, it was customary that the Saturday before the wedding would be the day that the female friends and relatives of the bride would bathe her. Water would be drawn from the wells and heated and wedding songs would be sung as the bride was prepared. This custom has not been followed for quite some time, instead, the bride is prepared on her wedding day.

The Bread Donations

The households' weekly bread supplies are baked on Saturdays by the village women. Traditionally, relations, friends and neighbors would contribute a fresh loaf of their own to the bridal family for it to be served at the wedding reception the next day. Fresh, right out of the oven loaves would be collected at the bridal home all during the day before the wedding. Friends and relatives would stop by and have a drink or a sweet and give a much appreciated gift.

Today, there is no need for the contribution of bread loaves because most island weddings have the bread ordered from a bakery or the caterer takes care of it. The Saturday before the wedding is spent in preparation for the big day and sometimes, as western cultures, bachelor and bachelorette parties are given.

Sunday - The Wedding Day

Getting Dressed

In Greek island weddings, even getting dressed has its customs and traditions that must be followed. Some villages simply let the bride and groom dress themselves while at their parental homes, where as others have more complicated ways of doing it.

Our village tradition is that neither, bride nor groom should get dressed in wedding clothes while in their own home and they not get dressed in the same house either although exceptions are sometimes made. This means their paternal homes as well as the new house that they will live in can not be used. In cases like this, homes of relatives, which may be next door to each other, are chosen in advance, and their clothing is waiting there for them. The wedding guests and families know where they will be getting dressed and meet them at the houses to begin the wedding ritual.

At the houses, the men with their violins have already begun their serenades of wedding songs as the bride and groom are escorted by their immediate families. Other guests and friends of the family are already there, filling the houses and streets as more continue to arrive. As the bride or groom arrives, each is taken to their designated house and the dressing begins.

This modern bride wears the traditional costume of the island of *Kárpathos*.

Once inside, the aunts, nieces and cousins as well as good friends are waiting for the *Stólisma tis Nífis* or to decorate the bride. The girls will wash and prepare the bride and do her hair. Each article of clothing is put on by a different person. For instance, the undergarments may be put on by her sister, the bridal gown may be put on by her mother, the shoes can be put on by her father, and her veil will be put in place by her best friend.

At the same time, the groom is going through the same ritual, next door. His relatives, friends and brothers wash and shave him, and piece by piece, they get him dressed.

Once the bride and groom have been dressed, they are taken to the living rooms of the respective houses where their family will begin adorning them with gold gifts. Just like the *hrísoma* of the engagement party, the bride and groom will stand as the family members put gold necklaces, bracelets and medallions on them. This is also the time that family heirlooms that have been given to them as babies or passed down from a grandmother are worn.

After the bride's family is finished putting on her gold, they will leave her and go next door to present the groom with his gifts. The same holds true for the groom's family. After they have completed the groom's trousseau, they too will go to the bride and dress her in the gold gifts. When the gifts have been given, both families will return to their son or daughter to prepare for the procession.

Both the bride and groom must show honor to their families and elders before they can being the procession to the church. They will genuflect to their parents, grandparents, brothers and sisters and kiss their hand. This is a gesture of respect and thankfulness for their blessing.

The Wedding Procession
Dressed and ready, the bride and groom can begin the walk to the church. The village orchestra leads the procession as an announcement that a wedding is following. The groom is escorted by his family and friends and is next in the procession towards the church. In his hands, he holds the bridal bouquet and he will carry it until they reach the church, at which time he'll give this as a gift to the bride.

The bride and her immediate family as well as the rest of the guests follow behind the orchestra and the groom. The bride is held by both arms as she is walking. Not only her father escorts her, but female friends as well as other relatives. Often, they will change places or let some one else have a turn.

At some point the procession will stop and gather together for the pre-wedding dancing. This can be in the village square or in the church courtyard, depending on its size. The guests will fill the surrounding area leaving room for a dance floor. Sometimes ouzo, *súma*, or *ráki* is passed around to heighten the party atmosphere. The orchestra will begin to play traditional songs and one by one, the family members will begin to join in dance. The bride's mother and father will start the dance with their in-laws and then the brothers and sisters will join in, followed by the aunts and cousins. This continues until almost the entire procession is dancing.

Now these are not slow dances. If you've had the chance to see the Greeks in action, you know that their dances are very fast and lively. This pre-wedding celebration is symbolic as the meeting and joining of the two families. The bride and groom can partake if they wish to but it's not mandatory.

For the most part, they will each dance once or twice with their immediate families and friends. The custom does take into consideration that the bride is loaded down in a heavy gown and veils, so the songs that are played for her dances, are slower paced, but the groom really gets the go of it.

His friends and the *koumpári* give him shots of ouzo and *súma*, then pull him to the front of the line to lead the liveliest displays. This pre-wedding ritual can last from twenty minutes to more than an hour, depending on the *kéfi* or party mood of the crowd. It's not unusual for the groom to be soaking in sweat and need a bit of a rest before the procession can continue.

The Wedding Ceremony

After the dancing of the families, the guests and relations will once again form together and continue the procession until the church is reached. In the courtyard, the groom will take his place in front of the church and the bride will walk to him. He gives her his gift of the bridal bouquet and hand in hand they enter the church.

On some occasions, there is a special prayer that is read to honor brides that are virgins. This may sound old fashioned to you, but it's a blessing that the bride herself can request to be read by the priest, if she chooses. To this day, many women are very proud of the fact that they are un-touched and want their families and in-laws to know it too. For this blessing to be read, the groom will continue to the altar while the bride waits in the back of the church. The priests will read the blessing, introducing her as "the virgin" and then she will take her place next to the groom.

The ceremony begins as the couple holds hands. The *koumpári* take their places at the sides or behind the couple as well as the parents and immediate family. In Greece, the churches are small. Other than the altar itself, guests will stand anywhere that they can find a spot, so there is always a crowd around a bride and groom.

At the beginning of the ceremony, the bride and groom walk together as they are escorted to the altar by the priest.

The priest will say the words "*Aravoniázete i doúli tou Theoú*" which translates to "the servant of God is becoming engaged." He will call the names of the bride and groom as he's holding the rings and making the sign of the cross over the couple. The priest will bless the wedding bands and slide them onto their fingers. Each of the *koumpári* are called to interchange the rings between the couple three times.

At the appropriate time in the ceremony, the priest will set the *stefánia* on the couples heads. Again, each of the *koumpári* will take a turn in this ritual and are called to stand in place. Holding a *stefáni* in each hand they cross their arms over the heads of the couple, exchanging the wreaths three times, symbolizing the Holy Trinity. The *stefánia* will remain on the couples heads until the end of the ceremony.

For a Rhodian wedding, the priest will wrap the couple together by throwing the piece of *Ífasma* or fabric over their shoulders, symbolizing their unity. A cup of wine is blessed by the priest symbolizing the blood of Christ and Holy Communion. The bride and groom are to take three sips each, although I know of nervous brides that took generous gulps to calm their nerves. The sharing of one cup is to remind the couple that they will share the rest of their lives together. After the bride and groom have had their three sips, the wine is also given to the *koumpári* to drink. As the *koumpári* will also play important roles in the couples life.

At the point in the wedding liturgy, when the priest reads:

Í gyný na fováte ton ántra
or
The woman to fear the man

it is customary that the groom gently step on his bride's foot when these words are spoken, displaying his dominance over her. Today, the custom has changed as the brides would rather step on the groom's foot. Attentively, the couple waits to hear the words spoken. Although, if they miss the line, their mothers or friends will give them a nudge anyway. The guests and families laugh as they see the couple almost kicking each other, trying to get their foot on top of the other's. Some somber priests are not happy about this display going on during their ceremonies and will ask the bride and groom to refrain from doing it before the ceremony begins. Others, will ask the couple to simply kiss each other at the appropriate time, and yet others, just go on with the tradition, letting the couple and guests have their fun.

I mentioned the Dance of Isaiah earlier in my discussion of Greek weddings, with enthusiasm simply because it's my favorite part of the ceremony and it's so much fun. In a village or island wedding, you may notice that at some time, the male friends and relatives begin to slowly move into place around the altar. This signals that the Dance of Isaiah is coming. This ritual does not involve dancing of any kind, as its name may mislead you. It's simply called this because of the words in the hymn.

The Profit Isaiah foresaw the coming of Christ, and this hymn describes the happiness and the celebration or "dance" that goes with a revelation of something new and forth-coming. Since the couple is starting a new life together, this is considered their first dance and celebration of their future happiness in marriage.

The traditional Dance of Isaiah around the altar.

While the couple is standing with the *stefánia* on their heads and fabric over their shoulders, the priest continues with the ceremony and begins the *Tropário* or hymn with the words "*Isaía Hóreve...*" or "Isaiah dance..."

Taking the groom by the hand, the priest will lead the couple and the *koumpári* to walk around the altar table three times. It is tradition that rice be thrown on the couple, symbolizing a well rooted and successful life with many children and often, the rice is mixed with Jordan almonds as well. The island customs take this tradition a step further by giving the couple and the *koumpári* strength for a solid beginning.

As the couple and *koumpári* walk past the crowd that has formed around the altar table, loving friends and family will smack and punch them on the back. Every time they go around, hands come out of the crowd, laying another blow. The guests cheer and laugh as the couple and *koumpári* huddle together, trying to avoid a face full of rice and Jordan almonds as well as a smack on the back from the new brother-in-laws. Even the little old grandmothers will make sure that they land at least one smack on the bride and groom's backs. The bride and the female *koumpáres* do get treated a little gentler, but the groom and the male *koumpári* are sure to get as much strength and solidity as possible.

The ceremony finishes with the bride and groom kissing each other. The attending priests will kiss the *stefáni* on each of their heads and wish them *kalorízíki* or to be well rooted. They remain standing at the altar along with the immediate family and the *koumpári* as the relatives and friends walk by to congratulate them. The guests continue to the church courtyard where family members hand out the *bounbouniéres*, and *melekoúni*.

The happy newlyweds after their wedding in 1948. Perhaps, you think they really don't look so happy. I'm told that the photographers of the time wanted a *sovaró* or serious expression from their subjects, so you will rarely find an old wedding photo that shows the couples smiling.

The Wedding Reception - The Bride's Dinner

In days of old, the bride would be put on donkey back and the groom would lead her through the village streets, showing her off as they proceeded to the house that was chosen for their newlywed dinner. Today, things are a bit more modernized. Although the Greek islands don't have limousines, a friend's car can be decorated just as western cultures do, to transport the couple to the reception hall or restaurant.

In a village wedding, the reception is held in the village square. All the surrounding cafes are employed for use of their tables and chairs. Where in the old times, the pots and pans of food, the stacks of breads and the flasks of drinks had to be delivered and distributed to these cafes early in the morning by the brides family, today, we can simply have the reception catered.

The village men with their violins and lyres are now teamed up with more musicians including *Bouzoúki* players and singers. They begin the music when the guests have begun to fill up the tables. Village receptions don't wait for the bride and groom to show up before they begin. Very often, the couple is busy with a photographer or taking a breather and freshening up. The guests are served the food and drinks and are often finished eating by the time that the newlyweds show up.

Once the couple arrives, they take their place with their immediate families and the *koumpári*. The orchestra will play a special song for the bride and groom to lead their families in a dance. After this, it is just like the pre-wedding dancing. Other family members will join in, one by one until all the guests are dancing. The reception is officially started and the music and drinking will continue for long into the night, sometimes until the morning. The bride and groom will go personally, to each and every guest and thank them for their attendance.

The Wedding Night

As you can imagine, the bride and groom are exhausted by the time that they can retreat from the reception, but the customs involved in the wedding process are still not over. It is tradition that the couple spends their first married night together on the bridal bed that was made up the week before the wedding.

Once the bride and groom reach their new home, they will find that their immediate families are waiting for them. The bride's mother stands in the doorway of the house and places a pomegranate on the floor of the entrance. Her new son-in-law must step on the pomegranate, crushing it with his right foot as he enters the house. Because this fruit has so many seeds, it is considered lucky for having lots of children.

On his wedding day, the groom has danced for an hour before even getting to the church. He's been assaulted by rice and Jordan almonds thrown at him and has been beaten with the love and kinship of his family and friends. Not to mention the fact that he has had to lead dance after dance at his own reception. Taking all this into consideration, it makes you wonder just what kind of wedding night the bride will have.

It is custom that the concerned bride's mother, looking out for her daughter's happiness, will stand in the living room with a dish of walnut meats covered in honey. Using a spoon, she will feed her new son-in-law this mixture so the groom can *kardamósi* or to become strong for his wedding night as walnuts and honey are considered an aphrodisiac by the Greeks.

With these small rituals, having been done, the bride and groom are finally left alone for some peace and quiet. This doesn't last long though, because early in the morning, the families will be back to visit them again.

Monday after the Wedding

The Sheets - *Ta Sentónia*

The day after a village wedding is also called the day of the sheets. Early in the morning, both mothers of the couple would be escorted by family members and the violin playing men to the home of the newlywed couple. They would stand outside of the house singing songs for the groom to open the door and let them come in.

Once inside the house, they would change the sheets of the bed, and make it up with fresh ones. This was done so they could see the stains of blood, proving that the bride was a virgin. If there was any sort of rumor in the village that the bride was not respectable, they would go as far as hanging the sheets outside for all to see.

There were times that the groom might have gotten friendly with his bride before the wedding. On the day that the sheets would be inspected, he would simply make a small cut on his finger and use the blood to make a stain, saving his bride from any embarrassment.

When the sheets were found clean of these blood stains, depending on the groom and his families reaction, the situation could become very severe and the families would go as far as separating the couple. The bride would be considered ruined and her fate undecided. For some girls, her family would wed her to a widower or a much older man who didn't care if his bride was a virgin or not.

Today, this does not happen in any of the islands or villages that I know. Although you may find some parts of the tradition still alive in the northern, remote areas of Greece, for the most part, our culture has become very modern in its thinking as far as bridal virgins are concerned.

The Week After The Wedding

The entire week after a wedding is spent celebrating with food and drinking. Everyday, there are dinner parties given at different homes of the family and *koumpári* of the newlyweds.

As you've already read, the Sunday wedding reception itself is known as the Bride's Dinner. On Monday, is the Groom's Dinner which is held at his parental home. Tuesday is the *Koumpáros* Dinner, Wednesday would be the Aunt's Dinner, Thursday would be the Cousin's Dinner, and on it would continue, with celebrations and drinking at the various family members homes until Saturday.

The Antígamo

The 8th day or Sunday that follows a wedding, is know as the *Antígamo* or "after wedding." On this day, the newlyweds will go to church together and receive Holy Communion for the first time as a married couple. After the church service, food and drinking are offered again, usually at the newlyweds home, as this is the final celebration of the wedding ritual.

What to Say?

When greeting a newlywed couple, use the Greek phrase "*Kalozíziki*" which means "may you be well rooted" or "*Na Zísete*" which means "may you live (long and happy)."

If you are greeting the parents, in-laws or immediate family, you can use the phrases "*Kalozíziki*" or "*Na Sas Zísoun*" which means "may they live (long and happy) for you."

When you are greeting an unmarried woman or man at a wedding, it is proper to say to them "*Ke Apó Ta Diká Soú*," which means "...and from yours," wishing them a happy wedding of their own.

If your friends are a married couple with children, you can greet them at the reception by saying "*Ke Apó Ton Paidión*," which means "...and from your children's," wishing their children a happy marriage too.

Of course, there is the traditional phrase that is used by the parents, *koumpári*, and most of the guests in attendance when toasting to the new couple.

"*Ke Me Éna Yió*" which means "... and with a son," which obviously wishes them a good and fertile honeymoon.

BAPTISMS

Baptism Preparations

Baptisms can be done at any time during the Greek calendar year. Unlike weddings, it is permissible to have a baptism during a fasting period, but unless there is a problem with the health of a baby, most parents will wait, so they can celebrate as well as serve meats and delicacies at the parties that may follow.

Children can be baptized at any age. Taking into consideration that the Greek Orthodox religion dips the entire child into the *kolimbíthra* or baptismal font, it's best not to wait for the child to get too big. Also, I have to mention that Greek baptisms can be scary ordeals for older children. The appearance of the priest with his long beard and the rituals of the actual ceremony itself can make even the calmest child scream and cry.

Baptism Invitations - *Prosklitíria*

Although not traditional, more and more parents are choosing to print invitations for their child's baptism. There is no rule as to who should be invited. A baptism can be very small, including the immediate family, the godparents and a few friends and would be an optimal choice if the baptism was being held in a small monastery. Other parents may choose to make the baptism an all out affair, such as a wedding would be and invite everyone they know. This would be acceptable as well.

When planning for invitations and parties, the guest count has to take into consideration the godparents invited guests as well. It is traditional that the godparents can invite whom ever they want to witness the ritual. This means giving them a stack of invitations to hand out on their own.

Godparents - *Noní and Koumpári*

Greek godparents are very respected and honored. Because they have in essence given the child's soul to Christ, they have an almost mystical responsibility for the child's well being and happiness and are second only to the parents as guardians of the child. And although technically, they do not anoint the child with the Holy Myrrh Oil or *Ágio Míros*, they are still considered as having *Mirósi* the child or aiding in its application.

Godparents give the child gifts for holidays such as Christmas, New Year's and Easter and are expected to celebrate the child's name day with a visit and more gifts. If for some reason the parents can not attend a church service, the godparents will take the child to receive Holy Communion in their place since it is their responsibility that the child grows up as a good Christian.

In many situations, you don't have the luxury of choosing who you want as a godparent. An example of this is for the first born of your children. You are expected to have as godparents the *koumpári* or best men and women of your wedding. The same people that put the *stefánia* or wreaths on you will also take the place of godparents to your first born child. If for some reason one of these *koumpári* can't do it, they can elect one of their own children to take their place or give you the green light to choose one of your own.

Some inventive Greeks have found a way to get around this tradition. They keep the mandatory godparent but add a couple of choices of their own. Few baptisms in the islands have less than three godparents and some have as many as six. Since it's the godparents responsibility to pay for most of the expenses of a baptism, this has worked out to their advantage because they can split the bill more ways.

When you have the choice for a godparent for your child, make sure that you choose wisely because the child's Godparent will one day be the *koumpáro* at its own wedding. It all goes around in a circle as he or she will put the *stefánia* on the grown child and be the godparent for their first born.

It's traditional to give the godparents gifts to show your respect and honor on the various holidays of the year. *Mbaniéria* or baskets are filled with home made cookies, wine, or ouzo as well as small gifts and are presented to them when they come to visit the child.

Just like the *koumpári* for a wedding, the godparents must pay for an assortment of traditional supplies that are needed for a baptism as well as the church service itself. The godparents will begin the baptism ritual by going shopping a month or so before the chosen date, sometimes including the mother of the child so she can choose what she would like for her baby.

Christening Clothes and Linens

A baby will go to church on its christening day dressed in simple clothing, but will leave in a completely new and elaborate outfit. Depending on what the godparents can afford, they will choose from many styles of christening clothes that can be plain or very elaborately embellished. The outfit consists of under clothes, shoes, a dress or suit and depending on the season, a coat and a hat. The entire ensemble can be found and ordered from the numerous boutiques that are available.

This is much more convenient than the days of old, when the young mothers would make the christening clothes for their babies by hand. Using plain white fabrics, a mother would adorn them with needlepoint, beads and charms to make simple outfits and linens for their babies. If a mother had no such fabrics available, then the godparent would help with the purchase and could ask another family member or friend to help with the task.

During the ceremony itself, a *mirópano* or white linen sheet or towel will be spread across the godparents arms and the baby laid onto it to be rubbed down with oil. After the child is dipped in the water and christened, it will be returned to the *mirópano* and dried off. This towel or sheet is also part of the godparents responsibility to supply.

Baptism Favors - *Bounbouniéres*

Traditionally, cookies, *melekoúni* and sweets were served to guests at the end of a baptism service, wishing the child a sweet life. Somehow through time, it has become customary to give out *bounbouniéres* instead. Although some families do keep the tradition and hand out individually wrapped pastries along with the favors.

The modern godparents can choose from the many favors available in the shops and don't have to stick to just sweets anymore. The traditional Jordan almonds are included, but today's *bounbouniéres* also contain small picture frames, toys or ornaments, which make them beautiful keepsakes.

The Baptism Candle - *Lampáda*

Symbolizing the light of God, the *lampáda* will stand at the altar until the appropriate time when it will be lit and lead the baby and the godparents in the procession around the altar table. As the wedding lampádes, this candle stands about four feet high and is elaborately decorated with fabrics and flowers. Some modern ones have stuffed animals tied onto them, making them very cute for a child's baptism.

The Gold Cross and Chain

This is one tradition that has remained untouched throughout the years. The godparents must purchase a gold cross and chain for the baby to wear when it becomes a Christian. The gift of gold can be very simple and small or very expensive, again depending on what the godparents can afford.

Olive Oil, Soap, and Holy Myrrh Oil - *Ágio Míros*

In the baptism ceremony, the baby will be rubbed down with oil by its godparents before it is dipped into the water. Many people believe that this is the Holy Myrrh Oil but it is not. It is simply a plain olive oil that the godparents will use to "protect" the child. Traditionally, a small flask of home-pressed olive oil would be taken to the church by the godparents to be used in the ceremony, but today there are elaborate decanters and bottles that are made just for this purpose and can be bought in the shops. A bar of soap must also be supplied as the godparents will use it to wash their hands after the baptism is finished.

The Holy Myrrh Oil or *Ágio Míros* is applied only by the priest when the baby has already been baptized and is still sitting in the baptismal font. This blessed oil is made in *Constantinoúpolis* and is kept by our Patriarchy who distributes it in small vials to the Orthodox churches. It is a mixture of olive oil, myrrh and 40 aromatic herbs and oils. Any water that contains the Holy Myrrh Oil, such as that of an Orthodox baptism, can not be poured down the drain or spilled outside where someone might step on it. Our village church has a special underground drainage reservoir called a *honevtíri* which is used only for collecting this Holy water.

The Baby's Gift
The godparents will begin their new duties by presenting the baby with a gift. This can be a lamp for their room, a wooden chest to use as a keepsake, or perhaps a dollhouse. The gift should be something that the child can keep through the years, remembering its christening.

The Godparents' Gift
It is customary that the parents present each of the godparents with a gift in appreciation for baptizing their baby. As in Greek weddings, these gifts will be wrapped like large favors and put on display for everyone to see. They can range from ceramic vases to very expensive gifts of gold. This will depend on what the parents can afford. Although the gift should be something that will last through the years, reminiscent of the baptism day, there is no rule that says what should be given.

The Baptism Ceremony - *I Váptisis*
Some islands keep the old custom of the families meeting at the baby's home and escorting it to the church. In a village, this would mean a small procession through the streets as they make their way to the church for its baptism. In the islands today, most modern couples just put the family in the car and drive to the church at the appropriate time.

The ceremony begins as the mother hands the baby to the godparents who are standing at the *pro naó* or pre-altar area of the church. The mother will not hold her baby again until after it has been baptized. In some villages, the mother is not allowed to go past the *pro naó* to see the baby either, totally entrusting her child to the godparents.

The priest stands with the godparents as they hold the baby, in the pre-altar area. The priest will make the sign of the cross over the child, symbolizing the Holy Trinity and will say its name out loud and read prayers from the *Euhológion*.

The baby is kept facing west as the *Apokírixi tou Sataná* is read, denouncing Satan and the priest will make blowing gesture in that direction, symbolically spitting on him. The baby is then turned to face east which is symbolic as the Kingdom of Christ. The priest reads on, giving the child's soul in the arms of Christ. He asks God to give the baby the Holy Spirit and to be *Áxios stis háres tou* or able to perform his God given talents. The godparents are asked to confess their belief in the church as guardians of the baby. It is said that the godparent must be good Christians, setting an example for the child to grow into a good Christian himself. The *Pistévo* or Orthodox Creed is read three times and the godparents speak the words along with the priest.

At the altar, the priest will continue with the ceremony as the child is taken to a small table at the side of the altar and is undressed. Water is poured into the *kolimbíthra* or baptismal font by an attendant and it is blessed as the priest makes the sign of the cross in it three times. Water is symbolic of being destructive as well as cleansing and giving life. As during his baptism, the believer is cleansed of his sins and is reborn into a new life as a Christian.

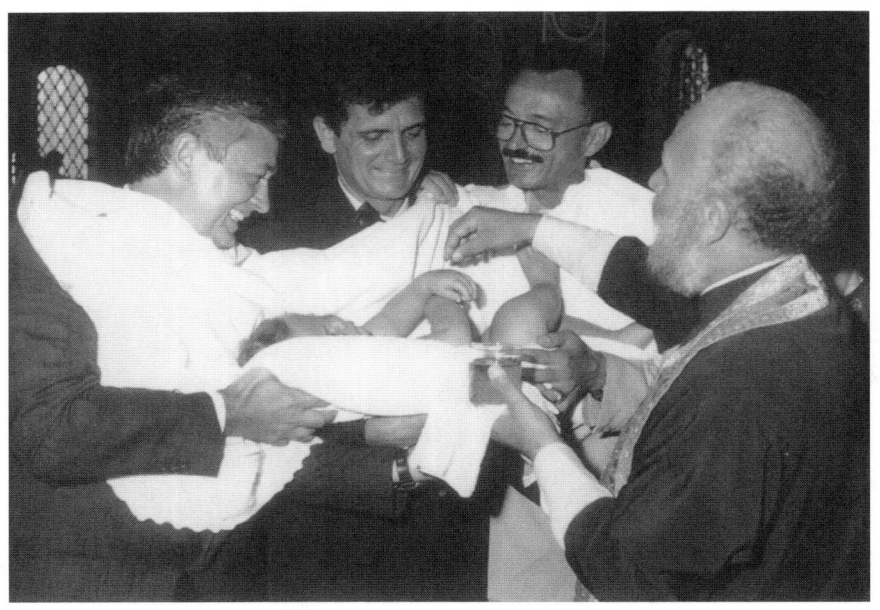

The godfathers of the child with the *mirópano* laid over them, preparing to anoint the child with oil.

The *mirópano* or white sheet is laid across the outstretched arms of the godparents and the naked baby is put into their embrace. Taking a small amount of olive oil, the priest will rub the baby with it and then the godparents will do the same. This is symbolic of ancient times when the warriors and athletes would be rubbed down with oil before a match. The church says that the baby will have to do battle between good and evil during its dipping in the water and the oil is rubbed on to protect it.

The baby is held up in the air by the priest and then lowered into the water as the priest calls *"Vaptízete o Doúlos tou Theoú..."* or "the servant of God is being baptized..." and then he calls out the given name of the baby. The baby will be dipped three times, symbolic of the three days of Christ's death to his resurrection, as the baby will be "reborn" a Christian.

After the third dipping, the priest will swab a small amount of the Holy Myrrh Oil or *Ágio Míros* on the babies forehead in the sign of the cross. Once the Holy Myrrh Oil has been rubbed onto the baby, it will not be washed off with soap for three days. Pieces of the baby's hair are cut and discarded in the water. The hair is cut in four places on the baby's head, making the sign of the cross. This symbolizes a small sacrifice made to his savior and that he belongs to his master, Jesus Christ. Once again, this dates back to ancient times when slaves would shave their heads, symbolizing their ownership to their masters.

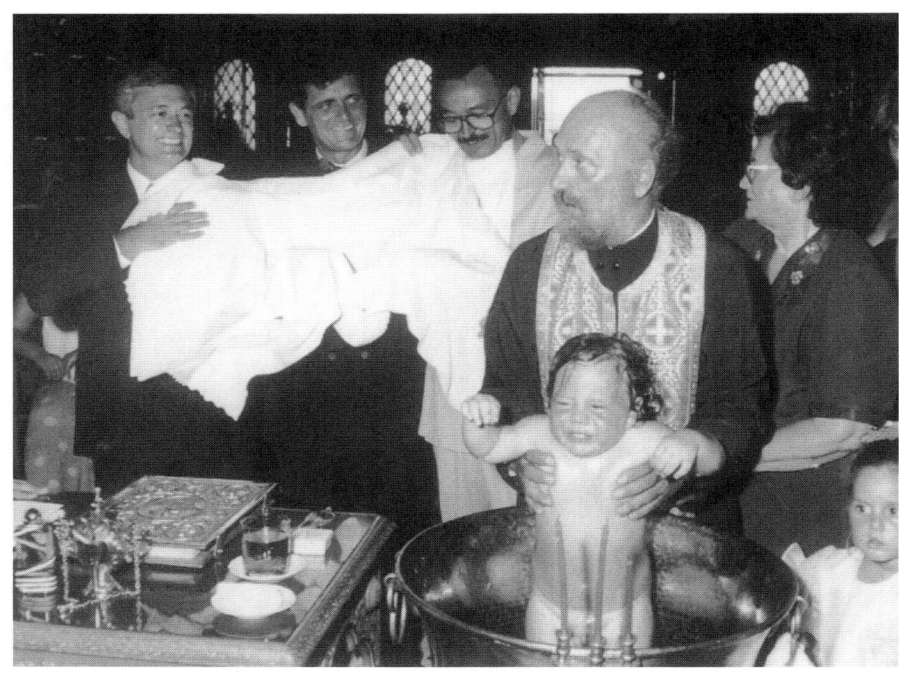

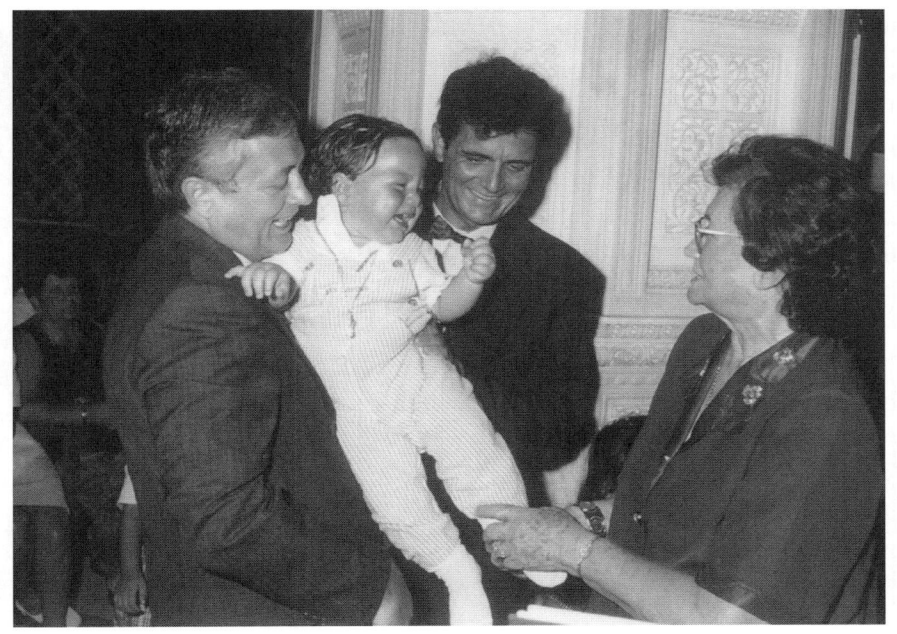

The child's grandmother helps the godfathers to dress him.

The priest gives the baby to the godparents who are waiting with the white towel laid across their outstretched arms. They dry the baby and take it to the side and dress it in its new clothes. The priest will continue with the ceremony as the godparents put the gold cross on the baby making it officially a Christian. From this time on, it is considered that the baby belongs to the church and Christ.

One by one, the godparents are offered soap to wash their hands. This is done over the *kolimbíthra* as an altar boy pours small amounts of clean water into their hands. Since the water in the baptismal font is blessed and contains Holy Myrrh Oil, it must be collected and disposed of properly.

The *lampáda* is lit and the altar boy leads the procession around the altar or *kolimbíthra*, depending on the size of the church. The priest and godparents follow, with the baby held in their arms. Although this is not the Dance of Isaiah as for a wedding, the symbolism remains almost the same. They will walk around the altar three times symbolizing the child's first spiritual "dance" at the revelation of a happy future as a Christian.

The godparents carry the baby to the back of the church, where the mother anxiously awaits. Before they give her the baby, she must genuflect to each of the godparents and kiss their hand, showing her honor and respect for giving her child to Christ. Once she has done this, they give her the christened baby and the ceremony is finished.

The baptism guests walk out to the courtyard where the *bounbouniéres* are given to them. Depending on the arrangements that have been made by the parents, the guests will either leave to go home, or continue to the village square or restaurant for eating, drinking and dancing.

Three Days after the Baptism

On the third day following a baptism, the new godparents will come to visit the child and give it its first bath, washing off the *Ágio Míros* or Holy Myrrh Oil. The clothes as well as any linens that have the Holy Oil on them will be washed also.

Just as in the church ceremony, the water that is used for this has to be collected. Since it contains Holy Myrrh Oil, it should be disposed of in a very careful manner. The islanders take the water to the sea and pour it into the surf. Once the task is finished, the parents present the godparents with a sit down dinner and they celebrate once more.

The Weeks Following a Baptism

For the next three Sundays following the child's baptism, the god parents must take the baby to receive Holy Communion. This is the same as for any Greek Orthodox service, consisting of a small spoonful of bread dipped in wine, symbolic of the body and blood of Christ.

The *lampáda* will also be taken to the church and held lighted for the duration of the liturgy. On the last Sunday, the *lampáda* can be left at the church, standing with the other candles that light the icons.

What to Say?

When greeting a couple, grandparents, family or the *koumpári* at a baptism, use the Greek phrase "*Kaloríziko*" which means "may it be well rooted" or "*Na Sas Zísi*" which means "may it live (long and happy)."

GREEK FUNERALS

The village church bell will clang loudly, once every few seconds. Its rhythmic sound is heard throughout the village and all the inhabitants recognize this slow ringing as a signal of death. The villagers will ask each other who died and it's by word of mouth that news of a death spreads through the village.

Greek village funerals are an exhausting experience as the mourning involved taxes your spiritual and physical being. Greeks believe in releasing all their sorrow at funerals and there is no such thing as "keeping up appearances." You will find that the men as well as women, cry over the loss of their loved ones fluidly. Even for very old people, whom the death was expected, the mourning is still filled with heart-wrenching cries of loss.

In tragic cases as when a young death is involved, doctors will often administer some kind of sedative to close family members, calming them enough to be able to attend the long processions to the church and cemetery as it's not uncommon to have people faint during these processions.

Funeral Dress

Greek women dress in black for funeral services. Some of the older village women keep to the tradition of wearing black scarves, covering their hair, while others don't. Women can wear pants, skirts or dresses as long as they are somber in fashion and don't reveal more than their calves and lower arms. And depending on the relation of the deceased, it is inappropriate for women to wear jewelry and make up or to be attired in any way that may show vanity during a funeral.

The Greek men don't have to change their wardrobes for a funeral. Although they do usually dress in dark clothes, light colored shirts can be worn. A male mourner wears a simple black armband that is pinned in place over a shirt or jacket sleeve. As for women, men are not to show vanity during a funeral or mourning period. This includes shaving and is why many Greek men will grow beards during their time of mourning.

Funeral Preparations

In most areas of Greece, the deceased's home is used as the funeral parlor. In the years that I have lived in the Islands, I have never been to a funeral parlor nor have heard of one's existence. There are funeral offices in the bigger cities that may provide this service as well as help with caskets and arrangements but in the villages of the islands, it's done at home.

The Greek Orthodox religion does not believe in cremation or embalming because Christ was not cremated nor embalmed. It is said that God made man from earth and water and therefore he should be returned to the ground at his death. Our religion sees death as a long sleep. Although the soul separates from the body, the two will be rejoined at the second coming of Christ.

Since mortuary practices are not followed, the human body is returned to the ground in it's natural state. It has only been in recent years that it has become common for village families to donate organs of the deceased to give a gift of life to some one in need. There is very little preparation done to the body itself. The family will wash the deceased with soap and water and if the mouth has remained open in death, the family will dip cotton into alcohol and use it to fill the opening.

A shroud or *sávano* is used for Greek funerals, symbolic of Christ's burial. Some people will wrap their deceased in the shroud where as others will use it to line the coffin and lay their loved one on it. This shroud is white in color and depending on the wealth of the family can be made from fine fabrics and embellished with needlepoint. Some of the old people will buy their own shroud and keep it for their burial day.

The deceased is dressed in their best suit or dress and their hair is combed and arranged. They are then laid in the coffin with the hands arranged over their chests.

The simple wooden coffin has a separate lid and is made by the village carpenter. There are fancier versions with satin linings, fine woods and metal trims just like they have in the United States that can be purchased from a funeral office, but more commonly, the plain caskets are used in the villages.

The coffin is set on a stand or chairs that have been arranged in the middle of the living room and family members gather around it. Coffee, soft drinks and cognac are served to the mourners as they mourn or *mirologoúne* for the deceased and keep vigil overnight. It is the law in Greece that the body must remain unburied for at least for 24 hours. This is done for *nekrofánia* or to insure that the person has really died and not in some comatose state.

It's also said that the dead body should not be left alone for this night because his soul will wander through the house and friends and relatives should keep him company. The doors of the house are left completely open and all the lights are turned on so his soul can roam around freely. All mirrors, TV's and radios are covered with white cloths, symbolizing the end of vanity and recreation because of the mourning period.

People will come to pay their respects bringing flowers or wreaths. The bouquets of flowers are disassembled and the flowers are arranged around the body, completely framing the departed loved one. The entire coffin is filled and the body itself is covered over with the flowers so only the face remains showing.

An icon of the Virgin Mary or Jesus Christ is laid upon the chest or torso area and it is proper when paying your respects to kiss the icon and then, depending on the relation, kiss the corpse. This is a little hard to do, especially for the squeamish, such as myself. Because of the lack of mortuary preparation, the skin of the deceased takes on a pale ashen to greenish tone. This is quite a contrast when compared to American mortuary practices where the corpse sometimes looks better in death than in life. Knowing my feelings about kissing a dead person, my mom once gave me a tip. Lightly kiss the hair of the deceased, just above the brow. This is not difficult to do and it's in keeping with the tradition.

When the deceased has been the victim of an accident or fire where the face has been scarred or damaged, a white cloth is used as a shroud to cover it. Again, the tradition is to kiss the icon and to kiss the hair even though it's covered with the shroud.

The Funeral

The next day, after at least 24 hours, the priest arrives and gives the *Triságio*. This is a short memorial service in the form of prayers for the salvation of the deceased that is performed in the home as a farewell. Once this ceremony is finished, the open coffin is picked up by family members and carried to the church in a procession of mourners, family members and friends.

They carry amongst themselves any flowers or wreaths that have been sent to the home and the coffin lid. An altar boy leads the procession with a cross or an icon and the priests follow with the mourners. Immediate family and grief stricken individuals are held by both arms, and escorted by other relatives. Depending on how far away the home is from the church, the walk can be a very long one and distraught mourners often need some help along the way.

At the church, the *Nekrósimi Akolouthía* or Death Service is given by the priest. At the end of the service you will again walk past the deceased and kiss the icon as well as the body in a last farewell. Once the mourners have finished, the open coffin is again carried by family members to the cemetery in a procession just like before.

Family Graves

Although cemeteries are sometimes called *nekrotafía*, or death tombs, they are also referred to as *kimitíria* or "sleeping places" which is the name that the village priests prefer. The island Greeks keep family graves. One grave is dug for an entire family and when someone dies, they are put into the same grave that contains other family members remains. The cemetery keeper will dig up the grave and remove any remnants of a coffin or simply the bones of an ancestor. These bones will be wrapped in a cloth and placed back into the grave at the foot of the coffin of the newly deceased.

Every Greek cemetery has a small church on its grounds. Within these churches, there is a small crypt like room which is also called the *osteofilákio* or "the bone keep." When there are too many bones in a family grave, they can be put into the crypt to be kept until the time when the soul will rejoin its body and be resurrected.

There should be a space of seven years between deaths before the family grave can be used, giving the coffin and human remains of a previous funeral time to disintegrate. If this is not possible, an other ancestral grave will be used or a new one dug up. For deceased young persons, sometimes new graves are made and kept only for them.

The Burial

When the procession reaches the grave area, the priest reads a short memorial service and then he pours some oil on the body while making the sign of the cross. This is symbolic of cleansing the body and protecting the deceased from evil. The priest will use a shovel and make the sign of the cross in the dirt and then spill some of the dirt into the coffin. This is symbolic of mans' return to the ground as in 'ashes to ashes and dust to dust'. The coffin is then hammered shut and lowered into the family grave. Every one in attendance takes a handful of dirt and throws it in as the men, usually family members, begin to fill the grave. Flowers and wreaths are then laid on the finished mound and oil burning candles are lit and placed within the head stone cabinets.

Funeral Reception

Once the funeral is finished, the mourners go to the family's home where coffee, soft drinks and cognac as well as food is served. Fish is symbolic as being the *lahtára* or longing of life. Again, because of the belief that the soul of the deceased is waiting to be resurrected, it is traditionally served for funerals, baked or as a soup.

Memorial Services

The memorial services of a deceased person continue on for one year.

It begins with the *Trímera* or the third day of remembrance. This ceremony is done at the church by the close family members and the memorial wheat or *kóliva* is given on this day. The next memorial service is performed on the ninth day of remembrance and is known as the *Eniámera*. Again, the family will make memorial wheat which is passed out to all in attendance and sometimes a small gift of a sweet cookie or pastry is given.

It is believed that a deceased person's soul wanders the earth for 40 days after his death. The memorial service that is performed for the end of this period is called the *Sarantámera* and is known as the day that his soul goes to God.

After these memorial services, there are the *Trímina* or three month, *Exámina* or six month, Eniámina or nine month and the *Chrónos* or one year. All of these memorial services are done in the same fashion as above, commemorating the deceased's memory with *kóliva*.

The Grave Caretaking

In the Greek islands, it's up to the family members to maintain and up keep the family graves. There are cemetery keepers that could be paid for helping out, but on the most part the immediate relatives of the deceased do the task.

Greek head stones are not simply engraved slabs as we have in the United States. The marble head stone of a village grave is made into a small cabinet like structure with a glass front opening door. Within this cabinet, the family keeps icons of Saints, a photo of the deceased, a *kantíli* or oil burning candle and a *thimiastíri* or incense burner. Some families will also place favorite keepsakes of the deceased in the cabinet as well.

The oil burning candle will always be checked and the oil replenished so the flame does not go out, symbolizing the eternal light of God. Flowers are freshened, and ritualistic incense is burned every day. Depending on the relation of the deceased and the circumstances of his death, this daily ritual can last from 40 days to years.

As holidays such as Easter or Christmas approach or perhaps the deceased's name day, family members will visit the grave and again refresh the flowers, fill the candles and visit with their loved one.

Young Deaths

The most distraught and painful funerals in the villages are for children and young people who have died in car accidents or very suddenly. In the cases when it's a young, unmarried person that has died, the body will be dressed in wedding clothes. Their godparents buy *stefánia* or wedding wreaths and they are placed on the head of the deceased. Jordan almonds are also bought and given out to the mourners just as they would have for a wedding.

Street Side Memorials

Driving through the islands, you will often see a small cabinet like stands off to the side of the road that flicker with candle light. These are street side memorials that are built when a person dies at the scene of a car accident. The memorials are very much like the headstones of the graves and are kept with oil burning candles, icons, photos and flowers inside them.

Mourning Period

The duration of the mourning period depends on the relation of the deceased. For widows, the mourning period was traditionally any where from five years to the rest of their lives, depending if they were young or old or had children that needed a father or a home. For close relations such as parents, in-laws, brothers or sisters, the mourning period would range between one to five years. Further relations and friends would be between 40 days to one year.

This time table is not a strict code as many Greeks today simply follow their feelings about the subject. One year is considered an appropriate amount of time for mourning close relatives and loved ones. Young widows may choose to mourn for more than five years where as others will re-marry within three.

During the mourning period, it is inappropriate to attend parties, go out to dances or socialize in the open. You can have visitors to your home or go on visits yourself, as long as it's done tamely so as not to disrespect the memory of the deceased. This is the reason that weddings and sometimes baptisms are postponed until the mourning period is over and a celebration can take place.

As for dressing for a funeral, during the mourning period, women always dress in black. Again, the clothing should be respectable by not uncovering too much of the body and large ornamental jewelry is avoided. In our modern times, it is alright to wear a little make up, but for the most part, a mourning woman should be simply adorned and dressed. The dress code for men remains the same also and the black armband and beard is worn through the mourning period.

What to Say?

The Greek phrase which is appropriate for a funeral or when meeting with a mourner who has recently lost a loved one is *"Zoí Se Sas"* or *"Zoí Se Lógou Sas."* Simply translated, it means "life unto you."

Memorial Wheat / *Kóliva*

Kóliva are whole-wheat kernels that have been boiled and sweetened. Fruits, nuts, Jordan almonds, herbs and spices are added to it and it is mounded onto a silver tray. The sign of the Cross is made with silver Jordan almonds or dragées in the center. On the upper side of the Cross, you will see the letters:

IC XC
NIKA

Which means "Jesus Conquers" and on the other side of the Cross, are the initials of the deceased.

The eating of *Kóliva* at church is to remember the departed soul and to pray for their forgiveness. Other than wheat, raisins and pomegranate seeds are usually amongst the ingredients. They symbolize the resurrection and the sweetness and abundance of life.

Most memorial services are performed at the end of the Sunday liturgy and the blessed *Kóliva* are put into small bags and handed out to the parishioners as they leave. For the Saturdays during lent that are known as *Psihosávato*, memorial wheat is made and is given out as all the dead are remembered. In Rhodes, these *kóliva* are also called *chrisó kouní* or golden kernels.

Kóliva or *Kouniá*
1 lb. whole wheat kernels
½ lb. toasted sesame seeds
2 cups sugar
1 cup pomegranate seeds
2 cups white seedless raisins
½ chopped fresh spearmint or parsley
½ cup flour
1 tbs. allspice
1 lb. powdered sugar
silver Jordan almonds or dragées
whole blanched almonds or walnut halves

Wash the wheat in a colander under plenty of running water. Put the wheat into a large pot and cover it with water. Bring it to a boil and reduce the heat so it simmers. Be sure to skim off any froth that collects on top with a spoon so the wheat won't sour. Keep simmering the wheat and adding more water as necessary until the kernels split in two - anywhere from 10 to 14 hours. Drain the wheat and rinse it under running warm water. Let it drain for one hour.

Cover a large table that is not in sunlight with thick towels and smooth a white sheet over them. Spread out the wheat on it to dry for 24 hours.

Collect the wheat into a large bowl. Using a blender or mortar and pestle, grind the sesame seeds. Heat a skillet and dry-fry the flour, stirring it with a wooden spoon until it turns a light gold color.

Toss together the wheat, sugar, pomegranates, raisins, spearmint or parsley, allspice and the flour until it is very well blended. Line a large silver tray or platter with wax paper or aluminum foil.

Spoon the wheat mixture onto the center of the tray and shape it with your hands so it's a smooth mound. Sprinkle the mound with the sesame seeds and and pat them down, using a piece of wax paper so you get a nice smooth finish.

Sift the powdered sugar over the mound and again, pat it down so it's smooth and about ¼ to ½ inch thick.

To decorate the *kóliva*, use a cardboard form or a knife, make a cross in the center of the mound and fill it with Jordan or blanched almonds, dragées, nuts or raisins.

On the either side of the upper part of the cross, indent the letters IC XC, NI KA, and on the bottom, write the initials of the deceased.

Use the decorations, nuts and raisins to fill in the indented letters and make it readable. You can decorate the rest of the mound by making borders or other simple designs using more of the same decorating ingredients.

Index

A

Aegean Pilaf 131
Agía Trápeza 503
Agiasmós 495
Agináres Avgolémono 145
Agináres me Tomáta 146
Agourákia Gemistá 53
Agriogoúrouno Krasáto 249
Ahinioús 452
Ahládi Glykó 390
Akoúmia 363
Aláti 506
Alisíva 463
Almond Cake in Syrup 364
Almond-Garlic Sauce 9
Amelétita 261
Amigdalópita Siropiastí me Sokoláta 422
Amigdalotá 381
Amygdalópita 364
Amygdalópita Ípirou Siropiastí 364
Amygdalópita Krítis 343
Amygdalópita Siropiastí 365, 422
Amygdalotá Tiganitá 357
Annunciation of the Virgin Mary 480, 511, 518
Anthónero 465
Anthoús Kolokithiás 60
Anthoús Kolokithiás Gemistá 60
Apokriés 513, 514
Appetizers 33, 35, 61
Apple Rings
   deep fried 355
Apricot Pit Liqueur 414
Apricots and Cream 349
Arakás Thessalías 155
Aravónes 551
Arnáki sta Kárvouna 196
Arní Exohikó 200
Arní Frikasé 199
Arní Giahní 202
Arní Kléftiko Paradosiakó 201
Arní Kléftiko se Hartí 199
Arní me Fasolákia 202
Arní Souvláki 215
Arní Soúvlas 197
Arní tou Foúrnou 203
Artichoke Salad 72
Artichokes
   cleaning fresh 434
Artichokes with Egg Lemon Sauce 145
Artichokes with Tomatoes 146
Ártos Kritikós 316

Ash Water 463
Aspic
   pork 192
Áspri Sáltsa giá Kréata 23
Áspro Psomí me Vótana 306
Assumption (Sleep) of the Virgin Mary 480
Asvestónero 464
Avgolémono 3
Avgolémono Kréma 4
Avgolémono Paradosiakó 4

B

Babies
   new born 460
   twin, in a swing 543
   village 525
Baby Cream
   wheat 408
Baby Goat
   pit roasted 237
   stuffed with rice 238
Bakaliéros Krokétes 45
Bakaliéros Skordaliá 44
Baked Beans in Tomato 147
Baked Beef Head 261
Baked Eggplant with Cheese 148
Baked Grouper 270
Baked Pork with Lima Beans 191
Baklavá 364, 366
Baptisms 571
Barbeque 473
   menu suggestions 473
   preparation tips for open pit 441
Barley Bread Wreaths 327
Bars 373
Basic Brine 404, 463
Basic Meat Pie 105, 210
Basic Meat Sauce
   for casseroles 16
Basil 459, 503
Basting Marinade
   for Game and Lamb 31
   for Goat or Kid Chops 32
Bat Bones 503
Batter 26
   Simple 26
   Spicy 26
Batter Fried Broccoli & Cauliflower 56
Bean & Rice Salad 85
Bean Soup 168
Beans 436

Béchamel Sauce 5
Bee and Wasp Stings 500
Beef
   and vegetable, boiled 189
   heads
      cleaning 439
   stewed with potatoes 186
   with orzo macaroni 185
Beef and Cheese Pie 107
Beef Rolls
   from Smýrni 208
   stuffed 187
Beef Soup 173
Beef Stew with Peas 186
Beef Stock 166
Beef Tongue with Olives 256
Beets
   in garlic sauce 72
   stuffed 73
Bergamot Spoon Sweet 386
Best Men 558
Best Women 558
Beverages and Bottling 409
Biscuits
   almond meringue 381
   Phoenician stuffed 378
   short bread 376
Bitter Orange
   in olives 401
Bitter Orange Spoon Sweet 386
Blossom Water 465
Blueberry Liqueur 414
Boar
   wild, in wine 249
Boiled Beef and Vegetables 189
Boiled Vegetables 144
   mixed 79
Boils 500
Bouillabaisse 176
Bounbouniéres 558, 572
Brains
   fried 262
Bread 295
   black garlic 307
   Christmas
      from Constantinople 310
   crusts 291
   Easter 312
      sweet 314
   fasting, sesame 304
   from Kárpathos 301
   glazes 293
   ground sesame 303
   herbal 306
   holiday & celebration 308
   Holy Communion 317
   lenten flat 313
   of Seven Fermentations 315
   pudding 352
   salt, fried 328, 329
   seven seed 305
   soggy 2
   stuffed olive 302
   sweet Christmas yeast 311
   sweet, fried 328, 329
   using left-over, mistakes 328
   village, making 288
      tips 291
   wedding 320
Bread Crumbs 328
Bread Pudding 328
Bread Stamp 297
Breads
   wedding 562
Breasts 500
Bridal Dowry 554
Bride's Bath 564
Bridesmaids 559
Broccoli
   batter fried 56
   cleaning fresh 434
Brooms 503
Bulgur Wheat 127
Burnt Thursday 514
Butter Pastry 332
Byzantine Rice Cake 343

C

Cabbage Rolls
   stuffed
      vegetarian 126
      with meat 126
Cabbage Salad 85
Cactus 503
Cakes 364
   almond 364
   almond-brandy 365
   Byzantine Rice 343
   chocolate almond 422
   lemon 344
   ouzo-coconut 345
   raisin 346
   short cut 423
      lemon 423
      raisin 423
      St. Fanourios 423
   short cut syrup 422
   St. Basil's 341
   St. Fanourios 340
      legend of 339
   walnut 371, 422
Carnival 513, 514
Casserole
   baked shellfish 276
   eggplant-potato 204
   macaroni 206

Cauliflower
	batter fried 56
	cleaning fresh 434
Cemeteries 518
Cheese and Honey Pie 347
Cheese Pie
	& beef 107
	fried 359
	plain 92
	ragged 94
	rich 93
	traditional 91
Cheese Saghanaki 52
Chestnuts 374
Chicken
	baked with vegetables 222
	herbed, breasts 224
	in tomato 221
	lemon baked 222
	livers in vinegar 257
	marinated 225
	pie, simple 95
	sesame fried 226
	stewed 227
	stuffed 228
	village 219
	with lentils 223
	with orzo 225
	with quince 224
Chicken Kebobs 215
Chicken Stock 166
Chickpea
	chili 170
	salad 84
	toasted 433
Chickpea and Sesame Sauce 13
Children 503
	Greek cooking for 419
	name day 478
		menu suggestions 478
Chili
	chickpea 170
Chocolate Chestnut Bars 374
Chrisómila Glykó 385
Chrisómila Poltós 349
Christmas 512, 520
	40 days before 480
	bread 310
	December 25th 520
	dinner 476
		menu suggestions 476
	fast of 520
	preparations 520
	sweet yeast bread 311
Christópsomo 311
Christópsomo Constantinoúpolis 310
Christoúgena 520

Chrímata 505
Church Altar 503
Church Bread
	from Crete 316
Clean Monday 514
	picnic
		menu suggestions 474
Cod
	salt 44
	salt, croquettes 45
Coffee 412
Colds and Flu 500
Colorful Salad 86
Constipation 501
Cookies 373
	moonshine 382
Corns and Calluses 501
Crab Salad 70
Crayfish
	steamed 275
Crescents
	cheese filled
		from Crete 360
Cretan Almond Torte 343
Cretan Lamb Torte 102
Croutons 328
Crows 503
Cure
	hangover 416
Cuttlefish
	in wine & sepia 269
	preparation 447
	stewed 269

D

Dandelion Salad 76
Desserts
	fried 355
Deutéra tou Pásca 519
Diarrhea 501
Díples 355, 356
Diskilióttita 501
Dolls
	grandmom's 543
	village rag 543
Dolmáthes 115, 119, 120, 124
	bulgur wheat 127
	cooking 122
	making 121
	serving 123
	tomato-onion 127
	village secrets 117
Dolmáthes me Pligoúri 127
Dolmáthes Nistísimi 127
Dolmáthes Pseútiki 124
Dough Balls

fried 358
Doughs
  fried 355
Dowries 554
Dressings 1
Dry Fruit Sweet 388
Duck
  with olive stuffing 229

E

Easter
  bread 312
  bread, sweet 314
  cookies 375
  lamb
    on a spit 197
    stuffed 198
  preparations 514
  soup, traditional 175
Easter Dinner 475
  menu suggestions 475
Easter Eggs 516
Easter Monday 519
Easter Sunday 516
Eau de Toilette
  village 502
Eel
  charcoal grilled 40
  moray
    in tomatoes 280
    preparation 450
  with eggs & vinegar 40
Efkiliótita 501
Egg Lemon Sauce
  creamy version 4
  traditional 4
  with artichokes 145
Eggplant 118
  cleaning 434
  pie 110
  roasted, salad 81
  spicy pickled 59
  spoon sweet 388
  stuffed, with quail 245
Egimosíni 505
Ekmék 422
Ekmék Kataífi 364, 368
Eláfi sto Foúrno 250
Eliés Nerantzátes 401
Eliés Tsakistés 400
Eliés Xithátes 399
Eliés Zoúpes 401
Eliópsomo Gemistó 302
Emoroídes 501
Engagements 551
Entóstia 255

Eortí ton Agíon Apostólon 480
Eortí Ton Vagión 480
Epiphany 520
  eve 480
  January 6th 521
Epitáphios 517
Eptásporo Psomí 305
Eptázima 315
Erethismoús ke Kapsímata 501
Evil Eye 489
Eye Infections 501

F

Fakés 169
Fakórizo me Sívrasi 133
Fanourópita 339, 340, 423
Farmer's Salad 82
Fasoláda or Lópia 168
Fasoláda tou Foúrnou 147
Fasolákia Giahnistá 150
Fasolákia me Kolokitháki ke Féta 151
Fasolákia Saláta 73
Fasólia me Rízi Saláta 85
Fast
  rigid
    sample menu 484
  semi-rigid
    sample menu 483
Fasting 474, 479, 517
  fish allowed 480
  menus 481
  rigid 480
  sesame breads 304
Favors
  baptism 572
  wedding 558
Feast of Lazarus 514
Feast of the Apostles 480
Feta
  &hot pepper dip 38
  home-made 406
  pie 100
Feta Cheese
  with fruit 82
Feta Salad
  & radish 76
  & tomato 69
Figs
  stuffed with nuts 353
Filahtá 492
Finíkia 378
Fish 503
  charcoal, tips 445
  cleaning 444
  defrosting 445
  filleting 444

fried, tips 445
grilled sun dried 44
in rosemary & garlic 272
large, serving 445
odors
   removing 446
preparation
   do's & don'ts 444
red sauce 22
roe fritters 39
shopping for 444
simple, poached 271
sinking sauce 405
spicy, in tomato sauce 272
spicy marinade 29
Fish Soup
  island 177
Fish Stock 167
Foúrno 283
Fried Almond Fingers 357
Fried Mussels 41
Ftárnisma 506
Ftísimo 506
Funerals 577

G

Galaktomboúriko 369
Galópites 421
Galopoúla Gemistí 231
Galopoúla me Patátes Stifádo 230
Game
  baked venison 250
Game Meats 235
Games 540
Garden Salad 86
Garídes Krasátes 49
Garídes me Agináres Saláta 71
Garídes me Kókkini Sáltsa 48
Garidosaláta 71
Garlic 460, 504
Garlic Sauce 8
Garlic Sauce -Thick Version 8
Garlic Sauce-Thin Version 8
Gémisi me Koukounária 128
Gemistá 115, 118, 119, 125
  vegetable preparation 118
Gemistá Pseútika 125
Giaprákia me Kréas 124
Giaprákia Pseútika 124
Gígantes Saláta 75
Glósa Moscarísia me Eliés 256
Glyká Koutalioú 384
Glykó apó Xirá Froúta 388
Glykó Fráoulas 391
Glykó me Kástana Attikís 374
Goat

heads
   cleaning 439
Goat Herder's Pie 207
Godparents 571
Good Friday 515
Gourounópoulo Gemistó 194
Grape Leaves
  stuffed
    vegetarian 124
    with meat 124
Grape Pudding 351
Grape Vine Leaves
  preparation 121
  preserved 121
  working with 120
Gravy
  village 21
Greek Independence Day 518
Greek Pantry 457
Greek Village Salad 67
Green Bean Salad 73
Green Beans 150, 202
  cleaning 435
  with zucchini & feta 151
Green Salad 86
Gýro 211
  dinner entrée 213
  from poultry 212
  making, ground meats 211
  pork 211
  traditional, pork 212

H

Halkítika Makarónia 139
Halva
  Macedonian semolina 370
Ham
  pie 420
Ham Pie 98
Hamburgers 210
Hands 504
Hare
  in garlic 240
  in onions 240
  spit barbequed 239
Headaches 501
Heads
  for soup & roasts
    cleaning & preparing 439
Héli me Avgá ke Xídi 40
Hemorrhoids 501
Herbal Basting Brushes 443
Herbs
  harvesting 459
Herbs and Spices
  for the Greek kitchen 459

Héria 504
Herring Salad 70
Hirinó me Gígantes 191
Hirinó Souvláki 214
Hirinó sto Foúrno 193
Holy Saturday 515
Holy Saturday Night 475
Holy Thursday 515
Holy Water 495
Honey Macaroons 380
Hortópita 112
Htapódi Krasáto 43
Htapódi me Makaronáki 275
Htapódi sta Kárvouna 42
Htapódi Xiró Skordaliá 42
Htípa Xýlo 504
Hummus 13

I

Ichthís 504
Icon Station 517
Iconostásio 517
Idrótas 502
Ífasma 558
Imam
    oven-baked 159
Imám tou Foúrnou 159
Incense Burning 494
Intestines
    cleaning 440

J

January Salad 84
Jordan Almonds 504

K

Kafés Ellinikós 412
Kakaviá 176
Káktos 503
Kalamarákia Gemistá 279
Kalámari Tiganitó 50
Kalámari Tiganitó Pikántiko 51
Kálous 501
Kaltsounákia Kritiká 360
Karavída 275
Karavóli Giahní 251
Karidáki Glykó 392
Karídia Glykó 393
Karidoskordaliá 10
Karpáthika Glykanálata Psomiá 301
Kataífi 364, 367
Katharí Deutéra 480, 514
Kathréftes 505
Katsikáki - Rifáki Kapamá 238
Katsikáki - Rifáki Soúvla 237
Kavourosaláta 70

Kavroumás 407
Kebobs
    chicken 215
    swordfish 215
Kefáli Gourounioú Psitó 260
Kefáli Moscarísia sto Foúrno 261
Keftédes 52
Kerási Glykó 387
Kerkiráiki Pastitsáda 190
Kidney Bean Salad 74
Kimíseos tis Theotókou 480
Kinígi 235
Kithóni Glykó 390
Knives 504
Knock on Wood 504
Knot Ropes 491
Kókala Nihterídas 503
Kokítis 502
Kókkines ke Prásines Piperiés Saláta 81
Kóliva 516
Kolokítha Tiganití 57
Kolokithákia Giahnistá 151
Kolokithokeftédes 61
Kolokithópita 113
Kolokithópites 58
Kolousafádes 263
Kolousafádes Skordáti 264
Kombológia 498
Komboskínia 491
Kopanistí 38
Korákia 503
Kóta Tiganití me Sisámi 226
Kotópita Aplí 95
Kotópites 420
Kotópoulo Gemistó 228
Kotópoulo Kokkinistó 221
Kotópoulo Lemonáto 222
Kotópoulo Marinátha 225
Kotópoulo me Fakés 223
Kotópoulo me Kidónia 224
Kotópoulo me Kritharáki 225
Kotópoulo me Makarónia 227
Kotópoulo Riganáto 224
Kotópoulo Souvláki 215
Kotópoulo sto Foúrnou 222
Kouféta 504
Koulourákia Ladioú 381
Koulourákia Pascaliná 375
Kouloúres tou Gámou 320
Kouloúria me Rakí 382
Koumpári 558
Kounéli Gemistó me Karídia 248
Kounéli me Yiaoúrti 247
Kourambiédes 376
Kourkoumpínia Thrákis 361
Kourkoúti 26
Kréas me Kritharáki Soúpa 173

Kréata 183
Kreatópita Aplí 105, 210
Kreatópita Kefalonítiki 101
Kreatópita me Tirí 107, 421
Kréma Bechaméla 5
Kréma gia Morá 408
Kremidokeftédes 58
Kría Sáltsa Tomátas 15
Kriologímata 500
Kritharáki 134
Kritharénies Kouloúres 327
Krithária 501
Ktipití 38

L

Ladolémono 6
Ladóxido 7
Lagána 313
Lagós me Skórda 240
Lagós Stifádo 240
Lagós stin Soúvla 239
Lahaniká 141
Lahanodolmáthes 126
Lahanodolmáthes Pseútiki 126
Lahanosaláta 77, 85
Lamb
  & feta pie 100
  Easter
    on a spit 197
    stuffed 198
  heads
    cleaning 439
  in paper 199
  in pastry 200
  Kleftiko, traditional 201
  leg, roasted 203
  pie
    from Cephalonia 101
  stew 202
  with green beans 202
  with Lettuce Fricassee 199
Lamb Chops
  charcoal grilled 196
Lambrí 516
Lambriátiko Arní Gemistó 198
Lambrópsomo 312
Lazarákia 319
Lazarus
  feast of 514
Lazarus Bread Cookies 319
Leafy Greens
  cleaning 435
Leek and Beef Pie 103
Leek and Egg Pie 104
Lemon Cake 344, 423
Lemon Oil Dressing 6

Lemon Pastry 333
Lemon Pilaf 132
Lemonópita 344, 423
Lenient Fast 482
  menu suggestions 482
Lenten Flat Bread 313
Lenten Spaghetti 138
Lentil Soup 169
Lentils
  with rice & onions 133
Lettuce Salad 75
Likér apó Diósmo 416
Likér apó Karídia 415
Likér apó Koukoútsia Veríkoko 414
Likér apó Mandaríni 414
Likér apó Portokáli 415
Likér apó Vatómoura 414
Likér apó Víssino 415
Lima Bean Salad 75
Lime Water 464
Liqueur
  apricot pit 414
  blueberry 414
  morello cherry 415
  orange 415
  raspberrry 414
  spearmint 416
  walnut 415
Liturgiá 317
Liver
  roúmelis in paper 258
  with leeks 259
  with rosemary 259
Logodósoume 552
Lópia 147
Loukanópites 99, 420
Loukoumádes 358
Loukoúmia 383
Lung
  stewed 262

M

Macaroni
  casserole 206
Macaroons
  honey 380
Magirítsa 175
Mahéria 504
Mahlep 462
Mahlépi 462
  liquid, substitute 462
Makaronáki Saláta 84
Makarónia Imám 135
Makarónia Nistísima 138
Makedonikós Halvás apó Simigdáli 370
Mandarin Liqueur 414
March Bracelet 513
Marídes Tiganités 47

Marinade
   for Beef Cuts 31
   for oven roasted lamb 32
   herbal, for roasts 30
   herbal, poultry 30
   lamb chops 29
   pork chops 29
   spicy fish 29
Maroulosaláta 75
Mártis 513
Mastic 462
Mastic Ice Cream 354
Mátsi 408
Matsógalo 350
Mávres 500
Mávro Skordópsomo 307
May Day 518
Mayonéza me Vótana 11
Mayonéza tis Stigmís 12
Mayonnaise
   herb 11
   minute 12
Mbámies me Patátes 152
Mbizélia me Ánitho 155
Mbougátsa 421
Meat Balls 52
   poached 209
Meat Pies
   fried sweet 108
Meatballs
   tomato gravy 20
Meats 183
Megáli Paraskeví 515
Megáli Pémpti 515
Megálo Sávato 480, 515
Melekoúni 377
Melintzanáki Glykó 388
Melintzánes Foúnou me Tirí 148
Melintzánes Gemistés me Ortíkia 245
Melintzanópita 110
Melintzanosaláta 81
Melomakárouna 380
Melon
   stuffed 353
Melópita Nisiótiki 347
Melópita Nissiótiki 421
Memorial Wheat 516
Menstruation 505
Mezé
   dinner party 471
     menu suggestions 472
Mezédes 33, 35, 61
Mialá Tiganitá 262
Mídia 452
Mídia Piláfi 274
Mídia Tiganitá 41
Míla and Tsirígia 407
Mirrors 505

Mizithrópites 359
Money 505
Moscári Giouvétsi 185
Moscári me Mbizélia 186
Moscári me Patátes Giahní 186
Moscári Tiliktó me Féta 188
Moscarísio Souvláki 214
Mountain Oysters 261
Mousaká 204
   with yogurt 205
Mousakás me Yiaoúrti 205
Moustoaleuriá 351
Mpiftéki 210
Mpougátsa 342
Muhlep 462
Mussels 452
   & feta 274
   fried 41
   with rice 274
Mustard Sauce 21
Mysterious Bean 436

N

Name Days 511
Nerantzáki Glykó 386
New Year 520
New Year's 521
   preparations 520
New Year's Eve 520
   party 477
Nistía 517, 520
Nistísima 481
Nistísmo
   meal, staples 481
"No" Day 522
Noní and Koumpári 571

O

O Evagelismós 518
O Koukoumás 518
October 28th 522
Octopus
   charcoal grilled 42
   in wine 43
   sun dried 42, 403
   with macaroni 275
Ohi Day 522
Oil cookies 381
Okra
   cleaning 435
   with potatoes 152
Olive Oil
   spicy 402
Olive Salad 78
Olives
   black wrinkled 401

fried, stuffed 54
  green, cracked 400
  green, in vinegar 399
  in bitter orange 401
Omelet
  tomato-egg 154
  village 154
Omeléta Horiátiki 154
Onion Fritters 58
Orange-Pepper Dressing 6
Orfós sto Foúrno 270
Organ Meats 255
Ortíka me Tomáta ke Krasí 246
Orzo
  in tomato sauce 134
Ouzo-Coconut Cake 345

P

Pagóni 505
Pagotó Mastíhas 354
Palm Sunday 480, 515
Pancakes
  savory pumpkin 58
  zucchini 61
Papádes 506
Pápies me Eliés 229
Papoútsia 506
Paramoní Protohroniá 520
Paramoní ton Theofaníon 480
Paránifes 559
Partridge
  in vine leaves 243
  with wheat stuffing 242
Pásca 516
Pascaliná Auyá 516
Pasta
  home-made 408
Pasta Imam 135
Pasta Pudding 350
Pastitsáda
  from Kerkyra 190
Pastítsio 206
Pastítsio me Pouré 207
Pastries
  syrup 364
Pastry
  crispy, in syrup 362
Pastry Dough 330, 333
  savory style 333
  working with 427
Patátes me Dendrolívano 157
Patátes me Diósmo 156
Patátes toú Foúrnou Kokkinistés 157
Patátes tou Foúrnou Lemonátes 156
Patatosaláta Attikís 80
Patatosaláta Vrastí 80
Patsás 176
Patsavoúra Tirópita 94

Patzária Gemistá 73
Patzária Skordaliá 72
Paximádi 323
Paximádia 321
Paximádia me Stafídes 324
Paximádia Nistísima 322
Peacock 505
Peas
  Thessalonian 155
  with dill sauce 155
Peasant Pasta Salad 84
Pediá 503
Pentárti 297, 316
Pepper Salad
  red & green 81
Peppers
  pickled 404
  stuffed, anchovies 404
  stuffed with feta 54
Pérdika Piláfi 241
Pérdikes Gemistés 242
Pérdikes se Ambelófila 243
Pergamónto Glykó 386
Períodos 505
Peristéria Gemistá 244
Phyllo
  fried 361
  home made, pastry sheets 331
    with egg 331
  pastry sheets
    working with 429
Phýllo Spitísio 331
Phýllo Spitísio me Avgó 331
Phytá 505
Piáse Kókkino 507
Pickled Peppers 404
Pies 420
  custard 342
  island cheese & honey 347
  lamb & feta 100
  milk custard 369
  short cut
    beef & cheese 421
    cheese 420
    cheese & honey 421
    chicken 420
    custard 421
    ham 420
    sausage 420
    spinach 420
    turkey 421
  wild greens 112
  yogurt 372
  zucchini 113
Pig
  stuffed suckling 194
Pig Heads 439
Pigeon
  stuffed 244

Pig's Head
   roasted 260
Pihtí 192
Pikántikes Melintzánes 59
Pikántiki Marináda gia Psári 29
Pikántiki Tomatosaláta 69
Pikántiko Eleólado 402
Pikántiko Psári me Tomáta 272
Pilaf
   Aegean 131
   bride's 132
   bulgur wheat 133
   heart & kidney 257
   lemon 132
   partridge 241
   pepper 136
Piláfi Lemonáto 132
Piláfi me Nefrá ke Kardiés 257
Piláfi me Piperiés 136
Piláfi tou Aegéou 131
Piláfia Ke Makarónia 129
Pilafs and Pastas 129, 139
Pine Nut Stuffing 128
Piperiés Gemistés me Antzoúgies 404
Piperiés me Féta Tiganités 54
Piperiés se Salamoúra 404
Piponáki Gemistó 353
Pita Bread 299
Píta me Arní ke Féta 100
Pitákia me Kimá 108
Pítes 87, 89, 299, 420
Plants and Cuttings 505
Pligoúri Piláfi 133
Pnevmóni Giahní 262
Podarikó 521
Ponokéfali 501
Poor Mans' Cabbage Salad 77
Pork
   preserved in lard 407
Pork Fats
   preserved 407
Pork Roast 193
Potato Salad
   island 80
Potato Salad from Attica 80
Potatoes
   lemon roasted 156
   mint roasted 156
   tomato roasted 157
   with rosemary 157
Pouleriká 217, 219
Poultry 217
Poutínga 352
Prasavgópita 104
Prasópita me Kréas 103
Pregnancy 505
Preserving and Pickling 395
Priests 506

Príka tis Nífis 554
Prósforo 317
Protimasíes 520
Protohroniá 521
Protohroniátikes Protimasíes 520
Protomagiá 518
Prozími 286
Prozími Horiátiko 287
Psári Vrastó 271
Psária 503
Psária Heliókafta 44
Psária Skordaliá me Dendrolívano 272
Psarósoupa 177
Psihosávato 513
Psomí Horiátiko 300
Psomiá 295
Pudding
   grape 351
Pumpkin
   fried 57
   pancakes 58

Q

Quails
   in tomato & wine 246

R

Rabbit
   in yogurt 247
   with walnut stuffing 248
Radíkia Saláta 76
Raisin Cake 346
Raisins
   village 407
Rakí 411
Rapanáki me Féta Saláta 76
Raspberry Liqueur 414
Renkosaláta 70
Revaní me Oúzo ke Karída 345
Revegión 477
Revíthia 170
Revithosaláta 84
Rice
   spinach 137
Rice Balls
   fried 363
Rice Pie 109
Rice Pudding 350
   traditional 349
Rice Salad
   herbal 85
Riganáda 323
Rízi me Vótana Saláta 85
Rizógalo Paradosiakó 349
Rizópita 109
Rose Water
   homemade village 465

Rosemary
   sauce 22
Rósiki Saláta 77
Rusks 322
   making 321
   oil 326
   raisin filled 324
   sesame 325
Russian Salad 77

S

Saint
   promise to 499, 528
Salad
   dandelion 76
Salads
   Attica green bean 74
   bean & rice 85
   cabbage 85
   chickpea 84
   colorful 86
   combinations 82
   farmer's 82
   garden 86
   green 86
   herbal rice 85
   January 84
   olive 78
   peasant pasta 84
   Russian 77
   shrimp 71
   shrimp & artichoke 71
   spicy tomato 69
   tamara (roe) 39
   tomato & feta 69
   tomato & herb 82
   tomato-green bean 83
   tuna-bean 83
   winter 83
Salamoúra - Álmi 463
Saláta Agináres 72
Saláta apo Eliés 78
Saláta apó Vrastá Kolokithákia 79
Saláta Chromatistí 86
Saláta Fasolákia Attikís 74
Saláta Himoniátiki 83
Saláta Laikí 82
Saláta Mavrofásoula 74
Saláta me Tóno ke Fasólia 83
Saláta Prásini 86
Saláta Taratór 78
Saláta tou Kípou 86
Saláta tou Yianári 84
Saláta Vrastí 79
Salt 506
Salt Cod with Garlic Sauce 44
Sáltsa Dendrolívano 22
Sáltsa gia Keftédes 20

Sáltsa gia Psári 22
Sáltsa Kimás 16
Sáltsa Kremidáti 19
Sáltsa Marináti 18
Sáltsa me Ánitho 18
Sáltsa me Hortariká 20
Sáltsa me Tahíni 13
Sáltsa me Tóno 273
Sáltsa me Yiaoúrti 24
Sáltsa Mídia ke Féta 274
Sáltsa Moustárdas 21
Sáltsa Pikántiki 17
Sáltsa Pipurioú me Portokáli 6
Sáltsa Psitoú 21
Sáltsa Savoúro 405
Sáltsa Tomatopiperiás 19
Sáltsa Yiaoúrti me Páprika 25
Sáltsa Yiaoúrti me Spanáki 24
Sáltses 1
Sardéla pou Keladái 46
Sardines
   "singing" 46
Saturday of the Souls 513
Sauces 1
   almond-garlic 9
   basic meat 16
   Béchamel 5
   chickpea & sesame 13
   cold tomato 15
   egg-lemon 3
      creamy 4
      traditional 4
   garlic 8
      thick version 8
      thin version 8
   mustard 21
   red, for fish 22
   rosemary 22
   sesame 13
   sinking, for fish 405
   tomato & rosemary 18
   tomato-dill 18
   tomato-onion 19
   tomato-pepper 19
   tomato-vegetable 20
   walnut-garlic 10
   white, for meats 23
   yogurt 24
   yogurt & mint 25
   yogurt & pimento 25
   yogurt-spinach 24
   zesty tomato 17
Sausage Pies 99
Sausages
   garlic rice 264
   pork & rice 263
Savory Pies 87, 89
Savory Pítes

short cut 420
Sea Urchins 452
   preparation 452
Seafood 267
Sesame Honey Bars 377
Sesame Rusks 325
Sesame Sauce 13
Sesame Soup 179
Sfouggáto me Maroúli ke Kremídi 153
Sfragítha 297
Shellfish
   baked, casserole 276
Shish Kebobs
   beef 214
   lamb 215
   pork 214
Shoes 506
Short Cut Sweet Pies 421
Shrimp
   in wine 49
   salad 71
Shrimp and Artichoke Salad 71
Shrimp Cocktail
   Greek style 48
Síka Gemistá me Xiroús Karpoús 353
Síko Gkykó 389
Sikotákia me Dendrolívano 259
Sikotákia tis Kótas Xitháta 257
Sikotariá me Prása 259
Sikóti se Hartí 258
Sisamotá Paximádia 325
Sisamotá Psomiá Nistísima 304
Sívrasi 144
Skartotséta apó Moscári 187
Skin
   rashes & burns 501
Skordaliá 8
Skordaliá Amygdálou 9
Skordaliá Lafriá 8
Skordaliá Pihtí 8
Skórdo 460, 504
Skoúpes 503
Smírna Plakí 280
Smyrnéika Paximádia me Ládi 326
Snails
   land, preparing 453
   land, stewed 251
Sneezing 506
Soggy Bread 2
Soup 161
   chicken egg lemon 172
   chicken-vermicelli 172
   cheese
      Santorini 178
   Easter 175
   fish & seafood 164
   hearty 163
   perfect 163

   poached meatball 174
   rooster 173
   sesame 179
   smooth 163
   tomato 171
   vegetable, village 171
   yogurt 178
Soup Stocks 165
Soúpa Avgolémono 172
Soúpa Fidés 172
Soúpa Horiátiki 171
Soúpa Petinoú 173
Soúpes 161, 163
Soupiés Giahní 269
Soupiés Krasátes me Meláni 269
Sour Dough 287
Souvláki
   making 214
Soúvles 441
Souvlomoutariá 40
Souzoukákia Smyrnéika 208
Spaghetti
   from Hálki 139
   Lenten 138
Spanáki Sívrasi 150
Spanakópita 111
Spanakópites 420
Spanakórizo 137
Spinach
   with onions 150
Spinach Pie 111
Spinach Rice 137
Spitting 506
Sponge
   with lettuce & onions 153
Spoon Sweets 384
   cherry 387
   eggplant 388
   fig 389
   grape 389
   green walnut 392
   pear 390
   quince 390
   strawberry 391
   walnut meats in syrup 393
Sprains 502
Squid
   preparation 447
   stuffed 279
Squid in Spicy Batter 51
Squid Rings 50
St. Basil's Bread 308
St. Basil's Day 521
Stafídes 407
Stafidópita 346, 423
Stafíli Glykó 389
Staples
   nistísmo meal 481

village meal 471
Stefánia 559
Stíthos 500
Stock
  beef 166
  chicken 166
  fish 167
  vegetable 167
Stomahikó 416
Stragália 433
Stravopátima ke Bríximo 502
Stuffed Cabbage Rolls with Meat 126
Stuffed Cucumbers 53
Stuffed Vegetables with Meat 125
Stuffed Zucchini Blossoms 60
Stuffing
  pine nut 128
  preparing 121
Súma 411
Sun Dried Octopus in Garlic Sauce 42
Sweat 502
Sweet Biscuits 373
Swordfish
  kebobs 215
Syrup Cakes 422

T

Ta Psomiá tou Gámou 562
Tahíni Dip 14
Tahinópsomo 303
Tahinósoupa 179
Talismans 492
Táma 499, 528
Taramokeftédes 39
Taramosaláta 39
Taratór
  Macedonian 78
Taratoúri 25
Tart
  sweet cheese 348
Tárta me Mizíthra 348
Táximo 499, 528
Télia Nistía 480
Thalassiná 267
Thalassiná tou Foúrnou 276
Thimíama 494
Thímiasma 494
Tiganitá 149
Tiganités Gemistés Eliés 54
Tiganítes me Míla 355
Tiganitó Mbrókolo & Kounoupídi 56
Tiganópsomo Almyró 329
Tiganópsomo Glykó 329
Tipári 297
Tirávgoulo Santorinítiko 178
Tirí Féta Spitísia 406
Tirí Saghanáki 52

Tirokauterí 38
Tirópita Aplí 92
Tirópita Paradosiakí 91
Tirópita Ploúsia 93
Tirópites 420
To Fotón 521
To Loúsimo tis Nífis 564
To Máti 489
To Piláfi tis Nífis 132
To Vagión 515
Tomáta me Avgó 154
Tomáta me Fasolákia Saláta 83
Tomáta me Féta Saláta 69
Tomáta me Vótana Saláta 82
Tomátes tis Ptolemaídas 55
Tomátes Xerés 402
Tomato - Green Bean Salad 83
Tomato Balls 53
Tomato Gravy
  for meatballs 20
Tomato Rice with Garlic 137
Tomato Sauce
  cold 15
  zesty 17
Tomato Soup 171
Tomato-Dill Sauce 18
Tomatoes
  Ptolemies' 55
  sun dried 402
Tomatokeftédes 53
Tomatórizo me Skórdo 137
Tomatósoupa 171
Tomb of Christ 517
Ton Mína tou Mélitos 557
Torte
  Cretan almond 343
  Cretan lamb 102
Toú Agíoy Vasíli 521
Toú Evangelismoú 480
Tou Lazárou 514
Touch Red 507
Toursés 395
Toúrta Krítis me Arní 102
Tripe
  cleaning 440
  preparing 440
  soup 176
Tríti Dekatrís 507
Tsiknopémpti 514
Tsimpímata Mélissas 500
Tsípouro 411
Tsouréki 314
Tuesday the 13th 507
Tuna
  in tomato sauce 273
Tuna-Bean Salad 83
Turkey
  holiday, stuffed 231

short cut, pies 421
with potatoes & onions 230
Tzatzíki 38

V

Vasilikó 503, 459
Vasilópita 308
Vasilópita Glýkisma 341
Veal Roll
with feta 188
Vegetable Stock 167
Vegetables 141
fried 149
preparation 118
stuffed 115
arranging for baking 119
making 118
vegetarian 125
with meat 125
Venison
baked 250
Véres 559
Village Bread 300
Village Cures 500
Village Salad 67
Vinaigrette Dressing 7
Vizantiní Rizópita 343
Vrastó Moscári me Lahaniká 189

W

Walnut Cake 371
Walnut-Garlic Sauce 10
Wedding Bands 559
Wedding Ceremony 566
Weddings 551, 556
honeymoon 557
presents 563
Saturday before 564
White Sauce for Meats 23
Whitebait
fried 47
Whole Apricot Preserves 385
Whooping Cough 502
Wild Greens 347
Wild Greens Pie 112
Wine
home-made 412
Wine Making 412
Worry Beads 498
Wreaths 559

X

Xifías Souvláki 215

Y

Yiaoúrti 466
Yiaoúrti Stragistó 466
Yiaourtópita 372
Yiaourtósoupa 178
Yogurt
home made 466
pie 372
soup 178
spinach sauce 24
strained 466
Yogurt and Mint Sauce 25
Yogurt Sauce 24
Youvarlákia 209
Youvarlákia Soúpa 174

Z

Zambonópita 98
Zambonópites 420
Zími me Lemóni 333
Zími Voutírou yia Pítes 332
Zomós Kótas 166
Zomós Lahanikón 167
Zomós Psarioú 167
Zomós Vodinoú 166
Zucchini
salad, boiled 79
stew 151
Zucchini Blossoms 60, 119
Zucchini Pancakes 61
Zucchini Pie 113
Zwieback 322
making 321

W

```
                              $39.95
641.5949 Atsaides, Susie
ATS      Greek generations :
         a medley of ethnic
  12/83  recipes, folklore, and
```

**PLEASE DO NOT
RETURN IN BOOK DROP**

THE BRUMBACK LIBRARY
OF VAN WERT COUNTY
VAN WERT, OHIO